THE KINGDOM OF QUITO IN THE SEVENTEENTH CENTURY

THE
KINGDOM
OF QUITO
IN THE
SEVENTEENTH
CENTURY

•

Bureaucratic Politics
in the Spanish
Empire

JOHN LEDDY PHELAN

THE UNIVERSITY OF WISCONSIN PRESS
Madison · Milwaukee · London
1967

Published by
The University of Wisconsin Press
Madison, Milwaukee, and London

U.S.A.: Box 1379, Madison, Wisconsin 53701
U.K.: 26–28 Hallam Street, London, W.1

Printed in the United States of America by
The Heffernan Press Inc.
Worcester, Massachusetts

Library of Congress Catalog
Card Number 67–25940

DMS

ERNST H. KANTOROWICZ
Magistri et Amici

PREFACE

The research for and the writing of this book were greatly facilitated by support from several foundations, and I am deeply grateful for all their assistance. A Guggenheim fellowship enabled me to spend a year in South America and Spain. An American Philosophical Society grant took me to South America again. A good deal of the writing was done during a year's leave of absence with funds provided by the Carnegie grant to the Comparative Tropical History Program and by the Ibero-American Ford grant to the University of Wisconsin. The Research Committee of the Graduate School frequently supplemented these grants.

I have received much assistance and unfailing courtesy in all the libraries and archives where I studied. I would like to express my appreciation to the directors and the staffs of the following institutions: the Archivo General de la Nación and the Biblioteca Nacional in Mexico City, the Archivo General del Gobierno (Guatemala City), the Archivo Nacional (Panama City), the Archivo Nacional de Colombia (Bogotá), the Archivo Nacional de Cali, the Archivo General del Cauca (Popayán), the Archivo

Municipal de Quito, the Archivo Nacional de Historia del Ecuador, the Archivo de la Corte Suprema (Quito), the Archivo Nacional del Perú, the Biblioteca Nacional (Lima), the Archivo de la Audiencia de Lima, the Archivo Municipal de Lima, the Archivo General de Indias, the Archivo Histórico Nacional and the Biblioteca Nacional (Madrid), the Museo de América (Madrid), the John Carter Brown Library, the Newberry Library, and the Library of Congress (Hispanic Foundation). Among the directors and staffs of those institutions, a special word of thanks goes to José María Arboleda Lorente, Howard Cline, Jorge A. Garcés, Fred Hall, and the late J. Joaquín Pardo. Among the many people who assisted me in the preparation of this volume, I would like especially to thank the following: Ruth Lapham Butler, Guillermo Céspedes, Philip D. Curtin, Justino Fernández, Andrew Gunder Frank, Robert E. Frykenberg, Robert Heussler, the late Ernst H. Kantorowicz, Frances Parkinson Keyes, Adele Kibre, James F. King, George Kubler, Santiago Sebastián López, Peter Marzahl, Luís Miranda, Marjorie Pettit, Juan Peréz de Tudela, doña María Josefa Muñoz y Roca Tallada de Martínez de Campos, Adam Szaszdi, James D. Thompson, José María Vargas, O.P., and Andy G. Wilkison. I did much of the writing of this book on the island of Ibiza. I am grateful to all my friends there who made my two stays so enjoyable.

Madison, Wisconsin JOHN LEDDY PHELAN
December, 1966

CONTENTS

ix

ILLUSTRATIONS

MAPS

INTRODUCTION

This book is not merely a biography of Antonio de Morga as such, nor is it intended only as a case study of the government of the *audiencia* kingdom of Quito from 1615 to 1636, when Dr. Morga served as president of that tribunal. The larger purpose is to explore the inner workings of the bureaucracy of the Spanish empire. A good deal but not all of the illustrative material comes from those two decades of the Morga administration.

This book falls into three sections. The first part deals with how an audiencia resolved some major problems as diverse as the conquests of frontier areas, the regulation of Indian labor, and defense measures against the Dutch. Some of the special characteristics of the colonial bureaucracy, such as graft and immorality, recruitment and promotion, crime and punishment, are the concern of the second section. The *visita general* system by which the central authorities in Madrid evaluated the conduct and the performance of magistrates overseas is the central focus of the last part.

A recurrent theme is the interaction of the magistrates in the audiencia with their superiors in Lima and Madrid and with their nominal inferiors

in the provinces. Another focus is the interrelationship between the bureaucracy and each major segment, as well as among segments, of that
multiracial society. The primary objective of the whole study is to unravel
the intricate web of authority, responsibility, and decision-making in that
governmental labyrinth. This book addresses itself to such questions as to
what extent magistrates overseas enjoyed some initiative without jeopardiz-
ing central control and in what manner various sectors in that heterogeneous
society influenced the decisions of regional magistrates in the audiencias
and the central authorities in Madrid.

This study comprises both social and institutional history. It seeks to
explore the interaction of law, *derecho,* and social conditions, *hecho,* by a
synthesis of divergent views. The Spanish school of the late Rafael Altamira
has stressed the study of colonial legislation in a somewhat narrow legalistic
context, whereas North American historians have usually concentrated on
the actual social conditions in the Indies, which often made an apparent
mockery of legislation. From a fusion of these two approaches may emerge
some fresh insights about the wide gap between the law and its observance
in the Spanish empire.

The presentation is comparative, influenced to some extent by the aims
of the Comparative Tropical History Program established by the Department of History of the University of Wisconsin in 1959 with support from
the Carnegie Corporation. Central to this program is the search for meaningful comparisons about the interactions between European and non-
European peoples in the southern latitudes of the globe with special emphasis on Latin America, Africa, south Asia, and southeast Asia. In
addition to the frequent comparisons between Quito and other regions of
the Spanish empire, I am interested in comparing the Spanish American
bureaucracy with the British system of administration in nineteenth-century
India. In the concluding chapter there are further comparisons of a more
abstract nature.

In this study the career of Antonio de Morga in Quito is examined carefully, not because he was a major actor in the drama of his own times,
but because he exemplified the vices and virtues, the strengths and weaknesses of an administrative system that governed a world-wide empire for
three centuries.

Antonio de Morga, Sánchez, Garay y López de Garfias was born in
Seville on November 29, 1559, of a Basque father and an Andalusian
mother. He died in Quito on July 21, 1636. Thus his life spanned the
reigns of the three Philips, during which time the fortunes of imperial
Spain disastrously declined.

Lawyers and Roman law dominated Spanish colonial administration, and Antonio de Morga was a jurist by training and a judge throughout his adult life. A student of the Universities of Salamanca and Osuna, he had earned by 1580 a doctorate in both *canones* and *derechos*.

After completing his academic training, Dr. Morga entered the service of the crown, in which he was to spend the rest of his long life. His career was typical of those of other middle-echelon magistrates in its empire-wide scope. He held several minor judicial posts in Spain between 1580 and 1593 before he left for service overseas. His first appointment in 1593 was in Manila, one of the least desirable stations in Spain's far-flung empire. In 1603 came a much-desired promotion to the audiencia of Mexico, where Dr. Morga served as *alcalde de crimen* for a decade. His presidency of the audiencia of Quito from 1615 until his death in 1636 climaxed his career.

Antonio de Morga was a bureaucrat of uncommon ability. Although a practicing jurist, he could transcend the cautious and conservative thinking of his fellow magistrates to offer bold solutions of vexing problems. An energetic magistrate, he was a zealous upholder of the authority of the crown. Yet he showed skill in harmonizing clashes of interests and personalities. He could be vindictive, but more times than not he was magnanimous and conciliatory. Above all, he personified that ideal of paternalistic service that often imbued the higher levels of Spain's colonial administration.

Although Dr. Morga was in many ways a representative figure of the Habsburg bureaucracy, he may also be considered to be a precursor of the Bourbon reforms of the eighteenth century. His opposition to monopolistic economic practices foreshadowed the economic reorganization of the empire, culminating in the enlightened despotism of Charles III. Secondly, Dr. Morga's tenacious battle with the viceroys in Lima to secure more autonomy for the audiencia reflected his conviction that the kingdom of Quito was a separate political, geographical, and economic entity whose problems could be better resolved in Quito than in Lima. By securing more self-government, he inadvertently contributed to the foundation of the independent Republic of Ecuador which emerged in 1830.

He was also a historian of distinction. His *Sucesos de las islas filipinas*, first published in Mexico City in 1609 and republished many times since, remains one of the most informative accounts we have of early Spanish colonization on those islands.

Yet for all his positive qualities as a magistrate, Dr. Morga ended his career in disgrace. Behind his white beard and his grave manner, he was a confirmed Don Juan. In addition he was avaricious. Nevertheless, the colorful vices of the Morga administration, which have attracted much attention from historians, should not obscure the solid accomplishments of that magistrate. The focus of this book is not so much on the man as on the governmental system he personified.

There is a considerable literature devoted to many aspects of Spanish colonial administration, but there are only a few studies concerned with how particular audiencias operated. From specific probing into the personalities and the politics of one audiencia tribunal during a relatively short period of time, I hope also to derive some generalizations of a wider scope in place and time.

I

THE THREE QUITOS

1.

ESMERALDAS: THE FAILURE OF
A CONQUEST

The Spanish conquest of the New World and the Philippines was a historical episode which began in the sixteenth century, but which had not yet culminated three centuries later when the empire had vanished.[1] On the Pacific coast of South America, for example, effective Spanish control was never established in certain areas. Vast zones of territory remained islands of resistance. The generation of Pizarro, Benalcázar, and Quesada during the 1530's accomplished the most dramatic exploits of the conquest by subduing the organized Indian resistance of the Incas and the Chibchas. Thus they placed under Spanish control the highland regions formed by the two chains of the Andes, an area stretching from central Chile through the modern republics of Bolivia, Peru, and Ecuador and north to the plateau of Bogotá. The subjugation of the coastal areas, however, was never as intensive or extensive as the conquest of the Sierra. In fact, many coastal regions remained unconquered until the nineteenth and twentieth centuries. One of these was Esmeraldas in the kingdom of Quito, whose successor state is the Republic of Ecuador.

3

Geographically, this part of South America is divided into three sharply contrasting zones: the coast, the Sierra, and the Oriente. During the colonial and early national periods, the Sierra overshadowed the other two regions. The coast has successfully challenged the domination of the Sierra only in the present century, when its bananas, cacao, rice, sugar, coffee, and toquilla palm became the nation's principal exports. The eastern zone of the Oriente, with dense tropical forests and flat jungle lands in the drainage basin of the upper Amazon River and its tributaries, never has played a significant role. First explored during the heroic age of the conquest, it became the site of a few missionary settlements in the seventeenth century, but its sweltering climate and its hostile natives have kept mastery of the upper Amazon country an unfulfilled dream exciting the imagination and the cupidity of merchants, conquerors, and missionaries from the sixteenth century to the present.

West of the Oriente lies the Sierra, or Andean plateau, about 390 miles long and a maximum of 45 miles wide, descending gradually toward the south from about 9,500 feet to 7,800 feet above sea level. Between the western and the eastern chains of the Andes with their snowcapped and volcanic peaks of 20,000 feet elevation, there are ten minor and three major basins arranged roughly in a line from north to south. Transverse ranges, the *nudos,* or knots, through which there are narrow passes, divide one basin from the next. In these valleys the Spaniards encountered dense Indian populations that had been brought under the sway of the Incas a few decades before the Spanish conquest.

Here the Spaniards established their principal settlements, encouraged by an abundant supply of labor and by a climate that tourist brochures still describe as "eternal spring." Less well advertised is the periodic occurrence of earthquakes. Ecuador is the only Andean country not endowed with substantial mineral resources, except for petroleum on the coast. The gold mines of the southern province of Loja could no longer be profitably mined by the end of the sixteenth century. In the Sierra the crops of the temperate zone, from maize and potatoes to wheat and other grains, were grown, and cattle and sheep were raised. A small group of Spanish colonists owned large estates, which were cultivated by the docile Indians.

The coast is a fertile alluvial plain lying at the feet of the Andes and varying in width from 12 to 100 miles. Mainly a lowland region less than 1,000 feet above sea level, it is cut by dozens of rivers which flow to the sea from the snowy peaks of the Andes. The two principal river systems are those of the Esmeraldas to the north and the Guayas to the south. On the right bank of the Guayas is located the port of Guayaquil, some 30 miles from the Pacific.

Although the equator crosses the Ecuadorian coast, the climate is significantly moderated by the Humboldt current. Europeans could become acclimatized to the coast far more readily than they could to the Amazon country. This is not to discount the very real health hazards and personal hardships that Europeans had to endure. Their buildings, made of wood in the years before the age of cement, were ravaged by fires and termites. Malaria and other diseases claimed many lives. But the existence of the port of Guayaquil is ample evidence that Europeans could live in the lowlands, with some discomfort, it is true, provided that they had sufficient incentive to do so.[2]

The Andes created a formidable barrier isolating the Sierra from the coast and the world beyond. The first and, even today, the most-used route for transporting people and goods between the inter-Andean valleys and the coast winds overland from Quito southward to Latacunga, Ambato, Riobamba, and Chimbo, down the steep western slope of the Andes to the Guayas River, and thence by water downstream to Guayaquil. The distance is some 240 miles. Virtually impassable during the rainy season, the Sierra's major lifeline to the outside world was kept open during the dry season by Indian porters and rowers, horses, mules, and donkeys. Far less used were the completely overland routes which linked the Sierra towns with Lima and Bogotá. The southern route, about 900 miles, passed through Cuenca, Loja, Piura, and Trujillo to Lima. The northern route, linking Quito to Bogotá and Cartagena, went via Pasto, Popayán, Cali, Cartago, and the Magdalena River valley. North-south travel from Quito on these two *caminos reales* was secondary to travel, by way of Guayaquil, north or south on the ocean. In the seventeenth century, maritime travel with all its inconveniences and hardships was still more rapid, more comfortable, and more economical than transportation overland. Against the southeastern winds, the sea voyage from Guayaquil to Callao took about forty days. The return trip took less than half that time.[3]

From the 1590's to the 1630's determined efforts were made in Quito to surmount the barrier of the Andes through explorations for alternate routes between the Sierra and the coast. The objective of these expeditions was to penetrate the Esmeraldas country, which then extended from the port of Bahía de Caráquez northward to the province of Barbacoas (today Nariño). The terminus of the first road opened between Quito and the northern coastal region was the port of Bahía de Caráquez (then called Bahía

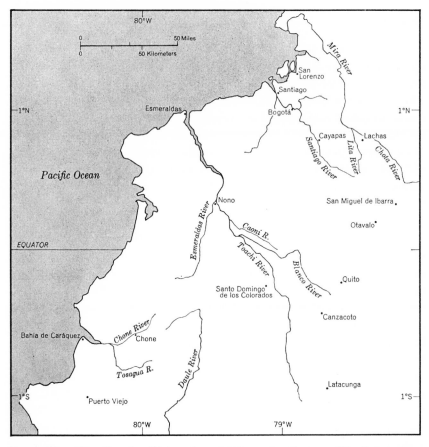

Esmeraldas. Map by the University of Wisconsin Cartographic Laboratory.

de Caracas), which is formed by the estuary of the Chone and Tosagua rivers. First explored by a Mercedarian friar, Diego de Velasco, in 1617, the path went from Quito through Canzacoto to Niguas, westward across unsettled country to the valley of the Tosagua River, and thence to Bahía de Caráquez.[4] The length of this overland trail was about 120 miles. The modern secondary road (Quito–Santo Domingo de los Colorados–Nueva Delicia–Flavio Alfaro–Ricaurte–Chone–Bahía de Caráquez) roughly parallels that old trail.

There were several possible routes into the heart of the northern or Esmeraldas country. The rivers rising in the western chain of the cordillera flow from the inter-Andean basins of Quito and San Miguel de Ibarra northwestward to the Pacific. Thus geography provided the conquistadores from the Sierra with many miles of river highways. There were two likely approaches from the basin of Quito to the estuary of the Esmeraldas River. One way was from Quito down the steep slopes of the Andes to the valley of the Toachi River, which flows into the Esmeraldas. This is the route of the modern highway. The other route, explored by Pedro Maldonado around 1738, went from Quito to Cotocollao to Nono, where the Caoni and Blanco rivers meet, and then down the Esmeraldas River to the sea. This was a distance of 138 miles, 72 miles overland and 66 miles by river.

The ports of Bahía de Caráquez, Esmeraldas, and Santiago were protected and deep, each possessing an abundant supply of nearby timber for building and repairing vessels.

Efforts in the seventeenth century, however, were concentrated on reaching the mouth of the Santiago River, whose estuary is about 42 miles north of that of the Esmeraldas. The basin of San Miguel de Ibarra, lying north of that of Quito, was the point of departure. The valley of the Chota River offered a convenient outlet from the Andes. Thence the trail led westward from Lachas across the Lita River to Cayapas and then northwestward through the valley of the Santiago River to Bogotá (then called San Ignacio de Montesclaros) where the Bogotá and Santiago rivers converge. From Bogotá the route followed the Santiago River to the Pacific. The distance was about 150 miles, requiring a minimum of ten days.

Still another possible route was from the Chota River valley northwestward through the valley of the Mira River to the sea. There was little interest in this route until the early nineteenth century. The San Miguel de Ibarra–San Lorenzo railroad, which was inaugurated in 1946, follows parts of both of these routes.

Neither geography nor climate, alone or together, can adequately explain the Spanish failure to conquer Esmeraldas. Historical and cultural factors were far more decisive. The abortive Esmeraldas enterprise ought to be viewed from the perspectives of the native population as well as from those of the vested interests in Lima, Guayaquil, Quito, and Madrid. Each of these factors in turn merits careful examination; it is the interaction of all of them that explains why the Spaniards failed.

At the time of the conquest, the Indian population along the coast was sparse in comparison with that of the Sierra, where there were about half a million people. After the arrival of the Spaniards, the scanty coastal population was decimated by the spread of diseases, such as malaria, yaws, intestinal ills, tuberculosis, smallpox, and measles.

The demographic character of Esmeraldas underwent a significant change after 1570, when a cargo of Negro slaves from the Guinea coast en route from Panama to Peru was shipwrecked off the coast. The ex-slaves encountered little difficulty in conquering the coastal area from Manta northward to the mouths of the Esmeraldas and Santiago rivers. The Africans killed or enslaved the Indian men and married their womenfolk. Within a generation of the shipwreck, a race of zambos (the usual Spanish term for people of mixed Negro and Indian descent) were masters of a goodly portion of Esmeraldas.[5]

The potential threat that this zambo republic posed was not lost on the Spaniards in Quito. An *oidor* of the audiencia, Juan del Barrio de Sepúlveda, traveled in and around San Mateo from 1597 to 1600 and claimed to have persuaded five thousand zambos to recognize the overlordship of Spain. He founded three pueblos. The judge persuaded two of the principal zambo caciques, don Francisco de Arobe and don Sebastián de Yllescas, to journey to Quito, where in solemn and picturesque ceremonies they formally recognized the sovereignty of the Spanish crown.[6] This scene is depicted in an oil canvas by an Indian artist, Adrián Sánchez Galque, in what is the earliest signed and dated painting from South America. It now hangs in the Museo de América in Madrid[7] (a reproduction of it is included in the illustration section of this book). Dressed as Spanish gentlemen, the zambos (incorrectly labeled "mulattoes") wore the golden nose- and ear-plugs of Indian chieftains.

This oath of fealty did not represent a step in the subjugation of Esmeraldas, although Yllescas died in 1607 as Spanish governor of San Mateo.[8] The zambo caciques had tasted liberty; they had every intention of preserving it. They had no objection to swearing an occasional oath of loyalty to the Spanish king or accepting an honorary title from him, provided the Spaniards made no attempt to enforce their overlordship in their villages by collecting tribute taxes or conscripting labor. Zambo leadership adroitly avoided actions which would provoke the Spaniards into dispatching punitive expeditions. Shipwrecked Spaniards, for example, were not killed or even mistreated. On the contrary, they were hospitably received and sent on their way to Quito with the necessary provisions.[9] The zambos went out of their way to reassure the Spaniards that they would do nothing to assist the Dutch fleets which were periodically infesting the Pacific.[10]

The zambos were willing to cooperate with the Spaniards to the considerable extent of receiving Catholic missionaries. In fact, they gradually became nominal Christians. The Mercedarians and the Dominicans sent some missionaries but never in sufficient numbers to carry out intensive indoctrination. With the notable exception of the Jesuits, the religious orders were demoralized by bitter strife between the Spanish-born and the American-born friars, a topic which will be discussed in Chapter 12. Had the Esmeraldas missions been assigned to the Jesuits, whose discipline and morale were far superior to those of the other orders (the Mercedarians, the Franciscans, the Augustinians, and the Dominicans), the results might have been different. The Jesuits, whose Quito contingent was less than forty men in 1615, administered the missions in the Amazon country from 1638, with their headquarters at San Francisco de Borja.

There is a graphic description of these zambo villages written in the 1820's by an Anglo-Irishman, William B. Stevenson. He served as the private secretary to one of the last Spanish presidents of the audiencia of Quito, Count Ruíz de Castilla, who rewarded him with the high-sounding but empty title of governor of Esmeraldas. Stevenson climaxed his distinctive South American career as private secretary to Lord Cochrane, the colorful if irascible British admiral who secured control of the Pacific for the American patriots during the war of independence in the early nineteenth century. "Governor" Stevenson thus described his ostensible subjects, as he found them in May, 1809:

The natives are shy with strangers, and particularly the females; they are however very ingenuous, which to some people appears indecent; and well it may, since cunning and craftiness are too often the handmaids of a high degree of civilization. They appear particularly attached to truth and honesty; their *yes* and their *no* bear the exact value of the words, and if at any time they are called upon to ratify them, or are induced to think that they are not believed, they leave in a very abrupt manner the person or the company. Their honesty is evinced by the exposure of what they possess, and by leaving it thus exposed when they go on their hunting and fishing parties. The houses, like those of the Puná, are not only without doors and windows, but without walls, and the only sign by which an inhabited house can be distinguished from an uninhabited one is, that the steps of the ladder in the latter are turned downwards, and no arguments whatever are sufficient to persuade an Esmeraldeno to enter a house when the ladder is thus placed.

It may with truth be asserted, that industry is certainly not a prominent feature in their habits; but where a sufficiency is easily procured, where luxury in food or clothing is unknown, where superiority is never contended for, and where nature appears not only to invite, but even to tempt her creatures to repose, why should they reject her offer. The excessive exercise taken in hunting and fishing is certainly a proof, that when exertion becomes necessary for the support of nature, it is resorted to with as much alacrity as in other countries, where labour is imposed either to support the pomp of superiority, or the whims of fashion. . . .

All the natives call themselves Christians, but they seldom conform to the ceremonies of the church, forming a very strong contrast to some others of the same denomination, who are really only Christians in the ceremonious part, and who are, I fear, more remote from loving God above all things, than those Indians are from loving their neighbors as themselves.[11]

The wandering Celt had evidently found his noble savages on the distant coast of Ecuador.

The zambo population, divided into small villages with few political ties among them, did not number as many as ten thousand. In the interior there were several small Indian groups who maintained their independence from both the Spaniards and the zambos. In contrast to the zambos, who took pains not to antagonize the Spaniards in order to preserve their independence, some Indian groups were fiercely bellicose. The Malaba Indians, numbering a few thousand people, became provoked by the harsh labor demands of the Spaniards and in 1619 sacked the new Spanish settlements at Bogotá and Santiago, killing the inhabitants. The road from San Miguel de Ibarra to the port of Santiago, which had been opened a few years before, was not reopened until the present century.[12] The hostility of the Malabas was a decisive factor but not the sole one.

When the Spaniards were united in purpose, they could wage a war of extermination with devastating success against small Indian groups like the Malabas. Such was the case in the province of Barbacoas, north of Esmeraldas, where a small expedition with units dispatched from both Quito and Popayán under the command of Captain Francisco de Parada crushed Indian resistance in 1600.[13] Just as topography was a significant obstacle to the conquest of Esmeraldas, so also was the resistance of the zambos and the Indians. Neither barrier, however, would have been impenetrable had the Spanish authorities been resolute. They were not. Thus the Spanish will to conquer Esmeraldas was fatally weakened.

The agents of the crown relied on a tried and proven instrument of conquest. An individual would sign a contract, or *asiento,* with the representatives of the crown, in which he received various political and economic benefits for exploring and maintaining a road. The contract received the joint approval of the audiencia of Quito and the viceroy in Lima. From the crown's point of view, the asiento system possessed the obvious advantage ordinarily of costing the already hard-pressed treasury little or nothing. On the road to Esmeraldas, however, the treasury did have to spend something. Between 1600 and 1611, before a suitable candidate appeared, the crown spent some 10,000 pesos.[14] On May 15, 1619, after the revolt of the Malabas, the treasury appropriated 800 pesos and authorized a loan of 1,500 pesos from the royal funds to help defray the expenses of a punitive expedition.[15] Except for these expenditures, most of the costs for exploration and conquest were borne by private individuals.[16]

Hence the effectiveness of the asiento system depended in large measure on the contractor. Above all else, he needed liquid capital of his own and a willingness to invest it. The crown offered immediate assistance as well as long-range benefits. The crown-administered *mita* system provided a supply of cheap Indian labor. Indians were required to clear the path, to build bridges over the rivers, to repair the trail, and to build the *tambos,* or rest stations, located at the end of each day's journey. The tambos had to be supplied with food, porters, rowers, and beasts of burden.

In 1611 the first asiento for a road through Esmeraldas was signed with Pablo Durango del Gadillo, who received the position of corregidor of the populous province of San Miguel de Ibarra for a five-year period with an annual salary of 1,000 pesos. He also received the office of governor of Esmeraldas, with the privilege of transmitting his office to two successive heirs. Martín de Fuica in 1617 received the administrative-judicial post of *alcalde* of Bahía de Caráquez, an office that he could transmit to two successive heirs. These political offices carried with them the right to name many minor officials. In addition the governor or alcalde received several lots in the port city that he was obligated to found and large tracts of rural land adjacent to the city.

The outstanding defect of the asiento system was that the private resources of one man were seldom sufficient to overcome the difficulties encountered. Nor was it easy to find a man of means who was willing to risk his capital on an enterprise if its history was one of repeated failures. Notwithstanding, the asiento system did produce some temporary successes. Between 1616 and 1619 Pablo Durango del Gadillo opened the road from San Miguel de Ibarra to the port of Santiago. Products were exchanged between Quito and Panama. The new bishop of Quito, Friar Alonso Fernández de Santillán, and the new oidor, Manuel Tello de Velasco, traveled from Panama to Santiago by sea and then overland to Quito on the new trail.[17] The Bahía de Caráquez road was in operation between 1626 and 1630. José de Arrazábal, who succeeded Martín de Fuica upon the latter's death from drowning in the Daule River, named the new port San Antonio de Morga de Bahía de Caráquez, in honor of the president of the audiencia.[18] President Miguel de Ibarra and Viceroys Montesclaros and Esquilache were similarly honored in the nomenclature of the new settlements whose conquest they patronized.

Many of the key decisions which partially determined the outcome of events in Esmeraldas were made not in Quito but in Lima. An overriding concern of the viceroys of Peru was the defense of the Pacific. Among the war theaters in the Hispano-Dutch global conflict, which ended in 1648, was the west coast of South America. Dutch squadrons entered Pacific waters in 1599, 1600, 1615, 1624, and 1643, seeking to capture the silver fleets plying between Callao and Panama or between Acapulco and Manila. Another objective of the Dutch was to acquire plunder from raiding the coastal settlements. In September of 1624 the Dutch succeeded in sacking and burning the port of Guayaquil. The viceroy was especially concerned with protecting the precious cargo of silver that sailed annually from Callao to Panama and thence to Spain: Peruvian silver was the very lifeblood of the imperial war effort. In viceregal terms the conquest of Esmeraldas therefore was subordinated to the overall strategy of defense against the Dutch.[19]

Don Juan de Mendoza y Luna, Marquis of Montesclaros and viceroy of Peru from 1606 to 1614, was an enthusiastic patron of the conquest of Esmeraldas. In 1611 he granted the contract to Pablo Durango del Gadillo, and he assigned the task of local supervision to the president of the audiencia of Quito. Montesclaros, a partisan of a mobile and aggressive strategy, favored the opening up of new ports as a means of providing the Spaniards with greater striking mobility against the Dutch.

During the administration of his successor, Francisco de Borja y Aragón, Prince of Esquilache (1614–21), the strategy of mobility fell into disfavor. The authorities in Lima began to question the desirability of new settlements along the coast. Not only would new ports have to be defended at considerable expense, but their very existence would provide the Dutch with inviting targets for plunder and provisions. Furthermore, new ports might facilitate invasions into the interior. The new strategy was static and defensive: starve the Dutch out of the Pacific coastal waters by restricting the coastal communities to a minimum, for the capture of a well-guarded silver fleet was chancy at best. It occurred only twice off the Pacific coast with Drake and Rogers each capturing a Manila galleon. The most damaging effects of "piracy" in the Pacific, as Peter Gerhard has suggested, may not have been so much the considerable inconvenience and financial loss it entailed at the time as the defense-inspired decision to discourage settlement along the coast. The long stretches of unsettled littoral along the Pacific in both Spanish North America and South America may be traced in part to this policy.[20]

The nonsettlement policy was gradually taking shape during the 1620's, at the very time when the fate of Esmeraldas was being decided. In fact, the plan to conquer this area was, at least partially, a casualty of the new defense strategy.

Viceroys Esquilache and Guadalcázar but not Viceroy Chinchón stressed the danger that new ports would provide the Dutch with springboards from which to attack the populous towns of the Sierra.[21] While this danger never materialized, the fears of the viceroys were not unjustified: in 1624 only incompetent leadership on the part of the Dutch high command prevented a landing at some point on the coast of Chile; in 1643 a Dutch expedition actually spent a few months in Valdivia in southern Chile. Evidently the Dutch had no territorial designs on the Esmeraldas coast, but the viceroys did not realize that.[22] In addition the viceroys pointed out that new ports might encourage the zambos to join forces with the Dutch. And, indeed, the Dutch expedition in Valdivia did place high hopes on exploiting Araucanian hostility against the Spaniards.

The audiencia of Quito and its president, Dr. Morga, doubted that the Dutch possessed sufficient manpower to conduct prolonged military operations in the interior. Even if their manpower were adequate, Dr. Morga was confident that the massive barrier of the Andes would guarantee the failure of any such attack.[23] By 1629 Viceroy Chinchón concurred in this judgment, although he opposed the conquest of Esmeraldas.[24]

Lima's disenchantment with the Esmeraldas enterprise gradually increased between 1617 and 1629. The Prince of Esquilache wrote the city council of Quito and Dr. Morga on October 6, 1617, voicing his uneasiness that the newly explored Bahía de Caráquez trail might facilitate an invasion of the Sierra and that the neighboring zambos might cooperate with the Dutch.[25] Yet he did not veto the project. Although on February 26, 1616, the viceroy had congratulated Dr. Morga on the opening of the Santiago road, within two years he made an about-face.[26] His recommendation to the Council of the Indies on April 16, 1618, was that the conquest of Esmeraldas be abandoned.[27] After the Malaba revolt, Esquilache wrote an "I-told-you-so" letter to the king, although he did authorize the audiencia of Quito to dispatch a punitive expedition.[28]

Before the Malabas closed the Santiago road, the viceroy undercut Governor Durango del Gadillo's position by replacing him as corregidor of San Miguel de Ibarra.[29] In addition to an annual salary of 1,000 pesos, the office of corregidor carried the necessary authority to conscript Indian labor and to mobilize Spanish soldiers and settlers. The city of San Miguel de Ibarra, located in the inter-Andean basin north of that of Quito, had been founded in 1606 as a base of operations from which to penetrate into

Esmeraldas. Furthermore a Spanish settlement had been considered desirable among the rather densely populated Indian communities north of Quito and south of Pasto.[30]

Upon the death of Governor Pablo Durango del Gadillo shortly after the revolt of the Malabas, Quito appealed to Madrid. The Council of the Indies supported Quito's argument that the conquest should be pursued.[31] The new viceroy, Diego Fernández de Córdoba, Marquis of Guadalcázar (1621–28), signed a contract with Captain Francisco Pérez Menacho, who in turn received the indispensable appointment of corregidor of San Miguel de Ibarra. Pérez Menacho, whose sister was married to Dr. Morga's son, a merchant in Lima, enjoyed the cooperation of both Morga and the audiencia in Quito.[32] Between 1623 and 1628 he spent 30,000 pesos of his own funds in the attempt to reopen the road.[33] But his efforts were not sufficient to overcome the hostile Malabas. Nor was he willing to seek an alternative route which would have bypassed the Malabas. It was Santiago or nothing.

When Pérez Menacho died in 1628, the audiencia of Quito recommended Captain Francisco de Frías as his successor. He had not only frontier military experience but also another necessary qualification: means of his own and a willingness to use them. Captain Frías traveled to Lima to secure confirmation of the contract that he had negotiated with the audiencia of Quito.[34] In Lima Frías met with disappointment. At a special junta convoked on November 29, 1629, to examine the Esmeraldas question, the audiencia of Lima not only rejected the proposed contract of Frías; they also vetoed the conquest of the province itself, citing the danger of Dutch penetration into the Sierra, the commercial prosperity of Guayaquil and Callao, the possible cooperation of the Dutch and the zambos, and the probable increase of the contraband trade.[35]

In the place of Captain Frías, Viceroy Guadalcázar appointed Captain Héctor de Villalobos as corregidor of San Miguel de Ibarra.[36] He was also given the title of governor of Esmeraldas. This, however, was a courtesy designation. Lacking means of his own, he could do little or nothing to further the conquest. This fact was appreciated in both Lima and Quito, but much less so in Madrid. Since the Council of the Indies had consistently supported Quito's desire to complete the conquest, the authorities in Lima had to evade Madrid's injunctions with caution. On the surface Villalobos' appointment looked favorable to the continuance of military operations, for he was a veteran of the war in Chile. Since he had no means of his own and owed his appointment to the authorities in Lima who had just vetoed further conquest, Villalobos' title as governor of Esmeraldas was mere window dressing.

Dr. Morga made one last attempt to have Madrid overrule Villalobos' appointment in favor of Quito's candidate.[37] However, the aged president's influence with the Council of the Indies was scant, since his administration was then undergoing a visita general in which a wide variety of abuses was being exposed. Madrid ultimately acquiesced in Lima's viewpoint.

Dominating all the thinking of the viceroys and their advisers was the Dutch threat. Yet there were other, more mundane considerations that stiffened Lima's opposition. The merchants of both Lima-Callao and Guayaquil saw a threat to their vested interests. When the Prince of Esquilache spent a few weeks in Guayaquil during September and October, 1615, on his way to Lima, the Guayaquil merchants probably did not lose the opportunity to fill his ears with anti-Esmeraldas talk. At any rate such was the charge of Dr. Morga. The merchants of Callao, the port of Lima, enjoyed a prosperous business exporting grain and cattle products to Panama. The Esmeraldas ports would reduce the shipping time by several days. Hence wheat from Quito could undersell that from Callao by some four pesos a *fanega* in Panama.[38] The merchants of Callao and Guayaquil brought pressure to bear on the November, 1629, junta of the audiencia, to protect their monopolies.

Another secondary factor that contributed to Lima's growing opposition to the Esmeraldas project was the contraband trade. By this time the monopoly system in which all trade between the peninsula and Spanish South America was channeled through Panama was proving increasingly difficult to enforce. China silks from the Philippines, which were confined to the Mexican market by countless royal edicts, commanded high prices when illicitly sold in Peru and in Quito. To prevent the expansion of the already-flourishing contraband trade, the viceroys were inclined toward restricting the number of functioning ports.

From 1611 to 1629, the attitude in Lima shifted from one of support to reluctance and finally hostility. In Quito, on the other hand, there was general enthusiasm for the project. The economy of the Sierra was largely agrarian, devoted to the production of cattle and sheep as well as the cultivation of corn, wheat, and barley. Quito lacked an export market for these products, whose prices were low as a result of their abundance. Hence the Spanish and creole landowners and the small class of merchants looked eagerly to Panama as a potential market. It is clear that the landowners and merchants in Quito were a significant factor in the audiencia's advocacy of the conquest.[39]

There is some evidence that the merchants and landowners in Quito were unduly optimistic about the Panama market. In contrast to the Santiago trail, which was blocked by the Malabas, the Bahía de Caráquez road was never threatened by hostile natives. Yet it fell into disuse after a few years of service in the 1620's, because the volume of trade apparently did not justify its continuance. As Dr. Morga argued with some cogency, however, the Santiago road possessed two striking advantages over the route to Bahía de Caráquez. The port of Santiago was 150 miles closer to Panama. Nearly half of the Santiago route was by river, whereas the Bahía de Caráquez trail was overland.[40] In the late 1730's, Maldonado avoided the Malabas by laying out a trail to the coast through the Esmeraldas River valley. Maldonado's road, closed by the viceroy in Lima after Maldonado died prematurely, was not in continuous operation long enough for its commercial potentialities to be tested. Certainly the trade possibilities were not as bright as the Quito merchants pictured them, although their prospects were not totally unfounded.

The Spaniards in the Sierra searched for an export market for the colony's agricultural surplus. They evidently did not contemplate any widespread development of the agricultural resources of Esmeraldas. To them, Esmeraldas was little more than a highway over which the products of the Sierra would pass to be exported overseas. Had the colonists in the Sierra been concerned instead with exploiting the agriculture, the effort to subjugate Esmeraldas would have had a stronger stimulus and perhaps a more positive result. The conquest of Esmeraldas had to wait until the twentieth century, when the incentives had broadened and deepened. Modern transportation made the bananas of the region a profitable export crop. In the seventeenth century, the potential products of Esmeraldas were too bulky, the ships too slow, and the adjacent export market too restricted to provide an economic incentive. Panama then did not need tropical products, but it could use wheat, cattle products, and gunpowder.

Although the hostility of the native population initially discouraged penetration, a greater deterrent may have been the very sparseness of the population.[41] The labor supply was not large enough to induce Spanish settlers to overcome native resistance. Labor would have to be imported. Negro slaves were costly, and Indians from the populous Sierra did not easily acclimatize to the lowlands. The crown, on humanitarian grounds, vigorously opposed transplanting highland Indians to lowland climates.[42] Had gold and emeralds, for which the province was inappropriately named, been found in abundant quantities, the Spaniards from the Sierra might easily have mustered sufficient force to subjugate Esmeraldas. The other participants in the conquest, the missionary orders, were demoralized by factionalism and poor discipline.

Moreover, rivalry was developing between the two cities of the kingdom—Quito and Guayaquil. As the capital and largest city in the kingdom, with some 50,000 people, Quito enjoyed prosperity and creature comforts far beyond the reach of Guayaquil. Many in Quito resented the Sierra's dependence on Guayaquil as its principal outlet for commerce. The political authorities in Quito pointed out the turbulent conditions in the port. Warehouses with Quito's merchandise were frequently raided by armed bands.[43] The populous Castro clan's virtual monopoly of municipal offices provoked riots and disorders. The Castros had emerged as the dominant faction in the port town after the Dutch had laid waste to the city in the summer of 1624. Guayaquil in those days was a rough, tough port town with about 152 Spanish property owners *(vecinos)* plus a Negro and mulatto population of a few thousand, among whom law and order were often the exception rather than the rule.

Around 1620 Viceroy Esquilache, who became hostile to the Esmeraldas project, had forbidden the export of cacao from Guayaquil to the ports of Central America and Mexico in the hope that the absence of legal maritime traffic at Guayaquil would reduce the opportunities for contraband. Thus the flourishing production of cacao in the Guayas lowlands, which had climbed to a million-peso-a-year business between 1600 and 1615, disappeared by the early 1620's. The value of cacao plummeted from 36 pesos per *arroba* to 3 pesos.[44] The collapse of the cacao boom hit Guayaquil with its full impact just as the Dutch arrived to burn the city to the ground. Hence these twin misfortunes drove the citizens of the port to cling with even greater tenacity to their last hope for prosperity—the near-monopoly of trade with the Sierra towns. Thus, although in regional terms Quito's rivalry with Guayaquil is understandable, from the viceroy's point of view it made no sense. Guayaquil's continued prosperity was essential to the defense effort, since the port was the principal shipyard in Spanish South America. According to mercantile principles, Guayaquil's quasi-monopoly of trade with the Sierra towns was desirable. Such concentration facilitated the viceroy's task of supervising licit commerce and suppressing contraband.

The initial push for the conquest of Esmeraldas came from the *cabildos* of Quito and San Miguel de Ibarra.[45] The town councils were the stronghold of the well-to-do and prominent citizens. The office of alderman, *regidor,* was apt to be hereditary, a status symbol purchased by an affluent citizen from the crown for prestige. The aldermen owned the farms and estates whose products needed an export market. The contract to open the Bahía de Caráquez-Quito road was first negotiated by the cabildo of Quito with Martín de Fuica, a merchant. The cabildo of San Miguel de Ibarra vigorously agitated for the conquest of Esmeraldas. But the cabildos lacked the resources and the political powers to carry out these projects.

When Dr. Antonio de Morga took possession of the office of president of the royal audiencia of Quito on September 29, 1615, the audiencia had already superseded the cabildos as the principal advocate of these enterprises. This was an inevitable development, since the conquest contracts had to receive the approval of the viceroy. The president of the audiencia was the viceroy's deputy for political and military matters. Although the audiencia had been involved in the Esmeraldas question prior to 1615, Dr. Morga made this cause peculiarly his own.[46] He argued for the project with conviction, eloquence, and persistence before the authorities in both Spain and Lima. He championed the viewpoint of the landowners and merchants as well as expressing his personal views on defense strategy against the Dutch.

Morga was in fact a partisan of the mobile and offensive strategy which was losing favor in the 1620's.[47] He stressed the positive contributions that the Esmeraldas road and port could make to the whole defense effort of the Spanish Pacific. Panama, which was then the west coast's link with Europe, had to import food and munitions from Peru. Quito could supply Panama with manpower, munitions, and provisions in sixteen days' time over the Esmeraldas road, several days sooner than it could be provisioned from either Guayaquil or Callao. At Latacunga, 36 miles south of Quito, there was a gunpowder factory, one of the major arsenals of the Pacific coast, from which munitions were dispatched annually to Panama via Guayaquil.[48] The viceroys took no heed of Morga's valid arguments.

Although Dr. Morga sincerely believed in the utility of the conquest of Esmeraldas on both economic and strategic grounds, he also had more personal reasons for favoring the project. Before arriving in Quito, he had served in subordinate posts in the audiencias of Manila and Mexico. He apparently enjoyed his new freedom in Quito, where he had no resident superior, and wished to extend it.

Throughout his correspondence with the king and the Council of the Indies in Spain during some twenty-one years in office, Morga betrayed his impatience with Lima's jurisdiction over the kingdom of Quito.[49] Stressing the distance between the two capitals, Morga argued that the viceroy in Lima lacked a realistic grasp of regional conditions. The president was not satisfied with being delegated limited authority by the viceroys in political matters. All his actions in this sphere had to be ratified in Lima.

As early as April, 1618, Morga recommended to the Council of the Indies that the kingdom of Quito be detached from the jurisdiction of the vice-royalty of Peru and made directly responsible to the Council of the Indies in Spain. What Morga was proposing was that the president of the audiencia should be made another viceroy. Morga justified his request on the grounds of greater administrative efficiency and the local magistrates' superior knowledge of regional conditions. In order to avoid the charge of personal ambition, Morga, citing his thirty-seven years in the royal service, asked to be retired if his proposal were adopted.[50]

Morga's proposal did not even merit a reply from the Council of the Indies, since it violated the very intent and spirit of the imperial bureaucracy. In an age of slow communications over great distances, the policy of the Spanish crown reflected an abiding distrust of its officers overseas. Each of the functions of government was deliberately divided among several agencies in order to curb the personal ambition of individual bureaucrats and to provide some check against corruption and malfeasance. Although the viceroy did exercise considerable supervisory control over Quito, the local audiencia could appeal directly to Madrid. And Madrid did side with Quito against Lima on several issues. In making his proposal, Dr. Morga, a career bureaucrat himself, was protesting against the system of checks and balances which was the very core of the bureaucratic structure.

Morga's suggestion also illustrates his personal reasons for advocating with such vigor the conquest of Esmeraldas. A secure road across the Esmeraldas country would put the kingdom of Quito in more rapid communication with Panama and Spain. An outlet on the coast of Esmeraldas would lend some geo-political reality to his pretension of the Quito tribunal's freedom from direct dependence on Lima.

When Dr. Morga died on July 21, 1636, the failure of the conquest of Esmeraldas was an established fact. The audiencia and the cabildo of San Miguel de Ibarra subsequently made sporadic efforts to breathe new life into the moribund project.[51] Abortive contracts were signed with Captain Juan Vicencio Justiniano in 1657,[52] Nicolás de Andagoya y Otalora in 1677,[53] and Fernando de Soto Calderón in 1713.[54] The corpse, however, could not be resuscitated.

In the eighteenth century, the little ports along the coast received only an occasional shipwrecked vessel or cargo of contraband goods. Perceptive observers like Jorge Juan y Santacilla (1712–73) and Antonio de Ulloa (1716–95) reversed the argument of the viceroys of Peru of the previous century: The failure of the Spaniards to establish a port in Esmeraldas and a safe road into the interior would invite foreign aggression against the towns of the Sierra.[55]

Success of a kind came at last. With the enthusiastic support of Dioniso de Alcedo, president of the audiencia, Pedro Vicente Maldonado y Soto-mayor took possession of the governorship of Esmeraldas on April 16, 1738. A native of Riobamba with private means, Maldonado was also a scientist who, along with Jorge Juan and Antonio de Ulloa, collaborated in the La Condamine mission (1734–40) to measure the arc of the earth at the equator.

It took several years to build the road. About 160 conscript Indians were required. The terminus of Maldonado's route was the mouth of the Es-meraldas River and not the estuary of the Santiago River, which a century earlier had been the objective of Pablo Durango del Gadillo. Thus Maldonado bypassed the territory of the hostile Malabas. Once again bad luck struck. Maldonado, who had gone to Spain on business connected with the road, died suddenly in London on his way back to Quito. The new president of the audiencia and the viceroy in Lima closed the road on the ground that the new port merely served to facilitate the contraband trade. Maldonado's legal heir as governor of Esmeraldas was his son-in-law, Manuel Díez de la Peña. But he was denied the governorship and compelled to accept the consolation prize of a five-year term as corregidor of San Miguel de Ibarra. Like Pablo Durango del Gadillo before him, Maldonado had spent most of his personal estate in the venture. Both men achieved momentary success, but their efforts came to nothing because of their sudden deaths.[56]

Two more fruitless attempts were made. Baron de Carondelet, president of the audiencia, signed a contract with Miguel Ponce in the early nineteenth century.[57] When Simón Bolívar passed through Ecuador on his way to Peru, he issued a decree on June 25, 1822, ordering the reopening of the Es-meraldas road, a project, he added, that "would rain a torrent of prosperity upon Quito."[58] The Liberator planted a seed in barren ground.

In summary, the failure of the conquest of Esmeraldas derived from a combination of delicately balanced factors. Of course, the towering barrier of the Andes was an obstacle, but topography itself was not invincible. Native resistance was another impediment. The Spanish colony in the Sierra, however, had sufficient resources to organize a prolonged offensive capable of crushing both the zambos and the Indians if the Spanish will to conquer had not been debilitated by disunity and insufficient incentive. The concern of the Spaniards in Quito was not to develop the resources of

Esmeraldas as such but merely to open up a road across the province to a
port on the Pacific. There was not enough in Esmeraldas itself to induce the
Spanish settlers and soldiers to undertake a territorial occupation in the
classic Spanish pattern with soldiers followed by missionaries. In the conquest of the Chichimeca country in north-central Mexico, the known existence of rich silver deposits stiffened the Spanish will to conquer the
militantly hostile Indians.[59] Had there been such a stimulus in the case of
Esmeraldas, nothing could have prevented the conquest. The negative attitude of the viceroys should be seen in this perspective. Enthusiastic support
from Lima during the 1620's would by no means have guaranteed the success of the project, although it might have helped. Dr. Morga's persistence
and eloquence notwithstanding, the incentives in Quito were too narrow to
offset the initial impediments of topography and native hostility. Although
there was no apparent alternative to the asiento system at the time, the
flaw was that it placed too much reliance on the particular man who possessed the temerity to risk his capital and sometimes his life in this uncertain venture.

The long-range consequences of the Esmeraldas project's failure were
momentous for the subsequent development of what was to become Ecuador. The Sierra remained virtually isolated from the rest of the world for
three hundred years. Behind the protective barrier of the Andes, a manorial-
type society, in which landownership was concentrated in the hands of a
small class of white colonists with a dense and docile Indian population providing cheap labor, consolidated itself. It was a hierarchal and paternalist
society, tradition-bound and tenaciously attached to the rituals but seldom
to the ethical spirit of Spanish baroque Catholicism. Not until the twentieth
century were the traditionalist patterns of the Sierra challenged by new
breezes of modernity coming from the metropolis of the coast, Guayaquil.
Had Esmeraldas been colonized in the seventeenth century, the subsequent
character of society in the Sierra might have been less tradition-bound and
therefore more receptive to novelty. Hence a more dynamic balance between
the Sierra and the coast might have emerged long before the present century.

A more positive and direct consequence was that the absence of functioning ports on the Esmeraldas coast helped to ensure Guayaquil's modern role
as the undisputed metropolis of the coast. Since there was no stable network
of towns along the coast and in the Sierra, Quito and Guayaquil in modern
times became the two dominant cities. Each controlled the economic life of
an extensive hinterland that was sparsely or unevenly settled and poorly
organized for commercial exchange.[60] Some of the origins for this modern

condition, I suggest, must be sought in the seventeenth-century failure to conquer Esmeraldas.

This study in failure throws some light on the decision-making process in the colonial bureaucracy. The imperial administration was not as tightly centralized as has often been assumed. A good many of the decisions were actually made in the Indies among several competing agencies, with local conditions and local interest groups playing a significant role. Although Madrid favored the conquest of Esmeraldas in principle, the authorities in the Indies had much more to do with directing the course of events than did the Council of the Indies. In part, at least, the abortive conquest of Esmeraldas became a struggle of wills between the viceroy in Lima and the audiencia in Quito. The viceroys not only had to take antagonistic vested commercial interests into account, they also had to weigh the relative importance of two injunctions issued in Spain: the defense of the Pacific coast against the Dutch and the acquisition of new coastal settlements. Lima concluded that the latter jeopardized the former. Madrid ultimately acquiesced. Thus decision-making in the imperial bureaucracy could be substantially decentralized.

2.

THE THRUST TO THE AMAZON:
SUCCESS AND FAILURE

The first half of the seventeenth century was a period of modest success for Spanish efforts to explore and to settle the "third Quito," that is, the upper Amazon basin with its dense tropical forests and flat jungle lands, which lay to the east of the cordillera. The unspectacular but real success of the Spaniards in the Oriente contrasts sharply with their more dramatic failure to subdue Esmeraldas.

Gonzalo Pizarro, brother of the conqueror of Peru and the first Spanish governor of Quito, sponsored the initial exploration of the Amazon in one of the most spectacular odysseys in the age of discovery. The expedition, consisting of two hundred Spaniards and several thousand Indians, left Quito in February, 1541. Pizarro's lieutenant, Francisco de Orellana, made the remarkable journey of more than 3,000 miles down the Amazon and then by sea to the Venezuelan coast. Some 2,000 miles separated Quito from the Atlantic. The feat was not to be repeated again for nearly a century.

Subsequent to the Pizarro-Orellana expedition, the Spaniards carved out the province of Quijos, to which Zumaco and La Canela belonged. This region lay directly opposite the city of Quito on the eastern side of the Andes. Baeza, its capital, was 60 miles from Quito. A small number of Spaniards settled in Baeza, Archidona, and Ávila. The Napo River, flowing through the province in a southeasterly direction, joins the main branches of the Amazon. Without significant minerals, that hot and humid land had, as its major resource, a sturdy cotton crop, which was in lively demand throughout the viceroyalty.

Following the general Spanish practice in the New World, the Indian population in Quijos was distributed among the colonists under the *encomienda* system. The *encomendero,* who received an annual tribute from his Indian wards, pledged in return to protect his wards and to prepare them to receive the Catholic faith. The Franciscan friars followed the encomenderos into the province. That the encomenderos abused their privileges over the Indians in a wide variety of illegal exactions is evident. Such was the tendency in encomiendas throughout the Spanish empire in their initial phase.

Settled by a mere handful of Spaniards, the province of Quijos was tenuously held. A general uprising of Indians in 1579 wiped out Spanish settlements at Archidona, Ávila, and Sevilla de Oro, thus confining the Spanish community to a small area around Baeza. All the contemporary sources place the blame for the revolt on the conduct of an oidor of the audiencia of Quito, Lic. Ortegón, who made a tour of inspection, a *visita de la tierra,* shortly before the Indians revolted. The mission of the judge was to correct abuses and to protect the Indians from illegal exactions by their encomenderos. During a whirlwind, forty-day visit in the area, he held forty trials against both the Indians and the encomenderos, collecting between 7,000 and 8,000 pesos in fines. Subsequent investigations of his conduct by the audiencia of Quito resulted in Lic. Ortegón's conviction for flagrant abuses of his authority, not the least of which was his pocketing some 4,000 pesos that belonged to the royal treasury. Although the audiencia fined him 3,000 pesos, the oidor managed to evade payment.

Reacting to the fines imposed on them by the judge-visitor, the encomenderos put pressure on the Indians to provide them with considerably more cotton than their customary annual allotment. The new exactions led the Indians to revolt. Although Oidor Ortegón may have set in motion a train of events precipitating the uprising, its success may be traced directly to the fact that the isolated province was weakly held by a few dozen Spanish encomenderos. While Ortegón was personally corrupt, he did uncover a number of abuses committed by the encomenderos against the Indians. In this respect he was acting well within the spirit and the letter of the law. By fining the encomenderos large sums, he prompted the latter to pass the burden on to the Indians. That action proved to be the proverbial straw that broke the overworked backs of the Indians.

The revolt spread through the province with the intensity of a tropical storm. Spaniards in isolated communities such as Ávila and Archidona were slaughtered by the enraged Indians in massacres whose gory details Spanish chroniclers recounted with pious horror. As generally happened with Indian uprisings, the revolt took the Spaniards completely by surprise.

Fearful that the uprising in the Oriente would spread across the Andes to nearby Quito, the audiencia undertook feverish precautions. Among them was to confiscate on sight all horses, reins, and arms possessed by Indians. In the valley of Quito there were only 1,200 Spanish vecinos and about 100,000 Indians. To be sure, the Sierra Indians were more docile than the lowland Indians, since the former had been subjugated by both the Incas and the Spaniards.

The audiencia also dispatched an expedition of three hundred horsemen and footsoldiers under the command of Captain Rodrigo Núñez de Bonilla, a son of the governor of Quijos who founded Baeza. This prompt military action managed to save Baeza as the last Spanish outpost in the province. A show of force, in addition to a general amnesty to all but the ringleaders, soon pacified the province.

Upon being captured, the four leaders of the revolt were dispatched to Quito for trial. The audiencia condemned them to death for treason and apostasy. Determined to strike sufficient fear into the hearts of the Indians to banish any thought of future rebellions, the audiencia compelled the caciques of both Quito and Quijos to witness the execution. The four condemned men were paraded through the streets of the capital in open carts in which they were being tortured by red-hot forceps. After they had been hanged until dead, their bodies were quartered and strewn on several highways outside the city. The heads of the dead men were left at the place of execution to rot.[1] Such was the time-honored punishment for those found guilty of treason.

The province of Quijos after 1579 languished in misery and poverty. From 1576 to 1608, the proprietary governor of the province was a well-to-do encomendero from Cuzco, Melchor Vázquez de Ávila. The government of the province, such as it was, lay in the hands of lieutenants appointed by the absentee governor. The fact that his brother was a prominent adviser to Philip II undoubtedly discouraged any sustained efforts to compel the absentee governor to perform the responsibilities of leadership.[2]

After the death of Melchor Vázquez de Ávila's grandson, who had succeeded the elder encomendero as proprietary governor, there was more direct royal control. In place of a proprietary governorship, the office became a five-year term filled by the king. The first of these royal appointees was Alonso de Miranda, who took possession on March 13, 1617. During the years of Dr. Antonio de Morga's presidency of the audiencia of Quito, at least two of the appointed governors sought to revitalize the province. Their activity, however, yielded meager results.

Alonso de Miranda concluded that a basic cause of the weakness of Spanish control was that the majority of the encomenderos did not reside in the province. Only five of the twenty-one encomenderos lived in Quijos. The rest were in Quito. Governor Miranda was not the first to point out this condition, but he was the most energetic in trying to change it. Royal legislation provided that encomenderos should not reside in the immediate vicinity of their Indian wards lest they be tempted to impose all kinds of illegal exactions on them. However, the law did require encomenderos to live in the capital of the province where they held Indians.[3] Among their obligations was one of feudal origin to serve as a militia at their own expense in times of war or rebellion. In a frontier area such as Quijos, the military services of the encomenderos were not merely *pro forma,* as they tended to be in the more settled provinces.

Governor Miranda appealed to the king and the Council of the Indies, with the result that a royal cedula on August 30, 1619, instructed the audiencia to order the encomenderos of Quijos to reside in the province. The encomenderos of Quijos who lived in Quito brought considerable pressure to bear on the audiencia. Using the "I obey but do not execute" formula, the audiencia suspended the execution of the cedula. The "I obey" phrase denoted the respect enshrined in Roman law for the legitimacy of the royal authority, which, if properly informed of all conditions, would never will an injustice. The "but do not execute" phrase represented the discretionary authority of subordinates.[4] The magistrates pointed out that there were plausible reasons for the absence of the majority of the encomenderos from Quijos: Some encomenderos held larger encomiendas elsewhere; some had urgent litigations before the audiencia which required their prolonged presence in the capital; others were in poor health, and some held "paper" encomiendas located in inaccessible places peopled by hostile Indians who were subjects of the crown in name only.[5]

This incident illustrates the decentralization of decision-making in the imperial bureaucracy, in which the lines of authority were intentionally kept vague by a crown suspicious of all its subordinates in the Indies. On one hand, the governor of an isolated frontier province had appealed directly to the crown over the head of his nominal superior, the audiencia. The king and the Council of the Indies had responded favorably to the governor's proposal and ordered the audiencia to enforce it. That tribunal, on the other hand, responding to the pleas of the absentee encomenderos of Quijos, set up an effective roadblock. Similarly, in dealing with the audiencia's advocacy of the conquest of Esmeraldas, we had occasion to observe how the viceroy of Peru, the ostensible superior of the audiencia, could thwart the recommendations of the Quito authorities who had enlisted the approval of the Council of the Indies in Spain.

However justified the audiencia may have been in refusing to impose the cedula of 1619, the fact that the majority of the encomenderos were absentees largely accounts for the feeble control the Spaniards exercised over Quijos. The audiencia did attempt to correct this situation by dispatching a small expedition of eighty soldiers. The rigors of the tropical climate and poor leadership soon reduced the expedition to thirty-four men who dejectedly complained they were abandoned to hunger and discomfort in isolated places by the governor and their commander living in Baeza.[6]

Álvaro de Cárdenas, who succeeded Alonso de Miranda as governor of Quijos, also sought to arrest the decay of the province. In 1625 there were five Spanish settlements with 27 vecinos and 1,934 pacified Indians. The governor claimed that the Franciscan friars had done little or nothing to indoctrinate the Indians but had concentrated on exploiting their charges. He urged the replacement of the Franciscans by the secular clergy on the grounds that the bishop might be able to exercise more effective supervision than had the superiors of the Franciscans. The bishop of Quito, on the other hand, argued that the most rapacious exploiters of the Indians were the governor and the encomenderos. In the face of these charges and countercharges, the Council of the Indies piously instructed the audiencia in 1627 to correct any abuses uncovered. The audiencia did little.[7] Its energies were absorbed by the bitter internecine struggle arising out of the visita general of Lic. Mañozca.

Several conditions explain the stagnation of Quijos during the Morga period. The torpor was well ingrained long before Morga arrived in Quito, for the province never did make a healthy recovery from the Indian rebellion of 1579. The only positive step Dr. Morga undertook to revive the area was to dispatch a small military force. His interest in Quijos was at best perfunctory and occasional.[8] His energies as a would-be conquistador were directed not inward toward Amazonia but outward toward the Pacific coast. Aggressive support from Quito might have contributed toward restoring the prosperity of the province during the early years of the Morga administration, when the governors were striving toward reform. But this argument cannot be carried too far. Troops, money, and settlers from either Quito or Lima or from both were not enough in themselves to guarantee success. Both Esmeraldas and Quijos lacked the natural and human resources to induce the Spaniards of the Sierra to mount a sufficiently sustained offensive to subjugate either region. The cotton of Quijos, some of which the Spaniards cultivated and exported to Peru in finished goods, was not a powerful enough incentive. Although Indian and zambo hostility initially discouraged the Spaniards in both areas, in the final analysis it was not the hostility but the paucity of the Indian population that was decisive. A dense aboriginal population capable of being reduced to a servile labor force or the presence of significant mineral resources might have aroused the Spaniards of the Sierra.

The paucity of Indians discouraged the missionaries also from going to Quijos in large numbers. The mere handful of Franciscans was never able to conduct a program of Christianization, comparable to the indoctrination of the Indians in the Sierra valleys, which would have reconciled the Indians to the new regime.

In the early seventeenth century, a somewhat more successful Spanish penetration toward the Amazon or Oriente occurred south of Quijos. The base of operations was Valladolid in the province of Yaguarzongo, which conquistador Juan de Salinas had carved out as his own government in 1560. Valladolid, capital of the province, lay on the eastern foothills of the Andes. From Santiago de las Montañas, near Valladolid, small groups of Spaniards debarked down the Santiago River to the Marañón River, which served as the highway for exploration and conquest. The Marañón River, some 1,000 miles in length, rises on the eastern slopes of the cordillera oriental in present-day Peru, flows north, veering northeastward just south of modern Ecuador, and turns east after it is joined by the Santiago River. Ultimately the Marañón joins the Ucayali and Napo rivers to form the Amazon. The Spaniards named this vast region Mainas, after a prominent Indian tribe living there.

The region of Mainas was first mentioned in the Jesuit annual letter of 1595, but no exploration took place until 1615 when a party of twenty soldiers and many more Indian auxiliaries "pacified" the region along the upper Marañón. The initial purpose of this Spanish expedition was to carry out reprisals on the Mainas Indians, who had sporadically raided adjacent Spanish-controlled settlements.

The expedition aroused the conquistador instinct of a rich and prominent citizen of the city of Loja. Don Diego Vaca de la Vega was sufficiently ambitious and bold to risk some of his own capital in the venture. Furthermore, he was a professional soldier who had served in garrisons in Panama and Callao. He had no illusions about the existence of precious metals in the area. His goal was to conquer for the sake of conquering, to carve out a government for himself. And he was motivated also by a genuine missionary fervor to convert the heathen.

Don Francisco de Borja y Aragón, Prince of Esquilache and then the viceroy of Peru, a scion of the famed Borja family, became the patron of this project to penetrate into the Amazon country. A minor lyric poet and a political protégé of the then all-powerful Duke of Lerma, the Prince of Esquilache was a great-great-grandson of Pope Alexander VI, who in turn was a nephew of Pope Calixtus IV. The viceroy was also the grandson of Francisco de Borja, Duke of Gandia, who after the death of his wife became the second general of the Society of Jesus; he was beatified by Urban VIII in 1624 and canonized by Clement XI in 1671.

The reasons which led several viceroys to oppose new settlements along the Pacific coast did not apply in the case of the Oriente. Since they were directed inward toward the interior of the continent, new settlements there could not provide the Dutch with bases. There were also no vested commercial interests such as those of Callao and Guayaquil whose comfortable monopolies would be jeopardized by the new conquest.

As in the abortive conquest of Esmeraldas, the viceroy used the tried and sometimes successful method of the *asiento*. Diego Vaca de la Vega became corregidor of Yaguarzongo for a five-year term. Among the customary privileges the crown granted to the new conquistador in a contract signed in Lima on September 17, 1618, was the proprietary governorship of Mainas during his lifetime and that of one heir. He also secured the privilege of distributing the Indians into twenty-four encomiendas. In return Diego Vaca de la Vega undertook to pacify the area at his own expense and to found a capital city of the province. The territory was bounded on the west and north by 450 miles of the Marañón River. A royal cedula in 1656 extended the boundaries of the province to include all territories covered by Jesuit and Franciscan missions.

Diego Vaca de la Vega left Santiago de la Montañas with sixty-eight Spanish colonists, one secular priest, four friars, and a large number of Indian auxiliaries. He established his capital at the foothills of the eastern slopes of the Andes on the left bank of the Marañón. The location of the city was east of the narrow and perilous strait in the Marañón, the Pongo de Manseriche. The formal founding was held on December 8, 1619. The name chosen for the city was San Francisco de Borja, in double honor of the viceroy and his grandfather, the future saint.

The isolated little colony, 900 miles from Quito and 240 miles from Jaén de Bracamoros, did not flourish. The governor distributed some seven hundred pacified Indians among twenty-one encomenderos. The Indians became increasingly restless under the harsh burdens imposed on them, and in February, 1635, they rose in revolt, nearly wiping out the struggling colony. As in the 1579 uprising in Quijos, the Spaniards were taken by surprise. A large number of the Spanish citizens—thirty-four of them— were outside the city of San Francisco de Borja at the time; they met death at the hands of the enraged Indians. Twelve Spaniards with their families managed to defend themselves in the hastily fortified parish church in San Francisco de Borja against a multitude of hostile Indians until reinforcements arrived from Santiago de las Montañas. Jesuit sources insist that those remaining in the city were secretly forewarned about the impending revolt by an Indian chieftain who was titular leader of the rebels but also was personally attached to the Spaniards.

Two factors saved the little colony from total extinction. One was the grim determination of the proprietary governor, Diego Vaca de la Vega, and his son and successor, Pedro Vaca de la Cadena.[9] Father and son also played a key role in attracting to Mainas the organization that did save the colony. More than any other single factor, the Society of Jesus was responsible for creating a modicum of stability in that isolated tropical outpost.

Unlike the Augustinians, the Franciscans, and the Dominicans in the seventeenth century, the missionary zeal and discipline of the Jesuits was not sapped by internecine struggles between American-born and Spanish-born priests, a topic which will be taken up in Chapter 12. The high level of Jesuit discipline was the consequence of their more selective recruitment, their more rigorous intellectual training, and the more authoritarian character of their government. In the eighteenth century, missionary zeal was renewed among the Franciscans, who developed a mission territory on the eastern slopes of the Andes, the Montaña region of upper Peru.[10]

The Jesuits needed all the discipline and dedication they could muster in order to maintain a chain of missions along the banks of Marañón, but succeed they did, at least for a while. The first Jesuit contingent of two priests arrived in San Francisco de Borja on February 6, 1638, four years after the rebellion of the Indians. The capital of the province was then a haphazard collection of miserable huts containing forty demoralized Spanish vecinos and several hundred sullen Indians.

Between 1636 and 1680 the Jesuit vice-province in Quito dispatched twenty-one missionaries. During these decades, the Jesuits claim to have baptized 107,035 natives. As a general rule, Jesuit baptismal records are extraordinarily accurate. Although the Franciscans founded some missions, the major responsibility for indoctrinating the Indians of Mainas was charged to the Society of Jesus. The Jesuits financed their missions in the Oriente with the profits coming from their efficiently operated estates in the Sierra.[11]

In terms of the number of missionaries, Spanish colonists, and Indians involved, this string of Jesuit missions represented a modest endeavor indeed. But the stakes were gigantic, for upon the outcome would depend the future control of one of the most fabled river valleys in the world, the Amazon.

According to the treaty of Tordesillas signed on June 6, 1494, the whole Amazon valley belonged to the crown of Castile. The Orellana expedition had solidified this claim. During the decades from 1580 to 1640, when the kingdoms of Castile and Portugal shared the same monarch, with Portugal retaining its separate government, the distinctions of the treaty of Tordesillas became blurred but not erased.

The conquering energy of the Spaniards on the coast of northern South America petered out at the mouth of the Orinoco River. By 1600 the Portuguese had established a chain of modestly prosperous sugar plantations along the northeast coast of Brazil from São Vicente in the south to the hump of Brazil in the north. As of 1600 the vast coastline of some 4,000 miles stretching from the hump of Brazil northwest to the mouth of the Orinoco was a no-man's land in which occasional English, Dutch, French, and Portuguese vessels traded with the natives.

The Portuguese filled this vacuum. In the course of one generation they pushed northwest along the coast for about 3,000 miles. The decisive result of this remarkable advance was that the mouth of the Amazon became Portuguese by virtue of prior colonization. The major stepping stones were the founding of Fortaleza in 1609, São Luis de Maranhão in 1612, and Belém in 1616. The expedition of Pedro Teixeira (1637–39) was a momentous move in which Portugal staked out a claim to the vast hinterland of the Amazon River valley, a region which belonged to Castile according to the treaty of Tordesillas. This was the first expedition from the mouth of the Amazon to Quito since Orellana a century before had journeyed in the opposite direction.

One contemporary source claims that the Council of the Indies sponsored this expedition in order to discover an inland waterway between the Atlantic and the Pacific oceans that was defensible against the intrusions of the Dutch. Other accounts flatly contradict this version. The audiencia of Quito was shocked by the unexpected arrival in Quito of the bedraggled members of the Teixeira expedition. The Spanish authorities hospitably received the Portuguese explorers and provisioned them for the return voyage, but the Spaniards politely told the Portuguese to go back from where they had come.[12]

Two Spanish Jesuits, who accompanied Teixeira on his return to Belém, journeyed on to Madrid where before Philip IV, king of Castile and Portugal, they claimed the whole Amazon valley as the missionary preserve of the Spanish Jesuits. A few days later on December 1, 1640, Portugal repudiated the sovereignty of the Spanish monarch. From that date onward, the ownership of the vast Amazon basin ceased to be a family quarrel between two peoples sharing the same king and became an international conflict between two sovereign powers often engaged in territorial and political disputes in both Europe and America.

How the Portuguese secured the lion's share of the Amazon valley was largely the consequence of a chain of events initiated by the Teixeira expedition. The underlying causes must be sought in the special character of missionary and nonmissionary penetration into the Amazon on the part of both the Spaniards and the Portuguese.

There were seldom more than one hundred Spanish colonists in the whole area at any one time during the seventeenth century. They were concentrated in and around the only Spanish town, San Francisco de Borja. The Jesuit missionaries therefore had a free hand to supervise the Indians. At its maximum extent, their string of missions served a vast area from the Pongo de Manseriche in the west to the mouth of the Negro River in the east, some 1,311 miles in length, and from the Napo River in the north to the upper Ucayali in the south for a distance of 725 miles. During the "golden age" of these missions, the Jesuits ministered to over 100,000 neophytes. Jesuit control, however, was more nominal than real. A series of events after 1680 led to the decay of the Spanish Jesuit "empire" in Amazonia.

The special character of Indian culture provides us with one explanation. Although the majority of these sylvan peoples belonged to the Tupí-Guaraní family, which stretched from Paraguay to the heart of the Amazon basin, there were 40 different languages and 140 dialects spoken. The missionaries communicated with their charges in the lingua franca of the Tupí-Guaraní, a not always satisfactory medium of communication. The linguistic diversity was in large measure a reflection of the decentralized character of settlement patterns. Among the Amazonian Indians, there were few political units beyond the extended family. These kinship units seldom consisted of more than six or seven families.[13]

There was only one feasible means for the Jesuits to overcome this geographical particularism. The Indians must be "congregated," in the official terminology, into compact villages varying in size between 2,400 and 5,000 people. Only thus could a few dozen Jesuits hope to reach the large numbers of heretofore scattered people. The Spaniards faced the same obstacle all over the Indies in one degree or another. Even in Mexico, where there were some large urban centers in the preconquest period, the Spaniards had to undertake a massive resettlement program.[14] The dispersal of the population, however, was much more extensive in the Philippines and in the upper Amazon valley. Hence some comparisons between the two areas are in order.

Inspiring the resettlement policies of the Spanish regime in all parts of the Indies was a common set of objectives. The natives could not be adequately indoctrinated in the Christian faith, the Spanish program of societal reorganization could not be implemented, or the material resources of the land effectively exploited, unless the Indians were congregated into large villages.

Population dispersal in both the Philippines and the Oriente violated an attitude deeply rooted in Spanish culture. As the heirs of Greco-Roman urbanism, the Spaniards instinctively identified civilization with the city, whose origins go back to the polis of ancient Greece. Man was not only a rational animal gifted with the capacity to receive grace, as defined by the medieval theologians; he was also the social animal of the ancient Greeks living in close communion with his fellowmen. Spanish chroniclers both in the Philippines and in Quito endlessly repeated that the natives in those regions lived without polity, *sin policía,* and for them that was synonymous with barbarism.

The Spanish Jesuits in the Amazon country enjoyed some momentary success in congregating the Indians into compact villages. Thirty-two pueblos were formed between 1638 and 1680. The Indians, however, tenaciously resisted resettlement. Those who were cajoled into the villages took the first opportunity to abandon them when epidemics struck. Economic or ecological conditions did not encourage the natives to settle in these villages.

Neither did they in the Philippines. In the traditional rice and fish economy of the islands, no compelling material inducement was offered by the new settlements that the clergy were seeking to organize around the parish churches. The Filipinos were subsistence not surplus farmers. Their adaptation to the environment required that they live adjacent to the land they cultivated. Fishing and hunting were important sources of food supply. The transfer to compact villages threatened to destroy the whole ecological balance of existence, a condition which aroused Filipino hostility to the resettlement policy of the Spaniards.

The clergy did manage to lure the Filipinos into the missionary-founded *cabeceras* on Sundays and major religious holidays, for they were genuinely attracted by the colorful rituals of Spanish baroque Catholicism. They even built Sunday houses in the cabecera towns, but most of them continued to live during the rest of the week adjacent to their rice paddies. Gradually small nuclei settled around the cabecera churches as new patterns of trade justified such a change. In time what emerged was an eclectic compromise between the highly decentralized pattern of preconquest settlement and the much more centralized pattern that the Spaniards wished to impose.[15]

In the Amazon country, conditions were somewhat similar. The Indians practiced a shifting cultivation of manioc and maize, which scarcely encouraged them to settle in one place for more than a few years. Yet the Jesuits achieved the remarkable feat of luring and cajoling 100,000 Indians into thirty-two pueblos by 1680.

In order to secure maximum benefit from their small numbers, the Jesuits divided the Amazon country into ten missions, or *partidos* as they were called, where a pair of Jesuits were stationed. From each mission one Jesuit was ordinarily on the circuit, spending several days or weeks in each pueblo. The ten missions covered the following regions: the upper Marañón or Mainas proper, Pastaza, south of the Huallaga River, north of the Huallaga River, the lower Marañón, Gran Cocoma, Upper Ucayali, Iquitos, Mayorunas, and Gran Omagua.[16]

The organization of this missionary dominion was so precarious that it fell apart after 1680 under the triple blows of epidemics, Indian revolts, and Portuguese invasions. The spread of European-introduced diseases was delayed for nearly thirty years. Once they arrived, however, they took a heavy toll in lives. In 1660 the first epidemic of smallpox killed about 44,000 people, that is, nearly half the mission population. Another epidemic in

Jesuit missions in the Amazon country. Map by the University of Wisconsin
Cartographic Laboratory.

1669 claimed 20,000 victims. The remaining Indians fled en masse from
the pueblos, where population concentration merely facilitated the spread
of epidemic diseases against which the Indians had no acquired immunity.
An epidemic of measles broke out in 1749 and recurred in 1756 and 1762.[17]

The Indians, many of whom were headhunters, were restless under the
guidance of their Jesuit mentors. Local revolts broke out periodically in
different areas. The most successful of these was the uprising in the Ucayali
region in which 40,000 Indians threw off Spanish missionary rule in 1742
under the messianic leadership of a semi-hispanized Indian from Cuzco,
Juan Santos Atahualpa.[18]

In the whole province of Mainas, all the Spanish laymen were concentrated in the valley of the upper Marañón around and in the city of San Francisco de Borja. This condition was both an advantage and a disadvantage to the missionary enterprise. It meant that the Jesuits had a free hand in organizing the Indians elsewhere in the hinterland. Missionary spokesmen all over the Indies often argued that the demands placed on Indian labor by the colonists clashed with the Christianization of the natives. In the Spanish Amazon and some other areas also this argument proved unrealistic. Without substantial Spanish colonization and some military force lurking in the background, it was almost impossible to keep the natives under missionary control, since most of them clung tenaciously to their old ways of life. A few dozen Jesuits, dedicated and skillful though they might have been, lacked effective coercive means to stifle revolts.

A minimum of Spanish military power was desirable, but large numbers of Spaniards meant that the clergy would lose effective control over the natives. Such was the case in the Sierra where Spanish colonists subjected the Indians to harsh demands. Unable to protect the Indians in the Sierra from being taken advantage of by the colonists, many of the regular clergy ultimately joined the colonists in exploiting them. From a missionary point of view, the ideal situation was that in upper California in the late eighteenth century. The area was sparsely settled with colonists, and attached to each mission was a very small garrison of professional soldiers. There were too many Spaniards in the Sierra and too few in the Oriente to enable the regular clergy in either area to create the kind of Utopia that the best among them ardently desired.

In the Seven Missions of Paraguay, the Spanish Jesuits allowed no colonists. They armed the Guaraní Indians against the incursions of the slave-hunting Paulistas from Brazil. The Guaraní Indians in Paraguay were much more docile than their Amazonian cousins; their ecology and their climate were suited to sedentary agriculture and hence to permanent, compact settlements easily supervised by the Jesuits. The contrary was true in the Oriente.

What made effective and permanent European settlement extremely difficult in the Amazon country was its tropical climate. Most Europeans could not live there in the seventeenth century, nor can many of them live there now, but a few did manage to survive in the face of severe hardship.

The almost total absence of Spanish military power left the missions on the lower Marañón a prey to the marauding forays of the Portuguese. Portuguese penetration into the Amazon basin from east to west contrasts sharply with that of the Spaniards from the foothills of the Andes eastward.

There were sufficient numbers of Portuguese colonists who demanded the labor services of the Indians. Desperately poor and hence unable to afford Negro slaves, they needed an inexpensive supply of Indian labor.

The Portuguese Franciscans initially fought the desire of the colonists to enslave the Indians. When they became discouraged, the Jesuits took up this cause with renewed determination. The battle seesawed between the two powerful antagonists until the compromise of 1686. Recognizing the need of the colonists for a supply of labor, the crown approved *entradas* or expeditions into the interior to capture Indians, and granted the religious broad powers to supervise the entradas. Captured Indians were congregated into villages or *aldeias* near the Portuguese settlements. The Portuguese missionaries supervised the administration of the aldeias. The compromise of 1686 laid down the conditions under which Indians in the villages might work for the Portuguese colonists. Paternalistically inspired regulations sought to afford some basic protection to the Indians in such areas as minimum wages and price controls. No Indian could work for a Portuguese colonist for more than six months out of each year. Nor could colonists live in the aldeias. From 1686 to 1755, when the Society of Jesus was expelled from the Portuguese empire, the Jesuit missions prospered. Disease, an unhealthy climate, and a scarcity of many resources, on the other hand, deprived the Portuguese colonists of any solid basis of prosperity.[19]

Given the pressure for fresh supplies of Indians, the Portuguese penetrated into the lower Marañón where the Spanish Jesuits had a precarious hold. As early as 1689, a German Jesuit, Father Fritz, who had been held captive by the Portuguese for several months, went to Lima and warned against Portuguese penetration into the Rio Negro.[20] Lima did not heed these warnings. In 1710 during the War of the Spanish Succession, when Portugal and Spain were in opposing camps, an expedition of 1,500 Portuguese and mestizos and 4,000 Indians plundered the Spanish missions. They pushed up the Amazon to the Yavarí River. Capturing thousands of Omagua Indians on the dubious pretext of cannibalism, they also destroyed several Spanish mission villages in an area stretching over 600 miles from the Negro to the Yavarí rivers.[21] Another mammoth Portuguese enslaving expedition in 1732 arrived at the Napo River itself. Only two Spanish Jesuits, one of whom the Portuguese captured, were in the area at the time.[22] They were powerless to organize any kind of effective resistance to the well-directed Portuguese attacks.

Thus the Spanish Jesuit missions disintegrated in the eighteenth century under the triple scourge of epidemics, revolts, and invasions. By 1762 there were only 18,000 neophytes confined to the upper Marañón and the upper Napo rivers. The struggle was no mere family quarrel between the Spanish and Portuguese Jesuits, as the famous French traveler La Condamine claimed in 1739.[23] The consequences were far-reaching, for the heart of the Amazon valley fell to Portuguese Brazil, with the Spaniards confined to only the upper drainage. The treaty of San Ildefonso, signed between the crowns of Portugal and Spain on October 1, 1777, merely confirmed the partition of the Amazon River basin which missionaries, explorers, settlers, and slavehunters had pragmatically worked out over the course of 150 years.

Not only was the basic partition of Amazonia between the Portuguese and the Spaniards determined by events going back to the time of Dr. Morga, but also the origins of one of the bitterest territorial disputes in contemporary Latin America may be traced to those remote happenings. The frontier quarrel concerns the republics of Peru and Ecuador.

Countless royal cedulas, the most important one being that of April 2, 1691, assigned the whole province of Mainas to the judicial and administrative jurisdiction of the audiencia of Quito and in the ecclesiastical sphere to the diocese of Quito. The boundaries of the province included the whole basin of the upper Amazon, over which the Spaniards exercised control or to which they laid claim. The Jesuit and Franciscan provinces in Quito supported and maintained their respective missions in Mainas.

It is a serious historical error to regard the audiencias in the Indies as merely judicial tribunals. That they were, but in Spanish juridical theory and practice, each audiencia was a kingdom, one of *los reynos de las Indias,* subordinate to and inalienable from the crown of Castile and León. The Spanish concept of the state was essentially medieval in that the administration of justice, not legislative or executive authority, was regarded as the highest attribute of sovereignty. Hence the chief organ of government in the overseas kingdoms was a tribunal of justice. Although each audiencia was a separate kingdom, not all the audiencias were equal among themselves. Quito, for example, was one of the "inferior" audiencias until 1720, for its jurisdiction was essentially judicial in character. The viceroy in Lima exercised political, administrative, and military control in theory, although in practice during the seventeenth century he tended to delegate a good deal of this authority to the tribunal in Quito. In 1720 the kingdom of Quito separated from the viceroyalty of Peru and joined the new viceroyalty of the New Kingdom of Granada with its capital in Bogotá. In the eighteenth century the audiencia of Quito enjoyed "superior" status, exercising *de jure* both military and political jurisdiction in the kingdom.[24]

When the Spanish empire dissolved in the early nineteenth century, the

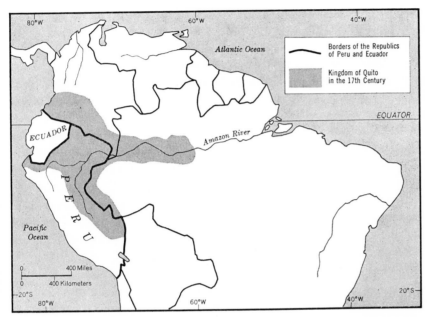

The republics of Ecuador and Peru today and the kingdom of Quito in the
seventeenth century. Map by the University of Wisconsin Cartographic
Laboratory.

smaller audiencia kingdoms and not the much larger viceroyalties, of which
there were four in 1810, became the nuclei of the independent republics.
After political emancipation, a host of boundary disputes, a few of which
erupted into war but most of which were settled by diplomatic negotiation,
arose because of vague demarcations between the audiencia kingdoms of
colonial times. According to the *uti possidetis* of 1810, which became the
generally accepted basis for solving boundary disputes, the province of
Mainas should have fallen to the Republic of Ecuador.

Ecuador would have had an irrefutable historical claim to the upper
Amazon valley but for the cedula of July 15, 1802. On that date Charles
IV detached both Mainas and Quijos from the audiencia of Quito, which
was then a component part of the viceroyalty of the New Kingdom of
Granada, and assigned those provinces to the viceroyalty of Peru. Another
cedula on July 7, 1803, included the province of Guayaquil in the kingdom
of Peru. In response to spirited protests from that port city, Ferdinand VII
rescinded this arrangement on June 23, 1819, the very eve of the dissolution
of the Spanish empire. Guayaquil returned to the jurisdiction of the audiencia kingdom of Quito.

The cedula of 1802 proved embarrassing to the Ecuadorian case. Some of their apologists denied that the cedula had ever been enforced. Peruvian scholars replied with documentary evidence that it had. Another unconvincing Ecuadorian argument was that the cedula applied exclusively to the ecclesiastical, not the political, organization of Mainas, for the cedula also created a separate diocese subordinate to the archbishopric of Lima. The Ecuadorians further contended that the cedula became null and void when the Republic of Gran Colombia, in declaring its independence, claimed as its territory the maximum extent of the former viceroyalty of the New Kingdom of Granada. At its creation in 1720, that viceroyalty specifically included the whole province of Mainas as a part of the audiencia kingdom of Quito. Thus according to the Ecuadorian argument, whatever validity the cedula of 1802 may have possessed was nullified by the treaty of 1829 between the new republics of Gran Colombia and Peru. Article 5 provided that their boundaries should follow those of the former viceroyalties and the component subordinate kingdoms.

While not denying the *uti possidetis* as a general frame of reference for settling disputed boundaries, the defenders of Peru's claims chose to place considerable emphasis on postcolonial conditions. On the basis of colonial precedents, Ecuador could lay claim to Túmbes and Jaén, since those provinces had been under the jurisdiction of Quito until 1821, when they elected to join the new republic of Peru. Lima, however, preferred to rest her historical claims to the upper Amazon valley squarely on the cedula of 1802; from Peru's point of view, the less said about earlier colonial precedents the better.

If Ecuador had the weight of history on her side, Peru had more material advantages. With three times the population of Ecuador and commensurately greater military strength coupled with more skillful diplomacy, Peru managed to secure most of the disputed area. The Peruvians explored and subjugated the region, and they buttressed their claims by their superior military force. Ecuador's pacific diplomacy relied on colonial precedents and abstract principles of international law. An attempted arbitration of the conflict by the queen-regent of Spain in the early 1890's failed to resolve the dispute, which continued to smolder. Actual military hostilities broke out in 1939. Mediation by the great powers of the western hemisphere headed by the United States, anxious to create a united front against the Axis powers in the wake of the Pearl Harbor bombing, resulted in the Protocol of Rio de Janeiro signed in January, 1942. Ecuador was compelled to recognize Peru's claim to most of the upper Amazon country.[25]

The modern border dispute, whose origins may be traced partially to

Dr. Morga's apathy toward the Mainas conquest, has left a deep imprint on the two neighboring republics. Ecuadorian nationalists bitterly, and understandably from their point of view, resent Peru's superior strength which deprived Ecuador of a vast territory which she could claim by reasons of history. Although the disputed zone is largely unpopulated and in many parts even unexplored, its potential wealth dazzles Ecuadorian patriots. With fierce pride the official stationery of the Republic proclaims: "Ecuador has been, is, and always will be an Amazonian country." The fiery and demagogic José María Velasco Ibarra, in his turbulent fourth presidential term (1960–62), made the recovery of the lost Amazon country one of the major goals of his administration.

The consequences of the boundary dispute are somewhat less profound in Peru. But they are not negligible. For one thing, the existence of a genuine frontier quarrel with a neighboring country has lent some ostensible justification for the military's large slice of the national budget. Although the decisive voice of the Peruvian military in political affairs is due also to factors other than the periodic recurrence of tension with Ecuador, that factor may not be discounted. Nationalism in Peru achieved substantially its goal and hence lacks the spirit that hurt pride has inspired in her smaller neighbor.

In 1618 when Viceroy Esquilache, scion of the famed Borja family, authorized Diego Vaca de la Vega to conquer Mainas, he inadvertently planted a seed which still bears bitter fruit.

The most obvious theme that emerges in these two chapters is the tenuousness of Spanish control over a considerable area of what was then the kingdom of Quito. Several thousand Spaniards ruled over a half million Indians in the high valleys of the Sierra. The semi-isolation of these communities was broken by only three routes to the outside world—that to the port of Guayaquil and the much less used caminos reales, one going north to Bogotá and Cartagena, and the other south to Lima. A good deal of the Pacific coast from Manta to Buenaventura remained in the hands of hostile Indians and zambos fiercely determined to maintain their own freedom. And on the other side of the Andes facing inward toward the continent, a corporal's guard maintained the frail authority of the king of the Spains.

In the frontier area of the Oriente, local circumstances determined events in a pragmatic fashion. In the last analysis the bureaucrats of the empire in Quito, Lima, and Madrid exercised little influence on the course of events. Their role was to give official sanction to what local conditions allowed, in contrast to the major centers of Spanish settlement where imperial bureaucratic control was usually more influential.

Regarding Esmeraldas, the bureaucracy played a much more positive role in shaping events. Local circumstances even there were all-important, but a contributing cause of the failure of that conquest was the inability of the authorities in Quito and Lima to agree on a common course of action. The passive attitude of the Spanish administration in the Oriente was largely due to their indifference toward that area. Vital and vested interests, such as the defense of the Pacific, the monopoly privileges of the Lima and Guayaquil merchants, and the ambitions of the Quito merchants, all of which encouraged the authorities in Quito, Lima, and Madrid to intervene in Esmeraldas, did not exist in the Amazon country. Hence local conditions were decisive.

The men on the frontier of the Oriente were the ones who had some control over events. Their freedom of action, however, was severely limited not by crown officials but by conditions of climate and environment. In this story of penetration into the Amazon on one of the "rims of Christendom," the key role lay with the Church, in this particular case, the sons of St. Ignatius Loyola. That the upper Amazon basin is today Spanish and not Portuguese is primarily the result of the efforts of a few dozen Jesuits. That their more grandiose dreams proved unattainable was the result of a combination of factors which even their intrepid zeal could not overcome.

The two Quitos that we have already discussed, the Quito of the coast and the Quito of the Oriente, were marginal to the third and most important Quito—the valleys in the Sierra lying between the two chains of the Andes, an area on which we must now focus attention.

3.

LA REPÚBLICA DE LOS INDIOS

Because of Elizabethan prejudice, the Anglo-Saxon countries used to make much of the atrocities of the Spanish conquest of America. There have indeed been few bloodless conquests in history, and this was not one. Wanton destruction of life and property there was. Yet the destructive aspect, which lasted in most cases for only a short span of time, should not obscure the constructive aspects of the conquest. Perhaps the most formidable obstacle blocking the creation of a stable new society based on a neomedieval corporate model was disease.

Isolated for countless centuries from direct contacts with the peoples of Europe, Africa, and Asia, the Indians of the New World had no acquired immunity against contagious diseases which the rest of the world had known from time immemorial. Malaria in the tropics and measles and smallpox in the highlands took a massive toll in lives. The greatest burden that the conquest imposed on the Indians was not Spanish cruelty, which was practiced but whose extent has been considerably exaggerated, nor even the cultural shock of the conquest, deep and penetrating though it was, but a series of epidemics. Those diseases would have been introduced by any European people who conquered the New World.

The demographic revolution varied in intensity from region to region in the New World. The most remarkable fact about the Indians of the Ecuadorian highlands during the three centuries of the Spanish colonial regime was that their numbers did not diminish appreciably. In central Mexico, on the other hand, the population precipitously declined from an estimated preconquest figure of 25.2 million in 1519 to 1.075 million by 1605. The 1519 figure should be understood as an estimate with a wide margin of error. The decline continued down to the middle of the seventeenth century, according to a series of demographic studies done by Lesley Byrd Simpson, Shelburne Cook, and Woodrow W. Borah.[1] Disruptive changes introduced by the conquest and harsh labor demands placed on the Indians by both the colonists and the clergy contributed to the woes of the Mexican Indians, but the principal explanation was the utter defenselessness of the Indians against the spread of epidemic diseases.

Deficient nutrition was unquestionably a contributing factor. Lower-class children in Chile today, for example, often die of measles. Children of the upper class seldom do. Malnutrition of the former is the probable explanation, according to some medical scientists. Although the lack of previous exposure to such diseases in the sixteenth century made the Indians pathetically vulnerable, it is reasonable to assume that malnutrition accelerated their death rate.

Spanish South America offers a significant contrast to Spanish North America. The population of South America was much less dense than that of Mexico at the time of the conquest, and the death rate among the Indians was much less in South America during the Spanish colonial period than it was in Mexico. The Indian population of the audiencia kingdoms of Lima, Charcas, and Quito was somewhere between 3.5 million and 6.75 million, compared with the estimate mentioned above of 25.2 million for Mexico at the time of the arrival of the Spaniards. Previous estimates of a population among the Incas of 10 million to 12 million must be treated with a large dose of skepticism until new evidence comes to light. Such a figure would presuppose a population for the audiencia of Quito of between 4 million and 6 million. There is little documentary evidence to justify a preconquest population beyond the 750,000–1,000,000 figure.[2]

In the audiencias of Lima and Charcas (present-day Peru and Bolivia) but not Quito, the Indian population under Spanish control declined from 1,490,137 in 1561 to 608,894 in 1796.[3] A steady recovery began in Mexico in the second half of the seventeenth century. By 1793 the Indian population had increased to around 3.7 million people. In Lima and Charcas, on the other hand, the decline was never as sharp as it was in Mexico, but it continued for some time into the eighteenth century without the demographic recovery that occurred in Mexico. Epidemic diseases never took such an overwhelming toll in lives among the Peruvians as they did among the Mexicans. In fact, diseases did not become a cause of mass deaths in Peru until the eighteenth century, some two hundred years after the Indians had first been exposed to them. By the eighteenth century the Mexican Indians had built up sufficient immunity so that the population steadily rose. Why the respective reactions of the Mexican and Peruvian Indians were so different has never been satisfactorily explained. The greater population density in Mexico over that in Peru may account for the more rapid and virulent spread of disease. And the earlier recovery of population in Mexico may be related to an expanding economy, during a time when Peru's economy was contracting, that led to better nutrition and health standards. Moreover, after two centuries of intense exposure to epidemic disease, the Mexican Indians may have developed some resistance.

The population decline in upper and lower Peru (the area of Peru and Bolivia), while less dramatic than that in Mexico, was still considerable. On the basis of the rather reliable 1561 population figure derived from tribute statistics, George Kubler estimates that the Indian population of the audiencias of Lima and Charcas declined between 1561 and 1796 from 1,490,137 to 608,894. His hypothesis is that the preconquest population was around three million. But he admits that the preconquest population might have been as high as six million.[4] This decline cannot be ascribed to any sharp increase in the death rate, since there was a relative lack of epidemics in the sixteenth century. The turmoil of the postconquest civil war was a contributing factor. Even more significant is the movement of people away from the Spanish-dominated Sierra to the more inaccessible montaña regions on the eastern slopes of the Andes, where Spanish control was not effective.

If the demographic changes in viceregal Peru present a foil to those in Mexico, another striking contrast is apparent within the viceroyalty of Peru between the northern audiencia of Quito and the southern audiencias of Lima and Charcas. The Kubler figures given above exclude Quito. The population of the kingdom of Quito, including the Pacific coast, the Sierra communities from Loja to the Cauca River valley, but not the Oriente, was between 500,000 and 750,000 Indians at the time of the conquest. The population of the Oriente did not exceed 200,000 people.[5] Hence the total population approached the one million figure. Most sixteenth century accounts point out that, in contrast to Lima and Charcas, the Indian population of Quito did not appreciably decline in the decades following the conquest.[6] Local epidemics did occur from time to time, but the death toll was not large.[7] There is no ready or facile explanation for this development. In the early seventeenth century, the audiencia repeatedly reported that the Sierra population was increasing not diminishing.[8] The consistency of bureaucratic reports cannot be treated lightly. The audiencia members were responsible and well-informed officials who had access to more demographic information than we do.

There were, of course, some islands of population loss. The indigenous peoples of the coast decreased drastically in number. The island of Puná, for example, located at the mouth of the Guayas River, became completely depopulated.

The Negro replaced the Indian in the coastal tropical lowlands[9] and proved remarkably adaptable. This adjustment cannot be explained solely by the similarity of the climates of central Africa and tropical America. More basic is the fact that the Africans had long been exposed to diseases such as smallpox and measles, to which both the Europeans and the Indians easily fell prey. Genetic adaptation made the Negroes less prone to malaria. Yet the Negro mortality rate was high, largely because they were underfed and overworked. The vacuum created by the disappearance of the Indians on the coast, however, was only slowly filled by the Negroes. The purchase of an African slave was an expensive capital investment, which the very modest economy of Guayaquil could not justify on a large scale. There were only a few thousand Negroes in the vicinity of Guayaquil during the Morga years. By 1802 there were about 60,000 Negro slaves and 42,000 zambos and mulattoes.[10] In the early nineteenth century, the African element constituted something less than one-sixth of the total population of the kingdom.

What happened in the area of Guayaquil also occurred along the tropical coastal areas bordering the Caribbean. Everywhere the coastal Indians disappeared, being replaced by the Negro and mulatto. In the tropical lowlands, malaria, which was unknown before the conquest, was particularly destructive. Furthermore, the social organization of the coastal Indians was of such a rudimentary sort that they found it impossible to adjust suddenly to the severe labor demands imposed by the Spaniards. The highland Indians with their well-developed forms of social organization, which reached the most mature expression among the Incas, were able to make the transition to the Spanish regime with far greater ease. Hence, because the coastal population was small initially, the sharp decline of the Indians on the coast did not appreciably affect the overall demographic picture of the kingdom.

Another tropical area where the Indian population declined precipitously was the Oriente. Epidemics did not devastate the population immediately. It was not until 1660, twenty-two years after the arrival of the Jesuits and forty-two years after the founding of San Francisco de Borja, that the first epidemics occurred. The fact that epidemics did not begin for several decades may be partially explained by the paucity of Spanish settlers and missionaries and the concentration of the colonists in and around San Francisco de Borja. Only a handful of itinerant Jesuits ministered to their charges periodically. The resettlement of large numbers of Indians into compact villages founded by the Jesuits ultimately served to facilitate the spread of epidemics. The Indian population on the Pacific coast disappeared more rapidly than that in the Oriente, since there were many more Spaniards in the coastal area and hence more vehicles for spreading disease.

Once the epidemics began in the province of Mainas, their impact was overwhelming. About 44,000 of the 100,000 partially Christianized natives died during the first epidemic of 1660. Another wave of smallpox occurred in 1669, killing 20,000 Indians. No more epidemics took place until 1749, when measles spread through the land, taking a massive toll in lives. Smallpox recurred in 1756 and in 1762, delivering the *coup de grâce* to the once-promising missions of the Jesuits in Mainas.[11] Along with Indian revolts and Portuguese slave-raiding expeditions, the epidemics reduced the missions to a scant 18,000 neophytes by 1762.

In only one area of the Sierra did the Indian population decline rapidly in the sixteenth century. The disruptive factors set in motion by the conquest, rather than epidemic diseases, were the cause. The province of Popayán, which extended from Esmeraldas to Buenaventura including all the territory from the city of Pasto to Cali, had a preconquest population of about 100,000 people.[12] Only superficially conquered by the Incas, many of these tribes resisted the conquest so ferociously that the Spaniards resorted to campaigns of extermination. In the province of Barbacoas, for example, a small expedition of soldiers dispatched from both Quito and Popayán under the command of Captain Francisco de Parada crushed Indian resistance with fire and sword brutality in 1600. Other hostile Indian groups were

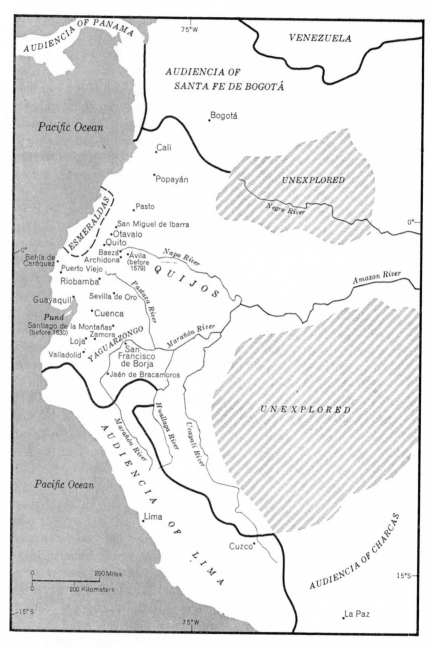

The kingdom of Quito and adjacent kingdoms in the late seventeenth century.
Map by the University of Wisconsin Cartographic Laboratory.

exterminated with equal severity. The population of the whole province of Popayán declined by approximately one-half during the first century of Spanish rule.[13]

Although the Sierra Indians of Quito managed to avoid the most catastrophic consequences of the Spanish conquest, namely, the epidemics, their burdens were not light. During the seventeenth century, a series of earthquakes and volcanic eruptions, followed by cycles of floods and droughts, caused many deaths. Earthquakes struck Riobamba in 1645 and 1698, Chimbo in 1674, and Latacunga and Ambato in 1698.[14] These events may have caused a slight but real drop in the population by 1700. If a modest decline did take place, the loss was recovered during the following century.

In the densely populated intermont valleys containing about a half million Indians, there were not more than 15,000 Spaniards and creoles before 1600. In addition to the vecinos, there were the *habitantes,* who were not freeholders. The number of habitantes may be arbitrarily estimated at 5,000. In 1576 López de Velasco reported that there were around 1,300 Spanish male homeowners, i.e., vecinos, in the whole kingdom.[15] The largest number resided in the city of Quito, where there were 600 Spanish households. It is impossible to project an accurate estimate of the mestizo population, but we may safely assume that it was several times that of the Spaniards. By 1650 the number of Spanish and creole households had risen to 2,500, and the mestizo and Indian population swelled the total population of the urban core of the city of Quito to about 50,000 souls.[16] That this small number of Spaniards managed to maintain control over the large Indian community is a remarkable fact.

In the course of one century, the inhabitants of the Ecuadorian Sierra underwent not one conquest but two conquests, beginning with the Inca conquest and culminating with the Spanish. Tupac Yupanqui began the Inca conquest around 1455. His son, Huayna Capac, completed the subjugation of the highlands some forty years later, shortly after Columbus had discovered the island of Hispaniola. The Inca advance into the Ecuadorian highlands represents the northernmost extension of Inca power, achieved on the eve of their conquest by the Spaniards.

Prior to the arrival of the Incas, there were several tribes and subdivisions among the highland Indians. The most important were the Cara, the Puruhá, the Cañari, the Panzaleo, and the Palta. Although loose confederations of villages covering limited territories for purposes of mutual defense did periodically emerge, there was no powerful centralization of political states comparable to the governmental machinery of the Inca empire.[17] The pre-

Inca "kingdom of Quito" of the Cara tribe, eloquently invoked by the controversial Jesuit historian Juan de Velasco, in the late eighteenth century, is largely a figment of his imagination.[18] He subconsciously sought to justify the nationalist claims of his own creole class by conjuring up the supposed glories of a remote preconquest past. The Mexican Jesuit Francisco Javier Clavigero did the same thing. Clavigero, however, was more fortunate than his Ecuadorian colleague, Velasco, in that he did not have to invent the Aztecs.[19] Velasco could not idealize the Incas, for, from a nationalist Ecuadorian point of view, the Incas were as much invading conquerors as the Spaniards were.

While the Inca conquest was brief in duration, in several spheres its impact was as profound as the subsequent Spanish conquest. Or put another way, the Spaniards completed what the Incas had begun. The foremost result of the Inca period was that it imposed a political unity on the highland communities, since the Incas introduced their own highly regimented social institutions. The Quechua language became the lingua franca of the whole Sierra. Although the pre-Inca languages did not disappear until the eighteenth century, Quechua had long since been the common tongue. The Spanish missionaries, who encouraged the spread of Quechua, did not convert the Indians to Catholicism in the pre-Inca languages. For the churchmen it was preferable to have to learn only one native language. Hence the Spaniards completed the task of political and social unification which the Incas had begun by encouraging the spread of a common language. The same practice was followed in other parts of the empire, most notably in Mexico where the missionaries extended the use of Náhuatl beyond the boundaries of the preconquest Aztec confederation.[20]

Apart from establishment of a common language, several other Inca policies promoted a greater degree of social cohesion among the highland tribes. The massive resettlement of people into strategically located colonies was one such factor. The raising of armies, the building of cities, fortresses, and temples, and the extension of the Inca road system all contributed mightily to promoting social unity. Because new imperial responsibilities were placed on the shoulders of the chieftains, social stratification became sharper. The upgrading of the prestige and authority of the curacas facilitated the Spaniards' task of finding appropriate intermediaries between themselves and the Indian masses. In religion and mythology Inca influence seemingly was scant.[21]

The initial unity created in the Inca conquest partially explains how chieftains such as Rumiñahui could raise large multilingual armies to oppose the Spanish invasion. Resistance was intense but brief. Pizarro's lieutenant,

Sebastián de Benalcázar, swept in from the south in 1534, receiving powerful Indian support from the Cañari tribe in the manner of Cortés. In broad strokes the Spaniards continued the aims of the Inca conquest. With its centralizing trend, Inca subjugation prepared the highland peoples to adjust to the new conqueror. The Spaniards had a far easier task in organizing the highland Indians than they did with the lowland peoples who were never effectively incorporated into the Inca regime. Lacking attractive resources, the coastal peoples were regarded by the Incas as brute savages scarcely worth the effort to civilize.[22]

The co-founders of the kingdom of Quito, of which the Republic of Ecuador is the successor state, were the Incas and the Spaniards. Ecuadorian nationalists may take offense at this statement, since they regard, quite correctly from their point of view, both the Incas and the Spaniards as alien conquerors. They prefer to base Ecuadorian nationality on the mythical pre-Inca kingdom of Cara, which Father Velasco fabricated out of whole cloth.

As befits two great imperialist powers, both the Incas and the Spaniards sought to impose their culture on the conquered and thus to reconcile them to the new regime. The missionary activity of the Spanish Catholic Church, more than any other single effort, was responsible for bringing the Indians into some sustained contact with Spanish culture. The hispanization of the Indians, although substantial, fell far short of the original goal.

The first generation of Franciscan missionaries, who arrived in Mexico during the 1520's, were under the influence of Erasmian humanism. Excited by the Indians' ready acceptance of Christianity, their simplicity of heart, and their lack of materialism, men such as Toribio de Motolinía, Archbishop Zumárraga, and Bishop Vasco de Quiroga plunged headlong into some remarkable social experiments. These churchmen sought to combine some features of Indian society, such as agrarian communism, with an emended and purified form of Spanish Christianity inspired by the Franciscan cult of poverty. Some of the bolder spirits among the Franciscans envisaged a simpler and more perfect form of Christianity emerging from a "terrestrial paradise" which the missionaries thought they could create among the Indians. One of the goals of this program, which was both neo-medieval and Renaissance in flavor, was the education of an Indian upper class in the precepts of Spanish humanism. From among them would ultimately come not only secular leaders but also a native Indian clergy.

This Erasmian project proved abortive, as the pages of Gerónimo de Mendieta's *Historia eclesiástica indiana* wistfully testify. A major cause for the ultimate failure of the Franciscans lay in the sharp decline of the Mexican Indian population, which accelerated after 1576. The acute and persistent pressure placed on the shrinking Indian population by Spaniards, creoles, and mestizos led not to a Utopia where agrarian communism and praises to God blended harmoniously together, but rather to debt peonage in which the Indians became an illiterate, alcoholic, and oppressed peasantry of quasi-serfs.

Fearful that the friars were acquiring a monolithic power over the Mexican Indians, Philip II deliberately set about to reduce the role of the regular clergy. The king sought to build up the secular clergy and the episcopacy as a counterweight for the same reason that a generation earlier his father had supported the friars as a counterbalance to the encomenderos. Under the double blows of royal disfavor and the spread of epidemic diseases among their charges, both the discipline and the idealism of the first generation of mendicant missionaries gave way to a more bureaucratic spirit of routine, if not discouragement. Inertia and caution replaced enthusiasm and innovation. Dissension between Spanish-born and American-born friars further sapped morale. The Indians, who were staunchly loyal to the friars in the sixteenth century, subsequently became indifferent to them.[23]

In Peru humanism exercised little influence. The postconquest civil wars delayed the effective beginning of the missionary enterprise there until the 1570's. In Quito, on the other hand, the Franciscans were inspired by the same humanist *philosophia Christi* pioneered by their Mexican confreres. But the efforts and the results in Quito fell far short of those in Mexico. In 1552 there were only twenty Franciscan friars and eight *doctrinas* in the whole kingdom.[24] The promising beginnings in Quito were cut short during the 1560's and 1570's. All over the empire there came to prevail the cautious and conservative spirit of the Counter Reformation, with little room for innovation and experiment. Rather than protecting their wards against excessive exploitation, the religious cooperated with the encomenderos. Religious instruction was inadequate. The avarice of the clergy led many of the Quechuas of upper Peru to view the major precepts of the Catholic faith with skepticism if not hostility. Until the end of the sixteenth century, many of the ethical, metaphysical, and ceremonial beliefs of the preconquest religion survived among the Quechuas beneath a not always opaque veneer of Spanish Catholicism.

Early in the seventeenth century, the Church threw its resources into an ambitiously systematic and largely successful campaign to uproot idolatry. By 1660 substantial progress had been achieved. The number of priests increased significantly; the clergy founded schools in the leading cities of the viceroyalty, including Quito and Cuenca, for educating the sons of the curacas. Efforts to teach the rudiments of the catechism to the people were intensified.[25]

A revealing description of the Indians' adaptation to Christianity emerges from the regulations adopted by a diocesan synod convoked by the bishop of Quito in August, 1596. All churches, for example, were to have doors which could be securely locked at night. No religious statue or image could be removed from the church unless carried in a religious procession during Holy Week under the supervision of the parish clergyman. The Spanish clergy disapproved of the fondness of the Indians for venerating sacred images in their homes, a practice done with "mucha indecencia."[26] A phobia of the religious was that the natives out of ignorance or malice would desecrate the sacred objects of the cult.

The presumption of some curacas that they should be exempt from obligatory attendance at mass, since their other privileges included being released from the mita and the tribute tax, was firmly rejected by the Church fathers. The clergy also sought to curb attempts by the curacas to secure divorces on the pretext they were not yet baptized. The synod did not prohibit outright the filthy pagan habit of smoking or chewing tobacco, which the Spaniards themselves were finding increasingly tasteful. But the Indians were admonished not to smoke inside the churches. The fathers frowned on the practice of holding a public market in the square outside the churches on Sundays on the basis that the affairs of Mammon might prevent the faithful from hearing mass. Another canon provided that each parish set up a school where the children of the curacas would be taught to read and write by the sacristan.

Yet another regulation sought to limit the *cofradías* or sodalities to a manageable number. The cofradía was a medieval Spanish institution combining religious worship and mutual aid for its members. The social and economic features, which were declining in importance in Spain itself during the sixteenth century, acquired a new vitality in the Indies. With the flux and insecurity of the new multiracial society emerging under primitive frontier conditions, there was an urgent need for the mutual aid features of the cofradías.[27] From the Philippines to Chile, sodalities arose in every Indian village. While the clergy encouraged this practice, they sought to regulate them.

The fathers of the synod of Quito were particularly anxious to curb drinking, not because they opposed the consumption of alcohol as such but because the imbibing of libations had been clearly identified with the performance of pagan religious rituals. The Indians were apt to drink wine and chicha on Good Friday, the feast of Corpus Christi, and the feast of the patron saint of the village, as well as at weddings, funerals, and baptisms. The synod gave the clergy rather sweeping authority to search for wine and destroy it. Curacas who were found drunk were to be lashed in public. For a second offense, deprivation of office for a year was the punishment. A third offense meant loss of office for life and one year's service without pay in the parish church. No libations were to be served at marriages. The parents of the bride and groom might invite the *ayllu* to a meal to celebrate the happy event, but everyone had to return home after the repast. The patronal fiesta was to be celebrated in the main square in front of the church and in the presence of the parish priest.[28]

The measures to stamp out ritual drinking adopted by the synod of 1596 reaffirmed in the main the celebrated ordinances that Viceroy Toledo had promulgated two decades previously.[29] The audiencia followed up Viceroy Toledo's ordinances in 1584 when the acting president, Lic. Pedro Venegas de Cauañeral, issued a code.[30]

The audiencia shared the determination of the Church to wipe out the identification between ceremonial drinking and pagan religious rituals, particularly on the feast of Corpus Christi, which the Indians associated with an Inca ritual. Unlike the churchmen, however, the secular magistrates did not propose to abolish drinking as such. Excessive drinking, they admitted, was harmful to the health and demoralizing to family life, but the audiencia added that moderate imbibing "contributes to preserving the health and the lives of these natives."[31] The tribunal flatly prohibited the Indians from manufacturing alcoholic beverages in their homes. They did allow the natives a rather generous daily ration of two pints of chicha which they could purchase only in licensed taverns. For the baptism of a child, an Indian might petition the corregidor for a larger ration in case he planned a celebration of the event in his home.

Both the Spanish clergy and the civil bureaucrats failed to understand ritual drinking in Indian terms. Ancient custom sanctioned these periodic orgies as a communal release, an act of self-protection, a propitiation to the supernatural powers, and a veritable affirmation of the community's being. As in the Philippines and Mexico, ritual drinking could not be abolished in Quito by mere legislative fiat. Imbibing libations gradually lost its pagan religious identification as the more elaborate ritual complex of Spanish baroque Catholicism, in which ceremonial drinking played no essential role, became part and parcel of the daily lives of the Indians.[32]

An impression of the morality of the Spanish clergy, on the other hand, can be gained from one regulation of the synod. Priests were forbidden to attend the baptisms, the weddings, or the funerals of their own children or grandchildren. Violation of this edict incurred a fine of 20 ducats.

The triumph of the Counter Reformation precluded the emergence of an Indian priesthood. In fact the Indians became second-class Catholics in that positions of leadership and responsibility inside the Church were denied to them. This condition explains many of the basic characteristics of Indian Catholicism. Among its outstanding features were outward ritual formalism rather than solid doctrinal knowledge, ceremonial performance rather than devotion to the ideal of the brotherhood of man, a tendency toward idolatry, superstition, and magic, and the infrequent reception of the sacraments. The Indians accepted Catholicism on their own terms, endowing it with a unique emotional and ceremonial flavor coming out of their own folkways.

From a Spanish viewpoint, this "Indianization" of Catholicism lay some distance from the norms laid down by the Church. The training of a select group of Indians from whose ranks a native clergy could have been recruited would have done something substantial to impart a firmer grasp of the doctrines, to eradicate superstitions, and to cause the sacraments to be received with much greater frequency. What resulted instead, not only in Quito but in other regions such as Mexico and the Philippines, was the emergence of virtually two religions. One was the Catholicism of the Spanish clergy and the Spanish citizens, and the other was the folk Catholicism of the Indians.[33] The Spanish clergy paid a heavy price for opposing the development of an Indian clergy.

The objection to an Indian clergy by all branches of the Spanish clergy stemmed from a selfish desire to preserve their lucrative Indian parishes as well as from genuine convictions. Although the Spanish-born and American-born clergymen engaged in bitter quarrels over who would dominate their particular ecclesiastical corporations, both groups closed ranks in their resolve to prevent the growth of an Indian clergy. An occasional mestizo and even a mulatto did manage to secure holy orders, but they were always a small minority. And they seldom received the more lucrative ecclesiastical benefices.

The Spanish clergy was not unaware of the universal character of its own creed, derived from the principle that all men are created equal in the image

of God, endowed by their Creator with a common origin and a common
end. It was in the service of this ideal that the Spanish missionaries had
journeyed to the New World to spend their lives among the Indians. Nor
was the Spanish clergy so parochial as to believe that God spoke only
Spanish. The clergymen preached the gospel in Quechua to the Indians of
Quito and in all the other major languages that the Indians of the New
World spoke. Catholic equalitarianism and universalism, however, were
essentially other-worldly, and this distinction cannot be stressed often
enough.

All men were created equal in the sight of God but certainly not in the
sight of their fellowmen. This-worldly inequalities in wealth, status, and
intelligence were viewed as a necessary consequence of man's imperfect
and sinful nature. In the Middle Ages, this principle of social inequality,
as expressed by Thomas Aquinas, applied to individuals and to groups
within a society but not to whole nations and races as such. Dante, both
one of the last exponents of medieval universalism and one of the first
spokesmen of modern statism and imperialism, extended the concept of
social inequality from individuals and groups to whole peoples and entire
nations. Dante set up a hierarchy of races with Rome as the pinnacle. The
Spanish humanist Sepúlveda molded this Dantean argument into a justification for Spanish imperialism overseas: The Spanish nation was con-
genitally superior to the Indian tribes "as adults are to children and as men
are to women."[34] This idea became characteristic of the colonialist
mentality, seldom challenged after the passing of the first generation of
Renaissance-oriented missionaries. In the late eighteenth century, a few
Jesuits, such as Clavigero in Mexico and Delgado in the Philippines, under
the influence of the Enlightenment challenged this *idée fixe*.[35] They made
little progress, however, in uprooting it.

Although the Spaniards cooperated with other races considerably more
than did the nations of northern Europe when they came in contact with
the peoples of the tropical world, the Spaniards also were racist and eth-
nocentric in their own fashion. But the Spanish version was different from
that of northern Europe. The Spaniards were willing to make concessions
to other races, but they never for a moment doubted their own superiority
over them. The European Spaniard not only regarded people of color as
grossly inferior but also arrogantly disdained the creoles, who were Spanish
in blood but born in the Indies. The peninsular Spaniards argued that the
alleged inferiority of the creoles could be traced back to the social en-

vironment of the New World. This cleavage sharply divided colonial society, as we shall have occasion to observe in Chapter 12.

The Spanish Church was catholic, that is, universal, in that it sought to encompass all groups and all races in society. The Anglican Church in Virginia in the seventeenth century provides a distinct contrast. The Church of England retained substantial elements of its Catholic heritage. It was universal, but its universe was more narrowly restricted to those whose origins went back to the British Isles. In Virginia the Church identified itself exclusively with the English planters and settlers. The Christianization of the slaves was positively discouraged. Both the Anglican and the Spanish Churches were tolerant and intolerant in ways that sharply complement each other. The Anglicans were internally far more flexible than the Spaniards in that they made serious efforts to reconcile their Catholic heritage with Calvinism. The Spanish Church of the Counter Reformation was rigidly inflexible about any doctrinal innovation, as the archives of the Holy Office of the Inquisition amply demonstrate. The Spaniards, on the other hand, were externally flexible in providing some place for all races inside the framework of their religion. Toward other races the English were as inflexibly intolerant as the Spaniards were toward other religious creeds.

The key to the Spaniards' willingness and capacity to accommodate other races within their religion lies in a special quality of Spanish society. The Spaniards recreated in the New World a version of the corporate society of the late Middle Ages. Hierarchically structured, it contained two kinds of associations: the primary estates and the functional corporations. The whites tended to dominate the latter. How they did will be discussed at some length in Chapter 10. One of the novel aspects of neo-medieval corporatism in the Indies was that the three primary estates were not the European trichotomy of the Church, the nobility, and commoners. In America an informal racial trichotomy emerged consisting of the whites, the mixed groups, and the Indians-Negroes at the bottom of the social pyramid. It was the neo-medieval corporate character of colonial society which enabled the Spaniards to find a place for the Indians. It was, however, an inferior place, for the only equality that the Spaniards were prepared to grant the Indians was equality in the next world. Spaniards, mestizos, and Indians were not equal, but they were organically interdependent. The Spaniards were the head of the body social, so to speak, and the Indians and Negroes were the arms and the legs. English-American society in the seventeenth century, on the other hand, was moving away from the medieval corporate model toward equalitarianism and individualism. In such a framework, there was no place for the Indian or the Negro except that of a nonhuman being.

The Spaniards came to regard the Indians as "gente miserable," in the precise canon law term. The Indians became wards, and the crown and the Church were their co-guardians. Such was the legal status of the Indians embedded in the *Recopilación de las leyes de los reynos de las Indias.*

For administrative purposes, the natives were treated as a separate commonwealth, *la república de los indios,* with its own code of laws and its own set of magistrates. The segregation of the Indians from the Spanish and mestizo communities gave the Indian commonwealth a kind of ethno-territorial reality, since most of the Spaniards lived in thirty-odd towns and cities of the kingdom. Inspiring the segregation of the Indians into separate villages was a humanitarian aim to protect them from what were regarded as demoralizing contacts with the Spaniards, mestizos, Negroes, and mulattoes.

The same corporate principle that applied to society as a whole extended into the internal organization of the Indian commonwealth. The curacas of preconquest times became a hereditary, privileged class, a kind of petty nobility from whose ranks local magistrates were recruited. The obligation of the curacas was to collect the tribute tax and to recruit quota labor gangs for the Spanish authorities. Royal law courts respected and protected preconquest property relationships, the most important of which were communal properties. The Indian community lands, however, became confined largely to the higher, barren, rocky terrain, with the much more fertile and arable valley bottomland falling under the control of the large estates owned by the Spaniards and creoles.[36] A standard practice of the colonial administration throughout the Indies was to recognize the customary law of the natives in all those situations which did not violate basic precepts of Spanish Catholic morality.

Neither the crown nor the Church would permit the colonists' maximum demand, which was wholesale enslavement of the Indians. The colonists could enslave Indians only in those cases where particular Indians in frontier areas were militantly hostile. Such cases were the exception and not the rule. Yet the colonists were able to exert sufficient pressure to secure a goodly number of their demands. The crown accepted their premise that the Indians had to offer their labor services to the Spaniards, who in turn accused the Indians of indolence. It would be fairer, however, to say that the Indians did not lack industry but that their employers would not adequately reward them for the toils of their labor. Indians all over the New

World adjusted rapidly to living as European wage earners in the cities where, as skilled craftsmen, they received adequate compensation. In agriculture and in unskilled labor, some form of compulsion had to be employed to make the Indians work for the Spaniards for only nominal wages.

The crown sought to reconcile its dual commitment to the natives, who, as "new Christians," merited some effective guarantees of their property rights and of the liberty of their persons, and to the colonists, who insisted that native labor be made available. The first workable compromise was the encomienda-tribute system. Originating in the Antilles, it was brought to Mexico and Peru by Cortés and Pizarro. This yearly tax collected from the Indians in labor services, goods, or specie was justified on juridical grounds as a concrete recognition of Castilian sovereignty and an acknowledgment of the temporal and spiritual services rendered by the Spanish administration. Its economic justification was the need of the colonists to gain access to a supply of cheap labor. The obligation of the encomenderos was to protect their wards and prepare them to receive baptism. One-third of the tribute went to the crown to defray the costs of religious instruction. All adult males between the ages of 18 and 50 paid the tribute. Nearly a sixth of the population, however, was exempt. Among the exemptions were the curacas, their eldest sons, and officeholders in the villages. Some Indians, especially in the cities, belonged to the crown encomienda, with the tribute collected by the royal treasury.

As late as the 1570's, the encomienda was a means of exploiting Indian labor, since encomenderos collected their tribute in the form of labor services from their charges. In response to pressure exercised by some factions among the regular clergy and determined to prevent the encomenderos from becoming a neo-feudal class with ambitions for political autonomy, the crown closed this loophole in the 1540's. Its enforcement, however, did not become effective in many areas for a few decades. Under the reformed encomienda, tribute could be collected only in goods and species, at a rate fixed by the audiencia, and not in the form of labor.[37] One of the first undertakings of the new audiencia set up in Quito in 1563 was to enforce this reform. That tribunal fixed the annual rate of tribute at three pesos and two tomines for the provinces of Quito and Loja and five pesos for Cuenca, one-half payable in gold and the other half in the abundant products of the locality. Judges of the audiencia, on their periodic tours of inspection, revised the tariff, the *tasación,* from time to time.[38]

The approximately 570 encomenderos in the kingdom received an income of between 1,000 and 5,000 pesos annually.[39] The majority of the encomiendas yielded closer to 1,000 pesos per year than 5,000, with the result that a Spaniard could not live well exclusively from the income of his encomienda. This meant that the encomienda provided him only with a welcome supplement to his income. Most of the wealth came from commerce and land.

Contrary to the popular notion which still persists despite the well-documented studies of Silvio Zavala, François Chevalier, and others, the large landed estates of the Spaniards seldom grew out of the encomienda.[40] The encomienda was never a land grant as such but merely the right to collect tribute from a certain number of Indians in a given locality. The law forbade encomenderos to live adjacent to their wards, but the encomenderos were required to live in the capital city of the province where they held a grant of Indians.[41] Although a few Spaniards may have violated this law, the majority of them preferred to live in the cities and towns with fellow Spaniards.

By the 1570's and 1580's, the encomienda in Quito had become "tamed," to use Lesley Byrd Simpson's phrase, into a not-too-onerous head tax on the Indians; it served as a convenient source of pensions for the crown and a desirable supplementary income for some of the well-to-do citizens. The number of Indians in the crown encomienda tended to increase between 1575 and 1625. Concomitantly, private encomiendas declined, for example, in New Spain from 721 in 1574 to 140 in 1602 and in Peru from 970 in 1574 to 695 in 1591.[42]

Royal legislation provided that encomiendas should be awarded to permanent residents in the Indies, with special consideration reserved for descendants of conquerors and original settlers.[43] In this fashion the crown hoped to create a modestly prosperous upper class. Although the majority of the encomiendas did go to residents of the Indies as the law provided, there were several exceptions during the reign of Philip III and that of his son, Philip IV. The viceroy in Lima assigned the encomiendas for Quito, with subsequent confirmation by the Council of the Indies, and over the years several viceroys granted encomiendas to nonresidents of the kingdom. The cabildo of Quito vigorously protested the practice.[44] Among the great nobles in Spain who held absentee encomiendas in Quito were the Duke of Uceda, the Prince of Esquilache, the Count of Castrillo, and the Duke of Medina de las Torres.[45]

Although curacas were never encomenderos as such, they did occasionally receive a special grant of the income from vacant encomiendas. This infrequent practice, however, was an extraordinary favor to a cacique who had rendered unusual services to the crown.[46]

After the reform and decline of the encomienda, the principal device for mobilizing Indian labor became the mita, institutionalized in the 1570's by Viceroy Toledo. Its guiding principles were compulsion and rotation. A certain percentage of the tributary population had to offer their labor services for hire periodically. The Quechua word "mita" meant "time" and hence "turn" or "spell." The Spanish mita supplied labor for the mines, agriculture, herding, building of houses and churches, textile workshops, and domestic service in addition to providing a general labor pool that was available weekly in the town squares for any work a Spaniard might care to have done. Viceroy Toledo stipulated that only one-seventh of the tributary population had to offer itself for hire at any one time. By 1620 this percentage had increased in several regions: the one-seventh figure applied only in the Sierra of upper Peru with the exception of the silver mines at Potosí, one-sixth for the coast of upper Peru, and in Quito, the most populous kingdom in the viceroyalty, the percentage was the highest, one-fifth. The viceroys and the audiencias set the general quotas, while the responsibility for providing the men rested with the curacas.

There were several regulations designed to protect the *mitayo* Indians. They were not to be taken long distances to work, nor to climates significantly different from their own. Curacas, their eldest sons, craftsmen, and artisans enjoyed exemption from serving in the mita. In contrast to the preconquest mita, the Indians did receive wages for their work on the supposition that such a practice would encourage the growth of a class of free, paid laborers. This was the solution that the crown preferred, but mita wages varying between 14 and 18 pesos annually for a work year of 300 days were far below what an Indian could earn in the free market.[47]

In the province of Riobamba, the salary for the agricultural mita was 15 pesos per year.[48] Out of this sum the Indian had to pay his tribute tax, seven to nine pesos. In the province of Quito, the mita wage was one peso and a half per month until 1587, when President Barros raised it to two pesos.[49] Under the Incas the maximum term was three months, but the Spaniards extended the tour of duty to a year for service in the mines and in the *obrajes,* the textile sweatshops. Shepherds served for three months.

The preconquest and the Spanish versions of the mita are only superficially similar. Before the conquest, the mita served rather limited purposes such as providing labor for the building and repair of roads and for sudden emergencies. Under the Spaniards the mita increasingly became the principal vehicle for the exploitation of all labor done by the Indians for the Spaniards. The essential difference between the preconquest and the postconquest mitas is one between a self-sufficient economy and a mercantilist economy based on the export and import of certain products. The demands placed on native labor after the conquest were far heavier than before 1533. The Indians had to grow food for the rapidly increasing number of Spaniards and mestizos. The textile workshops came to employ large numbers of people in both upper Peru and Quito, whereas obrajes as such did not exist under the Incas. Silver mining became one of the mainstays of the colonial economy, requiring the labor services of multitudes of mitayo Indians under harsh working conditions. Mining in preconquest times was a minor economic activity, since the Incas valued silver only as a form of ornamentation and not as currency.

Under the Incas there were built-in mechanisms which softened the system of quota labor. Furthermore, the fields of the men serving in the mita were cultivated in turn by others in the allyu. The Spaniards never exercised as tightly centralized control over the Indians as the Incas did with their monolithic bureaucracy, large army, and decimally organized population. Moving from one's habitual residence without official permission was a capital offense under the Incas. After the Spanish conquest, the Indians became rather mobile. Not only could Indians move from one village to another with relative ease, but also many natives chose the option of flight into inaccessible areas.[50]

Shortly after the ascension of the weak-willed but well-intentioned Philip III to the throne of Spain, his advisers made a frontal attack. A royal cedula issued in Valladolid on November 24, 1601, entitled the real ordenanza del servicio personal, virtually abolished the various systems of quota paid labor throughout the empire. The Council of the Indies underestimated the furious protest that greeted the arrival of this cedula in the New World. It remained a dead letter. Invoking the discretionary authority contained in the "I obey but do not execute" formula, the viceroys in both Mexico City and Lima suspended the execution of the royal ordinance. They dispatched spirited pleas to the king that the cedula be drastically modified if not withdrawn.

In Mexico demographic conditions made the cedula unenforceable. During the first administration of Velasco the Younger (1590–95), the repartimiento, the Mexican version of the mita, was failing to draft enough labor from the steadily diminishing Indian population to meet even those demands which crown officials recognized as having a priority on what labor was available. Although genuinely alarmed over the decline of the Indian pop-

ulation, the viceroys, the Count of Monterrey and the Marquis of Montesclaros, forcefully pleaded with the council that the demands on the
Indians could not be lightened without worsening an already grave economic crisis.[51]

Although Peru's demographic situation was not as critical as that of
Mexico, the labor force had appreciably declined. The viceroys, Luis de Velasco the Younger and his successor, the Count of Monterrey, mustered a
host of economic facts to demonstrate that the enforcement of the royal
ordinance of 1601 would destroy the already precarious colonial economy.
They laid particular stress on the need for draft labor in the silver mines of
Charcas, whose continued production was essential to the empire-wide
economy.[52]

In the face of this solid opposition to the suppression of the mita and the
repartimiento, the seldom courageous administration of the Duke of Lerma
retreated. Philip III issued a cedula at Aranjuez on May 26, 1609, which
provided for the continuation of the mita and the repartimiento.[53] But the
monarch instructed both the viceroys and the audiencias to take gradual
steps leading toward the ultimate abolition of the mita-repartimiento. In
1601 Philip III contemplated the immediate extinction of the system. In
1609 he had to settle for piecemeal abolition. The ordinance of 1609 also
reaffirmed previous legislation providing that the Indians receive wages
and that their working conditions be humane. Had even this legislation been
systematically enforced, the lot of the average Indian would have been considerably improved.

Between 1609 and 1633, a major shift took place in the recruitment of
labor in Mexico. Debt peonage replaced the repartimiento in agricultural
labor. Compulsory quota labor in the cities was gradually eliminated by
actions of the viceroys and the audiencia. By 1633 this change was nearly
complete so that the viceroy could formally abolish the repartimiento except
for service in the mines. The vehement protests that had greeted the cedula
of 1601 were absent in 1633. Mexico had simply outgrown the repartimiento.[54]

The progression from encomienda to mita to debt peonage took place
much more slowly in the viceroyalty of Peru. In Quito, where the Indian
population was still abundant, mita labor was economically efficient and
dependable. Hence local interests tenaciously resisted any change in the
status quo. The mita continued to supply a good deal of labor in the textile
obrajes. It was not until a cedula of December 31, 1704, that the crown

made a concerted effort to abolish the mita in the obrajes.[55] The mita in agriculture continued all during the seventeenth century. Bureaucratic action after 1609 was successful, however, in abolishing the urban mita, although even this modest reform met stiff resistance.

In conformity with the cedula of March 26, 1609, Viceroy Montesclaros (1606–14) abolished the mita under which one-fifth of the Indians living within the jurisdiction of the city of Quito had to offer their labor services for hire. The city limits of Quito covered a large area from Rumichaca in the north, where the jurisdiction of the city of Pasto began, to the village of Tiquicambe, the limits of the city of Cuenca, in the south. The capital Indians were subject to three kinds of mita: (1) public and private works, (2) fields and herds, (3) wood and fodder. The first and third were abolished by Montesclaros. In 1589 the mita quota for pastoral work was 5,000 Indians, with a tour of duty lasting a year. Another 1,000 Indians provided wood and fodder every two months. From July to September an additional 1,300 mita workers were required to repair private homes and public buildings. The mita also provided several thousand more Indians for sowing and harvesting for periods of two months.

The viceroy justified his action on the grounds that the density of the Indian population made voluntary paid labor feasible. In place of the mita, he ordered that each Indian village provide a weekly allotment of wood and fodder for sale in the city. The leading citizens of the capital soon complained that under the new arrangement they lacked sufficient labor, wood, and fodder. What they really meant was that these products cost more with free market prices for labor. The cabildo of Quito, which was the stronghold of the prominent and well-to-do citizens, consistently lobbied before the viceroy and the Council of the Indies for the restoration of the mita. The council expressed moderate sympathy with the viewpoint of the city council, but successive viceroys adamantly opposed the restoration of the mita.[56]

In his official correspondence, Dr. Morga remained strangely silent about the agitation of the cabildo. A likely surmise is that the president considered silence the most prudent course to follow. He did not want to alienate the well-to-do citizens in the capital by opposing their request. Several aldermen were his allies in the struggles arising out of the visita general. He apparently agreed with the reasoning behind the decision of the viceroy, for he did not oppose the action. Dr. Morga was seldom bashful about voicing his disagreement with the viceroys, for his settled conviction was that Quito could not be governed well from Lima.

Two factors facilitated the viceroy's action. One was the demographic stability in the Sierra, and the other was the urban character of Quito. Paid voluntary labor at free market prices existed usually only in metropolitan cities with their money economies, such as Lima, Quito, Mexico City, and Manila.

In the countryside, rural labor continued to be coerced under the mita, with wages considerably less than the free market rate. As the seventeenth century gave way to the eighteenth century, the mita degenerated into an informal system of debt peonage in which the principle of rotation disappeared. Juan and Ulloa, who traveled through the kingdom of Quito during the late 1730's and early 1740's, wrote a graphic description of how the mitayo had become a debt peon earning far less and working under much harsher conditions than the rural peasant in contemporary Spain.[57]

Although the drastic decline in the Indian population was a powerful obstacle to a workable compromise beneficial to the Indians, the demographic factor was not in itself all-decisive. In the kingdom of Quito, where there was population stability, the lot of the Indian was somewhat less harsh than it was in the audiencias of Lima, Charcas, or Mexico, where the decline was very much sharper. Yet the difference between Quito and the other regions was not very great. The pre-industrial technology, in which manual labor predominated, and the heavy demands placed on the slender economic and natural resources of the land both contributed to making the lot of the Indians in the kingdom of Quito scarcely enviable.

4.

THE SWEATSHOP OF SOUTH AMERICA

The Indians of Quito did not have to bear the heavy burdens of mining, with its inhumane working conditions that caused disease and took a heavy toll in lives. The Ecuadorian Sierra is the only major region in the Andean highlands not generously endowed with precious minerals. A blanket of recent volcanic rock covers most of the mineral-bearing strata. Some gold but very little silver did exist in the southern provinces of Cuenca and Loja. For a few decades, gold mines in isolated parts of these two provinces, principally near Zamora in Cuenca and San Antonio de Zaruma in Loja, yielded unpretentious but solid deposits. Annual gold production varied between 200,000 and 400,000 pesos.[1] This was a modest return in comparison with the lucrative silver mines of Mexico and Peru, but production from these mines represented a not insignificant item in the economy of Quito. By 1600 production had fallen off to a mere trickle.[2]

The mines themselves were not especially rich. In the twentieth century, even with improved technology and foreign investment, these same mines have not proved profitable.[3] Furthermore, located in isolated and almost inaccessible sites on the eastern slopes of the cordillera, the mines were in the territory of a small, belligerent Indian population. They were not the docile tribes of the high Sierra, previously subjugated by the Incas, but primitive folk fiercely determined to maintain their freedom from the intruders. The tribe of the Jívaros, for example, laid waste the small mining communities at Logroño and Sevilla de Oro and forced their abandonment.[4] If the mines had been lucrative, the Spaniards would have had the incentive to crush Indian resistance, as they did in the Chichimeca country in north-central Mexico.[5]

If mining did not impose heavy burdens on the Indians of the Sierra, textile manufacturing did. During the seventeenth century, the Sierra of Quito became the sweatshop of Spanish South America. The region produced high quality wool and cotton in great abundance.[6] Secondly, cheap labor was plentiful. The cotton came from the province of Quijos on the eastern slopes of the Andes. The fertile mountain valleys of the Sierra rapidly became grazing grounds for vast herds of wool-producing Merino sheep, as well as horses, mules, and cows. The sudden development of pastoral farming, which the Spaniards introduced, created a veritable ecological revolution. While on occasion the herds damaged the corn and potato fields of the Indians, the new pastoral economy also created a new source of food, clothing, and transportation.[7] By 1585 there were 150,000 head of sheep and goats, 30,000 head of cattle, 12,000 pigs, and 2,000 horses and mules in the valley of Quito. In the valleys of Latacunga and Riobamba, there were as many as 600,000 sheep. The province of Chimbo raised mules, for these patient, surefooted, and hardy animals were the principal beasts of burden along the treacherous paths of the Sierra.[8]

The obrajes produced a wide variety of textile goods. Among their products were coarse brown sackcloth, wadding, white or black woolen cloth, blankets, cordova hats, straw hats, fiber sandals, and ship riggings of high, medium, and ordinary quality. Although both men and women valued contraband Chinese silks for their exotic beauty, the cool climate of the highlands made woolen clothing and blankets a necessity.

Sheepgrazing and the obrajes provided modest fortunes for Spaniard and creole alike. Although owning a sweatshop lacked the social prestige of landownership, many prominent citizens were obraje owners. Andrés de Sevilla, Diego de Valencia León, Lic. Alonso de Carvajal, and Diego de Niebla, who will figure prominently in this study, were obraje owners.[9] The Church depended heavily on the textile industry for its income. A significant portion of the tithes, which were the principal rent for the secular clergy, came from sheepgrazing. All the religious orders held substantial herds as well as operating many obrajes, often illegally. These obrajes also contributed substantially to the income from the *alcabalas,* the sales tax which furnished a significant portion of the royal revenue. President Munive estimated in 1681 that the obrajes produced an average annual net profit for their owners of some 300,000 pesos.[10]

This pre-industrial system of manufacturing, which never recovered from the flood of cheap English textiles introduced after independence, was the basis of colonial Quito's export trade. Quito shipped its textile products all over the viceroyalty of Peru, from Panama and Cartagena in the north to Chile and Charcas in the south. Between Quito and Peru there was a very lively trade in which the Sierra exchanged her textiles not for the silver of Peru but for wines.[11] Today Ecuadorians quench their thirst with domestic-made beer and soft drinks, but, in the seventeenth century, Peruvian wines served this purpose. Chilean wines, which today are more potable than Peruvian beverages, were then not exported. Although Spain shipped her wines across the Atlantic and some entered Quito, they were scarce and expensive.

According to the mercantilist notions of the day, this export trade ought to have been suppressed, since Spanish manufacturers should have supplied the textile needs of South America. The textile industry in the peninsula, however, could not possibly produce the quantity of goods of all qualities for this immense market. They had all they could do to supply high-quality textiles. The Andalusian merchants, fearful of the competition from Chinese silks, were powerful enough to secure royal legislation prohibiting the export of Chinese silks to South America from either the Philippines or Mexico. This prohibition, however, was more honored in its breach than in its observance.[12] Andalusian textile interests never made sustained efforts to abolish the obrajes in Quito. The products of that remote Andean kingdom only partially competed with the manufactures of the peninsula. Although some of the Quito textiles were of high quality, the bulk of them were coarser, low-quality goods.

The prosperity of textile manufacturing in Quito was precariously balanced. An increase in Chinese contraband silks, satins, and taffetas or a larger supply of Spanish-made textiles could suddenly and drastically undercut the market for Quito's wares. Such a collapse occurred in the 1620's, causing a major economic depression in the Sierra.[13] In upper Peru itself there were many obrajes, whose owners resented the competition from Quito.[14] The wool from Quito was of higher quality than that from Lima, and labor costs in the Sierra were less than those in Lima. The obraje owners in Lima were powerful enough to persuade the viceroy, the Count of Chinchón, to impose on the existing tariff an additional 2 per cent tax on Quito imports into the port of Callao.[15]

In the face of all of these factors, the continued modest prosperity of the sweatshops in the Sierra depended in the last analysis on a ready supply of very cheap labor. The sweat of the Indians provided the difference between profit and loss.

There were several kinds of obrajes, the most basic categories being legal and illegal ones. Legal obrajes were those licensed by the viceroy. The license could be limited to a span of years, but many had no time limit. The most important distinction among the legal obrajes was that some received the highly valued privilege of a certain number of mitayo Indians. The others had to depend on voluntary labor. Among the legal obrajes, there were twelve which belonged to the Indian villages in their corporate capacity and thirty-two whose owners were individual Spaniards or creoles. Of the private obrajes, twelve had assigned quotas of mitayo labor and twenty operated with so-called voluntary labor.[16] There were two obrajes in the province of Otavalo enjoying a unique status, since those Indians were royal tributaries.

A minimum of 7,261 Indians were employed in the legal obrajes.[17] The province of Riobamba with the largest herds of sheep in the Sierra had nineteen obrajes, the valley of Latacunga south of the capital had ten obrajes, and in the valley of Quito there were some twenty licensed sweatshops. The obrajes near the capital tended to be smaller, employing on an average one hundred Indians, while those in Latacunga and Riobamba had twice as large a labor force. In the valley of Cuenca there was only one legal obraje and none in the valley of Loja. The majority of the legal obrajes received their licenses between 1610 and 1630, during the administrations of Viceroys Montesclaros, Esquilache, and Guadalcázar.[18]

The number of Indians in the licensed obrajes represents only a fraction of the total labor force employed in this manual industry. If there were fifty-one licensed sweatshops by 1681, it is not rash to estimate that there were 150 illegal workshops. The *fiscal* of the audiencia reported that in 1603 there were sixty illegal obrajes in the vicinity of the capital.[19] There were many more in the valleys of Latacunga and Riobamba. Many of the workshops in and around the capital were quite small. Called *chorrillos,* they sometimes employed as few as ten or twenty people. In the capital, much weaving was done by the Indians in their homes, whereas in the provinces the work was done in primitive factories that also housed the labor force.

If about 7,200 Indians were employed in the fifty-one legal obrajes and if we project a figure of 150 illegal obrajes, the total labor force must have approximated 28,800 Indians. In view of the facts that the woolen and cotton goods were manufactured with manual labor and that the products of Quito were in demand throughout all of Spanish South America from Panama to Buenos Aires, the estimate of 28,800 Indians is rather conservative.

The extent of textile production in Quito comes into perspective by comparison with that in the valley of Mexico. In the early seventeenth century, 2,205 Mexican Indians were employed in forty-nine factories. In Mexico City itself there were twenty-five obrajes making cloth and ten making hats. There were fourteen other shops in adjacent communities in the valley. Puebla was the other major textile center, with thirty-two obrajes employing an estimated work force of 1,440 laborers.[20] Not only was the total work force employed in Mexico much less than that in Quito, but the factories in Mexico were also much smaller. The average work force consisted of forty-five laborers. The largest obraje employed 120 workers and the smallest about thirty.[21]

The largest obraje owner in the kingdom of Quito was none other than Dr. Morga's patron, the Duke of Uceda, son of the Duke of Lerma. In the province of Riobamba, he held three licensed obrajes, with a quota of 782 mitayo Indians, yielding an average annual net profit of something less than 40,000 pesos.[22] The multiple holdings of the Duke of Uceda are exceptional. Ownership of the obrajes tended to be highly diversified, as is usually characteristic in the textile industry.

Coercion of various kinds had to be employed in order to recruit labor. In the mitayo obrajes, it was the responsibility of the curacas to provide the prescribed quotas of rotating labor. The vast majority of the obrajes, however, could not call on the mita to supply their labor needs. They depended on allegedly voluntary labor. In this case such a term was a euphemism for debt peonage. The corregidores and the audiencia itself enforced the validity of debts incurred by the Indians to their employers. Since wages in the shops varied between 20 and 30 pesos annually, the temptation for the Indians to borrow money was inevitable and irresistible. Another device the employers or their foremen used to ensure a sufficient labor supply was to sell their workers goods at inflated prices. Thus debt peonage provided the obrajes with a steady supply of labor.

In Mexico repartimiento labor was seldom used in the obrajes. The law required that Negro slaves and not Indians be employed, but this regulation was a dead letter. Since a Negro slave sold for about 400 pesos, an obraje owner would have had to invest between 15,000 and 20,000 pesos alone for his labor supply. Freed mulattoes were often employed as foremen and supervisors. The Mexican entrepreneurs relied to some extent on Indians convicted of crimes by the courts. But they depended even more on free labor by making contracts with Indians. In view of the venality of the lower courts, however, such free labor could easily degenerate into debt peonage and coercion.[23] By the seventeenth century, wages in Mexico varied between 36 and 48 pesos annually in contrast to those in Quito, where the wage scale varied between 36 and 40 pesos. In terms of real wages, the Quiteños were better paid, since the cost of living was much lower than in Mexico.

The regulation of working conditions and the general administration of the sweatshops were constant causes of concern to the crown and its representatives. In 1577 Viceroy Toledo issued the first general code to regulate the industry.[24] Among its provisions was the stipulation that no obraje could operate without a license from the viceroy. Mitayo Indians could not be assigned to the obrajes for a period of more than one year. In order to prevent graft on the part of the curacas, workers were to receive their salaries directly from their employers. Each Indian could be assigned to only one task in the workshop. Salaries varied between 20 and 24 pesos per year in addition to a small weekly supply of food. In the early seventeenth century, the salary rose to between 35 and 40 pesos for a work year of some 312 days.[25]

Mitayo Indians worked twenty-six days a month for nine hours a day. They were released from work for three weeks in October, two weeks in February, and another week at the end of their tour of work so that they might plant and harvest their own plots. Oidor Matías de Peralta, who conducted an extensive inspection of the obrajes in 1621, drew up a new code embodying the basic principles of Toledo's earlier ordinances. The Peralta code was still in force in 1681.[26]

That many Indians were brutally overworked can be amply documented. In place of the nine-hour day set by law, they often worked from dawn until dusk, sometimes chained to the weaving and spinning looms in buildings that were dimly lit. Sanitary conditions were primitive even by seventeenth-century standards.

In 1687 Oidor Matías Lagúnez visited one obraje in Quito and found that the Indians had been imprisoned there for small debts of less than ten pesos. They were not even allowed to leave the sweatshop to attend mass on Sundays. The oidor visited the obraje one Sunday morning at 11 and released the Indians to attend mass at noon. They, of course, did not bother to return to the shop. The owner, Bernardo de León, moved to Latacunga, where he continued to prosper in another sweatshop. Bernardo de León fed his workers roasted hides of beef, animal fodder, and uncooked tails of bulls, and their beverage consisted of their own urine.[27] Oidor Lagúnez admitted that working conditions were somewhat better in other obrajes. Conditions in the obrajes in Mexico were similar.[28] Although the cedula of 1609 had laid down regulations regarding the obraje working conditions,[29] obraje owners clearly did not abide by them fully. Another cedula in 1612 provided that Negroes could not work in the same obrajes as Indians on the grounds that the former would oppress and demoralize the latter. Neither Negroes nor mestizos worked in the obrajes of Quito.[30] Indian labor was more plentiful and much cheaper.

In his first general report to the king, Dr. Antonio de Morga pointed out that the colonists did not derive great prosperity from their extensive herds of sheep and cattle. Supply far exceeded demand. The president saw one solution in opening up the road to Esmeraldas and thereby creating a new market in Panama for the agricultural products of the Sierra. He realistically recognized that the whole export economy of Quito rested on the production of the obrajes. He stereotyped the Indians as indolent, mendacious, and alcoholic. Dirty wretches though the Indians may have been in his opinion, they were still human beings and vassals of the crown who merited some paternalistic protection.[31] His twin goals, therefore, were to restore the prosperity of the obrajes and to improve working conditions of the Indian laborers.

Dr. Morga believed that the principle justifying the community obrajes was sound in that these workshops provided the Indians with a steady source of income from which to pay their tributes and helped to finance activities beneficial to the villages. What aroused his concern was that these aims were not being achieved. He sought to improve the administration of the obrajes by reducing graft. He seldom wavered in his conviction that the basic cause could be traced back to the authority exercised by the viceroy in Lima. The administrators of the community obrajes were viceregal appointees, with an annual salary of 800 pesos. The lack of effective supervision gave the administrators ample opportunity for peculation. Dr. Morga regarded these posts as a means of patronage by which the viceroys could reward the many retainers who accompanied them from Spain to Lima and for whom they felt an obligation to provide. Special inspectors dispatched

by the viceroy periodically to investigate the obrajes performed usually perfunctory visitations.

The Morga solution was to transfer the responsibility for supervising
the obrajes from the viceroy in Lima to the audiencia in Quito.[32] In response to a chapter-and-verse chronicle of abuses in the workshops, the
king instructed the Prince of Esquilache to exercise more effective supervision over his appointees. The viceroy reacted to this mild admonition by
proposing that the task of supervising the obrajes be transferred to the oidor
in Quito, who by ordinance would conduct a tour of inspection, a visita de
la tierra, of one of the provinces every two years.[33] Dr. Morga greeted this
proposal with enthusiasm, since it coincided with his conviction that the
audiencia of Quito should have more autonomy from Lima. Esquilache
was one of the few viceroys to share this view. He deliberately delegated to
the audiencia much more political administration than his predecessors had.
He reasoned that granting the audiencia administrative and political responsibilities would encourage that tribunal to become more cooperative in enforcing his policies.[34]

The king and the Council of the Indies accepted the recommendation
of the viceroy. Special judges of inspection, heretofore dispatched by the
viceroy, were expressly forbidden.[35] Viceroy Esquilache's more vigorous
successor, the Marquis of Guadalcázar, simply ignored the cedula, and
he continued to send his own appointees to inspect the obrajes. In response
to a spirited protest from the audiencia, the king ordered the zealous viceroy to desist.[36] He ultimately complied, but his successors did not.

In 1678 the city council of Quito bitterly complained to the king that,
in violation of repeated royal cedulas, viceroy after viceroy continued to
send inspectors from Lima to the obrajes. The cabildo wearily requested
yet another cedula.[37] The inability of the viceroys to resist the temptation
of sending inspectors was due not only to their real need to provide patronage for their numerous retainers. Lima had justification for not trusting the
authorities in Quito to furnish adequate supervision. However, there is no
evidence whatsoever that the Lima appointees were any more resistant to
the opportunities for graft. It was in the nature of the Spanish bureaucracy
that the same functions were performed by several agencies, a condition
which tended to institutionalize mutual suspicion.

Dr. Morga's most solid victory in his campaign to eliminate the control
of Lima over the obrajes occurred on December 14, 1634, when the office
of administrator in the community obrajes was abolished by royal decree.
The crown accepted Dr. Morga's solution, which was to lease the Indian

community obrajes to private individuals.[38] The leaser signed a six-year contract with his administration, subject to periodic inspections from the circuit judge and the more regular supervision of the corregidor of the province. Prior to 1634, the crown had expressed some uneasiness about leasing the community obrajes for fear that the lessees would be driven to brutal exploitation of the Indian workers.[39]

In persuading the crown to adopt the leasing system, President Morga used two arguments, one negative and the other positive. Under the system of Lima-appointed administrators, the community obrajes had not even been able to pay the tribute tax, let alone provide any services for the benefit of the Indian workers. Profits there were, but neither the Indian village treasuries, the *cajas de comunidad,* nor the royal treasury received these earnings. They were siphoned off by the corrupt administrators.

President Morga's positive argument was that he had already experimented with the leasing system in one obraje with success. By 1615 the once-prosperous crown obraje in Otavalo was so corruptly and inefficiently administered that the Indians in that crown encomienda were 107,435 pesos in arrears in the payment of their tribute. This royal encomienda, which had formerly yielded an annual rent of 20,000 pesos a year, was then earning only 5,000 pesos.[40] The stormy residencia of Corregidor Pedro de Vergara, in which it was demonstrated that he had indulged in massive graft, left the whole province in a sorry state.[41] In order to correct such abuses, the audiencia drew up a comprehensive plan to reorganize the royal encomienda. One of its major provisions was to lease the already licensed obraje at San Luis and to establish another one at Peguchi. Unable to spare an oidor to undertake the assignment, the president appointed Pedro Ponce Castellejo, an alderman of Quito. This choice proved a happy one, for Ponce Castellejo was efficient, practical, and experienced. He had made a small fortune running an obraje whose license he obtained in 1609. In a period of five years, Pedro Ponce Castellejo reduced the amount owed in tribute arrears from 107,435 pesos to 39,903 pesos. The obraje at San Luis began to yield an average annual net profit of between 10,000 and 12,000 pesos.[42] These spectacular results in the early 1620's ultimately persuaded the crown in 1634 to accept the leasing arrangement advocated by Dr. Morga. In all matters dealing with making money either for himself or for his king, Dr. Morga usually displayed sound judgment. Dr. Morga himself made a small profit by retailing manufactures from the obrajes, for which illegal practices he was ultimately fined.[43]

In response to a royal cedula of October, 1627, the viceroy instructed

Dr. Morga to convoke a junta in Quito. Present at the conference were the oidores, the royal exchequer officials, and the newly arrived *visitador general*, Lic. Galdós de Valencia. The junta confirmed the major lines of the policy that the president had been developing. Among its conclusions and recommendations were (1) that the six licensed community obrajes were useful and desirable; (2) that in other areas where there were large numbers of crown tributaries, especially in Quito, Otavalo, and Riobamba, new obrajes should be created; (3) that all the community obrajes should be operated under the leasing system and not by Lima-appointed administrators.[44] The tenor of these recommendations prepared the ground for the crown's abandoning its latent opposition to leasing in 1634.

The junta of 1630 did not advocate the abolition of the licensed and unlicensed obrajes owned by individuals lest the economy of the land be thrown out of balance. Dr. Morga, however, was adamant in opposing the granting of any new licenses on the grounds that additional private obrajes would place an intolerable burden on the Indians. Many fewer licenses were granted by the viceroys after 1630 than before.

The Morga administration did undertake a concerted drive to compel the Franciscans and the Augustinians to give up a series of unlicensed obrajes that they operated in their parishes.[45] Some witnesses claimed that the friars did not pay their Indian workers any wages. It is not a proven fact that the Augustinians and the Franciscans treated their Indians any more harshly than the lay obraje owners did. The suspicion cannot be forborne that the nonecclesiastical sweatshop owners may have viewed with ill-grace the competition provided by the illegal religious obrajes.

Using all the legal machinations that the slow-moving Spanish judicial system provided, those two religious corporations tenaciously fought the efforts of the audiencia to make them close down their obrajes. Dr. Morga complained about the ire directed against him by the Augustinians. The vigor of the Morga administration's campaign was partially a retaliation against the animosity displayed by some factions in the Augustinian order against the audiencia.[46] Some obrajes closed down but not many. The religious orders were too deeply entrenched to be deprived of such lucrative investments. Although the results were not very lasting, no administration in the seventeenth century made a more consistent attempt to curb the illegal ecclesiastical-operated sweatshops than did the Morga administration.

The reorganization of the obraje at Otavalo was part of a much larger program designed by Dr. Morga in 1620 to restore the prosperity of the whole province, most of whose Indians were crown tributaries.[47] Among the principal aspects of this program was legislation providing that the Indians should be returned to their habitual place of residence. Every native was to be given a house and a small plot adjacent to it. All community lands and individual holdings acquired by Spaniards even by purchase should be returned to the Indians on the grounds that the audiencia had not given its consent. The prices paid had been low and unjust. No Spaniard or mestizo might live in an Indian village. All non-Indians, save the clergy, must reside in the Spanish town of San Miguel de Ibarra. No traders were allowed to visit the Indian villages. The Indians of the province were exempt from service in the mita. In order to reduce the cost of local government, each village was to have only one governor, whose principal responsibility was to collect the tribute. A whole group of minor officials called *mandones* was abolished. Several provisions dealt with attempts to improve the honesty of the viceregal-appointed corregidor of the province. The corregidor could not collect his salary until all the tribute money had been received. Nor was he to own any form of real estate or receive presents from the Indians.

The reform project of Otavalo was perhaps the most successful program that Dr. Morga sponsored in the general area of Indian legislation and administration. It was realistic, practical, and business-like. The immediate results were solid. Not only did the reorganization of the obrajes result in the decline of tribute in arrears, as mentioned previously, but also in subsequent years the arrears were totally liquidated. The obrajes continued to produce a steady income for the crown. The other provisions of the reform, although not totally enforced, did nevertheless contribute toward restoring the modest degree of prosperity for the whole province.

Over the course of the centuries, Otavalo has remained the most prosperous Indian community in the whole Sierra. The hand-loomed textile goods of the province, in particular their blankets, are still produced in the valley. They are rightly prized for their beauty and gracefulness of design as well as for their durability. While many conditions were responsible for the relative well-being of the province throughout the centuries, the administration of Dr. Antonio de Morga deserves some credit for its modest and realistic efforts to promote the prosperity of that Indian enclave.

The last ambitious effort under the Habsburgs to legislate the abuses out of the obrajes did not occur until the decade of the 1680's.[48] In response to a crescendo of protests over flagrant violations of the law, the decrepit government of Charles II (1665–1700) acted with a vigor for which it is seldom credited. The cedula of February 22, 1680, provided for the continued operation of the Indian community obrajes and the licensed private obrajes that had no time limit. The king ordered the immediate demolition of all unlicensed obrajes and all licensed obrajes whose time span had expired. The bulk of the licensed obrajes came under this category. No new obraje could be founded without the prior approval of the king. No Indian could be imprisoned in an obraje for debt. Labor by children from 12 to 17 years of age was to be abolished.

The crisis facing the then-president of the audiencia, Lope Antonio de Munive (1677–89), was of the acuteness which demonstrates the high degree of political skill that was required of an audiencia president. The career of that magistrate is reminiscent of that of Dr. Morga. Both men possessed more than average administrative ability and both were corrupt, but Munive escaped the wrath of a visitor general by his timely death.[49] President Munive had, on the one hand, been given a royal mandate; on the other, he had to face the irate cries from the leading citizens and corporations of the kingdom who faced bankruptcy if the cedula were enforced. It would reduce the number of obrajes from two hundred to about twenty. The whole economy of that not-too-prosperous kingdom would come crashing down. Severe dislocations would also ensue throughout the viceroyalty from Panama to Buenos Aires, wherever people depended upon Quito woolens. A solid phalanx of opposition pleaded with the audiencia to suspend the execution of the cedula. At the head of the opposition were the cathedral chapter, the city council of Quito, and the religious orders.

In those situations where royal mandates sharply conflicted with local conditions or where enforcement might create an injustice, the viceroys and the audiencias possessed discretionary authority. They could suspend the execution of a law. In a picturesque ceremony in which the president kissed the royal cedula, he invoked the "I obey but do not execute" formula. Upon applying the formula, the audiencia was required to submit to the Council of the Indies concrete proposals by which the suspended legislation might be improved or modified. Thus the viceroys and the audiencias were given an articulate voice in the formulation of subsequent legislation.

In view of the long distances and the slow communications requiring two years for an exchange between the Old and the New Worlds, some such device was a practical necessity. But the formula had to be invoked with discretion lest its too reckless use provoke the ire of the central authorities in Madrid. Penalties ranging from dismissal from office to the arrival of an always much-feared visitor general might be the answer of Madrid. The president and his colleagues on the bench had to cultivate a sensitivity to the

78   THE THREE QUITOS

real wishes of their superiors in Spain, which were not always expressed in the language of the royal cedulas. Upon this skill depended survival if not promotion on the bureaucratic ladder. The cedulas themselves were often the result of conflicting pressures inside the royal Court and the Council of the Indies. Since the explicit aims of royal legislation were often contradictory, subordinates in the Indies had to work by intuition to guess the real priority among the goals.

The conduct of President Munive in this crisis attests to his ability. He concluded that he had little alternative but to bow to the overwhelming local pressure by suspending the execution of the law pending an appeal to Spain. Failure to yield to the populace might have provoked civil turmoil if not open rebellion. Had such an event occurred, the president would have been held responsible. Subsequently, on July 30, 1681, he dispatched to the Council of the Indies a long memorandum which remains the single most informative document we have about the operation of the textile industry.[50]

He was adamant in his insistence that upon the obrajes depended the frail prosperity of the land. Their sudden abolition would damage every group in the kingdom and create a severe shortage of woolen goods throughout the viceroyalty. Obraje owners and sheep grazers would go bankrupt; the tithes would sag, and royal revenues would decline. Even the Indians would not benefit, for they would lack the wherewithal to pay the tribute. Although the president acknowledged that there were some grave abuses committed against the Indians, he pointed out that over the course of the years the audiencia had quietly made genuine efforts to bring about some corrections. He admitted that some further remedial legislation was in order. He urged the king and his advisers to recognize quite realistically that Indian labor had to be coerced in one fashion or another. The position of the president was that the imperial administration should concentrate on correcting some of the most flagrant abuses and not abolishing the industry as such.

After a careful and critical examination of the report of the president, both the fiscal of the Council of the Indies and then the council itself recommended that the views of the audiencia be accepted with some modifications. On September 5, 1684, Charles II withdrew the cedula of 1680 ordering demolition of all unlicensed obrajes.[51]

Not only did the sheep grazers and the millowners win significant concessions from the crown, but also the conduct of the audiencia in suspending the execution of the cedula of 1680 was vindicated. Madrid, however, exacted a price for its acceptance of Quito's recommendations. Among the reforms that the king ordered was that audits of both the community and the private obrajes were to be taken by royal bureaucrats every six months, so as to reduce any arrears in the payment of wages due the Indians. Prior to this date, only the community obrajes had been subject to audits. The king also accepted the proposal of the audiencia to limit the number of the small obrajes in the capital, the chorrillos, to forty.

The monarch also approved of the president's decision to close the royal obraje at Peguchi in the province of Otavalo. This sweatshop, founded by Dr. Morga's deputy, Pedro Ponce Castellejo, employed two hundred Indians. In contrast to the older obraje at San Luis, which was located on the main square of a densely populated village, the shop at Peguchi had to draw Indians from a radius of eight miles.

The king made one important change at the obraje at San Luis. The net annual profit, averaging between 10,000 and 12,000 pesos thanks to Dr. Morga's reorganization, was henceforth to be deposited in the village treasury, not in the royal exchequer. Long after the Indian arrears in tribute had been liquidated, the royal treasury had continued to receive the annual net profit. This reform too helped solidify the modest prosperity of Otavalo.

President Munive complained that the corregidores in the provinces, who had a wide variety of duties, lacked the time to supervise the obrajes adequately. The response of the king was that a variant of the pre-Morga system of Lima-appointed inspectors should be restored, the system which President Morga had successfully managed to get abolished.

The council rejected one recommendation of the audiencia. The president had defended the practice of employing boys between the ages of 12 and 17 as apprentices in the obrajes on the grounds that they were learning a useful trade. In 1609 royal orders had sanctioned this practice.[52] However, in 1684 the king forbade child labor in any form whatsoever. The cedula of 1684 closed with the customary admonition that all laws and ordinances providing for the humane treatment of the Indians should be scrupulously enforced.

Subsequent mandates from Spain sought to buttress the resolve of the crown to protect the Indians. The king granted the president, and not the audiencia as a body, exclusive jurisdiction with full powers as judge conservator over all cases involving Indian labor in the obrajes. Motivating this innovation was the belief that it was easier to hold one man accountable for the protection of Indian rights than a whole tribunal.

Oidor Matías Lagúnez took issue with this argument. He urged the council to give the Indians freedom to choose the judicial authority to whom they would appeal. It could be that an oidor or a corregidor might be a more zealous magistrate. Pointing out that the president had a host of other duties, Lic. Lagúnez also implied that President Munive lent greater weight to the pleas of the millowners than he did to the suffering of the Indians.[53]

This particular magistrate was indeed an ardent advocate of the Indians. Uncovering some lurid evidence about the mistreatment of obraje labor, he showed scant sympathy for the efforts of the president to work out a compromise in which the prosperity of the textile industry would be harmonized with the need to protect the Indians. Oidor Lagúnez was the "left wing" in this crisis, just as the sheep grazers and the millowners were the "right wing." The report that Lagúnez sent to Madrid, sharply but politely critical of the conduct of the president in the obraje crisis, was just another one of the pressures to which the chief magistrate of the kingdom had to adjust. Ordinarily the council lent much more weight to the views of the president, especially if a majority of the oidores sided with him, than to the dissenting opinion of an individual oidor. Such dissents, however, could undermine the credit and influence of the president before the council. If disunity on the bench became persistent and acrimonious, Madrid might adopt the drastic solution of sending a visitor general. In this particular case, the president prevailed over his colleague. In a series of carefully constructed arguments, the president had convinced the council about the desirability of his compromise approach.

While the sincerity of Oidor Lagúnez' concern for the plight of the Indians should not be doubted, his zealous attitude might also have been intended to attract the attention of the Council of the Indies for a much desired promotion. And promotions did come his way, first to fiscal and later to oidor in the audiencia of Lima.[54]

The most basic reform in the cedula of 1680 that was retained in the revised cedula of 1684 was the provision to abolish debt peonage in the obrajes. According to that ordinance, Indians could not be held against their will in the obrajes, and they were free to change their place of employment. No mill operator was to lend one of his workers more than six pesos. Any sum beyond that amount would not be a legally binding debt. Under no circumstances could an Indian be sentenced to work in the sweatshops for reasons of debt. The enforcement of this order would have substituted voluntary labor for debt peonage; as a result, wages inevitably would have risen. The increased labor costs probably would have driven several of the marginal sweatshops out of business.

The audiencia raised the maximum loan figure from six to ten pesos, and they continued to apply judicial machinery to enforce payment of debts up to that amount.[55] By Spanish standards, ten pesos was not a great deal, but that sum to an Indian worker was a fourth to a third of his annual salary. An ambitious, intelligent Indian might resist the temptation to borrow from his all-too-willing employer. Such foresight was not a characteristic of the less crafty native. To celebrate the baptism of a child or the wedding of a daughter, most Indians were driven to their employers for a loan. And once in debt, they found it difficult if not impossible to get out of debt.

The crown continued its efforts to improve working conditions among the Indians. On December 31, 1704, a cedula abolished mitas in the obrajes of the kingdom.[56] But this particular royal order was conveniently ignored, according to the account of Juan and Ulloa.[57] A similar royal attempt in 1720 to abolish the mita service in the silver mines of Potosí was equally unsuccessful.[58]

The crown's efforts to improve the lot of the Indians failed in that debt peonage was not abolished, although it is undeniable that the condition of Indian labor would have been worse if the crown had not made those efforts. The failure of the central authorities in Spain was largely the result of intransigent opposition by the sheep grazers and millowners who believed, and not without some justification, that very cheap Indian labor made the difference between operating at a loss and making a profit.

The reform measures contained in the New Laws of the 1540's, the cedulas of 1601 and 1609, and the cedulas of the 1680's share several characteristics. In each situation the crown did succeed ultimately in drastically modifying the institution that oppressed the Indians, be it the encomienda, the mita, or the obraje. But each time another almost equally oppressive device emerged as a replacement. The mita succeeded the encomienda, and debt peonage filled the vacuum created by the emasculated mita. In all these cases, the central authorities in Spain undertook bold and sweeping reforms which would have radically changed labor conditions. In all three cases, the colonists reacted so vigorously that the crown felt obliged to retreat. Madrid underestimated the intensity of the pressures that could be applied by the colonists when they felt their vested interests were in jeopardy. The complex and delicate responsibility of the viceroys and the audiencias was to interpret the vested economic interests of the colonists to the crown and to explain to the colonists the paternalistic idealism of the crown. The viceroys and audiencias demonstrated remarkable mediating skill. In only a few situations, such as the revolt over the alcabalas in Quito in the early 1590's, the disturbances in Potosí in the early 1620's, and the revolt of Tupac Amaru in Peru during the 1780's, were they unable to dominate a crisis.[59]

Although the crown retreated from its strongest humanitarian stand under the pressure of local vested interests, it never withdrew totally from its responsibility as the guardian of its Indian wards. By piecemeal legislation in the 1540's, the 1600's, and the 1680's, the crown exacted, as its price for abandoning wholesale reform, the discontinuance of the most flagrant forms of exploitation. That these compromise laws were never systematically enforced by local authorities should not obscure the fact that they were at least partially effective. The Indians did receive some protection from royal legislation, although not as much as the laws required.

The Spanish administration of her empire overseas can be summed up in a Hegelian formula. The thesis is the wishes of the crown, contained in Indian legislation whose tone was one of paternalistic humanitarianism. The antithesis is the complex of local pressures, personified by the colonists who demanded Indian labor at the lowest possible price. The synthesis was an eclectic compromise between idealism and realism, that is, a subtle and intricate synthesis between the *derecho* of royal legislation and the *hecho* of actual social conditions.

The Spanish monarchy was absolute only in the original medieval sense. The king recognized no superior inside or outside his kingdom; he was the ultimate source of all justice and all legislation. The late medieval phrase was, "The king is emperor in his realm." The laws that bore the royal signature, however, were not the arbitrary expression of the king's personal wishes. Legislation in fact reflected the complex and diverse aspirations of all or, at least, several groups in that corporate, multiracial society. The monarchy was representative and decentralized to a degree seldom suspected. Although there was no formal representative assembly or *cortes* in the Indies, each one of the major corporations, all of which enjoyed a large measure of self-government, could and did speak for its own constituents. Their views reached the king and the Council of the Indies, transmitted directly by their accredited representatives or indirectly by the viceroys and the audiencias. The aspirations of each of these corporations profoundly shaped the ultimate decisions.

The most influential of these corporations was apt to be the city council of the viceregal and audiencia capitals. Having purchased their positions from the crown at considerable cost as status symbols in a status-dominated society, the regidores or aldermen were the leading citizens of the community both in wealth and in social position. The town councils were apt to be dominated by American-born Spaniards, the creoles, although well-to-do European Spaniards were always in their ranks. The heirs of the late medieval municipal tradition which had declined in the peninsula by the time of Ferdinand and Isabella, the municipalities, like many other late medieval institutions, took on new vitality in the Indies.

Some useful research has recently been done on how effective the cabildos were in colonial society.[60] The discussion unfortunately has been limited to the performance of their rather narrow legal responsibilities such as policing, controlling prices, administration of justice, etc. Some have suggested that the cabildos in the seventeenth and eighteenth centuries became less effective instruments of government as their membership became increasingly oligarchic in character. But it was the very oligarchic character of the cabildos that enabled them to play a heretofore little-suspected but rather dynamic extralegal role in the larger political spheres. The cabildos, like the parliaments in northern Europe in the seventeenth century, represented property, in particular the new wealth, never people. Granted that they could not legislate about property but could only petition the audiencia, the viceroy, or the king; nonetheless, these petitions always received a hearing and often influenced the outcome of royal legislation. A formal representative assembly was in one sense superfluous. Through the municipalities, the new wealth in the Indies acquired a loud voice in influencing the policies of the state. The new wealth in England and Holland in the seventeenth century, on the other hand, played a similar role through representative assemblies.[61]

In 1594, as a punishment for its participation in the revolt over the alcabalas, the viceroy deprived the city council of Quito of the privilege of electing annually its two executive magistrates, the *alcaldes ordinarios*.[62] Although the cabildo deeply resented this humiliation, the city council throughout the seventeenth century continued to be an articulate and energetic agent of the wealthy creole and Spanish colonists. It often sent duly elected representatives, *procuradores,* to both Lima and Madrid to make known its views on major matters of public policy.

The ecclesiastical cabildo, the cathedral chapter, performed the same role as agent of the secular clergy. The regular clergy also dispatched procuradores from time to time to both Madrid and Rome. What the crown never would permit was that the representatives of the various corporations ever become a formal representative assembly meeting periodically with the power to legislate.[63] The crown jealously guarded its role as the "honest broker" among the aspirations of all the corporations.

In adjusting to the conflicting pressures of all groups in this corporate society and in making some concessions to each one, all the corporations were continually reminded of their dependence upon the throne as ultimate arbitrator. Thus we have the paradox that royal authority was maintained under a bureaucratic system where specific royal wishes were often disregarded. The government of the Spanish empire was in theory highly centralized in the person of the monarch, but in practice it was significantly decentralized. The "absolute" monarchy of the Habsburgs was a limited government in which local property interests exercised considerable influence.

Not only did the actions of corporate groups outside the bureaucracy contribute to the decentralization of decision making, but inside the bureaucracy itself other factors were working toward that end. When the tribunal of Quito was set up in 1563 as an inferior audiencia, the viceroy in Lima continued to exercise political, administrative, and military authority in the kingdom. The broad range of his duties, the distances involved, and the distinct regional characteristics of the land soon forced him reluctantly to delegate piecemeal some of his responsibility to the audiencia. During his twenty years as the head of that tribunal, Dr. Morga was a tireless and articulate champion of more autonomy for Quito. He saw the president as the chief executive officer of the kingdom and not merely as the viceroy's deputy. In some cases he almost managed to make that pretension real. In other cases he failed, but he persisted.

Although personal ambition and vanity may have inspired this attitude to some extent, Dr. Morga had a more positive vision. He clearly saw that geography and history had made the kingdom of Quito into an entity, separate from Peru, with its own set of problems that could be more efficiently resolved in Quito than in Lima. Although the crown never would separate Quito from Lima, for checks and balances were the very foundation of the administrative system, Dr. Morga did in fact enjoy more autonomy than his predecessors had. His grasp of the problems facing the land and his administrative ability demonstrated the feasibility of his pleas for more independent authority.

Buttressed by Dr. Morga's example, the audiencia in Quito did gradually acquire more autonomy during the rest of the seventeenth century.[64] In the obraje crisis of the 1680's, for example, the viceroy in Lima played no substantial role. In Dr. Morga's time, such passivity from Lima would have been unthinkable. The *de facto* detachment from Lima that Quito was acquiring during the seventeenth century became *de jure* in 1720, when that audiencia joined the new viceroyalty of the New Kingdom of Granada.

Dr. Morga thus made a modest contribution to the founding of the independent Republic of Ecuador in the early nineteenth century. He certainly was not a precursor of political emancipation. His clear conception of the audiencia kingdom of Quito, however, as a separate geographical entity whose administration could best be conducted from Quito itself contributed toward solidifying the steady growth of autonomy in the seventeenth century. Such administrative dissociation was one important step on the road that would ultimately end with political independence.

The bureaucracy fashioned by Charles V and Philip II proved remarkably effective even under incompetent kings. The last Habsburg king, Charles II, while not lacking in intelligence, was physically degenerate, the pathetic victim of generations of inbreeding in the Habsburg dynasty. Unable to play any sustained role in the affairs of state, he ruled over a Spain that was militarily, economically, and intellectually prostrate. Yet even under those appalling conditions, the bureaucracy was able to function, as the litigation over the obrajes in the 1680's demonstrates. Obviously its efficiency would have increased with improved leadership from the throne.

Such were the strengths and weaknesses of the three Quitos. Despite its modest resources, the kingdom could produce a surplus for the royal treasury. In 1624 there were, for example, some 250,000 pesos in Guayaquil belonging to the royal fisc ready for transshipment to Spain.[65] In 1626 the treasury in Quito dispatched 12,490 pesos to the metropolis and in 1630 some 25,600 pesos.[66] The assets and liabilities of the kingdom were to be put to a severe test during the years of Dr. Morga's administration when the Dutch boldly sailed through the Strait of Magellan to dispute Spain's supremacy in the Pacific.

5.

THE DUTCH CHALLENGE IN THE SPANISH PACIFIC

On June 3, 1621, barely two months after the death of Philip III of Spain and the ascension of Philip IV, the States General of the Dutch Republic chartered the Dutch West India Company. This action represents the Dutch answer to the celebrated donation of Pope Alexander VI in 1492, modified by the treaty of Tordesillas of 1494, in which Spain and Portugal divided between themselves the nonwestern world. Although the English and the French had made some spectacular incursions into the colonial world of the Iberian powers during the sixteenth century, it was the activity of the Dutch West India Company and the Dutch East India Company, chartered in 1602, which broke the colonial monopoly of Castile and Portugal.

The origins of the Hispano-Dutch conflict go back to the time when Philip II of the Spains inherited the Low Countries from his father, Charles V, who had abdicated his several crowns in the mid-1550's. Inspired by nationalism, the northern portion of the Low Countries, dominated by the maritime provinces of Holland and Zeeland, began the revolt in 1566. The Dutch rebelled against a foreign prince who, in their view, was seeking to replace the loose control of an aristocratic local oligarchy with alien Castilian forms of centralization. The Dutch revolt was also a rebellion of a highly sophisticated capitalist economy against a more backward, semicapitalist economy, which, by political and dynastic accident, could dominate the former. The fact that significant groups in the northern Netherlands, especially in the maritime provinces of Holland and Zeeland, although not the majority of the population, adopted the Protestant creed of John Calvin of Geneva added an acute religious dimension to the Hispano-Dutch conflict. Philip II committed himself to wiping out Protestantism in his own hereditary dominions. He was, however, far more flexible in dealing with Protestants in other lands. National and dynastic interests, which might or might not coincide with the advancement of Roman Catholicism, determined the policy of the prudent king.

The conflict between the Spains and the Dutch extended overseas after Philip II united the crowns of Castile and Portugal in a personal union in 1580. All during the sixteenth century, Dutch merchant vessels had picked up in Lisbon the lucrative cargoes of spices transported by the Portuguese from the spice islands of southeast Asia. From the bustling cities of the Low Countries, the Dutch had distributed the spices to northern and central Europe. The threat of Philip II to interfere with this trade, which he never succeeded in totally abolishing, provoked the Dutch into a momentous countermeasure, whose consequences drastically altered the history of the western and the nonwestern worlds. Dutch ships for the first time went directly to the Orient to dispute the Portuguese monopoly at the very source of the spice production.

The first Dutch fleet sailed around the Cape of Good Hope in 1595. After the chartering of the Dutch East India Company in 1602, the Dutch inflicted a series of blows upon the Iberian powers. The imprudent decision of Philip II to dispatch the Invincible Armada against England had been inspired largely by his belief that the subjugation of that island kingdom was a necessary prerequisite for the destruction of the Dutch republic. When England and Spain ceased fighting in 1604, the Dutch continued to win major victories against the Hispano-Portuguese. They destroyed a powerful Portuguese fleet off Malacca in 1606 and a Spanish armada off Gibraltar in 1607. By 1605 the Dutch had established factories on Java, Sumatra, Borneo, the Moluccas, and the coast of India. Dutch squadrons returned annually with valuable cargoes of spices, porcelains, and silks, rivaling those of Castile's American galleons.

The courtly, corrupt, and lazy favorite of Philip III, the Duke of Lerma, realistically recognized the fact of Spain's exhaustion, and he concluded peace with England in 1604. However, the Spaniards could not bring themselves to recognize the *de jure* independence of the Dutch republic, which had been a fact, and a painful one at that to the Spaniards, since the 1580's. In lieu of a formal treaty of peace, a twelve-year truce was drawn up, which implied only a *de facto* recognition of Dutch independence. The major obstacle in the negotiations was the Dutch insistence on their right to trade in both the East and the West Indies. Diplomatic double-talk eventually led to a face-saving formula. The fourth clause in the treaty left the Dutch with a relatively free hand in the East Indies but implied that the West Indies were to be regarded as a Spanish preserve. The peace party in Holland, headed by Johan van Oldenbarnevelt, found the formula acceptable, and the truce was signed in 1609.

The Dutch subsequently interpreted the fourth clause to suit their purposes. In 1615 a hostile Dutch fleet attacked the west coast of Spanish America. Even though peace parties were in power in both the Dutch republic and the Spanish monarchy, conflict in the tropical world could not be totally eliminated. Under the truce, however, it did diminish considerably.

The outbreak of the Thirty Years' War in Bohemia in 1618 set in motion a chain of events which swiftly led to the resumption of hostilities between the Iberian kingdoms and the Dutch. The Duke of Uceda, who had succeeded his father, the Duke of Lerma, in power in 1618, plunged the Spains into the war on the side of the Austrian Habsburgs for both dynastic and religious motives. As of March 30, 1621, when Philip IV succeeded his father, the Count-Duke of Olivares, who became virtual dictator of Spain, took up the aggressive foreign policy begun by the Duke of Uceda. The Dutch, on the other hand, were sympathetic to the German Protestants and militantly opposed to the Catholic party with which Castile had just allied herself. The twin goals of the Habsburg emperor were to re-Catholicize Germany and to create a strong centralized government, both of which were pointed threats to the Dutch. Thus, upon expiration of the Hispano-Dutch twelve-year truce, shortly after Philip IV's succession in Spain, war parties replaced peace parties almost simultaneously in both Madrid and Amsterdam. The Dutch counterpart of Olivares was Prince Maurice of Nassau, who came to power after the execution of Oldenbarnevelt, the embodiment of the twelve-year truce, upon a trumped-up charge of high treason. Prince Maurice lost no time in actively aligning the Low Countries with the German Protestants.

During the 1620's, the Spaniards won their most glittering victories against the Dutch in Europe. The spectacular triumphs of Spínola at Breda, immortalized by Velázquez, and Fadrique de Toledo's defeat of the Dutch fleet off Gibraltar in 1626 counted for little in the final outcome. The war was not going to be decided in the Low Countries or off the coast of Spain. In Europe the principal theater of operations became Germany, with the France of Richelieu and not the Dutch cast in the role of the successful challenger of the Habsburgs. The decisive theater of conflict between the Dutch and the Iberians was the tropical world.

Prior to 1621, William Usselinx (1567–1647) had advocated in a series of influential pamphlets that the Dutch establish a colonizing and trading corporation for America. Exceedingly hostile to Negro slavery on the grounds that it was both inhumane and inefficient, Usselinx favored free labor in the form of Dutch farmers emigrating to the New World. Although he wished to avoid war with the Iberian powers by colonizing areas not effectively occupied by them, such as Chile or Rio de la Plata, Usselinx insisted that the Spaniards recognize the freedom of the Dutch to settle in the Americas. The Dutch pamphleteer evidently advocated a policy of "peaceful coexistence" between the Dutch and the Spaniards in the New World.

The militant Calvinists, the Counter Remonstrant party, who favored the resumption of hostilities with the Spains even before expiration of the truce, took up Usselinx' proposal; but they subverted it to their own partisan ends. They formed the Dutch West India Company, which was chartered on June 3, 1621. It was not primarily a peaceful colonizing or trading company, but rather it was a corporation whose central purpose was to promote colonization by conquest. Although its charter was modeled after that of the earlier East India Company, its commercial aspect was clearly subordinated to military requirements. The company, whose stocks were held by the leading merchants of the Dutch republic, was capitalized at seven million florins. The States General provided an annual subsidy to help defray the expenses of military operations. Because of the dual operations of the company, encompassing the military as well as commercial interests, the military took a triple oath of allegiance—to the States General, to the stadholder as commander-in-chief of the armed forces of the republic, and to the company.

The great offensive of the Dutch against the Iberian tropical world falls

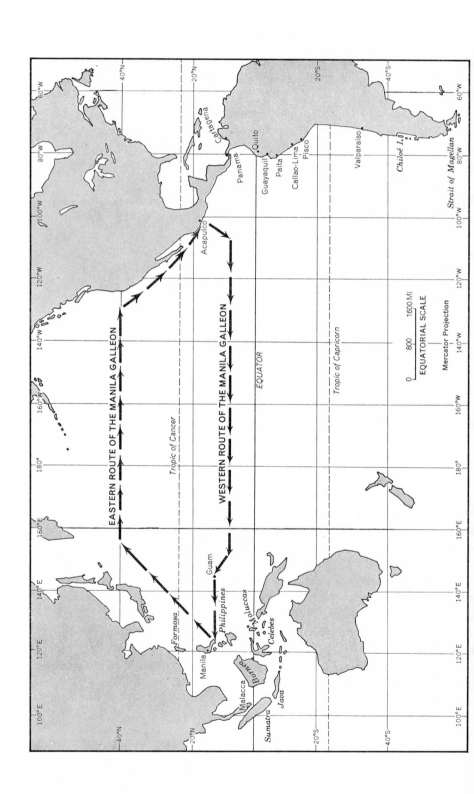

into two periods, the 1620's and the 1630's. The theaters of operations were the west coast of Africa, the Caribbean, the northeast coast of Brazil, the west coast of South and North America from the Strait of Magellan to Acapulco, and southeast Asia. During the 1620's, the Dutch attacked in several places, but the Iberians managed to put up an effective defense of their far-flung and isolated possessions. Although a Dutch fleet of twenty-six ships and 3,300 men captured Bahía, the capital of Brazil, in May, 1624, a mighty Spanish-Portuguese armada consisting of sixty-three ships and 13,000 men under the command of the great Spanish admiral, don Fadrique de Toledo, recaptured Bahía from the Dutch in the following year.

Simultaneously with the attack of the Dutch West India Company on the northeast coast of Brazil, the Dutch East India Company boldly carried the offensive into the Spanish Pacific. The Nassau expedition, as it came to be called, under the joint sponsorship of the States General and the East India Company, yielded disappointing results to its backers. In the Far East, Dutch successes were of a more solid variety. In 1624 a Dutch squadron played havoc with Spanish commerce off the bay of Manila. An Anglo-Dutch squadron inflicted a defeat on a Portuguese fleet off Ormuz in the Persian Gulf. The Dutch also occupied a part of Formosa.

The outstanding successes of the Dutch West India Company were in privateering in the Caribbean. Piet Hein in 1626 audaciously sailed under the guns of Bahía to seize twenty-three vessels loaded with sugar. In the same year the Dutch captured a Honduras galleon, a feat that they repeated the following year. Piet Hein won a dazzling victory when he captured the entire Mexican silver fleet on September 7 and 8, 1628, in the Cuban port of Matanzas. His fleet consisted of twenty-one ships with crews totaling 4,000. A happy combination of good fortune, able seamanship, and inspired leadership yielded Piet Hein a cargo worth 15 million florins. Not only was the Dutch West India Company able to liquidate all its debts and declare a 50 per cent dividend to its shareholders, but also enough remained to help finance a major offensive on the northeast coast of Brazil.

The decade of the 1630's was a period of uninterrupted successes for the Dutch West India Company. The decade began with the capture of Pernambuco by Hendrik Loncq in an expedition composed of sixty-five ships and 8,000 men. Under the humane and adroit leadership of the Governor General of Dutch Brazil, Count John Maurice of Nassau, New Holland by 1641 extended a distance of some 1,000 miles from the São Francisco River to the Amazon. In the climactic year of 1641, the Dutch captured the slave depot of São Paulo da Loanda on the coast of Angola and the sugar islands of São Thomé and Annobom in the Gulf of Guinea.

In the Orient the Dutch East India Company pushed on to even more notable triumphs. Dutch fleets blockaded Goa and the entire Malabar coast, thus isolating Goa from both Portugal and the Spanish Philippines. Profitable trading stations were set up along the Indian coast from Surat to Bengal. Between 1637 and 1640, the Dutch drove the Portuguese out of the cinnamon-rich island of Ceylon. In 1641 Malacca, the key Portuguese base on the Malay peninsula, fell to the Dutch after a siege of 165 days.

At the same time, the Spains made one last supreme effort in Europe to reverse the tide of mounting Dutch successes. In October, 1639, a Dutch fleet under the command of Admiral Maarten Harpertszoon Tromp inflicted a humiliating and decisive defeat on a Portuguese-Spanish armada of sixty-seven galleons with a combined crew of 24,000 men, commanded by don Antonio de Oquendo, off the Downs in the English channel. The battle of the Downs finished the work that had begun with the defeat of the Invincible Armada; Spanish naval power was expelled from the north Atlantic. A second Spanish-Portuguese fleet of eighty-six vessels and 12,000 men, which had crossed the Atlantic to Brazil, met defeat in a four-day running battle in January, 1640, from a squadron of forty-one vessels of the Dutch West India Company.

Referring to the chain of events culminating in 1641 with the capture of Malacca and Loanda, Engel Sluiter adds:

This was unmistakably the end of an epoch, not only in the Far East but in world history. A half century of vigorous, aggressive Dutch expansion had done more than anything else to shatter the ancient status quo, the Iberian colonial monopoly. Masters of the East, with vast territorial holdings in the West, enjoying commercial and naval supremacy in Europe, and recognized as leaders in the sciences and art, the United Netherlands had virtually reached the crest of its power and influence.[1]

This is not the place to chronicle the story of Dutch decline in the 1640's and the 1650's, the cause and consequence of which made England and France the principal beneficiaries of the Dutch destruction of the Iberian monopoly of the nonwestern world. Rather, within this broad perspective of the struggle during the 1620's and the 1630's, the strategic and tactical problems facing the Spaniards in their defense of the Pacific need to be scrutinized.

With its 70 million square miles of water and its thousands of islands, the South Sea, as the Pacific was then known, was the most spacious domain claimed by the kings of Castile and León. Although the donation of Alexander VI and the treaty of Tordesillas lent some juridical and theological foundation to this grandiose pretension, all the non-Iberian powers, including Catholic France, refused to recognize the validity of either document. Castile therefore sought to supplement her claim by an appeal to the principle of *mare clausum* in international law. As one Spanish commentator, Father Medina, asserted, the Pacific was a Spanish sea just as the Mediterranean had been the *mare nostrum* of the ancient Romans. The Spanish claim of a closed sea ran counter to the new international law whose outstanding formulator was the Dutch scholar, Hugo Grotius (1583–1645). "The seas and the oceans by reason of their immensity are not subject to the particular use of any one power against the rights of the rest," was the doctrine laid down by Grotius.[2]

The Spaniards did buttress their extensive claims, based on theoretical principles of theology and international law, by the more substantial rights of discovery and colonization dating back to 1513, when Vasco Núñez de Balboa crossed the narrow isthmus of Panama to become the first European to lay eyes on the Pacific. Clad in the ceremonial armor of a medieval knight, he entered the water, unleashed his sword, and declared the sea and its islands and all its contiguous territories to be the property of the crown of Castile and León. "Then before another decade was gone," in the words of the late William Lyon Schurz, "the epic voyage of Magellan gave heroic substance to the sweeping claim so lightly made by the conquistador on the shores of Darien."[3] As a result of the conquests of Mexico and Peru in the 1520's and 1530's, the authority of the Castilian crown covered broad stretches of the Pacific coast with various degrees of intensity from the Bio-Bio River in central Chile to Cape Mendocino in North America.

After 1564 the Spaniards extended their control westward across the Pacific to the Philippines until they reached the frontiers of the Japanese and Chinese empires. The Manila-Acapulco galleons, on which Mexican silver was exchanged for Chinese silks, became the economic lifeline of the Philippines. With the personal union of the crowns of Portugal and Castile in 1580, the Portuguese empire in the Orient, whose most lucrative source of wealth was the spices of the Moluccas and the Celebes lying south of the Philippines, became an appendage of the Castilian empire in that area.

The main artery of commerce along the west coast of South America was the sea route from Callao, the port of Lima, to Panama. Along this watery highway plied the galleons transporting the silver of Peru to Panama and thence across the Atlantic to Spain, and from Panama European goods were shipped down the coast to Callao, where they were distributed to all parts of Spanish South America. South of Peru lay the struggling Spanish colony in the central valley of Chile. The hostile Araucanian Indians stopped the Spanish advance at the Bio-Bio River for 250 years. Imperial Spain held Chile for the defensive purpose of keeping foreigners out of the area, thus providing a buffer for upper and lower Peru.

Along the coasts there were several ports of secondary importance. Arica, south of Callao, served as an outlet for some of the silver production of the audiencia of Charcas, now the republic of Bolivia. The port of Paita, north of Callao, had some commercial importance. Along with Callao, Panama, and Acapulco, Guayaquil was one of the four most strategic ports on the whole west coast. Guayaquil served as the gateway to the towns of the Ecuadorian Sierra. It was also the most active shipbuilding center on the west coast of South America. The munitions factory at Latacunga was a major source of firearms for the defense of the coast from the Bio-Bio to Panama.[4]

The major thrust of the Dutch challenge to the Spanish Pacific was not around Cape Horn and the Strait of Magellan but the opposite approach around the Cape of Good Hope into the Indian Ocean and thence to the Pacific. To a large extent, geography favored the Spanish defense of the southern gateway around South America. The winds and waves of those savage seas took a heavy toll in ships and lives of all nations. Their very remoteness discouraged foreign intrusions. The hardship of an unbroken voyage was a supreme test of endurance and discipline, for mutiny and debilitating diseases such as scurvy were daily contingencies. There were no convenient ports-of-call where a ship might safely refit and reprovision its stores between St. Catherine's Island off the southern coast of Brazil and the well-defended Spanish ports on the west coast.

Formidable though these obstacles were, they were overcome, first by Sir Francis Drake in 1579 and later by Cavendish in 1587. After 1600, however, the Dutch were more successful than the English. On five occasions, in 1599, 1600, 1615, 1624, and 1643, Dutch fleets made this perilous voyage. Between 1578 and 1594, the English sailed into the Pacific three times for a total of five ships weighing 670 tons with a combined crew of 250 men. Between 1599 and 1615, the Dutch sent twelve ships through the Strait of Magellan for a total tonnage of 4,200 tons and a combined crew of 1,000 men.[5]

The first Dutch expedition to sail around the Horn into the Spanish Pacific in September, 1599, was a fleet of five ships with a total crew of five hundred men under the joint command of Jacob Mahu and Simon de

Cordes. Mahu died in the Atlantic. Cordes and fifty of his men were killed by the Araucanians in southern Chile. Weakened by scurvy, hunger, and cold, the Dutch lost the smallest of the vessels to the Spaniards. In November, 1599, two of the Dutch boats crossed the Pacific from southern Chile. A third ship captured a few small Spanish vessels before it left the coast of Peru in June, 1600, for southeast Asia.[6]

A few months later the second squadron, composed of two large and two small vessels, was a more successful enterprise. Its commander was Olivier van Noort, a tavern keeper from Utrecht. He was also an experienced sailor. He financed the venture by organizing a joint stock company. Van Noort on the *Mauritius* and his associate, de Lint, were separated in March, 1600, in southern Chile, never to be reunited. De Lint cruised northward to the coast of Mexico before he sailed to the Far East. After the *Mauritius* had inflicted some damage on Spanish shipping in the port of Valparaíso, van Noort received news that the viceroy of Peru had just assembled a defense squadron, and therefore abruptly abandoned his original plan of sailing northward to California.[7]

Crossing the Pacific via the Ladrones Islands, he sighted the Philippines. In October, 1600, he lay off the coast of Capul, hoping to capture the two galleons coming from Acapulco "laden with friars and silver." Unsuccessful in this endeavor, he moved up the straits toward the bay of Manila, capturing several small vessels engaged in intra-island trading and plundering some coastal settlements in the Bisayas Islands. Van Noort lay off the bay of Manila hoping to intercept either the Chinese junks laden with precious silks plying between the south China coast and Manila or the even more desirable Manila galleon with its cargo of Mexican silver.

Inside the walled city of Manila, the Spanish authorities made frantic efforts to take the offensive against the intruder. Since this was the first Dutch vessel to appear around the harbor of Manila, the Spaniards were caught off guard. Most of the colony's armed forces were engaged in a punitive expedition against the Moros, the Muslim-Malay inhabitants of the southern Philippines. After some political skirmishes, Governor Tello appointed Dr. Antonio de Morga, then the senior oidor of the audiencia, as commander-in-chief of the fleet.

The appointment was certainly an unusual one, since the senior oidor was a lawyer and bureaucrat with no military experience in his background. Although naval warfare at that time was at best semi-professionalized, the appointment of Dr. Morga was a political decision largely divorced from military considerations. A better qualified candidate, and the first appointee, was Juan Ronquillo de Castillo, commander of the galleys. Although then in his early twenties, he was already a seasoned commander. This same Juan Ronquillo won a brilliant victory over a much larger Dutch fleet off Playa Honda seventeen years later. The governor dispatched Ronquillo to the near-by port of Cavite to supervise the construction and outfitting of a few vessels. Returning to Manila within a few days, Ronquillo, according to Morga, made a series of impossible demands, which Morga adroitly used as evidence of Ronquillo's "incompetence" in the crisis. On these grounds the governor dismissed Ronquillo and gave the command to Dr. Morga. It is fair to surmise that Ronquillo may have been inept or inexperienced in supervising the building of ships. Dr. Morga did have the energy and administrative know-how to perform this task, but the oidor proved himself incompetent at commanding in the fire of battle. From a Spanish point of view, it was a misfortune that Morga's assignment was not confined to building the fleet while Ronquillo was given its command. Thus the talents of the two men would have been better utilized.

If Ronquillo were an unsuitable candidate, which is highly questionable, the governor might have given the command to someone else with more military experience than Dr. Morga. Some of the professional military were appalled at the choice of Morga. Restless and unhappy in Manila, Dr. Morga saw the command of the fleet as a golden opportunity to achieve a spectacular success which would facilitate his much-desired promotion to the audiencia of Mexico. Although the ineffective governor and the more energetic judge had engaged in the normal amount of political in-fighting, Governor Tello at this time needed to conciliate Morga. As senior oidor, Morga would probably conduct Tello's *residencia* when the governor's term expired.[8]

Whatever he lacked in naval experience Antonio de Morga made up in enthusiasm and administrative talent. Within thirty-two days, three small vessels were being built under his direction. The judge-turned-admiral was so impatient to lock horns with the enemy that he sailed out of Cavite harbor without advising his second vessel. It could be that he wanted all the glory for himself, or that he was fearful the Dutch would elude him. The squadron consisted of the flagship, the *San Diego,* weighing some two hundred tons, and a much smaller vessel, the *San Bartolomé,* under the command of Captain Juan de Alcega.

Two days later on December 14, 1600, the Spaniards encountered the Dutch. The first battle was between the two opposing flagships, the *San Diego* and the *Mauritius.* For six hours the battle raged. The Spaniards clamped the two vessels together with grappling irons, and they boarded the deck of the enemy flagship. But the Dutch fought back with the rage of despair. From the waist of their ship, where netting protected them from above, the Dutch resisted the invaders with well-directed musket fire and with pikes and halberds. The Dutch ultimately forced the Spaniards to retreat to their own flagship.

Just when the Spaniards were boarding the deck of the *Mauritius,* the *San Bartolomé* approached the fray. Rather than joining in that combat, the *San Bartolomé* went off in pursuit of the second Dutch vessel. However, before leaving Cavite, Alcega had received written instructions from Morga to accompany the flagship at all times. Thus Dr. Morga later complained bitterly that Captain Alcega had deliberately disobeyed instructions when he left the *San Diego* locked in combat with the *Mauritius.* Alcega's defense was that he had no longer been needed on the scene, since the Spaniards on the deck of the enemy flagship were shouting cries of victory. Moreover, Alcega overtook the smaller enemy vessel, the *Eendracht,* captured it, and triumphantly brought it back to Manila as a prize of war.

Dr. Morga, on the other hand, did not win the glory he anticipated. Victory came very close, but it eluded him. As the Dutch were furiously driving the Spaniards off the deck of their flagship, the heavier artillery of the *Mauritius* punctured the hull of the *San Diego* below the waterline. The hull of the Spanish flagship began to fill with water, and the dispirited commander, now driven back to his own ship, had no alternative but to order his sinking *San Diego* to head for the island of Fortuna which lay four or five miles away. Before reaching its destination, the *San Diego* sank. The bulk of the officers and crew of some two hundred men drowned before reaching the shore.[9] But not Dr. Antonio de Morga, age 41, who swam to safety. He was then indestructible.

As the sinking *San Diego* foundered off, a fire broke out midship on the *Mauritius.* Van Noort managed to put out the flames. After repairing his vessel in Borneo, he sailed around the Cape of Good Hope and reached Rotterdam on August 27, 1601, with forty-seven bedraggled men. Thus Olivier van Noort, ex-tavern keeper from Utrecht, joined the illustrious company of Ferdinand Magellan and Sir Francis Drake. The *Mauritius* was the first Dutch vessel to circumnavigate the globe.

Dr. Morga had become enough of a sailor to feel himself disgraced. He had lost his ship. What especially rankled the new admiral was that his second-in-command had captured the other Dutch vessel. That it was a smaller vessel than the flagship provided little comfort. Dr. Morga charged

Alcega with insubordination. The oidor proposed to refight the naval engagement in the law courts where he was more competent than he was on the high seas in the heat of battle. Alcega briefly landed in jail, but he was never brought to trial. All of Dr. Morga's somewhat legalistic arguments could not obliterate the fact that Alcega was a hero for having captured an enemy vessel.[10]

Although due credit should be given to Dr. Morga for the energy and dispatch with which he built the needed vessels at Cavite, he evidently lost effective command during the battle. Some of his detractors even accused him of cowardice. Such a charge is manifestly unjust. He was, however, indecisive and confused. His officers regarded him as a political appointee, which indeed he was. His lack of cool judgment in the midst of combat merely reinforced the contempt of the officers for their commander.

In addition to the deep personal humiliation he suffered at the hands of the Dutch, Dr. Morga feared that this episode might cost him the coveted promotion to Mexico. Before news reached Spain of the encounter with the Dutch, the Council of the Indies approved his promotion to the audiencia of Mexico. Nonetheless, he indefatigably refought the battle in his correspondence with the Council of the Indies. Several years later in 1609, when he was comfortably situated in the audiencia of Mexico, he published his *Sucesos de las islas filipinas.* This book, which is a revealing account of early Spanish colonization in the islands, was inspired partially by his deeply felt desire to vindicate his conduct in the encounter with the former tavern keeper from Holland. In contrast to his correspondence immediately after the event, when he displayed vitriolic hostility toward Alcega, he used more restrained language in the *Sucesos.* Censorship standards required that authors avoid *escándalo.* It could be also that his bitterness against his former subordinate had subsided with the passing of the years and possibly with his remarriage in November, 1609, to a lady who was probably a relative of this same Alcega.[11]

The van Noort expedition was not a shattering success from either the Dutch or the Spanish viewpoint. Both sides came out rather bloody and battered. Although the Dutch did manage to get seven ships into the Pacific, bad weather soon dispersed the fleet. The Spaniards never had to face a united enemy. To be sure, the Dutch did do some damage to Spanish shipping. The most durable result of the expedition, however, was that van Noort's associate, de Lint, reached Ternate in the *Hendrik Frederik,* where he laid the basis for subsequent trade in spices. The victory of van Noort over Dr. Morga had far-reaching symbolic implications. As Engel Sluiter has remarked, "That a Rotterdam innkeeper should impudently sail in and out of Spanish waters without being chastized for his temerity hurt Spanish prestige."[12]

Although fortunately for Spain Dr. Morga was never to command another squadron against the Dutch, he had a second very close call with the seafaring sons of Holland. On July 16, 1615, Dr. Morga, his large family, and an inordinate amount of luggage departed from Acapulco on the small vessel, *Nuestra Señora del Rosario,* en route to Guayaquil, where he was to take up his new assignment as president of the royal audiencia. On August 27, as the little vessel was passing the Cape of Santa Elena north of Guayaquil, a fleet of six well-armed Dutch warships under the command of Joris van Speilbergen sighted *Nuestra Señora del Rosario.* The log of the Dutch fleet recorded, "August 27, 1615—we still kept the same course until the evening when we sighted a vessel in front of us, and made every endeavor to overtake it, but the darkness of the night caused us to lose sight of it."[13] Had the Dutch captured the Spanish vessel, they would have found an agreeable surprise. *Nuestra Señora del Rosario* contained a cargo of contraband Chinese silks worth one million pesos. Part of the cargo belonged to Dr. Morga, who listed his share of the contraband in the official registry of the vessel as his personal library. These same silks were to plague him for the rest of his bureaucratic career. He managed to escape exposure and punishment in 1615, but in 1636 the law finally caught up with him.[14]

One reason why the Dutch fleet tarried off the coast of Peru was the desire to capture the new viceroy of Peru, the Prince of Esquilache, who, Dutch intelligence had learned, was sailing down the coast from Panama. Esquilache managed to evade capture because his vessel hugged the coast, whereas the Dutch fleet was in the open ocean. The Dutch hoped to exchange the viceroy for the Dutch warrior Paulus van Caerden, who had been captured by the Spaniards for the second time in 1610 and was held prisoner in the Philippines. The hard-headed Dutch balked at paying the ransom of 40,000 pesos requested by the Spaniards.[15]

However, the main reasons the Dutch were in the Spanish Pacific were not merely to capture Esquilache and chase Morga's little ship. Their other objectives were to develop a strong aggressive force in the Far Eastern Pacific and secondarily to intercept the Manila galleons laden with silver and other precious cargo. Thus, early in 1614, apparently disregarding the twelve-year truce, the Dutch East India Company organized a fleet of six vessels, under the command of Joris van Speilbergen, a veteran Dutch seaman, which set sail in August, 1614, for the distant Spanish Pacific. On

July 17 and 18, 1615, he inflicted a humiliating and severe defeat on a Spanish fleet off Cañete. The Castilian losses included two warships and 450 dead. Van Speilbergen lost only forty men, and his vessels suffered scarcely any damage. After sacking the port of Paita and pursuing the *Nuestra Señora del Rosario* off the Cape of Santa Elena, van Speilbergen boldly sailed into the unfortified harbor of Acapulco, where he negotiated an exchange of Spanish prisoners for badly needed provisions. War, however, is not all fighting.

For a week Acapulco was the scene of a rare social mingling between the Dutch and Spanish officers, each side observing the strictest ceremony and punctilio. Many "captains and cavallieros" visited the pirate ships, where they were treated to ample Dutch hospitality and allowed to examine the armament and fittings. On the fifteenth, Speilbergen received a visit from Fernández de Córdoba, the Spanish commander. For such a distinguished guest the Dutch admiral had his troops drawn up in full parade uniform with muskets and swords. At the same time, to guarantee the safety of Fernández, Speilbergen's young son went ashore and spent the day with the *alcalde mayor* by whom he was "very honorably received and entertained."

Meanwhile the Dutch sailors, working shoulder-to-shoulder with the citizenry of Acapulco, were busy bringing out to their ships casks of fresh water, wood for the cooking fires, and a good supply of food, principally meat and fowls, vegetables, oranges and lemons. On October 16, while the provisions were still being brought out, the Dutch set ashore their twenty Spanish prisoners. The next day, having received all the supplies agreed on, the pirates took leave of their new friends with many expressions of mutual esteem.[16]

At the end of the week's truce, the grim business of war replaced social pleasantries. Van Speilbergen set out to capture the Manila galleon. He cruised along the coast of Jalisco for a couple of months until the end of November. Despairing of meeting his prize, he sailed across the Pacific to the Philippines, where he blockaded the port of Manila briefly before he retired to the Moluccas.

The years of 1615 through 1617 were decisive for the outcome of the struggle in the Far East. In 1616 Governor Silva mustered the largest armada that heretofore had sailed out of the bay of Manila. The bold objective of this fleet of sixteen large vessels was nothing less than to expel the Dutch from southeast Asia, while the van Speilbergen expedition of 1615 was planned to strengthen the Dutch forces in the Far East against that expected offensive of the Spaniards. Van Speilbergen's depredations along the west coast of Spanish America had been of secondary importance in the Dutch scheme of things.

The achievements of the Silva armada were disappointing. While relieving the besieged Portuguese fortress at Malacca on the Malay peninsula, Governor Silva suddenly died. His death and the failure of Portuguese reinforcements to arrive from India led to an abandonment of the general offensive against the Dutch. "The débacle of this expedition," according to Schurz, "is as important in the history of the East Indies as was the failure of the 'Invincible' in 1588, for it definitely settled the question as to who should dominate that region."[17]

While the Silva expedition was away, Joris van Speilbergen arrived off Manila, where he did no extensive damage. The next year the Dutch admiral returned to Philippine waters, where a decisive battle took place on April 13 and 14, 1617, off Playa Honda in the vicinity of Corregidor. Under the command of the veteran Spanish commander, Juan Ronquillo, whom Morga had replaced in 1600 in the battle with van Noort, seven Spanish galleons and two galleys engaged the Dutch squadron in a bitterly fought two-day battle. On the second day, the Spaniards boarded several of the Dutch vessels and overwhelmed their defenders with the sword. The Dutch lost three ships including the gigantic forty-seven gun flagship, the *Sun of Holland*. The Spaniards also captured two Dutch warships.[18]

If the failure of the Silva expedition foreshadowed the inability of the Spaniards to mount a successful general offensive to drive the Dutch out of southeast Asia, the Spanish naval victory at Playa Honda the next year foreshadowed the failure of the Dutch to expel the Castilians from the Philippines. After 1617 the Dutch did make several attempts to seize the Philippines, but they failed. Dutch strategy was to blockade the port of Manila periodically for several months and, by cutting off the silk trade with south China and preventing Mexican silver from reaching Manila, to force Spanish withdrawal from the islands. Although they inflicted severe economic dislocations on the Philippines by this strategy, the Dutch underestimated the pride and the valor of the Castilians. The latter were prepared to pay the heavy cost of defending the archipelago, an attitude that the Dutch never quite understood.[19] Although the events of 1616 and 1617 had suggested the ultimate outcome of the struggle, both sides relentlessly fought each other for two more decades, with the offensive passing to the Dutch.

After the twelve-year truce expired in 1621, the Dutch determined to mount the offensive against the Hispano-Portuguese empire on several fronts, in both the Atlantic and the Pacific. Prince Maurice of Nassau and the States General lent energetic support to the Dutch East India Company's plans to take the offensive along the west coast of Spanish America. The largest Dutch fleet ever to enter the Pacific waters of Spanish America, the so-called Nassau fleet, consisting of eleven ships and 1,650 men, had much more ambitious plans than previous expeditions. Not only did they seek to engage in contraband trade and to seize the silver galleons plying between Callao and Panama or between Acapulco and Manila, but also they had territorial ambitions in the New World.

The first misfortune to befall the ill-starred expedition occurred when its commander, Jacques l'Hermite, died off the coast of Peru. He had been in failing health since passing the coast of Sierra Leone. His successor, Hugo Schapenham, was much inferior in qualities of leadership. His first blunder was not to chase the treasure fleet loaded down with the accumulation of two years of silver, which had left Callao five days before the Dutch arrived. Instead Schapenham blockaded the port of Callao for three months. Although he inflicted some damage on Spanish shipping, he was unable to make any progress against the well-defended fortress of Callao.

Dutch strategy vainly envisaged that the blockade would encourage the Indians and the Negro slaves to revolt. In order to avert such a possibility, the viceroy disarmed the Indians and placed most reliance on the Spanish citizens. He did raise, however, two companies of freed Negroes who fought valiantly for the king of the Spains, since the Spanish authorities persuaded them that the Dutch would enslave them.

While off the Peruvian coast, units of the Dutch fleet sacked Guayaquil twice. Schapenham then sailed northward to Acapulco, where, to his acute disappointment, he found no Manila galleon. The growing scarcity of his water supply forced him after a month to abandon his plan to lie in wait along the coast of Jalisco to intercept the Manila galleon. He sailed westward across the Pacific to the safe haven of Java. The comment of Burney merits repetition: "Thus cheaply were the Spaniards freed from the most formidable armament that ever at any time before or since threatened their possessions in the South Sea."[20] Schapenham himself died off the island of Java toward the end of 1625, shortly before his fleet ingloriously disbanded.

In terms of the heavy expenditures involved, the "Nassau Fleet" was a dismal failure. This failure accounts for the fact that the Dutch did not dispatch another fleet around Cape Horn for nineteen years. The lack of success of the Dutch thrust along the Pacific coast of Spanish America cannot be ascribed merely to the inept leadership of Schapenham. Although he obviously failed to exploit his advantages, there were many conditions favorable to the Spanish defense and inimical to the Dutch offensive. The remoteness of the area from the Dutch bases in the Atlantic and in the Orient and the perils of that extended voyage, inviting disease, ill-discipline, even mutiny, were all powerful factors working in favor of the Spaniards. To capture one of the well-protected silver fleets either on the Callao-Panama line or on the Acapulco-Manila run was improbable at best. The Dutch never succeeded, but two Englishmen—Drake and Rogers—each captured a galleon. The paucity of flourishing settlements did not provide inviting targets for plunder. However feasible Dutch colonization may have been on the northeast coast of South America, such an enterprise on the Pacific coast was a chimera. The Dutch historian Pieter Geyl has even suggested that the Dutch unwisely neglected their position in North America by concentrating on Brazil, only to lose both.[21]

To stress the folly of the Dutch attempts at colonization on the west coast of South America does not mean to imply that there were not serious weaknesses in the Spanish position there. Spanish control was indeed imperfect. The Araucanians in southern Chile, the zambos in Esmeraldas, the Indian tribes in Buenaventura, and the enclaves of rebellious slaves in Panama, known as the cimarrones, amply demonstrate the existence of several islands of resistance to the Spaniards. But the Dutch were notoriously unrealistic in thinking that these anti-Spanish groups would cooperate with them against the Spaniards. The fierce determination of the Araucanians, the zambos, and the cimarrones to maintain their freedom would scarcely have encouraged them to give to the Dutch the obedience which they had militantly refused to grant to the Spaniards. The acuteness of the conflict between the Spaniards and the Dutch made little difference to the nonwhite enemies of the Castilian monarch.

Prince Maurice's instructions reflect the woeful ignorance of the Dutch about actual conditions on the west coast. He ordered the expedition to capture the port of Arica and, in alliance with the Indians, to march inland to occupy the fabled silver mines of Potosí. Once on the Peruvian coast, the leaders of the expedition soon learned the folly of such a plan. As one of them commented, ". . . all the fine projects of Indian conquests formed in Holland appeared to them romantic dreams that neither they nor anyone else could execute."[22] The sons of Holland learned from experience that the Spaniards were able to mount an effective defense of unfortified ports such as Arica, Pisco, and Guayaquil. The fortress of Callao was impregnable.

The Dutch did acquire for the first time some accurate information about the successful resistance of the Araucanians against the Spaniards south of the Bio-Bio River. In 1624 they considered making a landing on the south Chilean coast. When they returned to the Pacific in 1643, the Dutch actually occupied a site near present-day Valdivia for three months. They abandoned it when they discovered that the Araucanians were no more friendly to them than they were to the Spaniards.[23]

The unwillingness of Spain's nonwhite enemies to cooperate actively with the Dutch was a negative factor of decisive importance. It foredoomed Dutch colonization on the west coast. Although success would not have been guaranteed had these nonwhite groups been willing to ally themselves with the invaders, Dutch prospects would have brightened considerably.

The fact that the Spaniards were not able to extend their control over the whole Pacific coast ought not to obscure the sources of Spanish strength. None of the islands of resistance was able to threaten the main centers of Spanish resources. Although the Spanish advance may have been stopped in specific localities on the periphery, they could muster both human and material resources at the centers of power in Lima, Quito, Panama, and Mexico City that were disproportionately far in excess of anything that their European or their American enemies could mobilize.

The responsibility for defending the west coast of South America from central Chile to the isthmus of Panama belonged to the viceroy of Peru, and the defense of the Mexican coast was in the hands of the viceroy in Mexico City. Their primary concern was to protect the silver fleets plying between Callao and Panama and between Acapulco and Manila. They discharged their responsibility with distinction. During the Hispano-Dutch war, which came to a close with the treaty of Münster in 1648, no fleet was intercepted.

As early as 1584, in response to English threats, the Spaniards sought to bar foreign access to the Pacific by creating a fortified settlement on the Strait of Magellan itself. Ill-luck, mismanagement, an inhospitable climate, and poor communications with the base of supply rendered this attempt abortive.[24] The revised defense strategy that evolved at the end of the sixteenth century made Callao the key naval base on the Pacific coast. The heavy fortifications of the port made it impregnable. There they maintained three or four armed galleons, usually constructed in Guavaquil, to form an armada available immediately for offensive action. As soon as enemy ships were sighted at Chiloé or the islands of Mocha or Santa María recuperating after the ordeal of the long voyage, news was carried to the mainland and then northward by swift small vessels or by runners and signal fires into the interior to alert all the coastal cities.[25] Thus the Spaniards managed to minimize the element of surprise.

Beginning in 1615 with stepped-up Dutch activity, Viceroys Esquilache and Guadalcázar further developed the defense strategy. It was a static concept in which they sought to confine Spanish settlements on the coast to a minimum. Hence they opposed Dr. Morga's ambition to subjugate Esmeraldas. Not only would new ports have to be defended at considerable expense to both the crown and the local inhabitants, but also their very existence would provide the Dutch with inviting targets for plunder and sources of badly needed provisions. Furthermore, new ports might facilitate invasions into the interior. The same no-settlement policy was followed along the western coast of Mexico, with Spanish settlement confined to the port of Acapulco. "Piracy" in the Pacific did less immediate material harm than it did damage to potential territorial expansion along the coast.[26] The long stretches of unsettled littoral along the coast of Spanish America may be traced, in part at least, to this policy.

Of the four major ports on the Pacific, Callao, Panama, and Acapulco had permanent fortifications. The building of the castle of San Diego in Acapulco began after 1615 in order to forestall subsequent visits such as the one van Speilbergen had paid that port. Guayaquil alone was unfortified.

In 1624 news reached Quito and Guayaquil of the appearance of the Dutch fleet off the coast of Peru. Feverish preparations were made to put the port in a defensive posture. The Spaniards evacuated all women, children, elderly persons, and priests, as well as 250,000 pesos belonging to the royal treasury ready for transshipment to Spain on the next boat to Panama. In Quito the audiencia and the treasury officials met several times a week in order to equip a relief expedition of one hundred soldiers.[27] On May 23, 1624, two vessels of the Dutch fleet appeared off Guayaquil. This was in the nature of a probing action. The Dutch undertook similar probing actions against the ports of Arica and Pisco.

The first battle of Guayaquil was a modest Dutch success. Under the command of Captain Schulte, they burned three small Spanish vessels off the island of Puná and captured another. The invaders landed with two hundred men. The Spanish casualties were one hundred men, with seventeen of the defenders taken prisoner. Their captors subsequently threw them overboard several miles out in the open sea. Since the small Dutch expedition could not hope to hold Guayaquil, they withdrew within a few days. Before they did, they set afire all the contents in the well-stocked warehouses. Textile goods worth over 100,000 pesos went up in smoke.

The success of the first attack encouraged the Dutch to return on August 25. This time the whole Dutch fleet appeared off the island of Puná. Four hundred well-armed Dutchmen sailed up the Guayas River to Guayaquil itself where a bloody street battle occurred, lasting three hours, with several wooden buildings going up in flames. On August 25 the invaders resumed the attack, and again on August 26 the battered city sustained another assault, this time with six hundred Dutchmen joining the fray.

Although the Dutch put three times as many troops into the second attack as they did into the first, the Spaniards were greatly strengthened by reinforcements of men and munitions from the Sierra. They killed or captured twenty-eight Dutch soldiers. The Dutch landing party withdrew to the fleet lying off Puná. Their morale broken by the repulse, the men of the once-proud Nassau fleet sailed northward to Acapulco, where further frustration awaited them. A measure of the massive failure of the Nassau fleet is that the most extensive damage it inflicted on the Spaniards along the whole west coast was the sack of Guayaquil.[28]

What was the military significance of the battle of Guayaquil? Dr. Morga exultingly claimed a victory. In Spain, too, it was regarded as one of the defensive successes of the 1620's in which the Spaniards managed to defeat several Dutch probing actions all over the tropical world. The president of the audiencia proudly proclaimed that the Spanish forces frustrated a Dutch attempt at a permanent occupation of Guayaquil. There is little evidence that this was the Dutch intention, but if it was, the effectiveness of the Spanish defense made any such attempt a vain hope.

In 1624 Dr. Morga showed the same organizing skill that he had demonstrated in 1600 at Cavite when he had his vessels built within a month. Unfortunately for the Dutch in 1624, he did not command the troops in person. Hence his skill in organizing logistical support for the defense of Guayaquil did make a solid contribution to the Spanish victory. The battle of Guayaquil was the closest that he ever came to securing revenge for the humiliation of his defeat at the hands of van Noort in 1600 and the indignity he suffered in 1615 when the Dutch fleet nearly captured him and his contraband silk. The defense of Guayaquil was the successful climax of his bureaucratic career. A few months later Lic. Mañozca, the visitor general, arrived in Quito. From then until his death in 1636, Antonio de Morga fought skillfully but vainly to save his career and his reputation.

Although the Spaniards in general and Dr. Morga in particular could take pride in the successful defense of Guayaquil, the city lay in ashes and its economy in ruins. A few years before, Viceroy Esquilache, in a move designed to curb the contraband trade, had prohibited the export of cacao from Guayaquil to the ports of Central America and Mexico. An incipient

cacao boom collapsed, with the price plunging from 36 to three pesos per
arroba. The decades of the 1620's and the 1630's became a grim period for
the rough-and-tough port town. The collapse of the cacao boom and the
depredations of the Dutch left the members of the numerous Castro clan in
control of the municipal government. Their administration provoked furious
enmity from their opponents.[29]

After the Dutch attack in the summer of 1624, the desirability of fortifying Guayaquil came up for serious discussion. Viceroy Chinchón realistically assessed the pros and cons of such a step in a report he submitted to
Philip IV on April 15, 1630. The strategic importance of Guayaquil was
twofold, he pointed out. It was the largest shipyard on the west coast of
South America, where most of the galleons of Peru were constructed.
Secondly, if Guayaquil or the adjacent island of Puná guarding the entrance
to the port should ever fall into enemy hands, the Dutch could literally
destroy the Spanish empire in South America by dominating its main artery
of trade, the Callao-Panama lifeline.

Both Viceroy Esquilache and Viceroy Guadalcázar stressed another
potential danger. Dutch occupation of Guayaquil or any other coastal settlement would provide them with a springboard for invading the towns of the
Sierra. The viceroys also feared that such an invading force might receive
assistance from the zambo communities along the coast of Esmeraldas.[30]
Viceroy Chinchón dismissed this possibility as quite improbable because
Dutch manpower would most likely be inadequate to overcome the mountainous terrain and the strength of the Sierra towns. Viceroy Chinchón
agreed with the assessment that Dr. Morga had often advanced.

The viceroy opposed permanent fortifications at Guayaquil. They would
be costly, and they were unnecessary. He estimated that the original cost
to the treasury would be 65,000 pesos, not to mention subsequent expenses
for maintenance of these installations. The initial cost of fortifying Acapulco
came to some 142,000 pesos.[31] The successful repulse of the Dutch from
Guayaquil in 1624 demonstrated that the port could be defended without
fortifications. There were between 100 and 150 freeholders in the city who
could immediately mobilize a militia of 350 men. Within twelve days reinforcements of men and munitions from the Sierra towns of Cuenca,
Riobamba, and Chimbo could reach the port. Further help could come from
Quito within a few weeks.

Chinchón was not unmindful that this strategy placed a heavy burden
on the inhabitants of Guayaquil, whose prosperity was slender at best. With-

out fortifications the Spaniards could not prevent the Dutch from landing, burning the bamboo and palm huts, and destroying merchandise in the warehouses.

The recommendations of the viceroy are an example of tough realism. Exercising overall responsibility for the defense of the whole coast of South America, he had limited resources that were often strained to the breaking point. If a port could be defended without fortifications, even though its inhabitants would suffer acute hardships, then the royal treasury should concentrate on military objectives of higher priority.

Dr. Morga in Quito voiced a different view. He was a spokesman of the kingdom's interests and sincerely anxious to preserve its modest prosperity. He urged that permanent fortifications be constructed at Guayaquil.[32] He also pleaded for more military hardware. His pleas have the familiar ring of the local commander asking for more men and supplies from the theater commander.

Military operations in the Spanish empire offer a vivid contrast to the conduct of other functions within the imperial bureaucracy. In all sectors save the military, there was no clearcut division among the various agencies, all of which shared the same responsibilities. Only in the military area was there a vertical chain of command. The viceroy as captain general was supreme commander-in-chief for all of Spanish South America. In Spain a *junta de guerra,* directly accountable to the king and composed of two representatives apiece from the Council of the Indies and the Council of War, directed the defense of the Indies.[33] The corregidor in Guayaquil was the local field commander. The responsibility of the audiencia was to provide the corregidor with logistical support. Although distance and slow communications gave both the audiencia and the corregidor some latitude, everyone knew a clearcut chain of command led directly to the viceroy in Lima and the junta de guerra in Spain, and all acted accordingly. The penchant of the crown for dividing the same responsibilities among different agencies of the government in a horizontal line, of course, would have led to disaster in the military sphere, where unity of command was indispensable.

Although the authorities in Quito reacted quickly and effectively in sending assistance to Guayaquil, there was a prolonged subsequent dispute about who should pay. In the heat of the crisis, the treasury assumed the expenses when the encomenderos pleaded poverty. In 1624 the treasury paid out 5,000 pesos for an expedition of one hundred soldiers.[34] A plainly worded cedula reminded the encomenderos that it was their traditional military and financial responsibility to go to the assistance of any city in the kingdom threatened by foreign invasion.[35] The encomenderos argued that their duties as militiamen did not extend beyond the particular province where they held an encomienda.[36] Thus the military-feudal aspect of the encomienda still had some pertinence in Quito long after it had ceased to have any in other parts of the Indies. The Guayaquil episode illustrates how undependable it was in a major crisis. Fortified ports, such as Callao, Cartagena, Acapulco, and Veracruz, had garrisons of professional soldiers with salaries paid by the royal treasury.

In order to gain additional revenue for the war effort, the king in 1629 decreed that encomiendas could be inherited by three successive heirs instead of two.[37] The encomenderos in turn presented Philip IV with a substantial gift of money.

The direct military obligation, however, was not the only burden that the subjects of the crown had to bear to support the war effort. In order to finance mounting military expenditures, the government increasingly resorted to forced loans. In the absence of a formal representative assembly or cortes in the Indies, which, according to medieval precedent, possessed the sole authority to levy new direct taxes—*servicio* as opposed to a *donativo gracioso*—some such device as the forced loan was necessary in order to meet extraordinary expenses.[38] Rates on customary and indirect taxes, however, could be raised by royal fiat alone.

There was little that was voluntary in the *donativo gracioso y préstamo,* and repayment was out of the question. The audiencia exerted effective pressure on its own members, the functional corporations, the Church, and the Indians to contribute. Anyone who sought favors from the crown, and that included everyone, found it expedient to give. Although forced loans had been resorted to by other kings from time to time, Philip IV put much heavier reliance on this device.

Thrice during the Morga administration, in 1621, 1625, and 1631, the crown appealed to its loyal vassals to grant a loan and gift. Thereafter for the rest of the seventeenth century, there was apt to be a forced loan every ten years or so. Dr. Morga organized the collection of the first appeal with a vigor that would do credit to the chairman of a present-day charity drive. He collected 102,852 pesos.[39] In contrast, only 21,149 pesos had been collected for the forced loan of 1590.[40]

The loan of 1625, however, was much less successful than that of 1621. Not only was the modest capital of the leading citizens frozen by the turmoil unleashed by the visita general, but also a series of other events, including the sack of Guayaquil, the ban on cacao exportation to Mexico, and a cyclical decline in textile exports, had produced a veritable economic depression after 1624. Hence the second loan of 1625 netted only 18,777 pesos.[41]

Dr. Morga's performance in the third appeal of 1631 was somewhat better, although he could not match his first drive. In 1631 he raised 35,030 pesos.[42]

Although the energy of the president as a tax collector should not be minimized, the response of isolated Quito conformed to the general trend throughout the empire. The whole monarchy enthusiastically subscribed to the first appeal. The second forced loan was received with coolness and the third with open hostility.[43]

In his correspondence with the authorities in Spain, President Morga repeatedly stressed his contribution as a collector of forced loans. The impression emerges that the aging bureaucrat, whose administration was under constant fire during the 1620's and 1630's while the visita general dragged on, sought to suggest to his superiors in Madrid that his vigor as a collector of forced loans might partially offset his peccadillos, if not his sins. As the Council of the Indies deliberated over the verdict of the visita general, Dr. Morga took pains to dispatch to the council a notarized statement from the treasury certifying that he had personally contributed 2,500 pesos to the three collections. It was one of the last letters he ever signed.[44]

The attitude of Dr. Morga and his colleagues on the bench, who contributed generously to the forced loans, was more medieval than modern. Francesco Taverna, chancellor of the duchy of Milan under Charles V, had a more modern view of a bureaucrat's responsibility. In refusing to contribute to a government loan, he argued that his salary was not a matter of the monarch's grace and that he should not be expected to pledge those earnings to the monarch in the hope of a future *grazie*. If he fulfilled his duties to the satisfaction of the governor general, he would expect to keep his office and to receive his salary. If he failed to perform his responsibilities well, then he would anticipate being dismissed.[45] Alongside their feelings of professionalism, the oidores in the Indies still retained an attitude reminiscent of the older medieval patrimonial state in which offices were the personal possessions of the king, to be granted as a reward for past and future services.

The generosity of the citizens of Quito cannot be ascribed solely to the energy of Dr. Morga as a tax collector; it was also the expression of a deeply felt patriotism. Although modern historians may stress the economic and territorial aspects of the Hispano-Dutch clash, in those days the Spaniards saw the struggle more in patriotic and religious terms than in economic or political terms. To all Spaniards, the Dutch, whom they nicknamed the "Pechelingues," were "pirates" and "corsairs."[46] By any objective standard of international law, this was not the case. The Dutch fleets entered the Pacific waters with letters of marque. They enjoyed the official support of the Dutch state, which was at war with the Castilian crown. Spanish patriotic enthusiasm, however, usually swept aside these legal distinctions. When the Spaniards did consider the matter, they might reply with the legalistic contention that the Dutch authorities lacked the right to issue letters of marque. According to the Spaniards, the Dutch themselves were engaged in an unjust and illegal revolt against their legitimate sovereign, who was also the king of Castile.

What aroused the Spaniards' deep-rooted hatred even more than the supposed "piracy" was that the Dutch were heretics in the Spanish view. On these grounds alone, Philip IV could appeal to his subjects in the distant kingdoms of the Indies to make renewed sacrifices. And they responded and responded as the economic foundations of the empire eroded away.

If Spanish emotion could be most deeply aroused by an appeal to their fierce attachment to Catholicism, so could the Dutch hatred against the Spaniards be kindled to a flaming heat by their equally militant belief in the creed of John Calvin. For every bit of damage they inflicted on the Spanish-American outposts, the Dutch did take satisfaction in having wreaked vengeance on the enemies of their religion. One of the factors maintaining the discipline of the Dutch crews on the long, perilous voyage into the Pacific was the genuine fear that, if they did not loyally follow their leaders, they would have to face the hated ministers of the Holy Office of the Inquisition.

Dr. Morga's contribution to the defense effort was not just that of tax collector, nor merely that of participating in the repulse of the Dutch from Guayaquil in 1624, significant though these activities were. He was also a strategist who thought in bold, imaginative terms about the defense of the Spanish Pacific. He had scant sympathy for the conservative, static strategy ultimately adopted to defend the west coast. His experience in the Philippines, Mexico, and ultimately in Quito made him view the Spanish Pacific as an organic whole. He saw the Pacific as a gigantic triangle, with Callao, Guayaquil, Panama, and Acapulco on the west coast of America forming interdependent links with Manila and the Moluccas. To him, the most effective defense both on the west coast and in the Orient was an aggressive offensive. On November 20, 1615, a few months after his arrival in Quito, Dr.

Morga wrote Viceroy Esquilache at the latter's request a long memorandum in which he outlined in broad strokes his concept of a mobile offensive which he believed could drive the Dutch from the whole Pacific.[47]

He saw the Philippines as the anchor of the Spanish position in the whole Pacific basin. The Spaniards must retain control of the Philippines, not merely because of the Spanish colonists and the Catholic missions there. The loss of the islands would probably lead to the ouster of the Iberian powers from the Cape of Good Hope to the shores of Mexico. If the Dutch occupied the Philippines, not only would the Moluccas be lost, but also the key Portuguese enclaves of Goa on the Indian coast, Macao, and Malacca could not long withstand the Dutch offensive. In 1615 Dr. Morga correctly predicted that the Dutch would make a supreme effort, which they had not yet done, to take the Philippines. To forestall such an attempt, the Spaniards should mount a massive offensive to drive the Dutch out of the Far Eastern Pacific.

In the 1615 memorandum, the new president of the audiencia of Quito expressed disappointment over the failure of the viceroy of New Spain to send Governor Silva of the Philippines the full reinforcements Silva had requested the year before, in 1614, so that he could undertake a general offensive. The viceroy sent only 400 instead of 1,500 men. A year later, in 1616, Governor Silva did take the offensive, in command of the largest Spanish fleet heretofore assembled in Far Eastern waters. His sudden death in Malacca and the failure of the Portuguese from Goa to join him led to the collapse of the general offensive. Never again were the Hispano-Portuguese able to muster an armada sufficiently massive to enjoy a realistic chance of expelling the Dutch from southeast Asia.

There is no evidence that the failure of the viceroy to send the reinforcements that Governor Silva had requested was a contributing cause for the lack of success of the expedition. What should be underlined here is that Dr. Morga enthusiastically supported the offensive aims of the expedition.

In 1615, several years before the sailing of the great Nassau fleet, Dr. Morga furthermore correctly predicted that the Dutch would step up their operations along the west coast of America. This conviction made him underscore the need to drive the Dutch out of the spice islands, for the terminus of the Dutch expeditions along the west coast was their stations in the Moluccas. Dr. Morga also pointed out that the earlier Dutch expeditions around Cape Horn in 1599 and 1600 arrived in the Spanish Pacific so weakened by the rigors of the sea voyage itself that their striking power was significantly diminished. As the enemy acquired more navigational experience, the Spaniards ought to expect that future Dutch fleets would arrive in the Pacific in much better condition.

To meet this threat, Dr. Morga proposed several measures. Among them was to fortify and garrison ports such as Arica, Paita, and Guayaquil. Although he recommended fortifications for several Pacific ports, he was not thinking merely in terms of static defense. Basic to his approach was the aim of increasing striking mobility. His twin proposals were the conquest of Esmeraldas and the re-establishment of trade between the viceroyalty of Peru and the Philippines. Quito could supply Panama with manpower, munitions, and food in sixteen days over the Esmeraldas road, several days sooner than Panama could be supplied from either Guayaquil or Callao. His other proposal, to open direct trade between the ports of Peru and the Philippines, was even bolder than his cherished conquest of Esmeraldas. The principal military justification was that galleons could be built in the islands at far less expense to the crown than in Guayaquil. Vessels of 1,000 tons could be constructed in the Philippines, where there was an abundant supply of durable wood, for about 20,000 *patacones.* The timber supply adjacent to Guayaquil was giving out, with the result that harsher burdens were being placed on the Indians to transport wood from longer distances to the shipyards. The president also bitterly complained that the shipbuilders in Guayaquil were more concerned with their own profits than with the welfare of the defense effort.

The specific proposals of Dr. Morga to increase Spanish striking power came to naught. The failure of the conquest of Esmeraldas has already been discussed in Chapter 1. His proposal to revive triangular trade among the Philippines, Acapulco, and Peru fell on deaf ears in the Council of the Indies. In 1591 the crown forbade direct trade between Peru and the Philippines. This prohibition was the result of a powerful lobby, sixteenth-century style, composed of the merchants of Seville, with their monopoly of the trans-Atlantic carrying trade, and the textile interests of Andalusia, anxious to preserve their monopoly of the American market. So powerful was this lobby that on three different occasions during the reigns of Philip II, Philip III, and Philip IV the Spanish Court seriously debated whether to abandon the Philippines themselves. Fearful that their monopolistic privileges would be undercut if Mexico and Peru were flooded with cheap Chinese silks, both interest groups secured only their minimum objective. The Philippines were not abandoned. But in 1591 the crown did restrict Philippine commerce to the Manila-Acapulco run and abolished outright trade between Mexico and Peru. The cedula of 1591 limited the total value of goods which could be shipped from Manila to Acapulco to 250,000 pesos annually, an amount sufficient to maintain the Philippine colony, yet small enough to be absorbed by the Mexican market and hence not be exported. In practice, however, the annual value of merchandise imported on the Manila galleons came closer to 2,000,000 pesos. The volume of goods came to be determined not by royal fiat but by the amount of shipping space available on the galleons.[48]

Dr. Morga's proposal in effect would have opened up Peru to the importation of Chinese silks. The merchants of Seville and their allies in the textile industry were powerful enough to ensure that any such suggestion would be filed in the archives without action.

Dr. Morga's thinking on economic matters paralleled that on military matters. His approach in both areas was flexible, mobile, and aggressive. Although he never spelled out his position explicitly, he implicitly opposed the narrow monopolist trend of his own time. Just as in war the most effective defense was the offense, so also the most effective means of promoting prosperity was to expand trade by breaking down restrictions and monopolistic practices. Antonio de Morga vaguely foreshadowed the reforms of Charles III (1759–88), who abolished trade barriers within the empire and thereby unleashed a wave of prosperity.

In his advocacy of giving the Spaniards greater mobility in the Pacific, President Morga came up with two basically sound proposals, but both of them aroused determined opposition from vested commercial monopolies. The force that these vested interests could muster might have been swept away if the static defense strategy had failed to produce results. In fact, it succeeded, as far as the west coast of South America was concerned. But the Spaniards paid a heavy price in that the economy of the Pacific coast contracted. The poor showing of the Nassau fleet of 1624 discouraged the Dutch from sending another armada around the tip of South America until 1643. The Dutch concentrated their efforts after 1624 on inflicting a series of crippling blows on the Spaniards and Portuguese in the Caribbean, the northeast coast of Brazil, and southeast Asia.

In this world war, in fact the first world war in the history of western Europe, in which the Dutch overthrew the Iberian monopoly in the tropical world, Dr. Antonio de Morga was indeed a minor figure. However inadequate a tactician he may have been in the naval engagement with van Noort in 1600, the memorandum of 1615 does demonstrate that he was a strategist of respectable stature who was capable of thinking in global terms. His importance lies not in what he did but in the attitude he represented. He was a child of the Spain of Philip II, having lived the first forty years of his life during the reign of that monarch. He shared the spirit of bold adventure and limitless confidence of the sixteenth century, which gave the Iberian powers their domination of the tropical world. It was his personal misfortune to witness the decline of that heroic spirit of relentless energy during the last years of his very long life.

The kinds of problems and the methods of resolving them that have been discussed in the last five chapters have already brought to light several characteristics of the imperial bureaucracy. A more precise focus on the bureaucrats, the law, and the society is now in order.

II

JUDGES, THE LAW, AND SOCIETY

6.

RECRUITMENT, TRAINING, AND PROMOTION

The most important elements of government in the Indies were the smaller territorial units known as audiencias rather than the larger, more prestigious viceroyalties. Like most colonial institutions, the audiencias had a Castilian prototype. Ferdinand and Isabella reorganized the audiencias of Granada and Valladolid as the next-to-highest judicial tribunals in the kingdom of Castile. The jurisdiction of Granada included all the territory south of the Tagus River, and that of Valladolid extended north of the Tagus. In time the audiencias in the New World acquired extensive administrative, political, and military functions that their prototypes in the peninsula never exercised. The latter remained exclusively law courts. There were eleven audiencias overseas: Santo Domingo (1526), Mexico (1527), Panama (1535), Lima (1542), Guatemala (1543), Guadalajara (1548), Santa Fe de Bogotá (1549), Charcas (1559), Quito (1563), Manila (1583), and Chile (1609); Buenos Aires (1661) was suppressed within a few years.

The audiencias were not equal in status or prestige. The audiencias in Mexico City and Lima, as the capitals of the two viceroyalties, were the highest in rank. There were two distinct categories among the nonviceregal audiencias. The superior or pretorial audiencias had as their presiding officer a president who was not a lawyer. He exercised supreme military command in his capacity as captain general. Although one of the two viceroys exercised nominal supervision over the superior audiencias, the chief magistrates of the latter enjoyed by right a considerable measure of autonomous military and political authority.

The presidents of the inferior or subordinate audiencias were *letrados,* i.e., lawyers. *De jure* the inferior audiencias were merely judicial tribunals. With time they acquired widespread, *de facto* authority in political, administrative, fiscal, and military matters but only by delegation from the viceroy. The viceroys exercised a tighter supervision over the inferior audiencias than they did over the superior tribunals. The viceroys also exercised much more patronage in filling local and provincial offices in the inferior audiencias than they did in the superior audiencias. In the viceroyalty of New Spain, which embraced all of Spanish North America north of the isthmus and also included the Philippines, Guadalajara was the only inferior audiencia. In the viceroyalty of Peru, the inferior audiencias were Quito and Charcas, and the superior tribunals were Bogotá, Panama, and Chile.[1]

The juridical ties uniting the overseas settlements to the peninsula were not, strictly speaking, those of colony and mother country. Each audiencia was in law a separate kingdom, united in a personal union with the crowns of Castile and León. Indicative of the sovereign status of the audiencias, those tribunals in their corporate capacity enjoyed the rank, title, and style of Highness. Prior to the election of Charles V as Holy Roman emperor, the kings of Castile were addressed as "Highness" and not "Majesty." All the audiencias in the Indies enjoyed the superior status of supreme courts, *cancillerías,* from whose verdicts appeals were strictly limited. In Spain itself the only cancillerías were those of Valladolid and Granada, the capitals of the ancient kingdoms of Castile and Granada. The Council of the Indies alone exercised jurisdiction over the kingdoms of the New World, to the total exclusion of the other territorial councils. Functional councils such as those of finance, war, and the Inquisition, on the other hand, had competence in all the dominions of the king.

Some modern scholars have asserted that the kingdoms of the Indies were co-equal with Castile and León.[2] This is misleading. In the sixteenth and seventeenth centuries, the kingdoms overseas were subordinate to and inalienable from the crowns of Castile and León. For purposes of simplicity, the sovereign was referred to as *rey de las Españas y de las Indias* and on coins as *rex Hispaniarum et Indiarum*.[3]

The Habsburg arrangement of a series of kingdoms in the Indies with gradations of viceregal, superior, and inferior audiencias, all subordinate to Castile, had a parallel in the peninsula itself. Castile, Aragón, and Portugal were the three principal kingdoms, just as Mexico and Peru were the two major kingdoms in the New World. Belonging to each one of these primary kingdoms was a whole series of subordinate kingdoms, the names of which were often meticulously listed in royal cedulas. Although there was a powerful trend toward political centralization from the time of Ferdinand and Isabella onward, the centrifugal forces could and did vigorously reassert themselves during the 1640's, the 1700's, the 1830's, the 1870's, and even as late as the 1930's. In 1624 the Count-Duke of Olivares urged Philip IV in a secret memorandum:

The most important thing in the monarchy of Your Majesty is for you to become king of Spain; by this I mean, Sire, that Your Majesty should not be content with being king of Portugal, of Aragón, of Valencia, count of Barcelona, et cetera but should secretly plan and work to reduce those kingdoms of which Spain is composed to the style and laws of Castile with no difference whatsoever. And if Your Majesty achieves this, you will be the most powerful prince in the world.[4]

One of the major themes of the history of the Iberian peninsula since the reign of Ferdinand and Isabella has been the grand design to convert Spain from a geographical expression into a centralized and unitary political organism.

The Habsburg theory of the kingdoms of the Spains and the Indies united under one royal head fell into disuse after the ascension of the Bourbon dynasty in 1700. The settlements overseas increasingly acquired the juridical character of colonies or provinces of the metropolis. The traditional Habsburg nomenclature of *rey de las Españas y de las Indias* gave way increasingly in the eighteenth century to *rey de España y emperador de las Indias* or *de América*, reflecting the Bourbon urge toward creating a unitary state out of the diverse dominions in the Old and New Worlds.

In a juridical view, the dominions overseas were colonies only in the classical Roman sense of transplanting people from one area to another. Not even a good case could be made for the argument that the kingdoms of the Indies were colonies in the more modern sense of exploitation of their resources for the benefit of the metropolis. Not until the late eighteenth century was there anything approaching an efficient capitalistic exploitation of the wealth of the Indies for the benefit of Spain itself.

The "federal" conception of the Habsburgs was revived in the late eighteenth century under the stimulus of the Enlightenment, as part of a much broader renewal of interest in the representative traditions of Spain's late medieval past. It also provided the early advocates of independence with a historic-legal argument to justify the creole claim that provisional regimes could be set up in the kingdoms overseas in the absence of the legitimate king of Castile. In the early nineteenth century, the claim was that the kingdoms in the Indies were co-equal with that of Castile, whereas under the Habsburgs they were considered subordinate kingdoms. One of the most articulate formulations of this argument can be found in the writings of Friar Servando Teresa de Mier, the colorful spokesman of Mexican independence.[5] The difference between the Habsburg theory of unequal but interdependent kingdoms and the independence notion of the equality of the kingdoms overseas with those of Spain is the contrast between the neo-medieval corporatism of the sixteenth and seventeenth centuries and the equalitarianism of the American and French revolutions.

The Spains of Ferdinand and Isabella were a diverse mosaic of medieval and Renaissance. One of the medieval traditions that Castile carried across the Atlantic was that the administration of justice was the highest attribute of sovereignty.[6] It was not until 1570 that the French theorist Jean Bodin developed the more modern conception that the fundamental character of sovereignty lay in the capacity to legislate. The king was absolute only in the original medieval sense of recognizing no judicial superior in temporal matters inside or outside his kingdoms.[7] Although he was not procedurally responsible to his subjects for his conduct, there were several limitations on royal authority. To be sure, the king was the source of all positive law, but the latter was a reflection of and subordinate to divine and natural law. Hence the monarch could not arbitrarily dispose of the life and the property of his subjects. Nor could he violate the traditional privileges of the various corporations which together formed the *corpus mysticum* of the body politic. Thus the essence of royal authority was jurisdictional, i.e., to provide all subjects with protection through the administration of justice.[8] It therefore followed that the principal organ of government in each of the kingdoms of the New World was a judicial tribunal which by derivation exercised executive and legislative functions.

It is well known that the audiencia kingdoms and not the larger viceroyalties became the nuclei of the independent republics and that the territorial limits of the audiencias became the basis for the frontiers of the national states.[9] The juridical theory just discussed was indeed an important factor, but geographical, economic, and ideological considerations also contributed to the disappearance of the viceregal boundaries and the transmutation of the audiencias into the independent republics of the national period.

In the Spanish empire, checks and balances were not achieved, as in modern states, by a division between executive, judicial, and legislative functions. The same agencies shared several of the same functions.[10] Responsibility was so highly diffused as to degenerate at times into bewildering confusion. The only real centralization was at the top of the pyramid in the person of the king. Underneath the monarch there was a whole series of royal councils.

The royal councils were of two sorts, territorial and functional or universal. The territorial councils were Castile, the Indies, Aragón, Italy, Flanders, and Portugal. There were functional councils for war, finance, the Inquisition, the military orders, the Cruzada, and for a time the Hermandad. A Council of State, which the king himself presided over, coordinated empire-wide policy on the highest level. In practice the king and a small circle of immediate advisers, who might or might not be members of the Council of State, had to make the final policy decisions from the multitude of recommendations coming from the territorial and the functional councils.

Although the sovereign often accepted the advice tendered, the king could act in opposition to the recommendations of the councils. The *Consejo Real y Supremo de las Indias,* formally established on August 1, 1524, consisted of ten members or fewer. The majority were middle-sector letrados, with a sprinkling of nobles and prelates. The presidency of the Council of the Indies was one of the most prestigious positions at the royal Court, since that council ranked third highest below the Council of State and the Council of Castile. A nobleman or a prelate usually held this post. Since the presidents served for many years, they were apt to exercise considerable influence on policy.

The most influential member of the council next to the president was paradoxically the junior member, who was the fiscal. The endless stream of reports from the Indies first came to his desk. It was his job not only to paraphrase briefly what the principal issues were in every case, but, more important, to make recommendations as to what action the whole council should take. The councilors seldom saw the reports coming from the New World but merely the summaries prepared by the fiscal.

In many more cases than not the council adopted the viewpoint expressed by the fiscal. A clear majority vote by the council determined the outcome. In case of a deep division inside the council, the minority might submit a report to the king. Wherever possible, the council made strenuous efforts to secure a unanimous recommendation. With the high premium placed on consensus in such a committee form of government, the council usually settled for recommendations involving the least possible change from traditional policies. The cautious character of this conciliar form of administration was reinforced by the advanced age of most of the councilors. By and large, they were lawyers who had served in the inferior tribunals. They seldom received a promotion to the councils until they had reached their sixties.

The recommendations of the councils, the *consultas,* went to the desk of the king. Only the sovereign could issue the royal cedulas which expressed law and policy. Understandably the views of the Council of the Indies bulked large in the wording and content of these royal cedulas, but not always. There were sharp differences of opinion at times between the council and the small circle surrounding the monarch.

The vital links between the councils and the crown were the royal secretaries. In the reign of Philip IV, there were two royal secretaries of the Council of the Indies, one for each of the two viceroyalties. Something more than chief clerks and something less than secretaries of state, the royal secretaries had the responsibility to keep the endless correspondence flowing between the monarch and his councils. The king attended only the sessions of the Council of State. The royal secretaries often exercised considerable influence not only on matters of patronage but also on matters of policy. Friction often occurred between the secretaries and the councils. Yet without the former, there would have been a paralysis of government.[11]

In theory the viceroy was the highest magistrate in the Indies. As the representative of the person of the king, the viceroy was surrounded with all the trappings and ceremonial of royal pomp. He did not, however, exercise the prerogatives of a king.[12] He shared most of his powers with the other branches of the administration, each one of which enjoyed substantial autonomy. Only in the military sphere did he have undivided authority. He was the nominal superior of the other agencies of administration. He served as vice-patron of the Church and president of the audiencia, without a vote in judicial decisions if he were not a letrado. The audiencia in turn acted as an advisory council to the viceroy. He was also the presiding officer of the *junta superior de hacienda,* the royal treasury.

A strong-willed viceroy with moderate political talent could usually exercise genuine hegemony over these agencies, but an intransigent audiencia could make life difficult for a less able viceroy. In the seventeenth century, the control of the viceroy over the administration was much firmer in the viceregal audiencia kingdom than in the outlying audiencias where his authority became increasingly one of nominal supervision, except during acute crises. Whenever he chose to exercise his legal powers in both the inferior and the superior audiencias, the viceroy had to take into account the viewpoints expressed by the magistrates in those tribunals. His failure to do so often resulted in local disregard for viceregal directives. Perhaps the greatest limitation on the authority of the viceroy was the privilege that the audiencias, the ecclesiastical corporations, and the exchequer officials enjoyed of corresponding directly with the king and the council.

The dilution of individual responsibility and authority was an expression of two axioms of colonial government. Several magistrates or agencies shared the same powers. But even more important, the conciliar principle prevailed, exemplified particularly by the Council of the Indies, the audiencias, and the treasury. The Spanish imperial administration was, in a phrase, government by committee. Although the presiding officer could exercise some initiative in influencing his colleagues, he was in the last analysis little better than a *primus inter pares*. Inspiring this intricate mosaic of checks and balances, with its blurred lines of authority, was the central authorities' profound distrust of all agents overseas. Madrid wanted multiple sources of information in order to curb graft and restrain the personal ambitions of its magistrates in the New World.[13]

In the administration overseas, the viceroys formed a kind of political bureaucracy, in José María Ots Capdequi's phrase.[14] Since they represented the person of the king, they invariably belonged to the high nobility of the peninsula. More times than not, they were the second sons or the scions of the cadet branches of the great noble families. Although aristocratic lineage was indispensable under the Habsburgs, but less so under the Bourbons where military officers were often given preference, ability and experience also counted for a good deal in the selection of the viceroys. All were veteran residents of the royal Court. The majority also had held responsible military and diplomatic assignments outside of the peninsula. Under the Habsburgs the informal custom was for a viceroy to serve a term of five years in Mexico before being promoted to the richer and more prestigious viceroyalty of Peru. Many received high posts upon their return to Spain. As a general rule, the viceroys were experienced and competent. Very few proved outright inept. Even the young Prince of Esquilache, who was a protégé of the

Duke of Lerma, was not incompetent, although he was not an outstanding success. The Council of the Indies had opposed his nomination on the grounds of his youth and lack of political experience.[15]

The Spanish-American viceroy bears a remarkable resemblance to the British viceroy of India in the nineteenth century. Neither one had previous experience in the colony, since in both cases it was desirable that the viceroy, as chief executive, have close associations with the main centers of power in the metropolis. The viceroys in each area were "outsiders" who presided over a professional bureaucracy of career officers. Both were surrounded with the trappings of royal ceremonial without the full powers of a sovereign. Councils restricted the authority of both potentates. The Spanish-American viceroy had to contend with the Council of the Indies, the audiencias, and the ecclesiastical and fiscal agencies. The freedom of action of the British viceroy was limited by his own council, the Secretary of State for India and his council, the cabinet, and ultimately Parliament. In order to exploit the mystique of royalty, both the Spanish-American and the British viceroys had to be recruited from the most aristocratic echelon of society.[16]

If the viceroys constituted the political layer of the imperial bureaucracy, the *ministros superiores,* i.e., the presidents, the oidores, and the fiscales, formed the professional echelon. During the two centuries of Habsburg rule, some 1,000 superior magistrates held office in the audiencias. The number of these posts was about ninety-four. More than any other group, these men were the real rulers of the Spanish empire. Serving indefinite terms of office, in contrast to the viceroys whose tenure seldom exceeded five years, they provided the viceroys with day-to-day technical and administrative assistance. In the nonviceregal audiencias, they were the highest agency of political administration. The audiencias performed the complex task of acting as intermediaries between the central authorities in Madrid and the king's vassals in the Indies. Few decisions in the New World came to pass without the heavy imprint of the audiencias.

Among the superior magistrates, there were distinctions of rank and privilege, with the president at the top. Although he possessed a vote equal to that of the oidores, the president, like the viceroy vis-à-vis his own audiencia, exercised considerably more influence than the other oidores. How much more depended on his political skill.[17]

That seniority was highly prized is indicated by the frequency of litigations on this question. Ordinarily seniority was determined from the date the officeholder actually took possession of his office. Hence oidores took great risks, in an age when travel under even the best conditions was hazardous, in order to arrive at their posts a few days before their colleagues. An oidor lost his seniority when transferred from either an inferior or a superior audiencia. One of the advantages of the viceregal audiencias was that oidores transferred from Mexico to Lima retained their seniority. The judges of the audiencias of Granada and Valladolid also enjoyed this privilege.[18]

Disputes about seniority arose from the conviction of many jurists that length of service ought to be determined from the date of appointment by the king if an appointee were performing official business elsewhere which made it necessary for him to postpone his departure for his new post.[19] On occasion the crown followed this procedure. Antonio Rodríquez de San Isidro Manrique, who was appointed oidor in Quito on February 20, 1630, was then serving as visitor general of the audiencia of Bogotá. The king issued a cedula on February 20, 1630, granting him possession of the office in the audiencia of Quito as of the date of his appointment. He did not take actual possession of his new office until January 7, 1636.[20] Another oidor, Lic. Alonso Castillo de Herrera, arrived in Quito without a duly notarized royal cedula. The audiencia would not allow him to take office for over a year, nor could he apply time toward seniority until the proper documents arrived from the peninsula.[21]

This was a hierarchal society in which status and rank in the corporations to which one belonged counted a great deal. The junior oidor often received some of the onerous assignments. The rank of senior oidor was prized, since that magistrate became acting president of the audiencia in the event of the death of the proprietary president.[22] These interim presidencies occurred frequently. They might last as long as two years, until the new appointee arrived from Spain. There are very few cases of the senior oidor's receiving the proprietary appointment.

Because of the greater volume of business, the viceregal audiencias had eight oidores, in contrast to the other tribunals whose usual complement was four or five judges. In Lima and Mexico City a separate inferior court, attached to the audiencia proper, exercised criminal jurisdiction. The four alcaldes de crimen, who formed the sala de crimen, were subordinate in status to the oidores. In the nonviceregal audiencias criminal jurisdiction was also the responsibility of the oidores.[23]

In Mexico City and Lima there were two fiscales, the junior serving in the sala de crimen and the senior being attached to the audiencia proper. The fiscal was a state attorney. His primary responsibility was to defend the interests of the royal fisc, hence the origin of the title. He also had special duties to defend the Indians and the real patronato. In the early decades of the sixteenth century, the junior oidor acted as fiscal, but in time a separate office emerged. Although his salary was the same as that of the oidores, he ranked below the junior oidor. He could not vote in those cases to which he was party as crown attorney, but, in those cases to which he was not, he could vote only to break a tie. The fiscal deliberated but could not vote, *con voz pero sin voto,* in the political and administrative actions of the tribunal.[24]

The machinery for filling audiencia appointments illustrates the quasi-professional character of this layer of the imperial bureaucracy. When a vacancy occurred, the Council of the Indies drew up a consulta, listing three or four candidates.[25] Always brief, these consultas included four types of information. One was the educational background, since a law degree, either a licentiate or a doctorate, was an indispensable qualification for these judicial offices. There were, of course, no competitive examinations as such. The British pioneered this procedure in the mid-nineteenth century for entrance into the Indian Civil Service. Even without competitive examinations, a law degree from a seventeenth-century Spanish university was not an insignificant professional qualification. Furthermore, the council lent much weight to the previous administrative and judicial experience of the candidates. Virtually every person listed on a consulta had held some minor judicial office in the peninsula. Inexperienced and uneducated youths seldom received consideration. The moral character and the family background of the candidates also received some attention in the consultas. The council ranked the candidates in terms of suitability.

The king usually appointed the first name on the list; however, sometimes he chose the third or fourth name. An aspiring bureaucrat who enjoyed the support of a powerful nobleman might use that influence with those around the king. Although an element of favoritism entered into the selection of magistrates, it should not be forgotten that virtually all the names presented to the king possessed solid professional qualifications. Thus recruitment on the oidor level was based on a mixture of modern professional qualifications with overtones of medieval patrimony, by which officeholders were members of the king's household and hence office was viewed as an expression of royal favor and royal largesse. Yet the principles of permanence in the service and promotion on the basis of merit and experience were deeply embedded in the Spanish political theory of the seventeenth century. This theory profoundly influenced practice.[26]

Philip II, a conscientious monarch, placed a high premium on the ability, previous experience, and moral character of candidates. During the reign of his son, Philip III (1598–1621), the government fell into the rapacious hands of the Duke of Lerma and his family. Generously endowed with elegant manners but possessing scant political ability, the Duke of Lerma had two aims: to dominate the weak and pious king and to increase the wealth of his own family and retainers. The rich mine of patronage in the Indies excited the cupidity of the all-powerful royal favorite. Early in the reign, in 1600, the Duke of Lerma set up a small committee of three members to exercise exclusive control over all appointments in the Indies. The Council of the Indies vigorously and successfully fought to retain its voice in making recommendations. Within a few years, on March 16, 1609, the king abolished the *cámara* of Lerma.

In 1644 Philip IV re-established the cámara of three councilors with exclusive jurisdiction to make recommendations for all offices in the Indies. The aged and deaf Juan de Solórzano led the bitter opposition of the Council of the Indies to this change. His ultimate defeat was one important consideration that led Solórzano to request an honorable retirement. The council published an anonymous treatise of eleven folios in 1644 or 1645, which is a revealing indication of the professional thinking of the conciliar layer of the bureaucracy. If Solórzano was not the author, the treatise certainly reflects his point of view.

The treatise argued that, although the king could create, modify, or even suppress royal councils at will, the sovereign was under some moral restraint not to do so while incumbents held office. This argument to place some limit on sovereign authority the kings would never accept, but the fact that the council advanced it demonstrates their articulate degree of professional esprit de corps. To deprive the council of its traditional voice in patronage would deal a crippling blow to its power, prestige, and authority. The change would be equivalent to depriving the College of Cardinals of its primate prerogative of electing a pope.

The councilors would be reduced almost to idleness since patronage matters figured so prominently in their daily proceedings. Furthermore, such a blow to their prestige and authority would make it difficult for the council to attract magistrates of outstanding stature. No longer would an appointment to the Council of the Indies be regarded as a promotion from one of the inferior councils. Endless delays would result while it was being decided what matters should be referred to the cámara, since, in practice, matters of patronage, government, war, and state were interdependent.

The council's treatise further argued that the cámara had proved ineffective during the nine-year period it previously operated. For that reason it was suppressed in 1609. Conservative and traditionalist, the council warned Philip IV about the dangers of an innovation which promised no obvious improvement over a system that had worked moderately well for over a century.

The cámara did, in fact, take away a significant portion of the authority of the council, but the dire predictions of the 1644 treatise did not materialize.[27] The council was not reduced to insignificance. In spite of losing most control over patronage, the Council of the Indies after 1644 continued to exert pressure in favor of the principle that all candidates for the office of oidor must meet substantial professional qualifications. After 1644 that pressure, however, was less effective, and the standards of the bureaucracy did decline. The deterioration was not arrested until the Bourbons undertook their cautious reforms.

As experienced bureaucrats living in the atmosphere of the royal Court, the members of the council were usually willing to make some concessions to those who exercised commanding influence around the person of the monarch. In 1601, for example, there was a vacancy in the sala de crimen of Mexico. Dr. Vergara, the physician of Philip III, asked the Duke of Lerma for the appointment of his brother-in-law, Lic. Manuel Madrid y Luna, who, although he had a law degree, was a youth of no previous experience in the Indies. The council vigorously opposed this proposal with the argument that posts in the viceregal audiencias should be reserved as rewards for experienced magistrates who had already served in the lesser audiencias. The council had recommended Dr. Antonio de Morga for the Mexican post on the grounds that he had already served for several years in the audiencia of Manila. Not daring to offend the Duke of Lerma, the council then recommended that the brother-in-law of the royal physician be given the Manila post vacated by Dr. Morga and that the latter be promoted to Mexico City as alcalde de crimen.[28] The view of the council prevailed. After serving in Manila for fourteen years, Lic. Manuel Madrid y Luna was promoted to Mexico as alcalde de crimen and subsequently oidor.[29]

This case illustrates the council's conviction regarding reward and incentive for worthy service. In order to defend the principle of promotion, the council shrewdly selected as their candidate Dr. Morga, who had close personal ties with the family of the Duke of Lerma. In this manner they conciliated the all-powerful royal favorite. It was Dr. Morga's good fortune that, at the time the decision was being made, the authorities in Spain had not yet received the news of his defeat at the hands of Olivier van Noort.

The principle of promotion from lesser to higher office was deeply embedded in the conciliar layer of the bureaucracy. Most of the councilors began their careers in the lesser tribunals in the peninsula before they received late in life a much desired seat in one of the councils at Court. They were ranked in prestige, with the Council of State, the Council of Castile, and the Council of the Indies heading the hierarchy. Members of the lesser councils aspired to and were often appointed to the more prestigious councils. Hence it seemed natural and useful to the Council of the Indies to nurture a system of promotion in the Indies.

Nevertheless, influence with the powerful at Court was very important. The sixth president of the audiencia of Quito, don Miguel de Ibarra (1600-1608), was a brother of don Juan de Ibarra, a bureaucratic favorite of Philip II and long-time secretary of the Council of the Indies.[30] Miguel de Ibarra's appointment to Quito, however, was not due solely to the important connections of his brother. He had spent several years as oidor in Bogotá.[31] What kind of connections at Court the seventh president of the audiencia, Dr. Juan Fernández de Recalde, was able to mobilize is not known, but his professional qualifications were ample. He had been the senior oidor in Lima.[32]

In the consulta of November 14, 1613, drawn up for the vacancy in the presidency of the audiencia of Quito, there were four nominees. The first was Dr. Alberto de Acuña, who had successively served as oidor in Panama, oidor in Quito, and alcalde de crimen and then oidor in Lima. The second candidate was Lic. Luis de Paredes y Tapia, oidor in Seville for seven years. The third name was Lic. Pedro de Otalora, oidor in Mexico and the son of a former member of the Council of the Indies. Dr. Antonio de Morga was the fourth candidate. He had earned a doctorate in laws from the University of Salamanca. He held several minor judicial posts in the peninsula from the 1580's until he was appointed to the audiencia of Manila in 1595. From 1603 onward he served in Mexico, where he eventually rose to senior alcalde de crimen.

All four candidates possessed very respectable professional qualifications. The man whom the council ranked as fourth in suitability, however, was the one who received the appointment, namely, Dr. Morga. Unlike two of the other candidates, he had not served as an oidor in one of the viceregal audiencias, but merely in the inferior criminal court. According to the criterion of promotion worked out informally by the council, one of the oidores in Mexico or Peru should have received the presidency of Quito. Dr. Morga as the senior alcalde de crimen should have been promoted to the rank of oidor replacing whoever was appointed the new president of Quito. It did not happen that way. Dr. Morga had influential friends very close to the throne among the family of the Duke of Lerma.

Although Oidor Pedro de Otalora was maneuvered out of his promotion to the presidency of Quito in 1613, he subsequently received his reward. In 1618 he became president of the audiencia of Guadalajara. In 1625 another of the candidates for the presidency of Quito in 1613, Dr. Alberto de Acuña, was offered the presidency of Guadalajara, but he declined it. He preferred to stay on the bench in Lima, where he was the senior oidor. The third candidate for the Quito vacancy enjoyed positive good fortune in not getting the appointment. Then an oidor in the audiencia of Seville, Lic. Luis de Paredes y Tapia subsequently served on the Council of the Indies from 1626 to 1636, when he was promoted to the Council of Castile. Had he gone to Quito in 1613, he probably never would have received these more desirable appointments in Spain.[33] Thus the subsequent careers of Dr. Morga's competitors in 1613 reveal that all of them suffered only momentary disappointment, if any, at their failure to secure the Quito appointment.

Although the patronage of men in power was a key factor in his appointment, Antonio de Morga also possessed substantial professional qualifications. Favorable recommendations from the viceroys of Mexico under whom he had served and his emergence from the visita general of 1607 unscathed were factors that his patrons at Court could exploit to advantage.[34]

Doña Juana de Briviesca Muñatones, the first wife of Dr. Morga, was a native of Uceda in the province of Guadalajara.[35] Dr. Morga dedicated his *Sucesos de las islas filipinas,* published in Mexico City in 1609, to the nobleman whom he considered his patron, don Cristóbal de Sandoval y Rojas, Duke of Cea.[36] In 1610 Philip III created the Duke of Cea Duke of Uceda, and it is under the latter title that he is best known in Spanish history. He was the son of the Duke of Lerma. Although father and son often quarreled, in 1618 the son replaced the father at the head of the administration. Dr. Morga could not have chosen a more influential patron.

It is even possible, but it cannot be proven, that Dr. Morga may have presented a substantial gift to his patron. Be this as it may, the Duke of Uceda had a personal interest in arranging that one of his protégés be placed in the presidency of Quito. He possessed a series of encomiendas and obrajes, yielding an annual revenue of 40,000 pesos, in the province of Riobamba.[37]

Favoritism and political patronage were apt to play a bigger role in the selection of the presidents of the superior audiencias, since a law degree was not a requirement. In the inferior audiencias neither the king and his favorites nor the council had much alternative but to appoint a judge from another audiencia.

The same principles operated in the selection of oidores as in the appointment of presidents. The Council of the Indies stood its ground in insisting that candidates be academically qualified and that due weight be given to previous experience. But the influence of the powerful also played a role. Of the nineteen oidores and three fiscales who served in the audiencia of Quito from about 1598 to 1636, every one had earned a licentiate in law. Three had acquired doctorates. Eight oidores and two fiscales had served in other audiencias in the Indies.[38] The others had held minor judicial offices in Spain.

Family connections were often a factor in appointments. Oidor Luis de Quiñones (1611–18) was the nephew of Toribio Alfonso Mogrovejo, second archbishop of Lima, a prelate with a saintly reputation that eventually led to his canonization in 1726.[39] Oidor Matías de Peralta (1610–24), who was a nephew of Friar Salvador de Rivera, bishop of Quito (1606–12), was the younger brother of the inquisitor in Mexico City who later became archbishop of Charcas (1609–11).[40] Oidor Juan de Valdés y Llano was a first cousin of the bishop of Teruel and a nephew of Archbishop Fernando de Valdés of Seville, inquisitor general and president of the Council of Castile.[41]

Without some influence it was difficult to secure an appointment to the professional bureaucracy. Yet the Council of the Indies often scuttled proposed appointments whose only recommendation was the naked use of influence. Such was the case of doña Catalina de Velasco, lady-in-waiting to the late queen, Isabel de Borbón. In 1646 she requested the post of oidor in the audiencia of Lima for her fiancé, don Antonio de Urrutia, solely on the grounds of the services her parents and grandparents had rendered the crown. Her young fiancé lacked a law degree as well as any previous administrative experience. The council recommended to Philip IV that the petition be rejected. Citing the youth's lack of qualifications, the council also pointed out that he was a resident of Lima, where his father held extensive properties, and that he was also the brother-in-law of one of the oidores there. The king accepted the recommendation of the council.[42]

Although many nonjudicial posts were publicly sold, both the crown and the council fought successfully to maintain the principle that judicial office could not be purchased. Much more difficult to determine is what role gifts and bribes played. During the reign of Philip II, sustained efforts were made to curb corruption. Bribery became widespread during the reign of Philip III, when the rapacious Lerma clan was all-powerful.

The enemies of Dr. Morga claimed that in private conversations he admitted having paid 10,000 pesos for the presidency of Quito.[43] At the time his antagonists made this charge, the Lerma family had fallen from power. Since the ties of Dr. Morga with the Duke of Uceda were well known and since the Count-Duke of Olivares had begun his administration with an anti-corruption campaign, hearsay evidence coming from personal enemies must be treated with extreme caution. Yet there is some reason to believe that the charge might have been true. The general greed of the Lerma family is well documented. Furthermore, the influence of the Duke of Uceda was evidently responsible for Morga's receiving the Quito presidency ahead of more senior candidates. Thirdly, Dr. Morga's venture of smuggling contraband Chinese silks into Quito in 1615 could have been prompted by his need to provide a present for his ducal patron. In this particular case the available evidence is inconclusive to establish either the innocence or the guilt of Dr. Morga.

During the subsequent Olivares administration, there was much less likelihood that the royal favorite received bribes. The count-duke lusted for power, not wealth. In every reign, however, the royal secretaries of the councils, through whom recommendations for appointments went to the king, were often venal.[44]

There was no set term for the offices of president and oidor. Attempts were made to establish limits, but they were never enforced. On the political level and on the provincial layer also, there were set terms. Viceroys and corregidores both served for five years. The Council of the Indies opposed a proposal of Olivares to restrict the term of professional magistrates to five years.[45] Juan de Solórzano y Pereira argued that the term of office should be at the pleasure of the prince. He was willing that the less professional presidents of the superior audiencias, who did not need a law degree, should serve for fixed terms of eight years. Since the oidores acquired their offices on the basis of their academic studies and their magisterial service, in his opinion they should not be deprived of their posts unless they were guilty of proven malfeasance. He feared that a time limit would make these posts less desirable and hence make it more difficult to recruit men of ability.[46]

In practice there was considerable rotation on the audiencia level. The axiom that no magistrate should have personal or economic ties in his district encouraged this trend. The oidores themselves were restless. They often pleaded for a change of assignment. The presidents of Quito in the seventeenth century served for an average period of five years. The term of Dr. Morga, spanning twenty-one years, was an exception that resulted in some measure from the duration of the visita general. Of the nineteen oidores serving between 1598 and 1636, eight served for more than ten years, six between five and ten years, and the remaining five for periods of less than five years. Of the three fiscales during the same period, one served for nine years, another for eleven years, and Lic. Melchor Suárez de Poago held office for a record-breaking twenty-eight years.[47]

The Council of the Indies consciously sought to encourage professionalization by promoting magistrates from lesser to higher audiencias. Thus they tried to provide a system of incentives which would motivate officials to perform their duties effectively and conscientiously. Positions in the inferior audiencias, such as Guadalajara, Quito, and Charcas, were considered less prestigious than those in the superior audiencias. To be sure, some of the superior audiencias were regarded as undesirable, for example, the audiencias of Manila, Panama, Chile, and Santo Domingo. Manila and Panama were undesirable for their hot and humid climates, Chile for its isolation, and Santo Domingo for its lack of importance. Hence many oidores considered it a promotion to be transferred from one of those superior audiencias to tribunals such as Quito or Charcas where the climate was thought to be more healthy or agreeable. Although Quito enjoyed the reputation of a climate of eternal spring, most magistrates subsequently complained about the hardships of the altitude. Among the bishops there was also an informal system of promotion in which the relative prestige of an episcopal see was equivalent to that of the corresponding audiencia.[48]

In the hierarchy of promotions, every oidor yearned for an appointment to one of the viceregal audiencias, with Lima outranking Mexico. Not only were the climates in both capitals moderately healthy, but also both cities possessed some of the creature comforts and a way of life reminiscent of what they had known in the peninsula. In fact, the overwhelming majority of oidores in both Lima and Mexico City had seen previous service in one of the other audiencias in the Indies.

Most professional magistrates nostalgically yearned to return to Spain itself. Few attained the goal, but it did exist as the highest promotion in the service. Between 1523 and 1600, only one oidor from an American audiencia received an appointment to the Council of the Indies. None was promoted from the Indies for the period between 1629 and 1700.[49] Yet during the years from 1600 to 1629 six oidores from the New World received seats in the Council of the Indies.[50] The most illustrious of them was, of course, Juan de Solórzano.

The rarity of councilors with experience in the New World may be traced back to the method of their appointment. A small committee of the Council of Castile drew up recommendations to the king for filling vacancies in all the councils resident at Court. The members of the cámara of the Council of Castile in more cases than not had no personal knowledge of or acquaintanceship with oidores serving in the far-off Indies. Hence they tended to recommend for the Council of the Indies magistrates serving in the peninsula, in particular, judges of the audiencias of Valladolid or Granada or magistrates serving in the fiscal service, the *contaduría mayor*.[51] Since the Council of the Indies was the third-ranking council, magistrates serving in the less prestigious councils were anxious for a promotion to the Council of the Indies.

That few magistrates overseas attained the prize does not alter the fact that the possibility of a seat in the Council of the Indies was a powerful incentive exciting the ambition of oidores in the New World. The career of Juan de Solórzano was exceptional in many ways. A brilliant student at the University of Salamanca, he won a chair at the age of 32. His appointment to the audiencia of Lima shortly afterward was due to the patronage of the Count of Lemos, then the president of the Council of the Indies, who recognized early the talents of the young man. Lemos promised Solórzano a seat on the Council of the Indies after a tour of duty in Lima. The president intended that Solórzano would subsequently edit the digest of Indian legislation, the *Recopilación de las leyes de los reynos de las Indias,* to whose formulation Solórzano ultimately made a major contribution. Before his stay in Lima ended, which he regarded as a veritable exile in spite of the fact that he had an unusually favorable opinion of the creoles for a Spaniard and was himself married to a criolla, Solórzano had to use all his considerable influence to secure his recall to Spain. He appointed attorneys to plead his case at Court. He sent an abject supplication to the king. A personal and frank appeal to the all-powerful Count-Duke of Olivares, with whom he had been friends at the University of Salamanca, was undoubtedly more efficacious. Another patron also intervened to bring about his recall to Spain. He was don García de Avellaneda y Haro, Count of Castrillo, twice president of the Council of the Indies, to whom Solórzano dedicated the *Política indiana*. Solórzano's intellectual gifts as well as his talent for choosing patrons made his bureaucratic career exceptional. His service reached its climax with an honorary appointment to the Council of Castile and a knighthood in one of the military orders. The example of his promotion, however, inspired his colleagues with the hope, usually vain, that they could follow in his footsteps.[52]

There were also promotions inside the audiencias themselves. Several magistrates started out at the bottom of the ladder as fiscal and subsequently received a promotion to oidor. Eventually the junior oidor might reach the rank of senior oidor. Those who were promoted to the viceregal audiencias from the inferior or superior tribunals often began their service in the inferior criminal court, the sala de crimen, and with good service and the right connections they might in time be promoted to the higher rank of oidor. The moderately ambitious were anxious to acquire a presidency. Not only was there a greater degree of responsibility and authority attached to this office, but also there were a larger salary and some perquisites, such as free housing in the casas reales.

All nine presidents of the audiencia of Quito from 1585 to 1653 were veterans of service in other audiencias. Two presidents had served in Charcas, four in Lima, two in Mexico, and one in Bogotá.[53] The presidency of the audiencia of Quito was in practice not often a stepping stone to further promotions. Of the fifteen presidents during the seventeenth century, only four received promotions. Seven died in office and the others retired. Of the twenty-five oidores and fiscales serving in Quito between 1589 and 1630, one had previously served in Bogotá, three in Santo Domingo, and five in Panama. Thirteen of these magistrates received promotions. Two went to Charcas, six to Lima, two to the Council of the Indies, and one each to Mexico, Guatemala, and Bogotá. Of these twenty-five, nine died in office in Quito.[54]

The career of Matías de Peralta illustrates how a magistrate of good family connections could rise in the bureaucratic hierarchy. A nephew of a bishop of Quito and the younger brother of an archbishop of Charcas, he began his career in Quito as an oidor (1610–26), serving long enough to become senior oidor. He spent the rest of his long career in the audiencia of Mexico. Beginning at the lowest rank as junior alcalde de crimen, he was promoted to the rank of oidor. He eventually became senior oidor and for a year was acting chief executive of the kingdom during a viceregal interregnum, before his suspension from office in 1654.[55] Dr. Juan García Galdós Galdoche de Valencia (1562–1640) began his bureaucratic career as fiscal in the sala de crimen in Mexico (1610–13), fiscal of the audiencia of Mexico (1613–16), and then oidor from 1616 to 1624. From 1624 to 1640 he served in the audiencia of Peru, where for many years he was the senior oidor. He was also visitor general of the audiencia of Quito (1630–32).[56]

If there was a pattern of promotion in the professional bureaucracy, the machinery available for attaining advancement was essentially the same as that used to secure an initial appointment, that is, a combination of academic training, previous experience, and influential patrons. The presidents of the audiencias were under standing instructions to make recommendations periodically to the council about oidores who merited promotion. The presidents conducted secret inquiries in which witnesses of repute testified under oath about the moral character and the official conduct of those oidores who were potential candidates for promotion.[57] Furthermore, standing instructions provided that the presidents conduct similar investigations of all the licensed advocates.[58] The crown in theory, but seldom in practice, was willing to consider recruitment to the bench from the bar. In addition to those secret investigations, every candidate for promotion prepared a public *información de oficio y partes* in which a series of witnesses testified to the moral, academic, and magisterial qualifications of the applicant.[59] The applicant sent these bulky informaciones to the Council of the Indies, where they were filed for future reference.

A significant factor in promotion was the recommendations of peers and superiors. Dr. Morga, for example, was twice recommended for promotion by Viceroy Montesclaros before he received the Quito assignment.[60] Although his ties with the Duke of Uceda were more important, the recommendations of the viceroys under whom he served certainly facilitated his promotion. Although the chances for a promotion were slight without the active support of peers and superiors, such recommendations in themselves were not sufficient. On several occasions the audiencia of Quito warmly recommended the promotion of Fiscal Melchor Suárez de Poago to the rank of oidor, but the council consistently refused to act.[61] There are examples of the audiencia's submitting recommendations sufficiently tepid to guarantee the failure of the candidate.[62]

The magistrates themselves literally bombarded the council with explicit requests for a change.[63] Moreover, they sought to enlist informally the support of key officials at Court. Lic. Mañozca twice tried such an approach when he wrote Antonio González de Legarda, who, as secretary of the Council of the Indies for the viceroyalty of Peru, could be very influential in matters of appointments. After assuring the secretary of personal loyalty to him, Lic. Mañozca provided a brief biographical sketch of himself as well as a defense of his controversial conduct as visitor general in Quito.

He concluded the letter by presenting himself as a suitable candidate for the vacant archdiocese of Lima. This letter did not then achieve the desired result, but in time Lic. Mañozca received more than his quota of promotions, including the mitre of archbishop of Mexico.[64]

The case of Dr. Morga is typical of the restlessness of the quasi-career bureaucrats. Although he was initially delighted with his promotion to Quito, within a very short time he requested a change of assignment. On May 30, 1623, he asked for the prized post of a seat in the Council of the Indies as well as a knighthood in the order of Santiago. He cited his four decades in the royal service and his having raised more than 100,000 pesos as a forced loan and gift to the king. The council curtly turned down the request.[65] A decision had already been made to send a visitor general to Quito. Dr. Morga apparently did not realize that the question under consideration was not whether he would be promoted but whether he would retain the office he already had. Upon receiving the news that the president of Charcas had just died, the old bureaucrat dispatched a letter in 1630 requesting the vacant post.[66] By 1634 ill-health, old age, and the turmoil of the visita general had so undermined his ambition that he meekly requested an honorable retirement.[67]

In his salad days, before reverses had dampened his high spirits, Dr. Morga played a trick on some of his colleagues. He forged a royal cedula containing a promotion for two oidores. What reaction those disappointed magistrates might have expressed when Dr. Morga exposed his practical joke is not known. The Council of the Indies "was not amused." In the sentence of the visita general, they fined him 600 ducats for that bit of facetiousness.[68]

Not only did a pattern of rewards, incentives, and promotions encourage professionalization, but so also did the concomitant system of penalties ranging from reprimands to fines to suspension and even loss of office. How these penalties functioned in practice is the central topic of Part III.

The preponderance of the oidores were Spaniards from the peninsula and not Spaniards born in the Indies, i.e., creoles. Discrimination against the creoles had no basis in law. The crown repeatedly urged that properly qualified Spaniards from the Indies be given consideration. Juan de Solórzano urged recruitment of the bench from the bar, that is, from among the lawyers, many of them creoles, who were licensed to practice before the audiencias.[69] Encomenderos and the descendants of the conquerors and the first settlers constituted a social grouping, *los beneméritos de las Indias,* who, according to repeated royal cedulas, should be given consideration for appointment to offices in conformity with their abilities and qualifica-tions.[70]

The crown and the council in practice gave preference to Spanish-born lawyers. They were closer to the seat of power. Few creoles could enlist the patronage of powerful nobles or bureaucrats at Court, since the former had no personal ties with the latter. Another factor inhibiting creoles from becoming oidores was the principle that no judge could own property in the kingdom where he exercised jurisdiction.[71] Hence any would-be creole oidor had to be prepared to leave the American kingdom where he was born and reared in order to undertake the peripatetic existence normal to such magistrates. A creole of means faced with obvious distaste the prospect of leaving his and his wife's property in the hands of an administrator. If he did not have some property, the chances were that he lacked the mini-mum social and educational qualifications for consideration as a candidate.

The *de facto* exclusion of the creoles from the ranks of the professional magistracy prevented the development of a tradition in which several gen-erations of a family would enjoy bureaucratic careers in the New World. The children and the grandchildren of oidores joined the ranks of the cre-oles. Thus the oidores never became a hereditary *noblesse de la robe* like that which developed under the ancien régime in France. It is possible that such a development did occur in the Spanish peninsula, but further study needs to be done. In British India, on the other hand, the children of Indian civil servants received their education in England. Admission into the service was by competitive examination. Consequently there developed a tradition, especially among some Scottish families, in which several generations served in the Indian Civil Service.[72]

The social origins of the professional bureaucracy were middle-sector, in contrast to the political bureaucrats on the viceregal level, who were of the landed and titled aristocracy. The oidores came from the urban middle groups or the country gentry for whom a university education was not merely an ornament, as it was for the nobility, but a necessary prerequisite to earn their kind of living. While some of them may have inherited modest means from their parents or their wives, as a group they were not independently wealthy. Many of them were not destitute, however. The first wife of Dr. Morga, for example, brought him a dowry of 10,000 ducats. Dr. Morga's father, don Pedro de Morga, was one of the leading bankers in Seville until the failure of his bank during the second royal bankruptcy of 1576.[73] Hence Dr. Morga inherited nothing from his father. In any case, few bureau-crats had enough property in the peninsula to make it worth their while to stay there. Accordingly they depended for their livelihood in large measure on the salaries they earned.

These men were not middle class in the modern sense of belonging to a class with self-identity and aspirations autonomous from those of other classes. Rather they lived in the orbit and by the favors of the monarchical and aristocratic society whose cornerstones were institutionalized inequality and hereditary privilege. It was, after all, a combination of aristocratic patronage, academic training, and previous experience which enabled them to acquire entrance into and promotions inside the professional bureaucracy in the Indies.

The failure to grant any high offices to the creoles in the Indies contrasts sharply with the practices followed in the European extra-peninsular kingdoms of the Habsburg monarchy. In Sicily, for example, the parliament successfully defended the principle that no Spaniard could fill any senior position previously reserved for citizens of Sicily. Thus the only Spanish officials were the viceroy, and some of them were Italians, and a mere handful of his close advisers. The Council of Italy resident at Court, of course, had a large Spanish membership. When Philip II reorganized the judicial administration in 1569, Sicilian pressure forced him to give up his original plan of appointing some Spanish judges, as was then being done in the adjacent kingdom of Naples.[74] Very few Spanish magistrates were appointed in the other European possessions of the crown, such as Naples, Milan, or the Low Countries.

These were not new kingdoms, as were the Indies, recently created by the efforts of colonization, but ancient states with long traditions of government which happened by dynastic chance to share a common monarch with Castile. Any massive attempt to hispanize their bureaucracies would probably have unleashed a series of convulsions comparable to the Dutch revolt. As it was, the exclusion of creoles from high office in the New World did create an acute source of tension that became a contributory factor leading toward political emancipation in the early nineteenth century.

Underneath the conciliar bureaucracy in Spain, the political bureaucracy of the viceroys, and the professional bureaucracy, there was a fourth layer which we may call the clerking bureaucracy. In contrast to the professional bureaucracy, the superior magistrates, where European Spaniards overwhelmingly predominated, creole officeholders were frequent on the clerking level, the *ministros inferiores,* as they were called.

A clear distinction should be made between the superior and the inferior magistrates. The former were appointive offices serving at the pleasure of the king, whereas the latter were usually positions purchased from the crown. The superior magistrates were salaried officers, in contrast to the inferior magistrates whose offices carried no salary or only a nominal one payable by the royal treasury. They rendered a wide variety of clerking services for the general public. Their compensation, in fees set by the audiencia, came from those who received their services.

Several of these posts yielded a comfortable income to their owners. The *alguacil mayor* of the audiencia, as the chief constable of the kingdom, ranked just below the fiscal. He was responsible for the execution of all court orders, the arrest of persons, and the general preservation of public order. And for all these duties he received fees from the public who required his services. The office also carried considerable patronage, since the alguacil mayor could appoint deputies in the capital city and in the rural hinterland. The adjective *mayor,* when attached to an office, implied powers of patronage.[75]

The alguacil mayor of the city of Quito was the chief constable for the municipal government, with duties and privileges similar to those of the alguacil mayor of the audiencia. The municipal post fetched between 20,000 and 25,000 pesos.[76]

All forms of evidence and every kind of documentation presented to any court had to be submitted in writing and signed by a notary public. His skill was needed in the drafting of all legal documents, and his signature was required to attest to their authenticity. An *escribano real de las Indias* was not an office but merely a license to practice. Although there were some minimum qualifications to secure such a license, the test was a good deal less than a professional examination.

The *escribano de cámara* of the audiencia, on the other hand, was an office. As chief clerk of the audiencia, the escribano mayor held a lucrative office. Most of the actual notarial work was done by a large staff of deputies whom he appointed, but the escribano mayor received a fee for every document submitted to the audiencia. Hence the post of escribano de cámara commanded a high price when purchased from the crown. That office fetched some 15,000 pesos in 1605.[77]

There were several minor clerking offices whose fees gave their owners a steady if only modest income. The *relator* was the most important. A lawyer, he acted as a court reporter who worked closely with the office of escribano mayor and who prepared reports for both the oidores and the litigants.[78] His salary payable by the treasury was only 400 pesos, but the fees of the office amounted to about 2,600 pesos annually.[79] The *receptor de penas* collected the fines imposed by the court. The *depositario de bienes de difuntos* was a public trustee.[80] Another office of prestige, carrying with it emoluments, was that of *canciller*. His primary responsibility was to hold custody of the royal seal, without whose stamp official business could not be transacted.[81]

No lawyer could practice before the audiencia without being licensed by that tribunal. A lawyer became a certified *abogado* of the audiencia by merely demonstrating that he had a law degree of either the licentiate or the doctorate. The degree of bachelor was not sufficient. The licensed advocates observed seniority among themselves, since they sat before the oidores in places in accordance with the date they obtained their licenses to practice.[82]

The audiencia had a substantial amount of patronage to distribute to the licensed advocates. Since tie votes among the oidores were not infrequent, the president had the authority to appoint from among the advocates a *juez de remisión* who would serve as a temporary judge to break a particular tie.[83] When there was a temporary vacancy in the office of fiscal, the audiencia usually appointed one of the licensed advocates as fiscal *ad interim*. Jealous of its powers of appointment, the crown granted the acting fiscal merely a half-salary.[84] There are very few cases when the acting fiscal received the proprietary appointment. The audiencia also made other temporary fee-carrying appointments to the advocates, such as conducting residencias in the provinces.

With the exception of the licensed advocates and the relatores, many other inferior magistrates purchased their offices from the crown. The relator had to be a letrado. No professional qualifications were required for the alguaciles, the receptores, the depositarios de bienes de difuntos, the canciller, etc. The escribanos mayores did not have to be notaries public at the time they purchased the office, although they had to take a rather nominal test within a certain period subsequent to the purchase of the office. Seats in the city councils were also for sale. Aldermen in Quito paid 1,500 pesos for this privilege.[85]

The income to the crown for the sale and transfer of all offices in the Indies averaged 38,000 ducats annually.[86] Although other forms of taxation were more lucrative, this item was a significant source of royal revenue. It had the advantage of producing a rather steady revenue in that the crown received one-third of the original purchase price at the time an heir inherited the office. In the seventeenth century, direct taxation was apt to be confined to emergencies and indirect taxation tended to be fixed by custom. Since the crown lacked a sufficiently wide tax base from which to pay the salaries of those who rendered clerical services to the public, there seemed no desirable alternative. Thus the state required the public to pay directly for clerking services which the state itself had insufficient income to provide.[87] Under no circumstances would the crown hand over to the viceroys and the audiencias the responsibility for filling these posts. Such political patronage would have made a mockery of the carefully contrived system of checks and balances, whose dual purpose was to expose corruption and restrain individual ambition.

The Habsburg kings sought to retain a firm, personal grip over patronage in all their dominions. They well knew that upon a judicious exercise of that right largely depended the loyalty and cooperation of their subjects. In the Low Countries, for example, Charles V refused to delegate patronage to the governors, most of whom were his close royal relatives. Yet the king's personal administration of patronage did not give him the degree of control over his servants that he hoped to exercise. In most cases he was dependent upon the advice of a particular council. Those who did receive the appointments were more grateful to the council than to the monarch. Government by consulta also gave vast influence to the royal secretaries who, as the links between the councils and the sovereign, had much to say as to what papers reached the royal desk. Some secretaries were wont to sell their influence to the highest bidder.[88]

Another advantage of the sale of municipal and clerking offices was that it provided the crown with a means of bringing new blood into the bureaucratic system from among middle groups and the new wealth. The latter were more amenable, initially at least, to the maintenance of royal authority than were the aristocratic groups. Philip III made purchasable offices renunciable in 1603. Since such officeholders could nominate a successor by paying one-third of the price of the office, these posts tended to become hereditary. In institutionalizing the sale of some offices, Philip II had strengthened royal control, but during the reign of his son, the crown virtually abdicated its influence over the filling of these posts, except through a theoretical veto power which it seldom invoked.[89]

There were three types of offices that were sold: ceremonial offices carrying prestige but no real authority, clerking offices in the audiencias and the city councils, and municipal offices. In fact there was little possibility that the clerking positions in the audiencias could escape for long from the network of daily control of the superior magistrates. On the other hand, the cabildos did have a separate sphere of jurisdiction; they needed some independence in order to act as the spokesmen of the new and the old wealth.

Nonetheless, the intricate web of checks and balances in the whole bureaucratic system was sufficient to limit but not to wipe out their freedom of action.[90]

In addition to the political, the conciliar, the professional, and the clerking layers of the imperial bureaucracy, there were two other echelons. The fiscal officers administered the royal treasury, and the corregidores and their staffs manned the provincial administration. These two layers will be considered in the next chapter, where attention will be focused on corruption.

On the conciliar, political, and professional levels, there was a substantial amount of professionalism. In the lower levels, professionalism scarcely existed. Some scholars have been led to speculate that the sale of some ceremonial, clerking, and municipal offices may have caused venality.[91] That graft was a part of the Spanish system is undeniable, but its origins and its causes are far more intricate than the mere sale of clerking offices. Those posts carried only very limited powers. The inadequacy of salaries paid to oidores, corregidores, and treasury officers provides a much more satisfactory explanation for the existence of venality. Furthermore, the ideal and the practice of an uncorruptible bureaucracy were only imperfectly understood in the seventeenth century.

The decision-making posts on the judicial, administrative, and financial levels were never put up for sale. To be sure, during the reign of Charles II, a mere handful of those positions were illegally sold, but for only one oidor, for example, is there documentary proof that he purchased his office.

There was a dualism in the attitude toward the holding of public office in the sixteenth and seventeenth centuries throughout western Europe. On one hand, the modern ideal of a salaried and disinterested magistracy, in which office is a public trust and not a piece of property, clearly emerged in the Spanish empire. No more articulate expression of this attitude can be found than in the writings of Juan de Solórzano.[92] Yet the conduct of countless individual magistrates reveals more than a trace of an older attitude, an inheritance from the medieval patrimonial state. The officeholder made the most of the opportunities, financial as well as social, which the office afforded him. To be sure, the sale of several kinds of nonjudicial offices may have contributed to the perpetuation of this proprietary attitude, but such an explanation does not get much below the surface. There was a deep-rooted dichotomy between office as a piece of property and office as a public trust. The roots of the former lay in the medieval patrimonial state out of which the more modern bureaucratic states of the sixteenth century had emerged.[93] Nowhere can we see more clearly than in the Spanish empire in America how these contradictory attitudes coexisted and clashed, a conflict which caused grief to many magistrates. The definitive emergence of the ideal of an uncorrupt, professional, and salaried bureaucracy did not come until the nineteenth century, a consequence in large part of the triumph of middle-class values, or, in Max Weber's term, the emergence of systems of legal domination.

7.

GRAFT

The crown and the Council of the Indies made sustained but frequently vain efforts to expose and punish corruption among magistrates overseas. The basic cause of the considerable avarice throughout the bureaucracy was the inadequacy of the salary scale rather than the custom of selling the nonjudicial clerking offices. The crown's efforts to eliminate corruption would remain fruitless as long as compensation failed to be realistic. Those officials who were better paid were less apt to indulge in illegal forms of self-enrichment. The viceroys were the least venal, the oidores and the exchequer officials much more so, and on the lower provincial level among the corregidores massive corruption prevailed. The salaries for each level were the decisive factors.

The annual salary of the viceroy of Mexico was 20,000 ducats, approximately 27,000 pesos, and the viceroy of Peru received 30,000 ducats or 41,000 pesos.[1] If the salaries of the viceroys were impressive by the standards of those times, so also were their expenses and obligations. The costs of maintaining the pomp and ceremonial of a viceregal court, part of which came out of the private purse of the viceroy, were onerous. As scions of the great noble families, the viceroys and their wives usually had substantial means of their own. Upon returning to the peninsula, a viceroy might reasonably expect to receive favors and emoluments from the king for himself or his children to compensate somewhat for the expenses incurred overseas. All of these conditions contributed toward making the viceroys as a group remarkably honest.

Institutionalized corruption began on the second level of the administration, among the superior magistrates. Coming from middle-sector urban or country gentry backgrounds, the judges seldom had substantial independent means. Unlike the viceroys, they could not look forward to the lucrative emoluments from the king that were ordinarily reserved for the high nobility. Royal largesse for the oidores was of a much more modest variety. The professional magistrates depended in large measure on their salaries for the wherewithal to support themselves and their often large families. The crown was not unmindful of this condition. Oidores accordingly received somewhat larger salaries than their peers in the peninsula. Bureaucrats in the Indies in another way were more fortunate than their colleagues in the Old World. The former received their salaries in silver and the latter in paper currency. The purchasing power of the paper currency declined precipitously under the impact of galloping inflation.[2]

In conformity with the greater prestige and authority of the office, the presidents received higher salaries than the oidores. They ranged between 3,500 and 6,000 ducats. The president of Quito received 4,800 ducats annually. Among the "fringe" benefits enjoyed by the presidents was free housing in the casas reales, where the audiencia held its sessions.[3] Oidores, on the other hand, had to pay rent for their housing out of their salaries. The salaries of the oidores and the fiscales were uniform in each tribunal although the former outranked the latter. They ranged from 2,000 to 3,000 pesos. The oidores of Quito received 2,400 ducats annually.[4]

The salary level was rigid. There was not even an embryonic system of merit raises by which magistrates might hope to receive periodic increments for length and merit of service. Only when an oidor received a promotion to president was there a modest salary increment. Variations in the salaries among the audiencias were equalized largely by the differences in the cost of living. There was a per diem expense account, an *ayuda de costa,* during the period that an official was traveling from one post to another and during the period that an oidor served as circuit judge in the provinces.[5]

Although in the initial determination of salaries the king and the council paid some attention to variations in the cost of living among the different kingdoms in the Indies, the salary scale once set tended to remain inflexible. There were no sustained efforts to adjust salaries to changing economic conditions such as inflation.

The rigidity of the salary scale can be traced directly back to the narrow tax base from which the crown derived its revenue and the rapidly progressing inflation which was aggravated by the expanding foreign commitments of the Habsburg monarchy. A further reduction of the slender tax base occurred with the contraction of the economy that overtook the Spanish world after the ascension of Philip IV in 1621, when the Iberian powers found themselves involved in a world war. After mounting military disasters in Europe and throughout the tropical world finally led to the Peace of Münster in 1648 and the treaty of the Pyrenees in 1659, the Spanish monarchy emerged economically shattered and reduced to the rank of a second-class power. During these years the volume of trade between the peninsula and the Indies drastically declined. Hence the treasury was under sustained pressure to reduce its salary commitments rather than to expand them.[6]

So hard-pressed was the royal treasury that it refused to grant the traditional royal gift of one-half salary for a year to the widows of superior magistrates until each widow could justify it on the basis of need. In practice every widow who requested the royal largesse received it. The oidores could be counted upon to testify to the poverty of their recently deceased colleagues, since the next year their wives might be the widows requesting the same royal bounty.[7]

Although an oidor was urged to avoid extravagance and luxury in his way of living, as the representative of the king he was expected to live decorously. Given the treasury's inability to be more generous and flexible about salaries, the essential question is whether an oidor could provide for his family solely from his salary. In Quito economic conditions were quite favorable. Regional products were relatively cheap, since the labor supply did not diminish sharply as it did in Mexico. The tight monopoly system regulating intra-imperial trade made goods coming from the metropolis scarce and expensive. The supply of contraband merchandise was irregular but more plentiful and somewhat less expensive.

If an oidor contented himself with consuming local products and avoiding European imports and contraband goods, he could with penny-pinching frugality just manage to live within his salary. Those who did left their widows and children destitute. The families appealed to the king. A royal gift was usually forthcoming, such as an ecclesiastical benefice for one of the sons, a modest dowry to enable a girl to enter a convent, or a scholarship to facilitate the education of a youth.[8] The temptation to augment one's income became stronger the longer a magistrate stayed in the Indies or the larger his family became. If an oidor took a mistress, which was not infrequent, he had no alternative but to engage in graft.

Not to be discounted are the roles of the wives of the oidores, many of whom became restless with their modest incomes when they compared themselves to the more affluent creole ladies with whom they associated. The magistrates were at the very top of the social ladder, but their salaries, of course, did not reflect this condition. Wealthy creole ladies were apt to spend extravagantly on clothes and jewels. At mass they wore on their bosoms a large portion of their own and their husbands' estates.

The central authorities in the peninsula made some effort to provide for the old-age security of their salaried magistrates. The king did grant on occasion an honorable retirement to one of his servants abroad. The retirement pension was full salary as well as emeritus status with the ceremonial privileges of the rank held. Lest the generosity of the house of Habsburg be extolled, it should be pointed out that there was no set age for retirement.

The magistrate himself might petition for emeritus status. Sometimes the audiencia took the initiative. The king might grant the request upon the advice of the Council of the Indies. All such requests stressed advanced age, long tenure in the royal service, and deteriorating health. The Council of the Indies seldom recommended retirement unless they had conclusive evidence from the audiencia that the magistrate's faculties had failed to the point where they impaired the minimum performance of duties. In terms of pesos and ducats, the pension system cost the treasury very little. Often when the king did grant an honorable retirement, the news reached Quito after the death of the would-be emeritus. Such was the case of President Morga, Oidor Manuel Tello de Velasco, and Fiscal Suárez de Poago.[9]

The relator of the audiencia, Juan Guerrero de Luna, did not enjoy the few years of his retirement as of March 19, 1622. The audiencia repeatedly recommended his retirement on the grounds that his advanced age and ill-health made it difficult for him to perform his duties, although they generously praised the quality of his past services.[10] The relator took his honorable retirement with ill-grace, for he received only 400 pesos in salary. He was no longer entitled to the additional 2,600 pesos in fees that the office ordinarily earned each year.[11] Lic. Guerrero actually sued Dr. Morga for allegedly writing a libelous recommendation to the king which resulted in his retirement. After hearing the case, Visitor General Mañozca absolved Dr. Morga.[12]

Thus the retirement and pension system in the Spanish empire was so administered that few lived to enjoy its seemingly generous benefits.

From the king came a ceaseless flow of edicts, laws, and regulations, whose purpose was to keep the salaried magistrates from straying from the straight and narrow path of honesty. Honest government meant disinterested government. The bureaucrats were to be isolated from the community where they were temporarily stationed. They were to have no personal, emotional, or economic ties with the people over whom they administered justice. The viceroys, presidents, oidores, and fiscales, as well as the corregidores in the provinces and the officers of the royal treasury, were specifically forbidden to engage in commerce either on their own or through intermediaries. Nor could they own in their names or in the names of others any kind of urban or rural real estate. They could not engage in either pastoral agriculture or any branch of mining. These prohibitions applied also to the wives of the magistrates and to all their unmarried children, even those who were not living with their parents.[13]

Another conscious aim of the Council of the Indies was to isolate socially the magistrates of the audiencia from the rest of the community. As spelled out in the ordinances of the *Recopilación,* the ideal oidor would be aloofly polite to everyone and friendly to no one. Oidores could not serve as godparents at the weddings or baptisms of permanent residents of the kingdom, nor could such *naturales* serve in those capacities for the oidores. *Compadrazgo* was something more in the seventeenth century than a form of ritual co-parenthood. It was a religious, social, and economic series of bonds linking the two families involved by mutual obligations and assistance.[14] For this reason the crown was anxious to isolate the magistrates from compadrazgo ties with residents overseas.

Superior magistrates could not attend weddings or funerals of residents of the kingdom.[15] In its corporate capacity, the audiencia could attend mass only on officially designated holidays. The magistrates, their wives, and their children could not receive gifts of any kind from those living in the kingdom. The Council of the Indies admonished bureaucratic families not to enter into close friendships with families of local origin. The wives of the magistrates were under standing instructions to abstain from any intervention in the official business of their husbands. Specifically, legislation ordered them not to influence their husbands on behalf of litigants, nor were the wives allowed to mingle socially with litigants. Another ordinance provided that no magistrate or member of his family should allow gambling at card games in their homes.[16]

Legislation relating to the marriages of the salaried bureaucrats reflected the same spirit. Virtually every oidor who came to the New World was already married. But the life span was short. Some oidores found themselves widowers, and the widows of magistrates abounded. The crown tenaciously clung to the principle that no oidor or his children could marry a resident and native of the particular audiencia kingdom in which the oidor served. A magistrate might marry a resident of another kingdom of the Indies. Before doing so, he had to secure the consent of the king and the council by demonstrating that the woman's family background was suitable. Yet there were some exceptions to the rules. Juan de Solórzano, when an oidor in Lima, secured royal permission to marry a creole lady from the kingdom of Peru.[17] Serious trouble was most apt to occur when a magistrate did not secure prior approval from the king. Under the circumstances, there was a natural tendency for oidores to take as their second wives the widows of their colleagues. Several such marriages took place in Quito.[18] Few aspects of royal policy created as much turmoil as the enforcement of these provisions. The marital difficulty of Oidor Diego de Zorrilla, which will be discussed in Chapter 10, is just one of endless examples that could be cited.

The same regulations also applied to the children of oidores. Being prohibited from marriage with permanent residents, los naturales, of the kingdom where their father served, the sons and daughters of magistrates were rather narrowly restricted in their choice of marriage partners. A not untypical consequence of these stringent regulations was the *escandalo* created by the eldest daughter of Dr. Morga. Doña Juliana fled her father's house in Manila in the dark hours of the night by climbing out of a window. Her father had adamantly refused her permission to marry a young man on the grounds that he was far beneath her station. The girl's persistence finally won out over her father's furiously melodramatic efforts to regain custody over her. The timely intervention of the civil and ecclesiastical authorities enabled her to marry the man of her choice. Her irate father, however, never forgave her for the rest of his long life.[19] Thus marriage regulations designed to isolate the magistrates and their immediate families could impose hardship and heartbreak.

In his desire to promote the disinterestedness of the oidores, the Count-Duke of Olivares proposed in 1627 that no oidor could marry any woman living in any part of the Indies. The council successfully blocked this proposal on the grounds that it would impose an unnecessary hardship on the magistrates. They would have to recruit their new wives from the peninsula. Olivares finally accepted the counterproposal of the council, which was a restatement of the traditional policy. No remarriage could take place without prior royal approval. No magistrate might marry a woman who was a resident of the audiencia kingdom in which he served.[20]

Spanish legislative codes envisaged the professional magistrates as Platonic guardians. Having no material or emotional ties with those over whom they ruled paternalistically, they were to be the repositories of the wisdom and courage of the state. Spanish mercantilism, neo-medieval corporatism, and Counter Reformation scholasticism have a distinct Platonic flavor, shocking though this statement may sound. In the ideal society of the Athenian philosopher, property did not change hands; anything new, even in poetry and music, was prohibited; and a rigid caste system kept everyone in his designated place. The caste of guardians, in which the older men trained the younger, was superior to the military. Philip Mason has suggested that the Indian Civil Service during the Victorian age approximated this Platonic ideal. It is clear that the Spaniards under the Habsburgs, whether consciously or not, also sought to govern the New World along Platonic lines.

The ideal proved too abstract. The salaried bureaucrats never in fact became the Platonic guardians envisaged in royal legislation. Had they been paid salaries substantially larger and had they been rotated from one post to another every five years or so, the oidores might have fulfilled the first prerequisite of Platonic guardians in having no personal, economic, or emotional ties in the community. No one in the seventeenth century advocated doubling the salaries of the magistrates. Such a proposal would have been a fiscal nightmare for the parsimonious royal treasury. The Count-Duke of Olivares once suggested that the superior magistrates be automatically rotated every five years. The Council of the Indies turned a deaf ear to this proposal, for it would have destroyed the informal system of promotion among the various audiencias.[21]

Because many oidores remained at the same posts for periods much longer than five years and because their salaries were scarcely adequate to live decorously and comfortably, it was inevitable for them to acquire close friendships and business associations. Their long tenure in the same posts made them not disinterested philosopher-kings but acute practical politicians, sensitive and aware of the special interests of the communities in which they served. They became, in effect, brokers with the complex responsibility of trying to work out an endless series of compromises between what the distant crown and council in Madrid advocated and what local pressures in the Indies would permit.

In rooting out corruption, the British began with a more formidable handicap than the Spaniards. The English East India Company was originally a commercial operation in which some of its employees prior to 1756 made substantial fortunes. From 1492 onward the Castilian crown, not a quasi-public and semi-private commercial company, exercised *de jure* sovereignty over the New World.

Insofar as the Indian Civil Service did approximate the Platonic ideal of a guardian race, they met the three conditions which were glaringly absent in the Habsburg monarchy: adequate salaries, frequent rotation in office, and periodic home leaves.

The Indian civil servants received material benefits that were generous for those times. Salaries ranged between 1,080 and 10,000 pounds annually. Other benefits created between the administrations of Lord Cornwallis and Lord Bentinck were merit increases, promotion by seniority (as some wits quipped, promotion by senility), pensions for civil servants and their widows, educational scholarships for children, and periodic home leaves. Like his counterpart in the Spanish service, no civil servant could own real estate in India. The law obligated him to invest his surplus capital in government bonds or bank stocks.[22]

Experience taught the British that their ideal of scrupulous honesty had to be extended downward to the very large clerking bureaucracy composed of Indians. It was not enough that the one thousand-odd British subjects in the Indian Civil Service should be disinterested guardians. The widespread venality among the clerking bureaucracy threatened to undercut the basic aims of the British administration. During the second half of the nineteenth century, the British did manage to instill their code of rectitude and honesty into the Indian clerks. The task of the British was facilitated by the introduction of the English language and educational system, coupled with the introduction of new schemes in transportation, communications, credit, banking, irrigation, famine relief, and public health as well as the entrance of the new technology, the rise of a market economy, and the application of English legal procedures.[23]

Some Indian civil servants complained about the frequency of their being rotated from one post to another, usually once every three years if not more often. From one point of view, such a practice may have been undesirable. As soon as a district officer was beginning to acquire a firm grasp of regional conditions, he received a transfer. For this very reason, the procedure fostered more disinterested government. The Indian civil servants did not have the time to acquire either material or personal ties in the district to which they ministered.

An expanding economy, new forms of technology, and a rational tax system, all of which were absent in the Habsburg empire, provided the British with the wherewithal to provide generous material benefits to their agents. Steamships and the opening of the Suez Canal in 1869 enabled the British to provide their civil servants with periodic home leaves, when they could renew contact with the values and standards of their own society. The Spanish bureaucrat in the seventeenth century became *déraciné*. Very seldom did he ever see his native land again after setting out for the Indies. The hazards of travel in the days of the sailing ship made periodic home leaves unfeasible. Surrounded by servile and obsequious populations of different skin pigments, administering a hierarchal society based on privilege and endowed with the ritual but never the full content of power, Spanish bureaucrats became exiles in an alien land. A moral decay set in, which most often expressed itself in avarice and licentiousness.

Countless royal ordinances seeking to convert the salaried bureaucrats into disinterested Platonic guardians reflect the lopsided faith that the Spanish authorities placed in the efficacy of legislation. What they failed to provide was the underpinning, in the form of adequate salaries, more frequent rotation in office, and occasional home leaves.

However important the material benefits granted to the Indian Civil Service were, they never could be sufficient in themselves to root out graft. Salaries, pensions, home leaves, etc., had to be buttressed by a moral ethos. Utilitarianism provided much of that ethos. Jeremy Bentham (1748–1832) espoused the doctrines of the greatest good for the greatest number, utility as the criterion of worth, and democracy as the most effective means to achieve those principles. His earlier works had already inspired men with a belief in rationalism as the guiding rule in politics, religion, economics, and law. Along with his disciple, John Mill, he formulated a political program which advocated a unicameral legislature, a secret ballot, annual parliaments, female suffrage, the appointment of the prime minister by Parliament, and a civil service recruited by competitive examination. Utilitarianism was an ideology of middle-class capitalists opposing the landed aristocracy in government and monopolistic commercialism in business.

This program deeply influenced the mentality of the Indian Civil Service and the goals of British policy there. A mature expression of this thinking emerged in the proclamation issued by Queen Victoria in 1858, after the suppression of the Sepoy mutiny, when the British crown formally assumed sovereignty over the subcontinent. The queen outlined the basic aims of British rule in India. They were the preservation of internal peace, toleration of all religions, equality before the law, a career open to talent, and protection of private property, as well as respect for the ancient customs of India. The queen promised that, after the restoration of domestic tranquility, "it is our earnest desire to stimulate the peaceful industry of India, to promote works of public utility and improvement and to administer the government for the benefit of all subjects therein."[24] Hence material progress was a major goal. Equally important was the rule of law through the introduction of English norms of justice. The spirit and intent of British rule in mid-Victorian and late-Victorian India was, in a phrase, enlightened despotism.

Education of the masses to prepare them for ultimate self-government had no place. English education for the Indian upper classes was motivated not by any aim to promote political progress through self-government but rather as a means of fostering material progress and administrative efficiency. These were some of the paternalistic ideals that inspired the "Platonic guardians" in the Indian Civil Service. It was this ethos coupled with adequate salaries and related material benefits that made institutionalized graft unheard of among them.

In seventeenth-century Spanish America there was also an ethos, but the absence of adequate salaries made corruption rampant. In their own fashion, the Spaniards were as paternalistic as the British were to become. The Spanish ideal also included material progress, since the conquest of America created several material improvements brought about by the introduction of superior technology. Religious and cultural ideals also inspired the Spanish ethos. They were extirpation of pagan idolatry and its replacement by Catholicism, the gradual education of the Indians in Hispanic norms of culture and behavior through the spread of Christianity and Roman law, and some protection of basic human and property rights for legally unequal races such as the Indians and the Negroes. The ideal of service, which formed the backbone of the Spanish imperialist ethos, found an eloquent spokesman in Juan de Solórzano y Pereira. Historians have argued endlessly as to how successful the Spaniards were in achieving those ends. The important thing to bear in mind is that this ethos did exist, it had some influence on the bureaucracy, and to a certain extent the Spaniards did achieve these goals.

The British obviously were far more successful, but their goals were more limited. Nietzsche was once supposed to have exclaimed, "Those Spaniards!

those Spaniards! Those were men who wanted to be too much."[25] The British, for example, did not interfere with the religions of India. They merely confined themselves to wiping out a few fringe practices, such as infanticide, suttee, and human sacrifice, all of which they regarded as abhorrent.[26] The central instrument of the Spaniards in hispanizing the Indians, on the other hand, was the total destruction of the preconquest religions and the adoption of Catholicism by Indian and Negro alike.

However much the British did succeed in wiping out graft among their civil servants and however much the Spaniards failed, the latter did make heroic efforts to suppress corruption. Their failure merits careful examination. One of the major responsibilities of a visita general, to which every audiencia was periodically subject, was to investigate charges of graft. The laborious procedures of a visita general provide the best documented accounts of the quality and quantity of corruption among the salaried bureaucrats. The rather lurid accounts of venality written by travelers such as Juan and Ulloa, who arrived in Quito in 1736, must be viewed with some skepticism. Juan and Ulloa were impressionable youths in their early twenties. The magistrates whom they accused of massive venality did not have an opportunity to defend themselves.[27] A visita general, on the other hand, provides much more reliable data. The procedure was a judicial investigation in which the accused received ample opportunity behind closed doors to defend themselves. In passing sentence, the Council of the Indies seldom convicted magistrates unless the evidence was conclusive.

The visita general of the audiencia of Quito (1624–37) was, in part, an outgrowth of the dynamic administration of the Count-Duke of Olivares. The real significance of this particular visita general can be grasped only inside the larger empire-wide context. One of the cardinal goals in his campaign to arrest the economic and social decline of the monarchy was to eradicate corruption, luxury, and immoral living by emphasizing honesty, simple living, and hard work. The count-duke set out to reverse the trend of the preceding reign of Philip III (1598–1621).

During Philip III's reign, a sharp contrast emerged between the gross fortunes accumulated by the few who enjoyed royal favor and the general decline of the national economy. Venality of some sort was a characteristic of all the European courts of that time. What distinguished the administration of the Duke of Lerma was the magnitude of corruption. While the claim that Lerma amassed a fortune of 44 million ducats must be dismissed as a wild expression of popular imagination, bribery and peculation in his administration reached ungovernable proportions. Several leading figures of the reign were arrested. Two were actually convicted. Alonso Ramírez de Prado of the Council of Finance had to pay back 398,671 ducats which he had obtained illicitly. The sentence of Pedro Franqueza, Count of Villalonga, was to return to the royal treasury 1,406,259 ducats of his ill-gotten gains as well as to be imprisoned for life. Most of the corruption went undetected.[28] While venality was greater at Court than in the kingdoms overseas, the low standards prevailing in the peninsula did much to encourage graft overseas, to be sure, on a smaller scale. It was this situation that the Count-Duke of Olivares sought to correct.

Upon assuming office in April, 1621, he opened his campaign against venality by putting on trial the principal figures of the preceding reign. He imprisoned the great Duke of Osuna, who was equally notable for his brilliant administration as the viceroy of Naples and Sicily as for his ostentatious way of living. He died in jail before being sentenced on several accusations of illegal enrichment in office. The Duke of Lerma found himself briefly incarcerated on the same charges, but he soon recovered his liberty. The Holy See intervened on his behalf, since in 1618 Rome had granted him the red hat of a cardinal. But the duke-cardinal did not escape punishment. The Council of Castile compelled him to pay the royal treasury 72,000 ducats a year, with arrears for twenty years, as compensation for illicit self-enrichment. The sentence of his son, the Duke of Uceda, was a fine of 20,000 ducats and exile from the Court for eight years. Another royal favorite of the preceding reign, Rodrigo Calderón, Marquis of Siete Iglesias, lost both his fortune and his head.

The offensive of the count-duke against the *privados* of Philip III was not motivated solely by personal vindictiveness, although this factor was not totally absent. His goal was the more positive one of attacking corruption and encouraging simple living as the most effective means of restoring the economic health of the monarchy. In 1622 he established a junta for the reformation of manners, *la junta de la reformación de las costumbres,* one of whose principal purposes was to prevent officeholders in the Spains and the Indies from illegally enriching themselves. The junta registered the property of all those who had held major office since 1592 in order to compare their net worth as of 1622 with the value of their estate prior to taking office. The difference between the two figures, it was somewhat fallaciously assumed, was the amount that they had defrauded the state.

The king issued a cedula in January, 1622, requiring all persons to submit an inventory of their property upon taking office. No promotions were to take place unless the inventory had been brought up to date. Another cedula of May 8, 1622, provided severe punishment for officeholders concealing from the authorities the true value of their holdings. On December 5, 1622, the king extended these requirements to include all judicial and treasury officials in the Indies. A series of sumptuary laws sought to reduce ostentatious living. The new monarch set the tone by reducing the number of offices in the royal councils by one-third and halving the expenses of the royal household.[29] The fact that this economy drive and anti-corruption campaign all but disappeared by the 1630's, under the pressure of the monarchy's involvement in the Thirty Years' War and Philip IV's irrepressible addiction to luxurious living, ought not to obscure the fact that Olivares, like many administrators after him, began his term of office as a zealous and economy-minded reformer.

The visita general of the audiencia of Quito was but a component of this larger program to root out venality not only in the Spains but also in the Indies. The intimate relationship of the anti-corruption campaign to the broader domestic, foreign, and colonial goals of the "grand design" of Olivares will be discussed in Chapter 10. Here attention will be focused on the anti-venality aspects of the visita general in Quito. Our concern now is not how the evidence was gathered, or the method by which the verdict was reached, or the effectiveness of the visita as an instrument for punishing graft. All these issues will be considered in good time. The present focus is on the depth and extent of venality that came to light during this particular visita general.

The principal culprit was, of course, Dr. Morga. Some thirteen of the seventy-three charges leveled against him in the final sentence dealt with violations of the laws designed to promote honest and disinterested government. These charges fall into three general categories: (1) dealing in contraband goods, (2) retail merchandising, and (3) close social ties with prominent citizens.

In July, 1615, when Dr. Morga traveled on the *Nuestra Señora del Rosario* from Mexico to Quito, he took with him about 40,000 pesos' worth of contraband Chinese silks, part of a silk cargo valued at one million pesos. The cargo ended up on the island of Puná, where someone denounced it to the public authorities as contraband.[30] An unusual glare of publicity shone on the illicit cargo, since the new viceroy, the Prince of Esquilache, happened to be in Guayaquil briefly en route to Lima. The viceroy placed the contraband under armed guard, but the latter proved to be unusually inept or venal. Within a few days most of the cargo had disappeared under circumstances that suggest collusion with the authorities.[31] Upon reaching

Lima, the viceroy instructed the incorruptible oidor, Juan de Solórzano, to conduct an inquest to expose and punish the culprits. A few minor offenders received light sentences, but the royal treasury recovered only a small fraction of the cargo.[32]

Shortly afterward, in a retail shop in Quito located in the casas reales where the audiencia held its sessions, a large number of Chinese silks and taffetas were put on sale. One of the owners of the store was Antonio de Morga, *hijo,* the son of the newly installed president of the audiencia. Among his partners were Pedro Sánchez Pericón, a member of the president's household, and Francisco Ponce, a merchant. Young Morga's interest in the retail store was a flagrant violation of royal edicts, several of which prohibited any commercial activity on the part of the unmarried children of magistrates or their servants.

Still another matter was the origin and the ownership of the contraband China silks sold in the store. The judicial investigations conducted in Lima by Oidor Solórzano never directly involved Dr. Morga, although the current gossip in Quito was that the president was the real owner of the silks. Within a few months after arriving in Quito, the new president asked to be reassigned to another post.[33] His rapid disenchantment was probably not the result of any major difficulty in adjusting to the high altitude of the capital, for that particular magistrate had the physical constitution of a bull. The mercantile operations of the Morga family had evidently aroused enough displeasure on the part of some citizens of Quito so that the president lost his enthusiasm for the post for which only a few months before he had profusely thanked the king.

There is no available documentary evidence to explain satisfactorily how Morga managed to stay beyond the reach of the law during the investigation conducted in Lima from 1615 to 1617. One is led to speculate about the role of the viceroy. The council had opposed the appointment of the Prince of Esquilache on the grounds of his youth and lack of political experience, but Philip III and the Duke of Lerma overrode these objections.[34] It could be that Esquilache used his influence to shield Dr. Morga. Morga's relationship with the Lerma family also may have encouraged the authorities in Lima, even the conscientious but worldly Solórzano, not to implicate the president.

Dr. Morga thus escaped, at least temporarily. Retribution came twenty years later, long after the Lerma clan had fallen from power. One of the principal items of investigation in the visita general was this incident. The Council of the Indies in 1636 meticulously examined all the evidence. Their considered conclusion was that Dr. Morga was indeed the owner of the contraband silk sold in Quito in 1615 and 1616. The council imposed a fine of 12,000 pesos or the approximate equivalent of his salary for two years.[35] A touch of bureaucratic justice was provided by the presence in the council, as a member of the jury, of the same Dr. Juan de Solórzano who, as oidor in Lima, had conducted the inquiry in 1615 and 1616.

The importation of contraband Chinese silks into the viceroyalty of Peru was a frequent occurrence.[36] The venture of Dr. Morga was unusual only for the amount of publicity attending its exposure. The extensive, poorly policed coastline, the almost insatiable demand for China silks, and the venality of the authorities all contributed to increasing the volume of this illegal trade.

Dr. Morga owned only a portion of the cargo of silks on the small vessel that took him from Mexico to the shores of Quito. The estimated value of the whole cargo was approximately a million pesos. His share was around 40,000 pesos, which he listed in the registry of the ship as his personal library. The Council of the Indies claimed that the president sold his silks in Quito for some 100,000 pesos, thereby netting a profit of some 60,000 pesos. The amount of the net profit is open to question. The story of how the bulk of the cargo disappeared after it was denounced in Guayaquil leaves one little alternative but to infer large-scale collusion in which the owners of the illicit goods must have provided handsome bribes.

Dr. Morga evidently never again imported China silks into the kingdom. The chase by the Dutch and the near-confiscation of the merchandise after its denunciation may have discouraged the president from other such ventures. If he had to pay substantial gifts to his patrons in Spain for the presidency of Quito, the trip from Acapulco to Guayaquil afforded the opportunity to gain the wherewithal.[37]

After settling in Quito, Dr. Morga soon discovered that there were other means of making money less risky and speculative than importing contraband goods. He became a successful retail merchant specializing in textiles manufactured in the obrajes. He was, of course, a silent partner in these business ventures. His son, Antonio, *hijo,* continued to operate the retail store, for which he paid rent, in the casas reales until 1623, when the coming of the visitor general made it desirable for him to move to Lima. The other partners of Dr. Morga were Francisco de Segura, Pedro Sánchez Pericón, and Miguel Ximénez de Armentaros. The Council of the Indies found Dr. Morga guilty of being a silent partner in retail merchandising, a flagrant violation of countless royal cedulas.[38]

That Dr. Morga accumulated capital far in excess of anything he could have saved from his annual salary of 4,800 ducats is well documented. Out of the investigations of the visita general came conclusive evidence that he had given rich presents of gold and silver to his wife. He provided his step-daughter with a dowry consisting partly of precious stones of considerable value. The Council of the Indies fined Dr. Morga 1,500 ducats, not for possessing gold and silver and diamonds in suspiciously large quantities, but for failure to pay the royal tax of one-fifth of the value of newly mined minerals.[39]

Dr. Morga's business acumen and his princely tastes may have been derived in part, at least, from his Basque father. Don Pedro de Morga was one of the leading bankers in Seville between 1553 and 1576. During those years he invested heavily in commerce with the New World, the slave trade, and maritime insurance. So well known was he that the street in Seville where he bought a palatial mansion was known as the *calle de Morga*. In the second royal bankruptcy of 1576, which shook the whole Spanish economy to its foundations, the Morga bank failed.[40] Although Pedro de Morga became bankrupt just a few years before his son completed his formal education, the son was probably influenced by his once-wealthy father's way of life.

Like many successful businessmen before and after him, Dr. Morga preferred, for reasons of prestige and as a safe haven for some of his capital, to invest in works of art. He owned one of the largest libraries in the kingdom, and he was also an avid collector of art.[41] On December 13, 1629, the president purchased a collection of Italian and Spanish paintings and other objects of art, some forty items, for 4,730 patacones in cash.[42]

Dr. Morga probably would have been a successful retail merchant had he been merely a private citizen. Be this as it may, his business activities were a flagrant violation of the Platonic ideal of disinterested guardians as affirmed in the *Recopilación*. The acumen he displayed in his own affairs also asserted itself in the manner in which he conducted the business of the king. His reorganization of the community obrajes and the royal encomienda of Otavalo and his collection of forced loans were the solid achievements of a hard-headed and experienced businessman.

The Council of the Indies also found Dr. Morga guilty of several infractions of the laws prohibiting salaried magistrates from developing close personal ties with prominent residents of the audiencia kingdom. For serving as godfather of the son of his close personal friend, Pedro Ponce Castellejo, who executed the reform program in Otavalo, Dr. Morga was fined 100 pesos.[43] For serving as godfather at the wedding of don Nicolás de Larraspuru and María de Vera, he received a stiff fine of 1,000 ducats.[44] The council suspected that the president's leniency with the criminal activities of don Nicolás was a result of that close association.

One of Dr. Morga's pursuits that the Council of the Indies found offensive concerned his social life at home. Dr. Morga and his wife received the leading citizens of the capital every evening in their apartment in the casas reales, where the principal form of entertainment was gambling at cards. Not only did the oidores regularly assist at these soirées, but also plaintiffs and defendants in litigations before the audiencia were encouraged to attend. The gentlemen of the cloth were well represented too. The president himself was an avid card player who lost a round with ill-grace. Dr. Morga usually won. The president's lady presided at these gatherings, which took on more the atmosphere of a gambling house than a *tertulia*. She parlayed the house's take into some 200,000 pesos over the course of the years. The señora not only received four pesos per round but also was accustomed to accepting a monetary gift from every guest upon his departure.[45]

At Morga's rented country house at Anaquito near the capital, the card games went on for days. It was not unusual for the oidores to go into the capital to put in a brief appearance of some thirty minutes on the bench before returning to Dr. Morga's estate to continue the game where they had left off.[46]

His enemies charged that Dr. Morga put pressure on the vice-provincial of the Society of Jesus to exile Father Pedro de Lira, whose sermons criticized the frequency of gambling in the homes of the prominent, presumably because the president interpreted these sermons as an implicit criticism of his conduct. The Council of the Indies dismissed this charge as not proven.[47] The clergy were split right down the middle on the issue of card playing for money, with many being avid addicts and many others denouncing such games as the work of the devil.

The three major social activities of the well-to-do in colonial society were attending mass, making love, and playing cards. The conduct of Dr. Morga was unusual only in the intensity with which he devoted himself to all three activities. Hence royal legislation aimed at curbing card playing, which always involved some betting for money, fell on stone-deaf ears. Ordinances restricted all gambling games to the "small stakes" variety, a maximum of ten pesos per twenty-four hours. Licensed gambling houses were outlawed in 1609 and 1618, but that legislation merely restricted gambling to the more hospitable atmosphere of private homes. Not only were salaried magistrates and their wives forbidden to play cards for money in their homes even on the pretext that the proceeds were for religious charity, but also the superior magistrates were flatly admonished not to play cards for money at any time or at any place.[48]

In the eyes of the Council of the Indies, Dr. Morga and his wife sinned on many counts. As the principal representative of the king, the president of the audiencia was obligated to set the moral tone of the community. Converting his home into a veritable gambling casino every night scarcely enhanced the moral leadership of the president. What agitated the council even further was that the discords and friendships between judges and litigants fostered at the card table threatened to obstruct the impartial administration of justice. The all-too-active social life of the Morgas made a mockery of the crown's ideal of the salaried bureaucrats as Platonic guardians.

The council therefore imposed a fine of 6,000 ducats, an amount equivalent to fifteen months of the president's salary.[49] Dr. Morga was not the only president of an audiencia to convert his drawing room into a gambling casino, but he had the misfortune to be caught.[50]

The business activities of the presidents were apt to be on a larger scale and more frequent than those of the oidores. The wife of one of Dr. Morga's predecessors, acting President Venegas de Cauañeral, was the owner of an obraje.[51] One of his successors, President Munive, was found guilty of simony, having accepted bribes for ecclesiastical preferment. The avarice of that magistrate's wife put to shame the greed of Morga's second wife. By his timely death in 1689, President Munive escaped Dr. Morga's fate of having to account for his actions to a visitor general.[52] These infractions by the presidents resulted in part from the fact that they had no resident superior in the kingdom. The more avaricious a president might be, the more apt he was to be all the more intolerant of the wrongdoing of the oidores, whose nominal superior he was. Since most judges were anxious for promotions, they were acutely aware that any exposure of their business connections might jeopardize their careers. As alcalde de crimen in the audiencia of Mexico, Dr. Morga emerged from the visita general in 1606 and from his residencia in 1614 with a clean bill of health. In fact he received several assignments that indicate the esteem in which he was held by his peers and superiors.[53]

Among the magistrates investigated by the visita general, only three received sentences for corruption. The Council of the Indies found Oidor Manuel Tello de Velasco guilty of several infractions of conduct, but none of the 147 charges against him included the kind of venality and corruption of which Dr. Morga was found guilty.[54] The council reached a similar con-

lusion on November 14, 1637, when they rendered a verdict on the conduct of Lic. Melchor Suárez de Poago, fiscal of the audiencia.[55] It is impossible to determine the extent to which Oidor Matías de Peralta involved
himself in mercantile operations. On February 22, 1638, the Council of the
Indies fined him 19,900 ducats.[56] The sentence itself has disappeared from
the archives. The charge against Lic. Peralta was serious, for the fine of
19,900 ducats represented an oidor's salary for eight years. In fact the
Peralta fine was two-thirds of what Dr. Morga was fined. Hence it is highly
probable that a significant portion of Peralta's misconduct came from indulging in trade.

There may have been some petty chiseling among the inferior magistrates
of the audiencia but very little massive graft. However commercial-minded
some of the salaried magistrates may have been, they saw to it that the clerks
who worked under their daily supervision kept to the straight and narrow
path of honesty. The clerks usually received only their nominal salaries and
the fees and tips set down by the audiencia. This state of affairs alone demonstrates that the sale of clerking offices in the Habsburg monarchy was not
in itself a major cause for the prevalence of venality.

There was one major exception to this rule. That concerned the office
of escribano mayor of the audiencia, a position which in 1607 was purchased for 15,000 pesos. Until 1619 an escribano mayor could invest his
fees and tips in commerce and real estate. In 1619 Philip III extended the
classic order prohibiting viceroys, presidents, oidores, fiscales, and treasury
officials from engaging in commerce or owning real estate either in their
own names or through intermediaries to include escribanos de cámara and
relatores of the audiencias.[57] The purpose of the cedula was to promote
more efficient and disinterested government by eliminating outside business
interests which would divert the attention of those inferior magistrates from
the performance of their official duties. However, the investigations of the
visita general uncovered conclusive evidence that Diego de Valencia León,
escribano mayor of the audiencia, and Andrés de Orozco Guzmán, escribano
mayor of the city of Quito, continued their extensive commercial operations
long after the cedula of 1619. Both men received gigantic fines of 20,000
ducats apiece for their disobedience.[58] A more detailed analysis of this
complicated case is presented in Chapter 11.

The graft practiced in the audiencia, significant though it was, was mild
compared to the corruption that prevailed in the provincial echelon of the
imperial bureaucracy. There were three types of provincial units in the
kingdom of Quito: *gobiernos, corregimientos de españoles,* and *corregimi-*

entos de indios. The three gobiernos were Popayán, Quijos, and Yaguarzongo (suppressed in 1623). The four corregimientos de españoles were Quito, Cuenca, Loja y Zamora, and Guayaquil, and the five corregimientos de indios were Chimbo, Latacunga, Otavalo, Riobamba, and Los Yumbos. Corregimientos were usually designated *alcaldías mayores* in the viceroyalty of New Spain.

The governorships were ordinarily located in isolated areas, which had originally been conquered by a special contract with the crown that guaranteed the governorship to the conqueror and one or two heirs. Such was the origin of both Quijos and Yaguarzongo. The territorial limits of the government of Popayán extended over a populous area of what is now southwestern Colombia, from Barbacoas in the south to the Cauca River valley in the north. As a consequence of its distance from the audiencia capitals of Quito and Bogotá and even more remote Lima, the governor in fact possessed considerable autonomy. Popayán belonged to the kingdom of Quito during the seventeenth century, since the audiencia exercised appellate jurisdiction over most of the province. The fact that the audiencia of Bogotá was the appellate court for the government north of the Cauca River was a jurisdictional factor which enabled the governor of Popayán to play one audiencia against the other.[59] Hence he could augment substantially the freedom of action he already had by virtue of Popayán's remoteness. In a sense the government of Popayán had as much autonomy vis-à-vis the audiencias of both Quito and Bogotá as the audiencia of Quito ultimately acquired vis-à-vis Lima.

Given the quasi-military character of these governorships and their size, they enjoyed the highest status among the units of provincial government. Hence governors' salaries were in the top bracket, from 4,000 pesos for Popayán to 3,000 for Yaguarzongo and 2,000 pesos for Quijos.[60] The king, with the advice of the Council of the Indies, made these appointments.

Ranking under the governorships were the corregimientos de españoles. Also appointed by the king and the council, the *corregidores de españoles,* that is, the officials of the corregimientos, received salaries mid-way between those of the governors and those of the *corregidores de indios,* with Quito at 2,000 pesos, Loja at 1,500 pesos, Guayaquil at 1,000, and Cuenca at 800 pesos.[61] Although the corregidores de españoles exercised jurisdiction over the Indians in their territory, a basic difference between the two kinds of corregimientos was that in the Spanish ones there was usually a significant population of Spaniards and mestizos whereas in the Indian corregimientos the non-Indian population was sparse.

The less prestigious corregidores de indios were appointees of the viceroys and received salaries somewhat less than those of their peninsula-appointed colleagues. The customary stipend was 500 pesos.[62] The governor of Popayán enjoyed the patronage of appointing four corregidores in his district, varying in salary between 100 and 500 pesos.[63] The corregimiento de indios was one of the major reforms designed by Viceroy Toledo in the 1570's. Its essential purpose was to set up a governmental institution on the provincial level effective enough to protect the Indians against the rapaciousness of both the encomenderos and their own curacas.[64] Although the early corregidores may have been effective, by the beginning of the seventeenth century the cure had proven as harmful as the disease. One fiscal of the audiencia, subsequently removed from office for gross dishonesty, quipped that the corregidores had become *cogedores,* i.e., "collectors [of graft]."[65]

Since the office of corregidor de españoles was judicial, the crown never permitted that it be put up for sale. When a vacancy occurred, a committee of the Council of the Indies drew up a consulta in which they listed three candidates in order of preference. The whole council would recommend one candidate to the king. In sharp contrast to the academic and administrative criteria the council used for selecting presidents and oidores, the council virtually ignored professional considerations in selecting provincial magistrates. There was a tacit understanding that those posts should be reserved for military officers who merited either a pension or a reward from the crown for services rendered in the European wars.[66] Recommendations from highly placed officials also counted a good deal. But chance too played a role.

Discouraged by the meager rewards for his literary efforts, Miguel de Cervantes Saavedra applied for a vacant post in the Indies, either as corregidor or as a paymaster in the fiscal service. This was in 1590, fifteen years before he published the first part of *Don Quijote.* His qualifications were far more impressive than those of most candidates for bureaucratic appointments, which, in Cervantes' words, were the "refugio y amparo de los desesperados de España."[67] Not only did Cervantes have influential patrons and a distinguished military career, including service at the battle of Lepanto and imprisonment in Oran by Algerian corsairs, but also he had practical accounting experience. He was then serving as an assistant to the purveyor-general of the fleets of the Indies. Philip II issued orders that the request be granted. But the future author of *Don Quijote* never received an appointment in the New World. Why? Everything seemed to be working in his favor. The most probable explanation is that he alienated some important figure in the Court bureaucracy. While universal literature was the beneficiary, the incident points up the element of chance as a factor in securing bureaucratic appointments. "Lady Fortune" usually played a larger role in recruitment on the more nonprofessional provincial and fiscal echelons than on the oidor level. Yet it was never totally absent in any appointment.

Corregidores appointed by the viceroys usually had fewer professional qualifications than did the appointees of the king. Every viceroy traveled to his capital with a large entourage of retainers for whom he felt a certain responsibility. And the temptation to use the corregimientos de indios as patronage for retainers was difficult to resist. The viceroy of Peru appointed fifty-two of the eighty-five corregidores in the whole viceroyalty. The viceroys lost this source of patronage in 1678 when the appointments began to be filled by the king and the council.[68] Along with the administrative positions in the obrajes, the corregimientos de indios had provided the viceroys with a modest amount of political patronage.

The audiencia of Quito periodically protested the predilection of the viceroys to appoint members of their own households to these positions and alleged that such a practice discriminated against qualified creoles and Spaniards. The insistence of the Council of the Indies that *los beneméritos de las Indias,* as they were called in official terminology, should be considered for these posts fell on the deaf ears of the viceroys.[69] They felt greater pressure from their retainers for patronage than they did from the admonitions of the crown to appoint qualified residents of the Indies. The behavior of the viceroys in this matter was scarcely different from that of the authorities at Court. Both were using the provincial administration as a source of patronage to special groups toward which each felt a specific responsibility. The concern of the crown was with military officers in Europe, whereas the viceroys were under pressure from their own entourages.

In an attempt to keep the political patronage of the Indies from the grasping hands of the Duke of Lerma and his family, the Council of the Indies urged Philip III that preference be given to residents of the kingdoms of the Indies for all positions of corregidores. They did exclude port cities with fortifications where military qualifications were desirable. This particular aspect of the report was ultimately adopted in 1627.[70] The council recommended that the viceroys and the superior audiencias submit a list of six qualified candidates for every vacancy and that the council reduce the number to three, with the king making the final choice. The Duke of Lerma showed scant sympathy for this recommendation, whose underlying aim was to protect the bureaucracy in the Indies from domination by his family. In

replying, Philip III made it pointedly clear that he intended to retain full
freedom of choice as to whether to appoint European Spaniards or creoles,
but he urged the viceroys and the audiencias to continue to recommend
worthy creoles.[71]

The consequences were that once again, this time on the provincial level,
the creoles were largely frozen out of a bureaucratic career in favor of
peninsular Spaniards. Occasionally a creole might receive one of these posts,
but not often.

The salient characteristic of the provincial bureaucracy was its almost
total lack of professionalism. There was little in the military background
of most of the governors and corregidores that equipped them to discharge
the responsibilities of the chief administrative and judicial officer of a rather
populous and extensive district. Since a corregidor seldom had legal training, he was obligated to appoint a letrado as his *teniente* or deputy.[72] Many
litigations began in the court of the corregidor before going to the audiencia
on appeal.

The deputy, who served at the pleasure of the corregidor, was usually
a creole graduate of the local law faculty. Paid a ridiculously low salary
varying between 200 and 300 pesos annually, the deputy had little alternative but to supplement his income by illegal means. Working closely with
his superior, to whom he owed his appointment, the deputy became, in
effect, the graft collector of the corregidor.

The general corruption of the provincial administration, like that of the
bureaucracy, was the direct consequence of a grossly inadequate salary
scale. If an oidor had difficulty maintaining himself with a modicum of
decorum on a salary of 2,400 ducats, it was virtually impossible for a corregidor to do so on a salary as low as 500 pesos annually. The temptation
to the corregidores of resorting to graft in order to supplement their incomes
was compounded by the temporary and nonprofessional character of their
position in the imperial bureaucracy. Only a minority were reappointed
after a term of five years, and never in the same locality. The corregidores
lacked the legal training and the professional esprit de corps of the oidores,
who were making life careers in a bureaucracy in which merit, seniority,
and promotion counted for something. What kept the presidents and oidores
as honest as they were, and indeed they were no paragons, was the quasi-
professional character of their posts. The lack of these professional standards, as well as the ineffectiveness of the audiencia in supervising the
magistrates in the provinces, merely served to intensify the drift toward
venality on the lower level.

The principal source of wealth for the corregidores and their deputies was exploitation of the docile Indian population. There were two forms of exploitation that weighed most heavily on the natives. The corregidores sold products to the Indians at prices far beyond the free market value. Even more profitable for the corregidores was to purchase the products of the Indians at low prices and retail them at a handsome profit. Several corregidores used Indian tribute revenue belonging to the crown as collateral to finance their retail merchandising. The supervision of the obrajes provided endless sources of unlawful self-enrichment.[73] Like the superior magistrates in the audiencias, the corregidores were forbidden to engage in any form of commerce.[74]

The two institutional devices developed by the crown in its abortive effort to enforce the trade prohibition among the magistrates in the provinces were the residencia and the visita de la tierra. Growing out of precedents in medieval Spain, the residencia was a judicial review of an official's conduct, held immediately after he left office. The major complaint against the corregidores was illicit commercial activity. The residencia judges, however, imposed only nominal fines on corregidores whom they found guilty. The fines varied between 500 pesos and 4,000 pesos.[75] Corregidores might well afford to pay these token fines, since an avaricious corregidor could clear as much as 20,000 pesos from his district.[76]

A basic defect was that the new corregidor conducted the residencia of his predecessor. Leniency and token punishments were the consequences. In response to repeated requests from the audiencia in Quito, the crown experimented with a different procedure between 1618 and 1625. An oidor or one of the licensed advocates conducted the residencia of outgoing corregidores. In 1625, however, the old system was restored.[77]

A classic example of a turbulent residencia was that of Pedro de Vergara, corregidor of Otavalo. Conclusive evidence emerged that this "merchant-corregidor" used Indian tribute money to finance his extensive mercantile operations. The audiencia, upon appeal, reduced the fine imposed by the residencia judge to a nominal 420 pesos. Visitor General Mañozca unsuccessfully tried to prove that the leniency of the audiencia was due to personal friendship between the oidores and the corregidor.[78]

Testy old Oidor Diego de Zorrilla once charged that corregidores usually had "godfathers" in the audiencia.[79] While there is no documentary proof that oidores ever received bribes from the corregidores, there were ties of friendship between the two groups of bureaucrats. The audiencia generally tended to reduce fines in reviewing the residencia sentences of corregidores de indios. Only the Council of the Indies could review the residencia sentences of the royally appointed corregidores de españoles.[80] Even more important than friendship was a general conviction on the part of many experienced oidores that evidence gathered in a residencia trial against a corregidor was sometimes inspired by personal antagonism. When doubt existed, leniency was the prudent course to follow. Instead of seeking to eradicate corruption in the provinces, the audiencia concentrated on confining venality to what they regarded as reasonable bounds.

Thus standing royal regulations providing that all corregidores file inventories of their estates prior to taking office and requiring each magistrate to post bond as surety against a possible residencia fine, when enforced at all, did little to discourage illegal self-enrichment.[81]

The complex relationships between the magistrates in the audiencia and the corregidores in the provinces received such superficial attention during the visita general of the 1620's that no sound conclusions emerge. Only a handful of indictments in the final sentences concerned the ties between the oidores and the corregidores. In most of these few cases the council absolved the superior magistrates.

The visita de la tierra, the other institutional device to enable the audiencia to supervise the conduct of the corregidores, was as ineffective as the residencia. One of the oidor-visitor's specific responsibilities was to protect the Indians from illegal exactions by the corregidores, the clergy, and the curacas.[82] While the circuit judges piously denounced the commercial dealings of the corregidores, there is little evidence that they did anything effective to curb these abuses.[83] In fact they may have made them worse. Dr. Morga claimed that several of his colleagues on the bench collected substantial graft while serving as circuit judges, but he offered no supporting documentation. At the time he made this charge, personal relations between the president and his colleagues on the bench were bitter.[84]

The abuses and the general ineffectiveness of the corrective measures in the kingdom of Quito were no less rampant in other kingdoms such as Mexico.[85] No one, however, proposed a solution that might have yielded impressive results, that is, to raise the salaries of the corregidores and their deputies.

On one point all observers were unanimous. The regular clergy, who held most of the Indian parishes in the countryside, rivaled the corregidores in exploiting the Indians. Given the immense moral authority of the Church, they could have provided the Indians with substantial protection against illegal exactions. Although some men of the cloth were true to their trust,

a careful examination of the documentary evidence permits no other conclusion than that the regular clergy by and large were found wanting.[8]
Instead of using their authority and prestige to protect the Indians, all too
many of the religious joined the corregidores in exploiting the Indians. The
underlying causes for the deterioration in the morale of the regular clergy,
which will be dealt with at some length in Chapter 12, revolve around
the acrimonious conflicts between the American-born and the peninsular-
born friars. At this point, the focus is merely on one consequence of the
decline in the morale of the regular clergy, that is, the economic burden
placed on the Indians by the illegal and burdensome exactions of the
religious.

The maintenance of the whole ecclesiastical establishment in the provinces
fell largely on the shoulders of the Indians. The treasury allocated to the
clergy one-third of the tribute paid by all Indians, and from this fund each
priest received 400 pesos for every four hundred tributaries.[87] Not only
did the Indians have to pay fees for receiving some of the sacraments, but
also they paid tithes, which were usually something less than the proverbial
10 per cent. This ecclesiastical income tax on agricultural production was
the principal source of support for the secular clergy. Law and custom
sanctioned all of these obligations.

There was, however, a wide area of extralegal exactions imposed by the
clergy on their charges, which, along with the legal obligations already
alluded to, placed a heavy burden on the Indians. The Augustinian and
Franciscan orders ran a series of textile obrajes which proved quite lucrative.[88] They were illegal, since none of them had licenses. Working conditions in these obrajes, as well as on the many landed estates owned by the
religious, were harsh and oppressive, if we can lend any credence to the
frequent complaints of the Indian workers themselves.[89] Many clergymen
compelled their parishioners to supply them regularly, at little or no payment, with large quantities of chickens, vegetables, and grain, which the
religious retailed in the cities and towns.[90]

The Jesuits were the most efficient and successful businessmen in the
kingdom of Quito. Their grain and cattle farms in the province of Quito,
of which they had eight in 1633, yielded a gross annual income of 42,621
patacones.[91] The Jesuits demonstrated the same entrepreneurial gift in
organizing and operating profitably large estates in such diverse settings
as the Philippines, Mexico, and Paraguay.[92] The profits made in the Sierra
enabled the Society of Jesus to subsidize the missions in the upper Amazon
valley in the province of Mainas.

Venality also existed at the very bottom of the imperial bureaucracy among the curacas in the villages. The major responsibility of this class of hereditary and privileged chieftains was to collect the tribute tax and to select Indians to serve in the mita. In view of the crown's failure to supervise adequately the corregidores and the religious, royal efforts to curb the excesses of the curacas yielded indifferent results.[93] In return for the curacas' performance of the duties of tax collecting, both the secular and the ecclesiastical authorities in the provinces evidently tolerated a little graft on the part of the chieftains. Such petty chiseling, however, was the least of the burdens the Indians had to bear.

Among the cabildos there was little graft as such. What authority they possessed was carefully supervised by the corregidores and the audiencia.

The most difficult and elusive branch in the whole imperial bureaucracy in which to pinpoint venality is that agency which collected and disbursed the revenues of the crown. The exchequer officials, the *oficiales reales,* were a semi-autonomous but coordinate branch of the administrative hierarchy. In the kingdom of Quito, there were treasury offices in the capital, Guayaquil, Puerto Viejo, Loja, and Cali-Popayán. A treasurer and a paymaster administered each office. The king, upon the recommendation of the Council of the Indies, made these appointments. Like the oidores, they served at the pleasure of the prince. In making recommendations to the king, the council placed some importance on the bookkeeping and accounting experience of the candidates.[94] The very modest salary of 500 pesos was so low that creoles sometimes received these appointments. Yet peninsular Spaniards often sought these offices.

A *junta de hacienda* consisting of the president, the fiscal, the senior oidor, the treasurer, and the paymaster met twice a week in the capital of the audiencia kingdom. These sessions coordinated matters of mutual interest to justice, political administration, and the royal fisc.[95] In 1605 Philip III authorized the setting up of *tribunales de cuentas* in Lima, Bogotá, and Mexico City in order to make periodic audits of the accounts of the various treasury offices. The tribunal in Lima audited the accounts of Quito.[96]

The visitor general of the audiencia of Quito, Lic. Mañozca, received a commission from Philip IV to investigate the practices and procedures of the five treasury offices in the kingdom.[97] With his customary vigor, the visitor general plunged into his task. He soon emerged with a whole score of charges against these officers, including faulty bookkeeping, inefficient procedures in collecting taxes resulting in widespread fraud, and illicit commercial activities by the paymaster.[98] Lic. Mañozca ended up incarcerating the treasurer, Pedro de Vera, and the paymaster, Juan Saenz de Gauna, embargoing their property, and appointing temporary substitutes in their offices.[99] It is impossible to measure the veracity of Lic. Mañozca's charges. His successor did not pursue them, for the Council of the Indies did not render any final verdicts. Both officers died a few years before the conclusion of the visita general.[100]

It was not the responsibility of a visitor general to conduct an audit of the treasury offices. That task was better left to the trained accountants of the tribunales de cuentas. The instructions to the visitor general were to learn whether the oficiales reales engaged in mercantile operations. Their lowly salary of 500 pesos per year virtually guaranteed that they did.

In summary, then, it is clear that the basic cause for the prevalence of graft at all levels was the inadequate and rigid salary scale. Corregidores and their deputies had little alternative but to break the law if they wished to support their families decently. And this example was before the oidores day in and day out. Although the latter received larger salaries than their colleagues in the provinces, the stipends of the superior magistrates were scarcely adequate. Venality on the lower levels tended to percolate upward to the oidores. More frequent rotation in office might have diminished this trend.

For all their cumbersomeness, both the visita general and the residencia did manage to expose a good deal of graft in high places. Although it is difficult to measure, the ethos of the Spanish bureaucracy with its pater-nalistic spirit may have partially restrained greed. Among the oidores the most effective brake against corruption was the semi-professional character of that echelon. They regarded themselves as career officers, each of whom was anxious for a promotion. None of these conditions, however, prevailed in the provinces, where the corregidores lacked professional qualifications or previous administrative experience. Devices such as the residencia and the visita general, which had some effect at the audiencia level, were totally ineffective in the provinces.

It was not until the late eighteenth century that a massive effort was made to reform the provincial administration. Inspired by the practical re-forming spirit of the French Enlightenment and reacting to the mounting expenses of imperial defense, Charles III (1759–88) gradually replaced the corrupt corregidores with a new officer called a *gobernador intendente*, an intendant. Paid a generous salary ranging between 5,000 and 8,000 pesos, plus incidental emoluments which raised the total considerably, the intendant ruled a much larger area. In New Spain, for example, twelve intendants replaced the two hundred corregidores and alcaldes mayores. Since the intendant exercised the political, judicial, and military functions of the old corregidores and had the financial jurisdiction of the royal treasury, a better trained and more professionally qualified person could be recruited for the office. The intendant was in fact the head of a complex department of government, with a large staff of secretaries, fiscal agents, and judicial officers. His major responsibilities were to promote economic development and make the fiscal administration more efficient. The intendant districts became in fact the nuclei for the states of the Mexican federation of the nineteenth century.

During the last decades of the Spanish empire, prosperity crescendoed as a direct result of the *reglamento* of 1778 establishing free trade within the empire. Royal revenues from the provinces steadily increased. It is difficult to pinpoint what role the new intendant system played in this result. First introduced into Cuba in 1764 as an experiment and gradually extended to other areas afterward, the intendant system did not become universal in theory throughout the empire until 1790.[101] In fact, the intendants never took office in the New Kingdom of Granada, to which Quito then belonged. Three such units were projected, for Quito, Cuenca, and Popayán, in place of two gobiernos and nine corregimientos.[102] There were eight intendants for the audiencia kingdom of Peru. The intendants did not really have an opportunity to prove their full worth, since the outbreak of the French revolution soon brought about severe dislocations within the imperial economy and the subsequent dissolution of the empire itself.[103]

There was one serious flaw in this grand design to professionalize the provincial administration. The deputy of the intendant, who was called a *subdelegado,* was poorly paid. In charge of a district as large as that of the suppressed corregidores, he could have become a vehicle for continued corruption. An attempt to remedy this weakness took place in 1803, when the intendant system was revised. In place of the ridiculously low salary of 3 per cent of tribute collected, royal legislation created three classes of subdelegados with annual salaries ranging between 1,200 pesos and 2,400 pesos. The ordinance of 1803, however, was suspended shortly thereafter.[104]

The intendant bears a remarkable resemblance to the district officer in British India during the Victorian age. Exercising broad authority over a populous and extensive district, the district officer was the head of a complex department of government, including a mere handful of British assistants and a large Indian bureaucracy. The Spanish-American intendant, like the Indian district officer, enjoyed a wide measure of responsibility, subject to the general supervision of his superiors. This represents a sharp departure from the spirit of the Habsburgs, in which a profoundly suspicious crown refused to delegate very much responsibility to any one agency of government. Much of the success of the Indian Civil Service was an outgrowth of the confidence that superiors reposed in the district officers. The Bourbons were moving toward this attitude and away from the ingrained distrust of the Habsburgs.

By fostering the centralization of governmental functions in the provinces, the intendants relieved the viceroys and the audiencias of much office detail. The creation of a colonial minister directly responsible to the king and the downgrading of the Council of the Indies to a mere consultative body also promoted centralization. The streamlining of the bureaucracy to relieve higher echelons of the minutiae of office detail was a sharp reversal of the spirit of Philip II, who insisted that the central authorities know all the details of happenings overseas. The Bourbon reforms were moving toward the kind of administrative system that the British subsequently created in India, a system in which the top echelons made basic policy decisions with administrative details delegated largely to subordinates.

The Habsburg monarchy did make energetic but abortive efforts to create a bureaucracy composed of Platonic guardians. Their massive failure should never obscure the sincerity or determination of their intentions. The intendant reform of the late eighteenth century promised an approximation of this ideal, but the turmoil of the American and French revolutions rudely closed the door to such an evolution.

8.

THE SINNERS AND THE SAINT

The moral decay that tended to set in among the Spanish bureaucrats of long residence in the Indies expressed itself not only in the practice of graft but also in the form of licentiousness. Moral standards were an expression of that complex series of attitudes which, for lack of a better term, we may call baroque Catholicism.

The religiosity of the seventeenth-century Spanish world stressed the pathos rather than the ethos of religion. Outward display rather than inner piety seemed to predominate. The splendor of the cult stood in naked contrast to widespread public and private immorality. It was a world of sharp contrasts in which the acts of men seemed to conflict with their professions of belief and in which gross sensuality coexisted with militant if at times morbid religiosity.[1]

Nowhere are these contrasts more poignantly personified than in the characters of the third and fourth Habsburg kings, Philip III and Philip IV. According to one anecdote, Philip II is supposed to have lamented on his deathbed, "God who has given me so many kingdoms has not granted me a son fit to govern them."[2] Philip III led such a blameless personal life that one modern scholar has quipped, "The absence of vice was his only virtue."[3] His religiosity, however, became so extremely morbid that he be-came paralyzed in undertaking even the most ordinary decisions. His con-fessors had to spend endless hours trying to persuade the pious monarch that he was being overscrupulous. As the morbid king tortured himself with self-doubts, the family of the Duke of Lerma continued to enrich them-selves at the expense of the state, which was rapidly sinking into economic and political decay.

Philip IV, on the other hand, was torn between his powerful inclination as a Don Juan and his political and religious responsibilities. The weak, sensual, but not unintelligent monarch eventually sought to secure moral support and consolation by confiding his doubts and his guilt to a mystic nun, Sor María de Jesús, with whom he maintained a long-standing spiritual relationship largely through correspondence.[4]

Many of his servants overseas shared the dilemma of their king. There was a chasm, at times almost unbridgeable, between sensual drives and the moral restraints imposed by religion and civic responsibility. There were a meticulous observance of religious rituals and a systematic disregard for the ethical and moral injunctions that those rituals symbolized. The cere-monial aspect of Catholicism overwhelmed its ethical and moral qualities. It was not what one did but what one performed that mattered.

The sharp contrasts in the baroque spirit found graphic expressions in Quito. Side-by-side with licentious living, the Quiteños produced some of the most perfect examples of baroque architecture and some of the most expressive and original examples of baroque sculpture in the Spanish-speak-ing world. The tortured pathos of baroque emotion still lingers in the finely chiseled statues of the Quito sculptors, some of whom were mestizos. The Quito school of painting was more academic and derivative than were the architecture and sculpture. Within half a square mile, the capital contained ten elegant churches and an equal number of magnificent monasteries and convents. They were so solidly built that they are still in use today earthquakes and civil turmoil notwithstanding. During the seventeenth cen-tury Quito acquired a reputation as the "Cloisters of America" and the "Sanctuary of Colonial Art." Thus the brilliance of ecclesiastical architecture in Quito provided the appropriate setting for the theatrical Catholicism of the seventeenth century.

Two buildings, one Franciscan and the other Jesuit, typify the baroque skyline of Quito. (Their façades are reproduced in the illustration section.) The Franciscan monastery, according to George Kubler, was the most im portant single edifice of the sixteenth century in Spanish South America, in size, influence, and quality. Founded in 1535 on the site of the palace of Huayna Capac, the aisled church, with the upper part of the nave, the transepts, and the choir, was completed between 1564 and 1575. The building of the Andalusian-inspired main cloister took place between 1573 and 1581. No American façade of the sixteenth century was more Italianate. Its rigorous symmetry, banded surfaces, and portal were imitated many times in Spanish South America.

The Jesuit church of La Compañía, begun in 1605 and finished in 1616, was built in the form of a basilica with domes over the aisles, a larger dome over the crossing, and a rectangular apse. The use of the domes was a derivation from the celebrated Gesù church in Rome. Many Jesuit churches in the Indies followed this model. The church of La Compañía in Quito was no mere carbon copy of the mother church in Rome. The two most outstanding features of La Compañía are its luminous interior and its intricate and elegant baroque façade. Referring to the *mudéjar* ornamentation of the interior, Harold E. Wethy points out that the sensuously beautiful patterns in gilded relief against a red background recreated in the New World the oriental sumptuousness of the Alhambra. The façade of La Compañía, which is dynamic, angular, and repetitive in contrast to the more tranquil compositions of the Renaissance styles, stands out as one of the most exquisite expressions of baroque decoration in the whole New World.

In the opinion of George Kubler, the colonial architecture of the kingdom of Quito was a relatively pure transfer from European sources, blending different regional styles with high success: Italianate forms of bookish origin, mudéjar ceilings, Sevillian cloisters, Valencian façade motifs, Granadine interior surfaces, and, in a later period, Apulian motifs of the Compañía façade. "The special quality of Quito architecture is its high technical finish; again and again the artisanship is of metropolitan excellence."[5]

The baroque love of ceremonial pageantry and gaudy display, for which the glittering churches provided the background, found an appropriate outlet when word reached Quito that the first wife of Philip IV, Isabel de Borbón, had given birth to Prince Baltasar Carlos. (The portrait of him by Velázquez is reproduced in the illustration section.) It took a month to prepare the fiestas which lasted for nine days, beginning on February 20, 1631. While the preparations were in progress, bullfights took place every afternoon. When Thursday, February 20, finally arrived, all the church bells of the city rang out to announce the beginning of the celebration. Every balcony in the main square was festively decorated with silks, taffetas, and satins, all of them presumably once contraband merchandise. On each corner of the main plaza an elaborately decorated altar had been erected. One thousand soldiers in colorful uniforms lent a martial note to the proceedings. The religious ceremony began with a splendid procession, in which the faithful carried the image of Our Lady of Copacabana through the main square. The secular clergy, the seminarians, the regular clergy, the cathedral chapter, and finally the bishop marched in front of the statue. Behind the image the civil authorities followed in order of increasing social importance, i.e., the city council, the inferior magistrates, the superior magistrates, and the president of the audiencia. After the procession entered the cathedral, Bishop Oviedo sang a solemn high mass at which Dr. Quiros of the cathedral chapter delivered the florid and lengthy sermon. As the mass was being celebrated inside the cathedral, the military in the square outside fired salvos of artillery.

For the next seven days, there were bullfights every afternoon. In the early evening, each of the functional corporations, such as the shopkeepers, the silversmiths, the wholesale merchants, etc., at their own expense provided the multitude with a pageant. On Friday, February 21, there was a splendid masquerade with grotesque costumes. On the following night the silversmiths entertained the capital with a pageant consisting of a cast of two hundred, who were dressed as Spanish, French, and German nobles and as bishops and cardinals. The climax of the evening occurred when an actor dressed as the Pope appeared.

On the eighth day it was the turn of the Indians to provide the entertainment. Their masquerade consisted of a mock battle in which the forces of the Inca army fought and vanquished the hosts of the queen of Cochasquí. The Indians used the dress, the arms, and the musical instruments of Inca times. Thus, a little less than a century after the conquest, the grandsons and great-grandsons of the conquistadores watched the descendants of the Incas and the pre-Incas dramatize the bygone splendor of preconquest America.

The gaudy luxury with which the Quiteños celebrated the birth of the ill-starred heir to the Spanish thrones cost the lavish sum of 50,000 pesos. Another such celebration occurred in July, 1603, lasting fifteen days, when Philip III ordered sumptuous ceremonies to be held in all the capitals of his kingdoms in honor of the canonization of Spanish-born Saint Raimundo de Peñafort. Royal funerals were celebrated with as much pomp and ceremony as were royal births, in particular, those of reigning monarchs and their consorts. In 1613 Quito conducted an elaborate funeral for Margaret of Austria, the consort of Philip III, and in 1621 even more magnificent ceremonies for the funeral of Philip III. Shortly afterward glittering rituals took place to swear allegiance to the new sovereign.[7]

The pomp and circumstance of these ceremonials not only fitted the pictorial mood of baroque society but also served a useful political purpose. They were, of course, the Spanish-American version of the Roman circuses. More important still, because the stability of the Spanish empire rested in large measure on the mystique and charisma of the king, the occasional personification of the monarchy in remote kingdoms served to strengthen the bonds of loyalty to the king.

No one enjoyed these ceremonies more than Antonio de Morga, who, as chief magistrate of the kingdom, played a leading role in the rituals. The religiosity of Dr. Morga was baroque in its contrasts. He became zealous in the performance of his outward religious duties after 1612, when he obtained permission from the Holy See to erect a chapel in his home where mass could be said. After 1612 all his letters began with the sign of the cross. In Quito he enjoyed visiting various monasteries and giving short sermons to the friars about love of God and loyalty to the king.[8] His relations with the Franciscans were particularly warm. On his deathbed he selected their church as the site of his burial, and he received the last rites from one of their friars.[9]

His cultivation of the regular orders had several motivations. It is clear that emotionally and intellectually he was drawn to the Church as he grew older. His vanity may also have been fed by the constant attentions and courtesies which he received at the hands of the regular clergy, who were grateful to the president for his many outward demonstrations of piety. The regular clergy also turned out to be welcome allies during the turmoil of the visita general.

Dr. Morga's quickening religiosity did not express itself in a mere outward submissiveness to the clergy, much though he cultivated the men of the cloth. He saw himself in a quasi-sacerdotal role, through which he could legislate in matters ecclesiastical. Inasmuch as the Church and state were interdependent and the Castilian crown, under the *real patronato de las Indias,* exercised vast powers over the administration of the Church, the selection of personnel, and the collection of ecclesiastical revenues, the line between civil and ecclesiastical authority was often blurred. Jurisdictional conflicts between the two powers were frequent. They could become embittered when both sides displayed intransigence. One way to avoid conflict was for one authority to submit meekly to the other, but this did not often happen.

Meek submission was the case in President Morga's relationship with Friar Alonso Fernández de Santillán, the seventh bishop of Quito, who held the see from 1617 until his death on October 13, 1622. A Spanish-born Dominican and a former provincial superior of the province of Andalusia, Santillán was full of charity, humility, and modesty. He had renounced a considerable inheritance from his parents when he took the Dominican habit.[10] His very virtues, however, were liabilities on the bishop's throne. The determined and proud Dr. Morga soon came to dominate the timid bishop. In his desire to promote harmony between the ecclesiastical and civil powers, the bishop meekly allowed the president to interfere in matters strictly ecclesiastical, where the jurisdiction of the president was questionable if not downright impertinent.

When Pope Clement VIII (1592–1605) ordered all churches that were subject to the Roman rite to observe the newly promulgated Roman liturgy, many Spanish sees protested that several of the practices in the new code conflicted with their ancient uses and customs. The Sacred Congregation of Rites made a concession to the Spanish viewpoint when they ruled that the purpose of the new liturgy was not to abolish laudable practices of sees as ancient as those of the Spains. The whole question directly concerned the dioceses of the Indies, since they had been erected on the model of Seville. Since Rome had granted the sees in the peninsula some latitude in reconciling the new ritual with their ancient customs, the Council of the Indies, which had jurisdiction in this matter according to the patronato real, temporarily suspended the promulgation of the new liturgical code in the Indies. In Quito, Bishop Santillán's predecessor, Bishop Arias de Ugarte, had convoked several sessions of the cathedral chapter in order to determine what practices divergent from the Roman code should be retained. No firm decisions had been reached when Bishop Arias de Ugarte received a promotion to the see of Bogotá.

President Morga stepped into this confused and uncertain situation about how liturgical ceremonies were to be conducted. Furthermore, he made his decisions stick. When the audiencia in its corporate capacity attended services at the cathedral, the sacristan according to custom extended the peace offering to the president. Dr. Morga changed the procedure by excluding the sacristan and assigning this role to the deacon, with the subdeacon performing the same ritual for the bishop. These changes had an important symbolism whose meaning was apparent in those times. The deacon is a clerical rank in the hierarchy just below that of a priest, whereas the subdeacon is the lowest of the minor orders leading to the priesthood.

The sacristan is a secular person whose primary responsibility is the care of the sacred vessels and priestly vestments. Dr. Morga's innovation of the deacon's extending the peace offering to the president and the sub-deacon's extending it to the bishop had the symbolic implication of upgrading the secular and downgrading the ecclesiastical power.

That the president consciously pursued this goal is evident by his insistence that, in the pontifical processions inside the cathedral, he, the president, should preside, and not the bishop, who had formerly done so by custom. The timid bishop was so cowed by the president that he even submissively accepted a rebuke administered by the fiscal of the audiencia. The latter, acting on orders from Dr. Morga, upbraided the bishop for failing to give the president a reverential bow of the head during the celebration of the mass.

Dr. Morga obviously exploited the excessive timidity of the bishop. Bishop Santillán was unable not only to prevent the president from interfering arbitrarily in strictly ecclesiastical matters but also to maintain minimum control over the cathedral chapter. The canons insolently and publicly defied the bishop.[11]

Although personal vanity figured prominently in Dr. Morga's conduct in these episodes, there were basic ideological issues at stake. The president was a regalist in that he believed that the crown should dominate the Church. The basic premise of regalism was that the extensive privileges of the real patronato were inherent rights of the crown rather than concessions of the Holy See. Rome merely acknowledged what de jure belonged to the crown. Regalism was a characteristic attitude of many royal bureaucrats of this time, but it was tenaciously rejected in ecclesiastical circles. Juan de Solórzano was such an articulate regalist that he aroused as much ire in Rome as he gained approval in Madrid.[12]

The president behaved with much more tact in dealing with the regular clergy. He studiously courted them. Adroitly he sought not to get too deeply embroiled in the bitter internecine rivalries between the American-born and Spanish-born friars, which periodically plunged the regular orders into turmoil. Dr. Morga might afford the luxury of arbitrarily interfering with the jurisdiction of an excessively weak bishop, but he could not do so with the regulars. Their wealth and influence were deeply entrenched. Creole and peninsular friars might fight each other unremittingly for control of the elective offices in their respective orders, but the factions could become united in the face of any attempt on the part of the crown or the episcopacy to infringe on what they regarded as their rights and privileges.

Dr. Morga's increasingly militant religiosity was accompanied by both a quickening desire to acquire material goods and an unbridled sensualism. There emerged in his personality a conflict, quite characteristic of the baroque age in which he lived, between outward profession of faith and inner action. It was the same kind of tension as that which tortured his royal master.

His first wife was doña Juana de Briviesca y Muñatones, whom he married in Ecija in 1582. In addition to bringing her husband a dowry of 10,000 ducats, doña Juana proved a fertile mate. She presented her husband with ten children. He did have at least one natural child in the Philippines.[13] While serving there and in Mexico, Dr. Morga evidently did not indulge in any flagrant *donjuanismo,* though he was not above an occasional peccadillo. In a subordinate official, lascivious conduct might have held up a promotion. Once seated in the casas reales in Quito, however, Dr. Morga abandoned his customary discretion.

The new president at the age of 56 became a veritable conqueror of ladies. This is not a case of gossip and innuendo. Spaniards then and now are notoriously careless about the charges they level at people against whom they feel a personal animus. In the face of mountainous evidence gathered during the visita general, in which Dr. Morga had ample opportunity to defend himself in secret testimony, the Council of the Indies in its final sentence fined him 2,000 ducats. The charge was "for having lewd relations with much publicity with many women after he became President, married, widows, and those enjoying the reputation of virgins, living with them in concubinage and thus causing scandal and creating an unfortunate example."[14]

One of the president's love affairs was with doña Francisca de Tapia y Calderón, who accompanied Oidor Manuel Tello de Velasco and his wife to Quito. Dr. Morga fell in love with the young girl when she visited his country estate with Oidor Tello de Velasco and his wife. The president persuaded doña Francisca to leave the household of his colleague in order to live in his home. While she continued to be his mistress, the president arranged her marriage with one of his retainers, Sebastián de Bobadilla.[15]

The virile president was apparently having a simultaneous affair with his stepdaughter, doña Catalina de Alcega y Bermeo. He did not try to conceal his anger when she abandoned his roof to marry the son of the corregidor of Quito, don Cristóbal Vela.[16]

The grand passion of his Quito years, however, was his love for Gerónima de Arteaga, the wife of Cristóbal Mexía, a merchant. She was called *La*

Pallasca. (In Peru the verb *pallar* meant to extract the richest metallic portion from minerals.) The affair lasted several years, both before and after her marriage, during which time Dr. Morga became the father of three of her children. One of the coups of Lic. Mañozca was to secure copies of the six love notes written by the president in his own hand to his mistress. The visitor general gleefully dispatched them to the Council of the Indies. Furthermore, he released them to the public. Whether the visitor general intimidated the unfortunate *La Pallasca* into surrendering the love notes by invoking his powers as inquisitor general, or whether his ubiquitous agents stole them, is not known. Either alternative was in keeping with his general procedure.

These love notes reveal, if nothing else, that Dr. Morga, then in his sixties, was romantically in love with *La Pallasca.* Wrote the lover to his beloved, not without a touch of poetry, "Darling: Your departure has caused me much pain, for you are more to me than my own sight [. . . *te quiero más que a mis ojos*] and my eyes will hurt until you return, and then I will be full of joy; and if I can today, I will pass by your house in order to enjoy the gift of seeing you. Think of me often and command me as a slave. Yours."

Somewhat less romantic is this note in which the president complains about his health: "For eight days I have had an infection in my arm. Because of this and since the nights are so bright I urge you not to see me here. At present my house is full of people, which makes our meeting still more unwise. Let me know what you think. In the meantime, preserve secrecy with everyone, later on I will tell you the person with whom you should preserve the greatest secrecy."

The following note seems to contain a veiled reference to their children: "My love, I hope you arrived safely. I miss you so much that your absence causes me sorrow. I hope that you and our partners [*la compañía*] are well. I kiss the hands of all [four] of you. Here everything is at your service, and I will do with pleasure anything that you order. Yours."

The haunting fear that they would be detected hovers over this love note: "My lady, I have not answered your last note, for it seemed better to wait until I see you next. Much more can be said person to person. Until then it is enough for me to know what is happening and to be sure that every precaution is being taken. I will do anything you order, believe me. Yours."

The impatient lover looks forward to yet another rendezvous: "My love, How much I enjoyed your last visit even though it had to be so carefully hidden, as it must be, and my pleasure will be no less when I see you next on Friday evening when I will be free and when there will be less moonlight.

Until then, I promise you that I will be there without fail. No one else will be here, and I will be waiting at the door as usual. Yours."[17]

The romance with *La Pallasca* did not come to a grinding halt even in the glare of the publicity which the visitor general cast upon it.[18] While it has always been a matter of pride for a Spanish male to enjoy the reputation of *muy macho,* the visitor general's handling of the matter was designed to destroy the bureaucratic career of President Morga. More magistrates than not may have had mistresses. But these affairs had to be private and not public. Their careers were in jeopardy if their love letters ended up in the hands of the council.

Dr. Morga became a Don Juan late in life. Behind the dignified mien and the patriarchal white beard by which he impressed people as serious and sober, he was virile and warm-blooded. These were qualities that were said to have derived from his Basque-Andalusian heritage. Although we know very little about the personality of his first wife, who died in Mexico City in 1605, doña Juana de Briviesca y Muñatones may have been a quiet and retiring woman, as Spanish wives traditionally are wont to be. Nevertheless, she evidently possessed a quiet strength of character sufficient to encourage her husband not to stray too often from the straight and narrow path of marital fidelity. The bonds between the couple were further strengthened by the ten children she bore her husband.

His second wife, doña Catalina de Alcega, apparently exerted no comparable moral influence. She was no longer a young woman, having buried two husbands. She was 36 years old and Dr. Morga 50 years old when they married in Mexico City in 1609.[19] The newly married couple could boast of fourteen children from their previous marriages, but their marriage was childless. The emotional bonds between them evidently were never strong. Both sought consolation elsewhere. In Quito the señora de Morga converted her drawing room into a gambling casino. She also busied herself with various other business enterprises, all of which were illegal for the wives of magistrates. While his wife devoted herself to the affairs of Mammon, her spouse became the slave of Venus.

If his first wife was the companion of his youth and the mother of his children, his second wife was his business partner and his third wife was the nurse of his old age. Within a year after the death of doña Catalina de Alcega, Antonio de Morga, at the age of 71, married a pretty, vivacious, young creole from Lima, doña Ana María de Rivera Verdugo.[20] For the remaining six years of his life, the septuagenarian magistrate remained faithful to his third wife. Ill-health and advancing old age evidently gave him little alternative. It was his third wife who acquired the bulk of her husband's large estate, to the keen disappointment of his children and of the royal treasury, which was able to collect only a small fraction of the stiff monetary fines imposed on the president.

While the contrast in the moral influences exerted by his first two wives throws some light on the change in his private life, equally important is the fact that in Quito, for the first time in his career, he had no resident superior. The restraining influence of his peers and superiors in Manila and Mexico tempered his warm-bloodedness and his avarice.

His only peer in Quito was the bishop. The pious but weak-willed Bishop Santillán lacked the strength of character to influence the private life of the president. Dr. Morga frantically intensified the performance of his outward religious obligations, as he surrendered himself to the joint pursuit of his business interests and his amorous adventures. Yet the varied private interests of Dr. Morga still left him adequate time for the conduct of official business. All the available evidence amply demonstrates that he did not neglect his official duties. Prior to 1621, he must have counted on his powerful patrons near the throne to provide him with immunity from punishment. What he did not anticipate was the sudden fall from power of his patrons and the subsequent arrival in Quito of a relentless visitor general in whose hands his private life would lose its privacy.

As chief magistrate of the kingdom, he was supposed to be irreproachable in his personal conduct. It was his duty to set the moral tone of the community. His own failings in this sphere made it difficult for him to correct the conduct of his colleagues on the bench. His attempts to break up the long-standing liaison between Oidor Diego de Zorrilla and his mistress, doña Thomasina de Esquivel, created much ill-feeling, which indirectly influenced the decision in Madrid to send a visitor general to Quito.

One of the causes for the growing bitterness between the president and Oidor Manuel Tello de Velasco, which created concern in the Council of the Indies, had its origins in an amorous adventure. Oidor Tello de Velasco never forgave the president for persuading doña Francisca de Tapia y Calderón to leave his household for that of Dr. Morga, where she became his mistress.[21] His *machismo* was affronted. While there is no explicit evidence that doña Francisca was the mistress of don Manuel, the intensity of his feelings against Dr. Morga suggests this probability. Furthermore, as a conqueror of young ladies, don Manuel Tello de Velasco was a worthy rival of Dr. Morga.

Of the 148 charges in the indictment of the visita general against Tello de

Velasco, 11 dealt with his amorous life. The Council of the Indies found don Manuel Tello de Velasco guilty of deflowering three virgins. One of his exploits was gaining entrance into the home of one of his victims, Juana de Moreta, on the ruse that he was a relative of her grandfather, Manuel Tello de Moreta. The oidor used the home of one of his servants as a rendezvous for his paramours. Don Manuel was not always successful in his campaigns. The wife of Diego de Avendaño, a prominent citizen, rejected his advances and testified against her would-be lover in the visita general.[22]

Not all the magistrates included in the visita general were accused, let alone found guilty, of extramarital adventures. The crusty old fiscal, Lic. Melchor Suárez de Poago, famous for his acid tongue and short temper, was blameless on this score. So were the escribanos de cámara, Diego de Valencia León and Andrés de Orozco.[23]

While it is not to the point to prolong this *chronique scandaleuse* of life in Quito during the 1610's and 1620's, it is clear that licentiousness among the rich and the important was an everyday reality. Nor can this state of affairs be ascribed solely to the sensuality of the Spanish temperament, important though this may be as a fact of Iberian life. In the peninsula, at least, there were bonds of morality that put some brakes on uncontrolled sensuality. The Spanish bureaucrats, however, were not in Spain living in towns and cities where their families had roots and reputations to preserve. The magistrates led a quasi-gypsy existence. Representing royal authority but exercising only very limited powers, they nevertheless enjoyed great prestige and influence in the communities where they were temporarily stationed. Theirs was but to command, especially if it were the favor of a lady of uncertain virtue or, more important, of flimsy means. Many bureaucrats became progressively less Hispanic as residence away from their native land lengthened.

Furthermore, unsettled economic conditions in the Indies tended to weaken moral restraints by offering increased opportunities for sexual license. Behind the glitter and pomp of the baroque façade of the capital of an audiencia kingdom such as Quito lay a crude, primitive frontier community. The silver mines of Mexico and Peru and the dazzling baroque altars of gold and silver merely concealed the fragility of the economic organization of the Indies. During the first half of the seventeenth century, this economy sustained harsh blows inflicted by the ruinous wars of the Habsburgs. The cities and towns were full of Spaniards who had no certain means of livelihood, who depended upon the rich and powerful by attaching themselves to them as retainers and servants. The social prestige of an oidor was often in direct ratio to the number of retainers he could muster when he appeared at mass or at the casas reales.

Amid this marginal, floating population of Spaniards, there were many girls of no means who were persuaded into the arms of a salaried bureaucrat in the hope that he would ultimately arrange a marriage for her with one of his retainers. Dr. Morga, for example, eventually found husbands for some of his mistresses. Even if these young girls wanted to take the veil, and not all of them did, they lacked the wherewithal to provide the dowry required for entering the convent. The convents were in practice reserved for the daughters of well-to-do citizens.

The multiracial character of society also weakened moral restraints. In that corporate organization, the nonwhites possessed a status of legal inferiority to Europeans, although they did not lack certain basic rights as human beings. The increasing numbers of mestizos and mulattoes were by and large the illegitimate products of the lust of Europeans.

There is a valid distinction between a man who has a serious, responsible extramarital relationship and a man who indulges in outright promiscuity without assuming responsibility for the offspring he has sired in rather casual unions. The salaried bureaucrats tended to indulge in the former, whereas many but not all of the mestizos and mulattoes were the result of the latter.

Although the British and Spanish bureaucracies shared a common problem in seeking to wipe out graft, the British encountered no serious difficulty in enforcing a rather straightlaced code of sexual morality on civil servants. Only a few civil servants took Indian wives or mistresses, and those unions occurred during the first decades of the nineteenth century, before the system had fully matured.[24] Informal unions between British army officers and Indian women may have been more frequent.

After making due allowance for the dangers of relying too heavily on national characterologies, one is nonetheless brought to consider the contrast in temperament and standards between the two imperialist peoples. The virility of a Spanish male was apt to be measured in terms of his amorous conquests whereas no comparable standard existed among the British. Victorian middle-class morality was another factor. Not to be discounted were the special attitudes of the British, who refused to admit openly any sexual attraction toward dark-skinned women. The solid and expanding economy of British India precluded the emergence of a large class of English women of marginal means who might have been tempted to settle for something less than a legal marriage. The more highly professional character of the Indian Civil Service tended to reinforce the premium placed on respectability. And although it may sound facetious, it appears that the more athletic British spent their excess animal energy in physical exercise or in literary or scholarly studies.

Although the professional bureaucrats in the Spanish Indies were educated men not only in the narrow legal sense but also in the broader humanistic values of Renaissance culture, there were very few scholars among them. They seldom wrote books of memoirs, let alone works of scholarship. Antonio de Morga, Juan de Solórzano, Pedro Pérez Landero Otáñez y Castro, Juan de Matienzo, and Juan Díez de la Calle are the exceptions, but none of them was a universal scholar. Each one wrote rather limitedly, on the basis of his own administrative experience.

The churchmen, not the civil bureaucrats, were the scholars of Spanish America, and sometimes very eminent ones. The Indian civil servants, on the other hand, were more productive in this sphere than were their Spanish confreres. The former produced, for example, a whole series of philological studies, which by any standard were of respectable quality.

That sexual mores in the Indies did not become even more lax than they actually were was due in large measure to the moral influence of the Church. This does not mean that every clergyman practiced restraint. Many followed the examples set by their turbulent parishioners.[25]

Periodically there would emerge someone who seemed the incarnation of the moral and ethical virtues that everyone professed and few practiced. Such a person was Mariana de Paredes y Flores (1619–45). She managed to arouse the religious conscience of the Quito where she spent all twenty-six years of her brief life. The daughter of a Spanish gentleman from Toledo, don Jerónimo Zenel Paredes y Flores, and a creole lady from Quito, doña Mariana Jaramillo de Granobles, she was orphaned as a small child.

Refusing to enter a convent, Mariana lived the life of a nun. She renounced her family name and adopted the religious name of Mariana de Jesús. Taking a vow of perpetual virginity and distributing her dowry to the poor, Mariana remained in the home of her sister and brother-in-law. She lived apart from the rest of the family on the second floor where she practiced her mortifications and disciplines. She spent six hours daily in prayer, meditation, and discipline. She reserved five hours daily for works of charity such as feeding the poor, teaching the ignorant, and nursing the sick. With one hour allotted for recreation, her rigorous schedule left her only four hours for sleep. For five years she reputedly ate no solid food except the bread of Holy Communion, which she received every day at the Jesuit church of La Compañía. Toward the Society of Jesus she showed a very special affection.

Her rigorous austerities and her unfailing modesty soon won for her a reputation for saintliness among all classes in the community. Miracles in profusion were ascribed to her, many of which were never verified. The following miracle throws more light on the popular mentality of the times than it does on Mariana herself. One day she called one of her servants to her rooms. She instructed him to go to an isolated spot on the banks of the nearby Machangara River where he would find the grave of an Indian woman who had just been murdered by her husband in a fit of jealous rage. The servant of Mariana returned to the house with the corpse. Mariana caressed dry roses against the rope marks where the Indian woman had been strangled. Under the stimulation of this spiritual medicine, the dead woman Lazarus-like returned to life.

The climax of Mariana's brief life came during the spring of 1645. It was a year of catastrophes for the kingdom of Quito. An epidemic of measles and diphtheria, which took the lives of 2,000 Spaniards and 10,000 Indians, followed a series of earthquakes killing more than 2,000 people. Scarcely a household in the capital did not have black crepe on its doors. The great volcano of Pichincha, whose snow-capped cone dominates the city of Quito, erupted for the first time since the days of the Spanish conquest. As its lava spread over the surrounding countryside, the anguish and the terror of the Quiteños rose to a fever pitch. The clergy and the popular imagination interpreted this chain of disasters as an expression of God's wrath against the vices of the sinful city. A feeling of mass guilt enveloped Quito as the Lenten season of 1645 approached.

As Mariana's most recent biographer, Frances Parkinson Keyes, tells the story:

On the Fourth Sunday of Lent, which that year fell on the twenty-sixth day of March, Alonso de Rojas, the confessor of Mariana de Jesús, ascended the steps of the beautiful carved pulpit at the Compañía with a fixed purpose: he would not only declare that all the disasters which had visited Quito had been caused by sin and call upon the people to repent; he would offer himself as a propitiatory victim and ask that he might die to save others from the punishment they had brought on themselves.

He was a forceful and eloquent preacher, and he spoke with such fire and vehemence that even the most indifferent and hardened of the many who thronged the golden church that morning could not listen to him unmoved. One of them took immediate action: this was Mariana de Jesús who, as usual, was quietly seated at the foot of the pulpit, listening intently to the sermon.

She rose, gracefully and without haste, and, speaking in a clear firm voice, audible in all parts of the crowded church, announced that she would ask God to take her life in offering in place of the priest's, who could so ill be spared from the city, because of his great goodness and his noble example to others.

Unworthy as it was, she hoped the Lord would accept it "in defense of her country, her compatriots and her kindred" and she besought Him "that she might be chastized for everything in the city which deserved chastisement." . . . After leaving the church, she went straight to her home and never left it again, for she was instantly stricken with mortal illness. But, from that day forward, the earthquakes ceased, the plagues abated and the deadly volcano was again quiescent.[26]

As she lay ill, her physician ordered, on Good Friday, that once again she be bled in order to lessen her fever. The blood was reverently poured into a corner of the patio where it moistened the ground on which grew a little-noticed green plant. Shortly afterward the nondescript plant turned into a lily, the flower with which Mariana has ever since been identified. Mariana de Jesús died within two months, on May 26.

Her death made a profound impression on her fellow townsmen. Bishop Oviedo sang the funeral mass, with the sermon delivered by her Jesuit confessor, Father Rojas. The audiencia as a corporate body, the municipal cabildo, leading citizens, and a large popular throng attended the services. As of that date, the people of Quito canonized Mariana. The ecclesiastical authorities in Rome with their customary caution acted much more slowly. Pope Benedict XIV raised Mariana to the status of venerable in 1757. Her beatification occurred in 1850, but it was not until 1950 that Pope Pius XII presided over the solemn ceremonies in the basilica of St. Peter which made Mariana de Paredes y Flores, the "Lily of Quito," a saint of the Roman Catholic Church. She was the first and, to date, the only saint of Ecuador.[27]

While our major concern is the view of her contemporaries, it is permissible to speculate on the timing of her canonization. Mariana's sainthood strengthened the current political position of the Church in Ecuador, where traditional anti-clericalism and more recent Marxism have posed serious challenges. Her canonization in 1950, in fact, belonged to a much broader policy of the present Roman Catholic Church, that is, to make the Church as geographically global as it has always been dogmatically universal. In recent years canonizations and red hats for cardinals have been much more liberally distributed in areas such as Latin America, Africa, and Asia as a conscious means of widening the appeal of the Church in those continents.

Mariana's contemporaries saw for her death a supernatural explanation. By offering herself as a sacrificial atonement, she appeased the wrath of God toward the wicked city. The contemporary interpretation of her life and death fitted the austere and sacrificial pattern which Mariana had chosen for herself. For us who live in an age that jokes about masochism, a genuine effort of imagination is required to understand the life and times of this baroque saint. As Mrs. Keyes has written:

From earliest childhood she had visualized herself as a *víctima:* that is, it was her soul's sincere desire not only to worship God, but to make her personal "Imitation of Christ" a literal one as far as suffering was concerned; nor was this solely for love of Him or with the feeling that she could best prove this love by sackcloth and scourging. The Deity of her faith was not a Loving Father; he was the Jehovah of Wrath, whose righteous anger must be continually appeased, lest sinful mankind should be visited with frightful forms of death and destruction. Fearless, as far as she herself was concerned, as to both life and death, she foresaw with dread the fate that she believed awaited her city and her country, as the result of widespread wrongdoing; and convinced that she could be instrumental in helping to avert this, she surrendered herself to penitential discipline.[28]

It is not very useful to argue that the death of Mariana can be explained in natural terms without recourse to the supernatural explanation with which her contemporaries endowed it. Admittedly, Mariana had for a long time suffered from intermittent illnesses which became more frequent with each passing year. Fevers, headaches, and digestive disorders plagued her. Frequent oral hemorrhages suggest that she was consumptive. Several references to the severe pain in her side indicate that she may also have suffered from pleurisy. She did not willfully injure her health, since she seldom disobeyed her confessors when they ordered her to modify her austerities. Nevertheless, corporal mortifications took their toll from her frail body. However well-intentioned and lovingly administered her medical treatment was, it obviously did her more harm than good.

Her attitude toward constituted authorities both ecclesiastical and civil was one of respectful aloofness. She wanted freedom to pursue her own vocation. Her refusal to enter either the Franciscan or the Dominican convent of nuns merits careful examination. Although the convents were not havens for licentiousness, neither were they centers of rigorous asceticism. Before a young woman entered a convent, her family customarily offered an elaborate series of entertainments. Her parents also presented the convent with her dowry, on the principle that the young novice was taking Christ as her mystical spouse. The atmosphere in the convents was genteel, with the nuns spending a great deal of time doing embroidery and making jams and jellies. Although some nuns did devote themselves to acts of penitence and social charity, many more ladies lived behind the cloisters with all the creature comforts, including being attended by their own staff of servants.[29]

In the 1670's and the 1680's, the Dominican convent of Santa Catalina was thrown into turmoil by a prolonged conflict between the elderly nuns who wished to continue under the jurisdiction of the Dominican friars and the younger nuns who favored episcopal supervision. For a decade the citizens of Quito observed such unedifying scenes as an invasion of the convent by Dominican friars, from which several nuns emerged with their garments torn and their bodies black and blue from the blows inflicted upon them by the friars.[30]

A substantial number of creole heiresses throughout the Indies preferred to spend their lives in convents. It is usually asserted that the Spanish and Portuguese men mixed with Indian and Negro women because there was a shortage of European women. Although the shortage did exist during the early decades of the sixteenth century, in due time creole women abounded. Many of them were from well-to-do families with dowries, but large numbers of these ladies made themselves unavailable by taking the veil. To be sure, their upbringing and education obviously encouraged them to take this step, but it also seems as if they may have been protesting in a quiet way, without violating the mores of their society, the man's world of donjuanismo.

The social stability of colonial society depended in great measure on the existence of a large class of well-to-do Spaniards and creoles. The fact that many girls from prosperous families entered the convents and hence did not contribute to setting up economically stable Spanish households helped to engender social instability. In 1607 there were about three hundred nuns in the kingdom.[31] The reduction in the supply of eligible wives in turn may have encouraged many young creole men without any strong religious vocation to enter the monasteries.

Be this as it may, Saint Mariana de Jesús and her contemporary, Saint Rose of Lima, were both women of intense religious vocations who deliberately avoided the cloisters. The convents, with their genteel atmosphere and comforts, if not luxuries, were not suitable places for those two baroque saints to pursue their spiritual development. Both women engaged in rigorous corporal mortifications, and both were driven by an intense desire to help their fellowmen by the performance of acts of social charity.

Mariana preferred to remain as distant from the civil authorities as she did from the convents. One day an oidor met Mariana in the streets. Long impressed by her virtuous life, he gave her a chaste embrace and asked her to pray for him, prayers which he may well have needed. Upon returning home, the future saint was deeply shocked that a man's hands had touched hers. As her reputation for saintliness grew, oidores, their wives, or leading citizens were apt to approach Mariana in the church of La Compañía and ask her to intercede for them in her prayers. On feast days, when such requests were more frequent, Mariana avoided her customary place in front of the pulpit in order to conceal herself in some obscure corner of the church. Because of her modesty she was embarrassed by these requests.[32] On her deathbed she refused to allow the oidores to pay an official call on her. Even the visit of the bishop embarrassed her.

There is no record that Mariana ever explicitly criticized the colorful vices of Dr. Morga and the circle around him. Mariana was 19 when the old president died. Although the more flamboyant vices of Dr. Morga's times occurred during the early years of his administration before 1624, there is little evidence that the visita general did much to raise the level of public and private morality during subsequent years. The conditions which produced the vices of the early Morga years continued and so did the vices. Certainly Mariana was painfully aware of the moral decay of her city, but she never attacked those abuses directly. Thus there never was a dramatic confrontation between the saint and the sinners. Yet her whole life, climaxed by her sacrifice to atone for the sins of her native city, was a telling if implicit condemnation of the upper echelons of the society into which she was born.

Antonio de Morga and Mariana de Paredes y Flores were both people of their own times. Each was a somewhat exaggerated expression of the contradictory tendencies of that milieu whose glittering baroque façade concealed a raw frontier community in which vice and virtue, sinners and saints, both flourished.

9.

JUSTICE

The Spanish concept of sovereignty held dispensation of justice to be the highest privilege of the ruler. The supreme organ of government in each of the kingdoms overseas was the audiencia, which was a judicial tribunal as well as a political and administrative board. The ordinances issued at Monzón in 1562 applied originally to the new audiencias of Quito and Charcas, but subsequently they were extended to all the nonviceregal audiencias in the Indies.[1] In a very real sense the ordinances of Monzón composed the first constitution of the kingdoms of the New World.

It is indicative of the emphasis the Spaniards placed on the administration of justice that only 15 of the 311 clauses of the ordinances dealt with political administration, i.e., *cosas de gobierno,* and the wording of even those provisions was vague. The most carefully spelled out clauses in the ordinances of Monzón were those dealing with the administration of justice. An equally detailed section concerned the royal exchequer. The first 37 clauses dealt with the jurisdiction of the presidents and oidores in civil and criminal cases, clauses 38–52 with political administration, clauses 53–57 with ecclesiastical matters, clauses 58–68 with the treasury, clauses 67–68 with fines,

196

clause 69 with probate matters, clauses 70–78 with protection of the Indians, clauses 79–307 with the inferior magistrates, clauses 308–309 with fees, and the last clause with the keeping of the records.

Two types of officials staffed the lower courts, over which the audiencia exercised appellate jurisdiction. The municipal judges, the *alcaldes ordinarios,* and the corregidores were courts of first instance. In order to investigate serious and notorious crimes in outlying provinces, the audiencia could send a *juez de comisión* to act as a judge of first instance in a particular case.

The ordinances of Monzón empowered the audiencia to hear both civil and criminal appeals from decisions of all secular courts in the kingdom. Not only was the audiencia an appellate court, but also it exercised first-instance jurisdiction in certain types of crimes. They were the ancient *casos de corte,* such as murder, rape, violation of truces, arson, treason, acts against widows and orphans, and crimes committed by inferior magistrates, as well as all criminal cases occurring within five leagues of the capital and all cases of debasement and counterfeiting of currency. The audiencia was the final court in criminal cases, but in civil cases an appeal could be made to the Council of the Indies, *en grado de segunda suplicación,* within a period of one year. The council sought to restrict its activities as the supreme court of the empire in order to concentrate on political administration. On February 13, 1620, a royal cedula provided that only suits involving 6,000 pesos or more could be appealed from an audiencia to the council. The council confined its verdicts to questions of law and not to those of facts unless new facts were uncovered.[2]

One oidor sitting alone rendered verdicts in civil cases involving less than 200 pesos and also in petty criminal cases. The custom was that each oidor served his turn as oidor of the week, *oidor semanero,* in order to handle the routine work of the tribunal and to issue writs in minor cases. Although one judge might preside at the preliminary stages of a hearing, the final verdict, the *definitiva,* required a quorum of two oidores. In suits heard on appeal, *en grado de suplicación,* all the resident judges cast a vote, with a simple majority determining the outcome. In case of a tie, the oidores co-opted one of the licensed advocates to cast the deciding vote.

The importance of the clerking level of the bureaucracy lay in the Spanish custom that all phases of litigations be committed to written testimony. From a judicial standpoint, the two most important clerking offices were the relatores and the escribanos de cámara. The relator, a lawyer by training, was a royal appointee. The important responsibility of the relator was to prepare summaries of the relevant facts from the bulk of the evidence furnished by the litigants and their witnesses. Upon his impartiality and competence depended in part the fortune of the litigants. If relatores were convicted of inaccuracies, they could be penalized by fines, suspension from office, or even imprisonment. The escribano mayor and his large staff of deputies managed the routine but almost endless amount of paper work of the court. All documents presented to the court passed through their hands.

A licensed advocate prepared his case by formulating a statement for his client, a *petición,* a list of witnesses whom he wished to question, and a series of questions, an *interrogatorio,* for the witnesses to answer. The primitive practice of oath swearing, whose origins are Visigothic, had left its mark on judicial procedures even in those countries, such as Castile, where the acceptance of Roman law was most complete. The tendency was to call the largest possible number of witnesses to testify to the same set of facts. Not altogether successful efforts were made to restrict the number to thirty witnesses testifying to any one set of questions. The skill with which the questions were framed could significantly influence the outcome of the case. The interrogatorio had three sections. The first consisted of a series of formal questions whose purpose was to establish the character of the witness, his interest in the case, and the credibility of his testimony. The second section sought to establish a body of facts involved in the dispute. And the third section concerned hearsay evidence under the general heading *de pública voz y fama.* One of the responsibilities of the relator was to determine that the interrogatorio did not violate accepted rules of evidence and that it contained no leading questions or irrelevancies.

After the attorney of the plaintiff submitted the petición and the interrogatorio to the escribano de cámara of the audiencia, the oidores instructed the relator to draw up a summary of the material presented, which was sent to the defendant. The defendant received notification to submit his reply, the *contesta,* with a list of witnesses and his interrogatorio within nine days.

After the necessary interlocutory decisions had been reached, the principal issues in the case were submitted to the attention of the court, the *recibida a prueba.* The notary of the case, and not the judges, examined the witnesses and asked them to answer the questions contained in the interrogatorio. If any witnesses were unable to be present in the capital, it was the responsibility of the interested litigant to pay for the services of a *receptor* to record the testimony of those witnesses at their place of residence. Excluded as witnesses were the parties involved and their near relatives. Indians were not allowed to present testimony under oath, since their legal status was that of minors. The testimony of six Indians was usually held to be equivalent to that of one Spaniard. All non-Indian witnesses had to offer testimony under oath.

Public discussion between the judge and the counsel on points of law and cross-examination of witnesses by the defense and prosecuting attorneys never became an integral part of the Spanish legal machinery, as it did in the Anglo-Saxon countries. Although there was a limited form of cross-examination, the *repregunta,* in some types of appeal cases, the judges preferred to confine themselves to evaluating written evidence. The examination of witnesses took place in private. Although neither the accused nor his lawyer might cross-examine witnesses, the defense did possess the right to object to the admission of evidence. An elaborate body of precedents provided for the disqualification of interested or untrustworthy witnesses. During his examination, the accused did not receive a copy of the interrogatorio. He was required to answer under oath each question as it was put to him. There was no rule by which he could avoid testifying against himself.

In brief, the Spanish system of justice was secret rather than public and inquisitorial rather than accusatory. Derived from canon law, this procedure of prosecution became standard in the civil courts of the Roman law countries by the sixteenth century. It was far less favorable to the defense than the accusatory procedure it had replaced. Only England preserved the accusatory and public procedure, of which trial by a jury of peers and broader rights for the accused were the cornerstones.[3]

Torture could be applied only upon the written order of a judge. Judicial torture might be invoked if the accused were suspected of perjury or in order to extract a confession if the evidence against him were considered nearly but not quite conclusive. Certain classes of persons—men of gentle birth, men of learning, pregnant women, and children—enjoyed exemption from the application of judicial torture ever since the promulgation of the *Siete Partidas.*

Legislation provided that the decisions of the appellate courts be rendered within twenty days after the completion of the hearings. Only the judges, the fiscal, and the notary could remain in the court chambers while magistrates deliberated over decisions. The *Libro de Acuerdos* kept by the president recorded all verdicts and summarized in one or two sentences the votes of the majority and the minority. All parties in a case received a duly notarized copy of the final sentence. Another copy was filed in the archives of the office of the escribano mayor of the audiencia.

Some protection against arbitrary arrest and confinement to jail did exist, but the regulations left something to be desired from the point of view of the accused. A single denunciation might be sufficient to justify arrest and detention. All persons arrested received a copy of their indictment and enjoyed the right to secure counsel. During the three days granted to a prisoner to prepare his defense, he could not be questioned or put to torture. The law required that an oidor inspect the prison once a week. His standing instructions were to give priority to hearing cases of prisoners. A prejudiced oidor sometimes abused his discretionary powers by releasing from jail notorious delinquents charged with crimes as serious as murder. Prisoners, on the other hand, might languish behind bars without trial for months if they had aroused the animosity of the magistrates.[4]

Security conditions in the audiencia jails were less than satisfactory. Several *alcaldes de la cárcel* were removed from office and fined for allowing their prisoners to escape. Standing instructions that there be separate quarters for the sexes were sometimes disregarded.[5] So inadequate was the royal jail that socially prominent prisoners were seldom detained there for more than a few days. Those undergoing trial were put under house arrest, and for less serious indictments under city arrest. Jails then did not serve as a place of penance and punitive incarceration. Judicial sentences took the form of branding, mutilation, public whipping, or service in the galleys for the lowly and humble. For the upper echelons of society, fines and exile were the usual punishments. Exile varied all the way from exclusion from the limits of the capital city for a certain period of time to temporary expulsion from the confines of the audiencia kingdom and, worst of all, banishment to remote and isolated Chile.

Although as early as the sixteenth century, jails in western Europe were beginning to be used as places of punishment and not merely for detention, it was not until the reformers of the 1700's fought against torture, branding, mutilation, and whipping that public opinion in the Old World forced the substitution of imprisonment, emphasizing work, penance, and the rational equation that the punishment fit the crime. In Spanish America these reforms, of course, were unheard of. The jails served only the ancient function of a temporary place of detention before the trial.[6]

A striking feature of Spanish justice is the relative infrequency of the death penalty. Homicides were common in that turbulent society, but seldom was there capital punishment. In some cases the lower courts did impose the death sentence. More often than not the audiencia on appeal commuted the sentence to a period of exile and some monetary compensation to the family of the victim.[7] Chilean exile was much dreaded by culprits and often imposed by the judges. In spite of its sunny Mediterranean climate, Chile was then the end of the world, a primitive frontier outpost hemmed in by the hostile Indians. In the seventeenth century, Chile was a penal colony for the criminals of Quito, much as Australia became for English criminals in a later period.

In those rare cases to which the death penalty was applied, the victim was of Indian or Negro descent and seldom of European background. In that corporate society with its built-in inequalities, a person's status in society had something, but not everything, to do with the treatment received from the bench. Europeans could avail themselves of the infinite resources of the law and the eager assistance of the gentlemen of the bar. Given the excessive reliance placed on oath taking and the imperfect machinery for testing the credibility of witnesses, socially prominent murderers could usually arrange, by pleading self-defense, to have a death sentence commuted to exile. The racy if prejudiced English observer Thomas Gage ascribed the infrequency of capital punishment in Guatemala to the venality of the oidores.[8] Such an explanation does not get below the surface.

The reluctance of Spanish justice to impose the death penalty, preferring monetary compensation by the murderer to the family of the dead man, like the emphasis on oath taking, apparently is a holdover from the Germanic customs of the Visigoths. The mercy that Spanish justice was capable of showing toward murderers never, of course, extended to unrepentant heretics, who met death at the stake. Thus this colonial tradition of remote Visigothic antecedents in turn prepared the ground for the deep-rooted philosophical opposition to capital punishment that is characteristic of contemporary Latin America.

Not only was the inquisitorial character of Spanish justice unfavorable to the defense, but it was also costly. In addition to lawyers' fees, litigants had to pay for the endless clerking services rendered by the inferior magistrates. Although the audiencia set the amount of these fees in an official tariff, the *arancel,* many litigants must have found the temptation almost irresistible to pay something more than the legal fee in order to expedite business. Thus the line between a legal fee, an extralegal tip, and an illegal bribe became blurred. It was even necessary for the person who won a favorable judgment from the court to pay a fee to the constable for executing the writ of the court.[9] Although the tips and bribes to the clerks represent only petty chiseling in comparison to the institutionalized graft in other echelons of the bureaucracy, such practices did noticeably increase the costs of defense for litigants.

A careful examination of a few criminal careers will reveal more about the strengths and weaknesses of the colonial system of justice and the special attitudes of the Spaniards toward crime and punishment than will a series of further generalizations.

Don Nicolás de Larraspuru used his prominent family connections in the peninsula to create for himself a position of wealth and social prestige in Quito. He arrived there a knight of the military order of Santiago, an honor that was coveted by the ambitious with even more ardor in the Indies than it was in the peninsula. Dr. Morga, for example, lusted in vain for this distinction.[10] Don Nicolás owed his knighthood to his father's prominence rather than to his own efforts.

He was the youngest son of General Tomás de Larraspuru, the admiral who skillfully conducted the Spanish fleets that plied between Tierra Firme and the peninsula carrying the silver of Peru and Mexico, without which Philip IV could not have continued his wars. The crown derived an average profit of only one million ducats from the Indies after deducting expenses. Yet this sum could be used to borrow many more times that amount.[11]

His father sent young don Nicolás, already the black sheep of the family, to Quito with the evident hope that the rebellious youth would settle down and carve out for himself a respectable situation with the help of his family's influence. He started out well by making a good marriage. Doña María de Vera y Mendoza, his wife, was the daughter of one of the richest men in the kingdom, Juan de Vera y Mendoza.

Hot-tempered and belligerent, don Nicolás de Larraspuru seriously wounded two people of prominence. One was Lic. Antonio Rodríquez de Lorencana, newly appointed acting fiscal of the audiencia. His other victim was don Fernando Ordóñez de Valencia. The fine for the clash with the acting fiscal was 3,000 pesos and two years' exile from the city limits of Quito. For his encounter with Fernando Ordóñez de Valencia, the fine was another 1,000 pesos and four years' exile.[12]

Don Nicolás took up his residence in Riobamba, where he soon found plenty of congenial companions with whom he could carouse. He quickly ran afoul of the constable of Riobamba, Pedro Sayago del Hoyo.

A native of Extremadura, Pedro Sayago del Hoyo originally settled in Potosí, Charcas. The raw and turbulent mining town was torn by bitter dissensions between the Basques who came to dominate production in the silver mines and the other races from the peninsula. The tension erupted into open civil war in the early 1620's.[13] During that turmoil, Pedro Sayago del Hoyo was equally famous for his physical brawn and his prankish sense of humor. In Potosí he humiliated a prominent Basque by forcing him to dress in the habit of a Franciscan monk, covering his face with a cowl, and putting him in an open coffin which Sayago del Hoyo paraded around the streets asking for alms to bury the supposedly dead man in the coffin. That Basque became such a laughing stock that he left Potosí for Lima.[14] In 1625 the same Basque, Pedro Sánchez de Mañozca, was in Quito serving as a member of the entourage of his uncle, the all-powerful visitor general.[15] Exiled from Potosí for his role in the civil turmoil, Pedro Sayago del Hoyo settled in Riobamba, where he bought the office of chief constable.

A clash between the rich and high-born ne'er-do-well, Nicolás de Larraspuru, and the burly constable was inevitable. There was the antagonism of nationality: Larraspuru was Basque, and Sayago del Hoyo was a native of Extremadura. In the seventeenth century, there were acrimonious tensions between Castilians, Basques, Extremeños, and Andalusians, all of whom on occasion quarreled and hated each other with lusty contempt. These antagonisms were an outgrowth of the crown's attempt to impose political unity on the peninsula. They sometimes culminated in the Indies in bloody street fights with several deaths or in bitter disputes that led even priests to violate the secrets of the confessional. The common contempt that all groups of European Spaniards felt for the creoles, a hatred which the latter cordially returned, tended to put a lid on these intra-peninsular feuds. Sometimes, however, the lid did blow off.

Not only did Larraspuru and Sayago del Hoyo have reason to hate each other as Basque and Extremeño, but also the two would inevitably collide in the small town of Riobamba. Larraspuru was addicted to carousing at night with his cronies. Sayago was the chief police officer whose duty was to preserve order in the streets after dark.

On the night of December 29, 1626, a bloody fight erupted in the usually quiet streets of Riobamba. While the constable was making his nightly rounds, a gang of thirty men led by Nicolás de Larraspuru attacked him. The burly, powerful constable fought his assailants with the courage of a lion. He left eight of them dead on the street, but the sheer force of numbers eventually wore him down. Mortally wounded, Pedro Sayago del Hoyo pleaded that a priest who had joined the crowd observing the bloody clash should hear his confession and grant him absolution for his imminent journey to the next world. Nicolás de Larraspuru showed no compassion on his fallen foe. He refused to allow the priest to approach the dying man. He yelled hoarsely, "Let him confess to Lucifer in the fifth hell."[16]

The news of this atrocious crime reached the visitor general at his lodgings in Quito on New Year's Eve. Lic. Mañozca was visibly shocked. He immediately realized that the sanguinary and public character of the murder could precipitate riots and violence of the type that had occurred in Potosí just a few years before. The blame for any such outbreak of lawlessness would probably be placed on him, since the majority of the audiencia had been suspended from office by his action eighteen months before. The visitor general's partiality for his fellow Basques and his close friendship with the father of Larraspuru, which led him to serve as godfather to one of the children of don Nicolás, were well known. The visita general itself, now entering its third year, had created such widespread dissatisfaction that the murder in Riobamba might provide the spark to ignite an explosion. His countless enemies in Quito were clamoring for his head in Madrid.

The visitor general may have taken some pleasure in the cruel treatment of the man who had humiliated his nephew in Potosí a few years previously, but he had no time to indulge in his usual vindictiveness. He had to take drastic steps to bolster his sagging position. With characteristic energy he took them. He restored to office all the members of the audiencia, save the fiscal.[17]

The restored audiencia met in an emergency session on January 1, 1627. Only an acute crisis could provoke such a session, for the inviolable custom was for the audiencia to adjourn from December 23 to several days after Epiphany. In order to forestall possible riots, the audiencia on January 1 dispatched to Riobamba Oidor Castillo de Herrera, armed with ample powers as a *juez pesquisidor*. So anxious was the audiencia that the oidor undertake his special mission immediately that he left Quito for Riobamba on that very day, before the notaries had drawn up his credentials.[18]

Lic. Castillo de Herrera conducted the trial in Riobamba during the month of January, 1627. The evidence began to mount that Nicolás de Larraspuru was the ringleader in a premeditated murder. Facing the grim prospect of conviction, the knight of the order of Santiago fled to Lima and thence to Spain.[19] Several of his closest cronies also escaped with him. To what extent the authorities acquiesced in his escape is uncertain. On one hand, escapes from colonial prisons were commonplace. Rare indeed is the case of the constables' recapturing an escaped prisoner, who usually headed for the next audiencia kingdom. Extradition procedures were cumbersome and seldom effective. In the case of Larraspuru, the audiencia did authorize a special posse of twenty men to recapture him, but without success.[20]

There is some evidence to suggest that both Dr. Morga and Lic. Mañozca were relieved by Larraspuru's escape. President Morga was a close friend of don Nicolás' father-in-law. In flagrant violation of the law, the president had served as a godfather at the wedding of Larraspuru. For so doing and also for allegedly acquiescing to his escape from Riobamba, Morga was fined 1,000 pesos by the Council of the Indies.[21] After 1627, when Dr. Morga finally became convinced of the criminal and incorrigible character of Larraspuru, he abandoned all efforts to help him out of his increasing difficulties with the law. The president then advised the Council of the Indies to banish his errant godson from the Indies.[22]

Lic. Mañozca was also relieved that the ne'er-do-well had fled, for the visitor was an intimate friend of the father of the murderer. General Tomás de Larraspuru reciprocated the friendship of his fellow Basque. The general sent by special courier from Cartagena the cedulas of March 7, 1627, dismissing Lic. Mañozca as visitor general a month before the news reached Quito by regular mail.[23]

A few days before Nicolás de Larraspuru fled to Lima, the Council of the Indies, with no knowledge of the bloody events in Riobamba and acting upon the request of his father, granted permission to the son to spend four years in the peninsula on business without being accompanied by his wife. As an encomendero, he had to secure the council's permission to absent himself from the kingdom.[24] After fleeing Riobamba, he headed for Spain to mend his dilapidated fortunes.

In the meantime Lic. Castillo de Herrera concluded his investigations in Riobamba. He found Nicolás de Larraspuru and several accomplices guilty of the premeditated murder of Pedro Sayago del Hoyo. The sentence was death by hanging, and his estate was to pay the widow of the murdered constable the sum of 9,000 pesos as compensation.[25]

Lic. Castillo de Herrera was more successful in punishing the less prominent accomplices in the crime. He convicted a Negro and a mulatto. Feeling in Riobamba was running so high among the Extremeños after the escape of Larraspuru and his principal accomplices that the oidor feared the mob would lynch the two hapless prisoners. On February 5, 1627, the audiencia ordered that the two culprits be brought to Quito under armed guard sufficiently strong to protect their lives.[26]

In response to a plea from the audiencia, the Council of the Indies on

April 12, 1628, authorized Lic. Mañozca's successor as visitor general to conduct a sweeping investigation and to punish Larraspuru for any crimes of which he might be found guilty.[27] The new visitor general, Lic. Galdós de Valencia, and Nicolás de Larraspuru arrived in Quito almost simultaneously. Don Nicolás brandished a cedula from the king in which he was allegedly pardoned for all his previous misconduct in recognition of the distinguished services of his father. In the meantime don Nicolás committed yet another homicide.[28]

Lic. Galdós interpreted his instructions literally. He refused to consider the two murders, since neither crime was specifically mentioned in the royal cedula. He did conduct an elaborate investigation in which he found Nicolás de Larraspuru guilty of a wide variety of crimes, ranging from failing to kneel at mass, to noisy carousing at night, to attempted homicides, assaults, and robberies. He had apparently committed every crime but deflowering virgins and raping married women.[29] Feeling in the city against don Nicolás was rising. In order to prevent an outbreak of violence, the visitor general prudently put him in jail. Spanish prisons being what they were and don Nicolás being what he was, he escaped and fled to Lima. He never returned to Quito.

Nicolás de Larraspuru, a knight of the order of Santiago, who had arrived in Quito little more than a decade before as a most eligible bachelor, found himself destitute and banished by the Council of the Indies from all the kingdoms of the New World and ordered back to Spain into the custody of his father.[30] Although the Council of the Indies sharply reprimanded the audiencia of Quito for its failure to punish the flagrant crimes of Nicolás de Larraspuru, the attitude of the council was gratuitous. They minimized the difficulties of the audiencia, and they ignored some basic weaknesses of the judicial system.

A modern psychiatrist would probably classify Nicolás de Larraspuru as a psychotic personality, but of course no such concept existed in the seventeenth century. Had he come from the lower echelons, the courts probably would have cut short his career of crime nearer to its inception. His career was prolonged for over a decade because he was his father's son. The son capitalized on this fact with cunning until his misdeeds mounted so in number and horror that he finally dissipated the influence of his father and his father-in-law. Furthermore, don Nicolás was able to exploit several defects of the Spanish judicial system, such as the widespread practice of false testimony, the poorly guarded prisons, the ineffectiveness of the police force, and the ease of flight.

His career also reflects the insecurity of social conditions. The companions of don Nicolás came from those marginal groups who had no secure footing in that tightly structured, neo-medieval corporate society. Those of them who became lawless and predatory threatened the stability of the established order. Many marginal individuals who were less disorderly attached themselves to a patron. Side-by-side with the "stable society," which was largely a transplant from Europe, there coexisted the "violent society." From the latter an alienated if not psychotic personality such as Nicolás de Larraspuru could recruit accomplices for his crimes.

If frontier conditions contributed to the existence of the "violent society" in the Indies, lawlessness could also prevail in the more established societies in the Old World. When Viceroy García de Toledo arrived in Sicily, he found the city of Palermo terrorized by armed gangs and thieves. The nobles maintained heavily armed retainers. Murder was an everyday occurrence. Private feuds often resulted in pitched battles in the streets. The authorities were reluctant to intervene, since the armed gangs enjoyed the protection of powerful nobles. Bandits infested the countryside. The judicial machinery was clogged by the prevalence of false testimony, which was a symptom of the people's profound distrust of the law.[31]

In contrast to Nicolás de Larraspuru, a disturbed personality from a prominent family, Diego de Niebla was a self-made man of humble origins who made a modest fortune, only to lose all he gained by allowing himself to be destroyed in the bureaucratic treadmill of Spanish justice. Born in Seville, he went to Quito as a penniless immigrant some time before 1593. He set up a grocery store where he sold wine, bacon, and butter. After he married the daughter of another grocer, his modest prosperity was threatened by his taking the wrong side during the petty civil war of 1593 which broke out in Quito when the crown sought to introduce the traditional sales tax, the alcabalas. Although he was fined 500 pesos and exiled temporarily to the neighboring city of Pasto, the talent of Diego as a retail merchant could not be suppressed. Returning to Quito, he expanded his grocery business by becoming involved in importing merchandise from Panama. He also made money by operating an obraje.[32] By dint of his industry and shrewdness, he became one of the richest men in the kingdom, amassing a fortune of some 40,000 pesos. The unprestigious source of his wealth excluded him from the upper echelons of society to which he aspired and to which, on the basis of his capital, he could reasonably expect to belong.

Diego de Niebla made the leap to upper-class status in his second marriage. His bride was Ana Ronquillo de Galarça, the 13-year-old daughter of Juan de Munoa Ronquillo, a well-to-do petty bureaucrat. As *escribano de visitas,* Juan de Ronquillo accompanied the circuit judges as their official notary. Several relatives and friends opposed the proposed marriage of his very young daughter to the middle-aged grocer. To them it was a mésalliance not merely because of the wide disparity in their ages but also because of Diego de Niebla's humble origins. What attracted Juan de Ronquillo was his capital of 40,000 pesos. Few men in Quito who might aspire to his daughter's hand possessed so substantial an estate. Juan de Ronquillo and his wife provided their daughter with a dowry of 12,000 pesos.

Agreeing to give up his grocery and retail business as a socially inferior occupation, Niebla bought from the crown the office of alguacil mayor of the city of Quito for the large sum of 25,000 pesos. Although the capital investment was heavy, the office of chief constable produced a steady and comfortable income from the collection of fees. Not only was the office lucrative, it was also socially acceptable. The chief constable was an ex officio member of the city council, the stronghold of the wealthy and prominent citizens. Although some brows were raised by the sudden transformation of the rich grocer into a member of the social elite, all went according to form. The impecunious crown, although periodically reasserting the desirability of selling offices to people of proper social background, readily accepted Niebla's cash. In due time doña Ana Ronquillo presented her husband with two children.

The career of Diego de Niebla is an arresting example of how a self-made man could carve out for himself a modest but secure niche in the upper echelons of society. Tranquility of mind and the pacific enjoyment of his new social status, however, were not to be the fate of this unhappy man.

From 1606 onward the new alguacil mayor became embroiled in a series of litigations and quarrels, which, over the course of the years, made him the principal litigant before the audiencia. In time he became the most unpopular man in the whole kingdom. He became involved either as a plaintiff or as a defendant in thirty-two suits before the audiencia itself, not counting several other litigations before the episcopal tribunal and the court of the corregidor. Some of the suits concerned the prerogatives and the perquisites of the office of alguacil mayor of the city. Niebla claimed the right to appoint deputies in the principal towns outside the capital, such as San Miguel de Ibarra, Latacunga, and Chimbo. The Council of the Indies eventually upheld the verdict of the audiencia, which was unfavorable to these claims. Sold separately, these posts could fetch between 5,000 and 9,000 pesos apiece.[33]

Although in this regard Niebla's pretensions may have been justified, he generally did not conduct himself with the decorum of one belonging to his station. Quarrelsome, hot-headed, and intemperate in language, he became embroiled in a host of incidents with his new social equals. In the main square of Quito, after a heated argument with his father-in-law, he drew his sword. The father-in-law escaped harm, other than an acid tongue lashing from his son-in-law, by the timely intervention of bystanders. Niebla's relations with his wife were no less bitter than those with his father-in-law. According to her testimony, her husband confined her in prison-like isolation in their home, where her diet often consisted of bread and water. After eight years of marriage, doña Ana fled his house and brought action before the court of the bishop for an ecclesiastical separation from her husband. She also brought civil action before the audiencia for separate maintenance for herself and her children.

This was a drastic step for those times. However abused wives may have been by their husbands, they usually preferred to suffer quietly behind the locked doors of their homes than to cause the commotion and scandal of seeking an ecclesiastical separation. The church authorities also discouraged such actions. Doña Ana Ronquillo was not the only person whom Diego de Niebla drove to desperation.

Whatever else he was, Diego de Niebla was no gentleman. In one of his suits, he charged that he had carnally known his bride before their marriage, although he subsequently withdrew this assertion. He refused to give testimony before the ecclesiastical court in regard to his wife's separation petition. He consistently evaded the orders of the audiencia to provide alimony to his estranged wife. In a series of legal actions, doña Ana managed to wrest her dowry from the control of her husband. When the ecclesiastical authorities went to his home in order to gather testimony, the fiery Diego de Niebla instructed his servants to bolt the doors and to refuse admission to everyone. A writ issued by the oidor of the week was required so the door could be broken down by force.

Diego de Niebla's relations with his newly acquired colleagues in bureaucratic officialdom were just as tumultuous and quarrelsome as those with his wife and father-in-law. In the main square of the capital, he drew his sword against a fellow alderman, Captain Juan Sánchez de Xerez, when the alderman charged that one of Niebla's slaves had murdered one of Sánchez de Xerez' chattels. Niebla used such abusive language against another regidor, Dr. Meneses, that the latter brought legal action against him. Niebla's sentence was a small fine of 30 pesos and deprivation of his right to vote in the city council for a year.

Imprisoned in 1616 because of action brought against him by his creditors, Niebla became seemingly paranoiac. He accused most of the judges of the audiencia, the episcopal tribunal, and the lower court of the corregidor of being prejudiced against him. A supposedly rich man, he refused to pay his creditors the debts which, by his own admission, were around 1,000 pesos. His creditors claimed some 5,000 pesos were due.

In August, 1619, the acting fiscal, Lic. Carvajal, brought criminal action against Diego de Niebla, indicting him on twenty counts. He sought to defend himself by asserting that he could not be tried, since he was unable to secure a lawyer. Niebla argued that no advocate would defend him because they were all intimidated by the oidores' hostility toward him. Niebla requested the audiencia to encourage some qualified lawyer to assist him. In the meantime he also asked for special permission to circumvent the established procedures of the courts by being allowed to present his own petitions rather than those composed by a notary.

The audiencia curtly dismissed this request. Obviously petitions written by him would be illegible and perhaps incomprehensible. Furthermore, this request, if granted, would create a dangerous precedent that would undermine the livelihood of the large number of notaries. The tribunal asserted that no lawyer would serve Niebla, not because of any alleged hostility of the judges toward the defendant, but because the legal community was all too familiar with the erratic behavior of the alguacil mayor. Not only did he not pay his bills, but also he did not accept the advice of the lawyers, nor would he conform to the established procedures of the courts.

A man of little formal education, Niebla had taken to booklearning with a vengeance. He acquired a large library of books in Spanish and Latin dealing with law and theology. The oidores, of course, poked fun at Niebla's clumsy efforts to use these learned treatises, which they claimed he did not understand. To them it seemed ludicrous and pretentious that the former grocer sought to use the language and concepts of academic culture.

The acting fiscal's series of twenty charges included most of the incidents that have already been recounted. One of the additional charges was that Diego de Niebla was virtually terrorizing the judges and corregidores by threatening to make charges against them during their residencias if they did not bribe him not to do so.

The initial reply of Niebla was that all these charges were calumnious and defamatory. He argued that the audiencia possessed no jurisdiction, since he had filed a declaration of prejudice against two of the oidores and the acting fiscal and had appealed all his litigations to the Council of the Indies. Secondly, without legal assistance he was unable to defend himself adequately. This maneuver was clearly illegal. The Council of the Indies never exercised original jurisdiction but only appellate jurisdiction in questions of law, not of fact, and all under rigidly prescribed conditions which Niebla ignored. The audiencia ordered him to answer the indictment. Eventually Niebla complied reluctantly.

He maintained that he was personally blameless even though his colleagues were often offended by his words. His words and actions were motivated not by any personal animus against the individuals toward whom they were directed but solely by his zeal to preserve the general welfare of the commonwealth. He made a flat denial of all charges involving mistreatment of his servants. He portrayed himself as having been a loyal subject of the king in the sales tax disturbances of 1593, which had resulted in his being exiled and fined. Diego de Niebla vigorously denied that he had abused his right to seek redress of grievances through the courts. He also repudiated the charge that he had incited others to make charges against officials undergoing the residencias.

Admitting his lack of a formal education, he insisted, contrary to the assertion of the acting fiscal, that his petitions to the magistrates were always respectful in tone and intent. He acknowledged that some may have lacked literary polish. At the conclusion of his reply to the fiscal's indictment, Niebla listed the names of dozens of citizens who were so prejudiced against him that they should be disqualified from the litigation. The list included virtually every major and minor officeholder in the capital.

On April 7, 1620, the audiencia confirmed the original sentence which provided that Diego de Niebla be deprived of the office of chief constable of the city of Quito without compensation, fined 2,000 pesos, and exiled for six years to Chile.[34]

While the original verdict was on appeal, Niebla took the offensive once again against his wife. He brought criminal action accusing her of having committed adultery with several leading citizens. The audiencia eventually cleared doña Ana, but only after she had spent a brief sojourn in jail.[35]

It is clear that the oidores had lost patience with Diego de Niebla when they handed down that stiff sentence. Yet their severe action was not totally groundless or arbitrary. Niebla's endless suits threatened to paralyze the wheels of justice, since the volume of his business alone was consuming a good deal of the court's time. Niebla had managed to alienate almost everyone of prominence in the community. The legal actions undertaken against his estranged wife, his passion to engage in law suits, and the perversity with which he prolonged his litigations all suggest that he had become unbalanced and reckless.

Diego de Niebla was resourceful and tireless in his grim determination to protect what he considered were his rights. As early as March 4, 1617, he had arrived at the conclusion that he could more effectively attack his enemies by appealing to the Council of the Indies to send a visitor general to Quito.[36] The Council of the Indies cautiously responded to these charges of venality and maladministration on November 1, 1619, when the king sent instructions to Dr. Morga. The president was to call Niebla into his private office to inform him in strict confidence that for the present there would be no visita general. But Niebla was given the option of becoming an accuser and a denouncer, i.e., a *delator* and a *capitulante,* with the right to make documented charges of misconduct against any official in the kingdom, provided that he would post bond in case these charges proved calumnious.

The crown usually granted this privilege upon the request of a private citizen. The posting of bond was meant to discourage slanderous attacks against the magistrates. By the time this royal cedula had reached Quito in August of 1620, the audiencia had already pronounced sentence. Dr. Morga obeyed the instructions. In the president's private office, Diego de Niebla, then an inmate of the royal jail, reaffirmed to the president his belief that the charges contained in his letters to the king were truthful. He declined, however, the opportunity of becoming an accuser.[37] He would have to post bond. He had already denied having the 2,000 pesos to pay the fine imposed by the audiencia. Hence his financial credit in the community was nil.

Shortly afterward Diego de Niebla under armed escort left Quito for Lima, where that audiencia received instructions from Quito to dispatch the prisoner to Chile to serve his sentence of exile. Misfortune aplenty occurred to Diego de Niebla, much of it of his own making, but he did manage to evade the penal colony in Chile. He persuaded the audiencia in Lima not to send him to Chile by citing the cedula granting him the opportunity of becoming an accuser.[38] The decision of the audiencia in Lima was based on the knowledge that the king had decided to send a visitor general to Quito. Lic. Mañozca in fact invited Diego de Niebla to return to Quito. His role in the visita general was inconsequential.

Although Niebla's accusation of corruption and maladministration was the first such charge to arouse the suspicions of the Council of the Indies, his personal claims never were vindicated. Dr. Morga sent a lengthy justification of the audiencia's conduct. After due deliberation, the council found no fault with their resolution of the matter.[39] Neither did the two visitors, the first of whom was decidedly unfriendly to the Morga administration and partial to its enemies.

Diego de Niebla, the self-made man and rich grocer who bought his way into upper-class officialdom, had abused the countless opportunities that the cumbersome machinery of Spanish justice provided.

There is a familiar observation that the measure of any civilization is the way it treats its criminals. Traditionally, criminal law enforcement has been assessed by the style and manner of its physical implementation. Coercion, invasion of privacy, and police lawlessness have aroused the most vehement criticisms of the criminal trial process.[40] On these scores the Spanish-American system left something to be desired by modern standards, but in the context of the seventeenth century, the procedures were probably no better and no worse than those in the other Roman law countries of western Europe.

There was, of course, no equality before the law. The individual was not the common denominator of society. The rights, the privileges, and the obligations of each person came from the functional corporations and the estate to which he belonged. And there were built-in inequalities between those corporations and estates. The social status of a culprit influenced the nature of his punishment.

Between members of the same corporation there was some equality. The vast majority of disputes were settled inside the corporate jurisdictions without recourse to the secular courts. The Church, for example, operated its own courts which exercised exclusive jurisdiction over those of clerical rank. Marriage, too, was regulated by the ecclesiastical tribunals. The functional economic corporations also operated their own tribunals to solve disputes relating to the exercise of their respective professions and trades. The primary purpose of the secular courts on the municipal, provincial, and audiencia levels was to adjudicate disputes and crimes involving members of different corporations and estates, where, of course, legal inequalities prevailed. The most equalitarian feature of the whole system was that the members of every corporation and estate had free access to the courts in order to protect what they thought were their privileges and obligations, however substantial or modest those rights might be.

The Indians, for example, who were regarded as legal minors, were encouraged to have recourse to the courts. For those who did not speak Spanish, the courts provided and paid for interpreters. And indigents could secure gratis the services of the *abogado de pobres,* whom the audiencia appointed and whose modest salary came from court fines.[41] Obviously the rich, who could afford their own counsel, probably received better treatment before the bench, but no one in seventeenth-century Spanish America had any illusion that he was living in an equalitarian society.

The United States, which prides itself that it is equalitarian, has only recently begun to recognize that it has an inherently unequal double standard of law enforcement for the rich and the poor. In a series of decisions since 1956, the United States Supreme Court has sought to correct this situation. The doctrine underlying these decisions was pithily summarized by Justice Hugo Black when he observed, "There can be no equal justice where the kind of trial a man gets depends upon the amount of money he has."[42] The Spaniards never pretended to provide equal justice, but they did make meaningful efforts to grant access to the courts to everyone.

Although it is traditionally assumed that Roman law established its unquestioned supremacy in Castile between Alfonso the Learned and Ferdinand and Isabella, its triumph was something less than complete. Originally designed for a society whose common denominator was the individual citizen, it became the vehicle for protecting corporate privileges in the Iberian peninsula.

Richard Morse captured the essence of this distinction when he wrote:

The *Partidas* [the *Siete Partidas*, the basic Roman law code drawn up *circa* 1260 and promulgated in Castile in 1348] assumed the nuclear element of society to be, not the Lockean atomistic man, but religious, societal man: man with a salvable soul (i.e., in relationship with God) and man in a station of life, i.e., having mutual obligations with fellow humans determinable by principles of Christian justice.[43]

The judicial machinery, with its slow-moving procedures but with some real if not always effective safeguards to protect the rights of litigants, obviously encouraged the litigiousness that became a salient characteristic of colonial society. For that matter, the whole bureaucratic administration with its vast network of checks and balances tended to create bitter personal animosities among both the magistrates and the subjects alike. Nowhere can we find a better documented insight into the character and the depth of factionalism than in the origins and the development of a visita general, the major theme of the rest of this study.

10.

THE COMING OF THE VISITA GENERAL—
THE GATHERING STORM

If the "I obey but do not execute" formula provided magistrates in the Indies with some measure of freedom to maneuver between the pressures created by the central authorities and local conditions, two other administrative devices, the residencia and the visita general, made these same officers sensitive to the wishes of their superiors in the peninsula. Historians have argued at some length about the differences between the two. Significant though they were, the contrasts were sometimes blurred. Both devices, however, had a common purpose. Each served as an agency of royal control over subordinates. Both provided subjects with periodic opportunities to seek redress of grievances, alleged or real, against magistrates.

The residencia was statutory. It was a judicial review of the conduct of a magistrate at the end of his term in office. All civil appointees of the crown were obliged to reside—hence the term *residencia*—in their districts for sixty days after leaving office. During this period a specially designated residencia judge, a *juez de residencia,* conducted a public court of inquiry in which he heard all charges of malfeasance against the former incumbent. After hearing the evidence presented by anyone in the district, the judge drew up a list of charges, *cargos,* together with the names of the accusers, which he presented to the ex-magistrate. The cargos were a kind of indictment. When he had heard the defense, the judge weighed the evidence and passed sentence. Dismissal from further officeholding, heavy fines, confiscation of property, and even imprisonment were possible sentences in cases of grave misconduct. The fact that sentences were often reversed or altered by the Council of the Indies on appeal does suggest that verdicts sometimes reflected the personal bias of the judges or that an official under investigation was able to bring to bear a commanding influence at Court.

As a measure to expose graft, personal immorality, maladministration of justice, or political ineptitude, the residencia left a good deal to be desired. One of its major weaknesses was that the residencia of a president or an oidor was usually conducted by that magistrate's replacement. In judging his predecessor, the successor tended to be lenient. Not only were both the judge and the judged colleagues in the same bureaucratic system where there was a certain esprit de corps, but also the judge was aware that sometime later his incumbency would be reviewed by another colleague.

This same defect became even more glaring in the residencias of the corregidores in the provinces. Massive corruption received only token punishments in the form of light fines. As we had occasion to observe in Chapter 7, the venality in the provincial layer of the bureaucracy may be traced back to the grossly unprofessional character of that service and the inadequate salary level. The residencia proved a frail instrument indeed for correcting abuses.

The visita general sought to compensate for some of the deficiencies of the residencia. The model of the civil visita was the episcopal visita of the Middle Ages, whose procedures and aims received their final codification at the Council of Trent. The historical origins of both the residencia and the visita general go back to the *Siete Partidas* of Alfonso the Learned. In the peninsula, oidores of the audiencias were not subject to residencias when they received transfers, but they were included in the periodic visitas generales.

In contrast to the residencia, which was an investigation of the conduct of a particular magistrate at the end of his term of office, the visita general applied to a whole body of magistrates, usually embracing the whole audiencia and the exchequer officials. Very infrequently did the visita general extend to provincial and municipal officials, all of whom, however, were subject to the residencia. The visita general could occur at any time. Although those being "visited" remained in office, the visitor general had discretionary authority to suspend from office any magistrate who impeded the work of the inquiry. Since magistrates under investigation usually remained in office, procedures existed to protect the anonymity of witnesses who testified against the incumbents. The content of hostile testimony was revealed to those being investigated in order to enable them to respond in their own defense, but the names of witnesses were never made known. All the proceedings of a residencia were public. Those of a visita general took place in utmost secrecy behind closed doors.

In contrast to the residencia, which had a statutory time limit of sixty days, the visita general had no fixed time span. Visitas usually lasted for a minimum of two years. Sometimes they dragged on for decades without ever being completed. The visita general in Quito began in 1624 and ended in 1637. In Mexico a similar inquiry lasted fourteen years, from 1640 to 1654, in Bogotá from 1630 to 1637, and in Lima from 1625 to 1638. The visita general in Charcas dragged on for twenty years.

Not only was a visita general of indeterminate duration, but those subject to its jurisdiction were held responsible for their present as well as their past actions. A visitor general usually received authority to investigate all actions of the audiencia from the end of the last visita general until the date he completed his findings. A residencia, on the other hand, concerned the past, since the official undergoing it no longer held office.

A visita general was expensive. The visitor general and his staff collected handsome salaries, far in excess of what ordinary magistrates received. Lic. Mañozca, for example, received 3,600 ducats per year in addition to his regular salary of 2,000 ducats as inquisitor of Lima.[1] In fact the three-year Mañozca mission cost the royal treasury 66,878 pesos.[2] The bishop of Puebla, Juan de Palafox y Mendoza, spent 32,000 pesos during the visita general in Mexico (1640–42).[3] Although the crown ideally hoped to pay for the heavy expenses of a visita general through the collection of fines, those revenues in practice often fell far short of the expenses of the visitas.

The salaries of those conducting the visita general were high in order to attract men of ability for these arduous assignments. A visita general, which usually engendered turmoil and conflict, was a purgatory for everyone involved. The munificent salary in itself was not sufficient. The Council of the Indies often had to entice an unwilling candidate by offering him a promotion as well.

In contrast to the residencia, the visitor general did not pass sentence. He heard complaints, he collected evidence, and then he allowed the visited to defend themselves. From these, the visitor general drew up a list of charges with the evidence attached. This material he forwarded to Spain. The king and the Council of the Indies then passed the only and final sentence from which there was no appeal.

The visita general was an extraordinary measure invoked when the authorities in Madrid were dissatisfied with conditions in an overseas kingdom. Only the king, after consultation with the council, could order a visita general, whereas a residencia was an automatic procedure when a magistrate left office. Between 1524 and 1700 there were sixty to seventy visitas generales.[4] Approximately one thousand residencias of superior magistrates occurred during that time.

Under the Habsburgs, a visita general was more apt to take place if complaints of malfeasance acquired increasing volume and if that particular audiencia had not been visited for two decades or so. During the reign of Philip II (1555–98), a visita general tended to be a rather orderly and sedate judicial inquiry completed within a few years. During the reign of his grandson, Philip IV, a visita general might drag on for decades while the administrative machinery was thrown into turmoil. Acrimonious conflict was frequent between the visitors and the visited and between those who defended and those who opposed the incumbents. During the reigns of the Bourbon kings in the eighteenth century, the visita general took on a more positive and dynamic role. Instead of being merely an instrument to expose and punish misconduct of officials overseas, the crown used the visita as a reforming instrument to impose a new set of policies. The most successful example of this dynamic role of the visita general was the mission of José de Gálvez to New Spain (1765–71). A dramatic failure was the visita general of Peru conducted by José Antonio de Areche in the late 1770's.[5]

The graft-ridden and do-nothing government of Philip III (1598–1621) obviously neglected to use the visita general as an instrument to expose corruption and maladministration. During those two decades, the viceroyalty of Peru received only two visitas, one in Charcas in 1604 and another in Bogotá in 1610. Only one took place in Mexico, with Lic. Diego de Landeras y Velasco as visitor general (1606–09).[6] The visita general became a major instrument of policy, however, in the succeeding reign of Philip IV.

On March 31, 1621, surrounded by a host of relics of saints, the melancholy and morbidly religious Philip III died, leaving all his crowns to his 16-year-old son, Philip IV. A sensual debauchee but not lacking in political intelligence, Philip IV spent more time on affairs of state than has been traditionally assumed. His outstanding weakness was a certain lack of self-confidence which made him lean on someone of stronger will. The Count-Duke of Olivares with his driving energy and his fixity of purpose was that man. From 1621 until 1643, Gaspar de Guzmán (1587–1645), Count of Olivares by inheritance and Duke of Sanlúcar la Mayor by favor of the king, held an almost hypnotic sway over the well-intentioned but weak-willed monarch.

Olivares contrasts sharply with the favorites of the preceding reign, the Dukes of Lerma and Uceda, whose overriding concern was the enrichment of their family. Power, not wealth, provided the fuel for the almost limitless ambition of Olivares. He was driven by a bitter resentment over the failure of his father to win the coveted rank of grandee from Philip II. The father had served that monarch as ambassador to the Papal court and later as viceroy of Naples and Sicily. The finest horseman in Spain, Olivares treated men as he treated his big-boned chargers, breaking them to obedience by force of will and persistence. A sharp foil to the lazy, courtly, and conciliatory Duke of Lerma, the count-duke was tireless, vehement, and arrogant. He was impatient even with the lazy king upon whom his power squarely rested. Intolerant of criticism and given to wild fits of rage, he alienated the independent-minded and increasingly surrounded himself with sycophants. The masterful portraits of Velázquez reveal him as a large, thick-set man with a square head and brilliant black eyes, long moustaches upturned, a broad chin, and a beard bristling with arrogance and authority. This man was born to rule or to be destroyed in the attempt.

Behind the façade of arrogance and vitality so well depicted in the portrait by Velázquez reproduced in the illustration section, mental and physical disorders began to sap Olivares' energies. The late Gregorio Marañón in his classic biography of the count-duke, which he aptly subtitled la pasión de mandar, describes the personality of the great minister as that of a manic depressive. Periods of inactivity and depression followed outbursts of furious energy and dynamic action. This cycle of behavior intensified in the 1630's as reverses at home and abroad eventually culminated in his fall from power in 1643. He died shortly afterward in Toro in a fit of violent madness, the victim of his manic-depressive temperament and the ravages of syphilis.

In contrast to his immediate predecessors, he had a policy. The monarchy ceased to drift. His foreign policy was an immediate inheritance from his predecessor, the Duke of Uceda, and an ultimate legacy from Charles V. In the last days of Philip III, Uceda plunged the Spains into the Thirty

Years' War on the side of the Austrian Habsburg emperor. This action made war with the Dutch inevitable when the twelve-year truce expired in 1621. The Spanish monarchy found itself committed to a war in central Europe on the side of the Austrian branch of the Habsburg dynasty against the Protestant forces in Germany, Holland, Sweden, and eventually France. Thus not only did the Court at Madrid contest for political domination in central Europe but also the Iberian powers found themselves involved in an equally significant conflict with the Dutch over the destiny of the tropical world.

Olivares was the heir of the tragic legacy of Charles V, who converted the Iberian kingdoms into the vehicle for imposing Habsburg domination over northern and central Europe. Such a goal might have served the dynastic and all-European interests of the Habsburgs, but it did in fact exhaust the resources of the Iberian states. The national interests of Castile and Aragón would have been better served by concentrating on North Africa and the tropical world.

Richelieu, whose foreign policy was also an inheritance from Francis I, Henry II, and Henry IV, saw the involvement of the Spains in northern and central Europe as a splendid opportunity to replace the hegemony of the Austro-Spanish Habsburgs with that of France. The impressive Spanish victories at Höchst, Fleurus, and Nördlingen gave way to a series of Spanish defeats, culminating in Europe at Rocroi and in the tropical world with the overthrow of the Iberian monopoly, which reduced the Spanish Habsburg monarchy to a second-class power by 1659.

In the early 1620's, Olivares was not deceived by the glitter of the façade of imperial Spain. Realistically assessing that the monarchy was far weaker than it appeared, he proposed a series of drastic and energetic measures to revitalize the government. The objectives of Olivares in northern and central Europe, the Iberian peninsula, and the Indies formed interdependent components of a larger whole. While attention will be focused largely on the New World, the Iberian and the European aspects of his policy deserve some attention, if only cursory.

In Chapter 7 his vigorous efforts to wipe out corruption and to replace ostentatious living with frugality and simplicity were mentioned. In the Iberian peninsula his aim was centralization, in short, to replace the Spains with Spain. Convinced that the greatness of the French monarchy lay in its centralization and that Castile was bearing a greater share of the tax burden than the outlying kingdoms of Portugal, Biscaya, Barcelona, and Valencia, he sought to create, for the whole peninsula, a centralized administration responsible to one monarch. In the place of six cortes, he wanted one. Above all else, his purpose was to impose a uniform tax policy on all the kingdoms. Olivares was no mere Castilian extremist. While he advocated that the laws for the whole peninsula should conform to those of Castile and that the tax burden should be equalized, he was also a partisan of breaking the Castilian monopoly of officeholding. As John H. Elliott has already suggested, the count-duke was groping toward some wider concept of Spanish nationality.[7]

The hispanization of the outlying kingdoms of the peninsula, which still retained a considerable amount of administrative autonomy, encountered increasing opposition. Not only did Olivares seek to trim the power of the cortes, but also he sought to circumvent the slow-moving councils by setting up smaller juntas which could act more rapidly. His ruthless and tactless methods, the strength of local particularism, and the pressure placed on the weakening economy by the ruinous costs of the wars in Europe and in the tropical world led to a series of revolts in the Basque country, Catalonia, Portugal, and the Sicilies. This quickening chain of disasters finally drove Philip IV to dismiss the count-duke in January, 1643.

The aims of Olivares in the Old World are better known than his objectives in the New World. His purpose in the colonies was not so much the negative one of eliminating corruption as it was the positive goal, like that for the peninsular kingdoms, of reasserting centralized control from Madrid over the whole colonial administration. Olivares saw corruption and venality as a consequence of the weakening of centralized control during the reign of Philip III. A revitalized colonial bureaucracy, more responsive to the wishes of the king and hence less prone to graft, would provide Spain with the wealth to pursue her grandiose objectives in Europe. The count-duke referred to the kingdoms of the Indies as *el imperio de las Indias*. Seldom used in those times, this term epitomized in a later age the Bourbon urge toward creating a unitary state. Olivares also called these kingdoms "colonies," another characteristic eighteenth-century attitude. Olivares' desire to "defederalize" the Habsburg monarchy makes him appear as a precursor of the Bourbons.[8] Thus the domestic, European, and American objectives of Olivares' policy are closely interdependent.

Within a few months after succeeding to power, Olivares assumed the initiative by proposing a visita general of the four major audiencias of the viceroyalty of Peru. Although as early as September 25, 1621, the king and the Council of the Indies had reached tentative agreement on the choice of personnel, opposition to the impending visita general gathered inside the council.

The council submitted a consulta on April 1, 1622, in which the councilors apparently raised some objections to the proposed visita general. The text has disappeared.[9] It is not clear whether the council recommended that the visita general be postponed or abandoned or drastically modified. Internal evidence from the subsequent consulta of July 1 suggests that the council recommended merely a delay on the grounds that the heavy expense to the royal treasury would be justified only after all the complaints emanating from the four audiencias had been carefully evaluated. The council was cautious for several reasons. They were appointees of the late king, and they had been in office for some time. Newly arrived to power, the vigorous and ambitious Count-Duke of Olivares must have struck the seasoned and conservative bureaucrats in the council as brash. The consulta of April 1 was a successful delaying action on the part of the council. A few days later in April, 1622, Philip IV ordered the suspension of the visita general until further notice.[10]

Olivares could not be thwarted that easily. He sent the council a fat dossier of complaints about the administration of the audiencia of Lima. When the council did not act swiftly, Olivares, in the name of the monarch, expressed his impatience and displeasure.[11] A few days later on July 1, 1622, the council did recommend that the proposed visita general be reactivated.[12] It was not that they opposed a visita general in principle, but they suspected that Olivares was being too impetuous in resorting to that extraordinary procedure without first weighing the need carefully. Experience had taught the council that a visita general was not a panacea which would cure misgovernment and graft. The consulta on July 1, 1622, pointed out that none of these audiencias had been visited for several years. The last visita to Lima had been twenty-eight years earlier, Charcas eighteen years earlier, Quito twenty-seven years, and Bogotá twelve years. The multitude of complaints against the incumbents suggested the need for an impartial investigation.

The majority of the council recommended that the four visitas be dispatched immediately and simultaneously. One member of the council, Lic. Francisco Manso y Cúñiga, dissented from the majority recommendation. While recognizing the need for a visita general in all four audiencias, he suggested that two visitas be postponed until the first two had been completed. Lima and Quito should have priority. Neither audiencia had been visited for over twenty years. The complaints against the magistrates of those two capitals were far more serious than those coming from either Bogotá or Charcas, which had both undergone visitas more recently. He added that the burden on the treasury would be stretched over a longer period.

The count-duke accepted this aspect of the minority report of Lic. Manso y Cúñiga. The visitas began in Quito and Lima in 1624 and 1625 respectively, whereas similar missions did not arrive in Bogotá and Charcas until 1630 and 1634 respectively.

A good deal of the minority report of Lic. Manso y Cúñiga dealt with his recommendation that Dr. Juan Gutiérrez Flores not be given the Lima assignment on the grounds that his affiliation with the Inquisition in Mexico did not give him the necessary stature and experience to conduct an investigation of the most prestigious audiencia in the Indies. Councilor Manso y Cúñiga was tactlessly adamant that the Lima assignment should go to one of the oidores in the audiencias of Valladolid or Granada, whose ability and qualifications were better known to the council.

Olivares curtly dismissed that part of the recommendation. Shortly afterward, the whole council received a reprimand from the king instructing them to submit their conclusions in brief form and to exclude lengthy justifications of how they reached them.[13] The handling of the consulta on July 1, 1622, by the count-duke was designed to teach the council who enjoyed the royal confidence. The king rejected the majority report, which recommended simultaneous visitas generales of the four audiencias, in favor of the minority report suggesting that only two visitas be conducted at a time; yet the author of the adopted minority report received a terse reprimand for his recommendation about personnel. In this manner both the majority and the minority in the council were firmly informed that the new, all-powerful royal favorite intended to select what recommendations the crown accepted from the council.

Among his many other roles in Spanish history, the Count-Duke of Olivares was a reformer of the colonial bureaucracy. During the 1620's, his reforming energies had not yet been sapped by the military reverses of the 1630's.[14] There was a basic disagreement between Olivares and the council as to the purposes of the visita general. The count-duke saw the visita general partly as a means to impose new centralizing policies, thus foreshadowing to some extent the later dynamic usage of the visita general by Charles III. The Council of the Indies, on the other hand, had the pessimism of experience and regarded the visita general merely as a vehicle to punish venality and misgovernment. During the 1620's, the restlessly optimistic count-duke and the wise and wary council engaged in a dialogue about the purposes of the visita general.

Events in the 1620's seemed to justify the reservations of the council. The two visitas generales of Lima and Quito proved disappointing. They did expose many abuses but at the heavy price of throwing the two audiencias into turmoil and bitter factionalism. The visita general in Charcas provoked endless strife.

The restless energies of the count-duke turned again to reform of the bureaucracy when, in June, 1627, he submitted in the king's name a sweeping series of proposals. Among the recommendations were that no oidor could serve in one post for more than a period of five or six years; that the property of any magistrate would be confiscated if the size of his estate were in gross disparity with his salary; that no magistrate would be allowed to marry a woman who resided in any kingdom in the Indies. Lastly Olivares advocated that a visita general of each audiencia be conducted every five years.[15]

These proposals were designed to implement the traditional objectives of the colonial administration by promoting disinterested government and eliminating graft. Inspiring the proposal for a statutory visita general was Olivares' desire to strengthen the centralizing control from Spain over the Indies, thus complementing his similar objective in the Iberian peninsula itself. The destruction of his personal papers makes it impossible to determine how privately committed he was to carrying out this program.[16] It could be that he deliberately framed his proposals in Draconian terms to shock the council into formulating some serious counterproposals.

After due deliberation, the council submitted a consulta to the monarch in which they carefully weighed the relative advantages and disadvantages of the Olivares program. The general tenor of their reply clearly indicates that they regarded the cure as worse than the disease. They pointed out that a five-year term for oidores would undermine the authority and prestige of the audiencias as institutions, which they described as *verdaderos presidios*, for maintaining royal authority overseas. Not only would a fixed term tend to attract men of lesser ability, but also automatic transfers would undercut the morale of the professional bureaucracy, because oidores would have to be shifted from superior to inferior audiencias. The council strongly recommended continuation of its traditional practice of promoting oidores from the inferior to the superior to the viceregal audiencias. A seat in the audiencia of Lima or Mexico must be held out as an incentive to the magistrate serving in a less prestigious and less desirable post.

If implemented, the Olivares proposal would have made the oidores more disinterested and hence less prone to graft and factionalism. As we observed in Chapters 6 and 7, the fact that oidores served in the same posts for periods much longer than five years made it increasingly difficult for them to fill

Dr. Antonio de Morga, president of the royal audiencia of Quito, as a young man. From a portrait at the University of Osuna.

Lic. Juan de Mañozca, inquisitor in Cartagena and Lima, visitor-general of the audiencia of Quito, and archbishop of Mexico. From a portrait in the Cathedral of Mexico City.

...ms of the city of Quito,
...anted by the Emperor
...arles V.

A present-day view of the presidential palace, Quito, seat of the royal audiencia from July 3, 1612, onward.

Zambo chieftains of Esmeraldas (1599). Courtesy of the Museo de América, Madrid.

The Count-Duke of Olivares, by Diego de Velázquez. Courtesy of the Museo del Prado, Madrid.

Philip IV, King of the Spains and the Indies, by Diego de Velázquez.
Courtesy of the Metropolitan Museum of Art (New York), Bequest of
Benjamin Altman, 1913.

Prince Baltasar Carlos, by Diego de Velázquez. Courtesy of the Museo del Prado, Madrid.

The Prince of Esquilache, viceroy of Peru, 1615–21. From a portrait in the Museo de la Historia, Lima.

The Marquis of Guadalcázar, viceroy of Peru, 1621–29. From a portrait in the Museo de la Historia, Lima.

The Count of Chinchón, viceroy of Peru, 1629–39. From
a portrait in the Museo de la
Historia, Lima.

Dr. Francisco de Sotomayor, bishop of Quito, 1623–28. From a portrait in the Cathedral of Quito.

Saint Mariana de Jesús, with her pupils. From a painting in the Carmelite Convent, in Quito. Courtesy of Frances Parkinson Keyes.

Façade, San Francisco. Courtesy of George Kubler.

Façade, La Compañía. Courtesy of George Kubler.

the role of disinterested Platonic guardians, as envisaged in royal legislation. Olivares, however, failed to face squarely the major weakness of the whole system of colonial administration, which was, of course, the inadequate salary scale.

The council also expressed misgivings about Olivares' proposal providing for the confiscation of estates which exceeded a certain value. They pointed out that any set ceiling would be arbitrary, in that the value of property varied considerably from region to region. Secondly, they mentioned that such an arrangement would discriminate in favor of those who spent their illicit gains and against those who did not. The council recommended the re-issuing of the cedulas prohibiting oidores from acquiring real estate or engaging in commerce. In order to tighten the existing regulations, the council urged that all magistrates be required to file upon their departure for the Indies and after their return to Spain a notarized inventory of their estates.

The council recognized that the visita general could be an instrument for correcting abuses, but they opposed Olivares' suggestion that each audiencia be visited every five years. They cited the heavy expenses to the treasury. Furthermore, all concerned at Court were painfully aware of the bitter strife that the visita general was engendering in Quito at that very time. The council urged the sovereign to reserve the visita general as an extraordinary measure to be invoked only periodically when conditions in a particular kingdom seemed to merit such a step.

Olivares accepted the counterproposals of the council in their totality. On December 2, 1627, the royal cedulas were issued.[17] Whatever may have been the intent of the original proposals of Olivares, in practice they would have been arbitrary and perhaps unworkable. The councilors skillfully but tactfully pointed out these defects to their own advantage. Why Olivares, who was never noted for his reasonableness, accepted the moderate if not conservative advice of the council is a matter of conjecture. His responsibilities were all-embracing, extending from affairs of state to arranging the endless nocturnal entertainments for the pleasure-loving Philip IV. Hence reforming the colonial bureaucracy was toward the bottom of his priority list. And he expended his energy erratically, oscillating between bursts of activity and inactivity. Yet Olivares should be recognized for what he was—a serious if somewhat overzealous and amateurish reformer of the colonial bureaucracy.

The dialogue between the council and the count-duke, the eternal debate between the experts and the activist, throws some light on the inner relationships between the crown and the Council of the Indies. In theory the crown was the source of all decision-making, with the council serving merely in an advisory capacity. In practice the authority of the council was far greater than that and in many cases decisive. During the time of Philip II, who completed his father's work of structuring the imperial administration, the relationship between the crown and the council was in dynamic equilibrium. The king diligently pored over the reports submitted to him by the council and the authorities in the Indies. Indeed, his major defects were the habit of allowing himself to get too deeply involved in minutiae and a tendency to procrastinate. Although the first bureaucratic king of modern times, Philip II never learned how to delegate authority and when to intervene. He reposed confidence in less than a handful of close advisers. His innately distrustful nature prompted him to fashion the elaborate system of checks and balances that was a characteristic feature of the Spanish administration. Yet for all his defects, the hard-working and conscientious Philip II was an effective partner with the council.

During the reign of his son, Philip III, the balance between the crown and the council broke down. Faced with a do-nothing king and venal favorites, the council had to exert authority. It managed to protect the colonial administration from the greedy grasp of the family of the Duke of Lerma. The council did a remarkable job, but there was something lacking. Able, conscientious, and experienced though the councilors were, they tended to be excessively cautious and prudent. They needed to be prodded and challenged by the king or by a single minister in whom he reposed confidence. Above all else, they needed to be pushed into re-examining their basic policies, which in their minds had become sanctified by precedent and long practice.

During the 1620's, the Count-Duke of Olivares restored some of the balance between the crown and the council. His brash aggressiveness was just what the conscientious but conservative council needed. Olivares and the council worked together creatively in the 1620's, with the count-duke asking the questions and the council providing serious answers. This equilibrium disappeared in the 1630's as the reforming energies of the frustrated Olivares dissipated themselves. In fact, the balance was not restored until the eighteenth century, when the Bourbon dynasty brought new vitality into monarchical leadership.

Olivares' goal of promoting more centralized control also applied to the viceroyalty of Mexico, although there he chose to employ a different method from that used in the other viceroyalty. Rather than sending a visitor general, the count-duke appointed the Marquis of Gelves as the new viceroy of

Mexico. Zealous reformer he was, but the marquis lacked political skill. He was as tactless as Olivares himself was, and he alienated every significant group in the community. Rather than restoring effective government after the easy-going Marquis of Guadalcázar (1612–21), Gelves' administration ended up in the bloody riot of January 15, 1624. The mobs sacked and burned the viceregal palace, and the viceroy himself sought refuge in the Franciscan convent.[18] Thus, Olivares' attempts to restore more effective centralized control over the viceroyalty of Mexico proved as abortive as were his efforts in Peru. But he did try.

Up to this point, attention has been focused on the Madrid-oriented factors which contributed to the king's decision to send visitas generales to the four audiencias in the viceroyalty of Peru. However, local conditions were also influential, for between central and local conditions there was a subtle and at times elusive interplay, without which the visita general to the audiencia of Quito, in particular, would not have occurred when it did.

As long as Philip III lived, and he was only 43 at his death in 1621, Dr. Morga was largely immune from serious reprisals from the Court. Morga himself was a protégé of the Duke of Uceda, who in 1618 had replaced his father as the head of affairs. Like his father, the new *privado* had no interest in reforms. But the Council of the Indies was concerned. Complaints against the Morga administration began to trickle into the council. Evidence began to mount that there might be something rotten in the kingdom of Quito.

The unfortunate Diego de Niebla, whose endless difficulties with the audiencia were recounted in the last chapter, was the first to make charges of corruption and misgovernment. His particular targets of criticism were Oidores Diego de Zorrilla and Matías de Peralta. Niebla urged a visita general, pointing out that the last one had taken place nearly thirty years earlier. The cautious reply of the council was that Diego de Niebla should be given the option of becoming an accuser, but he declined the invitation by refusing to post bond.

Increasing factionalism among the oidores themselves seemed to lend substance to the charges of Niebla. It began to appear to Madrid as if Dr. Morga was unable to maintain order and control over his colleagues on the bench. Heated controversy raged around two oidores, Diego de Zorrilla and Manuel Tello de Velasco. Both cases merit careful examination.

The acknowledged mistress of Oidor Zorrilla was doña Thomasina de Esquivel, the wife of Lic. Francisco Rodríquez Plaza, a licensed advocate and twice appointed by the audiencia as fiscal *ad interim*. A dedicated Don Juan himself though more discreet in his public conduct, President Morga assumed the delicate assignment of trying to persuade his colleague to discard his mistress of many years.[19] Whether because of Morga's persuasions or other considerations, Lic. Zorrilla suddenly married the very recent widow of a fellow oidor, Lic. Antonio de Villareal y Leuía, who had died in Quito en route from his post in Bogotá to a new assignment in Lima.

A serious question arose as to whether this marriage violated the cedulas which provided that a magistrate must secure the prior consent of the king. Lic. Zorrilla had not requested royal approval, contenting himself merely with seeking the permission of the bishop.[20] A second possible violation revolved around the residence of the new wife of the oidor, doña Catalina de Hospina y Medinilla. Lic. Zorrilla claimed that she did not qualify as a resident of Quito in that she and her first husband were transients in Quito en route from Bogotá to Lima when her first husband suddenly died. This was a plausible argument as far as it went. Since her first husband's estate came under the probate jurisdiction of the audiencia in Quito, where the will was contested, a clearcut conflict of interests arose.

Dr. Morga appealed to the viceroy in Lima for specific instructions. The viceroy admitted that Lic. Zorrilla had some justification in claiming that his bride was not a resident of the kingdom of Quito, but he added that the magistrate had violated the law by failing to secure the prior permission of the king. On the conflict of interests issue the viceroy showed no hesitation. He ordered Oidor Zorrilla not to sit in judgment on any litigation before the audiencia involving the estate of the first husband of his new wife.[21]

The instructions from Lima proved superfluous, for within a few months after marrying, Oidor Zorrilla died suddenly. But the pot continued to boil. The little community of Quito was shocked when the widow of Lic. Zorrilla brought charges before the audiencia claiming that her husband's sudden death was caused by sorcery and witchcraft practiced by doña Thomasina de Esquivel, his rejected mistress.[22]

The efforts of Dr. Morga to break up the liaison between Oidor Zorrilla and Lic. Plaza's wife embittered the relations between Zorrilla and the president and also the relations between the president and Oidor Matías de Peralta. Peralta, who had arrived in Quito at about the same time as Zorrilla, was Zorrilla's close friend. They publicly demonstrated their displeasure in the spring of 1620 when the new fiscal of the audiencia, Lic. Melchor Suárez de Poago, formally took possession of his office. The standard ceremonial was for a new magistrate to pay a protocol visit to the president in his official residence before retiring to his own lodgings. Oidores Zorrilla and Peralta met Suárez de Poago at the entrance to the city, where they sought to persuade him not to pay a courtesy call on the president, who was awaiting him, but to go directly to his lodgings. The new fiscal, a veteran of many bureaucratic contretemps in Cuba and Panama, was much too experienced to snub the president by such a gesture. The fiscal repaired directly to the casas reales. The two oidores publicly registered their ill-humor by refusing to enter the palace, while the fiscal exchanged social pleasantries inside with Dr. Morga.[23] Morga subsequently complained to the king. The council mildly reprimanded the oidores, reminding them to observe the customary courtesies with the president.[24]

In this corporate privileged society, questions of protocol assumed an importance that seems ludicrously exaggerated. Etiquette, however, was a reflection of status in society. These European-born bureaucrats were Europeans in quasi-exile to whom minor questions of social precedence, which at home might not have arisen at all, became in the Indies proverbial tempests. Similar incidents were not unknown even to the more placid Britishers in twentieth-century Africa. It is not surprising that such tempests were frequent in Spanish America, in view of the rigid hierarchal character of society and the more acute sense of "honor" among the Spaniards.

Dr. Morga's resentment toward his two colleagues revealed itself in a letter addressed to the council in which he accused them of indulging in wholesale graft on their recent tours as circuit judges. Since the president offered no supporting evidence, his charges were reckless if not unwise.[25] They would only serve to arouse the suspicions of the council about conditions in Quito.

Although the marital and extramarital relations of Oidor Zorrilla created genuine ill-feeling between the president and Oidores Zorrilla and Peralta, much of this bitterness disappeared after the sudden death of Zorrilla. Cordial relations between Peralta and his colleagues resumed. A much more significant legacy of the Zorrilla matter was the mortal hatred of Lic. Rodríquez Plaza toward Dr. Morga. He apparently became deeply embittered with the president over the latter's role in breaking up his wife's affair with Zorrilla. Only a few years before, Plaza had been on excellent terms with the magistrates, for twice the audiencia had appointed him fiscal *ad interim*. Lic. Rodríquez Plaza, who came to the Indies in 1588, was a would-be oidor who never quite made the grade. His ambition was frustrated for a variety of reasons. Among them were his lack of influential connections at Court, his conviction as a murderer in 1601, the mestizo background of his second wife, and her public liaison with Oidor Zorrilla. From 1620 on, he was a sworn enemy of the Morga administration.[26]

On April 25 and April 28, 1620, two letters were dispatched to the king, both of which were frontal attacks on Dr. Morga and his associates on the bench. The signatures on the letters were those of Juan García de Solís and Pedro de Espinosa Pacheco. Private individuals writing to the council customarily identified themselves, if only to establish the credibility of their testimony. However, in those letters neither correspondent identified himself.[27] This fact lends support to the contention of Dr. Morga and the fiscal that neither person existed. In all the mountainous correspondence of this period, the names of the two gentlemen in question never appeared again. Dr. Morga and the fiscal asserted that the real authors of the two letters were none other than Oidor Zorrilla and Lic. Rodríquez Plaza[28] and that they had invented fictitious names in order to protect themselves against reprisals. The Council of the Indies probably would have informed Dr. Morga about the contents of the letters and the names of the two correspondents. Since neither Zorrilla nor Rodríquez Plaza could anticipate that the letters would help provoke the visita general, although that was their purpose, they might have chosen to hide behind the cloak of fictitious names.

Dr. Morga and his colleagues had every reason to be concerned about the two letters, whoever their authors may have been. Diego de Niebla previously had made rather vague charges of corruption and maladministration against the audiencia as a whole. His target was not Dr. Morga so much as Oidores Zorrilla and Peralta. The García de Solís–Espinosa Pacheco letters, which were almost identical in wording, were much more damagingly specific. In the case of Dr. Morga, they cited chapter and verse of his misdeeds both real and invented. They cited the president's illegal importation of contraband silks in 1615 as well as the semi-public gambling house he maintained in his home. Few details were spared in describing his amorous adventures.

This is not the place to discuss the energetic countermeasures that Dr. Morga took against Lic. Plaza and his alleged confederates during the spring of 1624, when he ascribed the forthcoming visita general to the García de Solís–Espinosa Pacheco letters. Here it should be emphasized that those letters were in the hands of the Count-Duke of Olivares and the Council of the Indies in 1621 and 1622 when the decision to send a visita general hung precariously in the balance. A consideration of how significant a factor they were should be delayed until we explore the rising controversy that swirled around another oidor, Manuel Tello de Velasco.

Manuel Tello de Velasco arrived in Quito in 1618. Within a period of two years, he aroused the militant hostility of all his colleagues on the bench. Receiving his law degree from the University of Alcalá de Henares, he served in Seville on the staff of Luis Méndez de Haro y Sotomayor, Marquis of Carpio.[29] This powerful nobleman, who was also a nephew of the Count-Duke of Olivares, ultimately became the chief minister of Philip IV in 1644. In addition to the support of the Marquis of Carpio, Tello de Velasco enjoyed the patronage of the hated but powerful Marquis of Siete Iglesias.[30] Tello de Velasco's appointment to the bench in Quito was typical in that it was due to a combination of professional qualifications and the patronage of the influential.

Given to extravagant display in his clothing and prone to make supercilious remarks about the noble lineage of his family in Spain, he surrounded himself with a large retinue of hangers-on when he appeared in public. What disturbed his colleagues was not so much his ostentatious style of living as his open friendships with litigants. His associates came to the conclusion that his judicial decisions were the result of caprice and ignorance, if not outright favoritism. Manuel Tello de Velasco's custom of keeping a notebook in which he recorded the peccadillos of his colleagues did nothing to close the widening breach between him and his associates.[31]

On April 15 and May 15, 1620, Dr. Morga wrote the Council of the Indies complaining in general terms about Oidor Manuel Tello de Velasco. He stressed his ostentatious manner, his illicit mercantile activities, his injudicious choice of friends, and the partiality of his decisions. He cited few specific examples of these general charges.[32]

In the face of any charge of misconduct, the instinctive response of the cautious council was to avoid hasty conclusions until all the evidence was carefully examined.[33] Just as the council initially suspended judgment on the accusations leveled against Dr. Morga, so it also held in abeyance the complaints of the president against Tello de Velasco. Dr. Morga received a curt but firm reprimand from the Council of the Indies on October 23, 1621. The council advised the president not to submit charges of such a general and unspecific character against any one of his colleagues. This cedula was subsequently circularized to all the audiencias of the Indies and included in the *Recopilación*.[34] The king and council further instructed Dr. Morga to conduct a formal but secret hearing, without the knowledge of Oidor Tello de Velasco, in which witnesses of the highest repute would specifically document the alleged misdeeds of the oidor.

Dr. Morga received another reprimand. The council expressed amazement that the president continued to assign important commissions, such as the recent residencia of the corregidor of Quito, to an oidor in whom he reposed such scant confidence. The council instructed Dr. Morga not to assign any further missions to Oidor Tello de Velasco until his status and reputation became clarified.[35]

On April 15, 1622, President Morga somewhat unconvincingly wrote the king that the projected visita general was really not necessary, because "since its foundation this audiencia has never been in a better and more tranquil state than it is now." The marginal comment of the fiscal of the council was a curt "no need to respond."[36] The king and the council had already decided upon a visita general. The machinery was slowly set in motion for the visita general which would make the alleged tranquility in the audiencia of Quito the proverbial lull before the storm.

The interaction of local and central factors in the decision to dispatch a visita general may be revealed if we examine the case of a visita general which did not occur in Quito during the administration of President Miguel de Ibarra (1600–1608). Conflict erupted between the president and the fiscal, Blas de Torres Altamirano, whom the president accused of a wide variety of violations, including several illicit love affairs, operating a gambling table in his home, illegal commercial activities, and an "unbridled tongue." Refusing to mend his ways after receiving several private admonitions from President Ibarra, the fiscal was suspended from office and put in jail. The president proceeded to conduct a public trial of the alleged abuses of the suspended fiscal.[37]

The authority of the president to suspend the fiscal from office was highly questionable. In justifying his action, President Ibarra proposed a sweeping change in administrative procedures. Arguing that a visita general was expensive, time-consuming, and often ineffective, he urged that the president of the audiencia be given broad powers to punish nefarious conduct of oidores and fiscales. Complaints against the president could be investigated not by a visitor general but by one of the oidores or prelates en route to Lima.[38]

This proposal received scant attention from the council. The president would be given too much authority. Experience had taught the council that the abuses of the presidents were often more serious than those of the oidores, since presidents had no resident superior. The council tenaciously clung to its conviction that a discreet use of the visita general was the only realistic method of uncovering misconduct.

On March 7, 1608, the Council of the Indies recommended to Philip III that Lic. Juan Páez de Laguna, an oidor of the audiencia of Lima, conduct a visita general in Quito. On December 22, 1608, the king and the council canceled the proposed visita general.[39] News had just reached Spain that President Ibarra had died. When the council examined the testimony taken by the late president against the fiscal, they concluded that Lic. Blas de Torres Altamirano was notoriously guilty. The council dispatched orders that he not be allowed to take up his duties as fiscal of the audiencia of Lima, a post to which he had been promoted before the controversy in Quito had erupted. The recommendation of the council was that the expenses and the inevitable turmoil of a visita general could be avoided, since the new president could conduct an investigation of any charges against Oidor Ferrer de Ayala during that oidor's residencia.

The council avoided recommending a visita general whenever possible, but they would not back away from one if it seemed necessary. If a controversial magistrate could be transferred to another post or if a key figure involved in a factional dispute died, the council willingly called off a visita general.[40]

If, for example, Dr. Morga had died in 1621, the Council of the Indies might have made the recommendation, as it did in 1608, to cancel the visita general on the grounds that the new president would be competent to handle factional disputes. But such a recommendation, if it had been made, might not have been accepted in 1621 and 1622. The authority of the Spanish crown was exercised in 1621 by the aggressive Count-Duke of Olivares and not by the courtly and lazy Duke of Lerma.

Of all the events leading to the visita general of the audiencia of Quito, the change of monarchs which brought Olivares to power was perhaps the single most decisive factor. Aggressive, calculating, and ruthless, he was determined to root out the graft in the Indies that was inherited from the previous reign and to strengthen central control from the peninsula over the Indies.

While experience had taught the council that oidores in the conscientious performance of their duties often were the object of slanderous and unfounded attacks, experience also had demonstrated that the judges on occasion abused their authority. The council and the crown both became alarmed when the presiding officer of an audiencia demonstrated his inability to maintain harmony among the judges. That was the situation in Quito in 1621 and 1622 when Olivares and the Council of the Indies were debating the desirability of a visita general. The disquieting reports from Quito provided Olivares with potent arguments to persuade the council out of its reluctance to recommend a visita general.

The crisis in Quito, which helped to precipitate the visita general, brought to the fore some of the tensions in that neo-medieval, corporate society. The society can be categorized by any one of three somewhat overlapping criteria: (1) according to primary "estates"; (2) according to functional corporations; (3) according to distinct and unequal juridical rights defined in general legal codes or specific legislation which granted each corporation considerable self-government over its members. In the multiracial society of the Indies, the estates were not the trichotomy of the Church, the nobility, and the commoners, as found in medieval Spain, but rather a racial distinction of Europeans, the castes, and the Indians-Negroes.[41] In America most Spaniards considered themselves nobles and were usually accepted as such. The Council of the Indies recognized this attitude when they once observed, "It is undeniable that in those kingdoms [in America] any Spaniard who comes to them, who acquires some wealth, and who is not engaged in a dishonorable occupation is regarded as a noble."[42]

Coexisting with these three primary estates were a multitude of functional corporations each possessing legally defined responsibilities, privileges, and immunities. Among the most significant of these were the cabildos, the various ecclesiastical corporations, the guild merchants (the *consulados*), the artisan guilds or *gremios,* the universities, etc. In theory purity of blood, *limpieza de sangre,* was a requirement for entrance into these corporations. The whites tended to monopolize the cabildos, the consulados, the universities, and the upper echelons of the church. The people of mixed blood were confined largely to the parish clergy and the craft guilds.

Our primary concern here is with the Spanish estate, just as in Chapters 3 and 4 the focus was on the Indian estate. Although the Spanish estate was the most privileged group in society, some Spaniards were more equal than others. The most basic cleavage, which cut across the whole corporate structure, was the distinction between those Spaniards born in the peninsula (*chapetones*) and those born in America (*criollos*). The superiority of the chapetones over the criollos was a matter of practice, not of law. Rivalry was acrimonious, beginning with the children of the first conquistadores and continuing to the wars of independence. The fact that European-born Spaniards monopolized the highest offices in the civil and ecclesiastical bureaucracies caused bitter resentment among the creoles.

All those magistrates who received their offices by appointment from the crown were at the top of the social pyramid. The superior magistrates, including the fiscal, the oidores, the corregidores, and the officers of the royal treasury, were only a handful, led by the president of the audiencia and the bishop. Bureaucrats who left Spain to spend the rest of their lives in the Indies might pine to return to their native land, but their careers in the New World provided them with positions of authority and social prestige that would be denied to them at home. Coming from the middle sectors of peninsular society where education and not wealth differentiated them from the lowest and the highest rungs, these jurists in the Indies found themselves at the very top of the social pyramid in the absence of a king, a royal Court, and an extensive hereditary and titled nobility.

Underneath the superior magistrates were the prosperous and prominent citizens, both Spanish-born and American-born, whose institutional stronghold was the cabildo. The wealth of the aldermen, who bought their posts from the crown as status symbols, was in both land and commerce. The city council had a lot to do with land grants. Land grants apportioned by the cabildo had to be "confirmed" by the Council of the Indies through the payment of a fee. What mattered was the payment to the hard-pressed treasury.[43] Confirmation was *pro forma.* The crown and its agents, however, never allowed the control and allocation of Indian labor to fall into the hands of the cabildo. Thus the professional bureaucracy and the cabildo between them administered the two keys to wealth and social prestige: labor and land. Hence these groups constituted a veritable upper class.

The members of the cabildo constituted a kind of elite based on wealth, just as the Spanish-appointed magistrates formed a bureaucratic elite deriving from royal appointment. Wealth in seventeenth-century Quito ought to be defined somewhat more precisely in order not to create misleading impressions. In comparison with the rich in the peninsula or even in the viceregal capitals in the Indies, the Quito magnates had only very modest wealth. No one there was worth more than 100,000 pesos. Diego de Niebla, a mere grocer, was able to buy his way into the cabildo elite and to marry into it, with a reputed fortune of 40,000 pesos.

Although land was the symbol and often the content of wealth, many of the cabildo elite, who disdained commerce, actually derived a good deal of their income and capital from trade. However socially unprestigious the obrajes were, they provided the basis for many small fortunes. As soon as anyone acquired either the capital or the desire to belong to the cabildo elite, he turned himself into a landowner. If he continued his commercial operations, he did it through intermediaries.

In Chapter 4 it was mentioned that the cabildo played an extralegal and political role as the agent of the vested economic interests of the well-to-do creoles. Although the viceroy deprived the cabildo of Quito of the traditional privilege of electing its own executive magistrates, the *alcaldes ordinarios,* the cabildo continued to represent effectively the point of view of the incipient creole oligarchy. The deprivation of the cabildo's right to elect alcaldes ordinarios meant that the city council exercised no judicial functions. Many viceroys argued that all cabildos should be deprived of their judicial officers and that first-instance jurisdiction should be exercised by the royally appointed corregidores. Viceroy Cañete acted against the cabildo of Quito as a punishment for its participation in the revolt over the alcabalas in 1593. As late as 1646, the cabildo's right to elect its own magistrates had not been restored, in spite of endless appeals to the king.[44]

If the imperial bureaucracy and the cabildo elite occupied the two highest rungs in the social ladder, the inferior magistrates in the audiencia constituted what we might call the "upper-middle sector" of colonial society. The alguaciles mayores, the escribanos de cámara, the escribanos de la vista de la tierra, the canciller, the receptores, and the notaries formed the clerking layer of the imperial administration. They earned a modest, or in some cases a prosperous, living from collecting fees from the public whom they served. Theirs was a much less privileged position than that of the superior magistrates, for they could not aspire to promotion to the professional magistracy whose offices were ordinarily monopolized by peninsular-born Spaniards with influential connections at Court. Those were the passports to advancement that the inferior magistrates usually lacked.

One group in the "upper-middle sector" could take advantage of one limited avenue for upward mobility. The more prosperous among the licensed advocates and the notaries might enter the ranks of the cabildo oligarchy if they were willing or able to pay 1,500 pesos for the post of alderman.

Although the licensed advocates' incomes, as proscribed fees from clients, were independent of the audiencia, their activities were under the constant scrutiny of the judges and they depended heavily on commissions distributed by the audiencia. Such assignments as holding the residencias of corregidores, conducting special inquests in the provinces, and working *ad interim* as acting fiscal or co-opting judge all together constituted a considerable amount of patronage that tended to make the licensed advocates dependent upon the good will of the superior magistrates. A lawyer such as Juan Alonso de Carvajal, for example, made a career out of these assignments before he purchased the post of alguacil mayor of the audiencia. So did Lic. Rodríquez Plaza until he began to feud with the oidores.

The creole lawyers who served as deputies to the corregidores also belonged to the upper-middle sector. They too enjoyed little independence of action, since they served at the pleasure of the corregidor who appointed them.

Given these limited opportunities, many creoles understandably chose careers in the secular or regular clergy. An Indian or a Spanish parish offered a comfortable living for someone who had no better prospects. Hence the clergy attracted many men of indifferent or weak religious vocations. This helps to explain the widespread immorality, venality, and factionalism among the clergy.

As mentioned previously, the marked tendency for many girls of the upper classes with dowries to take the veil rather than marry also increased the social instability in that the number of girls whose dowries could contribute to setting up additional economically stable Spanish households was greatly reduced.

Those Spaniards who did not have careers with the professional bureaucracy, the cabildo elite, the clerking administration, or the Church had only a few restricted opportunities for self-advancement. To be sure, an unusually industrious Spaniard could start with nothing and make a modest fortune, as did Diego de Niebla. But not all Spaniards and creoles had the industry or the business acumen of Diego de Niebla. The empire-wide depression, whose repercussions began to be felt everywhere by the 1630's, did not provide a favorable economic climate.

With the fertile bottomland of the Sierra valleys largely pre-empted by the creole elite and the Church, the more adventurous among the Europeans could go out to remote frontier areas such as Esmeraldas and Mainas. Some did follow the conquerors and would-be conquerors of those two remote provinces. None achieved prosperity, since the conquest of Esmeraldas proved abortive and the pacification of Mainas created few economic opportunities.

The less adventurous remained in the cities, where they formed a parasitic group. They were the habitantes, having no fixed occupations, in contrast to the vecinos who owned their own homes in the urban nucleus. In order to survive, many attached themselves to the wealthy as retainers. Others were the predatory elements who formed the periodically lawless street gangs. From among them Nicolás de Larraspuru recruited his cronies. The girls from this group often became the mistresses of the more affluent members of the magisterial bureaucracy and the cabildo elite.

The second "estate" consisted of the mestizos, the mulattoes, and the zambos. Although they belonged to the república de los españoles and in law enjoyed the same rights as whites, the castes were in fact socially inferior to those of European descent. Upward social mobility, however, was not totally closed to them. Those few who made outstanding achievements in wealth or education could blend into the white community. In the eighteenth century, a prominent mulatto could even secure legal recognition as a white by paying a fee to the crown through the device known as *gracias al sacar*.[45] But in general there was a virulent prejudice against them. A Spaniard such as Solórzano, who had an unusually favorable opinion of the creoles, had no sympathy at all for the castes.

Enough mestizos did become encomenderos, aldermen, and clerking bureaucrats so that spokesmen for the Spanish community protested to the king. A sharp reprimand from Philip III in 1601 telling the audiencia not to sell or grant such offices to mestizos "since they are restless trouble-makers" brought a prompt reply from the audiencia. That tribunal indicated that, while it did not wish to deprive the mestizos of the positions that they had already purchased in good faith, their posts, when vacant, would be redistributed to "Spaniards and honorable folk."[46] In the seventeenth century, fewer mestizos entered the ranks of the clerking bureaucracy as the competition for those positions grew keener among the rapidly expanding creole population.

The alienated group recruited its members not only from marginal Spaniards and creoles but also from the rapidly multiplying mestizos.[47] The more industrious and stable mestizos were engaged in the skilled crafts and service occupations, each organized into a separate guild or gremio. In the rural areas, the mestizos found employment as foremen and overseers of the Indians in the obrajes and on the Spanish-owned estates. The more stable mestizos constituted what we might call the "lower-middle sector," with the Indians forming the base of the social pyramid. On the coast, the mulattoes, most of whom were freedmen, and the Negro slaves occupied roughly analogous positions to those of the mestizos and the Indians in the Sierra.

In contrast to the medieval cities where there were both political and economic conflicts between the artisan guilds and the rich merchants, such clashes did not occur in the Indies.[48] The artisan gremios exerted no significant political influence in the New World, largely because they were dominated by the mestizos and in some cases by the Indians, who formed the socially inferior "second" and "third" estates, respectively. Between the gremios and the rich merchants was a wide gap created not only by economic disparity but by racial differences. The craft guilds enjoyed no representation in the Spanish-American city councils as they sometimes did in the municipalities of the Portuguese colonial world.[49]

The conventional view that colonial society was static and ponderously stable can no longer be accepted. From the conquest until independence, society was experiencing a steady rhythm of development. To be sure, the velocity of change may not have been spectacular. The formation of the American variant of estates, the growth of mixed groups, and the existence of some upward and downward social mobility are significant expressions of the kind of social change that was occurring.[50]

Behind the façade of hierarchally structured corporate society, there were lurking predatory elements that menaced its stability. The arrival of a much-feared visitor general allowed these immiscible forces to come to the surface to vent their dissatisfaction. These predatory groups—the parasites living on the margin of the professional bureaucracy, the cabildo oligarchy, and the upper-middle sectors—could not have asserted themselves as much as they did if there had not been some basic weaknesses in the upper echelons upon which they could prey. Among those weaknesses was the deep-rooted antagonism between the European and American branches of the Spanish estate. Both the bureaucratic and the cabildo elites were small groups of proud individuals with a keen sense of their own importance and status in the community. Frequent contacts with each other created a certain esprit de corps, but also their closeness provoked bitter clashes of personality.

Thus the storm provoked by the visita general was intensified by factionalism between the two elites and by the restlessness among the parasitic groups. The nature of the visita general as an instrument of government and the personality of the particular visitor general added to the fury.

III

THE JUDGES JUDGED—
A VISITA GENERAL

11.

A ZEALOUS VISITOR GENERAL

Among the people inconvenienced by the Dutch fleet off the coast of Peru during the spring and summer of 1624 was the newly appointed visitor general of the audiencia of Quito, Lic. Juan de Mañozca y Zamora. After having overcome the hazards of travel between Panama and Callao, during which journey the main mast of his sailing vessel broke in two, he had still to postpone his voyage from Callao to Guayaquil for several months until the Nassau fleet withdrew. He arrived in Quito on October 28, 1624.[1]

The man chosen to conduct the visita general belonged not to the secular bureaucracy but to the Holy Office of the Inquisition. Both the king and the council preferred to recruit visitors from among the judges of the Holy Office. It was hoped that they might be more impartial, since they had no built-in ties with the civil bureaucracy. The inquisitors also had a reputation of stern determination in probing misconduct.[2] Inquisitors, however, were not always available, and on occasion the independent-minded Holy Office refused to lend its personnel to the crown for this purpose. On September 15, 1621, when the Council of the Indies recommended visitas generales

for the audiencias of Quito, Bogotá, Lima, and Charcas, two of the pro
posed visitors general were inquisitors.[3]

Lic. Mañozca was truly a child of the Inquisition. He was the nephew o
one inquisitor and the uncle of another. Although he was born around 157
in Marquina in the Basque country of a Castilian father and a Basqu
mother, he was reared in Mexico City in the household of his materna
uncle, Pedro Saenz de Mañozca, senior inquisitor of the Holy Office. Ou
of apparent affection for his maternal uncle, he used the maternal nam
of Mañozca and not his father's name of Zamora.

After Juan de Mañozca had taken a bachelor of arts degree from th
University of Mexico in 1596, his uncle sent him to Spain to complete hi
education. He received a licentiate in both canon and civil law at the Uni
versity of Salamanca.[4] His presence in Spain and his uncle's long servic
in the Inquisition in Mexico were responsible for his appointment to th
newly established tribunal of the Holy Office in Cartagena.

During his service in Cartagena from 1609 to 1622 Lic. Mañozca ex
hibited some of the characteristics that were to mark his subsequent career
his inexhaustible energy, his seldom-concealed arrogance, and his irascibilit
against those who did not bend to his will. Militantly devoted to his friends
he was an implacable enemy to his opponents. His choice of friends wa
sometimes injudicious in that several were marginal people of dubious repu
tations. Once he reposed confidence in a friend, he seldom withdrew tha
loyalty, even when mounting evidence suggested that his loyalty had bee
misplaced.

Some have ascribed his arrogance and irascibility to his Basque tempera
ment.[5] National characterology is too facile an explanation, although th
temptation to indulge in it is irresistible on occasion. However, there ar
much more revealing explanations for Lic. Mañozca's temperament tha
his national origin. In any event, he was only one-half Basque. His fathe
was Castilian. Dr. Morga also was one-half Basque, yet temperamentall
he was a perfect foil to the inquisitor. Moreover, Lic. Mañozca spent onl
his earliest infancy in the Basque country. He was educated in Mexico Cit
and Salamanca. Finally, the hot-tempered severity that he exhibited was n
monopoly of the Basques.

The inquisitional environment in which he was reared and to which h
returned after completing his formal education, rather than his Basque her
tage, was perhaps responsible for his austere temperament. Living in th
shadow of the tribunal to whose care was commended not only the purit
of the faith but also the regulation of private morality, Lic. Mañozca spe

his formative years in an environment hostile to any spirit of humility or
real compassion for the weaknesses of men.

These qualities began to show themselves when he was in Cartagena.
With his vitality and intelligence he soon completely overshadowed his
senior and older colleague. Gathering around him a band of fiercely loyal
partisans, he also aroused deep antagonisms. He alienated the bishop. He
treated the city council with disdain. He finally made an enemy of the
easy-going governor, Diego Fernández de Velasco, whose more influential
brothers were the Count of Nieva and the Marquis of Villamanrique. After
three years the young inquisitor so exhausted the patience of the governor
that the governor complained to the king, ". . . that this tribunal [the Holy
Office] has sought to become so much the master of everything that this
republic and province are terrorized . . . ."[6] He had intimidated the cathedral
chapter into greeting the inquisitors at mass before extending greetings to
the governor. Dr. Morga acted in a similar fashion, except that Morga was
a regalist and Mañozca the exact opposite. The inquisitor set the prices he
would pay for food. If the tradesmen did not acquiesce gracefully, the inquisitor threatened to call them before the Holy Office. He did the same
when he compelled a slave trader to sell him slaves at a price below their
market value.

When one of his slaves who was caught bearing arms at night was punished by one hundred lashes, as the law required to preclude possible revolt
by the 14,000 Negroes in Cartagena, the inquisitor exploded in wrath. Sum-
moning to his residence the soldiers who had administered the lashes to
his slave, the inquisitor ordered them lashed in turn and then exiled them
from the city limits of Cartagena.[7]

The most savage attack on the private and official life of Lic. Mañozca
came in 1619 from a Franciscan friar, Sebastián de Chumillas, who cited
chapter and verse of Mañozca's alleged affairs with women. One of the most
dramatic incidents presumably occurred when one of those mistresses married. Anxious to get her out of the reach of her former lover, the inquisitor,
her husband departed with his bride for Bogotá. Before they had reached
the city limits of Cartagena, the ubiquitous agents of the Inquisition intervened. Her husband went on to Bogotá alone to secure the assistance of the
audiencia in regaining control over the person of his young bride.

Lic. Mañozca emphatically denied these charges. He insisted that he
was "as chaste as a Carthusian monk." He did admit visiting one woman
from time to time but without immoral intent. She was middle-aged, "de
edad."[8] It should be pointed out that the most devastating attack an antag-

onist could make on a clergyman was to charge violations of celibacy. I
some cases the charges were true. In regard to Lic. Mañozca, they cannc
be proved. In his subsequent career he did not exhibit the inclinations of
Don Juan. What is beyond dispute, however, is that the inquisitor by hi
imperious manner had aroused militant hostility.

These reports filtered back to Spain. In July of 1615, Viceroy Esquilach
en route to Lima stopped off in Cartagena, where, at the request of the king
he administered a mild reprimand to Lic. Mañozca. The complaints con
tinued to pour into Madrid. Finally the inquisitor general ordered a full
scale investigation, and he summoned the inquisitor to Madrid to defen
his conduct. Mañozca arrived in Spain in October, 1620.

His career was in jeopardy. The charges against him were serious, an
many were well documented. This was not to be the only time that h
managed to extricate himself from possible disgrace. His customary energ
and intelligence did not fail him. Before leaving for Spain, he secured letter
from a wide variety of organizations, both secular and religious, praisin
him as an upright and zealous judge who led an exemplary life. The fac
that some extolled the inquisitor for "the mildness of his comportment
suggests that their authors wrote these letters with tongue in cheek.[9] It i
tempting to speculate to what extent these testimonials were extracted b
the threat of reprisals from Mañozca if he returned to Cartagena exonerated

The actual deliberations of the Inquisition in this case have not survivec
He was exonerated and returned to Cartagena in July, 1621. José Toribi
Medina argues that the decision was designed to save the face of the Hol
Office by ostensibly allowing him to return to his post.[10] Within tw
years, on February 18, 1623, Lic. Mañozca received a new assignmen
a promotion to the Inquisition of Lima. When the Spanish bureaucracy wa
confronted with diametrically opposed sets of evidence about the conduct o
a controversial magistrate, whose guilt or innocence could therefore not b
clearly established, their sensible response often was to shift the individua
in question to another post.

Lic. Mañozca happened to be at Court at the beginning of the reign o
Philip IV. He had occasion to meet and make contacts with those wh
were in positions of power and to assess the aims and the spirit of the ne
regime. Among the contacts he made was Antonio González de Legarda
who, a few years later, received the key post in the Council of the Indie
as secretary for the viceroyalty of Peru.[11]

His contacts, if any, with the Count-Duke of Olivares must have bee
casual. Temperamentally Lic. Mañozca was a carbon copy of the ne

master of the Spanish monarchy. Both men were intelligent but totally unable to tolerate opposition. Hence they tended to surround themselves with sycophants. Both were ruthless, ambitious, arrogant, and energetic. The very qualities that had made Mañozca such a controversial figure in Cartagena may have persuaded those around the count-duke that the inquisitor would implement the anti-corruption drive of the new administration with relentless determination in Quito.

Olivares had a tendency to appoint to high office in the Indies men who reflected his own strengths and weaknesses. The Marquis of Gelves, who took office as viceroy of Mexico in the fall of 1621, possessed uncommon energy and ability, but his monumental tactlessness alienated everyone. His intolerance of opposition contributed mightily to the outbreak of the bloody riots of January 15, 1624.

Mañozca was exonerated just before the death of Philip III on March 31, 1621. As early as September 25, 1621, the council recommended him for the assignment of visitor general to Quito.[12] The approval of the Inquisition was not difficult to obtain; the continued presence of Lic. Mañozca in Cartagena was not desirable. Between September 25, 1621, and July 1, 1622, when the final decision to dispatch the visita was reached, the Inquisition in Madrid ordered the transfer of Lic. Mañozca to Lima.

Before he took up his post, the Council of the Indies drew up a set of instructions for the benefit of the visitor general. Unfortunately they cannot be located. A good number of these instructions can be pieced together from subsequent documents. The commission of the visita general included an investigation of the conduct of all audiencia and treasury officials since 1590 when the last visita general occurred. The visitor general also received copies of all the recent correspondence between the audiencia and the council.[13] There is little doubt about the procedural instructions Lic. Mañozca received, for by this time they were well standardized. We may infer that several additional instructions ordered the visitor general to investigate the welter of charges and countercharges arising out of the turmoil of the Morga administration.

Although Lic. Mañozca arrived in Quito on October 28, 1624, the visita general did not formally begin until December 2, when he published his edict. It was posted in the principal squares of every city in the kingdom, announcing to the populace his commission from the king. The edict invited all and sundry to submit testimony, even anonymously.[14] According to the experienced bureaucrat Juan de Solórzano y Pereira, a visitor general should not receive anonymous complaints, which merely opened the door to

calumny.[15] From the day he began his investigation, the visitor general mad
it plain that he was looking for abuses and that the means by which he un
covered them were not especially important.

On the day following the proclamation of the visita general, Lic. Mañozc
paid his first formal call on the audiencia. He asked to inspect the officia
records. The ordinances of Monzón required each audiencia to keep a libr
de acuerdos in which they recorded the date, a brief description of the litiga
tion, and the vote of each oidor with his signature for all cases involvin
more than 100,000 maravedís.[16] Lic. Mañozca reported that the libro d
acuerdos was in complete chaos. The volume covering the years from 159:
to 1610 was missing and presumed lost. Between 1610 and 1624 the au
diencia had made 1,874 decisions, but only 120 votes had been recorded i
the libro de acuerdos.[17] Many of the records were incomplete even fo
those cases. On December 7, 1624, the visitor general issued an edict order
ing the president and the oidores to comply with the ordinances of Monzó:
in regard to keeping official records. And from that day on, the record
were meticulously kept.[18]

On the following day, the visitor general paid his first formal call on th
treasury officials. He was severely critical of their bookkeeping and account
ing methods. His most notable discovery was that the records of the junt
de hacienda were as incomplete as the libro de acuerdos of the audiencia.[19]
The junta de hacienda, consisting of the president, the senior oidor, the fisca
the treasurer, and the paymaster, met once a week to coordinate matters c
mutual interest to justice, political administration, and the royal fisc. Onc
again the visitor general issued an edict that the meetings and the record
of the junta de hacienda be kept according to standing regulations.[20]

Lic. Mañozca expressed horror at discovering that the royal seal, whos
custodian was the chancellor, was not in the casas reales, where the lav
required it to be kept at all times. The aged chancellor, Juan de Beraír
alleged that the room reserved in the casas reales for the royal seal wa
damp and dark and that it could be more decorously housed in his ow
home. The stern visitor wasted no patience on this explanation. He ordere
the return forthwith of the royal seal to the casas reales. A few days late
the servants of the ubiquitous visitor caught a Negro slave of the old chan
cellor carrying the royal seal concealed in his clothes from the casas reale
to the home of his master. The visitor acted swiftly. He immediately sus
pended the chancellor from office. He appointed Juan Vera de Mendoza
the father-in-law of don Nicolás de Larraspuru, as his temporary replace

ment. After trial, the chancellor was deprived of his office and exiled five leagues from the city limits of Quito for a period of two years.[21]

By deposing the chancellor, Lic. Mañozca hoped to ingratiate himself with the Count-Duke of Olivares, who could now name a deputy for that post in the audiencia of Quito. On November 5, 1623, Philip IV had appointed the count-duke grand chancellor of the Indies, giving him the right to nominate a deputy in each audiencia whenever the office became vacant.[22]

The royal seal was a mystical symbol of the majesty of the king. Legislation required that it be treated with the utmost respect and veneration.[23] Acting on his conviction that the disrespect shown to the royal seal required public atonement, Lic. Mañozca organized a solemn ceremony, attended by the oidores, the clergy, and the leading citizens, to carry the royal seal in state through the streets back to the casas reales. The visitor general at his austere best presided over the act, which climaxed with his genuflecting before the royal seal in its refurbished chamber.

While one is tempted to poke fun at his sanctimonious solemnity, it should not be forgotten that the royal seal was then the object of as much emotional veneration as the flag is today in the United States. Yet there is little doubt that his exposure of the rather careless custody of the royal seal put him in the role he loved to play as the zealous servant of the king.

This incident, as well as his discovery of the inefficient and incomplete record-keeping of the audiencia and the treasury, served to strengthen his conviction that the administration of Dr. Morga was riddled with abuses. From his first letter he expressed this conviction. His initial exposures, for which the Council of the Indies ultimately reprimanded the audiencia in the final verdicts, were still minor offenses, however. With all the energy at his command he was determined to ferret out major abuses. Such an aim also fitted the reforming zeal of the new Olivares administration. A well-documented exposure of widescale abuses in Quito would facilitate the promotions that the ambitious visitor general ardently desired. An archbishop's mitre was his goal.[24] He had to wait nearly twenty years, however, to realize that ambition.

His first attempt to document major abuses was an assault on the audiencia's decision in the spring of 1623 to reduce the fines imposed in the residencia sentence of Pedro de Vergara for misdeeds as corregidor of Otavalo. Lic. Mañozca conducted a lengthy investigation during which he charged the president and the oidores with criminal failure to punish adequately the misdeeds of Vergara. He accused them of allowing personal friendship to influence their judicial conclusions and permitting the royal treasury to be defrauded of tribute money. Lic. Mañozca found the oidores guilty. He allowed them to appeal the sentence to the Council of the Indies after they had posted a bond amounting to 24,000 pesos.[25] This litigation, finished by March, 1625, did not bring the results anticipated. The Council of the Indies in the final sentences took no action whatsoever in regard to the role of the oidores in the Vergara residencia.

Partly as a result of the abuses uncovered in the Vergara residencia, Dr. Morga undertook a systematic and rather successful reorganization of the province. This reform, discussed in Chapter 4, was one of the solid accomplishments of his regime. The Vergara case illustrates a basic contrast in the approach of these two administrators. Lic. Mañozca, a product of the Inquisition, firmly believed that the most effective means of eradicating abuses was to castigate rigorously those who violated the laws. Dr. Morga, on the other hand, was less optimistic about the efficacy of this approach. He put more faith in promoting, through realistic legislation, conditions which would make such abuses more difficult to commit in the future.

If Lic. Mañozca could not make his charges in the Vergara case stick, he was much more successful in regard to Diego de Valencia León, who had purchased the office of escribano mayor of the audiencia in 1607 for 15,000 pesos. It was a lucrative office, since all documents submitted to the audiencia went through the office of the escribano mayor, who then collected a set fee from the litigant. Diego de Valencia León had been in Quito for more than thirty years and had become modestly rich from his notarial office as well as from his business enterprises as a retail merchant and an obraje owner. He made a good second marriage with Juan de Manoa Ronquillo's widow, the mother-in-law of Diego de Niebla. An intimate friend of Dr. Morga, he was fair game for the inquisitor.

His conduct in office was open to criticism on several counts. When he purchased the office, he did so not for himself but for his son, with the condition that he could hold the position until his son reached the age of 25. Diego García de Valencia became 25 in 1616, but then the father refused to turn over the profitable office to his son, who sued for possession. The audiencia, under its somewhat partial president, Dr. Morga, ruled that the father could continue to hold the position.

The visitor general reversed this ruling. His investigation also exposed the escribano's failure to secure a license as a royal notary before he had taken possession of his office. This was a standard requirement. Far more serious was the proven fact that Diego de Valencia León had violated the royal cedula of April 19, 1619, which had extended the prohibition on commercial activities to include both the escribanos de cámara and the relatores. A cedula as early as May 3, 1605, directed specifically to Quito, had prohibited all inferior magistrates of the audiencia from indulging in commercial operations.[26] The audiencia, however, made no sustained attempt to enforce it.[27] The cedula of 1619 was a more serious effort on the part of the crown to professionalize the lower echelons of the bureaucracy, for it applied to the whole empire.[28]

Both Diego de Valencia León and his colleague, Andrés de Orozco Guzmán, escribano de cámara for the city of Quito, freely admitted that they were also retail merchants. They requested the visitor to postpone action on this count until they could appeal to the Council of the Indies. They argued that they could not support their families decently merely on the income from their notarial offices. What they meant, but did not dare to make explicit, was that they could make a good deal more money by investing their official income in their business enterprises. Conveniently ignoring the cedula of 1605, they also contended that they were the victims of an *ex post facto* situation. They had purchased the offices several years before the 1619 cedula had specifically included their offices in the trade prohibition.

The verdict of the visitor general was that both Diego de Valencia León and Andrés de Orozco Guzmán should be deprived forthwith of their notarial offices.[29] Although both men returned to office in the summer of 1627 following the dismissal of Lic. Mañozca, the position of the visitor general in this matter was ultimately vindicated. In 1632 the Council of the Indies in blunt language ordered the audiencia not to allow Diego de Valencia León to continue to exercise the office of escribano mayor, since he had violated several of the conditions under which he had purchased the office.[30] In 1636 and 1637 the council dealt severely with both Dr. Morga and the escribanos mayores when they handed down the final verdicts. Dr. Morga received a severe reprimand for his decision of 1616 allowing Diego de Valencia to continue in office.[31] The council held both escribanos mayores responsible for their mercantile activities since the cedula of 1619. Each fine amounted to 20,000 ducats.[32]

During the spring of 1624, before the arrival of the visitor general in Quito, President Morga had initiated a series of legal actions clearly designed to persecute Lic. Francisco Rodríquez Plaza, whom he believed to be the real author of the complaints influencing the council's decision to dispatch a visita general to the kingdom. Although Morga's belief grossly oversimplified the complex interplay of events that led to the decision, it contributed to the already embittered relations between the president and Lic. Rodríquez Plaza—bitterness due to Dr. Morga's attempts to break up the affair between Oidor Zorrilla and the wife of Rodríquez Plaza.[33] Several others whom the audiencia regarded as Plaza's allies, such as Juan Serrano del Valle and Juan de Ibarra, fled to Lima, but Lic. Rodríquez Plaza chose to fight it out in an obviously unfriendly court.

On March 26, 1624, the president issued six decrees ordering Lic. Rodríquez Plaza to show cause why he should not be prosecuted by the audiencia for a number of complaints, among them that he, Juan de Ibarra, and Juan Serrano del Valle had conspired to discredit the judges of the audiencia by dispatching slanderous reports to Spain. Several decrees dealt with whether the defendant had fulfilled the sentence imposed upon him by the audiencia for the murder of Domingo de Agurto in 1601, twenty-three years before. The court in Loja had sentenced him to death, but on appeal the audiencia had reduced the sentence to exile from the kingdom for eight years and a fine of 600 pesos. The defendant admitted the homicide but pleaded self-defense. When Lic. Rodríquez Plaza was unable to produce his copy of the notarized documents, President Morga put him in jail.

Lic. Rodríquez Plaza produced witnesses on April 12 who provided sworn testimony that he had fulfilled all the conditions of the verdict of the audiencia of May 22, 1601. Dr. Morga intervened again on May 14, 1624. He presented three letters from Cuenca and Loja alleging that Lic. Rodríquez Plaza on his way from Loja to Quito had falsified the proceedings of his trial and that the audiencia's repeal of the death penalty was based on this falsified testimony. Lic. Rodríquez Plaza replied that the audiencia issued the edict ordering him to go to Quito on June 15, 1601, and that the audiencia had handed down its verdict rescinding the death sentence on the preceding May 21. Dr. Morga allowed him to leave the royal jail, but he placed him under city-wide arrest, with a bond of 2,000 pesos.

The president was on weak ground in trying to demonstrate that Lic. Rodríquez Plaza and his friends had protested against Morga's administration. That was the privilege of any citizen. The visita general, not Dr. Morga, would determine whether these attacks were slanderous. In seeking to conduct an inquiry into the sentence of 1601, Dr. Morga was obviously harassing him. The real purpose was to remind the authorities in Spain that the defendant had been convicted of murder. Thus Dr. Morga sought to undermine the credibility of the unfavorable testimony that Lic. Rodríquez Plaza allegedly submitted to the council.

Lic. Rodríquez Plaza could not defend himself effectively against this judicial harassment by the president, since he had lost his copy of the notarized documents. The other certified copy was in the archives of the escribano mayor of the audiencia. Diego de Valencia León claimed that the papers had been mislaid or had disappeared during the tenure of his predecessor. Be this as it may, Rodríquez Plaza suspected foul play. The escribano mayor was a close personal friend of Dr. Morga. Moreover, Lic. Rodríquez Plaza had served as the lawyer for the son of Diego de Valencia León in his unsuccessful suit to take over the office of escribano mayor from his father.

The tables were turned when Lic. Juan de Mañozca arrived in Quito shortly afterward. The visitor general was as partial in the litigations of Lic. Rodríquez Plaza as Dr. Morga had been hostile. Lic. Mañozca allowed Lic. Rodríquez Plaza to bring before his court two criminal actions. One was against Diego de Valencia León and the other against the president and the oidores. Alleging that Diego de Valencia León was motivated by personal hatred against him for having served as the son's lawyer, he accused Valencia León of deliberately removing from the archives the key documents relative to his murder conviction so as to embarrass him in his litigation with Dr. Morga. Lic. Rodríquez Plaza produced three witnesses who were minor functionaries of the office. They swore under oath that the missing documents had been in the archives shortly before the litigation with Dr. Morga developed.

On March 5, 1625, the visitor general ordered Diego de Valencia León to pay Rodríquez Plaza the sum of 800 pesos as compensation. On November 20, 1625, the visitor general ordered the judges to pay the plaintiff 1,000 ducats as compensation for his illegal imprisonment during the spring of 1624. The judges were also fined an additional 2,000 ducats, payable to the royal treasury. Dr. Morga had filed a countersuit before the visitor general, accusing Lic. Rodríquez Plaza of conspiring to discredit his administration by sending false reports to Spain. Lic. Mañozca absolved Lic. Rodríquez Plaza.[34]

Dr. Morga and his colleagues, of course, posted bond and appealed their cases to the Council of the Indies. The council refused to hear the appeals and referred the whole matter back to the audiencia.[35] By that time Lic. Mañozca had been deposed and Dr. Morga was still president. The matter therefore languished.[36]

In his handling of the litigations of Lic. Rodríquez Plaza, the visitor general allowed his zeal to overcome his prudence. It would have been far wiser for him to have refused to hear the suits of Lic. Rodríquez Plaza against the audiencia. Had he confined this matter to the secret aspect of the visita general, Lic. Mañozca could have proved that the audiencia had deliberately persecuted Rodríquez Plaza during the spring of 1624. Because of Mañozca's public ruling in favor of Rodríquez Plaza, the audiencia in turn could make out a creditable case that they were humiliated by an over-zealous and prejudiced visitor general, thus obscuring the fact that they had been quite obviously prejudiced against Lic. Rodríquez Plaza.

On several occasions Lic. Mañozca confused the procedures of a residencia and a visita. One of their essential differences was that the residencia was a public investigation occurring immediately after an official had left office, whereas the visita general was held during the tenure of the magistrates and the testimony taken was necessarily secret. On his own initiative, Lic. Mañozca superimposed the procedures of a residencia on those of the visita general. Any citizen might request the judge of the residencia to re-examine any judicial sentence rendered by the magistrate being investigated. The residencia judge could not receive complaints after the sixty-day period of the inquiry.[37] The demandas públicas de mal juzgado constituted one method of determining whether the oidores had administered justice impartially by observing all the safeguards and procedures established by law to protect the rights of the king's subjects. It could be assumed that many verdicts had aroused resentment. Much depended upon the fairness and impartiality of the residencia judge, who was under standing instructions to give the oidores some benefit of the doubt in view of the real danger that litigants would seek to secure revenge on judges who had merely conscientiously done their duty.[38]

The visitor general issued a public ordinance inviting any citizen in the kingdom to bring suit before his court against any or all the judges for any alleged miscarriage of justice. Between July 1, 1625, and March 27, 1627, the visitor general received seventy-nine complaints. By March 27, 1627, he had handed down sixty-seven sentences. Of this total number, twenty were sentences involving complaints directed against the audiencia as a whole. Eight suits concerned Oidor Peralta, and three involved only Dr. Morga. Dr. Morga alone had passed judgment or issued writs in some twelve hundred cases. Oidor Peralta had been involved in many more, since he had been serving on the bench since 1611.[39] These statistics suggest that the oidores, with just a few exceptions, had administered justice to the satisfaction of the people over whom they exercised jurisdiction. In view of the ill-concealed hostility of the visitor general for the incumbent magistrates, it is highly doubtful that anyone who felt grossly aggrieved by the judges would not have stepped forward and claimed retribution. A further examination of the thirty-one complaints directed against the superior magistrates reveals that Lic. Mañozca found them guilty in only seven cases. Fourteen complaints came from sworn and proven enemies of the magistrates.[40]

These figures superficially suggest that the visitor general made an honest effort to render impartial verdicts. The fact that only one person issued a complaint against Lic. Manuel Tello de Velasco casts some doubts on the impartiality of the whole procedure. Oidor Tello de Velasco, who was a militant enemy of his colleagues on the bench, allied himself with the visitor general.

For the seven suits in which the audiencia as a whole was found guilty the visitor general showed little mercy in inflicting pecuniary punishment. The total fines amounted to 4,500 ducats. The plaintiffs also received 1,656 pesos from the defendants. None of the fines or the damages, however, ever reached the treasury or the plaintiffs. Legislation provided that the oidores could appeal the verdicts to the Council of the Indies by posting bond.

Upon examining Lic. Mañozca's use of this procedure, the Council of the Indies concluded that the visitor general had acted imprudently and harshly. Juan de Solórzano y Pereira reflected their thinking when he warned visitors general about abusing their right to hear demandas públicas de mal juzgado. They should elect to hear only those cases where there was substantial evidence that the judges had been motivated by prejudice or bribery. Solórzano advised visitors whenever possible to include such cases in the secret proceedings where the magistrates would have an opportunity to defend themselves in private session.[41] The cautious approach of Solórzano, however, evidently taxed the not very ample patience of Lic. Mañozca. The Council of the Indies instructed Lic. Mañozca's successor not to hear any public cases and to confine such matters to the secret proceedings.

The defects of the system of subjecting the judicial decisions of the oidores to a public review during a visita general came to the fore with Juan Serrano del Valle, a former obraje overseer. He was the most persistent accuser of the magistrates, being the plaintiff in twelve of the sixty-seven cases. Before the arrival of the visitor, the audiencia had sentenced him to four years of exile and a fine for attempted homicide.[42] Lic. Mañozca recalled him to Quito. The visitor general initially viewed Juan Serrano del Valle with favor. He evidently ignored the fact that Juan Serrano del Valle had been sentenced by the audiencia in Lima several years before for recruiting false witnesses. When Lic. Mañozca became convinced that Serrano del Valle had bribed witnesses to testify falsely and deliberately concealed official documents that might prejudice his case, the visitor turned on his erstwhile friend with a vengeance. On January 29, 1627, Lic. Mañozca sentenced Juan Serrano del Valle to six years' exile in Chile and a fine of 1,000 pesos.[43]

The oidores bitterly criticized the visitor general for his massive use of the demandas públicas. They asserted that his real motive was to humiliate them in public. They also argued that such a procedure should be used selectively. Its wholesale application would only invite malcontents to use it as a vehicle for vengeance and slander. Finally the magistrates protested that most of their energy and all of their estates were consumed in the effort to protect themselves.[44]

Lic. Mañozca scoffed at this reasoning. His major responsibility was to gather evidence as to how well the oidores had administered justice. The most direct means of acquiring such information was to provide everyone who had received justice at their hands with an opportunity to protest.[45]

What aroused the ire of the magistrates was that the visitor lent credence to their sworn enemies. Furthermore, many who protested the sentences were people of little or no social standing, in some cases individuals found guilty of base crimes. The magistrates never tired of pointing out that Juan Serrano del Valle was a convicted perjurer. The only social equal among their enemies was Lic. Rodríquez Plaza, and he was an alienated member of their class.[46] What the oidores implied was that, as magistrates, they could not be convicted merely on the basis of testimony of people who either had criminal records or were their social inferiors. Such evidence must come from their peers. As members of a corporate society, the privileged were to be judged by the privileged, according to their view.

Lic. Mañozca, as a product of the Inquisition, did not share this attitude. In matters of morality and purity of the faith, the privileges of class and caste disappeared. The evidence of one man, no matter what his social background might be, was as good as another man's. Servants could testify against employers, social inferiors against social superiors, and slaves against masters. Like most authoritarian organizations, the Holy Office was equalitarian, certainly much more so than the corporate society in which it functioned.

In response to a mild and friendly expression of concern from some members of the clergy about the dangers of using witnesses of dubious reputation, Lic. Mañozca was reported to have replied that, in discharging his duty of exposing the misdeeds of the magistrates, he would use all means at hand. He likened the humiliation that these people of humble origins were causing the magistrates to the torture that the devil, with the permission of God, inflicted on human souls in order to test their merit.[47]

The man who became the principal lieutenant of the visitor general was Juan de Ibarra. To the critics of Lic. Mañozca, Juan de Ibarra was the evil genius of the visita general. The oidores vented their frustration at the visitor general on the underling whom they accused of being the "bag man." They charged that Juan de Ibarra accepted bribes and sold his influence with the visitor general as if it were an article of merchandise. They made much of his unsavory background. Several years before, he had been an employee in the office of the relator. The audiencia convicted him of gross misconduct, not the worst of which was accepting bribes.[48] Exiled, he happened to be in Lima during the brief stay of Lic. Mañozca there in 1624. The visitor general took him in his entourage to Quito, where he soon made himself indispensable to his new employer.

Lic. Mañozca's choice of Juan de Ibarra as one of his principal deputies was grossly imprudent.[49] In Quito as in Cartagena, Lic. Mañozca was the friend of his friends and the foe of his enemies. He evidently felt more secure reposing confidence in assistants of somewhat unsavory backgrounds.

Another characteristic of Lic. Mañozca was that the more power he possessed, the more he wanted. Broad though his authority as visitor general was, it did not encompass every citizen in the kingdom. By invoking his authority as inquisitor, he could claim jurisdiction over everyone on the pretext that he was seeking to expose crypto-Jews. Jew-baiting was a major activity of the Inquisition. All cases involving the Holy Office in the kingdom of Quito were referred to the tribunal in Lima. His presence in Quito enabled Lic. Mañozca to set up a special court of the Inquisition. Those whom he could not arrest on secular grounds could be detained under the writ of the Holy Office.[50] The Inquisition was genuinely feared by all, and with good reason. Combining the authority of visitor general and that of inquisitor, Lic. Mañozca had some potent weapons with which to cow the opposition.

The techniques of Lic. Mañozca as an interrogator of witnesses came from his long service in Cartagena. They inspired fear in those whom he questioned. The sessions lasted for hours. The inquisitor probed relentlessly, asking the same questions time and time again in order to observe whether there were any important variations in testimony. He could be quite arbitrary in selecting what evidence was pertinent. All testimony deemed impertinent was not recorded by the notary. Stern, severe, and irascible, he seldom showed any patience with uncooperative witnesses. A cooperative witness by the standards of the Holy Office was one who freely admitted his guilt. The visitor general seldom restrained his acid tongue with refractory witnesses. They in turn were expected to exercise infinite patience as the visitor general bored in unremittingly.[51]

Lic. Mañozca was unsure that even the potent authority of visitor general and inquisitor would enable him to consummate his mission, so deep ran his lust for power and his inner sense of insecurity. In the summer of 1625, six months after he had begun his inquiry, Lic. Mañozca took a momentous step. On July 22, he suspended from office President Morga, the senior oidor, Lic. Matías de Peralta, and Oidor Manuel Tello de Velasco.[52] A few days earlier he had suspended the fiscal.[53] The edict instructed each of the suspended magistrates to depart within eight days to separate and designated places of exile at some distance from the urban nucleus of the capital, although within a few weeks all were allowed to return.

Lic. Mañozca justified this drastic step on the grounds that few people dared to testify against the oidores while they were still sitting on the bench.[54] The validity of his argument is questionable. In order to protect witnesses during a visita general, the strictest secrecy surrounded the investigation. Although the incumbents were informed of the content of adverse testimony, they never received the names of witnesses.[55] In a residencia, on the other hand, there was no need to protect the anonymity of witnesses since the official under investigation no longer held office. Lic. Mañozca once again confused the procedures of a residencia and a visita.

In suspending the majority of the audiencia, the visitor general violated his instructions. Because of the factionalism in and beyond the audiencia, the council had warned the visitor to proceed with caution and prudence. Standing instructions were that no magistrate should be suspended from office until the visitor general had drawn up charges and until the visited officials had been given an opportunity to defend themselves. Then might the visitor use his power of suspension, but only in those cases where the evidence indicated "notorious guilt." A magistrate might also be suspended if he actively impeded the work of the visita.[56] On neither grounds did Lic. Mañozca justify his action. He even allowed the suspended magistrates to retain their salaries, an unusual move.[57]

Those procedures which the crown and the council had devised, on the basis of long experience, to protect the rights of the defendants required too much restraint for Lic. Mañozca. Zealous inquisitor that he was, he considered the defendants already guilty. Their rights could be abridged in order to facilitate his task of demonstrating their guilt.

The Council of the Indies reacted indignantly to the visitor general's rather high-handed disregard for the established procedures. In fact, a major justification for his later dismissal was his wholesale suspension of the audiencia before the magistrates had been given an opportunity to defend themselves in secret session. What also aroused the concern of the council was that such a massive suspension within six months after the start of the visita general discredited the institution of the audiencia.[58] The council always made a sharp distinction between the misconduct of individual judges and the prestige of the tribunal as a corporate body.

Not satisfied with stripping the audiencia of independent authority, the visitor general also suspended the paymaster and the treasurer. He put both officers in jail, placed an embargo on their property, and replaced them in office with his appointees.[59]

From July 22, 1625, to February 26, 1626, only the two junior oidores, Lic. Castillo de Herrera and Espino de Cáceres, and an acting fiscal served on the bench. From February 26, 1626, onward, only Oidor Espino de Cáceres signed the decisions. After a clash with the visitor general, Lic. Castillo de Herrera found himself no longer sitting on the tribunal.[60] Although the truncated audiencia continued to meet and hand down verdicts, usually co-opting one of the licensed lawyers, there was no doubt where the seat of justice really was. It was not in the casas reales but at the residence of the visitor general.

There were bound to be conflicts between the extraordinary jurisdiction of the visitor general, with the rather sweeping powers of his commission, and the ordinary jurisdiction of the regular magistrates. Visitors did sometimes suspend one or two officials at the very most, but seldom did a visitor general go to such extremes as Lic. Mañozca in suspending five out of six magistrates, in addition to the officers of the treasury. From July 1625 onward, there were no further conflicts of jurisdiction, since all authority lay in the firm hands of the now completely powerful visitor general.

Lic. Mañozca soon realized that the suspended president and the oidores were still a formidable opposition that could do him some damage in Spain. Their unity must be broken. An unexpected opportunity presented itself shortly after the suspension of the judges. The situation concerned the clash between Lic. Manuel Tello de Velasco and his colleagues on the bench.

Dr. Morga's dissatisfaction with the private and public conduct of Lic. Tello de Velasco was one of the factors that persuaded the council to send a visitor general to Quito. The council expressed annoyance with the un-specific character of Dr. Morga's critique of his colleague. The president received instructions on October 23, 1621, to conduct a formal but secret hearing, unbeknownst to Oidor Tello de Velasco, in which witnesses of the highest repute would specifically document the alleged misdeeds of that judge.[61] The president complied with these instructions in April, 1623. Interpreting his orders to mean the greatest possible secrecy, Dr. Morga invited only seven witnesses to present testimony. They were Oidores Peralta and Castillo de Herrera, the fiscal Suárez de Poago, Lic. Juan Alonso de Carvajal, Lic. Luis de Montesinos, Lic. Agustín Moreno, and Diego de Valencia León. All of the non-oidores were close friends of the magistrates on the bench. While Dr. Morga may be accused of "packing" the inquiry with critics of Tello de Velasco, the only means by which the secrecy of the inquiry could be preserved was to select witnesses who were in basic agreement.

The testimonies of the seven witnesses differed only in detail.[62] They accused Oidor Tello de Velasco of speaking in public against his colleagues who differed with him in regard to judicial sentences. He also made uncom-plimentary remarks about the wives of the other oidores. Vain and boastful, he dressed extravagantly. Both in the audiencia chamber and outside of it, he surrounded himself with litigants and people of questionable character. Women of the demimonde regularly visited his home. The most serious set of charges was not that the oidor did not conduct himself with the dignity and decorum befitting a royal magistrate but that he was an incompetent and dishonest judge. He favored certain litigants. He once created a public scene when he stormed into the royal jail and compelled the warden to re-lease Juan Serrano del Valle, who had been imprisoned on the charge of attempted homicide. The audiencia subsequently intervened and reversed the action.

Having come to Quito poor, Lic. Tello de Velasco lived with such osten-tation that all the witnesses concluded that he engaged in illicit business enterprises on the side. His salary as oidor was not sufficient to support his lavish household.

Upon receiving this report, the Council of the Indies recommended that it be turned over to the visitor general, with instructions for him to investi-gate the truth or falsity of the charges as a part of the secret proceedings of the visita general.[63] The council was acutely aware that publication of the charges would damage even further relations among the magistrates. One of the major stipulations in the instructions to the visitor general was that all charges relating to the oidores be investigated in complete secrecy, lest the publication of derogatory information against magistrates, however true or false it might be, would damage the prestige of the audiencia as an institution.[64]

These new instructions reached the visitor general on August 29, 1625, less than two months after he had suspended the majority of the audiencia. Lic. Mañozca heretofore had not been aware of the hostility that all of the other magistrates felt toward Manuel Tello de Velasco. Neither was don Manuel. On March 4, 1625, Oidor Tello de Velasco had joined his colleagues in writing to the king protesting against the procedures of the visitor general. He felt as threatened as his colleagues.[65]

A whole new range of possibilities opened up to Lic. Mañozca. With his usual dispatch, he began secret hearings on September 8, barely a week after the receipt of the royal cedula. The visitor general allowed the president, the fiscal, and Oidor Peralta to return immediately to the capital in order to present testimony. Lic. Mañozca extended the scope of the inquiry to include the testimonies of some 100 witnesses. From October 21 to October 30 he questioned Oidor Tello de Velasco.[66]

Lic. Mañozca or a member of his staff presented Manuel Tello de Velasco with a copy of the Morga investigation of April 15, 1623. This was a flagrant violation of instructions. The inquiry could have been conducted without the names being revealed. The procedure of the visitor general ran counter to the style of both the visita general and the Inquisition, where the accused never knew the names of his accusers. The opponents of Lic. Mañozca claimed that he did it in order to aid the defense of Tello de Velasco and thus to place Tello de Velasco in his debt. According to them, the visitor general exclaimed, when he published the Tello de Velasco proceedings, "What a bull I have hurled into the ring."[67] Faced with proof that his colleagues had accused him of being incompetent, dishonest, and immoral, don Manuel had little alternative but to become a willing ally of the visitor general and reveal what he knew about his colleagues. By this maneuver Lic. Mañozca broke the united front of the audiencia.

The acid hostility between Manuel Tello de Velasco and his associates on the bench, which became public as a direct consequence of Lic. Mañozca's act, lent apparent justification to Lic. Mañozca's contention that none of the suspended judges should return to the bench in Quito.[68] Thus the visitor hoped to force the temporary suspension of the oidores to become permanent.

The motives of the visitor general, however, were too transparent for this maneuver to pay him the dividends that he had anticipated. For one thing, although Oidor Manuel Tello de Velasco did cooperate enthusiastically in the visita general, he evidently was unable to provide the visitor general with additional documentary evidence of major importance against his colleagues. Furthermore, the obvious partiality of the visitor toward don Manuel was a fact that President Morga and his friends were able to use with telling effectiveness to discredit the visita general. Thirdly, the deliberate conversion of the Tello de Velasco case from a secret to a public inquiry, which further embittered the relations among the magistrates, was such a flagrant violation of instructions that the Council of the Indies subsequently regarded it as a major justification for Lic. Mañozca's dismissal.[69]

On February 11, 1626, Lic. Mañozca handed down his verdict. He absolved Oidor Manuel Tello de Velasco of all the accusations contained in the Morga inquiry of April 15, 1623. Phrasing his statement carefully to avoid prejudicing any charges that might result from the visita general, the visitor general declared don Manuel "a good, upright and clean-living judge."[70]

Fearful that Oidor Tello de Velasco would be restored to the bench, where he would seek to inflict vengeance on his enemies, the city council of Quito took alarm. Their procurador, Pedro de Arellano, on February 19, a few days after the publication of the verdict, respectfully requested the visitor general not to restore don Manuel to the tribunal in view of the inflamed state of factionalism. Lic. Mañozca responded in hot anger. He ruled the petition impertinent, and he imposed a fine of 500 pesos on the procurador.[71] The Council of the Indies ordered the fine rescinded.[72]

Once the sentence had been handed down, Oidor Manuel Tello de Velasco brought countercharges against all seven witnesses of the Morga investigation of 1623. Adding more fuel to the flames, the visitor general agreed to hear this suit. Don Manuel accused the defendants of engaging in a deliberate and sinister conspiracy, using slander and perjury, to destroy his reputation before the king. He regarded Dr. Morga as the architect of the plot and the other witnesses merely as willing accomplices.

After hearing testimony for several months, Lic. Mañozca declined to render a verdict. He sent 4,200 pages of written testimony to the Council of the Indies for that tribunal to make the decision.[73] The council filed the testimony, for its patience with the iron-willed visitor general was almost exhausted.

By March, 1627, Lic. Mañozca became sensitive to the decline of his influence in Spain. He finally became aware that he had overplayed his hand. The same magistrate who had declared Manuel Tello de Velasco an "upright judge" a year before admitted on March 20, 1627, that the original charges leveled against don Manuel by Dr. Morga on April 15, 1623, were substantially true. Lic. Mañozca confessed that don Manuel was brazen about his love affairs and vindictive and arrogantly partial in his judicial decisions. His only qualification was that Dr. Morga had not sufficiently documented these charges.[74]

While the Tello de Velasco investigation dragged on with charges and countercharges, imprisonments, and embargoes engendering more bitterness each day, Lic. Mañozca continued to hear testimony and to question witnesses in the secret proceedings of the visita. On December 19, 1626, the visitor general hit what a modern investigator would call "pay dirt." He secured the six love letters written by Dr. Morga in his own hand to his mistress, Gerónima Mexía, La Pallasca.[75]

The visitor general had little time to rejoice over that result of his constant probing. He had alienated most of the prominent citizens and corporations in the kingdom, all of whom were deluging the Council of the Indies with requests that he be recalled. For two years he had held almost undisputed sway. No longer was he feared, for he had done as much damage to the leading citizens as he could with his considerable powers.

On New Year's Eve, 1626, a special messenger brought to the lodgings of the visitor general the shocking tale of the bloody murder that had just taken place in Riobamba. Nicolás de Larraspuru and a gang of cronies had murdered the constable of Riobamba, Pedro Sayago del Hoyo, in a street brawl which took several more lives. The murdered constable was an Extremeño, and his assassin was a Basque. Animosity between the two Iberian nationalities had erupted into bloody riots in Potosí a few years before. Not only was Lic. Mañozca an intransigent partisan of his fellow Basques, but also he was a close friend of the father of the presumed assassin.

The visitor general immediately recognized that the atrocity of the murder could be the spark that would ignite a violent explosion of lawlessness. The land was already seething with unrest. The blame for any outbreak of violence would fall squarely on his shoulders, for there was then only one judge sitting on the bench. For the first time in two years, the principle of sharing authority seemed attractive to Lic. Mañozca. Although a few months earlier the viceroy had suggested that the suspended magistrates be restored to office, Lic. Mañozca refused to act.[76] He stubbornly held to his conviction that none of them should ever hold office again in Quito. On New Year's Eve his recalcitrance was swept away by the threat of a civil war. On January 1, 1627, President Morga and Oidores Tello de Velasco and Castillo de Herrera, but not the fiscal, were restored to office after an absence of eighteen months.

In an unprecedented session on January 1, 1627, the restored magistrates took emergency measures. To head off further bloodshed, the audiencia dispatched one of its members, Alonso Herrera de Castillo, to Riobamba with ample authority as *juez pesquisidor* to sentence the culprits. So concerned were the oidores that Lic. Herrera de Castillo departed immediately for Riobamba, before the notaries had drawn up the official documents.[77]

The judges were back on the bench. The visitor general continued to visit, but his days of power were drawing to a close. Protests against his conduct were before the Council of the Indies. In February, 1627, the council evaluated those documents. Not only did they examine his handling of the Tello de Velasco inquiry and his wholesale suspension of the magistrates, but also they recognized that the visitor general had become embroiled in an acrimonious dispute with the Augustinian and Dominican orders. To this sorry tale of ecclesiastical factionalism we must now turn.

12.

THE BIRTH OF NATIONALISM

Perhaps the most controversial action of the strife-torn *visita general* of Lic. Juan de Mañozca was his unwise if not reckless intervention in the triennial elections of the Dominican order. In the early seventeenth century, there were about three hundred regular clergy in the audiencia kingdom of Quito, divided among the Mercedarians, the Augustinians, the Jesuits, the Franciscans, and the Dominicans.[1] They were usually referred to as the religious or *los religiosos* in contrast to the two hundred secular priests under the immediate supervision of the bishops. The religious orders held the majority of the Indian parishes, whereas many parishes of the secular clergy were in the Spanish and mestizo communities.[2]

While there were still many priests of high standards among the religious, morals had noticeably declined by the beginning of the seventeenth century. The evidence is overwhelming that infractions of the monastic vows of obedience, chastity, and poverty were frequent and often flagrant. One bishop of Quito estimated that about one-third of the Augustinians had left their religious community as apostates.[3]

That the Society of Jesus managed to avoid this decline in discipline may be ascribed to their more selective recruitment, their more rigorous intellectual training, and the more authoritarian structure of their government. The inability of the mendicant orders to discipline themselves was a consequence of their decentralized organization. Provincial superiors and definitors, the governing council, held office for only three years. They were reluctant or unable to take effective punitive measures against misconduct, since they themselves would soon return to the status of subjects. The inspection system whereby a visitor from outside the province received broad powers of investigation, the system after which the secular system of the visita general was patterned, did not prove very effective in rooting out abuses. The powers of the superiors in Rome were not very extensive. The governmental structure of the Franciscans and the Dominicans goes back to the thirteenth century, when the federal and representative structure in monastic organization was in vogue. The government of the Society of Jesus, on the other hand, emerged during the more authoritarian time of the Counter Reformation. Rome appointed the provincial superiors of the Jesuits, in contrast to the intraprovince election of superiors of other orders. Because of the highly centralized if not quasi-military character of the Jesuit organization, Rome could intervene in any province before the abuses got out of hand. With the mendicant orders, Rome could step in only after the abuses had been publicly exposed, and by then the intervention was often ineffective. Finally, the Jesuits avoided the major cause of the factionalism that plagued the other orders in the New World by restricting the membership of creoles to a controllable minority.[4]

In the sixteenth century, the religious born in Spain dominated all the orders, but the balance changed sharply by the beginning of the seventeenth century when the creole friars constituted majorities in many kingdoms. Feeling between these two branches of Spaniards soon became acrimonious, especially within the Dominicans, the Franciscans, and the Augustinians. The Mercedarians, like the Jesuits, were European-dominated. The rivalry was not confined to religious organizations, for it was rampant in all sectors of colonial life.[5]

The Spanish friars argued that the creoles were ill-trained, ill-disciplined, and by inclination lascivious. The Spanish-born religious accused the creoles of being ungrateful for the great efforts they had made in organizing and developing the missionary provinces. The attitude of the Spanish clergy had unmistakable overtones of innate superiority. The creoles could not be trusted, for they had acquired the vices of the land.

Lic. Mañozca expressed harshly but vividly the deep-rooted suspicion that European Spaniards felt toward their American-born cousins when he observed, "Even though the creoles do not have Indian blood, they had been weaned on the milk of Indian women, and hence the creoles like the Indians are children of fear."[6] The intensity of his feelings may result in part from the fact that, although he was born in the peninsula, he spent his childhood and youth in Mexico City, where he was surrounded by creoles. His Spanish birth gave him a feeling of superiority to which he arrogantly clung.[7] The creoles returned the disdain of the Spanish-born. They accused the latter of being misfits or laggards unable to adapt to different conditions in the New World. The creoles contemptuously referred to the Spaniards as *chapetones*, i.e., tenderfoots.[8]

Given the limited economic opportunities and the proclivity of creole heiresses to take the veil, many young creole men of indifferent religious vocation entered the orders, where they were guaranteed a comfortable living. The tension with the chapetones offered an outlet for that large part of their energies not absorbed by religious duties. While we cannot accept the generalization of the Spanish-born friars that the creoles as a group were licentious and ill-disciplined, it is apparent that many creole men entered the orders not out of any compelling religious dedication but out of a feeling that the habit represented a comfortable and secure career.

There is no evidence that the friars who came from Spain were any more virtuous as a group than the creoles. Many Spanish religious chose the habit for the same worldly reasons that the creoles did. An arrogant bigotry underlay the contempt of the Spaniards for the creoles.

The weight of evidence suggests that the clergymen in the New World were more licentious and ill-disciplined than were their brethren in the peninsula. This generalization, however, applied to secular society also. The laxity of moral standards in the Indies grew out of unique social conditions. The existence of large groups of Indians, Negroes, and mixtures with legally defined positions of social inferiority encouraged the spread of moral laxity on the part of the legally superior race—be they European or American Spaniards, be they men of the cloth or laymen. Fragile economic conditions also encouraged this trend. While it is clear that the vow of chastity had some restraining influence on the clergy, immorality and materialism were nevertheless widespread among them. In the last analysis, the clergy could not escape from being influenced by the society in which they lived.

The focus of conflict between the European-born and the American-born religious centered on the chapter elections, held every three years, in which the provincial superior and definitors were chosen by all those of priestly status. In most orders the creoles constituted a clear majority. If they had had their way, they would have monopolized all the offices in the order as well as the most desirable parishes. The peninsular-born religious appealed to the crown and the Council of the Indies, who came forth in the early seventeenth century with the compromise of the *alternativa*. Every other triennium the offices of provincial superior and definitors were to rotate between religious born in the Indies and those born in Spain. Selection of superiors was to be determined not on the basis of numbers or any principle of merit but rather by accident of birth. The alternativa was actually a formula developed in late medieval Spain to soothe the differences among various nationalities in the peninsula.[9]

As it worked out in the Indies, the alternativa was a device to protect the minority against the majority; where the Spaniards were the majority in some orders in the Philippines and Guatemala, they adamantly refused to grant the alternativa to the creole minority. The creoles bitterly resented the forced imposition of the alternativa. They argued, not without some cogency, that this device would intensify the ill-feeling between the two groups.

The wise and experienced Juan de Solórzano disagreed with the settled policy of Madrid and Rome of imposing the alternativa. He observed that the creole friars were "often not inferior in virtue, religious observance, prudence and learning to those of Spain."[10] He expressed genuine sympathy with the creoles' resentment at having to suffer being lorded over in their own land by outsiders. His conclusion "that such alternativas should not readily be granted" did not prevail.[11] Very few Spaniards were as generous in their opinion of the creoles as was the Spanish-born Solórzano, who served for many years in the audiencia of Lima and whose wife was a criolla from Lima. Madrid and Rome imposed the alternativa all over the empire wherever the creoles were a majority. Its application created some of the bitterest disputes in the history of the Spanish colonial world. Chapter meetings often degenerated into brawls and pitched battles in which troops were required to restore a modicum of order. So unrestrained did factionalism become that on occasion partisans resorted to murder. Some of the less turbulent chapter meetings required the presence of an oidor to help calm the more agitated spirits.

These faction-ridden elections actually had social repercussions that extended beyond the walls of the monasteries. Most creole families had a son or two in one of the orders. The families became identified with the creole group inside the order. As Friar Antonine Tibesar has observed, "Thus the chapter meetings of the religious orders may be regarded as the first forum in which the creole was able to state for the first time his preference in regard to a ruler."[12] In this connection, the genesis of modern democracy goes back to the monastic orders of the Middle Ages even more than to the example of the ancient Greeks, whose democracy was direct and not representative. The regular clergy of the Middle Ages pioneered the procedures of representative institutions. The chapter election in Spanish America was one of the first experiments with representative government. It was not a happy one. The representative character was considerably diluted by the desire of Madrid and Rome to protect the Spanish-born minority. There is no doubt that the imposition of the alternativa did much to accentuate the feelings of hostility between Spaniards and creoles. Hence the bitter monastic feuds in the seventeenth century planted some of the seeds out of which grew the movement for independence at a later time.

The Dominicans of Quito adopted the alternativa in 1617 and made one of the first attempts in the Indies to apply it. Its turbulent results foreshadowed the bitter controversy that arose wherever the alternativa was imposed. The Dominicans administered about thirty parishes in the kingdom. In the order were thirty-four Spaniards and about eighty-five creoles, although only forty-one of the latter had the right to vote in the chapter election. In the election of 1621 the creole group received all the offices, for the Spaniards had elected their partisans in the previous triennium. The creoles were so numerous in the chapter meeting held in September, 1624, that they disregarded the alternativa. A creole friar from Pasto, Sebastián Rosero, won twenty-seven votes to the fourteen votes for his Spanish opponent, Gaspar Martínez.[13]

The Spaniards appealed to the audiencia to intervene, with the charge that the creoles had violated the alternativa. Recognizing the explosive potential of disputes among the friars, Dr. Morga came forth with a compromise that demonstrates his political skill. His personal sympathies were with the Spanish faction, but he refused to allow his own inclinations to interfere with his role as an honest broker between the two parties. In the final verdict of the visita general, Dr. Morga received a mild reprimand for preferring to appoint Spanish-born clerics over creoles to secular benefices.[14] While in office, however, he managed to conceal his anti-creole prejudice.

His primary concern was to work out a face-saving compromise. Since the creoles had a clear majority, he persuaded the Spanish group to recognize the creole provincial superior, Rosero, on condition that this recognition would not prejudice any subsequent ruling from Rome as to which candidate was the legitimate prelate. The crisis eased. Friar Sebastián Rosero remained in possession of his office for eight months.

Two events occurred which were destined to make the triennium of Friar Rosero the most turbulent in the history of the Dominican order in Quito. Barely a month after the disputed election, the formidable Lic. Mañozca arrived in Quito. In May, 1625, a letter arrived from the minister-general of the Dominican order in Rome. This communication ordered the Dominican province in Quito to observe the alternativa, but the language employed was ambiguous as to its retroactivity. The minister-general had not yet received the news of the disputed election of the previous September. When Rome did receive the accounts, the minister-general ruled that Father Rosero, the creole candidate, was the winner, and he admonished the Dominicans to observe the alternativa in the future.[15] Although Rome did not intend that the alternativa should be retroactive, this intention was not known in Quito during the spring of 1625.

The Spanish party led by their defeated candidate, Gaspar Martínez, appealed to the audiencia to enforce their interpretation that the ruling of the minister-general was retroactive. The Dominican order was thrown into a turmoil. Both the creole and the peninsular friars abandoned their parishes in the provinces and rushed to Quito to agitate for their respective candidates. Once again Dr. Morga offered his assistance in working out a compromise. He proposed a conference of prelates from all the religious orders and the secular clergy in order to persuade the Dominicans to accept a temporary provincial superior until new orders came from Madrid and Rome clarifying the ambiguous language of the minister-general.

It was at this point that the visitor general intervened. He was not a compromiser by temperament. He insisted that the audiencia take definite action on the petition of the Spanish group. Had the visitor general supported the conciliatory efforts of Dr. Morga, the subsequent fracas might have been avoided. Lic. Mañozca was harshly hostile to the creoles as a group, regarding them as little better in the social scale than people of mixed blood. He often referred to the creole friars as mestizos and mulattoes. During his term as inquisitor in Cartagena, he had boldly intervened in the internal affairs of the Dominican order.[16] Not only did Lic. Mañozca have a grudge against the Dominicans, but also he had clashed with the creole leader, Father Rosero. The latter had refused to grant the lucrative parish at Pintag to one Friar Sebastián Maldonado, a personal friend of the visitor general. Rosero's refusal to grant this request was reasonable. Maldonado did not belong to the Dominican province of Quito. He had been expelled from the province of Lima for gross misconduct and sentenced as a galley slave.

After he had been deposed as visitor general, Lic. Mañozca published a tract in Lima defending his conduct in this episode. He claimed that he had observed strict neutrality in the disputed election. His correspondence in 1625 and 1626 contradicts this assertion.

Compelled by Lic. Mañozca to act on the petition of the Spanish party, the audiencia delayed handing down its verdict until July 10, 1625. With the exception of Oidor Peralta, all the magistrates reluctantly voted to grant assistance to the Spanish candidate, Martínez.[17] He was duly installed as provincial superior, but only after twenty of the more spirited young creole friars were taken in custody and scattered among the monasteries of the other orders. One of the first acts of the new provincial superior was to assign to the somewhat dubious friend of Lic. Mañozca the lucrative parish he coveted.

Seven days after the audiencia handed down its decision, the visitor general issued his edict suspending the majority of the magistrates and leaving the bench in the hands of the two junior oidores. Pressure from Lic. Mañozca was largely responsible for the ruling of July 10. By his own admission, one of the factors that led him to suspend the magistrates was their obvious reluctance to vote in favor of the Spanish candidate. Left to their own bureaucratic ways and under the experienced direction of Dr. Morga, the audiencia judges would have done what comes naturally to most bureaucratic agencies. They would have solved the problem by postponing its solution with some *ad hoc,* face-saving compromise.

Much of the responsibility for subsequent events fell on the willing shoulders of the now all-powerful visitor general. His defense of his conduct published after his dismissal as visitor general was that the audiencia took most of the actions in the controversy. This argument is highly questionable. The two remaining oidores possessed little freedom of action. They were, in the words of Fiscal Poago, "a couple of miserable constables executing the orders of the visitor general."[18]

The dispossessed creole majority appealed their case to the viceroy in Lima. After consulting a junta of theologians, the viceroy accepted their recommendation that the creole candidate, Rosero, was the canonically elected provincial superior. The viceroy instructed the acting fiscal in Quito on November 20, 1625, to lend all possible legal assistance to Sebastián Rosero.[19] The two remaining oidores were in a quandary. They were caught between the orders of the viceroy and the adamant hostility of Lic. Mañozca toward restoration of the creoles to office. They procrastinated. They wrote to the viceroy on December 3 justifying their action in recognizing Martínez and stressing the factionalism and lack of discipline among the creoles.[20] The viceroy replied on January 20, 1626, rejecting these arguments and firmly insisting on the reinstatement of Rosero.[21]

The viceroy's letter of November 20, 1625, ordering the reinstatement of Rosero had caught everyone in Quito by surprise. The creoles acted swiftly and recklessly. They received the news from their friends in Lima before the official communication reached Quito. The Spanish provincial superior, Martínez, was in the provinces and so was Father Rosero. The sudden death of the ranking Spanish friar in the capital, Marcos Flores, who was prior of the convent, facilitated a creole coup d'etat. Under the leadership of Friar Gaspar Manrique de Lara they seized control of the main convent in Quito in order to restore to office the board of definitors elected by the creoles in the election of September, 1624.

Friar Sebastián Maldonado rushed back to Quito to protect the interests of the Spanish party. He frantically appealed to the audiencia to put down "the revolt of the creoles." But the triumphant creoles gleefully cited the orders of the viceroy. On December 1, 1625, Maldonado sought refuge in the *portería* of the convent of the nuns of St. Catherine of Siena. The creole party sent a group of six young friars to the convent to take Maldonado by force back to the Dominican monastery. The charge was disobedience. The convent of St. Catherine happened to be located next to the lodgings of the visitor general.

Maldonado resisted arrest. The young friars used force. According to the account of Lic. Mañozca, the *frailecitos* were armed with swords and daggers. Hearing the noise of the fighting, the visitor general appeared on the balcony and ordered his retainers to arrest all those involved in the turmoil and to bring them by force if necessary into his lodgings for questioning. In the meantime, a crowd of three hundred people had gathered to watch the spectacle of the fighting clergymen.

What happened inside the house of the visitor general is the subject of contradictory testimony. Father Maldonado, according to Lic. Mañozca, was more dead than alive. After disarming the young creole friars, the visitor general arrested them in the name of the Inquisition. On any trumped-up charge of heresy the jurisdiction of the Holy Office superseded that of all the other secular and ecclesiastical tribunals. It was only by invoking his authority as inquisitor that Lic. Mañozca could exercise jurisdiction over the friars. The visitor general questioned them for more than six hours. According to the anti-Mañozca accounts, the visitor general used harsh words, denouncing them as "brigands, infamous ones, and Indians in the habits of monks."[22] Lic. Mañozca subsequently denied these accusations. After the questioning was completed, the Holy Office placed the Dominican friars under house arrest. During the interrogation, the visitor general was reputed by his opponents to have said, "I am like a flash of lightning. I strike suddenly. No one is going to escape from my hands . . . even if I have to pursue him into the bowels of the earth in order to drag him out and punish him."[23]

The prior of the Dominican convent refused the summons of the visitor general to report to his lodgings. He regarded the arrest of the friars as a sacrilegious act meriting automatic excommunication. With the visitor general's encouragement, the two remaining oidores then led a large delegation of citizens to the Dominican convent, whose premises they invaded searching for arms. Finding none, they withdrew but not before admonishing the friars to continue to obey Martínez as provincial superior.

It is clear that the attempt to arrest Maldonado was reckless and provocative. If the creole leader, Rosero, had been in Quito at the time, he might have been able to restrain the young hotheads. Such an attempt was bound to evoke a sharp retaliation from the quick-tempered visitor general. The Dominican creoles had a favorable ruling from the viceroy. The visitor general ultimately would have to enforce it, but a little patience was required. However, neither side was in a mood to wait. Lic. Mañozca was equally rash in arresting the friars in the name of the Inquisition. Whether he verbally or physically mistreated the friars is unimportant. The fact that he arrested them gave the extremists among the creoles a pretext to claim that the traditional privileges of the order were being violated. They invoked a legal weapon of great potency by setting up a special ecclesiastical tribunal called a *conservatoría* (conservatory).

Pope Pius V and then Gregory XV in 1621 had granted permission to the regular orders to set up conservatories in those situations where their privileges were challenged by the bishops or other ecclesiastical corporations. Among the traditional privileges was immunity from arrest. As one of the "estates" in a corporate society, each of the various components of the Church enjoyed autonomous jurisdiction over its own members. The crown recognized the need for conservatory tribunals, provided certain conditions were met. A special tribunal could not function without the prior permission of the audiencia and without a definition of the scope of its jurisdiction.[24]

On December 2, 1625, the day after the fracas at the convent of St. Catherine, the Dominicans notified the audiencia that they wished to set up a conservatory. They were nebulous about the scope and purpose of the tribunal, merely citing something vague about preserving the good government of the province. The two judges took no action. They hoped that procrastination would give them some time to work out a compromise. But the time for conciliation had passed.

The suspended fiscal went to the convent of the Augustinians, who had agreed to staff the conservatory. He assured them that they did not need the approval of the audiencia in order to set up a conservatory. He also informed the friars that the visitor general could be excommunicated on the testimony of others without being given an opportunity to defend himself. The opinion of the fiscal about the role of the audiencia was based on his interpretation that, since the two remaining oidores were included under the visita general, they had no real freedom of action. As a "rump tribunal," their permission was not necessary. The conservatory was legal in that its sole purpose was to deal with a clearcut case of physical violence perpetrated by ecclesiastics against ecclesiastics.

Somewhat questionable though that opinion was, the fiscal was on even shakier ground when he argued that an excommunication could be pronounced without the visitor's being allowed to defend himself. The Spanish legal system meticulously guarded the right of defendants to testify on their own behalf before being sentenced.

Melchor Suárez de Poago came from Asturias, a land that borders on the Basque country of Lic. Mañozca. Like Mañozca, he was a man of vibrantly intense emotions. In Panama, where he served as fiscal from 1613 to 1619, he feuded so furiously with his colleagues that the Council of the Indies decided to send him to Quito in 1619, and thus he escaped the devastating earthquake that destroyed Panama City on May 2, 1621.[25] But he could also be staunchly loyal to his friends. He never wavered in his friendship for Dr. Morga. Stubborn, cantankerous, and tireless, he was an enemy worthy of Lic. Mañozca. Their first meeting in Cartagena in 1613, when Lic. Suárez de Poago was passing through en route to his new post in Panama, was also their first clash. In Quito they were implacable enemies from the beginning.[26] There are no more fiery indictments of the conduct of Lic. Mañozca than the ones penned by Lic. Suárez de Poago.[27] Lic. Mañozca paid him back with the same coin. The more often the visitor general arrested the fiscal and the more fines he imposed on him, the more tenaciously the stubborn fiscal fought back. On one occasion Lic. Mañozca paid a left-handed compliment to his foe when he observed, ". . . his boldness which some call courage and others call want of prudence and recklessness . . . ."[28]

With the willing assistance of the suspended fiscal, the conservatory held secret hearings during the month of December in which some twenty witnesses solemnly swore that the agents of the visitor general had physically maltreated the six Dominican friars in front of the convent of St. Catherine on December 1. The Dominican creoles won the support of the large Augustinian order, whose provincial superior was then Friar Francisco de la Fuente y Chaves. The large creole contingent of the Augustinians willingly allied themselves with the Dominican creoles by lending the services of one of their most respected members as judge conservator. Friar Fulgencio de Araujo, twice provincial superior of the Augustinian province, was then prior of the convent in Quito.[29]

On December 26, 1625, the Dominican creoles delivered their counter-blow. And it was a telling one. On all the main squares of the capital the friars posted notices excommunicating Lic. Juan de Mañozca and his staff for physically abusing the six Dominicans on the previous December 1. This act created a major scandal. If the excommunication could be enforced, no one would be obligated to obey the orders of the visitor general.

Lic. Mañozca mobilized all his energies and his considerable powers to get the edict of excommunication withdrawn. Deeply mortified by the temerity of an attempt to excommunicate an inquisitor in his own district, and by creoles at that, he publicly proclaimed that the act was brazenly illegal.

On the very day that the bans of excommunication were posted, the audiencia issued an edict exiling the Augustinian friars composing the con-servatory. Those friars, of course, were in hiding. The visitor general moved swiftly and simultaneously against the two men whom he regarded as the real architects of his excommunication, i.e., the provincial superior of the Augustinians and the suspended fiscal.

The Augustinian provincial superior and five other friars were arrested in the name of the Inquisition. They were in custody for several days.

When the fiscal was arrested in his home, he refused to put on street clothes. The agents of the visitor general escorted him in his undergarments through the streets. The old but agile fiscal managed to escape from his police escort and flee into the cathedral, where he could not be arrested.

After three days he surrendered to the authorities. Placed in jail for six days, he was questioned by the visitor general every day from 3 P.M. until 10 or 11 P.M. When he was released from jail, he was placed under house arrest. His property (what there was left of it) was embargoed.

The principal aim of the visitor general was to capture the judge conservator and get his hands on the testimony submitted to the conservatory. His agents tirelessly searched every convent and many private homes day and night. The audiencia issued an edict exiling from the kingdom anyone who provided food or shelter to the judge conservator and his two notaries. In one of the searches of the Augustinian convent, the agents of the visitor general inspected the archives, from which they removed and published secret investigations of the misconduct of the friars, much to the mortification of the Augustinians.

Once again Lic. Mañozca used his inquisitional authority to strike a blow against the Augustinians. He ordered the Holy Office to conduct a secret investigation of the life and morals of the Augustinian provincial superior, Friar Francisco de la Fuente y Chaves. His bitter enemies among the Spanish faction in the order abundantly documented his shortcomings. Among their allegations were that he failed to confess for long periods, that he won his election by simony, that he received women in his cell, and that he did not punish the wrongdoings of his friends in the order. While the subsequent career of Friar Francisco de la Fuente y Chaves suggests that these charges in the main were not inaccurate, Lic. Mañozca's motive was clear. He sought not to expose wrongdoing as such but to punish the Augustinian creoles for their alliance with the Dominicans against him.[30]

In the absence of the bishop from the city, Lic. Mañozca requested the provisor of the see, Gerónimo Burgazes, to lift the ban of excommunication. As the chief deputy of the bishop, he granted only a conditional removal of the ban. The provisor argued quite correctly that only the bishop had the authority to issue an unconditional removal. Anticipating the wrath of Lic. Mañozca, the provisor had the good sense to request the bishop to reassign him to another post.

The bishop of Quito, Francisco de Sotomayor (1623–28), whose portrait hanging in the Cathedral of Quito is included in the illustration section, was not unclever. Correctly sizing up the personality of the visitor general, he chose to leave the capital in order to make a year-long pastoral inspection of his diocese. He was a placid soul who had no stomach for controversy and turmoil. Since his brother was the confessor of Philip IV, and therefore both he and Lic. Mañozca were identified with the Count-Duke of Olivares, there were sound political reasons for him not to get involved in the turmoil of the visita general. The good bishop was scarcely courageous, but his long absence from the capital preserved his peace of mind.[31]

The visitor general then turned to the pliant audiencia. On the basis of the conditional lifting of the ban by the provisor, the two oidores declared the ban lifted on January 8, 1626. They asserted that all the acts of the conservatory tribunal were null and void, since the audiencia had not granted a license for the establishment of that tribunal.

Friar Fulgencio Araujo, the fugitive judge conservator, and his two notaries managed to remain in hiding for fifteen days. The Holy Office appointed a host of deputies, *familiares,* who searched homes and buildings for these friars "as if they were hunting for lions."[32] Friar Fulgencio's brother Leonardo, who was also an Augustinian friar, arranged for Friar Fulgencio to surrender to the visitor general and to hand over the testimony collected by the conservatory tribunal.

Punishment was swift. The judge conservator, Fulgencio Araujo, the provincial superior, Francisco de la Fuente y Chaves, and one of the notaries of the conservatory were exiled by the audiencia to the penal colony of Chile. Like others before and after them, they remained in comfortable Lima by appealing to the viceroy.

The friars were determined to squeeze every drop of melodrama out of the order of expulsion. Dressed in their white habits, they were escorted by guards while the whole of Quito silently congregated in the square overlooking the monastery of that order. Friar Francisco de la Fuente y Chaves raised his voice and said, "This is the justice that Lic. Mañozca administers to these three humble Augustinian friars for having defended the authority of the Roman pontiff: he who acts in such a fashion ultimately will have to pay."[33]

Not the bitterest pill that Lic. Mañozca had to swallow was ultimate compliance with the orders from Lima. Friar Sebastián Rosero returned to office as provincial superior, with the visitor general personally pleading with the Spanish group to grant him obedience. Rome and Madrid eventually confirmed the decision.[34] After completing his strife-torn triennium, Sebastián Rosero received an isolated missionary parish in the province of Quijos, where he died in 1628.[35]

In the heat engendered by this controversy, all parties to the dispute acted rashly and twisted the law to their own partisan purposes. To argue the legal pros and cons would be pointless. More significant are the political implications. The intensity of the hatred between the Spaniards and the creoles precluded any permanent solution except avoidance of direct confrontations, whenever possible, by means of artful compromises. As the French say, there is nothing so permanent as a temporary arrangement. That there were not even more violent explosions between the creoles and the Spaniards (and there were many indeed in all parts of the empire) was due to the political skills of magistrates like Dr. Morga. Lic. Mañozca, on the other hand, was one of those forceful, arrogant officials who erroneously believe that there is a solution for every problem—their own solution. Dr. Morga and many of his colleagues had the wisdom to realize that there is no solution to some problems but skillful procrastination.

The major blunder of Lic. Mañozca was to allow himself to get involved in the controversy. His commissions to investigate the audiencia and the royal treasury did not include any authority to intervene in the affairs of the religious orders. When the viceroy received accounts of what had happened in Quito, he sharply rebuked the visitor general for meddling in the dispute and curtly reminded him to confine himself to carrying out his commissions.[36] As one result of the whole fracas, circular cedulas applicable to all the kingdoms of the Indies were issued, upon the suggestion of the viceroy, ordering that no audiencia henceforth should give legal assistance in a disputed election among the friars without first securing the approval of the viceroy.[37] The aim of such legislation was to limit the number of conservatories, for those extraordinary ecclesiastical tribunals could create genuine social disturbances by an indiscriminate use of their authority to excommunicate.

The ill-concealed hostility of Lic. Mañozca toward the creoles and his obvious partiality toward the Spanish party aroused fierce resentment in the large and influential creole community of the capital as well as in the religious orders. Although he may have gained some support among the Spanish-born residents, his alienation of the creoles proved to be a major error. Moreover, his arbitrary actions lent support to the assertions of the suspended magistrates that he was tyrannical, ruthless, and capricious.

In the course of one year, the visitor general had aroused a formidable coalition against him, consisting of the suspended magistrates, the religious orders, and the creoles. The combined efforts of these diverse elements were to bring about his fall.

13.

THE FALL OF A VISITOR GENERAL

The enemies of Lic. Mañozca combined forces in the winter of 1626. He was no longer feared; he had already shot his bolt. What the anti-Mañozca coalition now needed was an appropriate emissary to carry their case to the authorities in Spain. The man chosen for this delicate mission possessed the necessary qualifications. He was Friar Leonardo de Araujo, the brother of the exiled judge conservator. After the exile of the Augustinian provincial superior, Friar Francisco de la Fuente y Chaves, Friar Leonardo had been placed in that office. On his mission to Spain he carried with him not only a memorial of fifty-four chapters outlining the creole position in the disputed election, which he published in Lima, but also letters from Dr. Morga, the other suspended magistrates, the city council of Quito, leading citizens, and the provincial superiors of all the religious orders.[1] This combined correspondence constituted a redoubtable indictment of the visitor general and vividly depicted the visita as a virtual reign of terror.

Lic. Mañozca allowed Friar Leonardo de Araujo to leave Quito for Europe in March, 1626, evidently without suspecting the true nature of his

279

mission. The rump audiencia could have prevented his departure.[2] Unquestionably Araujo reassured the visitor general of his good intentions toward him. His arranging the surrender of his brother, the judge conservator, and his role in restoring a modicum of tranquility in the Augustinian order lent some substance to his protestations of friendship for the visitor general. The letters of Lic. Mañozca at this time depict a man who was supremely confident that he had vanquished his foes. Ordinarily suspicious of all but his closest collaborators, he let his defenses down when he allowed Friar Leonardo de Araujo to depart peaceably for Spain with his explosive baggage.

A year before the Araujo mission, the suspended magistrates had already begun their offensive to undermine the position of Lic. Mañozca before the king and the Council of the Indies. As early as March 4, 1625, barely three months after the beginning of the visita general, the audiencia dispatched to Spain an articulate protest. The magistrates denounced the visitor general's treatment of Diego de Valencia León, his acceptance of testimony from convicted criminals, his partiality toward Lic. Rodríquez Plaza, and his abuse of the demandas públicas de mal juzgado.[3] The magistrates also pointed out the sharp decline in the prosperity of the land.

In fact the conduct of the visita general coincided with an economic depression. The collapse of the cacao boom and the sack of Guayaquil by the Dutch in the summer of 1624 sent that whole province into an economic tailspin.[4] The economy of the Sierra was hard hit by one of the periodic drops in Peru's demand for Quito textiles.[5] The nearly 100,000 pesos raised by the forced loan of 1621 had further drained the slender resources of the land. The actions of the visitor general merely worsened an already bad situation. Many of the richest citizens found themselves embroiled in the countless litigations arising out of the visita general while their liquid capital was tied up by fines, embargoes, and bonds. The visitor general managed to immobilize most of the liquid capital of the kingdom.

The audiencia pointed out the bleakness of economic conditions. Lic. Mañozca, whose forte was not economics, dismissed their account as a plot hatched by Dr. Morga to shift attention away from his own misdeeds.[6] But the state of the economy in the remote mountain kingdom was a matter of some concern to the Council of the Indies.

Of even greater concern to the council was the mounting cost of the visita general. The officers of the exchequer, both of whom had been briefly jailed and then suspended from office, took malicious pleasure in reporting to the king that, in a period of fourteen months, the treasury had paid out 29,978 pesos, 7 reales, and 3 quartillos for the expenses of the visita general.[7] By the date of his dismissal, Lic. Mañozca and his staff had spent 66,878 pesos in two and a half years.[8] It was one of the most expensive visitas generales in the history of the Spanish empire. Although the royal treasury was responsible for paying the salaries of all officers of the visita general, it was hoped that each mission would be self-supporting from the fines collected. In practice, however, the fines were difficult to collect, as we shall see in Chapter 15. Hence the Council of the Indies observed with increasing distress the mounting expenses of the visita general.[9] The enemies of Lic. Mañozca exploited the council's concern to the maximum.

In order to secure prompt action from the overworked council, the suspended judges, minus Manuel Tello de Velasco, hired an agent-lawyer, an *agente de negocios,* to represent their interests. Some magistrates also sent personal emissaries, often one of their relatives who happened to be at Court. Oidor Peralta and the fiscal, Suárez de Poago, and Diego de Valencia León had personal representatives. So did the visitor general.[10]

On January 15, 1626, the agente de negocios, Francisco Juárez Arguello, submitted a memorandum on behalf of his clients, the oidores. He was apparently unaware that the visitor general six months before had suspended his clients.[11] The memorandum requested that a date be set for termination of the visita general; that the visitor general be ordered to end the demandas públicas; that the visitor be forbidden to receive anonymous testimony; that Lic. Mañozca be prohibited from imposing fines on the judges or embargoing their property; that the visita general of the treasury be confined to investigation of the conduct of treasury officers and that the auditing of their books be done by the tribunal de cuentas in Lima; that convicted criminals and people of questionable and humble origin not be allowed to testify; and that no residencia sentences be reviewed by the visitor general.

The second offensive of the audiencia produced few tangible results. Just as the council refused to take any hasty action against the audiencia when the first wave of protests against the Morga administration began to arrive, so now the instinctive reaction of the council was to postpone taking any action against the visitor general. The decision to dispatch a visitor general to Quito had been reached after mature deliberation. Without prejudging the Morga regime, the council had become convinced that the complaints required a careful examination. Hence they were determined to give Lic. Mañozca a free hand to conduct his inquiry.[12]

The mood of the correspondence of Lic. Mañozca with the Council of the Indies falls into clearly defined periods. In April, 1625, his letters brim with the confidence of a man who dominates all he surveys: The audiencia of Quito is a nest of corruption and sin, and he is diligently setting it to rights. In February of 1626, the mood of exultation and optimism reaches its climax: He has just rendered his verdict that Manuel Tello de Velasco is an honorable and upright judge,[13] and he erroneously thinks that he has crushed, a few months earlier, what he considers the insolent insubordination of the creole faction in the Dominican order. By September of 1626, his mood of confidence has disappeared, and he is no longer on the offensive. The bitterness provoked by the Tello de Velasco affair and the turmoil revolving around the friars have brought a profound sense of insecurity and uneasiness to the once-indomitable visitor general. At last he is learning that a visita general can be a purgatory for the investigator as well as the investigated. He complains to one important official in the council, "I am alone here and so many are against me."[14]

In the late fall of 1626, Friar Leonardo de Araujo arrived at Court with his shocking picture of a Quito fallen into turmoil. The charges were so serious that they could not be brushed aside, since every major corporation joined the chorus of protest. The Count-Duke of Olivares, in the name of the king, requested the Council of the Indies to make a formal evaluation of these charges. Lic. Mañozca's agent at Court made feverish efforts to protect the interests of his client. He urged the council to re-examine all Lic. Mañozca's correspondence and not only the accounts critical of his conduct.[15]

The consulta that ensued merits careful examination. The council recommended that Lic. Mañozca be removed as visitor general and someone else be appointed to conclude the inquiry.[16] That the audiencia of Quito had committed abuses was not questioned. What disturbed the council were the procedures the visitor general was employing to uncover these abuses. From Madrid it looked as if the visitor had committed three major blunders: (1) his suspension of the magistrates, (2) his handling of the Tello de Velasco case, and (3) his intervention in the disputed election of the Dominican order. The visitor general had proved himself harsh, prejudiced, and capricious. He had allowed his investigatory zeal to override the traditional legal rights that all defendants possessed.

In suspending the majority of the judges barely six months after the beginning of the visita general, Lic. Mañozca had violated his instructions. The visitor general had been ordered to make every effort to include all matters relating to the president and the oidores in the secret aspect of the visita general lest public exposure of the misdeeds of individual judges tarnish the prestige of the tribunal as an institution. Under no circumstances were any of the superior magistrates of the audiencia to be suspended until the visitor general had drawn up charges against them and allowed them to present testimony in their own defense. Lic. Mañozca had not followed these instructions. His justification for the suspension, that people would be afraid to testify even in secret against the incumbent judges, was considered unsatisfactory and inadequate.

In leaving only two and then only one judge on the bench, Lic. Mañozca had virtually abolished the audiencia. Thus he had usurped for himself the ordinary jurisdiction reserved for that tribunal. The extraordinary authority of the visitor general was supposed to complement, not supersede, the ordinary jurisdiction of the audiencia.

The Council of the Indies also had harsh words for the way in which the visitor general had conducted the Tello de Velasco inquiry. He had misinterpreted his instructions to investigate the Morga report of 1623 when he conducted a public trial in which he revealed to Lic. Tello de Velasco all the contents and the names of the Morga report of 1623. The investigation of the Morga charges should have been included in the secret proceedings of the visita general. To give Manuel Tello de Velasco access to the Morga report merely widened and deepened the factional feud dividing the audiencia, a condition which had been one of the major reasons for dispatching the visita general in the first place. To pass a public sentence declaring Manuel Tello de Velasco "a good, upright and clean-living judge" and then to allow him to file a criminal suit against all the signatories of the 1623 report was irresponsible usurpation of authority. In a visita general only the Council of the Indies rendered verdicts. The responsibility of the visitor general was to collect the testimony and draw up the charges.

The council in its consulta furthermore stressed that the intervention of Lic. Mañozca in the disputed election of the Dominican order was unwise. Instead of rushing into the center of the controversy, he should have avoided getting involved in it at all, since his commissions did not include such matters. If he had to play any role, it should have been that of honest broker to conciliate, not expand, the dispute. The council realistically recognized that all parties in the clash had behaved recklessly, but they directed their hottest anger at the conduct of Lic. Mañozca.

While the consulta of the council concentrated on the three factors just described, other aspects of the conduct of the visitor general came under pointed criticism. Subjecting the magistrates to the demandas públicas was an unnecessary harassment. His massive imposition of fines, bonds, and embargoes brought about needless harm and humiliation. His reliance on the testimony of convicted criminals and sworn enemies of the magistrates also came under attack. And finally the council pointed out to the king that the visita general was proving quite costly.

The council also took a dim view of the visitor general's using his authority as inquisitor without expressed permission. The authority of a visitor general was extensive enough without the additional, dreaded power of the Holy Office. Lic. Mañozca, however, was not the only person to use the Inquisition as a means of circumventing other courts. In any matter of alleged heresy, the authority of the Holy Office overrode that of all other tribunals. Even Philip II, with his profound respect for the laws and the courts, resorted to the Inquisition in a trumped-up charge of heresy in order to wrest Antonio Pérez from the court of the *justicia mayor* of Aragón.[17]

The recommendation of the council was that not only should Lic. Mañozca be replaced as visitor general but also he should be deprived of his regular position in the Inquisition in Lima. His proven inability to maintain harmonious relations with the regular clergy made him unsuitable for the Holy Office. This part of the recommendation of the council never was enforced. Lic. Mañozca did retain his post in the Inquisition of Lima. It could be that the independent-minded authorities of the Inquisition refused to comply, for their motive was to salvage the career of one of their own members.[18]

On March 7, a mere two weeks after the council had submitted its advisory consulta, the king acted. The royal cedula provided for the termination of Lic. Mañozca's commission as visitor general within three days after its publication in Quito. The cedula contained a series of orders designed to repair some of the damage inflicted by the visitor general.[19] The suspended magistrates were restored to their posts with full salaries for the whole period of their suspension. It so happened that they had not been deprived of their salaries by the visitor general. On March 7, 1627, Madrid, of course, did not know that on the previous January 1 Lic. Mañozca had restored several judges to office. The fiscal, however, did not resume his post until September 20, when the royal cedula arrived in Quito.[20]

In contrast to the extensive analysis contained in the secret consulta of the council, the published royal cedulas dispatched to Lic. Mañozca and the audiencia only very briefly outlined the reasons for the royal action. The king tersely expressed his displeasure over the visitor general's suspension of the magistrates and his role in the alternativa controversy.

On September 18, 1627, the official courier arrived in Quito with the news. Lic. Mañozca had already learned of his fate a few weeks before by a special courier dispatched from Cartagena by his old friend, General Tómas de Larraspuru, commander of the fleet and father of the notorious don Nicolás.[21] On the first night after the publication of the cedulas, a group of more than slightly irreverent friars serenaded the visitor general in front of his lodgings. Playing funeral music, they jested with the liturgical office of the dead, ending with the imprecation, "A porta inferi . . . nunquam eruas, Domine, animam Joannis . . . ."[22]

Dr. Morga, on the other hand, was guilty of no disrespect to his fallen foe. He showered on Lic. Mañozca all the courtesies that the latter, during his days of arrogant power, had failed to render to the president. He frequently visited Lic. Mañozca in his lodgings. On the day of departure, the president led a large group of notables in bidding Lic. Mañozca good-by with ceremony and courtesy.[23] During his journey to Guayaquil, the ex-visitor general penned in his own hand a series of amicable notes to the president.[24] The polite behavior of Dr. Morga made Lic. Mañozca appreciate an aspect of the president's character that he had perhaps not previously noticed. Antonio de Morga could be a Spanish gentleman—unfailingly courteous and quietly dignified in most of his social dealings.

Although Lic. Mañozca made clear from the beginning his determination to document the abuses of the Morga administration, the visitor general had no personal animus against the president similar to the hatred and contempt he felt toward the fiscal. While serving as alcalde de crimen in Mexico City, Dr. Morga had also been a part-time legal consultant to the Inquisition, a *consultor*. The senior inquisitor then was Pedro Saenz de Mañozca, the uncle of the future visitor general. There is no evidence that they did not enjoy polite and friendly relations. Dr. Morga would not have received the post of consultor without the positive support of the senior inquisitor. Dr. Morga did not know the youthful Lic. Mañozca in Mexico, for the latter had left for Spain a few years before Dr. Morga arrived in Mexico from the Philippines.[25]

Fiscal Suárez de Poago was neither as prudent nor as gentlemanly as President Morga. The fiscal tried to gain access to the documents of the visita general on the pretext that Lic. Mañozca possessed some of the audiencia records. But the ex-visitor general tenaciously protected those mountainous bundles. The king had explicitly instructed Lic. Mañozca to hand over to his successor in Lima all the secret and confidential testimony he had collected.[26]

Although Dr. Morga insisted that the deposed visitor general be treated with every possible courtesy, such compassion did not extend to the staff of Lic. Mañozca. They were the victims of a series of imprisonments and legal harassments that fell little short of persecution. Among those who bore the full brunt of the wrath of the audiencia were Juan de Ibarra, the principal deputy of Lic. Mañozca, and Lope de Bermeo, his notary.[27]

As visitor general, Lic. Mañozca overplayed his hand. He was accumulating considerable evidence that there were serious abuses in the audiencia. But prudence was not a part of his make-up. Instead of confining himself to proving certain misdeeds, he wanted to expose Quito as a den of iniquity. Even more than the secular courts, this particular inquisitor believed a man guilty until proven innocent. Hence he displayed a notorious bias against all those whom he was investigating. Intolerant of opposition and intransigently partial in his friendships and animosities, he sought to terrorize all those who would not bend to his will. He intimidated them to the point that they fought back. At stake were their careers, their estates, and their honor. The friars also returned the fire with the same vehemence that the laymen displayed. But the friars had an additional weapon which in desperation they employed —excommunication. In treating the political and ecclesiastical authorities in Quito as if they were behind the closed doors of an inquisitorial chamber, Lic. Mañozca learned to his sorrow that the whole bureaucratic structure of government was a complex web of checks and balances in which no one possessed clearly defined authority. The visitor could investigate the visited, but the conduct of the visitor in turn was subject to review by his superiors in Madrid.[28]

However different Dr. Morga and Lic. Mañozca were in temperament— the former courteous and dignified and the latter irascible and arrogant— they shared one important trait. Both men degenerated in positions where they lacked resident superiors. Dr. Morga served with distinction in the audiencias of Manila and Mexico, where he was surrounded with peers and superiors. In Quito, on the other hand, where he was the dominant figure in the absence of a strong bishop, his sensuality and avarice came to the fore. Lic. Mañozca also served with distinction in Lima, Madrid, Granada, and Mexico in positions of responsibility. In those posts his powerful urge to command arbitrarily was held in check, to some extent at least, by the presence of magistrates who were his equals or his superiors. In Cartagena and Quito, on the other hand, there were no such restraints placed on his zeal. However inefficient the Spanish bureaucratic system of checks and balances may have been, it did manage to put some limits on the arbitrary extremism of strong-willed personalities such as Antonio de Morga and Juan de Mañozca.

If the visita general of Lic. Mañozca proves anything, it is the danger of entrusting that delicate mission to a man of overzealous temperament. And the rapidity with which he was dismissed in those days of slow communications points out how swiftly the crown and the Council of the Indies could intervene to restore the balance.[29]

Juan de Solórzano, who had a wealth of practical experience with visitas generales from his service in both Lima and the Council of the Indies, laid down some guidelines which, if followed, might guarantee something like an impartial execution of justice: A visitor general should give the benefit of the doubt to those magistrates under investigation. A visita general should have a set time limit. A visitor general should seek to ascertain the virtues as well as the faults of those being visited. A visitor general should be chosen with care so that he could be given the benefit of the doubt in the face of charges made by his critics. A visitor general should restrict to a minimum a review of the regular judicial decisions of an audiencia. Solórzano probably had in mind the particular visita general in Quito, which was still going on while he was writing his observations.[30] It is clear that Lic. Mañozca violated those precepts. His successor made a conscientious effort to observe them.

14.

A CAUTIOUS VISITOR GENERAL

However displeased the king and the council were with the manner in which Lic. Mañozca had conducted himself, the authorities in Madrid were grimly determined that this visita general, once begun, should be brought to a conclusion. Quito waited anxiously for three years until the successor of Lic. Mañozca finally arrived. The first appointee, Juan Ximénez de Montalvo, oidor in Lima, died before he could assume the post.[1] Both the viceroy and the audiencia of Lima delayed taking action. The nervous audiencia in Quito blamed the alleged intrigues of Lic. Mañozca in Lima for the delay, when in reality none of the oidores in Lima wanted the thankless assignment. Perhaps the authorities in Lima intentionally dragged their feet in the vain hope that the death of a few key magistrates in Quito would make the completion of the visita general unnecessary.[2]

Reluctantly Dr. Juan García Galdós Galdoche de Valencia, senior oidor in the audiencia of Lima, accepted the task. He was a veteran of thirty years of service, divided between the audiencias of Mexico and Lima.[3] He was then 68 years old, experienced and prudent but in poor health.

On February 5, 1630, he formally resumed the visita general. The situation he found in the capital was disturbing, with the city divided into two factions. One was identified with President Morga, Oidor Castillo de Herrera, and the fiscal, and the other party rallied around the standard of Oidor Manuel Tello de Velasco. Street fighting and violence had not yet broken out, but the stage was set for just that. Personal relations among the judges were so bitter that the ordinary administration of justice was impeded. Among the ranks of the two bands were the principal leaders of the community. Since the less well-to-do had attached themselves as informal retainers to the more prosperous while some 2,500 mestizos of indifferent means and status lurked as potential opportunists, the danger that the factionalism would erupt into violence was real.[4]

Much of this ill-feeling went back to the decision of Lic. Mañozca to publish the secret testimony collected by Dr. Morga in 1623 against the conduct of Oidor Manuel Tello de Velasco. The split between him and his colleagues on the bench, which became increasingly bitter after the departure of Lic. Mañozca in the fall of 1627, was not diminished by royal instruction to the magistrates to preserve harmony.[5] In verdicts handed down by the audiencia, Oidor Tello de Velasco was often a minority of one.[6] The arrival of a new oidor, Diego García Maldonado, did not help to decrease the tension, for he died shortly after his arrival.[7] With the death of Oidor Espino de Cáceres on August 27, 1629, only Morga, Castillo de Herrera, Suárez de Poago, and Tello de Velasco remained on the bench, glowering with hatred at each other.[8]

Continued turmoil among the friars aggravated the dissensions inside and outside the audiencia. The Augustinians were torn apart by a battle for leadership between the followers of Francisco de la Fuente y Chaves and those of Leonardo de Araujo. Friar Francisco de la Fuente y Chaves, whom Lic. Mañozca had exiled, repudiated his role in setting up the conservatory tribunal. The visitor allowed him to return to Quito. Joining the pro-Mañozca party, he became a bitter enemy of his erstwhile friend, Leonardo de Araujo, whose journey to Spain in 1626 provided the ammunition for the dismissal of Mañozca. Re-elected provincial superior of the Augustinians, Francisco de la Fuente y Chaves systematically discriminated against the followers of Leonardo de Araujo.[9] When the audiencia began an investigation of the illegal obrajes operated by the Augustinians, they uncovered documentary proof that the provincial superior was pocketing some 30,000 pesos annually from an illegal obraje in Latacunga.[10] It is possible that this investigation by the audiencia was inspired by the known friendship of Dr. Morga with Leonardo de Araujo. Yet the evidence is overwhelming that the Augustinian order, under the leadership of Fuente y Chaves, had sunk into a morass of immorality and worldliness. In 1631 the special emissary of Francisco de la Fuente y Chaves in Spain, Friar Francisco de Herrera, published in Madrid a tract of twenty-four folios in which he lavishly praised the conduct of Lic. Mañozca and savagely attacked the audiencia. Never shying away from a polemic, Fiscal Suárez de Poago replied charge-by-charge in a counterattack bristling with indignation.[11]

It would be pointless to assess the charges and the countercharges. What is significant is that the bitter dispute between the two parties within the Augustinian order added more fuel to the flames of partisanship raging in Quito. The group supporting Friar Francisco de la Fuente y Chaves lent support to the faction headed by Oidor Manuel Tello de Velasco, and those friars backing Friar Leonardo de Araujo looked to the party identified with President Morga.

This was the situation that confronted the new visitor general. A prudent man by temperament and aware of the unfortunate example of Lic. Mañozca, Lic. Galdós de Valencia avoided any intervention in the disputes among the friars. He did, however, seek to lessen the tension among the magistrates. As an old bureaucratic veteran, he had witnessed countless instances of personal antagonism on the bench. They occurred with the periodic regularity of epidemics in every audiencia. His first reaction was to advise the king to transfer all the judges with the possible exception of Dr. Morga.[12] Such a solution had often been adopted in single cases. Fiscal Suárez de Poago, for example, had been transferred from Panama to Quito because of mutual incompatibility with his colleagues.[13] The initial solution of Lic. Galdós de Valencia was the same as that of his predecessor but with one important difference. Lic. Mañozca deliberately brought the antagonism among the magistrates into the open. The new visitor general realized that his advice, however sensible, could not be accepted at once. The king and the council were grimly determined to complete the visita general before they would consider the transfer of any of the magistrates.

Although one side identified itself with President Morga, the visitor general felt that the president had neither created nor encouraged the factionalism. He would have kept Dr. Morga in his post. He remarked, "I consider Dr. Morga very capable and one of the most experienced and sagacious magistrates in the Indies."[14] His favorable opinion of Dr. Morga, however, did not prevent him from probing deeply into the less respectable corners of Morga's public and private life.

In order to diminish the tension between the two parties, the visitor general first called in the leaders. He sought to persuade them not to hold meetings in their homes.[15] Determined at all costs to avoid his predecessor's mistakes, which he believed were the root causes of the prevailing factionalism, he decided to confine his inquiry to the secret proceedings. He refused to hear any public cases, demandas públicas de mal juzgado.[16] He carefully avoided the penchant of Lic. Mañozca for intervening in litigations that were not directly connected with his commissions. On January 13, 1631, he issued an edict specifically forbidding any member of either faction from presenting testimony before his court.[17] For a year or so, at least, the visita general proceeded calmly in comparison to the turmoil created by Lic. Mañozca.

Drawing up charges, cargos, from the testimony submitted, Lic. Galdós de Valencia then allowed the judges and lesser magistrates to present their defenses, descargos. As his instructions provided, he observed the strictest secrecy, with only himself, the notary, and the witness present. The audiencia, which had bitterly denounced the capriciousness of Lic. Mañozca, sang the praises of his successor. They lauded his "rectitude, Christian zeal and learning."[18] In contrast to his predecessor, Lic. Galdós de Valencia sought to maintain harmonious relations with the incumbent magistrates.

The resolve of the visitor general weakened under the pressure of events. He came to the conclusion that the two principal instigators of discord were Oidores Manuel Tello de Velasco and Alonso Castillo de Herrera. Their removal from the bench, he observed, would destroy the roots upon which this factionalism fed.[19] He could not act immediately. The removal of those two judges would leave on the bench only the president, then an old man. The arrival of two new oidores in April, 1632, eliminated this obstacle.[20] But the cautious visitor general proceeded slowly.

Lic. Galdós de Valencia arrived at the same conclusion that Dr. Morga and his colleagues had reached by 1623, an opinion reluctantly shared even by Lic. Mañozca. Manuel Tello de Velasco was vain, ostentatious, and systematically partial in his judicial decisions. Frequent threats by members of his immediate family against anyone who presented testimony against him in the secret proceedings and the public assertion by don Manuel that the authority of the visitor general would terminate at the end of one year gave the cautious visitor general a justification for acting. On January 6, 1632, he suspended Oidor Manuel Tello de Velasco on the grounds that his numerous acts of hostility were impeding the work of the visita general.[21] The visitor general ordered him to leave the capital forthwith. He still retained his salary, at least for a few months more.

The visitor general did not suspend the other instigator, Alonso Castillo de Herrera, until he had heard his descargos. His unfavorable opinion of Castillo de Herrera rested on his conviction that the oidor allowed his personal friendships to color his votes on the bench. The visitor general was also critical of the oidor's mercantile activities and his amorous adventures. Oidor Castillo de Herrera's harsh stand in voting to expel the Augustinian friars in the alternativa crisis lowered him further in Galdós de Valencia's estimation.

The reluctance which Lic. Galdós de Valencia showed in using his authority to suspend the magistrates stands in sharp contrast to the eagerness with which his predecessor used the same power. The instructions to both visitors included discretionary authority to suspend any magistrate who impeded the performance of the visita general or any official who, after presenting his defense, was "notoriously guilty" in the opinion of the visitor general.[22] Lic. Mañozca violated the stipulations. Lic. Galdós de Valencia observed them to the letter.

On July 24, 1632, the eve of his departure for Lima, the visitor general suspended from office a whole group of officials belonging to both parties. The suspension included not only Manuel Tello de Velasco (who had already been suspended as of the previous January 6 but not deprived of his salary) but also Oidor Alonso Castillo de Herrera. Both judges lost their salaries. Both were ordered to leave the capital. The visitor general did give them the rather costly option of going to Spain where they could appeal their suspension before the Council of the Indies. Neither magistrate could return to the bench until the king ordered otherwise. The same prohibitions applied to the inferior magistrates whom he suspended. Among them were Andrés de Orozco, Diego de Valencia León, and Cosmé de Oliva, escribanos mayores, Rodrigo de Ocampo and Diego Gómez Morcillo, royal notaries, and Hernando Zurita, Francisco Navarro, and Bartolomé Marín.[23]

In the edict of suspension, he justified his action on two grounds. The officials in question were the principals in the discord. Moreover, after hearing their defense, he found them "notoriously guilty."

For those magistrates who were not suspended the visitor general issued a series of twenty ordinances intended to lessen factionalism.[24] The visitor prohibited the audiencia from appointing any one of several leading partisans as fiscal ad interim in case that office became vacant or from co-opting any of them as juez de remisión to break a tie. Those singled out were Juan de Carvajal, a staunch friend of Dr. Morga, who, before purchasing the post of chief constable of the audiencia, made a career out of commissions he received from the audiencia, and Pedro Ortiz de Ávila, appointed fiscal *ad interim* by Lic. Mañozca and a leading partisan of the Tello de Velasco faction. Silvestre de Pineda, Hernando Serrano, and Juan de Valencia also fell under the ban. Regarding the fiscal, Melchor Suárez de Poago, as one of the instigators of factionalism, Lic. Galdós de Valencia specifically enjoined the audiencia not to allow him to cast a vote in any cases not involving the royal fisc or the Indians.

The majority of the twenty ordinances instructed the audiencia and the royal treasury to observe a series of standard regulations which had not been honored.

A stunned Quito received these edicts a few days before the ailing visitor general set out on his journey for Lima to prepare his final report for the Council of the Indies. Drastic though the actions were, they were not hasty or capricious. They were the decisions of a prudent, even overly cautious man who temperamentally found such Draconian measures distasteful. For want of a better alternative, he adopted them. That they accomplished their primary purpose is evident. The more rebellious spirits were cowed. While all was not peace and quiet, factionalism significantly diminished after the departure of the visitor general. There was no longer the real danger that dissensions on the tribunal would generate a wave of street fighting or even open rebellion. The overriding aim of Lic. Galdós de Valencia was to avoid bloodshed and tumult. Only six years before going to Quito, he had observed as an oidor in Mexico how the bitter clash between two equally intransigent personalities, the viceroy and the archbishop, had led to the bloody riot of January 15, 1624, when Indians, Negroes, and mestizos pillaged the viceregal palace. Although he never mentioned the uprising of 1624 in his Quito correspondence, it is fair to infer that that event had a profound influence on the conduct of that naturally cautious bureaucrat. In fact, the king had fined him 100 ducats for an action closely connected with the outbreak of the riot. He had voted to allow a close personal friend, Melchor Pérez de Varáez, a merchant dealing in the resale of corn, to hold simultaneously the offices of corregidor of Mexico and alcalde mayor of a province, a violation of countless royal cedulas.[25]

Lic. Galdós de Valencia completed his mission in Quito with substantial success. He showed the courage to take drastic action, but only after mature deliberation. He completed his hearings in Quito in less than two and a half years. During several months of that period, however, he had to suspend the visita general because of ill-health. The king had directed Lic. Galdós de Valencia to complete his hearings within the period of a year if at all possible. Upon his request, the king granted an extension of one year.[26] The costs of the visita general were far less than under Lic. Mañozca, for Lic. Galdós de Valencia avoided granting commissions to agents in the provinces.[27] By a combination of tact and firmness the visitor general managed to curb factionalism.

From the point of view of Madrid, the visitor general's chief liability was the slowness with which he made his final report to the Council of the Indies. Returning to Lima in August, 1632, he took nearly four years to write up the results of his findings, which he sent to Spain in the spring of 1635.[28] Although Viceroy Chinchón had released him for long periods from his regular duties on the bench, the poor health and advanced age of the visitor made him work so slowly that his seeming inactivity aroused much impatience in Spain and anguish in Quito.[29] It was not until 1636 and 1637 that the king and the Council of the Indies were able to render final verdicts.

However slow Lic. Galdós de Valencia may have been in submitting his final report, the material he sent to Spain was sufficiently documented that the Council of the Indies could render responsible and humane verdicts. His most controversial act, however, suspension of the two oidores, was not ratified by the council. While the councilors recognized that both magistrates were guilty of serious offenses meriting reprimands and fines, their considered view was that the oidores' misconduct did not call for such a drastic punishment.[30] The decision of the council was based largely on a consideration of the evidence presented against their behavior in office and in their private lives. The Spanish authorities seemingly lent no weight at all to the major reason for the visitor general's action, namely, that the two oidores were the principal practitioners of factionalism. Neither had the authorities in Spain witnessed, as Lic. Galdós de Valencia had, the riot of January 15, 1624, in Mexico City.

The decision of the council was partially influenced by the vigorous and effective measures undertaken by the two suspended magistrates to rehabilitate their careers. Don Manuel Tello de Velasco did not leave Quito to appeal his case, for he had powerful patrons in Spain. Rather than being dismissed from the bureaucratic service, he was promoted to the audiencia of Guatemala.[31]

Not as confident of his patrons in Spain as don Manuel, Alonso Castillo de Herrera took the expensive expedient of traveling from Quito to Spain to plead his own cause in person. Leaving his wife and a brood of nine children scattered among several convents in the capital, Castillo de Herrera spent two years lobbying in the antechambers of the council. In Lima he published a tract justifying his position.[32] It was an effective job of special pleading. He minimized the dangers of factionalism, which had loomed so large in the mind of the visitor general, and stressed that the charges brought against him in the visita general were not even as serious as those leveled against magistrates who were still serving on the bench. From Lima on March 24, 1637, Lic. Galdós de Valencia wrote a rebuttal to the tract, but it arrived too late to be effective.[33] On December 25, 1635, the council recommended that Castillo de Herrera be restored to his post with full payment of his salary from the date of his suspension.[34] The wording of the consulta slyly suggests that sending the oidor back to Quito would rid the councilors of an importunate pest.

Vindicated at last, Alonso de Castillo de Herrera resumed his duties in Quito on February 3, 1637. As the senior oidor, he had the responsibility of collecting the fines imposed on his colleagues in consequence of the visita general. Whatever satisfaction he may have derived from this task was short-lived. On the following December 17 he died.[35]

However responsibly the visitor general may have conducted his mission in Quito, both the investigator and the investigated were made aware that the king and the Council of the Indies constituted the court from whose verdicts no appeals could be made. Instead of receiving a thank-you for a job reasonably well done, the 77-year-old magistrate received a fine on April 26, 1639, of 500 ducats. The specific justification for the fine cannot be determined. Perhaps the fine reflected the council's displeasure with his slowness in submitting a final report and its dissatisfaction with his decision to suspend the two oidores. The old bureaucrat promptly paid his fine. He wrote the king expressing his mortification and proclaiming the rectitude of his conduct during forty years of service.[36] He survived this personal humiliation for only a short time. He died on June 8, 1641.[37]

15.

THE VERDICT

The responsibility of a visitor general never extended to passing sentence on the magistrates being investigated. His duty was to take secret testimony, to draw up a list of charges, and to allow the investigated officials to defend themselves against those charges. From the welter of evidence thus collected, the visitor general then drew up an indictment which he presented to the Council of the Indies, along with supporting evidence. It was the council and the king that rendered the verdict. Once approved by the king, it could not be appealed to a higher court. At the request of the convicted officials, the council on occasion might reduce the monetary fines as an act of compassion, but they would not reverse the verdict as such.[1]

The council examined and weighed the evidence submitted by the visitor general with meticulous care. Anything but a kangaroo court, the council demanded convincing documentary evidence and dismissed hearsay and gossip. If the evidence was not conclusive, the council did not hesitate to render the negative verdict of "not proven," as opposed to the positive verdict of innocent. The magistrates undergoing judgment usually received the benefit of the doubt. The council did recognize the real dangers of their being victims of slander and innuendo.[2] For those charges of which the defendant was found guilty, the punishment ranged from a mild reprimand to stiff monetary fines, suspension from office for a certain period of time, or outright expulsion from the service.

In the case against Dr. Antonio de Morga, the council examined seventy-three charges. Although it absolved him on several counts and on others mildly admonished him to observe the laws, the council found him guilty on many others. Out of a total of seventy-three charges, the council declared the president innocent or absolved for lack of sufficient proof on only seventeen counts. Three charges concerned the semi-public casino his second wife operated in her drawing room, for which the fine was 6,000 ducats. Five charges dealt with his having illegally imported into Quito on his voyage from Mexico a large amount of contraband Chinese silk, listed as "books" in the registry of the ship, from which he allegedly netted a profit of 60,000 pesos. The fine was 12,000 pesos. Seven charges concerned his failure to pay the tax of one-fifth the value on all the precious metals which he had acquired. The penalty was an additional 1,500 ducats. For his amorous adventures, which were meticulously documented, the president received yet another fine of 2,000 ducats. For his close personal relations with the family of the notorious Nicolás de Larraspuru, the council imposed a penalty of 1,000 pesos.

These five sets of charges represent the bulk of the fines assessed against Dr. Morga, but there were many accusations of lesser misdeeds of which he was found guilty and for which he was heavily fined also. The council "was not amused" by his prank of forging royal letters to two oidores announcing promotions. That joke cost him 600 pesos. The council also convicted Dr. Morga of being a silent partner in the merchandising business of his son and of being a silent partner of other merchants as well. Punishment for that violation of the law was a part of an additional 6,000-ducat fine which covered several other charges also.

A whole string of charges involved his failures to observe the standard procedures and regulations set down in the ordinances governing the non-viceregal audiencias in the Indies. Although the council admonished the president to observe the laws, it imposed no fines. The specific infractions were failure to reserve one day a week for cases involving the royal treasury, failure to set aside one day a week for the meeting of the junta de hacienda, failure to name a fine collector, failure to keep the audiencia records in proper order, failure to provide a clock in the audiencia chambers, failure to keep the royal seal in the casas reales, failure to provide separate quarters in the audiencia jail for men and women, and failure to observe the regulation that each judge should spend three hours daily in his own chambers.

The council refused to pass judgment in the thorny dispute as to whether Dr. Morga persecuted Juan Serrano del Valle, Lic. Francisco Rodríquez Plaza, and others for having complained about the conduct of the magistrates to the council. The council ruled that such a question could best be decided in Quito in a separate trial at which these gentlemen could bring a complaint of mal juzgado against Dr. Morga.

The council convicted the president on very few counts concerning the actual administration of justice. They were that he had unlawfully allowed Diego de Valencia León to retain the office of escribano mayor after his son reached the age of 25, that he had demonstrated some partiality in the residencia verdict of Eugenio de Ávila, corregidor of Chimbo (200 pesos), and that he had named his servants to minor positions.

The final verdict was a massive condemnation of Dr. Morga for both his personal and his official conduct. The total fine amounted to 31,300 ducats, the approximate equivalent of the president's salary for six and a half years. Moreover, the king forbade him to hold office for a period of six years and deprived him of all emeritus honors and pension rights.

The king signed the cedula containing the sentence of Dr. Morga on October 26, 1636, but the laborious work of the council in sentencing the other magistrates had scarcely begun.[3] It was not until November 14, 1637, that the council recommended to the king the sentences of Oidor Manuel Tello de Velasco and the other major figures of the visita general. One hundred and forty-eight charges were considered. In order to expedite matters, the council divided the charges into two groups and set up two separate subcommittees, each to consider one group of charges. The total fine imposed on Lic. Tello de Velasco was 1,920 ducats, in contrast to Dr. Morga's fine of 31,300 ducats, 480 ducats less than the annual salary of 2,400 ducats paid to each oidor. Furthermore, the council reluctantly recommended that he could take up his duties as oidor in the audiencia of Guatemala, an appointment that had been suspended pending the outcome of the visita general.

Of the 148 indictments, the council found Tello de Velasco innocent or absolved for lack of sufficient proof on 49 counts. In its meticulous attempt to judge the magistrates on specific evidence, the council rejected such vague accusations as that, within a few years of his arrival in Quito, he was reputed to be worth a fortune of 50,000 pesos. Eleven charges involved amorous adventures. He was found guilty and fined 500 pesos. Perhaps the most serious charges of which he was found guilty concerned the efforts he, his wife, and his nephew made to intimidate witnesses not to give testimony against his conduct in the secret proceedings of the visita general. One of the accusations most frequently leveled against Tello de Velasco was his partiality and friendship for certain litigants. On only two counts, however, did the council convict him. He received a fine of 300 pesos for accepting small gifts, such as eggs, chickens, and honey, from one Alonso González who had litigations before the tribunal. And he was found guilty of caprice in seeking the release of Juan Serrano del Valle from jail when there were serious criminal accusations pending against the latter.

No charges were brought against Manuel Tello de Velasco for illicit commercial operations. The council, however, did fine him 100 ducats for using unpaid Indian labor in his household. This was a common practice; both Dr. Morga and the fiscal had received similar fines. A whole series of accusations against Tello de Velasco dealt with his conduct as a circuit judge in the provinces and with his administration of probate matters. In both activities he was found guilty of several minor infractions of the standard regulations and was admonished to observe the laws.[4]

On the same day that the council approved the sentence of Oidor Manuel Tello de Velasco, they also formally ratified the sentence of his bitter enemy, Fiscal Melchor Suárez de Poago. Of all the superior magistrates of the audiencia, the fiscal emerged with least damage, but few managed to come out of a visita general totally unscathed. His was the smallest fine, a mere 900 ducats, amounting to about two-fifths of his annual salary. Furthermore, the council recommended that he continue to serve as fiscal.[5] The council, however, was sufficiently concerned about the fiscal that the king dispatched a letter to the audiencia reprimanding him for his "shortcomings and excesses."[6] The cedula instructed that this letter should be read to the fiscal at a closed meeting of the audiencia, at which time the president and the oidores were to admonish Lic. Suárez de Poago to correct those defects or face subsequent and more severe punishment. What the fiscal did not pay in fines he paid for in humiliation. A proud if irascible man and a long-time member of a bureaucratic organization in which personal dignity counted for a good deal, the private session of the audiencia when he received the reprimand was a humiliating ordeal for him.

The "shortcomings and excesses" which vexed the council were his furious Asturian temper and his apparent inability to control it. The fine for his periodic outbursts of rage, which spared neither his colleagues nor the litigants, amounted to 300 of the total fine of 900 ducats. On one count alone, the council fined him 100 ducats—for hurling insults of "thief" and "assassin" at a certain Captain Pedro Martín Navarro. The council admonished the fiscal to show more patience, tact, and simple politeness in his official dealings.

Of the sixty-eight charges considered, the council declared him innocent or absolved for lack of sufficient proof on thirty counts. Only five charges involved a fine. There were two kinds of charges for which the council often convicted him, but the punishment in most cases was a relatively mild reprimand and reminder to observe the laws. Those charges concerned the special responsibility of the office of fiscal for the administration of the royal treasury and the defense of the rights of the Indians. Some twelve counts involved his negligence to observe the regulations about keeping the official records of the junta de hacienda, his laxity about retaining one of the three keys to the royal chest, and his violation of various regulations about the administration of property held in probate. The fiscal also received a reprimand for his failure to enforce the standard regulations which provided that no Spaniard or mestizo might live in an Indian village or the laws prohibiting Indians from drawing up wills in the presence of a parish priest lest the priest exercise undue influence.

In contrast to many of his colleagues, the brusque old fiscal was never accused of donjuanismo. The council did fine him 200 ducats for allowing his slaves to compel passing Indians to carry—without any compensation—the sedan chairs of his wife and daughters who were going to hear mass.

There is no available record of the charges and the sentences rendered for Oidor Alonso Castillo de Herrera. Other documents reveal that he received only a small fine. The council rescinded his suspension from office, ordered by the visitor general in 1632, and restored the salary withheld during the period of his suspension.[7] This decision suggests that the charges leveled against Castillo de Herrera were perhaps no more serious than the ones brought against the fiscal.

It is unfortunate that the sentence of Oidor Matías de Peralta could not be located, since his fine amounted to a substantial 19,900 ducats. In one sense, Peralta's fine was heavier than Morga's fine of 31,300 ducats. The Morga fine was the equivalent of six and a half years of the annual salary of president, whereas the Peralta fine amounted to more than eight times the smaller annual salary of an oidor. It is reasonable to infer that Oidor Peralta, who served in the audiencia of Quito from 1611 until 1625, was found guilty of misdeeds far in excess of those of his fellow oidores and more approximate in seriousness to those of President Morga. The stiff fine suggests that he was guilty of illegal practices of self-enrichment. In view of the magistrates' modest salaries, the council seldom imposed heavy fines on them unless it had conclusive evidence that they were guilty of massive graft. The slowness of the whole visita system placed the council in a difficult position. Oidor Peralta had left Quito in the winter of 1626 to take up his duties as alcalde de crimen in the audiencia of Mexico. Promoted subsequently to the post of oidor, he was apparently performing his duties satisfactorily. The council recommended clemency, at least to the extent that he not be dismissed in 1638 from the audiencia of Mexico for errors that he had committed much earlier in his career. They did recommend, however, that he not be allowed to continue in office unless he paid the stiff fine of 19,900 ducats within a period of six months. The king sent instructions that the viceroy and the four senior oidores should summon their colleague, Peralta, to a closed meeting, "at which time you should reprimand him in the strongest and severest language for the wide variety of excesses for which he was found guilty in the visita general and at the same time you should inform him that in view of his improved conduct, his long years in my royal service and for other just motives it is my royal will not to suspend him from his present office."[8]

The two officials who received the heaviest fines after Dr. Morga's were not superior but inferior magistrates. They were Diego de Valencia León, escribano de cámara of the royal audiencia, and Andrés de Orozco Guzmán, escribano de cámara of the city of Quito. The former received a fine of 26,100 ducats and prohibition from ever holding office again, and the latter's fine was 24,200 ducats. Although the council found that both officials had been delinquent in the performance of some of their notarial duties, those charges accounted for only a small fraction of their total fines. What incensed the council was that both notaries, by their own admission, had openly engaged in commerce. On these grounds alone, Diego de Valencia León was fined 16,000 ducats. An additional fine was imposed on Diego de Valencia León for illegally exercising the office after 1616 when his son had reached the age of 25. The fine of Andrés de Orozco Guzmán for his commercial activities was 20,000 ducats.[9] Both notaries evidently confined their energies to commercial rather than amorous enterprises; neither one was accused of licentiousness.

Many other minor magistrates were also fined, but in several cases the fines or the charges cannot be located. Lic. Juan de Carvajal, then the chief constable of the audiencia, for example, received a fine of 7,281 pesos, but the text of the sentence is not available.[10]

The magistrates of the royal treasury were also included under the visita general. Evidently the council rendered no verdicts in their cases, for both magistrates had died before Lic. Galdós de Valencia had completed his investigations in Quito. It was difficult enough for the royal treasury to collect the fines of the living, but it was virtually impossible to collect the fines from the estates of the dead.

There was, however, a wide chasm between the fines the council assessed and the money that actually came into the coffers of the royal treasury. The total amount of the fines imposed on this particular visita general came to about 116,614 ducats. The amount collected did not exceed 43,896 ducats.[11] The salaries of all the agents of the visita general cost the treasury something in excess of 78,000 ducats.[12] The implications of these figures are revealing. Among the many justifications for the council's firm conviction that a visita general should be used only occasionally was its knowledge that the investigations placed yet another burden on the treasury. In theory a visita general was supposed not only to pay for itself but also to add something extra to the royal coffers. The inquiries took place only in cases of glaring abuses when the probability was that considerable fines would be assessed.

One major explanation for the defectiveness of the collection system lies in the slowness of the whole procedure. The visita general in Quito began in 1624, but the council did not pass the final verdicts until 1636 and 1637. Some visitas were more rapid, but others were even slower. The probability was that some of the magistrates would die before the verdict could be handed down and therefore their fines would never be collected. Both Dr. Morga and Andrés de Orozco Guzmán, whose fines amounted to more than half of all the fines assessed, were dead before the verdicts reached Quito.

Thus Dr. Morga was spared the final humiliation. When his bull-like constitution began to fail, he requested on April 30, 1634, an honorable retirement and the customary full salary until his death.[13] The following year he repeated the request, in which he cited his poor health and his forty years of service in three different posts in the Indies, during which time he had buried two wives and lost two sons in military campaigns.[14] On November 10, 1635, the council recommended to the king that Dr. Morga be retired as president of the audiencia but that consideration of his request for an honorable retirement at full salary should be postponed until the verdict of the visita general had been rendered.[15] On July 17, 1636, the council voted on the sentence of Dr. Morga, but it was not until October 22 that the king signed the cedula.[16] Four days after the council had voted on the Morga verdict, in far-off Quito the senior oidor notified the council,

"Our Lord was served to take away from us, Dr. Antonio de Morga, president of said audiencia, an eminently satisfactory and experienced magistrate."[17]

The council had suspected that death might cheat the treasury of the fine. For this reason the king approved publication of the Morga fine before the other verdicts had been handed down.[18] The estate of Dr. Morga was considerable at one time, but by June 10, 1637, eleven months after his death, it had largely evaporated. His widow, Ana de Rivera Verdugo, had returned to her native Lima shortly after the death of her husband, carrying with her everything that was movable or liquid. Once under the jurisdiction of another audiencia, she could more easily evade the efforts of the authorities in Quito, for the transference of litigations from one audiencia to another provided endless opportunities for delays. Furthermore, the widow could claim that whatever property she then held belonged to her dowry and not to the estate of her husband. She did, however, leave behind his extensive library, which the audiencia ordered sold. The children of the president, who were his principal heirs, began a suit alleging that much of Dr. Morga's property was a part of the dowry of their mother, who was Dr. Morga's first wife. According to custom, it was not considered a part of the estate of their father. The senior oidor, whose statutory responsibility was to collect the fines of a visita general, managed to collect a mere 6,069 pesos of the total fine of 31,300 ducats.[19]

A similar situation occurred in the case of Andrés de Orozco Guzmán, the escribano mayor of the city of Quito, who died before the verdict arrived in Quito. His children successfully managed to exploit the machinery of the courts to avoid paying the bulk of the heavy fine of 24,200 ducats. Their major argument was that most of the estate, valued at the substantial sum of 78,369 pesos, belonged to their mother's dowry and its increment. Hence, they argued, it was exempt from the payment of their father's debts. The senior oidor collected only 8,584 ducats from the Orozco estate.[20]

Diego de Valencia León, the ex-escribano mayor of the audiencia, had the misfortune of living on to spend his last years in penury and humiliation, his once prosperous and successful career shattered. He managed to avoid paying the bulk of his fine, but in the process he was stripped of everything he owned. The treasury eventually collected 4,400 ducats out of the total fine of 26,100 ducats.[21]

The easiest fines to collect were those assessed against magistrates still holding office. They were usually given six months to pay or face automatic suspension. Hence the fiscal paid promptly. So did Lic. Juan de Carvajal.[22]

Presumably Oidor Matías de Peralta did also.[23] Manuel Tello de Velasco failed to pay his fine on the grounds that he was destitute. The senior oidor charitably allowed him to leave Quito to take up his post in Guatemala with a written promise that he would eventually pay. Whether he ever did is not known. He died a few years later.[24]

The poor record of the Spaniards in collecting fines in the seventeenth century is not particularly surprising. In the United States today, with its sophisticated machinery of tax collection, Assistant Attorney General William Brady recently estimated that 110,000 individuals and firms around the country owed the federal government more than 200 million dollars in judgments.[25] Most of the debts are probably uncollectable, since those involved are indigent.

That the Council of the Indies did a conscientious job of assessing the evidence is apparent. There were no convictions which were not well documented. There were, however, many large categories of activity in which the magistrates were not convicted of extensive wrong-doing. For example, in very few cases were the judges found guilty of making serious errors in judicial decisions. The military role of the audiencia did not come under the purview of the visita general. Review of the military functions of the viceroys and the audiencias was under the exclusive jurisdiction of the residencias.[26] The more political functions of the audiencia emerged from the visita general with very few indictments. The role of the audiencia in promoting the abortive conquest of Esmeraldas and the more successful thrust to the Amazon, the audiencia's jurisdiction over the Indian community, and its undoubted energy in collecting forced loans all received scant attention. Yet in those activities the administration of Dr. Morga had made substantial and positive accomplishments. Although Juan de Solórzano admonished visitors general to stress the virtues as well as the defects of magistrates, the emphasis in fact was on punishing abuses, to the exclusion of rewarding accomplishments.[27] The visita general directed most of its attention to two areas. The private morality of the magistrates and violations of the rather rigid concept of conflict-of-interest actually account for the bulk of the fines.

That Dr. Morga was guilty of the abuses for which he was convicted cannot be questioned, but, in all fairness to him, it should be pointed out that he received no credit for his very real achievements. The evidence is conclusive that his second wife ran a semi-public gambling casino in her drawing room, that he did import contraband Chinese silks in 1615, that he was a silent partner in a commercial house, and that he was a gentleman who enjoyed considerable success with the ladies. His fine of 31,300 ducats represents about one-third of the total fines assessed. The loss of his pension and the ban against his holding office for a period of six years seem severe. In 1636 Dr. Morga was 77 years old. The council apparently used the sentence of Dr. Morga as an object lesson for his younger colleagues.

The punishment of Oidor Peralta lends some credibility to this conjecture. His fine of 19,900 ducats suggests that he was found guilty of abuses approaching the same magnitude as those of Dr. Morga. Yet he retained his post in the audiencia of Mexico. He was younger than Dr. Morga, a fact which may have encouraged the council to show some clemency. Moreover, because Dr. Morga was not merely an oidor but the presiding officer whose conduct was supposed to set the tone for his colleagues, the council may have decided to make his punishment an object lesson. Lic. Peralta received lenient treatment in 1636. But twenty years later, in a visita general of the audiencia of Mexico, the same Lic. Peralta, then as old as Dr. Morga was in 1636, was the sacrificial victim who ended his long career in disgrace. It was his conduct as acting president of the audiencia (1649–50) that caused the visitor general to suspend him from office.

The older men were expendable but not the younger ones who, for all their shortcomings, were experienced bureaucrats and could not be easily replaced. It was this factor more than any other which accounts for the relative leniency of the king and the Council of the Indies in sentencing many magistrates, who indeed were guilty of massive violations of instructions and laws.[28]

The visita general was a judicial proceeding from the point of view of those magistrates whose conduct was under investigation. The perspective of the king, however, was different. Cardinal Granvelle, Philip II's trusted minister, pithily expressed the real view of the monarch toward the visita general when he observed, "It seems to me that they do not understand what is the purpose of a visita general. It is not to conduct a formal legal investigation upon which to pass sentence, which is the aim of ordinary justice, but merely to inform the mind of His Majesty . . . ."[29] To inform the king of the actual conditions in the Indies was the inner, deeper meaning of the visita general. Hence the monarch and the council could afford to be lenient or harsh, as circumstances dictated, in meting out punishments.

That the visita general was an imperfect instrument to achieve its stated purposes ought to be abundantly clear by now. While it is reasonable to assume that the abuses which the visita general sought to correct would have become more flagrant had that device not been invoked periodically, sexual license and venality continued to flourish. For the Spanish crown to attempt to legislate monogamous abstinence among its representatives overseas was a quixotic venture doomed to failure. The roots from which graft continued to grow could only have been removed if the Habsburg monarchy had been prepared to pay larger wages and give its servants in the Indies more ample authority. Such was the intent of the intendant system at the end of the eighteenth century. Had the empire survived longer, the colonial bureaucracy might have evolved along the lines of the Indian Civil Service.

For all its failure to achieve its stated goals, the visita general, nevertheless, served several useful purposes. It did provide the crown with a documented survey of bureaucratic administration in its distant dependencies, conducted by a source independent of the regular administration. The visita general also gave the king's subjects a vehicle to protest against abuses, real or fancied as the case might be, committed against them by the professional magistrates. In a sense the visita general acted as a safety valve by which subjects could periodically release pent-up resentments against bureaucrats. Thus the loyalty of the king's subjects was reinforced.

A visitor general performed some of the same functions that the celebrated *ombudsman* does in modern Scandinavia. That officer is a public investigator whose job is to look into complaints from individual citizens about the manner in which they are being treated by government agencies. The visitor general, like the ombudsman, could be approached directly by any citizen with a complaint or a claim of inefficient or unjust handling by the administration. Although the similarities between the two institutions are real, so also are the differences. The office of ombudsman is permanent; that of visitor general was occasional. The role of the ombudsman is to persuade bureaucrats to make adjustments and concessions to aggrieved citizens if the laws so justify. The visitor general, on the other hand, sought to document malpractices for which the council might impose punishments. Yet both devices have provided citizens with a means to redress grievances over arbitrary actions of bureaucrats.[30]

Viceroy Montesclaros once likened the visita general to one of "those occasional gusts of wind encountered in the streets and squares which accomplish nothing but to raise the dust and refuse and to cause everyone to cover his head."[31] This may be an apt contemporary evaluation of the institution from the viewpoint of bureaucrats subject to investigation, but it misses the point. The visita general was a boom that could be lowered whenever Madrid so chose. It was bound to hit many. The professional magistrates dreaded its coming, and their apprehension kept them painfully aware that, regardless of the limited authority and prestige they enjoyed in their respective posts in the Indies, the real locus of power was with the king and his advisers at Court. Because the long tenure of the professional bureaucrats in the same posts induced a progressive dehispanization and fostered close relations between them and many creoles, the audiencias might have become converted into nuclei for movements leading to political separation from the metropolis. This did not happen for three centuries, at least partly because of the visita general. That device was a sword of Damocles, ready to fall to remind viceroys and oidores alike of the tenuous nature of their authority.

16.

AU PLUS CELA CHANGE,
AU PLUS C'EST LA MÊME CHOSE

"The more things change, the more they stay the same"—the old French adage characterizes in general the subsequent careers of the principal actors in the visita general of the audiencia of Quito. In particular the futures of the fiscal, Lic. Melchor Suárez de Poago, Oidores Manuel Tello de Velasco and Matías de Peralta, and Lic. Juan de Mañozca y Zamora merit our attention, for they reflect the continuity within the bureaucratic system.

Oidor Alonso Castillo de Herrera, whom visitor general Galdós de Valencia suspended in 1632, was reinstated by the Council of the Indies in December, 1635. Resuming his position early in 1637, he enjoyed his vindication for less than a year before his sudden death.[1]

The only major figure who remained for any length of time in Quito was Fiscal Suárez de Poago. He held that office until his death in 1648. All the evidence suggests that the blustery fiscal just became more cantankerous as he pushed into advanced old age. He evidently paid scant attention to the sharply worded reprimand, contained in his sentence, that he should exhibit more patience and tact with both his colleagues and the litigants. His sharp tongue, his iron will, and his explosive temper seldom failed him. Not long after his reprimand, the fiscal discovered that Oidor Prada had permitted his only daughter to marry a resident of Quito without first securing the permission of the king. This act, of course, was a flagrant violation of the laws. Oidor Prada and the old fiscal mixed like oil and water. They became such uncompromising enemies that their hatred exploded into a fist fight in the audiencia chambers; their colleagues had to separate them. Oidor Prada turned out to be the Manuel Tello de Velasco of the 1640's, and he managed to arouse the verbal hostility of most of his colleagues. No other magistrate besides Suárez de Poago allowed his hostility to express itself in physical combat, but no other magistrate possessed the explosive temper of the irascible fiscal from Asturias.[2]

Stone-deaf and his other faculties failing also, Lic. Suárez de Poago was recommended to the king by the audiencia for honorable retirement at full salary. On June 28, 1647, Philip IV issued a royal cedula granting the request. As often happened with the retirement system in the Spanish service, Lic. Melchor Suárez de Poago died in Quito several months before the arrival of the cedula.[3]

Oidor Manuel Tello de Velasco was broken in spirit and body, destitute, and burdened with a large family when he took up his duties as oidor in the audiencia of Guatemala in 1639. The records indicate that he played a rather inactive role in the conduct of official business. Seldom does his name appear on the letters that the audiencia dispatched from time to time to the Council of the Indies.[4] When he became virtually blind, the king and the council granted him an honorable retirement at full salary on November 23, 1643. Like his former colleague in Quito, the fiscal, Oidor Manuel Tello de Velasco died before the royal cedula reached him in Guatemala.[5]

Thomas Gage, the celebrated English traveler who for a few years was a Dominican friar, actually visited Guatemala during the time that Manuel Tello de Velasco served on the bench there. He has left us a sprightly account of the Guatemala of those times. The president of the audiencia, Álvaro de Quiñones y Osorio, prohibited gambling in all private homes. He insisted that all such diversions be concentrated in his own residence where, according to Gage, the leading citizens of the capital gathered every night, with the president collecting a percentage of all the money waged. Although reminiscent of Dr. Morga, Álvaro de Quiñones had no visitor general with whom to contend. Instead of being castigated, he received a promotion to the presidency of Charcas. The enjoyment of this honor escaped him. He died in a shipwreck en route to his new post.[6]

Thomas Gage recounts with relish and not without an anti-Spanish malice the venality of the audiencia. Judges received bribes and actively participated in various business enterprises.[7]

It is doubtful that don Manuel Tello de Velasco, in broken health and nearly blind, had the opportunity or the inclination to engage in the activities zestfully described by the wandering Englishman.

Some twenty years after the death of his father, the son, Manuel, *hijo,* appealed to the king in 1661 to grant him the vacant post of principal sacristan in the cathedral of Guatemala. The bishop had already turned him down. In justifying his request for royal intervention, the younger don Manuel cited in glowing terms the distinguished services of his father in the audiencias of Quito and Guatemala. He had the good sense not to mention the visita general, which made his father's career then look something less than distinguished.[8]

Of all the magistrates investigated in the visita general of the audiencia of Quito, Matías de Peralta had the most distinguished subsequent career. He managed to hold onto his seat in the audiencia of Mexico in spite of the heavy fine imposed on him. He enjoyed as bull-like a constitution as Dr. Morga. He lived until 1654. The storm provoked by the visita general of Lic. Mañozca to Quito was a mere squall compared to the hurricane that swirled around the audiencia of Mexico from 1640 to 1654.

During that period, Matías de Peralta was senior oidor and a prominent actor in the bitter clash between Bishop Juan de Palafox y Mendoza (who was incidentally a member of the Council of the Indies when the Quito verdicts were reached) and the Society of Jesus. The climax of Peralta's career began on April 22, 1649, when the governor of the viceroyalty, don Marcos de Torres y Rueda, bishop of Yucatán, died. Pending the arrival of a new viceroy from Spain, the audiencia as a corporate body exercised the functions of that vacant office. As senior oidor, Matías de Peralta became acting president of the audiencia, so that he was in fact the ranking civilian magistrate in the viceroyalty of New Spain.[9] He enjoyed this honor for fourteen months, until the arrival of the new viceroy, the Count of Alba, on June 13, 1650. A veteran of forty years in the bureaucratic service, Oidor Peralta demonstrated a singular lack of political skill in his climactic year of power. He acted imprudently and harshly, stirring up a hornet's nest of opposition which ultimately led to his disgrace.

Relations between the audiencia and the bishop-governor had long been strained. Thus Peralta did not wait until the bishop-governor had died before he placed an embargo on Rueda's estate, with a charge of simony. Late at night, as soon as the chief magistrate had died, the new acting president compelled the testamentary executor of the estate, don Nicolás Romero de Melba, to surrender, under threat of jail, 150,000 pesos. Oidor Peralta alleged that the late bishop-governor, either out of ignorance or poor health, had allowed his private secretary and nephew by marriage, Juan de Salazar, to abuse his confidence by openly selling both ecclesiastical and civilian appointments.

Oidor Peralta was in grave difficulty if he could not prove his charges. The dead magistrate's secretary appealed to the king to vindicate the memory of his uncle, for simony was one of the most serious crimes with which to charge a prelate. But even if the charges could be documented, the procedures employed by the senior oidor had been arbitrary and harsh. After four decades in the royal service, Peralta evidently had forgotten that anything he did was subject to review by several agencies. And in the shadows lurked another visitor general.

The visita general of the audiencia of Mexico, begun in 1640 by Bishop Palafox but interrupted by his boisterous clash with the Jesuits in 1647, was resumed in 1649 with the arrival of Pedro de Gálvez, alcalde de crimen of the audiencia of Granada. The bitterness engendered by Peralta's conduct as acting president of the audiencia focused the attention of the visitor general on him. On November 16, 1650, Lic. Gálvez suspended Oidor Peralta from office and exiled him to the nearby village of Coyoacán. Coincidentally, on December 12, 1650, Lic. Peralta's old acquaintance of Quito days, Lic. Juan de Mañozca y Zamora, who had been serving as archbishop of Mexico since 1645, died in Mexico City. The visitor general allowed Lic. Peralta to resume his post on January 2, 1651. On January 16, the oidor accompanied his colleagues to the solemn funeral ceremonies held in the cathedral for the repose of the soul of the late archbishop. We do not know what thoughts passed through his mind as he attended the funeral of his old foe— perhaps compassion, for there is no indication that the oidor and the archbishop clashed in Mexico.

The second and final blow fell ten months later. On November 10, 1651, Lic. Gálvez again suspended Oidor Peralta along with Oidor Gómez de Mora. On June 1, 1652, the visitor presented the oidor with a series of charges, concerning which Peralta was invited to present testimony in his own defense. A major reason for the visitor general's decision to suspend Oidor Peralta was the latter's harsh actions and accusations against the late

Bishop Rueda.[10] Oidor Peralta was never to return to the bench, although, by orders of Lic. Gálvez, he received his salary until his death on May 22, 1655.[11]

Even had he lived, it is doubtful that Lic. Peralta could have cleared his name. No sentence was handed down in his particular case because his death made that procedure unnecessary. After a careful examination, the Council of the Indies did exonerate the late Bishop Rueda of the charge of simony. This action constituted an implicit condemnation of the conduct of Lic. Peralta. As it did for his former colleague, Dr. Morga, death mercifully intervened to spare him further humiliation. And like Dr. Morga, he was an able and conscientious subordinate who deteriorated when he found himself without a resident superior or any bureaucratic peers who could put a brake on his rashness. A friendly but firm archbishop might have persuaded him to act less arbitrarily in proceeding against the memory of the late bishop-governor, but this role obviously could not be filled by Lic. Mañozca. Thus Lic. Peralta, who barely managed to salvage his bureaucratic career from one visita general, saw it shipwrecked in another.

The subsequent career of Lic. Juan Galdós Galdoche de Valencia was uneventful. He continued to serve in the audiencia of Lima until his death on June 8, 1641, at the venerable age of 79.

Of all the actors in the Quito drama, Lic. Juan de Mañozca was the one official whose subsequent conduct was somewhat sobered by his experience in Quito. Although he was involved in several controversies (and this was unavoidable in seventeenth-century Spanish America), he never again aroused the intense personal hatred and animosity that he had provoked in both Cartagena and Quito. This change had several origins. His later career took place during his fifties and sixties. A factor even more mollifying than increasing age was that in his posts after 1627 he was surrounded by several competing authorities to whom he had to accommodate himself. In both Lima and Mexico, there were viceroys, audiencias, and other peers, secular and regular clergy and occasional visitors, whose opinions, prerogatives, and sensibilities he had to take into account. His arbitrary and dictatorial tendencies came to the fore in both Cartagena and Quito, for there were no bureaucratic peers who were either willing or able to stand up to this strong-willed son of the Basque country.

During the decade from 1627 to 1638 when he was in the Inquisition in Lima, Lic. Mañozca became a firm friend of the viceroy, the Count of Chinchón (1628–38), who recommended his promotion.[12] Lic. Mañozca confined his bountiful energies to his inquisitional duties. The climax of his career in the Holy Office in Lima occurred during the auto-da-fé of August 17, 1636, when a large number of Portuguese merchants were convicted of being crypto-Jews. Because these Portuguese-Brazilian merchants, who played a major role in the commercial life of Lima, were wealthy, considerable sums poured into coffers of the Holy Office with their convictions.[13]

Lic. Mañozca's Jew-baiting zeal was partially responsible for his promotion in 1638 to a seat on the governing board of the Inquisition in Spain, the Suprema. By that time the verdicts of the visita general had been handed down, and the sentences seemed to vindicate the conclusions of the ex-visitor general, although not necessarily his methods. By 1638, however, the conclusions seemed more important than the methods. Lic. Mañozca was now a resident at Court near the real sources of power and patronage. A series of distinguished appointments came his way. In 1642 the king named him president of the royal audiencia of Granada, one of the two major tribunals of justice in the kingdom of Castile.[14]

Lic. Mañozca remained in Granada for less than two years. In 1643 there was a vacancy in the archepiscopal see of Mexico. This see, ranking just below Lima in prestige, had been vacant for nearly eleven years. Juan de Palafox y Mendoza, the bishop of Puebla, had turned down the appointment. Lic. Mañozca accepted it with alacrity. Ever since the 1620's, he had aspired to an archepiscopal mitre.[15] His ambition was finally fulfilled in his sixty-eighth year. Thus his career would end in the Mexico City where he had spent his youth. Bishop Juan de Palafox y Mendoza of Puebla solemnly consecrated Juan de Mañozca on February 24, 1645. He was the first archbishop of Mexico to be installed in the present cathedral of Mexico, although the cathedral itself was not formally dedicated until February 2, 1656.[16]

The new prelate at the age of 68 had lost none of his characteristic vitality. From January 24 until June 1, 1646, he undertook an extensive tour of his diocese, visiting sixty-eight communities to administer the sacrament of confirmation to 72,375 people.[17]

Nor had the old archbishop lost his zest for a quarrel or his impatience with those who disagreed with him. Given the special assignment by the Suprema in Madrid to conduct a visita of the Holy Office in Mexico City, the archbishop suspended from office Antonio de Gaviola, fiscal of the Holy Office, on the grounds that he had advised the Inquisition to influence a compromise settlement between Bishop Palafox and the Jesuits. An implacable foe of Palafox, the archbishop bitterly resented the advice of the fiscal. The archbishop also clashed with Bartolemé de la Cerda y Benavides, bishop of

Oaxaca, over some question concerning the jurisdiction of the Inquisition. The bishop appealed to the audiencia for assistance. When the suspended fiscal of the Inquisition sided with the bishop of Oaxaca, Archbishop Mañozca promptly excommunicated the fiscal for disobedience. A street brawl threatened when the fiscal of the archbishop sought to remove the suspended fiscal of the Inquisition by force from the convent of San Sebastián where he had taken refuge. A large crowd gathered at the convent entrance, determined to protect the unhappy Gaviola. The timely intervention of the governor of the viceroyalty, Bishop Rueda, and the audiencia, backed up by soldiers, prevented a riot. The secular authorities managed to arrange a face-saving compromise which permitted the suspended fiscal to retire to the village of Tepotzotlán until the Suprema in Madrid handed down a decision.[18]

This incident demonstrates not only that Archbishop Mañozca was capable of provoking intense wrath, but also that his virulent temper could be restrained by the presence of bureaucratic peers who had the authority and prestige to save him from his own anger. During the encounter, the thoughts of the senior oidor of the audiencia, Lic. Peralta, must have returned to the years when he and Lic. Mañozca were locked in combat in Quito.

Although no longer a member of the Holy Office, the archbishop continued to take an active and sustained interest in the affairs of that tribunal, in which he had served for many years. His nephew, Juan Saenz de Mañozca, was an inquisitor. Moreover, during his term as archbishop, the long dormant Inquisition came to life again, and some of the most spectacular autos-da-fé ever conducted by the Holy Office took place. The resurgence of the Inquisition was not attributable solely to the zeal of the archbishop, although the role of his enthusiasm should not be discounted. The revolt of the Portuguese in 1640 incited a wave of persecution by the Holy Office against the Portuguese Jews in both Mexico and Peru.[19]

All the other controversies in which Archbishop Mañozca was involved were minor compared to that concerning the bishop of Puebla and the Society of Jesus. Although Lic. Mañozca had no responsibility for the origins of the clash—one of the most complex and controversial jurisdictional conflicts in the history of colonial Spanish-America—the archbishop became a major actor in the drama that unfolded.

Juan de Palafox y Mendoza (1600–1659), natural son of Jaime de Palafox y Mendoza, Marquis of Ariza, studied law and theology at the Universities of Salamanca and Alcalá before being ordained in 1629. After serving in the household of the empress Margaret, he received a seat on the Council of the Indies. On December 27, 1636, he was consecrated bishop of Puebla. The king and the council gave him the additional assignment of visitor general to the viceroyalty of New Spain.

Arriving in Mexico in June, 1640, he was largely responsible for persuading the king to dismiss the Duke of Escalona as viceroy on the grounds that his favoritism toward the Portuguese community indicated an intention to lead a revolt against the crown. The Duke of Escalona was a close blood relative of the Duke of Braganza, who was proclaimed King John IV in 1640 during a coup in which the Portuguese recovered their independence. The charges of Palafox ultimately turned out to be without foundation. When the Duke of Escalona returned to Spain, the king declared him innocent and appointed him viceroy of Sicily.[20]

For five months, from June 10 to November 1, 1642, Bishop Palafox held two positions: those of viceroy of New Spain and visitor general. He turned down the offer of the archbishopric of Mexico. The Count of Salvatierra soon replaced Palafox as viceroy, for clerics usually served only as interim viceroys, and besides it was not desirable to concentrate the offices of viceroy and visitor general in one person for any length of time. Intelligent, energetic, and strong-willed, Bishop Palafox effectively exposed abuses in the administration. Yet he behaved with sufficient tact and caution that he did not provoke undue opposition. He showed himself a vigorous and effective defender of the Indians.[21] One of his major achievements was to complete the process that Philip II had begun in 1583 of replacing the regular clergy with the secular clergy in many of the Indian parishes and bringing all the parishes that the regular clergy still retained under the direct supervision of the local bishop.[22]

The conflict between Bishop Palafox and the Jesuits pitted an exceptionally able and vigorous prelate against a religious community of extraordinary intellectual talents which enjoyed widespread respect and popularity among all classes. Bishop Palafox enjoyed friendly relations with the Jesuits at the beginning of his stay in Mexico. The clash originated in the bishopric of Puebla over whether the Jesuits were obligated to pay the tithes on the income from a farm which the Society had received as a bequest. The cathedral chapter of Puebla initiated the suit before Palafox' arrival in Mexico. Although he was convinced that the cathedral chapter was justified, the new bishop was initially conciliatory toward the Society. He urged them either to await the verdict of the courts or to offer to compromise.

The tithes constituted the major source of revenue for the bishops and the secular clergy. All over the Indies the bishops heatedly complained that the increasing concentration of farm property in the hands of the regular clergy threatened to deprive them of the needed revenues with which to operate their sees and parishes.[23] Anxious to strengthen the bishops, the crown threw its weight on the side of the episcopacy. The regular clergy, however, fought a tenacious rear-guard battle to avoid paying the tithes.

The Jesuits expressed their ill-feeling toward the bishop in petty discourtesies, including vituperative sermons. Palafox struck back on Ash Wednesday, March 6, 1647, when the vicar general of the diocese, Juan de Mero, prohibited some Jesuit fathers from preaching or hearing confessions unless they secured a license from the bishop. The dispute over the tithes, important though it was, faded into the background with the emergence of this larger and more basic jurisdictional issue.

On one hand, the bishop was asserting the prelate's prerogative to license all priests exercising care of souls within his see. Various decrees of the Council of Trent supported the position of Bishop Palafox. The Jesuits, on the other hand, claimed that such a pretension would undercut the obedience they owed to their own superiors. They further argued that the claim of the bishop conflicted with the special privileges that various popes had bestowed upon the Society.[24]

When a Jesuit priest delivered a sermon without securing a license from the bishop, Juan de Palafox promptly excommunicated him and others for violating the canons of the Council of Trent. Although the Jesuit community in Puebla bowed to the edict of the bishop, the provincial superior in Mexico City refused. Asserting that their traditional privileges were being violated, the Jesuits established in the capital a conservatory tribunal staffed by two Dominican friars.

If the secular and episcopal authorities in Mexico City had not approved the establishment of this special tribunal, a great deal of bitterness and unhappiness might have been avoided. The dispute thus would have gone directly to the Council of the Indies and to the Holy See for a settlement. But both the viceroy and Archbishop Mañozca recognized the legality of the conservatory. The viceroy arbitrarily and illegally excluded the audiencia from taking a stand in the matter.[25] He accepted the petition of the Jesuits that the audiencia was prejudiced, but refused to accept the counterpetition of Palafox' representative that the viceroy himself be excluded from jurisdiction because he was prejudiced against the bishop of Puebla.[26]

After the viceroy and the archbishop recognized the conservatory, the Jesuits took the offensive. They demanded that the Jesuit fathers be restored to their public ministries. Bishop Palafox obviously rejected the demand.

Both sides hurled excommunications at each other. Fearing for his life and anxious to avoid bloodshed, Bishop Palafox went into hiding for several months. The Jesuits pressured the frightened cathedral chapter of Puebla into withdrawing the obnoxious decrees of the absent bishop. Bishop Palafox resumed his office in November, 1647. The Jesuits rejoiced when letters arriving from Spain released Palafox from his position as visitor general of the kingdom.

Both sides appealed their cases to Madrid and Rome. In scarcely temperate language, Bishop Palafox assailed the Jesuits, whom he accused of trying to make themselves masters of the wealth of the kingdom and to undermine the authority of the bishops. The decision in both Rome and Madrid was in the main favorable to Bishop Palafox. The council did reprimand him for his intemperance and admonished him to be more conciliatory and tactful in the future. Yet the council supported his basic position. It ordered the Jesuits to disband the conservatory tribunal forthwith.[27] The king upbraided the Dominicans for promoting scandal by staffing the conservatory.[28] Archbishop Mañozca received a sharply worded reprimand for his pro-Jesuit stand.[29] So did the viceroy. And the audiencia, which had been excluded from jurisdiction by the viceroy, was scolded for not informing the king immediately about this matter.[30]

On May 14, 1648, Pope Innocent X handed down a decision which also vindicated the position of Bishop Palafox. The Pope informed the Society of Jesus that they could not preach or be confessors to the laity even inside their own churches without notifying the bishop, nor could they in any other church without securing his consent. The Holy See forbade the Jesuits to set up another conservatory or to excommunicate Bishop Palafox or his vicar general.[31]

The general of the Jesuit order, Father Vincencio Caraffa, wrote to Father Pedro Velasco, provincial superior of Mexico, "Although I would like to exonerate your conduct, I cannot."[32] In polite but firm language, he pointed out that the Jesuits in Puebla had been disrespectful to the bishop of Puebla by not showing him their credentials to preach. They had also demonstrated a lack of prudence in setting up the conservatory tribunal.

The Jesuits then and through the centuries have deeply resented the vigorous and, at times, intemperate language with which the bishop of Puebla fought his case against them. Jesuit hostility played an important role in preventing Bishop Palafox from securing the prestigious bishopric of Cuenca in Spain. He spent his last days as bishop of the much less important diocese of Osma.[33]

In the eighteenth century, Juan de Palafox y Mendoza was a serious candidate for canonization by the Roman Catholic Church. His prolific writings on a wide variety of religious and pastoral subjects earned for him a loyal band of admirers long after his death. Among his most zealous advocates was King Charles III of Spain (1759–88).[34] His vigorous defense of episcopal authority, which in effect meant royal supremacy over the Church, was one of the factors which led Charles III to champion ardently the cause of the Palafox canonization before the Papal curia. Jesuit opposition in Rome, however, proved more effective than the diplomatic intervention of the Spanish Court. Juan de Palafox was not canonized. That opposition to his canonization was a minor irritant in the growing alienation between the Spanish crown and the Jesuits. The estrangement culminated in 1767 with the momentous decision of Charles III to expel the Society of Jesus from all the Spanish dominions.[35] The principal cause was the feeling on the part of the government of Charles III that the Jesuits, with their fierce loyalty to Rome and with their efficient and well-disciplined organization, constituted a "state within a state," a potential if not actual threat to the supremacy of the crown over all groups and corporations within Spanish society.

Therein lies the real meaning of the boisterous clash between Bishop Palafox and the Jesuits a century earlier. Their conflict was but a chapter in the long struggle of the Spanish crown to assert its jurisdictional control over the Spanish church. Ferdinand and Isabella laid the foundation when they wrested from the Holy See permission to re-establish the Inquisition under royal control and gained the privilege of presenting three candidates to the Pope for every vacant ecclesiastical benefice. The bishops, in effect, became royal appointees. In insisting that the rural property of the Jesuits be subject to tithes and that Jesuit priests administering to the laity secure permission from the bishop, Juan de Palafox was defending not only episcopal authority but also royal supremacy over the Church.

The specific role of Archbishop Mañozca in the controversy can only be understood inside the much larger perspective that has just been outlined. The king and the council sharply upbraided him for his lack of neutrality in siding openly with the Jesuits against Bishop Palafox.[36] What the crown was saying was that the archbishop should have used the prestige of his high office to work out a compromise between the two contenders and not to side openly with one of them. In recognizing the legality of the conservatory tribunal established by the Jesuits, the archbishop intensified the conflict by allowing the Society to take the offensive against Bishop Palafox.

According to the crown, the conservatory was illegal and unnecessary. The dispute should have been referred directly to the Council of the Indies and to the Roman curia for a settlement. The viceroy, the archbishop, and the audiencia should have prevailed on both parties to accept some kind of face-saving truce until Madrid and Rome reached a verdict.

The Council of the Indies was asking Archbishop Mañozca to be something that by temperament he could not be. A man of strong convictions, he was driven to taking sides. He never was and never could be impartial, neutral, or, for that matter, judicious. He was by nature a partisan from the first day in 1610 when he took up his duties in the Inquisition in Cartagena until his death thirty-nine years later.

His stand with regard to the conservatory in Mexico contrasts with his actions during the visita general in Quito. In Mexico he sanctioned the Jesuit-sponsored conservatory manned by the Dominicans, while in Quito he denounced the conservatory tribunal sponsored by the Dominicans and staffed by Augustinians. To be sure, the Dominican conservatory in Quito was aimed squarely at him. From one point of view, at least, it is surprising that Archbishop Mañozca supported the Jesuit conservatory, since it was directed against a fellow bishop. Why then did he not side with Bishop Palafox in defending episcopal jurisdiction over the regular clergy? Admittedly, Lic. Mañozca had joined the episcopal ranks barely two years before, but many ecclesiastics recently arrived at the episcopal dignity rapidly became vigorous defenders of their new authority. However, in the Palafox-Jesuit collision, Lic. Mañozca acted more as a representative of the Inquisition than as an archbishop.[37] The Society of Jesus and the Holy Office had long been intimately tied together. This tradition of close cooperation encouraged the archbishop to side with the Society. In addition, the archbishop's nephew, Juan Sáenz de Mañozca, was then serving as an inquisitor.[38] If one of the mendicant orders and not the Jesuits had clashed with Palafox, Mañozca undoubtedly would have stood by his fellow bishop. He was a zealous admirer of the Jesuits, who, incidentally, were dominated in the New World by Spanish-born priests. The mendicants had large contingents of creoles, for whom Lic. Mañozca never concealed his contempt.

From the preceding sketches of the subsequent careers of the principal participants in the visita general of Quito, it is apparent that most of the magistrates did not change in temperament or conduct. Some became a little more subdued, others scarcely at all. They were all formed in the same bureaucratic milieu. Some final reflections about the nature of that system are now in order.

17.

A WEBERIAN ANALYSIS OF
THE SPANISH BUREAUCRACY

In dealing with any kind of bureaucratic organization, no historian can afford to neglect the central contribution of the German sociologist Max Weber. Only very recently, however, have Weber's ideas been applied to the Spanish colonial administration, in a series of studies by S. N. Eisenstadt, Richard Morse, and Magali Sarfatti.

Historians would agree that detailed data on many phases of the Spanish colonial administration are still meager. That is one justification for the present book. More such studies need to be done. While monographic work continues, the larger comparative and theoretical focus cannot be neglected. Although historians will place much emphasis on a particular space and time dimension, they have much to learn from the sociologist's and the political scientist's quest for the abstract and the general. Any Weberian analysis of the bureaucracy of the Spanish empire must be viewed as tentative. Its usefulness lies in the possibility that it may stimulate a broader and deeper understanding by placing the Spanish empire in a larger comparative and theoretical framework.

Weber used historical data with skill and imagination to illustrate his models. He admitted that in history his pure or ideal types of political domination never existed. They could, however, be found in various combinations. His approach was typological, not developmental. He did not analyze how the mixture of feudal, charismatic, and patrimonial elements characteristic of the West during the late Middle Ages led to the modern state.[1] That was the sphere of the historian, he thought.

The Spanish-American system of administration lends itself to such an analysis. Since the Spanish monarchy grew out of medieval origins, the feudal, charismatic, and patrimonial elements bulked large. But in the novel attempt to govern a world-wide collection of states, the Spanish monarchy pioneered new procedures of bureaucratic control. In so doing, the Spanish empire foreshadowed the Weberian model of legal domination that did not become triumphant in the West until the nineteenth century.

Rulers usually develop some myth of superiority to legitimate their authority, the essential characteristics of which are the power of rulers to command and the duty of subjects to obey. Every form of domination develops a corresponding governmental apparatus to justify and to implement its power to command. Weber concluded that there were three principal forms of domination that have occurred in historical time: (1) charismatic, (2) traditional, and (3) legal.

Charismatic domination emerges in times of trouble and stress. Hence it is a uniquely personal and emotional response to a crisis situation. Legal and traditional domination have solved the problems of succession and everyday routine, but both systems can be ineffective, if not paralyzed, in a time of acute crisis. Charisma, meaning "gift of grace," is a term that Weber adopted from the early Christian Church. For Weber, charisma represented the magic power of an individual leader to command the intense loyalty of his followers.

The successors of a charismatic leader have always sought to institutionalize and depersonalize the emotional quality. Charisma became familial in the medieval monarchies and institutional with the Roman Catholic Church. The European monarchies possessed an element of familial charisma, based on the mystique of royal blood and hereditary succession. The Church transmitted charisma by education, consecration, and organization. The distinction which the Church made between the office and the officeholder enabled it to preserve some institutional charisma. The difference between personal and institutional charisma is the contrast between Christ and the ecclesiastical organization that followed him or, another example, between Saint Francis of Assisi and the Franciscan order.

Charismatic features—personal, familial, and institutional—were not absent in Spanish America. For example, conquistadores such as Cortés and Pizarro were, in part at least, dynamic leaders who aroused the kind of blind loyalty that only charismatic figures can command among their followers. Charismatic leadership does much to explain the rapidity of the conquest.

Familial charisma also existed in the Habsburg monarchy. While Ferdinand and Isabella constantly worked to create stable, depersonalized institutions of government, they were, among many other things, charismatic rulers. In unifying the Spains around the crusading ideal of religious uniformity, they inspired deep-rooted loyalty among their subjects. Their example cast a charismatic glow over all their royal successors, best symbolized in the phrase "Their Catholic Majesties." Nowhere is this trend more graphically reflected than in the contemporary chronicles of the Indies.

The vision of a universal monarchy, in which Ferdinand and Isabella and their successors were cast in the role of messiahs destined to unite all mankind in the millennial kingdom on the eve of the end of the world, also enriched the charismatic aura that enveloped the crowns of the Spanish Habsburgs.[2]

Institutionalized charisma, of course, existed in the Church centuries before the conquest. But there were some unique American experiences that fortified this trend. The remarkable exploits of the first generation of missionaries in converting the Indians to the Catholic faith took on heroic qualities of charismatic proportions in the minds of their successors, as the pages of the *Historia eclesiástica indiana* of Gerónimo de Mendieta wistfully testify.

All of these charismatic features lent stability to the Spanish-American kingdoms. The example of the conquistadores gave to Spaniards and creoles alike a sense of security, confidence, and accomplishment. This feeling served to counteract to some extent the bitter feud dividing the peninsular Spaniards from the creoles. One can scarcely exaggerate the central importance of the mystique of the monarchy. That institution's partially charismatic quality served to buttress the loyalty that the magic symbol of the crown evoked in the Indies. The bureaucracy could exploit it to administer the empire on a day-to-day, year-to-year basis. Along with the monarch, the Spanish Catholic Church—and it was more Spanish than Roman—was the other institution that was primarily responsible for preserving stability in that society where disruptive forces were not lacking. In view of the bitter hostility between creole and Spaniard in the religious orders and the Church's great difficulty in enforcing even minimum standards of morality among the clergy, it is clear that the Church's personal and institutionalized charisma was an endless source of strength.

Equally significant is the fact that the Habsburg system resembled what Max Weber has identified as the traditional form of political domination. Traditional domination springs from a belief in the legitimacy of an authority "that has always existed." The rulers are masters who have exercised authority by virtue of inherited status. Feudalism and the patrimonial state are the two subdivisions of traditional domination. Common features of these two forms are the arbitrary power of the rulers and the limitation of that power by sacred tradition. In medieval Europe, the patrimonial state grew out of feudalism, although some features of the feudal heritage never were totally obliterated until the French Revolution.

In a feudal society, government officials are not the personal dependents of the ruler, as they are in patrimonial states, but socially prominent allies who have given an oath of fealty to the monarch. The possession of landed wealth is accompanied by the exercise of governmental authority over retainers, as defined in a grant or a contract. Feudal lords are men of wealth who are capable of equipping themselves and their retainers for warfare. The legal order becomes a collection of assorted privileges, and administration and law become fused. The royal councils of the late Middle Ages were both administrative agencies and law courts.

While Ferdinand and Isabella and their immediate successors succeeded in destroying the autonomous political authority of the landed nobility, some feudal elements persisted in the peninsula. Some feudal features were not even lacking in the New World, specifically as feudal attitudes rather than feudal institutions. The Castilian crown studiously prevented the emergence of a feudal system as such in the Indies.

The encomienda was not the most significant example, although that institution contained an obvious feudal core. Encomenderos were obligated to arm themselves at their own expense to defend the kingdom from either foreign attack or local uprisings.

A far more significant feudal legacy was a basic principle of the whole system of government in the Indies, namely, the corporate principle that the individual's rights, privileges, and obligations were derivative from the particular estate and functional corporations to which that individual belonged. Built-in inequalities characterized the estates and corporations, whose privileges and responsibilities were usually spelled out in specific charters. As in feudal society, the whole legal order in the Indies was a mere bundle of privileges. Administration became adjudication. That principle, of feudal origin, was also incorporated into the patrimonial state of the late medieval period. The patrimonial ideal was that the administration of justice was the highest attribute of sovereignty. The king was the supreme judge. Hence legislative and executive functions were outgrowths of judicial authority. Every major agency of government from the Council of the Indies to the audiencias, town councils, and corregimientos combined both judicial and administrative authority.

In both feudal society and the society in the Indies there was an exaggerated sense of honor and personal dignity. An obsession with status was a dominant characteristic of these magistrates, who saw themselves as quasi-nobles. The absence of a large titled nobility and of a royal Court in the Indies encouraged magistrates to adopt the pretensions and the attitudes of the nobility. In that corporate, privileged society, questions of protocol took on a tremendous importance, for the magistrates' concern with etiquette reflected their hypersensitivity about their place in society. For the displaced Europeans in the Indies, minor matters of social precedence, which might not even arise in the peninsula, could become causes of bitter personal dissensions. The acute sense of pride and the obsession with status were further intensified by the built-in suspicion characteristic of the Spanish bureaucracy and the somewhat vague overlapping of jurisdictions. The endless feuds among the magistrates are reminiscent of the constant clashes among the feudal nobility. The Spanish bureaucrats fought with words, insults, and intrigues; the feudal nobles with arms.

Another arresting resemblance between the feudal nobility of late medieval times and the Spanish-American society is the style of life of the wealthy creoles. The poorer creoles entered the lower echelons of the bureaucracy and the Church. The upper ranks were in effect closed to them. Thus they were deprived of a natural outlet for their energies. The wealthy creoles lived lives of ostentatious display, filled with baroque pomp and circumstance, in an endless round of attending mass, making love, and playing cards. Their attitude toward consumption was anti-utilitarian. For that matter, the whole style of life of the richer creoles was anti-utilitarian. Their aristocratic life was self-contained, lacking a goal or purpose. The disdain that creole aristocrats felt toward those engaged in commerce was the same contempt that feudal groups have usually showed toward the bourgeoisie for being devoted to utilitarian pursuits.

The resemblances between the colonial bureaucracy and the other form of traditional domination, the patrimonial state, are even more striking than those with feudalism. Under patrimonial administration, there is no clearcut division of authority among the various officials. An official derives whatever authority he enjoys from the ruler's confidence and favor. Office is a privilege and a grace from the monarch which he can grant and withdraw at his personal pleasure. Magistrates do not receive annual set salaries but stipends from fiefs, allowances in kind, fees paid by subjects, or graft. The patrimonial ruler acts arbitrarily within certain limits that do not violate sacred tradition. In their relations with subjects patrimonial officials act as capriciously as the ruler does with them without violating the norms of sacred tradition.

While a patrimonial state of the ideal form described in Weber's model never existed in history, the late medieval kingdoms of Western Europe had pronounced patrimonial characteristics: All government offices originated and belonged to the personal household of the king. Officials became more independent as their distance from the center of authority increased. Patrimonial rulers resorted to a whole series of devices in order to prevent a further fragmentation of their authority. Invariably in medieval Europe the kings made periodic visits to different parts of their realm. Moreover, they appointed officers who could supplement their own personal jurisdiction, such as the circuit judges in medieval Europe or the *missi dominici* of Charlemagne. The oidores who conducted a visita de la tierra served the same purpose in the Indies. The patrimonial rulers sought to preserve authority by the following practices, aimed partly at preventing the emergence of an independent landed aristocracy with inherited privileges. Benefices or prebends were given to individuals as a reward for services rendered, with the income remaining as an attribute of the office and not of the incumbent as a person. Time limits were placed on the tenure of royal officials. Magistrates could not marry or own property in their jurisdictions. Spies or inspectors were employed to supervise the performance of regular magistrates. Because judisdictions among the various agencies were deliberately unclear, they in turn supervised each other.

Although the patrimonial ruler derives his legitimation from sacred tradition, he also lays claim to a substantial amount of independent if not arbitrary personal power. The administration of law is on an *ad hoc* basis from case to case. Justice becomes a series of individual decisions, not necessarily as interpretations of "law" but as gifts of grace from the ruler that do not create binding precedents.

Richard Morse has observed, "This typology of the patrimonial state describes with surprising accuracy the structure and the logic of the Spanish empire in America. It also assists us to understand why chaos ensued when the ultimate authority for the system, the Spanish crown, was suddenly removed."[3] My quarrel with this arresting hypothesis is not with what it says but with what it does not say. That the Spanish empire was profoundly patrimonial is a discerning insight, but the system also contained pronounced characteristics of feudal, charismatic, and legal domination.

As historians, we should never ignore Weber's own warning that none of his models ever occurred in a pure or ideal form in history but in various combinations or mutations. In the Spanish empire, charismatic, feudal, patrimonial, and legal features meshed together in a unique combination. The responsibility of the historian is to analyze that combination.

To what degree did the Spanish empire approximate the patrimonial model? That corporate state with its built-in inequalities was a deeply traditional society. Although significant social change was taking place, the central goal of the whole regime was to preserve a traditional order. The monarchy itself derived its legitimation from a combination of charismatic and patrimonial ideals.

The notion did survive that the members of the royal councils, the viceroys, the bishops, and even the oidores belonged to the royal household. But this was more fiction than fact. There was a dualism in the attitudes toward the holding of public office during the sixteenth and seventeenth centuries. This dichotomy prevailed not only in the Spanish empire but throughout western Europe. On one hand, the modern ideal of a salaried and disinterested magistracy with clearly delimited responsibilities did exist. Yet the conduct of countless magistrates demonstrates the persistence of an older tradition whose origins are recognizably patrimonial. The officeholder exploited to the fullest every opportunity, financial as well as social, that the office afforded. That very dichotomy brought grief to many magistrates, for corruption and sexual license accounted for the bulk of the fines in a visita general.

As mentioned earlier, a basic cause of the Spanish failure to wipe out corruption was the inadequate salary scale on several levels. The better compensated officials were much less apt to indulge in illegal forms of self-enrichment. The Spanish imperial bureaucracy was midway between a patrimonial bureaucracy in which officials were paid in kind, in tips, and in graft and a modern administration with regular, monetary salaries paid by the state.

Although magistrates held office at the pleasure of the prince, there was considerable security of tenure on several levels. Job security was characteristic at the conciliar layer of the bureaucracy. The viceroys, of course, were political appointees who served five-year terms. The viceroy of Mexico was often promoted to Peru and then perhaps to a prestigious post in Europe. The corregidores also served five-year terms, but most were not reappointed to other posts.

Among the superior magistrates in the audiencias, professional qualifications counted for much in recruitment, although influence-wielding did play a role. The president and the oidores had substantial job security. Most of them remained in the imperial service, being promoted from one post to another until they died. There was even an embryonic retirement system. Their job security, however, was not *de jure* but *de facto*. The king could remove them at his pleasure, but he seldom did in fact. Even in those cases where magistrates were found guilty of serious misconduct, the few who were dismissed were aged officials. The punishments for most were sharply worded reprimands and monetary fines.

A basic feature of the patrimonial state is a division of authority among the several agencies so that, in effect, they become mutually supervisory. Although there was some rational division of authority among the various agencies in the government of the Indies, there was also a great deal of overlapping. The conciliar or collegiate principle tended to reinforce the tendency. Because several agencies shared the same responsibilities and because a wide variety of pressures both inside and outside the bureaucracy had to be taken into account, no one magistrate or agency had *de jure* the final word. Neither did the king and his immediate advisers, although no decision became final until the monarch ratified it. The final outcome of any event was the result of an endless tug of war among the various echelons of the bureaucracy, all of whom were influenced by pressures from the divergent interest groups in the Indies. The views championed by a viceroy or an audiencia or a provincial governor might prevail, depending on the circumstances of a particular case.

The high degree of flexibility in the Spanish system has clear patrimonial features. So does the Spanish system of law. While the king recognized limitations of his authority imposed by divine and natural law, the monarch was in fact the source of all written law. Also the monarch was morally if not legally obligated to respect the privileges and charters of the various corporate groups. The king, however, wished not to be bound by the fetters of written law in the sense that a specific interpretation of the law became a binding precedent. The monarch preferred to adjudicate each dispute as an independent expression of royal grace and favor. But the particular rulings of the monarch did establish precedents that were binding to some extent. The very fact that the great digest, the *Recopilación,* was finally published in 1681 indicates that the monarch was not as free of binding precedent as he ideally might wish to be.

Yet the king did not lack freedom to act arbitrarily as long as he did not violate the basic precepts, i.e., the sacred tradition of that corporate society. The wide gap between the law and its observance gave the monarch some choice in determining when to attempt to enforce the law and when to tolerate noncompliance.

Every cedula in the *Recopilación* was originally issued to correct a specific abuse in a certain place at a particular time. Hence the cedulas in the *Recopilación,* on one level at least, have an *ad hoc* flavor. But beneath this apparent hodgepodge, there was a coherent world view—a vision of society as it ought to be, a pale but nevertheless recognizable reflection of the ideal world encompassed in divine and natural law.

The crown's Platonic ideal of magistrates as disinterested guardians and the twin devices of the visita general and the residencia are all patrimonial in spirit and intent. Yet a system of inspectors to review the conduct of regular magistrates is not a monopoly of patrimonial administrations.

It is clear that the Spanish administration contained a wide variety of features characteristic of patrimonial states. What remains to be seen is in what ways the Spanish administration foreshadowed the model of legal domination as envisaged by Weber.

Under legal domination, which did not come to prevail in the West until the nineteenth century, those who exercise command, whether appointed or elected, do so by legally sanctioned procedures. Persons under the legal jurisdiction obey the "law" rather than those who administer it. The apparatus of administration is continuous. Controls over the exercise of authority exist such that the private person is separated from the performance of his official duties.

The rule of law presupposes (1) a legal order, subject to change by legislation, (2) a bureaucracy conducting official business in accordance with legislative regulation, (3) a binding authority over all persons who obtain membership in the community at birth, and (4) the government's monopolization of the legitimate use of force. The specific duty of each official is delimited in terms of impersonal criteria. Each official is given sufficient authority to carry out his assigned functions. The means of compulsion at his disposal are strictly limited, and the conditions under which its employment are legitimate are clearly defined.

The responsibilities of each official belong to a hierarchy of authority in which the higher officials supervise the lower ones, but the latter have certain rights of appeal. The officials do not own the resources necessary for the performance of their duties, but they are accountable for the use of those resources in official business. Private affairs, official revenue, and private income are quite separate. Public office cannot be appropriated by incumbents as a piece of private property that can be sold or inherited. Pensions, dismissal procedures, and discipline techniques are not property rights but incentives to promote better performance. All official business is conducted on the basis of written documents. In contrast, official business in patrimonial regimes is transacted through personal encounters and oral communications, not through impersonal documents. In regimes of legal domination, an official receives his appointment by contract. His appointment and his job placement are dependent upon his technical qualifications. His rewards are a regular monetary salary with a life-time career and prospects for promotion and retirement benefits.

The Spanish bureaucracy contained both patrimonial and legal features in a bewildering combination. In the appointment of magistrates on the oidor level, technical qualifications, such as a law degree and previous administrative experience, bulked large, but so did favoritism and influence-wielding. Promotion by merit and even some retirement benefits were not totally absent. Officials were paid fixed salaries but in many cases not enough. The result was the widespread corruption which in patrimonial states is "simply a matter of the disorganization of an unregulated system of fees."[4] Clerking offices in the audiencia, some ceremonial offices, and municipal posts were sold and could be inherited for the payment of a fee. While this practice had the obvious merit of bringing new blood into the system, it also had the grave disadvantage of making certain offices private property and hence less subject to government regulation. This, in effect, was a throwback to the patrimonial state.

The Spanish administration to a limited extent foreshadowed the modern concept of a hierarchy of offices with the lower ones subject to the supervision of the higher ones, i.e., the king, the Council of the Indies, the viceroy, the audiencia, the treasury, the corregidores and municipalities, etc. But this ostensibly vertical chain of command became at least somewhat horizontal, since every agency could correspond directly with the king and the Council of the Indies. While Madrid recognized the existence of the formal hierarchy, the authorities in Spain often sided with the lower agency. The overlapping of jurisdictions, such that several agencies shared a voice in decision-making, added a patrimonial dimension to the whole bureaucratic apparatus, with the consequence that there was a good deal of room for arbitrariness. Yet all official business in the Spanish administration was conducted through an endless mountain of written documents, a characteristic feature of legal domination.

S. N. Eisenstadt in a stimulating comparative study, *The Political Systems of Empire,* has supplemented Max Weber's three categories of charismatic, traditional, and legal domination with a fourth category. He calls it the "historical bureaucratic polities."[5] These administrative systems fall somewhere between the traditional and charismatic states on one hand and the regimes of legal domination on the other. Basing his hypothesis on a wide and intensive use of historical data, he compares and contrasts systematically the following societies, which he considers to be examples of historical bureaucratic polities: the Inca empire, ancient Egypt, Sassanian Persia, several Chinese dynasties, the Ottoman empire, the Roman empire, absolutist Europe (pre-French Revolution), and the Spanish-American empire. His focus is on these polities as distinguished from pre-bureaucratic societies, such as the Mongols, feudal Europe, and the Carolingian empire, and from the modern bureaucratic societies that Weber classifies as regimes of legal domination. Eisenstadt's approach is comparative and historical, whereas Weber, using history to illustrate his models, had a topical, not developmental, focus.

In the historical bureaucratic polities, the rulers were the protagonists in the political struggle while the antagonists were the major groups in the society, i.e., the bureaucracy, the aristocracy, the professional, religious, and cultural elites, the upper, middle, and lower urban groups, the landed gentry, and the peasants. The rulers and their immediate advisers largely created the framework inside of which the political struggle took place. The initiative lay with them, as they were the most dynamic element in the political equation. But the bureaucrats and the members of the upper strata were active participants in the political struggle, with a voice in determining the outcome of events.

Among the goals that the rulers of the historical bureaucratic polities sometimes shared with those of patrimonial states were territorial expansion, economic development, and the preservation of a given cultural pattern. The heads of historical bureaucratic polities also possessed unique goals. Their most basic objectives were to create and preserve a unified and centralized polity subject to their personal control and to ensure that they could continuously recruit the necessary financial resources from every section of society. Only thus could the rulers have the freedom to pursue other more particular objectives.

Monarchs in historical bureaucratic polities and in patrimonial states both had a great deal of personal, arbitrary power. A patrimonial king, however, did not possess the capacity to pursue long-range political goals. A patrimonial ruler, for example, simply would lack the power to conduct the sustained and ambitious foreign policy pursued by the Spanish Habsburgs.

A basic contradiction in all of these historical bureaucratic polities was that the rulers' goal of mobilizing "free-floating resources" could be blocked by the immense power that the traditional elements wielded. A great deal of wealth was in agricultural land, held by traditional groups such as the Church and the aristocracy. They enjoyed tax exemption by virtue of ascriptive rights founded in medieval precedent. That is a fundamental difference between those societies and modern bureaucratic states where economic activities have tended to revolve around market exchange, hence greatly facilitating the rapid mobilization of resources on the part of rulers.

In the Spanish empire, for example, the *donativo gracioso,* or forced loan, took on a special importance. This device enabled the crown to mobilize substantial resources independent of the fixed ascriptive rights of the upper classes. But it was a poor substitute for an annual system of direct, regular taxation.

The freedom of action of the Spanish kings was limited not only by the ascriptive privileges of traditional groups but also by the monarchs' continued reliance for their legitimation on symbols which were essentially traditional and charismatic in nature. The Spanish monarchs were expected to uphold a given cultural tradition. While they sought to limit the power and influence of the aristocracy and the Church by creating new and more flexible status groups, they continued to use the symbols of status identified with the religious and aristocratic elites. An entirely new, secular and "rational" type of legitimation, based on the positive support of nontraditional social groups and oriented toward universalistic symbols and values, was never instituted in any of the historical bureaucratic polities, least of all in the Spanish empire.

Why? Such a legitimation would require a massive broadening of the base of political participation to include politically passive groups, such as the lower urban population and the peasantry, and an upgrading of the political roles of the middle and upper urban groups. A change as drastic as that would also entail the ultimate destruction of the whole corporate society with all its built-in inequalities. Hence the monarchs were unable to transcend the symbols of hierarchal stratification and legitimation represented by the aristocratic groups whose very influence they sought to curtail but never to abolish.

The consequences of this inner contradiction were momentous. For one thing, it limited the mutual identification between the rulers and the lower classes, thus restricting the possibility that the latter could appeal to the former. The best that these politically passive groups could obtain was some paternalistic protection of their basic interests inside the framework of an aristocratic and hierarchal society in which their rights were narrowly defined. Such was the case of the Indian population of Spanish America.

The second consequence of the traditional nature of legitimation was that, given the emphasis placed on the superiority of aristocratic values, nonaristocratic groups aspired to obtain "aristocratization" by identifying themselves with those symbols and values. This tended to limit the opportunities for social mobility and advancement of the middle and lower groups. Thus the power that the central political institutions had for attracting the more dynamic elements among the nonaristocratic groups was narrowed appreciably.

Another facet of the trend toward aristocratization was that overevaluation of landed property as a symbol of status tended to restrict economic growth. Economic growth was a major goal in most historical bureaucratic polities.

The bureaucracies played a mediating role in the conflict between the goal of the kings to generalize power and the desire of the traditional ascriptive groups to maintain the *status quo*. In the formative stage of a bureaucracy's development, the major preoccupations of the magistrates were "bread and butter" issues— salaries, emoluments, job security. Once the bureaucracy had evolved into a somewhat autonomous body with its own traditions, broader and deeper conflicts could develop between them and the monarchs. The most acute source of tension centered around the desire of the bureaucracies to preserve and even expand their autonomy in the areas of political decision-making, the acquisition of status, and certain sensitive issues of economic policy.

Bureaucracies fought for and usually attained a legitimation distinct from that of the ruling elites, mostly of a "legal-rational" or professional nature in contrast to the more traditional and charismatic variety of the old elites. In the Spanish bureaucracy, there were also pronounced aristocratic overtones. An ideology eventually emerged in which the bureaucracies stressed their ethical, professional, and legal responsibility for implementing the chief values and goals of society. Implicit in this rationale was the contrast between the bureaucratic administration as the embodiment of government by laws and the predilection of the rulers toward arbitrariness.

In Byzantium, China, Rome, and absolutist Europe, such ideologies were well developed. So were they in the Spanish empire. Juan de Solórzano was perhaps the most systematic spokesman, but there were countless others who voiced the ideology and whose official conduct was in part motivated by it. Nowhere is the existence of that professional, if semi-aristocratic, ideology more apparent than in the struggle between the Council of the Indies and the king over the control of patronage in 1600–1609 and again in 1644.

The particular conflicts in the Spanish bureaucracy were typical of those in most well-developed historical bureaucratic polities. At stake were the political autonomy of the bureaucracy itself and the degree of control that the kings could exercise over the administration. Conversely the issue was to what extent the upper echelons could determine the basic policies governing their own activities.

There were several concrete issues within this broad spectrum of conflict. One was the extent to which the king's personal officers could effectively determine the making of decisions in the royal councils, i.e., the influence wielded by the presidents and the secretaries of the councils as opposed to the councilors themselves. In the Spanish councils there was an endless tug of war between those two sets of officials.

Another more specific issue was the extent to which the king could act through independent agencies outside the regular administrative organization. The Count-Duke of Olivares often used special committees or cámaras to circumvent the more slow-moving councils.

The third concrete source of conflict was the struggle of the bureaucracy to determine the criteria governing recruitment of its members. In Chapter 6 much was said about how the Council of the Indies fought to maintain high professional standards in recruitment and how the king and his immediate circle were more apt to be influenced by favoritism. The pendulum swung backward and forward. What emerged was an ever-changing balance between professionalism and favoritism. After 1644, when the council as a body lost most of its control over patronage, the latter tended to predominate over the former. Professionalism, however, was never completely abandoned. Professional standards were revitalized in the eighteenth century as a consequence of the cautious and gradual reforms of the Bourbons.

Because the monarchs were dependent on the bureaucracy on a day-today basis, they needed to maintain an intimate group of advisers who were independent of the regular administrative system. Strong-willed sovereigns, such as Charles V and Philip II, relied on the Council of State. Weaker monarchs, like Philip III and Philip IV, reposed much confidence in a particular minister.

Another device used by most of the monarchs in the historical bureaucratic polities was a system of inspectors, which in the Spanish empire took the form of the visita general, as a means of supervising the conduct and performance of the regular magistrates.

Questions of status involved the kings and the bureaucracies in further conflict. In addition to its "legal-rationalist" ideology, the bureaucracy sought to acquire aristocratic or semi-aristocratic symbols of status and in some cases even to establish their hereditary transmission. A basic instrument of the royal policy in regard to social stratification was the granting of titles. The monarchs sought to preserve a clear distinction between the functions within the administration and honorific titles denoting the general status of officials in the social hierarchy. While there was usually some correspondence between the two, they seldom became identical. The maintenance of this distinction enabled a king to exercise some control over both the bureaucracy and the aristocracy and thus to make each group dependent upon him as the ultimate arbitrator.

However much the Spanish bureaucrats sought to copy the attitudes and to acquire the symbols of the titled nobility, the king seldom granted hereditary titles of nobility to magistrates below the rank of viceroy. The latter usually had inherited titles. The Spanish kings used the three military-religious orders of Santiago, Calatrava, and Alcántara to reward the upper echelons of the bureaucracy. Juan de Solórzano received a knighthood at the end of his career. Dr. Morga was ambitious to receive this honor, as were many other magistrates. The military orders became a kind of aristocracy of bureaucratic merit. These honors were ad personam and not hereditary. But they carried with them certain privileges of minor nobility. The monarchs' use of this source of patronage proved to be an effective means of keeping the upper echelons of the bureaucracy sensitive to royal control and of preserving the distinction between the bureaucracy and the nobility.

While caution is advisable in generalizations about the political orientations of bureaucratic states, one trend seems to stand out. That is, they were legalistic and bound to tradition. Their instinctive attitude was toward maintaining the status quo rather than championing changes. With their close ties to the legal profession and with their ingrained respect for legal tradition and codification, the bureaucrats were intuitively distrustful of *ad hoc* measures coming from the kings and their executive ministers. The cautious and legal-minded attitudes of the Spanish bureaucrats came to the fore during the dialogue between the Count-Duke of Olivares and the Council of the Indies in the 1620's.

The Spanish administration was perhaps even more conservative than other bureaucratic systems. The traditional-minded attitude of the Spanish bureaucracy stems from the legal training of the conciliar layer of the bureaucracy as well as from the principle of collegiate responsibility. The custom of appointing men of advanced age to the councils strengthened the conservative trend. The executive ministers of the king or the presidents of the audiencias were usually more willing to champion moderate change, but the council was often unsympathetic. Olivares and Dr. Morga are cases in point.

If the bureaucracies fought to maintain their own identity and autonomy vis-à-vis the king and his immediate circle, they also refused to be absorbed by the upper strata of society. That they did not become mere echos of the professional and traditional elites was due in some significant measure to their lack of homogeneity. In the Spanish bureaucracy, the political, conciliar, and professional levels and the aristocratic, country gentry, and bourgeois elements were complexly meshed together, with large numbers of creoles in the lower ranks. It was this very lack of homogeneity in composition and social outlook that enabled the bureaucracy to maintain a certain distance from those upper strata to which they had originally belonged. The bureaucrats tended to see themselves as a group apart from the rest of society. In a paternalistic fashion, the bureaucracy sought to provide some protection to the lower strata against the excessive demands of the upper classes. Obviously the bureaucracies tended to favor the interests of the upper strata over those of the lower. Their deep-rooted conservatism never allowed them to question the rightness of the built-in inequalities of the social order. But they also were not unmindful of the need for some protection to lower groups.

The lower groups were politically passive in absolutist Europe. They were even more so in Spanish America, where wide differences of culture and race separated the Indians and the Negroes from the dominant white minority. Yet even these groups did not lack the mechanisms or the inclination to make known their aspirations to every level of the bureaucracy. In several cases the Indians actually won modest redresses of their grievances.

The fact that the decision-making echelons of the Spanish bureaucracy were formed of peninsular Spaniards served to strengthen the separation of the magistrates from the creoles. A qualification is in order. The viceroys and the Council of the Indies were indeed independent-minded. The audiencias, on the other hand, tended to be more sympathetic toward the aspirations of the creole elite, but they seldom abdicated their independence of judgment. The audiencias actually played the difficult role of seeking to reconcile the point of view of the crole elite with that of the central authorities in Spain in an endless series of compromises.

In the Spanish colonial administration, there was some balance between the principles of authority and flexibility. The highly centralized decision-making vested in the king had a counterbalance in the substantial measure of decentralized decision-making exercised by various bureaucratic agencies from the council downward. The council fought a constant tug of war with the king and his immediate advisers and also often clashed with the magistrates in the Indies. What enabled the viceroys and the audiencias to play a creative role vis-à-vis both the king and the council in the ultimate formulation of policy was the "I obey but do not execute" formula. If the officials in the New World thus had some room in which to maneuver, the visita general periodically reinforced the principle of centralized authority.[6]

The dialectic of Spanish bureaucratic politics can be summed up in the Hegelian formula noted previously. The thesis is the wishes of the central authorities in Spain, embodied in their instructions to the magistrates overseas. The antithesis is that complex of pressures in colonial society which the royal bureaucrats had to take into account. The synthesis is what actually happened: a seldom mutually satisfactory but usually workable compromise between what the central authorities intended and what local pressures would permit. In more cases than not, local pressures played a more decisive role than did the intentions of the central authorities. This Hegelian formula does much to explain the wide gap between the law and its observance.

It also illustrates the intensity and the depth of the political struggle in this particular historical bureaucratic polity. Although the king and his immediate circle largely created the framework inside of which the political struggle unfolded, the various layers of the bureaucracy and the upper strata had much to say about the ultimate development. And even the lower groups were not totally excluded from participation in the political struggle.[7]

Insofar as the administration in each bureaucratic polity could maintain a "middle position" between the rulers and the various social groups and thus preserve some independence from both, they contributed mightily to the efficient functioning of the whole system. Any one of these bureaucracies could become corrupt, inefficient, and self-aggrandizing. They could develop tendencies which restricted the rulers' generalization of power and thus dry up the flow of free-floating resources.

A characteristic feature of the historical bureaucratic polities was that, when an administrative system became corrupt, inefficient, and dominated by one social stratum, reforming movements arose to correct those abuses. The reforming impulse came either from the kings and their executive ministers or from the bureaucracy itself, sometimes in the face of opposition from the king. In the Spanish empire, the reforming drive came from the kings and their executive ministers rather than from within the ranks of the bureaucracy.

Although during the second half of the seventeenth century the Spanish bureaucracy declined in standards and efficiency, as did monarchical leadership also, the administration was still able to preserve some of its basic mediating function. The obraje reforms of the 1680's support such a conclusion. A more sustained and more effective reforming drive had to wait until the advent of the Bourbon dynasty. The full impact of those changes, however, did not begin to be felt until the eve of the dissolution of the Spanish empire.

REFERENCE MATERIAL

SPANISH TERMS

SPANISH CURRENCY

The basic unit of Spanish currency was the *maravedí*. Ferdinand and Isabella created the *excelente de Granada,* better known as the ducat, modeled after the Venetian coin of that name. A ducat was 23.75 carats of fine gold, worth 375 maravedís. In Spanish America the *escudo,* created by Charles V in 1537 with a value of 350 maravedís but subsequently raised to 400 maravedís by Philip II in 1566, never did replace the ducat as a unit of calculation.

The most commonly used unit of currency in the Indies was the *peso,* in whose terms the treasure of America was usually calculated. A peso was the equivalent of 450 maravedís or 1.2 ducats. There were two kinds of pesos, the *peso de oro* and the *peso de plata.* The latter was much more common because silver production under the Habsburgs was nearly ninety times as great as gold production. There were two kinds of silver pesos. The Mexican silver peso was divided into eight reales; from it the United States dollar originated. A *patacón,* on the other hand, was worth nine instead of eight reales.

John Lynch has written a brief but useful account of Spanish currency, *Spain under the Habsburgs* (2 vols., New York: Oxford University Press, 1964—), I, 349. For a more extensive account see Felipe Mateu y Llopes, *La moneda española* (Barcelona: Editorial Alberto Martín, 1946), pp. 231–74.

GLOSSARY

abogado. A lawyer.

alcabalas. The traditional Spanish form of sales tax.

alcalde de crimen. A judge of a lower court, the *sala de crimen,* attached to the *audiencias* of Mexico and Lima to exercise criminal jurisdiction.

alcalde ordinario. An executive and judicial magistrate elected annually by the aldermen of a city council.

aldeia. Portuguese word for a village.

alguacil mayor. A constable with certain powers of patronage.

alternativa. The rotation of offices among different regional groups.

asiento. A contract granted by representatives of the crown authorizing a private individual to conquer and pacify a frontier area.

audiencia. The highest tribunal of justice in a Spanish-American kingdom, acting also as a general administrative board.

ayllu. The basic social, political, and economic unit of pre-conquest Inca society, retained with modifications during the Spanish regime.

ayuda de costa. A per diem expense account paid to magistrates traveling on official business.

cabecera. A principal village with several villages subordinated to it.

cabildo eclesiástico. A cathedral chapter.

cabildo secular. A city council.

casas reales. The seat of an *audiencia* where the president of that tribunal also resided.

canciller. The chancellor and keeper of the royal seal in each *audiencia.*

cancillería. An *audiencia* which enjoyed the rank of kingdom.

cofradía. A sodality or religious fraternity.

compadrazgo. Ritual co-parenthood.

consulta. A recommendation of a royal council to the king.

consultor. A civilian jurist who served in an advisory capacity to the Inquisition.

contaduría mayor. The royal fiscal service.

corregidor. The governor of a province.

corregimiento. A provincial unit of administration.

criollo. A person of European descent born in America.

curaca. The Peruvian term for an Indian chieftain. The Mexican equivalent, *cacique.*

demandas públicas de mal juzgado. A review of the verdicts of a judge, ordinarily confined to a *residencia.*

encomienda. A system under which Spanish colonists collected tribute tax from the Indians in exchange for providing their charges with some protection.

entrada. A military expedition into an unconquered province.

escribano de cámara. The head of the notorial office of an *audiencia* or a *cabildo secular.*

escribano real. A notary licensed to practice.

fanega. A unit of measure, approximately equal to 1.60 bushels, or 116 lbs.

fiscal. A crown attorney serving as one of the superior magistrates of an *audiencia* and overseeing the royal treasury.

gobernador intendente. A governor of a provincial unit of administration larger than a *corregimiento,* established in the late 18th century.

gobierno. A governorship.

habitante. A Spaniard who is not a freeholder, in contrast to a *vecino* who is.

juez de comisión. A temporary judge appointed to make a specific investigation.

juez de remisión. A licensed advocate co-opted by the *audiencia* to break a tie.

juez pesquisidor. A special judge appointed by the *audiencia* to conduct an investigation of a particular crime in the provinces.

junta de guerra. A subcommittee of the Council of the Indies which coordinated military operations in the overseas empire.

letrado. Someone possessing a university law degree.

ministros inferiores. The clerking level of an *audiencia.*

ministros superiores. The president, *oidores,* and *fiscal* of an *audiencia.*

mita. A system of compulsory Indian draft labor.

obraje. A textile shop in which Indians provided the manual labor.

oficiales reales. Officers of the treasury.

oidor. A judge of an *audiencia.*

patronato real. Laws and customs regulating relations between church and state.

procurador. A duly accredited agent or emissary from one corporation or governmental agency to another.

regidor. An alderman.

relator. An *audiencia* official whose duties were principally clerical.

repartimiento. A quota system of draft labor.

residencia. A judicial review of the conduct of a magistrate after he left office.

sala de crimen. A branch of the *audiencias* of Mexico and Lima exercising criminal jurisdiction.

tambo. A way-station on an isolated road.

tribunal de cuentas. A board set up by the *contaduría mayor* to audit the accounts of the local office of the royal exchequer.

vecino. A freeholder.

visita de la tierra. A periodic tour of a province by an *oidor.*

visita general. An occasional investigation of the conduct of an *audiencia* upon authorization of the king.

CHRONOLOGICAL CHART

KING	VICEROY	PRESIDENT	EVENTS IN THE EMPIRE
			Inca Conquest, 1455–95
Charles V, or Charles I, 1516–56			Spanish Conquest, 1533
Philip II, 1556–98			Dutch War, 1566–1609
Philip III, 1598–1621 (Lerma, 1598–1618)	Montesclaros, 1606–14	Ibarra, 1599–1608 Recalde, 1608–12	Twelve-Year Truce, 1609–21
(Uceda, 1618–21)	Esquilache, 1614–21	Morga, 1615–36	
Philip IV, 1621–65 (Olivares, 1621–43)	Guadalcázar, 1621–28 Chinchón, 1628–38		Dutch War, 1621–48 Visita general of viceroyalty, 1621–50
			Treaty of Münster, 1648
Charles II, 1665–1700		Munive, 1677–89	

EVENTS IN QUITO	ECONOMY	THE CHURCH AT LARGE	THE CHURCH LOCALLY
		Humanism ↓	
	Encomienda ↓	Counter-Reformation (Council of Trent, 1545–63)	Conversion of Indians ↓
Audiencia of Quito, 1563	Mita, 1570's	(Inquisition)	
Revolt of Quijos, 1579	↓	↓	
Sales Tax Revolt, 1593			
Esmeraldas, 1594–1629	Debt peonage ↓		Synod, 1596
Mainas, 1619	Otavalo reform, 1619		Mariana de Jesús, 1619–45
	Textile & cacao depression, 1620's		
Sack of Guayaquil, 1624			
Mañozca, 1624–27			Alternativa, 1625
Galdós de Valencia, 1630–32	Indian labor reform, 1630		
Revolt, Mainas, 1635			
Visita sentences, 1636–37			Jesuits, Mainas, 1639
Earthquake, Riobamba, 1645			
Epidemic, Mainas, 1660, 1669			
Earthquake, Chimbo, 1674			
Portuguese invasion of Amazonia, 1689	Obraje reform, 1680–84		Decay of Jesuit missions, Mainas
↓			
Earthquakes, 1698			

NOTES

ABBREVIATIONS USED IN THE NOTES

AGI/AQ: The Audiencia de Quito section of the Archivo General de Indias (AGI), Seville.
AGI/AL: The Audiencia de Lima section of the AGI.
AGI/EC: The Escribanía de Cámara section of the AGI.
ANH: The Archivo Nacional de Historia, Quito.
AMQ: The Archivo Municipal de Quito.
ACS: The Archivo de la Corte Suprema de Justicia, Quito.
AGC: The Archivo General del Cauca, Popayán.

CHAPTER 1: ESMERALDAS: THE FAILURE OF A CONQUEST

1 For a discussion of the continuing character of the conquest in the Philippines, see my *The Hispanization of the Philippines: Spanish Aims and Filipino Responses, 1565–1700* (Madison, 1959), pp. 136–44. This chapter, before modification, first appeared under the title "The Road to Esmeraldas, The Failure of a Spanish Conquest in the Seventeenth Century," in *Essays in History and Literature: Presented by the Fellows of the Newberry Library to Stanley Pargellis,* ed. Heinz Bluhm (Chicago, 1965), pp. 91–108.

2 For succinct accounts of the geography, see the admirable book of Lilo Linke, *Ecuador, Country of Contrasts* (London and New York, 1960), pp. 1–5; and Robert C. West, *The Pacific Lowlands of Colombia: A Negroid Area of the American Tropics* (Baton Rouge, 1957).

3 President Antonio de Morga to king: April 20, 1620, AGI/AQ 10. This document was published by José Rumazo González, ed., *Documentos para la historia de la audiencia de Quito* (8 vols., Madrid, 1948–50), IV, 230–40. Rumazo's collection contains many but not all of the archival documents relating to Esmeraldas. Hence, I am also giving the AGI reference.

4 Investigations conducted by audiencia *re* contract with Martín de Fuica: 1616–17, AGI/AQ 10.

5 Most of the Negro population in Esmeraldas today is descended not from these zambos but from recent migrants from coastal Colombia during the last 100 years. West, *Pacific Lowlands*, pp. 101–8. Norman E. Whitten, Jr., *Class, Kinship, and Power in an Ecuadorian Town: The Negroes of San Lorenzo* (Stanford, 1965), pp. 22–25.

6 "Relación del Pedro de Arévalo . . . ," December 2, 1600, AGI/AQ 25, and Rumazo, ed., *Documentos,* IV, 15–37. "Asiento hecho con Alonso de Yllescas . . . ," July 13, 1600, AGI/AQ 9. "Conversión y población de ynfieles, el estado que tienen y otras cosas . . . ," July 9, 1600, AGI/AQ 9. Also see Viceroy Velasco to Viceroy Monterrey: Lima, November 28, 1604, in *Colección de las memorias ó relaciones que escribieron los virreyes del Pirú acerca del estado en que dejaron las cosas generales del reino* (2 vols., Madrid, 1921–30), I, 139.

7 George Kubler and Martin Soria, *Art and Architecture in Spain and Portugal and their American Dominions, 1500–1800* (Baltimore, 1959), p. 319.

8 Hernando Hincapie to audiencia: Puerto Viejo, March 23, 1607, ANH, I, No. 12.

9 "Relación del Arévalo," December 2, 1600, AGI/AQ 25. Rumazo, ed., *Documentos,* IV, 15–37.

10 See note 9. Morga to king: April 20, 1620, AGI/AQ 10, and Rumazo, ed., *Documentos,* IV, 230–40. Morga to viceroy: April 1, 1630, and Morga to king: April 20, 1630, AGI/AQ 11, and Rumazo, ed., *Documentos,* IV, 258–59, 225–27.

11 William B. Stevenson, *Historical and Descriptive Narrative of Twenty Years' Residence in South America* (3 vols., London, 1829), II, 390–92.

12 ACS, *Libro de acuerdos de hacienda, 1601–57:* May 15, 1619. Morga to king: April 20, 1620, AGI/AQ 10, and Rumazo, ed., *Documentos,* IV, 230–40. Morga to king: April 20, 1630, AGI/AQ 11, and Rumazo, ed., *Documentos,* IV, 225–27. Viceroy to king: April 29, 1619, AGI/AL 38. At that time San Ignacio de Montesclaros or Bogotá had 22 property owners (*vecinos*) and the port of Santiago had 30.

13 Antonio Olano, *Popayán en la colonia, bosquejo histórico de la gobernación y de la ciudad de Popayán en los siglos xvii y xviii* (Popayán, 1910), pp. 8–11.

14 Oidor Diego de Zorrilla to king: April 1, 1612, AGI/AQ 9.

15 ACS, *Libro de acuerdos de hacienda, 1601–57:* May 15, 1619, and August 4, 1619.

16 For the texts of the contracts of Martín de Fuica (April 12, 1616), and Francisco Pérez Menacho (November 7, 1622), see AGI/AQ 10. For an analysis of the juridical character of these contracts, see José María Ots Capdequí, *España en América: Las instituciones coloniales,* 2nd ed. (Bogotá, 1952), pp. 55–57. For royal legislation governing these contracts, see the *Recopilación de las leyes de los reynos de las Indias* (4 vols., Madrid, 1681), Bk. IV, Titles i–vii.

17 Morga to viceroy: January 15, 1616, AGI/AQ 10, and Rumazo, ed., *Documentos,* IV, 240–43. Morga to king: April 20, 1620, AGI/AQ 10, and Rumazo, ed., *Documentos,* IV, 230–40.

18 Cabildo of San Antonio de Morga de Bahía de Carácas to Morga: January 2, 1629, AGI/AQ 11, and Morga to king: April 25, 1629, *ibid.;* and also Rumazo, ed., *Documentos,* IV, 222–24. ACS, *Libro de acuerdos de la real audiencia, 1630–41:* September 9, 1630.

19 See Chapter 5 for a broader view of the Hispano-Dutch conflict.

20 Peter Gerhard, *Pirates on the West Coast of New Spain, 1565–1742* (Glendale, 1960), p. 242.

21 Viceroy to king: April 16, 1618, AGI/AL 38, and Rumazo, ed., *Documentos,* IV, 229–30. Cedula to Morga: October 23, 1621, AGI/AQ 10, and Rumazo, ed., *Documentos,* IV, 192–97.

22 See Chapter 5, notes 22–23.

23 Morga to king: April 20, 1620, and April 20, 1630, AGI/AQ 10, 11, and also Rumazo, ed., *Documentos,* IV, 230–40, 225–27.

24 Viceroy to king: April 15, 1630, AGI/AQ 11.

25 Viceroy to cabildo of Quito: October 6, 1617, AMQ, V, fol. 60.

26 Morga to viceroy: January 15, 1616, and viceroy to Morga: February 26, 1616, AGI/AQ 10, and also Rumazo, ed., *Documentos,* IV, 240–44.

27 Viceroy to king: April 16, 1618, AGI/AL 38, and Rumazo, ed., *Documentos,* IV, 229–30. King to Morga: March 17, 1619, AGI/AQ 10, and Rumazo, ed., *Documentos,* IV, 228.

28 Viceroy to king: April 29, 1619, AGI/AL 38, and Rumazo, ed., *Documentos,* IV, 229–30.

29 Zorrilla to king: April 30, 1619, AGI/AQ 10. Morga to king: April 20, 1620, *ibid.*

30 Federico Gonzáles Suárez, *Historia general de la república del Ecuador* (7 vols., Quito, 1890–1903), IV, 9 ff.

31 King to Morga: October 23, 1621, AGI/AQ 10, and Rumazo, ed., *Documentos,* IV, 192–97. King to Morga: December 7, 1626, AGI/AQ 10, and Rumazo, ed., *Documentos,* I, 83–84.

32 Fiscal Melchor Suárez de Poago to king: October 20, 1622, AGI/AQ 10.

33 Morga to king: April 20, 1630, AGI/AQ 11, and Rumazo, ed., *Documentos,* IV, 225–27. Morga to king: April 25, 1629, AGI/AQ 11, and Rumazo, ed., *Documentos,* IV, 222–24.

34 Captain Francisco de Frías to viceroy: November 1, 1629, AGI/AQ 11,

and Rumazo, ed., *Documentos,* IV, 260–61. Morga to king: April 25, 1629, AGI/AQ 11, and Rumazo, ed., *Documentos,* IV, 222–24. Morga to viceroy: April 1, 1630, AGI/AQ 11, and Rumazo, ed., *Documentos,* IV, 258–59. Morga to king: April 20, 1630, AGI/AQ 11, and Rumazo, ed., *Documentos,* IV, 225–27.

35 Auto of the audiencia of Lima: November 29, 1629, AGI/AQ 11, and Rumazo, ed., *Documentos,* IV, 261–62.

36 For Villalobos' appointment of January 26, 1628, see AMQ, XIX, foll. 208–12.

37 Morga to king: April 15, 1631, AGI/AQ 11.

38 Morga to king: April 20, 1620, *ibid.* 10, and Rumazo, ed., *Documentos,* IV, 230–40. Morga to king: April 25, 1621, AGI/AQ 10, and Rumazo, ed., *Documentos,* IV, 186–88. Morga to king: April 20, 1630, AGI/AQ 11, and Rumazo, ed., *Documentos,* IV, 225–27. González Suárez puts too much emphasis on the role of the merchants of Guayaquil and not enough on the other factors: González Suárez, *Historia,* IV, 104–10.

39 In his first general report to the king after arriving in Quito, Dr. Morga expressed concern about creating new export markets for the agricultural products of the land. Morga to king: April 20, 1616, AGI/AQ 10.

40 Morga to king: April 20, 1620, *ibid.;* Rumazo, ed., *Documentos,* IV, 230–40. Morga to king: April 20, 1630, AGI/AQ 11; Rumazo, ed., *Documentos,* IV, 225–27. Morga to king: April 15, 1631, AGI/AQ 11.

41 Oidor Zorrilla, the only critic of the Esmeraldas project in the Quito administration, had a more realistic grasp of the meaning of the sparse population than did Dr. Morga. Zorrilla to king: April 1, 1612, *ibid.* 9. He ascribed past failures to hostile geographical conditions created by mountain barriers and the tropical climate. He made light of Indian-zambo resistance: Not the hostility of the natives but their paucity made it difficult to provision the tambos. In 1619 he no longer minimized Indian resistance, for the Malabas had just revolted, but he blamed Viceroy Esquilache for weakening Governor Durango del Gadillo by replacing him as corregidor. Zorrilla to king: April 30, 1619, *ibid.* 10. Lic. Zorrilla's increasingly acid personal relationship with Dr. Morga was not a primary cause of his opposition to the Esmeraldas venture, for his skepticism pre-dated Dr. Morga's arrival in Quito. For the Morga-Zorrilla feud, see Chapter 10, notes 19–24.

42 *Recopilación,* Bk. VI, Title xii, laws 29 and 38.

43 Morga to viceroy: May 10, 1620, and viceroy to Morga: July 20, 1620, AGI/AQ 10; and also Rumazo, ed., *Documentos,* IV, 189–90. Morga to king: April 25, 1621, AGI/AQ 10, and Rumazo, ed., *Documentos,* IV, 186–88.

44 González Suárez, *Historia,* IV, 103–4. ACS, *Libro de acuerdos de la real audiencia, 1630–41:* August 2, 1632.

45 Cristóbal de Troya, the founder of San Miguel de Ibarra, first undertook the exploration of the Santiago route. See his letter of May 3, 1607, in Rumazo, ed., *Documentos,* IV, 40–53. Also see AMQ, XIV, foll. 236–37;

and *Libro de cabildos de la ciudad de Quito, 1610–16,* ed. Jorge Garcés (Archivo Municipal, Vol. XXVI, Quito, 1955), pp. 420–22. The cabildo of Quito initially sponsored the Bahía de Caráquez enterprise before the audiencia took over: Garcés, ed., *Libro de cabildos,* pp. 417, 470.

46 The audiencia replaced the cabildo of San Miguel de Ibarra in 1611 when Pablo Durango del Gadillo received his contract. President Fernández de Recalde to king: March 12, 1612, AGI/AQ 9.

47 From Morga's point of view, it was a misfortune that the Marquis of Montesclaros left office as viceroy of Peru in 1614 shortly before Morga's arrival in Quito. Montesclaros had formed a favorable opinion of Morga's abilities when the latter served in the audiencia of Mexico and the former was viceroy of Mexico. Montesclaros had enthusiastically recommended Dr. Morga for promotion: W. E. Retana, "Estudio preliminar," in Antonio de Morga, *Sucesos de las islas filipinas* (Madrid, 1909), p. 118. Furthermore, both officials shared the conviction that the Spanish Pacific could best be defended against the Dutch by the adoption of a mobile and offensive strategy. Hence Dr. Morga's task might have been facilitated with Montesclaros in Lima, but even a sympathetic viceroy would not have guaranteed the success of the conquest of Esmeraldas.

48 *Recopilación,* December 15, 1607, Bk. III, Title v, laws 6 and 7. The most carefully spelled out exposition of his defense strategy is Morga's letter to Viceroy Esquilache: November 20, 1615, in the appendix to the Retana edition of Morga's *Sucesos,* pp. 347–59. See Chapter 5 for a more extensive discussion of Morga's strategic plans. For some eighteenth-century accounts of the Morga period, see the following. Juan de Velasco, S.J., *Historia del reino de Quito en la América meridional* (3 vols., Quito, 1946), III, 145–52. Juan de Velasco, S.J., *Historia moderna del reyno de Quito y Crónica de la provincia de la compañía de Jesús del mismo reyno,* ed. Raul Reyes y Reyes (Biblioteca Amazonas, Vols. IX–X, Quito, n.d.), IX, 181–84. Antonio de Alcedo, *Diccionario geográfico-histórico de las Indias occidentales ó América* (5 vols., Madrid, 1786), I, 76–77, 370. Jorge Juan and Antonio de Ulloa, *Noticias secretas de América . . . ,* ed. Rufino Blanco-Fombona (Biblioteca Ayacucho, Vols. XXXI–XXXII, Madrid, 1918), XXXI, 181–88.

49 For an example, see Morga to king: April 20, 1616, AGI/AQ 10.

50 Morga to king: April 15, 1618, *ibid.*

51 AMQ, XIX, foll. 213–14, 231–34.

52 President Pedro Vázquez de Velasco to king: July 10, 1657, AGI/AQ 13, and Rumazo, ed., *Documentos,* IV, 263–66. That magistrate used the same arguments to justify the route as Dr. Morga had. Also see Rumazo, ed., *Documentos,* I, 48–82, 92.

53 AGI/AQ 34, and Rumazo, ed., *Documentos,* IV, 267–437.

54 Rumazo, ed., *Documentos,* I, 24 ff.

55 Juan and Ulloa, *Noticias secretas,* XXXI, 181–88.

56 González Suárez, *Historia,* V, 466–78. Rumazo, ed., *Documentos,* Vols. I, III, and VII, contain a rich collection of primary materials on the Maldo-

nado period. *Plan del camino de Quito al río Esmeraldas según las observaciones astronómicas de Jorge Juan y Antonio Ulloa, 1736–42*, ed. Jorge Garcés (Archivo Municipal, Vol. XIX, Quito, 1942).

57 Garcés, ed., *Plan del camino*, pp. 85 ff. Stevenson, *A Historical and Descriptive Narrative*, II, 358–407. Rumazo, ed., *Documentos*, VII, 1–136.

58 Garcés, ed., *Plan del camino*, pp. 236–37.

59 For the Chichimeca story, see Philip Wayne Powell, *Soldiers, Indians, and Silver, The Northward Advance of New Spain, 1550–1600* (Berkeley and Los Angeles: University of California Press, 1952).

60 For a stimulating analysis of urbanism in Spanish America, see Richard Morse, "Some Characteristics of Latin American Urban History," *American Historical Review*, LXVII, No. 42 (January, 1962), 317–38.

CHAPTER 2:   THE THRUST TO THE AMAZON: SUCCESS AND FAILURE

1 For a Mexican example, see Diego Muñoz Camargo, *Historia de Tlaxcala* (Mexico, 1892), p. 264. For the revolt of 1579, see José Rumazo González, *La región amazónica del Ecuador en el siglo xvi* (Seville, 1946), pp. 238–42. Toribio de Ortiguera, "Jornada del río Marañón" in the *Nueva Biblioteca de Autores Españoles: Historiadores de Indias*, II (Madrid: Bailly, Bailliére é Hijos, 1909), 406–22.

2 Rumazo, *La región amazónica*, pp. 231–47. Agustín Bustos to audiencia: February 4, 1609, ANH, I, No. 21. Francisco de la Serna to audiencia: February 6, 1610, *ibid.*, No. 26.

3 Richard Konetzke, *Colección de documentos para la historia de la formación social de Hispanoamérica, 1493–1810* (4 vols., Madrid, 1958–62), II, 112. AGI/AQ 209.

4 Clarence Haring, *The Spanish Empire in America* (New York, 1947), pp. 122–23. Jerónimo de Castillo de Bovadilla, *Política para corregidores y señores de vassallos en tiempo de paz y guerra . . .* (Barcelona, 1916), Bk. II, Ch. x, sec. 77, p. 440. *Recopilación de las leyes de los reynos de las Indias* (4 vols., Madrid, 1681), Bk. II, Title i, laws 24 and 26.

5 Governor Alonso de Miranda to king: March 15, 1617, and audiencia to king: April 15, 1621, AGI/AQ 10.

6 Soldiers to audiencia: October 2, 1621, ANH, I, No. 55.

7 Governor Álvaro de Cárdenas to king: November 12, 1625, AGI/AQ 10. Antonio de Morga, ed., "Recopilación de cédulas despachadas en diferentes tiempos por S. M. . . . para la real audiencia . . . del Quito del Pirú, 1589–1632" (ms. [1632], Biblioteca Nacional, Mexico City), No. 130, No. 134.

8 President Antonio de Morga to king: April 25, 1629, AGI/AQ 11.

9 For the role of the first two governors, see the following. "Relación de la entrada que hizo el gobernador d. Diego Vaca de Vega al descubrimiento y pacificación de las provincias de los indios Maynas . . . ," *Relaciones geográficas de Indias*, ed. Marcos Jiménez de la Espada (4 vols., Madrid, 1881–97), IV, cxxxix–clxii. Julio Tobar Donoso and Alfredo Luna Tobar,

Derecho territorial ecuatoriano (Quito, 1961), pp. 1–15. José Jouanen, S.J., *Historia de la compañía de Jesús en la antigua provincia de Quito, 1570–1696* (2 vols., Quito, 1941), I, 334–40. Pío Jaramillo Alvarado, *Historia de Loja y su provincia* (Quito, 1955), pp. 153–60. Morga to king: April 25, 1629, AGI/AQ 11.

10 See the introduction of Lino G. Canedo to Fray Isidro Félix de Espinosa, O.F.M., *Crónica de los colegios de propaganda fide de la Nueva España,* 2nd ed. (Washington, D.C.: Academy of American Franciscan History, 1964).

11 The principal Spanish Jesuit sources are the following. Jouanen, *Historia.* Bernardo Recio, S.J., *Compendiosa relación de la cristianidad de Quito* (Madrid: Consejo Superior de Investigaciones Científicas, 1947). Juan de Velasco, S.J., *Historia del reino de Quito en la América meridional* (3 vols., Quito, 1946). Francisco de Figueroa, *Relación de las misiones de la compañía de Jesús en el país de Maynas* (Madrid: V. Suárez, 1904). José Chantre y Herrera, *Historia de las misiones de la compañía de Jesús en el Marañón español* (Madrid: A. Avrial, 1901). Pablo Moroni, S.J., "Noticias auténticas del famoso río Marañón y misión apostólica de la compañía de Jesús de la provincia de Quito," in Marcos Jiménez de la Espada, ed., *Bolétin de la Sociedad Geográfica de Madrid,* XXVI–XXX (Madrid, 1889–92). *Journal of the Travels and Labours of Father Samuel Fritz in the river of the Amazons between 1683 and 1723,* ed. George Edmundson (The Hakluyt Society, 2nd series, No. 51, London, 1922). For the Franciscan missions in the Montaña region in southeastern Peru, which lay south of the Jesuit missions, see Diego de Córdoba y Salinas, O.F.M., *Crónica franciscana de las provincias del Perú,* ed. Lino G. Canedo, O.F.M. (Washington, D.C., 1957; 1st ed., Lima, 1651). ANH, I, No. 85.

12 Marcos Jiménez de la Espada, *Viaje del capitán Pedro Teixeira* (Madrid, 1889). Jaime Corteso, "O significado da espedicão de Pedro Teixeira a luz de novos documentos," *Anais de IV congreso historico nacional* (Rio de Janeiro, 1950). For the viceroy's displeasure about the expedition, see Viceroy Mancera to Viceroy Salvatierra: October 8, 1648, in *Colección de las memorias ó relaciones que escribieron los virreyes del Pirú acerca del estado en que dejaron las cosas generales del reino* (2 vols., Madrid, 1921–30), II, 205–6. For the Spanish-Jesuit expedition, see Cristóbal de Acuña, S.J. *Nuevo descvbrimiento del gran río de las Amazonas . . .* (Madrid, 1641).

13 See the Jesuit sources cited in note 11. Larger villages were characteristic among the Omagua and Cocoma tribes of the upper Amazon River basin. Ecological factors, such as their river habitat, facilitated farming on banks and flood plains, thus lessening the labor of slash and burn horticulture. For the ethnography of the tribes of the Montaña region and the upper Amazon basin, see the monographs of Julian H. Steward, Alfred Métraux, and Curt Nimuendaju in the *Handbook of South American Indians,* ed. Julian Steward (7 vols., Washington, D.C., 1946–59), III, 507–762.

14 Howard Cline, "Civil Congregations of the Indians of New Spain, 1598–1606," *Hispanic-American Historical Review*, XXIX (August, 1949), 349–69.

15 John L. Phelan, *The Hispanization of the Philippines: Spanish Aims and Filipino Responses, 1565–1700* (Madison, 1959), pp. 44–49.

16 Velasco, *Historia del reino*, III, 268.

17 *Ibid.*, pp. 323–28. Steward, ed., *Handbook of South American Indians*, III, 512.

18 Velasco, *Historia del reino*, III, 319–22.

19 My account of the Portuguese penetration into the Amazon closely follows that of Mathias Kiemen, O.F.M., *The Indian Policy of Portugal in the Amazon Region, 1614–1693* (Washington, D.C.: Catholic University of America Press, 1954), pp. 181–86.

20 Tobar Donoso and Luna Tobar, *Derecho territorial*, pp. 15 ff.

21 Velasco, *Historia del reino*, III, 310.

22 *Ibid.*, p. 313.

23 *Ibid.*, p. 312.

24 For a more extensive discussion, see Chapter 6.

25 The historical and juridical arguments are contained in the following sources. *Ecuador: Ministerio de relaciones exteriores, litigio de limites entre el Ecuador y el Perú* (2 vols., Madrid: El Liberal, 1910). *Perú: Ministerio de relaciones exteriores: Memorias y documentos diplomáticos sobre la negoción del tratado del limites entre el Perú y el Ecuador* (Lima, 1892). Tobar Donoso and Luna Tobar, *Derecho territorial*, Julio Tobar Donoso was foreign minister of Ecuador at the time the Protocol of Rio de Janeiro was signed. For a recent and the most objective account of the controversy, see David H. Zook, Jr., *Zarumilla-Marañón: The Ecuador-Peru Dispute* (New York, 1964). Zook regards Peru's policy as more realistic. She supported her claims by settlement and military force while Ecuador policy relied on colonial precedents, abstract principles of international law, and pacific diplomacy.

CHAPTER 3: LA REPÚBLICA DE LOS INDIOS

1 Sherburne F. Cook and Lesley Byrd Simpson, *The Population of Central Mexico in the Sixteenth Century* (Ibero-Americana, No. 31, Berkeley and Los Angeles, 1948). Woodrow W. Borah and Sherburne F. Cook, *The Population of Central Mexico in 1548* (Ibero-Americana, No. 43, Berkeley and Los Angeles, 1960). Woodrow W. Borah and Sherburne F. Cook, *The Indian Population of Central Mexico, 1531–1610* (Ibero-Americana, No. 44, Berkeley and Los Angeles, 1960). Woodrow W. Borah and Sherburne F. Cook, *The Aboriginal Population of Central Mexico on the Eve of the Spanish Conquest* (Ibero-Americana, No. 45, Berkeley and Los Angeles, 1963). For a concise summary, also see Woodrow W. Borah, "¿América como modelo? El impacto demográfico de la expansión europea sobre el mundo no europeo," *Cuadernos americanos* (November–December, 1962),

pp. 172–85. There is a considerable difference between the original 1948 Cook-Simpson estimate and the 1963 Borah-Cook estimate.

The 1948 estimate		The 1963 estimate	
1519	11,000,000	1519	24,200,000
1540	6,427,466	1532	16,800,000
1565	4,409,180	1548	6,300,000
1597	2,500,000	1568	2,650,000
1607	2,014,000	1580	1,900,000
1650 (*ca.*)	1,500,000	1595	1,375,000
1700	2,000,000	1605	1,075,000
1793	3,700,000		

2 Cieza de León estimates that the preconquest population of the Sierra Quito was approximately 500,000 people: Pedro de Cieza de León, *La crónica del Perú*, in *Crónicas de la conquista del Perú*, ed. Julio J. Le Riverend Brusone (Mexico: Editorial Nueva España, n.d.), Chs. xxxvi–lvi. According to López de Velasco (*ca.* 1576), the total Indian population under Spanish control was 400,000 people: Juan López de Velasco, *Geografía y descripción universal de las Indias* (Madrid, 1894), pp. 404–6. The Cook-Borah-Simpson studies reveal that the early chroniclers in Mexico, both religious and lay, were far more reliable about the demographic situation than many modern historians have held.

3 George Kubler, "The Quechua in the Colonial World," *Handbook of South American Indians*, ed. Julian Steward (7 vols., Washington, D.C., 1946–59), II, 334–39.

4 Kubler, "The Quechua," pp. 334–39. John Rowe estimates that the total population of the three audiencias at the time of the conquest was closer to six million persons: John Rowe, "Inca Culture at the Time of the Conquest," in Steward, ed., *Handbook of South American Indians*, II, 184–85. For a convenient summary and an evaluation of the printed demographic sources, see Ángel Rosenblat, *La población indígena de América desde 1492 hasta la actualidad* (Buenos Aires, 1945). The latter studies are thoughtful and carefully done, but they rely almost exclusively on published primary sources. What is urgently required is a more extensive study based on tribute rolls and other manuscript data, similar in scope and intensity to the series of monographs Cook, Borah, and Simpson have written concerning Mexico. Until such an investigation is completed, anything said about the demographic history of Spanish South America must be considered tentative. In order to arrive at total population figures using tribute statistics, it is necessary to multiply the number paying tribute by four (average size of family), and to assume that at least one-sixth of the tribute population was exempt from payment, i.e., curacas, their eldest sons, village officeholders, Indians employed in the service of the Church, etc.

5 The Jesuit sources provide the only reliable data for the population of the

Oriente, and the figure that emerges is very much an estimate. See Chapter 2, note 11 for the Jesuit sources.

6 Marcos Jiménez de la Espada, ed., *Relaciones geográficas de Indias* (4 vols., Madrid, 1881–97), III, 24. Also see "Anonymous Account of the City of Quito" (1582), in Eliecer Enríquez, *Quito a través de los siglos* (2 vols., Quito: Imprenta de la Universidad Central, 1938), I, 65–66.

7 *Libro de cabildos de la ciudad de Quito, 1610–1616,* ed. Jorge Garcés (Archivo Municipal, Vol. XXVI, Quito, 1955), pp. 107, 394–95. Audiencia to king: April 24, 1618, AGI/AQ 10.

8 President Antonio de Morga to king: April 20, 1616, and April 30, 1629, AGI/AQ 10, 11. Fiscal Suárez de Poago to king: May 2, 1634, *ibid.,* 12.

9 "Descripción de la gobernación de Guayaquil" (*ca.* 1606), *Colección de documentos inéditos relativos al descubrimiento, conquista y organización de las antiguas posesiones españolas de América y Oceanía* (42 vols., Madrid, 1864–84), X, 247–309.

10 Oscar Efrén Reyes, *Breve historia general del Ecuador* (2 vols., Quito: Imprenta de la Universidad Central, 1938), I, 373–74. His figures come from Alexander von Humboldt.

11 Juan de Velasco, S.J., *Historia del reino de Quito en la América meridional* (3 vols., Quito, 1946), III, 323–27.

12 Antonio Olano, *Popayán en la colonia, bosquejo histórico de la gobernación y de la ciudad de Popayán en los siglos xvii y xviii* (Popayán, 1910), p. 8.

13 Cieza de León, *Crónica,* Ch. xxxvi. Audiencia to king: January 15, 1564, AGI/AQ 8. López de Velasco, *Geografía,* pp. 406–13. Rosenblat, *Población,* pp. 77–78. Gregorio Hernández de Alba, "The Highland Tribes of Southern Colombia," in Steward, ed., *Handbook of South American Indians,* II, 923. Jaime Arroyo, *Historia de la gobernación de Popayán* (Popayán: Imprenta del Departamento, 1907), pp. 286 ff.

14 Federico González Suárez, *Historia general de la república del Ecuador* (7 vols., Quito, 1890–1903), IV, 415–21.

15 López de Velasco, *Geografía,* pp. 406–40. Jiménez de la Espada, ed., *Relaciones geográficas,* III, 24. Enríquez, *Quito,* I, 65–66.

16 Augusto Albuja Mateus, "El obispado de Quito en el siglo xvi," *Missionalia hispanica,* XVIII (May–August, 1961), 161–209.

17 John Murra, "The Historic Tribes of Ecuador," in Steward, ed., *Handbook of South American Indians,* II, 785–821.

18 *Ibid.,* pp. 792–93. For a recent survey of this controversy, see Adam Szászdi, "The Historiography of the Republic of Ecuador," *Hispanic-American Historical Review,* XLIV, No. 4 (November, 1964), 508–10.

19 John L. Phelan, "Neo-Aztecism in the Eighteenth Century and the Genesis of Mexican Nationalism," in *Culture in History, Essays in Honor of Paul Radin,* ed. Stanley Diamond (New York: Columbia University Press, 1960), pp. 760–70.

20 Robert Ricard, *La "conquête spirituelle" du Mexique* (Paris: Institut d'Ethnologie, 1933), pp. 66–69.

21 Murra, "Historic Tribes," pp. 808–12.

22 *Ibid.*, p. 809.

23 John L. Phelan, *The Millennial Kingdom of the Franciscans in the New World: A Study of the Writings of Gerónimo de Mendieta, 1525–1604* (University of California Publications in History, No. 52, Berkeley and Los Angeles, 1956). Charles Gibson, *The Aztecs under Spanish Rule: A History of the Indians of the Valley of Mexico, 1519–1810* (Stanford, 1964), pp. 110–12.

24 George Kubler and Martin Soria, *Art and Architecture in Spain and Portugal and their American Dominions, 1500–1800* (Baltimore, 1959), p. 87. José María Vargas, O.P., *Historia de la iglesia en el Ecuador durante el patronato español* (Quito, 1962), pp. 39–44.

25 Kubler, "The Quechua," pp. 400–401.

26 Luis Lopes de Solís, "Constituciones sinodales del Quito," MS, Univ. of Wisconsin Library, Ch. 55. (This is a late 18th-century copy of the 1596 MS.)

27 George M. Foster, "Cofradía and Compadrazgo in Spain and in Spanish America," *Southwestern Journal of Anthropology*, IX (Spring, 1953), 10 ff. Kubler, "The Quechua," pp. 405–6.

28 For the societal meaning of the patronal fiesta, see my *The Hispanization of the Philippines: Spanish Aims and Filipino Responses, 1565–1700* (Madison, 1959), p. 73.

29 Roberto Levillier, ed., *Gobernantes del Perú* (14 vols., Madrid: Sucesores de Rivadeneyra, 1921–26), VIII, 1 ff.

30 "Autos y capítulos de la audiencia de Quito en favor de los naturales," August 20, 1584, AGI/AQ 8. Alberto Landazuri Soto, *El régimen laboral indígena en la real audiencia de Quito* (Madrid, 1959), pp. 37–52.

31 See note 30.

32 Phelan, *Hispanization*, pp. 23, 74, 76–77. For some discerning comments on ritual drinking in Mexico, see Gibson, *The Aztecs*, p. 133.

33 Phelan, *Hispanization*, pp. 79–80.

34 Phelan, *Millennial Kingdom*, pp. 61–64. For the failure of a native clergy to emerge in other regions of the empire, i.e., Mexico and the Philippines, see Ricard, *La "conquête spirituelle,"* pp. 260 ff., and Phelan, *Hispanization*, pp. 33, 42, 84–89, 160.

35 Phelan, *Hispanization*, p. 86. Phelan, "Neo-Aztecism," pp. 765–66. Juan and Ulloa, who visited Quito in the early 1740's, shared the same environmentalist view. Jorge Juan and Antonio de Ulloa, *Noticias secretas de América . . .* , ed. Rufino Blanco-Fombona (Biblioteca Ayacucho, Vols. XXXI–XXXII, Madrid, 1918), XXXI, 289 ff.

36 Kubler, "The Quechua," p. 367. The most succinct contemporary statement of the juridical status of the Indians in colonial society is that of Juan de Solórzano y Pereira, *Política indiana* (5 vols., Madrid, 1647) Bk. II, Ch. xxviii.

37 The classic study of the encomienda is by Lesley Byrd Simpson, *The*

Encomienda in New Spain (Berkeley and Los Angeles: University of California Press, 1950).

38 Aquiles R. Pérez, *Las mitas en la real audiencia de Quito* (Quito, 1947), pp. 232–33. Enríquez, *Quito,* I, 65–66. Francisco de la Serna: February 6, 1610, ANH, I, No. 26. Oidor Matías de Peralta to audiencia: July 18, 1614, ANH, I, No. 37. Lic. Antonio de Calatayud to Pedro Lema de Carvajal: 1622, ANH, I, No. 57. Governor Álvaro de Cárdenas to king: November 12, 1625, ANH, I, No. 57. Cárdenas to king: November 12, 1625, AGI/AQ 10. Pedro Pérez Landero Otáñez y Castro, *Práctica de visitas y residencias de los reynos del Perú* . . . (Naples, 1646), pp. 208 ff.

39 Enríquez, *Quito,* I, 65–66. Suárez de Poago to king: May 2, 1634, AGI/AQ 12.

40 Silvio Zavala, *La encomienda indiana* (Madrid: Imprenta Helenica, 1935). François Chevalier, *La formation des grands domaines au Mexique, Terre et société aux xvie–xviie siecles* (Paris: Institut d'Ethnologie, 1952). Phelan, *Hispanization,* pp. 116–67.

41 Cedula: May 3, 1605, AGI/AQ 209; Richard Konetzke, *Colección de documentos para la historia de la formación social de Hispanoamérica, 1493–1810* (4 vols., Madrid, 1958–62), II, 112.

42 Kubler, "The Quechua," pp. 364–67.

43 Solórzano, *Política indiana,* Bk. III, Ch. vi, Nos. 38 ff.

44 *Ibid.* AMQ, XIII, foll. 168–70, 170–76. Cedula to viceroy: April 26, 1618, AGI/AL 571. Konetzke, *Colección,* II, 198.

45 Duke of Lerma to president of Council of the Indies: February 17, 1615, AGI/AQ 1. Indians of Latacunga to Suárez de Poago: 1636, *ibid.* 12. President Lope Antonio de Munive to king: July 30, 1681, *ibid.* 69, and Landazuri Soto, *Regimén,* pp. 110 ff.

46 Diego Sancho Acho to king: August 2, 1607, and María Cauchu to king: October 30, 1626, AGI/AQ 1.

47 For the postconquest mita, see the following primary sources. Solórzano, *Política indiana,* Bk. II, Ch. vii, Nos. 3 ff. *Recopilación de las leyes de los reynos de las Indias* (4 vols., Madrid, 1681), Bk. VI, Title xii. Audiencia to viceroy: 1612, ANH, I, No. 23. Cedula to audiencia: October 28, 1612, AGI/AL 571. Juan López de Cañizares to audiencia: ANH, II, No. 116. Cristóbal López to audiencia: April 2, 1639, ANH, III, No. 126. The most informative secondary accounts are the following. Kubler, "The Quechua," pp. 372 ff.; Pérez, *Las mitas.* The latter is especially useful for the ample citations of primary sources, but his unsophisticated Marxist bias, which leads him at one point to view the mita as a sixteenth-century version of a Nazi concentration camp, leaves something to be desired.

48 Cedula to audiencia: October 18, 1865, AGI/AQ 210.

49 President Manuel Barros to king: May 12, 1589, *ibid.* 8.

50 Cedula to audiencia: March 15, 1609, *ibid.* 209. Konetzke, *Colección,* II, 146. Oidor Diego de Zorrilla to king: April 30, 1619, AGI/AQ 10. Suárez de Poago to king: May 2, 1634, AGI/AQ 12. For the Inca mita, see Bernabé

Cobo, *Obras* (2 vols. Madrid: Atlas, 1956), II, 129–32. Pedro de Cieza de León, *The Incas*, ed. Victor von Hagen, trans. Harriet de Onis (Norman: University of Oklahoma Press, 1960), p. 95. Luis Valcárcel, *Ethnohistoria del Perú antiguo* (Lima: Universidad de San Marcos, 1959), p. 95.

51 Woodrow W. Borah, *New Spain's Century of Depression* (Ibero-Americana, No. 35, Berkeley and Los Angeles, 1951), p. 36.

52 Viceroy Velasco to Viceroy Monterrey: Lima, November 28, 1604, *Colección de las memorias ó relaciones que escribieron los virreyes del Pirú acerca del estado en que dejaron las cosas generales del reino* (2 vols., Madrid, 1921–30), I, 120.

53 The texts of the ordinances of November 24, 1601, and May 26, 1609, are in the *Recopilación*, Bk. VI, Titles xii and xiii.

54 Gibson, *The Aztecs*, pp. 226–36. The mita in the silver mines at Potosí was abolished by royal cedula in 1720, but it was not enforced: Kubler, "The Quechua," p. 373.

55 Pérez, *Las mitas*, p. 200. The Mexican obrajes, in contrast to those of Quito, did not rely on repartimiento labor. Gibson, *The Aztecs*, pp. 243–46.

56 Pérez, *Las mitas*, pp. 67, 87–90. AMQ, XIII, foll. 163–67, 168–70, 170–76; XI, fol. 41. Viceroy Esquilache to Viceroy Guadalcázar, *Memorias de los virreyes que han gobernado el Perú durante el tiempo del coloniaje español* (6 vols., Lima, 1859), I, 23–24, 127–28.

57 Juan and Ulloa, *Noticias secretas*, XXXI, 289 ff.

CHAPTER 4:   THE SWEATSHOP OF SOUTH AMERICA

1 Treasury to king: April 20, 1618, AGI/AQ 19. President Antonio de Morga to king: April 20, 1622, *ibid.* 10. Audiencia to king: April 24, 1618, *ibid.* Alonso Rodríquez to Lic. Juan de Valdez y Llanos, ANH, II, No. 105. Alonso Anda Aguirre, *Zaruma en la colonia* (Quito: Casa de la Cultura Ecuatoriana, 1960), pp. 38, 40–41. Lilo Linke, *Ecuador, Country of Contrasts* (London, 1960), pp. 141 ff. Aquiles R. Pérez, *Las mitas en la real audiencia de Quito* (Quito, 1947), pp. 251–52.

2 Pérez, *Las mitas*, pp. 251–52.

3 Linke, *Ecuador*, pp. 141 ff.

4 Anda Aguirre, *Zaruma*, pp. 40–41, 59–61, 82–83. Pío Jaramillo Alvarado, *Historia de Loja y su provincia* (Quito, 1955), pp. 112, 115–17.

5 Philip Wayne Powell, *Soldiers, Indians and Silver, The Northward Advance of New Spain, 1550–1600* (Berkeley and Los Angeles: University of California Press, 1952).

6 Antonio Vásquez de Espinosa, *Compendio y descripción de las Indias occidentales* (Washington, D.C., 1948), pp. 336–37.

7 For the ecological changes created by the conquest in Mexico and the Philippines, see Lesley Byrd Simpson, *The Exploitation of Land in Central Mexico in the Sixteenth Century* (Ibero-Americana, No. 36, Berkeley and

Los Angeles, 1952); John L. Phelan, *The Hispanization of the Philippines: Spanish Aims and Filipino Responses, 1565–1700* (Madison, 1959), pp. 105 ff.

8 Vásquez de Espinosa, *Compendio,* p. 334.

9 President Lope Antonio de Munive to king: July 30, 1681, AGI/AQ 69, and Alberto Landazuri Soto, *El régimen laboral indígena en la real audiencia de Quito* (Madrid, 1959), pp. 110 ff. Munive's letter is the single most informative account of the obrajes. Landazuri Soto's collection of primary sources from the AGI is invaluable.

10 Munive to king: July 30, 1681, AGI/AQ 69, and Landazuri Soto, *Régimen,* p. 146.

11 Morga to king: April 20, 1616, AGI/AQ 10. Fiscal Melchor Suaréz de Poago to king: April 15, 1630, *ibid.* 11. Antonio de Alcedo, *Diccionario geográfico-histórico de las Indias occidentales ó América* (5 vols., Madrid, 1786), IV, 369 ff. Ricardo Cappa, *Estudios críticos sobre la dominación española en América* (20 vols., Barcelona, 1895), VII, 70 ff. Vásquez de Espinosa, *Compendio,* pp. 349 ff.

12 Woodrow W. Borah, *Early Colonial Trade and Navigation Between Mexico and Peru* (Ibero-Americana, No. 38, Berkeley and Los Angeles, 1954), pp. 126–27. Phelan, *Hispanization,* pp. 13–14.

13 See Chapter 13, note 4.

14 Antonine Tibesar, O.F.M., *Franciscan Beginnings in Colonial Peru* (Washington, D.C.: Academy of American Franciscan History, 1953), pp. 86–87. George Kubler, "The Quechua in the Colonial World," *Handbook of South American Indians,* ed. Julian Steward (7 vols., Washington, D.C., 1946–59), II, 363. Vásquez de Espinosa, *Compendio,* pp. 455 ff. Alonso de la Peña Montenegro, *Itinerario para párrocos de Indias* (Antwerp, 1698), p. 382. Guillermo Lohmann Villena, *El corregidor de indios en el Perú bajo los Austrias* (Madrid, 1957), pp. 227, 244, 321, 438, 439, 568. Fernando Silva Santisteban, *Los obrajes en el virreinato del Peru* (Lima, 1964).

15 *Libro de cabildos de la ciudad de Quito, 1638–46,* ed. Jorge Garcés (Archivo Municipal, Vol. XXX, Quito, 1960), pp. 398–99.

16 Munive to king: July 30, 1681, AGI/AQ 69, and Landazuri Soto, *Régimen,* pp. 110 ff.

17 This is an approximate figure based on the assumption that the nonmitayo obrajes employed the same number of workers as the mitayo workshops.

18 Munive to king: July 30, 1689, AGI/AQ 69, and Landazuri Soto, *Régimen,* pp. 110 ff.

19 See note 18. Federico González Suárez, *Historia general de la república del Ecuador* (7 vols., Quito, 1890–1903), IV, 472 ff. Cappa, *Estudios críticos,* VII, 63–64.

20 This figure is an estimate based on the assumption that the average work force in the Puebla factories was about the same as that in the valley of Mexico (45 workers). In 1603 there were 33 factories in Puebla, but the number declined to 22 in 1622. Jan Bazant, "The Evolution of the Textile

Industry of Puebla, 1544–1845," *Comparative Studies in Society and History*, VII, No. 1 (October, 1964), 63–64. Querétaro was another textile center, but I have no figures available.

21 Charles Gibson, *The Aztecs under Spanish Rule: A History of the Indians of the Valley of Mexico, 1519–1810* (Stanford, 1964), pp. 243–46. William H. Dusenberry, "Woolen Manufacture in Sixteenth-Century New Spain," *The Americas*, IV (1947–48), 223–34. The carefully documented findings of Gibson supersede the older account of Luis Chávez Orozco, *Historia económica y social de México* (Mexico: Ediciones Botas, 1938), pp. 30–50.

22 Munive to king: July 30, 1689, AGI/AQ 69, and Landazuri Soto, *Régimen*, pp. 110 ff. In 1704 the Duke of Uceda, who was then about to be promoted from ambassador in Rome to president of the Council of the Indies, petitioned the Council of the Indies to abolish all unlicensed obrajes on the grounds that the production of the latter was unjustly reducing the income of the legal obrajes. Duke of Uceda to council: April 3, 1704, AGI/AQ 69, and Landazuri Soto, *Régimen*, pp. 174–80.

23 Gibson, *The Aztecs*, pp. 243–46.

24 Roberto Levillier, ed., *Gobernantes del Perú* (14 vols., Madrid: Sucesores de Rivadeneyra, 1921–26), VIII, 400–406.

25 González Suárez, *Historia*, IV, 472 ff.; Pérez, *Las mitas*, pp. 172 ff.

26 See note 25. Report of Oidor Matías de Peralta: 1622, ANH, I, No. 57. Munive to king: July 30, 1681, AGI/AQ 69.

27 Oidor Matías Lagúnez to king: March 16, 1687, and "Testimonios sobre agravios de indios en la obrajes de la ciudad de Quito," March, 1687, AGI/AQ 69; and also Landazuri Soto, *Régimen*, pp. 200–206, 166–74. For other lurid descriptions of abuses in the obrajes, see Jorge Juan and Antonio de Ulloa, *Noticias secretas de América . . .*, ed. Rufino Blanco-Fombona (Biblioteca Ayacucho, Vols. XXXI and XXXII, Madrid, 1918), XXXI, 297–316. Pérez's account is a rehash of Juan and Ulloa's: Pérez, *Las mitas*, pp. 171 ff. For a balanced contemporary account, see Juan de Solórzano y Pereira, *Política indiana* (5 vols., Madrid, 1647), Bk. II, Ch. 12. *Recopilación de las leyes de los reynos de las Indias* (4 vols., Madrid, 1681), Bk. IV, Title xxvi. González Suárez, *Historia*, IV, 472–78. Audiencia to king: September 23, 1586, AGI/AQ 8. Caciques to audiencia: November 1, 1608, ANH, I, No. 19. Oidor Sancho de Mujica to king: April 27, 1619, AGI/AQ 10. Francisco Maldonado to audiencia: October 4, 1619, ANH, I, No. 52. Caciques of San Andrés to king: 1625, AGI/AQ 30. Francisco Camonal y Angulo to audiencia: October 21, 1626, ANH, I, No. 72. Suárez de Poago vs. Indians of San Andrés: December 23, 1627, and March 27, 1628, ACS, *Libro de acuerdos de la real audiencia, 1610–30*. Suárez de Poago to king: April 15, 1630, AGI/AQ 11. Viceroy to king: May 5, 1630, AGI/AL 43. Morga to king: April 20, 1631, AGI/AQ 32.

28 In 1660 Oidor Andrés Sánchez de Ocampo visited six obrajes in the suburb of Coyoacán where he found working conditions tolerable in five. In the sixth one, owned by Melchor Díaz de Posadas, he uncovered a whole series of flagrant abuses, including beatings that caused the death of one

worker. Edmundo O'Gorman, ed., "Visita a los obrajes de paños en la jurisdicción de Coyoacán, 1660," *Boletín del archivo general de la nación,* XI (1940), 33–116.

29 See Chapter 3, note 53.

30 Cedula to viceroy: October 28, 1612, AGI/AL 571. Richard Konetzke, *Colección de documentos para la historia de la formación social de Hispanoamérica, 1493–1810* (4 vols., Madrid, 1958–62), I, 184.

31 Morga to king: April 20, 1616, and April 15, 1620, AGI/AQ 10.

32 See note 31. King to viceroy: March 7, 1617, in "Recopilación de cédulas despachadas en diferentes tiempos por S. M. . . . para la real audiencia del Quito del Pirú, 1598–1632," ed. Antonio de Morga ms. (1632), Biblioteca Nacional, Mexico City, No. 21. Morga to viceroy: March 10, 1620, AGI/AQ 10. Audiencia to king: April 25, 1620, AGI/AQ 10. Suárez de Poago to king: April 23, 1620, AGI/AQ 10.

33 Viceroy to king: April 23, 1620, AGI/AL 39. Cedula to audiencia: October 17, 1622, AGI/AQ 10.

34 Viceroy Esquilache to Viceroy Guadalcázar in *Memorias de los virreyes que han gobernado el Perú durante el tiempo del coloniaje español* (6 vols., Lima, 1859), I, 103.

35 Cedula to audiencia: October 17, 1622, AGI/AQ 10. For the procedures of inspection, see Pedro Pérez Landero Otáñez y Castro, *Práctica de visitas y residencias de los reinos del Perú . . .* (Naples, 1646), pp. 228 ff.

36 Audiencia to king: April 25, 1625, AGI/AQ 10.

37 Cabildo of Quito to king: May 27, 1678, *ibid.* 69, and Landazuri Soto, *Régimen,* pp. 97–100.

38 ACS, *Libro de acuerdos de hacienda, 1601–57:* January 12, 1636.

39 *Recopilación,* February 22, 1602, and March 28, 1618, Bk. IV, Title xxvi, law 6.

40 Morga to king: April 15, 1622, AGI/AQ 10. Audiencia to king: April 20, 1622, *ibid.* Morga to king: April 15, 1623, *ibid.* Treasury to king: April 20, 1625, and king to Morga: June 13, 1627, *ibid.*

41 For documentation of the Vergara residencia, see Chapter 11, note 25.

42 Munive to king: July 30, 1681, AGI/AQ 69, and Landazuri Soto, *Régimen,* pp. 143 ff.

43 See Chapter 7, note 75.

44 Audiencia to king: May 15, 1630, AGI/AQ 11. Morga to king: February 1, 1630, *ibid.* Viceroy to king: May 5, 1630, AGI/AL 43.

45 The voluminous documents are in AGI/AQ 11.

46 See Chapter 14, notes 9–11.

47 Morga to viceroy: March 10, 1620, AGI/AQ 10.

48 Landazuri Soto has published the key documents, which have been often cited.

49 González Suárez, *Historia,* IV, 361–66.

50 Munive to king: July 30, 1681, AGI/AQ 69, and Landazuri Soto, *Régimen,* pp. 110–58.

51 AGI/AQ 210, and Landazuri Soto, *Régimen,* pp. 58–62. Charles II to

audiencia: March 21, 1689, AGI/AQ 210, and Landazuri Soto, *Régimen,* pp. 215–17; and August 28, 1689, AGI/AQ 210, and also Landazuri Soto, *Régimen,* pp. 163–65.

52 *Recopilación,* May 26, 1609, Bk. VI, Title xiii, law 10.

53 *Ibid.* Lagúnez to king: March 16, 1687, Landazuri Soto, *Régimen,* pp. 200–206.

54 Ernesto Schäfer, *El consejo real y supremo de las Indias* (2 vols., Seville, 1935–47), II, 485, 491, 515.

55 Lagúnez to king: March 16, 1687, Landazuri Soto, *Régimen,* pp. 200–206.

56 Pérez, *Las mitas,* p. 200.

57 Juan and Ulloa, *Noticias secretas,* XXXI, 288–316.

58 Kubler, "The Quechua," p. 373.

59 The three principal subdivisions of expressions of social discontent were revolts arising out of the conquest, agitation within the lower classes, and protests brought on by dissatisfactions among the creoles. For this typology, see Lincoln Machado Ribas, *Movimientos revolucionarios en las colonias españolas de América* (Buenos Aires: Editorial Claridad, 1949).

60 Constantino Bayle, S.J., *Los cabildos seculares en la América española* (Madrid, 1952). John Preston Moore, *The Cabildo in Peru under the Habsburgs: A Study in the origins of town councils in the viceroyalty of Peru, 1530–1700* (Durham: Duke University Press, 1954). Frederick Pike, "The Municipality and the System of Checks and Balances in the Spanish Colonial System," *The Americas,* XV, No. 2 (October, 1958), 139–58.

61 Woodrow W. Borah, "Representative Institutions in the Spanish Empire: The New World," *The Americas,* XII, No. 3 (January, 1956), 256.

62 See Chapter 10, note 44.

63 For a discerning analysis of the failure of formal representative assemblies to emerge in the Indies, see Borah "Representative Institutions," pp. 246–57.

64 From 1636 to 1700 the correspondence of the viceroys of Peru seldom mentions Quito matters. Out of a total of 444 letters, only 13 contain any significant references to Quito, AGI/AL 46–49.

65 González Suárez, *Historia,* IV, 97–98.

66 Treasury to king: March 10, 1626, AGI/AQ 20. ACS, *Libro de acuerdos de la hacienda, 1601–57:* September 14, 1630.

Chapter 5: The Dutch Challenge in the Spanish Pacific

1 Engel Sluiter, "Dutch Maritime Power and the Colonial Status Quo, 1585–1641," *The Pacific Coast Historical Review,* XI (March, 1942), 41. Among the other works consulted for my general discussion of the Hispano-Dutch rivalry are the following. Charles R. Boxer, *The Dutch in Brazil* (Oxford, 1957), pp. 1–32. Peter Gerhard, *Pirates on the West Coast of New Spain, 1565–1742* (Glendale, 1960). William L. Schurz, *The Manila Galleon,* 2nd ed. (New York, 1959), pp. 287–302, 342–57, 361–87. Pieter Geyl, *The Revolt of the Netherlands* (New York, 1958), pp. 250–59. Pieter Geyl,

The Netherlands in the Seventeenth Century (2 vols., New York, 1961–64), I, 158–208. Reginald Trevor Davies, *The Golden Century of Spain, 1501–1621* (London, 1961), pp. 227–60. Reginald Trevor Davies, *Spain in Decline, 1621–1700* (London, 1961), pp. 1–22.

2 Schurz, *Manila Galleon,* p. 288. Francisco Javier de Ayala, *Ideas políticas de Juan de Solórzano* (Seville, 1946), pp. 467–70.

3 Schurz, *Manila Galleon,* p. 288.

4 Audiencia to viceroy: November 7, 1602, and March 15, 1604, ANH, I, Nos. 6 and 7. Viceroy to king: April 15, 1630, AGI/AQ 11.

5 Engel Sluiter, "The Dutch on the Pacific Coast of South America: 1598–1621," Ph.D. thesis, Univ. of California, Berkeley, 1937, pp. 233–36.

6 Gerhard, *Pirates on the West Coast,* pp. 101 ff. Schurz, *Manila Galleon,* pp. 342 ff.

7 See note 6. Sluiter, "The Dutch on the Pacific Coast," pp. 160 ff.

8 W. E. Retana has published several key documents from the AGI dealing with this whole episode. W. E. Retana, "Estudio preliminar," in Antonio de Morga, *Sucesos de las islas filipinas* (Madrid, 1909), pp. 72 ff. Also see appendix to Morga's *Sucesos:* Morga to governor: February 5, 1601, pp. 271–310. Also consult Emma Blair and James Alexander Robertson, *The Philippine Islands, 1493–1803* (55 vols., Cleveland: A. H. Clark, 1903–9), XI, 140–48, 149, 166, 173–86.

9 For the Spanish side, see note 8. Sluiter has a graphic account of the battle. Sluiter, "The Dutch on the Pacific Coast," pp. 160 ff. I do not read Dutch; hence I could not consult Dutch sources which had not been translated.

10 See note 8.

11 For Morga's account, see his *Sucesos,* pp. 112 ff. For a discussion of the Philippine content of Morga's book, see Luis Miranda, "Primera historia de Filipinas," and "Sucesos de las islas Filipinas," in *Boletín bibliográfico,* Nos. 155 and 156 (May 15, 1959, and June 10, 1959), pp. 2 and 6, and pp. 2 and 8. John L. Phelan, *The Hispanization of the Philippines: Spanish Aims and Filipino Responses, 1565–1700* (Madison, 1959), 201–2.

12 Sluiter, "The Dutch on the Pacific Coast," p. 235.

13 *The East and West Indian Mirrow, Being an Account of Joris van Speilbergen's Voyage Around the World: 1614–17* (The Hakluyt Society, 2nd series, 1906), p. 102. The first edition in Dutch was published in Amsterdam, 1621.

14 See Chapter 7, notes 30–36.

15 Sluiter, "The Dutch on the Pacific Coast," p. 221.

16 Gerhard, *Pirates on the West Coast,* pp. 115–16. For the Spanish defense, see ACS, *Libro de acuerdos de la real audiencia, 1610–30:* August 6, 1615. Corregidor of Guayaquil to audiencia: August 25, 1615, ANH, I, No. 39, and audiencia to corregidor: August 31, 1615, ANH, I, No. 41.

17 Schurz, *Manila Galleon,* p. 347.

18 *Ibid.,* p. 348.

19 For the effect of the Dutch war on the Philippines, see my *Hispanization,* pp. 8, 12–13, 70–72, 99–106, 110, 113–36, 138, 140–42, 146, 148, 156–57.

20 James Burney, *A Chronological History of the Discoveries in the South Seas or Pacific Ocean* (5 vols., London, 1803–17), III, 32. Burney's account of the Nassau expedition is a reprint from John Callender, *Terra Australis Cognita* (3 vols., Edinburgh, 1766–68), II, 287–334. Callender translated into English the Dutch account of Adlop Decker, who was an officer in the expedition. Also see Schurz, *Manila Galleon,* p. 350, and Gerhard, *Pirates on the West Coast,* pp. 101–34.

21 Pieter Geyl, *The Netherlands in the Seventeenth Century,* I, 197.

22 Callender, *Terra Australis,* II, 300.

23 Gerhard, *Pirates on the West Coast,* pp. 131–32. Burney, *A Chronological History,* III, 142–44.

24 Sluiter, "The Dutch on the Pacific Coast," pp. 92–93.

25 *Ibid.,* pp. 91–101.

26 Gerhard, *Pirates on the West Coast,* p. 242. For a succinct defense of this strategy, see Viceroy Mancera's letter to his successor in *Colección de las memorias ó relaciones que escribieron los virreyes del Pirú acerca del estado en que dejaron las cosas generales del reino* (2 vols., Madrid, 1921–30), II, 176 ff.

27 ACS, *Libro de acuerdos de hacienda, 1601–57:* May–August, 1624.

28 Callender, *Terra Australis,* II, 287–327. President Antonio de Morga to king: September 20, 1624, AGI/AQ 10. Audiencia to king: April 25, 1625, AGI/AQ 10. Morga to king: April 15, 1625, and April 30, 1629, AGI/AQ 10, 11.

29 Francisco Pérez de Naverrete to audiencia: June 6, 1628, ANH, I, No. 79. Fr. Diego de Martínez to audiencia: March 19, 1630, *ibid.,* No. 90. Fr. Luis de Aranda to audiencia: March 18, 1630, *ibid.,* No. 89. Pérez de Navarrete to audiencia: January 4, 1631, *ibid.,* II, No. 94. Toribio de Castro to audiencia: January 3, 1632, *ibid.,* No. 98. ACS, *Libro de acuerdos de la real audiencia, 1630–41:* August 2, 1632. Federico González Suárez, *Historia general de la república del Ecuador* (7 vols., Quito, 1890–1903), IV, 100–102. Dora León Borja y Adam Szaszdi Nagy, "El Comercio del Cacao de Guayaquil," *Revista de Historia de America,* Nos. 57– 58 (January–February, 1964), 1–50.

30 See Chapter 1, note 10.

31 Viceroy to king: April 15, 1630, AGI/AQ 11. Engel Sluiter, "The Fortification of Acapulco, 1615–1616," *Hispanic-American Historical Review,* XXXIX (February, 1949), 69–80. Gerhard, *Pirates on the West Coast,* p. 242.

32 Morga to viceroy: November 20, 1615, AGI/AQ 10. Morga to king: September 20, 1624, *ibid.* Audiencia to king: April 25, 1625, *ibid.* Morga to king: May 15, 1628, April 30, 1629, *ibid.* 11.

33 Ernesto Schäfer, *El consejo real y supremo de las Indias* (2 vols., Seville, 1935–47), I, 165 ff. and 198 ff. Juan de Solórzano y Pereira, *Política indiana* (5 vols., Madrid, 1647), Bk. V, Ch. xviii. *Recopilación de las leyes de los reynos de las Indias* (4 vols., Madrid, 1681), Bk. II, Title 11. *Ordenanzas de la junta de guerra de las Indias* (Madrid, 1634).

34 ACS, *Libro de acuerdos de hacienda, 1601–57:* May-June, 1624, May 20, 1626, and September 30, 1630.

35 King to audiencia: October 19, 1629, and October 15, 1630, AMQ, X, foll. 11, 69, 79, and 96.

36 *Ibid.*

37 Viceroy to audiencia: May 20, 1632, "Recopilación de cedulas despachadas en diferentes tiempos por S. M. . . . para la real audiencia del Quito del Pirú, 1589–1632," ed. Antonio de Morga, ms. (1632), Biblioteca Nacional, Mexico City, No. 166.

38 Woodrow W. Borah, "Representative Institutions in the Spanish Empire: The New World," *The Americas,* XII, No. 3 (January, 1956), 253.

39 Morga to king: April 15, 1624, AGI/AQ 10. Fiscal Melchor Suárez de Poago to king: April 14, 1623, *ibid.* Treasury to king: March 17, 1629, *ibid.* 11.

40 President Manuel Barros to king: February 15, 1591, *ibid.* 8. President Miguel de Ibarra to king: 1603, *ibid.* 9.

41 Morga to king: November 15, 1625, *ibid.* 61. Treasury to king: April 27, 1635, *ibid.* 12.

42 Morga to king: April 30, 1634, and April 30, 1633, *ibid.*

43 Antonio Domínguez Ortiz, *Política y hacienda de Felipe IV* (Madrid, 1960), pp. 298 ff.

44 Suárez de Poago to king: April 14, 1623, AGI/AQ 10. Morga to king: April 15, 1623, and April 15, 1624, *ibid.* Morga to king: April 30, 1634, and April 27, 1635, *ibid.* 12.

45 Helmut G. Koenigsberger, "Patronage and Bribery during the Reign of Charles V," *Anciens pays et assemblées d'états,* XXII (Louvain and Paris, 1961), 167.

46 Engel Sluiter, "The Word Pechelingue: Its Derivation and Meaning," *Hispanic-American Historical Review,* XXIV (November, 1944), 683–98.

47 Morga to viceroy: November 20, 1615, AGI/AQ 10, and Morga, *Sucesos,* Appendix, pp. 347–59.

48 Woodrow W. Borah, *Early Colonial Trade and Navigation Between Mexico and Peru* (Ibero-Americana, No. 38, Berkeley and Los Angeles, 1954), pp. 126–27.

CHAPTER 6: RECRUITMENT, TRAINING, AND PROMOTION

1 Juan de Solórzano y Pereira, *Política indiana* (5 vols., Madrid, 1647), Bk. IV, Chs. iii–iv, xii, xv. *Recopilación de las leyes de los reynos de las Indias* (4 vols., Madrid, 1681), Bk. II, Titles xv and xvi; Bk. III, Title iii. Ernesto Schäfer, *El consejo real y supremo de las Indias* (2 vols., Seville, 1935–47), II, 3–156. Clarence Haring, *The Spanish Empire in America* (New York, 1947), pp. 119–37. Francisco de Pelsmaeker é Ibáñez, *La audiencia en las colonias españolas de América* (Madrid, 1925). Carmelo Viñas Mey, "El régimen jurídico de responsabilidad en la América indiana," *Revista de las Españas,* III and IV (January–February and August, 1928,

and January–February, 1929), 17–21, 362–69, 36–54. Enríque Ruíz Guiñazú, *La magistratura indiana* (Buenos Aires, 1916).

2 Ricardo Levene, *Historia del derecho argentino* (11 vols., Buenos Aires: Editorial Guillermo Kraft, 1945–58), II, 26 ff.

3 *Recopilación*, Bk. II, Title iii, law 1, and Title xv, law 17. Solórzano, *Política indiana*, Bk. IV, Ch. xix, No. 37; Bk. I, Ch. xi, Nos. 38–39; Bk. V, Ch. viii, No. 2; Bk. V, Ch. xv, No. 6; Bk. V, Ch. xvi, No. 12. Haring, *The Spanish Empire*, p. 7. Haring's account is excellent as far as it goes, but he does not take into account the juridical ties between the audiencias and the viceroyalties.

4 As quoted in John H. Elliott, *The Revolt of the Catalans: A Study in the Decline of Spain, 1598–1640* (Cambridge, 1963), p. 200. The original is in the Biblioteca Nacional in Madrid, ms. 9893. Elliott has a succinct analysis of the juridical pluralism of the peninsular kingdoms. *Ibid.*, pp. 8–12.

5 *Antología del pensamiento político americano, Servando Teresa de Mier*, ed. Edmundo O'Gorman (Mexico: Universidad Nacional Autónoma de México, 1945), Prologue, p. xxxiii. Servando Teresa de Mier Noriega y Guerra, *Historia de la revolución de Nueva España* (2 vols., Mexico: Cámara de Diputados del Congreso de la República de México, 1921; 1st ed., London, 1813), II, Bk. XIV. "Ideas de la constitución dadas a las Américas por los reyes de España," in *Escritos inéditos de Fray Servando Teresa de Mier*, ed. J. M. Miguel Vergés and Hugo Díaz-Thomé (Mexico: Colegio de México, 1944), pp. 249, 279–81. Servando Teresa de Mier Noriega y Guerra, *Memorial político-instructivo enviada desde Filadelfia* (Philadelphia, 1821), p. 31. Mier tried to demonstrate that in the laws of the Indies there was an implicit "social contract" or an embryonic constitution defining and limiting the mutual rights and obligations of the crown and its subjects in the overseas kingdoms. While he was obviously twisting Habsburg theories for his own partisan ends, Mier was on firm historical ground in distinguishing between the more limited and decentralized form of government under the Habsburgs and the more autocratic and unitary trends under the Bourbons. For a useful general discussion of some juridical aspects of the independence movement, see Alfonso García Gallo, "El derecho indiano y la independencia de América," *Revista de estudios políticos*, XL, No. 60 (November–December, 1951), 157–80. But García Gallo does not focus sharply on the one issue I stress. See in particular García Gallo, "El derecho," pp. 169–70, 172–73.

6 John H. Parry, *The Audiencia of New Galicia in the Sixteenth Century* (Cambridge, 1948), p. 3.

7 R. W. Carlyle and A. J. Carlyle, *A History of Political Thought in the West* (6 vols., Edinburgh and London: W. Blackwood and Sons, 1903–36), V, 143. Pope Innocent III first enunciated this doctrine in his often-quoted letter, *Per venerabilem.*

8 Francisco Javier de Ayala, *Ideas políticias de Juan de Solórzano* (Seville, 1946), pp. 184–204. Mario Góngora, *El estado español en el derecho*

indiano; época de fundación, 1492–1570 (Santiago, Chile, 1951), pp. 35, 303.

9 See Chapter 2, note 25.

10 Haring, *The Spanish Empire*, p. 122.

11 Schäfer, *El consejo*, I, 114–15. John Lynch, *Spain under the Habsburgs* (2 vols., New York, 1964——), I, 184 ff. For the duties of the secretaries of the Council of the Indies, see the *Recopilación*, Bk. II, Title vi. Also see Helmut G. Koenigsberger, *The Government of Sicily under Philip II of Spain: A Study in the Practice of Empire* (London and New York, 1951), Foreword by J. M. Batista I. Roca, pp. 9–35, 59–73. For the more abstract views of the role of the councils by peninsular political theorists in the seventeenth century, see José Antonio Maravall, *La teoría española del estado en el siglo xvii* (Madrid, 1944), pp. 275–317.

12 *Recopilación*, Bk. III, Title iii. Solórzano, *Política indiana*, Bk. V, Chs. xii–xiv. Haring, *The Spanish Empire*, pp. 119 ff.

13 Haring, *The Spanish Empire*, p. 122.

14 José María Ots Capdequí, *El estado español en las Indias*, 3rd ed. (Mexico, 1957), p. 54.

15 Schäfer, *El consejo*, II, 29. For a list of the viceroys, see *ibid.*, pp. 439–42.

16 Sir Edward Blunt, *The Indian Civil Service* (London, 1937), pp. 68 ff.

17 *Recopilación*, Bk. II, Title xvi. Solórzano, *Política indiana*, Bk. V, Ch. iv.

18 *Recopilación*, Bk. II, Title xvi, law 25.

19 *Ibid.* Solórzano, *Política indiana*, Bk. V, Ch. iv, No. 24.

20 Solórzano, *Política indiana*, Bk. V, Ch. iv, No. 24. ACS, *Libro de acuerdos de la real audiencia, 1630–41:* December 7, 1635. Audiencia to king: April 15, 1636, AGI/AQ 12. Juan de Mañozca, *El lic. Mañozca . . . con los señores doctores d. Andrés de Reuda Rico . . . sobre la precedencia que pretendo me toca en el asiento y demás actos como más antiguo* (Madrid, 1640).

21 Solórzano, *Política indiana*, Bk. V, Ch. iv, No. 25. Morga to king: April 15, 1623, AGI/AQ 10.

22 *Recopilación*, Bk. II, Title xvi, law 16.

23 *Ibid.*, Title xvii. Solórzano, *Política indiana*, Bk. V, Ch. v.

24 *Recopilación*, Bk. II, Title xvii. Solórzano, *Política indiana*, Bk. V, Ch. vi. ACS, *Libro de acuerdos de la real audiencia, 1610–30.*

25 Antonio Rodríguez de León Pinelo, *Autos, acuerdos i decretos de gobierno del real i supremo consejo de las Indias . . .* (Madrid, 1658), May 23, 1625, No. lix.

26 *Ibid.*, April 9, 1605, No. xvi. The *consultas* dealing with the appointments of the following magistrates for the period 1610–30 are in the AGI/AQ 1 and 2: Luís de Quiñones, Juan de Licarazu, Juan Fernández de Recalde, Pedro de Vergara, Antonio de Morga, Sancho de Móxica, Melchor Suárez de Poago, Espino de Cáceres, Justino de Valdés. Many, of course, are missing. Maravall, *Teoría*, p. 301. Solórzano, *Política indiana*, Bk. V, Ch. xiv, Nos. 21–32. Among the Spanish political theorists who championed bureaucratic professionalism were Francisco Bermúdez de Pedraza, *El*

secretario del rey (Granada, 1637); Juan Alfonso Rodríquez de Lancina, *Comentarios políticos a los anales de Cayo Vero Cornelio Tácito,* ed. José Antonio Maravall (Madrid, 1945); and Diego Saavedra Fajardo, *Idea de un príncipe político christiano* (Monaco and Milan, 1640).

27 Schäfer, *El consejo,* I, 175 ff. and 227 ff. Consejo real de las Indias, *Sobre que se debe escusar el de cámara en que se ha de tratar de formar* (Madrid, 1644?).

28 W. E. Retana, "Estudio preliminar," in Antonio de Morga, *Sucesos de las islas filipinas* (Madrid, 1909), pp. 104–5.

29 Schäfer, *El consejo,* II, 455, 460.

30 *Ibid.,* pp. 115, 181, 357. At the time of his brother's appointment to the presidency of Quito, Juan de Ibarra was secretary of the Council of the Indies. Subsequently from 1604 until 1611 he was a member of the council.

31 *Ibid.,* p. 500.

32 *Ibid.,* p. 481.

33 Consulta: November 13, 1613, AGI/AQ 1. Schäfer, *El consejo,* I, 359, 453, 493.

34 Retana, "Estudio," pp. 118, 125, 126.

35 The will of the first señora de Morga can be found in "Autos hechos por el s. Lic. d. Alonso de Castillo . . . sobre los bienes de Dr. Antonio de Morga," AGI/AQ 12.

36 Morga, *Sucesos,* pp. 9–10. Retana uncovered evidence that, at the last moment, Morga changed his dedication from Philip III to the Duke of Cea. Retana, however, confused his genealogy. He claimed that the Duke of Cea was the father of the Duke of Uceda, when in fact Cea and Uceda were one and the same person, the son of the Duke of Lerma. Retana, "Estudio," pp. 174–75. For the correct genealogy, see Julio de Atienza, *Nobiliario español* (Madrid: Aguilar, 1948), pp. 843, 892, 992.

37 See Chapter 4, note 22.

38 For a list of these magistrates, see Schäfer, *El consejo,* II, 511–16, Also see the consultas in the AGI/AQ 1 and 2.

39 Consulta: January 15, 1611, AGI/AQ 1.

40 Oidor Matías de Peralta to king: April 20, 1622, AGI/AQ 10. Lic. Juan de Mañozca to king: March 27, 1627, AGI/AQ 62. For Salvador de Rivera's controversial career as inquisitor in Mexico City, see Henry Charles Lea, *The Inquisition in the Spanish Dependencies* (New York, 1908), pp. 207–8.

41 Consulta: June 3, 1630, AGI/AQ 2.

42 Consulta: July 2, 1646, AGI/AL 7, and Richard Konetzke, *Colección de documentos para la historia de la formación social de Hispanoamérica, 1493–1810* (4 vols., Madrid, 1958–62), II, 402–4.

43 See Chapter 7, note 37.

44 See Chapter 7, note 29. Also see note 88, this chapter.

45 King to council: June 3, 1627, AGI/Indiferente General 755. Council to king: June 3, 1627, *ibid.*

46 Solórzano, Bk. IV, Ch. iv, No. 33.

47 Schäfer, *El consejo,* II, 511–16.

48 For a clear expression, see Consulta: June 23, 1627, AGI/Indiferente General 755. For a list of the bishops, see Schäfer, *El consejo,* II, 565 ff.

49 Schäfer, *El consejo,* II, 359–66. Lic. Pérez de Salazar served in the council first as fiscal and then as Councilor from 1589 to 1596, after having served in the audiencias of Bogotá and Mexico City. *Ibid.,* I, 356, 367; II, 157, 453.

50 *Ibid.,* I, 353 ff. Their names were Dr. Eugenio de Salazar (Mexico), Dr. Francisco Alonso de Villagra (Mexico), Lic. Rodrigo de Aguiar y Acuña (Quito), Lic. Alonso Maldonado de Torres (Lima), Lic. Fernández de Boan (Lima), and Dr. Juan de Solórzano y Pereira (Lima). The king rejected the request of Oidor Rodrigo de Aguiar y Acuña for a per diem expense account (*ayuda de costa*) to defray his travel costs from Quito to Madrid on the grounds that his promotion to the council was ample reward. León Pinelo, *Autos,* Consulta of May 12, 1607, No. xxii.

51 Schäfer, *El consejo,* I, 113, 134.

52 Ayala, *Ideas políticas de Juan de Solórzano,* pp. 45, 48. José Torre Revello, *Ensayo biográfico sobre Juan de Solórzano y Pereira* (Buenos Aires: Imprenta de la Universidad, 1929). Juan Manzano y Manzano, *La incorporación de las Indias a la corona de Castilla* (Madrid: Cultura Hispánica, 1948), pp. 279–80, 284–85. José María Ots Capdequí and Javier Malagón, *Solórzano y la Política indiana* (Mexico and Buenos Aires, 1965), especially pp. 23–25. This is the most recent and very concise synthesis on the life and the political thought of the Spanish jurist-magistrate.

53 Schäfer, *El consejo,* II, 511.

54 *Ibid.,* p. 513.

55 *Ibid.,* pp. 142, 456, 461, 513.

56 *Ibid.,* pp. 454, 460, 463, 465, 482.

57 *Recopilación,* Bk. III, Title iii, law 6; Bk. II, Title xxiii, laws 1–16.

58 *Ibid.,* Bk. III, Title iii, law 8.

59 For some samples, see the Informaciones of Lic. Espino de Cáceres, AGI/AQ 11; of Lic. Francisco Rodríquez Plaza, Pedro de Vera, Lic. Melchor Suárez de Poago, *ibid.* 50; and of Juan Sánz de Gauna, *ibid.* 51.

60 Retana, "Estudio," p. 125.

61 Audiencia to king: April 28, 1621, and April 21, 1624, AGI/AQ 10.

62 For some examples, see audiencia to king: April 19, 1620, *ibid.* Audiencia to king: March 23, 1609, and March 31, 1612, *ibid.* 9.

63 Peralta to king: April 20, 1622, *ibid.* 10. Fiscal Melchor Suárez de Poago to king: April 20, 1621, *ibid.* Pedro Ortiz de Ávila to king: 1626, *ibid.* 31. Antonio Rodríquez Moniño, *Catálogo de memoriales presentados al real consejo de Indias, 1626–1630* (Madrid: Editorial Maestre, 1953). There are 430 requests of bureaucrats or would-be magistrates requesting appointments or promotions, 24 of which deal with Quito.

64 Mañozca to Antonio González de Legarda: February 28, 1627, AGI/AQ 62. In view of the controversy surrounding his mission to Quito, Lic.

Mañozca's name did not even appear on the Consulta for the vacant see of Lima. Consulta: August 31, 1627, AGI/AL 5.

65　President Antonio de Morga to king: March 15, 1614, and May 30, 1623, AGI/AQ 10.

66　Morga to king: October 1, 1630, *ibid.* 11.

67　Morga to king: April 30, 1634, *ibid.* 12. For the recommendation of the council, see November 10, 1635, *ibid.* 2.

68　Cedula: October 22, 1636, *ibid.* 12.

69　Solórzano, *Política indiana,* Bk. V, Ch. iv, No. 4.

70　Góngora, *El estado,* p. 186. León Pinelo, *Autos,* Consulta of March 18, 1594, No. 2.

71　Solórzano, *Política indiana,* Bk. V, Ch. iv, Nos. 29–30.

72　L. S. O'Malley, *The Indian Civil Service, 1601–1930* (London, 1931), pp. 228–57. Oidor Diego de Zorrilla, who was in Quito from 1608 to 1620, was the son of Oidor Pedro de Zorrilla, who had served in the audiencias of Bogotá, Quito, and Charcas. Such cases of father-and-son magistrates in the Indies, however, were rare, although they may have been more frequent in Spain itself.

73　See note 35. Ruth Pike, *Enterprise and Adventure: The Genoese in Seville and the Opening of the New World* (Ithaca, N.Y.: Cornell University Press, 1966), pp. 93–94.

74　Koenigsberger, *The Government of Sicily,* pp. 73–97. Some viceroys were non-Sicilian Italians. The Duke of Terranova, a Sicilian, served as president (acting viceroy) from 1571 until 1577.

75　*Recopilación,* Bk. II, Title xx, laws 1, 2, 5, 7, 9, 11, 12, 16, 22. Parry, *The Audiencia,* pp. 40, 162.

76　Fiscal Blas de Torres Altamirano to king: April 17, 1606, AGI/AQ 9. Suárez de Poago to king: April 29, 1622, *ibid.* 10.

77　*Recopilación,* Bk. II, Title xxiii. Parry, *The Audiencia,* pp. 154–55, 164–65. Consulta: May 17, 1607, AGI/AQ 1.

78　*Recopilación,* Bk. II, Title xxii. Parry, *The Audiencia,* pp. 154, 157–58.

79　Morga to king: April 15, 1620, AGI/AQ 10.

80　*Recopilación,* Bk. II, Titles xxv and xvii.

81　*Ibid.,* Title xxi.

82　*Ibid.,* Title xxiv.

83　For examples, see ACS, *Libro de acuerdos de la real audiencia, 1610–30.*

84　*Recopilación,* Bk. III, Title ii, law 51.

85　Suárez de Poago to king: April 29, 1622, AGI/AQ 10.

86　John H. Parry, *The Sale of Public Office in the Spanish Indies under the Habsburgs* (Ibero-Americana, No. 37, Berkeley and Los Angeles, 1953), pp. 69–73.

87　*Ibid.,* pp. 6–20.

88　Helmut G. Koenigsberger, "Patronage and Bribery during the Reign of Charles V," *Anciens pays et assemblées d'états,* XXII (Louvain and Paris, 1961), 168. Also see his *Government of Sicily,* p. 65.

89　S. N. Eisenstadt, *The Political Systems of Empires* (New York, 1963), pp. 152–53. John H. Parry, *The Spanish Seaborne Empire* (New York, 1966), pp. 208–9, 273–80.

90 I disagree with Woodrow Borah's emphasis in his provocative essay: "Representative Institutions in the Spanish Empire: The New World," *The Americas,* XII, No. 3 (January, 1956), 256. I think that it is desirable to distinguish between the clerking municipal offices and the royally appointed magistrates. Although wealth did profoundly influence decision-making, its voice was not as all-decisive as Borah seems to imply.

91 My minimizing the importance of the sale of offices as a cause of graft runs counter to prevailing opinion. Both Ramón Menéndez Pidal and John Parry put great emphasis on the sale of offices. See Parry's latest book, an elegantly written and thoughtful synthesis: Parry, *The Spanish Seaborne Empire,* pp. 208–9, 273–80.

92 Solórzano, *Política indiana,* Bk. V, Ch. iv. Also see the *Recopilación,* Bk. II, Title xvi; and note 26, this chapter.

93 For some discerning comments, see Koenigsberger, "Patronage and Bribery," p. 169, and his *Government of Sicily,* p. 65.

CHAPTER 7: GRAFT

1 Antonio de León Pinelo, *Autos, acuerdos i decretos de gobierno del real i supremo consejo de las Indias* . . . (Madrid, 1658), fol. 7. Ernesto Schäfer, *El consejo real y supremo de las Indias* (2 vols., Seville, 1935–47), II, 27–30.

2 Schäfer, *El consejo,* II, 119–21.

3 Consulta: November 13, 1613, AGI/AQ 1.

4 Consulta: July 20, 1622, *ibid.* Consulta: January 15, 1611, *ibid.*

5 *Recopilación de las leyes de los reynos de las Indias* (4 vols., Madrid, 1681), Bk. II, Title xvi, laws 30 and 31.

6 Pierre Chaunu and Huguette Chaunu, *Seville et l'Atlantique, 1504–1650* (9 vols., Paris, 1956–59).

7 *Recopilación,* Bk. II, Title xvi, law 95. Consulta: March 7, 1623, AGI/AQ 1. Consulta: February 19, 1633, AGI/AQ 2. Consulta: December 18, 1621, AGI/AQ 1. This policy is similar to the custom of the United States Senate, which ordinarily grants to the widow of a senator dying in office an amount equal to his salary for one year.

8 See Fiscal Melchor Suárez de Poago to king: April 6, 1625, and April 13, 1630, AGI/AQ 10, 11. King to Suárez de Poago: November 12, 1635, *ibid.* 12. The fiscal reported that his three daughters were in a convent. One-half of his salary had gone to pay for part of their dowries, but he still owed the convent the other half. He requested from the king a benefice in the cathedral of Quito for his son who was a secular priest. For the case of an oidor who died leaving behind many debts and eight minor children, see audiencia to king: April 20, 1638, *ibid.*

9 Consulta: November 10, 1635, *ibid.* 2. For Oidor Tello de Velasco's retirement, see Archivo General de la Nación (Guatemala), Al. 23, exped.

39223, legajo 4568, fol. 23. For the retirement and death of Suárez de Poago, see cedula to audiencia: June 28, 1647, AGI/AQ 209, and President Martín Arriola to king: August 17, 1648, AGI/AQ 13.

10 *Recopilación,* Bk. III, Title iii, law 7. Audiencia to king: March 22, 1611, March 31, 1612, and April 20, 1613, AGI/AQ 9. President Antonio de Morga to king: April 25, 1621, AGI/AQ 10. Consulta: March 9, 1622, AGI/AQ 1.

11 Morga to king: April 15, 1620, AGI/AQ 10.

12 Morga to king: February 28, 1626, *ibid.* Lic. Juan de Mañozca to king: March 27, 1627, *ibid.* 62.

13 *Recopilación,* Bk. II, Title xvi, laws 53, 54, 57, 58, 59, 60, 65, 66, 69, 70.

14 *Ibid.,* law 48. Also see Chapter 3, note 27.

15 *Recopilación,* Bk. II, Title xvi, laws 49 and 50.

16 *Ibid.,* laws 53, 67, 68, 69, 70, 75.

17 Juan de Solórzano y Pereira, *Política indiana* (5 vols., Madrid, 1647), Bk. V, Ch. ix, Nos. 10 and 68. José María Ots Capdequí and Javier Malagón, *Solórzano y la Política indiana* (Mexico and Buenos Aires, 1965), pp. 16–17.

18 The recent widow of Oidor Alonso de Castillo, doña Graviela Bravo de Olmedo, married Oidor Juan de Valdés y Llano: President Alonso Pérez de Salazar to king: May 30, 1639, AGI/AQ 12. For another example, see Chapter 10, notes 19–23.

19 W. E. Retana, "Estudio preliminar," in Antonio de Morga, *Sucesos de las islas filipinas* (Madrid, 1909), pp. 93–104.

20 Consultas: June 23, 1627, and December 2, 1627, AGI/Indiferente General 755.

21 *Ibid.*

22 My account of the Indian Civil Service is based on the following sources. Sir Edward Blunt, *The Indian Civil Service* (London, 1937). M. Ruthnaswamy, *The Political Theory of the Government of India* (Madras, 1928), and M. Ruthnaswamy, *Some Influences that Made the British Administrative System in India* (London, 1939). L. S. O'Malley, *The Indian Civil Service, 1601–1930* (London, 1931). Philip Mason, *The Men Who Ruled India* (2 vols., London, 1953). G. O. Trevelyan, *The Competition Wallah,* 2nd ed. (London, 1866). J. C. Curry, *The Indian Police* (London, 1932). Joseph Chailley, *Administrative Problems of British India* (London, 1910). B. B. Misra, *The Central Administration of the East India Company, 1773–1834* (Manchester, 1959). Jadunath Sarkar, *Mughal Administration,* 4th ed. (Calcutta, 1952). *Bombay in the Days of George IV: Memoirs of Sir Edward West,* ed. F. Dawtrey Drewitt (London, 1907). Sir Evan Maconochie, *Life in the Indian Civil Service* (London, 1926). George Campbell, *Modern India: A Sketch of the System of Civil Government* (London, 1853). John Beames, *Memoirs of a Bengal Civilian* (London: Chatto & Windus, 1961). Percival Spear, *Twilight of the Mughuls* (Cambridge, 1951).

23 Robert E. Frykenberg, *Guntur District, 1788–1848: A History of Local*

Influence and Central Authority in South India (Oxford, 1965), pp. 230–44.

24 Ruthnaswamy, *Political Theory*, p. 3. Many of the accounts listed in note 22 discuss the influences of utilitarianism, but Ruthnaswamy's is the most concise.

25 José Ortega y Gasset's essay "Meditation in the Escorial," in Ortega's *Invertebrate Spain*, trans. Mildred Adams (New York: W. W. Norton & Co., 1937), p. 208.

26 Mason, *Men Who Ruled India*, I, 248–65.

27 The *Noticias secretas de América* of Jorge Juan and Antonio de Ulloa was first published by David Barry in London in 1826 with the apparent intent to discredit the recently overthrown Spanish colonial regime. The *Noticias americanas,* published in Madrid in 1772, contained none of the explosive material criticizing the conduct of the bureaucracy and the churchmen, for the *Noticias secretas* was a "top-secret" report submitted to the king and never intended for publication. Liberal Hispanists, led by the late, distinguished Rafael Altamira, in their purpose of stressing the constructive role of Spanish colonization, were the first to warn that the *Noticias secretas* cannot be accepted uncritically. Rafael Altamira y Crevea, *La huella de España en América* (Madrid: Editorial Reus, 1924), pp. 101–6. Carmelo Viñas Mey, *El estatuto del obrero indígena en la colonización española* (Madrid: Compañía Ibero-americana de Publicaciones, 1929), pp. 245 ff. The latter author's emphasis on legislation to the total exclusion of actual social conditions makes his view as lopsided as the "black legend" he seeks to refute.

28 Antonio Cánovas del Castillo, *Historia de la decadencia de España desde el advenimiento de Felipe III al trono hasta la muerte de Carlos II* (Madrid, 1854). Reginald Trevor Davies, *The Golden Century of Spain, 1501–1621* (London, 1961), pp. 227–60. Schäfer, *El consejo,* I, 175–267.

29 In addition to the sources in the preceding note, consult the following. John H. Elliott, *The Revolt of the Catalans: A Study in the Decline of Spain, 1598–1640* (Cambridge, 1963), pp. 182–207. Reginald Trevor Davies, *Spain in Decline, 1621–1700* (London, 1961), pp. 1–33. Antonio Domínguez Ortiz, *Política y hacienda de Felipe IV* (Madrid, 1960). Cedula: December 15, 1622, Richard Konetzke, *Colección de documentos para la historia de la formación social de Hispanoamérica, 1493–1810* (4 vols., Madrid, 1958–62), II, 271. Gregorio Marañón, *El conde-duque de Olivares, la pasión de mandar,* 4th ed. (Madrid, 1959). Martin Hume, *The Court of Philip IV: Spain in Decadence* (New York: Brentano, 1927).

30 Also see Chapter 5, notes 14–17 for the Dutch sources. Morga to king: February 20, 1616, AGI/AQ 10, and *Calendar of Philippine Documents in the Ayer Collection of the Newberry Library,* ed. Paul Lietz (Chicago: The Newberry Library, 1956), No. 23, and also Retana, "Estudio," pp. 130 ff. Morga to king: April 20, 1616, AGI/AQ 10.

31 Audiencia of Lima to king: May 9, 1616; and viceroy to king: May 10, 1616, AGI/AL 37.

32 "Memoria y relación cierta de algunos excesos que el príncipe de Esquilache, virrey del Perú, ha hecho en el tiempo de su gobierno" (n.d., *ca.*
   1621), *ibid.* 96. Audiencia to king: April 14, 1617, and April 10, 1617,
   ibid. 96, 37. For a contemporary overview of the contraband trade, see
   Solórzano, *Política indiana,* Bk. VI, Ch. x, Nos. 24 and 31. *Recopilación,*
   Bk. VIII, Title xvii. Woodrow W. Borah, *Early Colonial Trade and Navigation Between Mexico and Peru* (Ibero-Americana, No. 38, Berkeley
   and Los Angeles, 1954).

33 In his letters of April 20 and 22, 1616, Dr. Morga does not mention the
   contraband episode, nor does he request a new assignment. Two months
   before, on February 20, 1616, he did ask for a new post. All three letters
   are in the AGI/AQ 10. Retana published only the letter of February 20.
   Retana, "Estudio," p. 130, and Lietz, ed., *Calendar,* No. 23.

34 Schäfer, *El consejo,* II, 29.

35 Retana has published the sentence of Dr. Morga. Retana, "Estudio," pp.
   148 ff. The original is in the AGI/AQ 12. Hereafter cited as "Morga
   sentence."

36 One of the oidores in the audiencia of Lima served as *juez privativo de la
   ropa de contrabando,* an assignment that Solórzano once held. Solórzano,
   Política indiana, Bk. VI, Ch. x, Nos. 24 and 31. On the continuation of
   this illegal trade, see viceroy to king: February 10, 1626, AGI/AL 40;
   ACS, *Libro de acuerdos de la real audiencia, 1630–41:* November 13,
   1633; and Jorge Juan and Antonio de Ulloa, *Noticias secretas de America . . . ,* ed. Rufino Blanco-Fombona (Biblioteca Ayacucho, Vols. XXXI–
   XXXII, Madrid, 1918), XXXI, 220 ff.

37 The allegation that Dr. Morga said in private conversation that the presidency of Quito cost him 10,000 pesos was made by one of the bitterest
   enemies of his regime. Juan García de Solís to king: April 28, 1620, AGI/
   AQ 29. On the disputed identity of the author, see Chapter 10, notes 27
   and 28. The available evidence is inconclusive.

38 Morga sentence, AGI/AQ 12, and Retana, "Estudio," pp. 148 ff.

39 See note 38.

40 Ruth Pike, *Enterprise and Adventure: The Genoese in Seville and the
   Opening of the New World* (Cornell University Press, 1966), pp. 93–94.

41 For a list of the contents of the library, heavily weighted toward theology,
   morality, history, and law, see Retana, "Estudio," pp. 158–59.

42 The bill of sale has been published by José María Vargas, O.P., *El arte
   quiteño en los siglos xvi, xvii y xviii* (Quito, 1949). The original is in the
   AGI/AQ 11. Retana published the inventory of Morga's extensive art
   collection taken shortly after his death. Retana, "Estudio," pp. 159 ff.

43 Morga sentence, AGI/AQ 12, and Retana, "Estudio," pp. 148 ff.

44 See note 43. For the criminal career of Nicolás de Larraspuru, see Chapter
   9.

45 Morga sentence, AGI/AQ 12, and Retana, "Estudio," pp. 148 ff. García
   de Solís to king: April 28, 1620, AGI/AQ 29.

46 Testimony of Cristóbal de Troya in the Morga-Velasco suit, AGI/EC 919.

Between card games the magistrates and their wives went into the adjoining garden where they observed or engaged in exercises with small bulls and calves.

47 *Ibid.* Morga sentence, AGI/AQ 12, and Retana, "Estudio," pp. 148 ff.

48 *Recopilación,* Bk. II, Title xvi, laws 74 and 75; Bk. VII, Title ii, laws 1–3.

49 Morga sentence, AGI/AQ 12, and Retana, "Estudio," pp. 148 ff.

50 The president of the audiencia of Guatemala, Álvaro Quiñones y Osorio, 1633–40, prohibited all card gambling in private homes so as to concentrate all such activity in his own drawing room. Thomas Gage, *The English-American, His Travail by Sea and Land; Or a New Survey of the West Indies,* 2nd ed. (London, 1648), p. 126. This practice was also common-place among the corregidores in the provinces. Juan de Aponte Figueroa, "Memorial que trata de la reformación del reino del Pirú," April 24, 1622, *Colección de documentos inéditos para la historia de España,* ed. Martín Fernández de Navarrete *et al.* (112 vols., Madrid, 1842–95), LI, 525.

51 Federico González Suárez, *Historia general de la república del Ecuador* (7 vols., Quito, 1890–1903), III, 115.

52 *Ibid.,* IV, 361–66.

53 Retana, "Estudio," p. 109. During the visita general of Lic. Diego Landeras y Velasco (1607–9), one of Dr. Morga's colleagues in the sala de crimen was suspended. Alcaldes de crimen to the king: April 25, 1607, AGI/Audiencia de Mexico 72. Indicative of the esteem in which he was held in Mexico, Dr. Morga received additional appointments such as *auditor de guerra,* administrator of the estate of the marquesado de Oaxaca, and *consultor* to the Holy Office of the Inquisition. Retana, "Estudio," p. 118. A consultor of the Holy Office was a lay magistrate who rendered occasional legal advice, not including religious doctrine, to the Inquisition. For Morga's activities, see Archivo General de la Nación (Mexico), Inquisición 274, exped. 16; 275, expeds. 1, 6, 14. For the marquesado de Oaxaca (the estate of Hernán Cortés), see Archivo General de la Nación (Mexico), Hospital de Jesús 434, expeds. 7 and 8.

54 Tello de Velasco sentence: November 14, 1637, AGI/EC 921a.

55 Sentence of Lic. Melchor Suárez de Poago: November 14, 1637, *ibid.*

56 King to viceroy of Mexico: February 22, 1638, AGI/AQ 209 (II, foll. 120–21). This cedula is also in the Archivo General de la Nación (Mexico), *Reales cédulas,* I, exped. 234, foll. 440–41.

57 Consulta: May 17, 1607, AGI/AQ 1. Cedula to audiencia: May 4, 1627, *ibid.* 87.

58 Sentences of Diego de Valencia León and Andrés de Orozco Guzmán: November 14, 1637, AGI/EC 921a.

59 In 1614, for example, there occurred a clash of jurisdictions in which the audiencia in Quito attempted to depose the governor of Popayán, Francisco Sarmiento de Sotomayor. The latter retired to the other side of the Cauca and continued to govern the province until his term of office expired. Gustavo Arboleda, *Historia de Cali* (3 vols., Cali: Universidad del Valle,

1956), I, 154–55. ACS, *Libro de acuerdos de la real audiencia, 1610–30,* March 6, April 6, April 30, August 14, September 1, 1614.

60 Guillermo Lohmann Villena, *El corregidor de indios en el Perú bajo los Austrias* (Madrid, 1957), pp. 308–14, 595–600.

61 *Ibid.* For the responsibilities of the governors and the corregidores, see *Recopilación,* Bk. V, Title ii.

62 Lohmann Villena, *El corregidor,* pp. 308–14, 596–600.

63 Antonio Vásquez de Espinosa, *Compendio y descripción de las Indias occidentales* (Washington, D.C., 1948), p. 721.

64 Lohmann Villena, *El corregidor,* pp. 421–47.

65 Fiscal Blas de Torres Altamirano to king: April 6, 1605, AGI/AQ 9. For that particular fiscal's own shortcomings, see Chapter 10, notes 37–39. Another contemporary, a retired military officer, wrote that the corregidores in upper Peru "are like the locusts in Castile; wherever they go, they consume everything and lay waste the land": Aponte Figueroa, "Memorial," p. 525.

66 See the following consultas involving appointments of governors and corregidores in the AGI/AQ 1: April 29, 1614, January 21, 1616, January 19, 1619, November 14, 1620, January 22, 1620, November 14, 1622, December 20, 1622, January 10, 1622, January 30, 1626.

67 As quoted in Martín Fernández de Navarrete, *Vida de Miguel de Cervantes Saavedra* . . . (Madrid, 1819), p. 76. For a discussion and the original documentation of the frustrated bureaucratic career of Cervantes, see *ibid.,* pp. 74–77 and 311–48.

68 Lohmann Villena, *El corregidor,* pp. 115–34. This study is meticulously and abundantly documented from the AGI for upper and lower Peru, but it contains only a handful of references to the audiencia kingdom of Quito. The same practice prevailed in the viceroyalty of Mexico. Pablo González Casanova, "Aspectos políticos de Palafox y Mendoza," *Revista de historia de América,* No. 17 (June, 1944), pp. 44 ff.

69 Cabildo of Quito to Gerónimo de Escobedo: March 3, 1616, AMQ, XIII, foll. 168–70. Cabildo of Quito to Alonso Vela: [1617?], *ibid.,* foll. 170–76. Morga to king: April 15, 1618, AGI/AQ 10. Cedula to viceroy: April 26, 1618, AGI/AL 571, and Kontezke, *Colección,* II, 198. Viceroy to king: March 27, 1619, AGI/AL 38. Lic. Merlo de la Fuente to king: April 24, 1619, AGI/AL 96. *Recopilación,* Bk. III, Title ii, law 27. Morga to king: April 15, 1622, and April 15, 1627, AGI/AQ 10, 11. Cabildo of Quito to Fr. Marcos de Valencia: March 10, 1628, AMQ, XIII, foll. 191–92. Cedula to the viceroy: July 20, 1629, AMQ, XI, fol. 73.

70 León Pinelo, *Autos,* Consulta of March 26, 1627, No. lxviii.

71 Consulta: May 17, 1607, AGI/AL 2, and Konetzke, *Colección,* II, 124–26.

72 Jerónimo de Castillo de Bovadilla, *Política para corregidores y señores de vassallos en tiempo de paz y guerra* . . . (Barcelona, 1616), Bk. I, Ch. xvi.

73 George Kubler, "The Quechua in the Colonial World," *Handbook of South American Indians,* ed. Julian Steward (7 vols., Washington, D.C., 1946–

59), II, 367–70. Lohmann Villena, *El corregidor,* pp. 421–47. Audiencia to viceroy: March 2, 1601, ANH, I, No. 3. Torres Altamirano to king: April 8, 1605, AGI/AQ 9. Caciques to audiencia: November 1, 1608, ANH, I, No. 19. Morga to king: April 20, 1616, AGI/AQ 10. Fernando de Cozar, O.F.M., to president of council: April 23, 1619, and Cedula to audiencia: October 20, 1621, "Recopilación de cédulas despachadas en diferentes tiempos por S. M. . . . para la real audiencia . . . del Quito del Pirú, 1589–1632," ed. Antonio de Morga ms. (1632) Biblioteca Nacional, Mexico City, Nos. 44 and 69. Viceroy to king: March 27, 1619, AGI/AL 38. Oidor Diego de Zorrilla to king: April 30, 1619, AGI/AQ 10. O.S.A. provincial superior to king: April 2, 1619, AGI/AQ 87. Convent of Chambo to king: April 23, 1619, AGI/AQ 87. Suárez de Poago to king: April 23, 1620, AGI/AQ 10. King to audiencia: July 15, 1620, AGI/AQ 209. Suárez de Poago to king: April 29, 1622, AGI/AQ 10. Residencia of Antonio de Villacis: 1622, AGI/EC 909. Lic. Mañozca to king: April 10, 1625, AGI/AQ 61. ACS, *Libro de acuerdos de la real audiencia, 1630–41:* February 6, 1634, January 31, 1636. Suárez de Poago to king: April 10, 1636, AGI/AQ 12. Aponte, Figueroa, "Memorial," pp. 521–25. For a pioneer monograph, see Carlos E. Castañeda, "The Corregidor in Spanish Colonial Administration," *Hispanic-American Historical Review,* IX, No. 4 (November, 1929), 446–70. Also see note 76.

74 Solórzano, *Política indiana,* Bk. V, Ch. ii, No. 52. For some comments on venality in the lower echelons of the administration in Mexico, see William Dusenberry, *The Mexican Mesta, The Administration of Ranching in Colonial Mexico* (Urbana: University of Illinois Press, 1963), pp. 172–73. His explanation of corruption, however, errs on the side of oversimplification. Also see González Casanova, "Aspectos políticos de Palafox," pp. 44–45.

75 Morga, ed., "Recopilación de cédulas," April 24, 1618, No. 10. Zorrilla to king: April 30, 1619, AGI/AQ 10. Suárez de Poago to king: April 29, 1622, AGI/AQ 10. Residencia sentence of Antonio de Villacis: 1622, AGI/EC 909. Residencia sentence of Sancho Fernández de Miranda: 1624, AGI/EC 909. Morga to king: April 19, 1624, AGI/AQ 10. Oidor Manuel Tello de Velasco, residencia sentences for 1632–34, AGI/Contaduría general del Consejo de Indias 10. For the formal procedures of a residencia trial, see Pedro Pérez Landero Otáñez y Castro, *Práctica de visitas y residencias de los reinos del Perú* . . . (Naples, 1646), pp. 164 ff. In Chapter 11 there is a discussion about the differences and the similarities between the residencia and the visita general. Also see *Recopilación,* Bk. V, Title xv.

76 Torres Altamirano to king: April 9, 1604, AGI/AQ 9. Morga to king: April 15, 1620, *ibid.* 10.

77 Lohmann Villena, *El corregidor,* pp. 463–505. Audiencia to king: April 20, 1606, AGI/AQ 9. Audiencia to viceroy: March 2, 1601, ANH, I, No. 3. Morga to king: April 20, 1616, AGI/AQ 10. Oidor Matías de Peralta to audiencia: July 18, 1618, ANH, I, No. 37. Zorrilla to king: April 30, 1619, AGI/AQ 10. Viceroy to king: March 27, 1619, AGI/AL 38.

78 Mañozca to king: February 28, 1625, AGI/AQ 61. Also see Chapter 11, note 25.

79 Zorrilla to king: April 30, 1619, AGI/AQ 10.

80 *Recopilación,* Bk. II, Title xv, law 68; Bk. V, Title xii, law 8, and Title xv, law 4.

81 *Ibid.,* Bk. III, Title ii, law 68; Bk. V, Title ii, law 8, and Title ii, law 9. León Pinelo, *Autos,* September 3, 1608, No. xxviii.

82 *Recopilación,* Bk. II, Titles xxxiii and xvi, laws 89–90. Pérez Landero, *Práctica de visitas,* pp. 228 ff. John H. Parry, *The Sale of Public Office in the Spanish Indies under the Habsburgs* (Ibero-Americana No. 37, Berkeley and Los Angeles, 1953), p. 17.

83 For two reports of oidores-visitors, see Peralta to audiencia: July 18, 1614, ANH, I, No. 37. Zorrilla to king: April 30, 1619, AGI/AQ 10.

84 Morga to king: April 15, 1620, AGI/AQ 10. Also see Chapter 10, notes 18–22.

85 Charles Gibson, *The Aztecs under Spanish Rule: A History of the Indians of the Valley of Mexico 1519–1810* (Stanford, 1964), pp. 92–93.

86 *Recopilación,* Bk. I, Title xiii. Also see notes 89 and 90.

87 *Recopilación,* Bk. I, Title xvi, law 16. Solórzano, *Política indiana,* Bk. II, Ch. xxiii. Torres Altamirano to king: April 17, 1602, and April 9, 1604, AGI/AQ 9. Audiencia to king, April 21, 1621, AGI/AQ 10. Fiscal vs. Bishop: October 4, 1657, AGI/AQ 13.

88 See Chapter 4, note 45.

89 Martín de Ocampo: April 24, 1608, ANH, I, No. 17. Francisco de la Serna to audiencia: February 6, 1610, *ibid.,* No. 26. Audiencia to viceroy: [1612?], *ibid.,* No. 23. Francisco Centeno Maldonado to audiencia: October 4, 1619, *ibid.,* No. 52. "Memorial de los Indios principales del pueblo de Zangolqui de agravios que reciban en las haciendas del valle de Chillo de la Compañía de Jesús": March, 1623, AGI/AQ 10. Fernando Gamonal to audiencia: October 21, 1626, ANH, I, No. 72. Indians of Chuacalle vs. Juan de Luna, O.S.A.: 1632, AGI/AQ 11.

90 Peralta to audiencia: July 18, 1614, ANH, I, No. 37. Zorrilla to king: April 30, 1619, AGI/AQ 10. Centeno Maldonado to audiencia: October 4, 1619, ANH, I, No. 52. Audiencia vs. Augustinians, 1620–31, AGI/AQ 11. Fr. Antonio Gracián de la Trinidad to king: September 9, 1624, AGI/AQ 61. Governor Álvaro de Cárdenas to king: November 12, 1625, AGI/AQ 10. Suárez de Poago to king: April 15, 1630, AGI/AQ 11. Indians of Chuacalle vs. Juan de Luna, O.S.A., 1632, AGI/AQ 11. Morga to king: April 15, 1636, AGI/AQ 12. Autos of the audiencia *re* doctrinas in Latacunga: 1636, AGI/AQ 12. Cristóbal López to audiencia: April 2, 1639, ANH, III, No. 126. Juan López de Canizares to audiencia: November 27, 1639, ANH, III, No. 130.

91 José Jouanen, S.J., *Historia de la compañía de Jesús en la antigua provincia de Quito, 1570–1696* (2 vols., Quito, 1941), I, 138–39.

92 John L. Phelan, *The Hispanization of the Philippines: Spanish Aims and Filipino Responses, 1565–1700* (Madison, 1959), p. 109. François Che-

valier, *Land and Society in Colonial Mexico, The Great Hacienda*, ed. and trans. Lesley Byrd Simpson (Berkeley and Los Angeles: University of California Press, 1963), pp. 239–50.

93 More archival research needs to be done on this topic before hard and firm conclusions can be drawn. For that matter, the whole area of provincial administration in the Indies has scarcely been touched by recent research. The notable exception is Lohmann Villena's study on the corregidores in Peru.

94 Consultas: March 15 and May 5, 1605, AGI/AQ 1.

95 For the minutes of this committee, see ACS, *Libro de acuerdos de hacienda, 1601–57.*

96 *Ordenanzas reales para el gobierno de los tribunales de la contaduría major:* Valladolid, 1606, in the *Recopilación*, Bk. VIII, Title i.

97 Cedula to Mañozca: October 2, 1622, AGI/AQ 61.

98 Mañozca to king: March 6, 1625, and April 10, 1625, *ibid.* Treasury to king: April 20, 1625, *ibid.* ACS, *Libro de acuerdos de hacienda, 1601–57:* January 16, 1625. Mañozca to king: March 6, 1626, AGI/AQ 61. Auto of Lic. Mañozca: 1627, AGI/AQ 62 .

99 Auto of Lic. Mañozca: 1627, AGI/AQ 62. Treasury to king: March 4, 1626, and April 26, 1627, *ibid.* 20.

100 Consulta: May 5, 1631, *ibid.* 2.

101 Clarence H. Haring, *The Spanish Empire in America* (New York, 1947), pp. 145–48. *Real ordenanza para el establecimiento é instrucción de in-tendentes de exército y provincia en el reino de la Nueva España* (Madrid, 1786); for an English translation, see Lillian Estelle Fisher, *The Intendant System in Spanish America* (Berkeley: University of California Press, 1929), pp. 93–331. Also see Alain Viellard-Baron, "L'établissement des intendants aux Indes par Charles III," *Revista de Indias*, XII (July-September, 1952), 521–46. The most thoughtful and best documented study of the intendant reform is that of John Lynch, *Spanish Colonial Administration, 1782–1810: The Intendant System in the Viceroyalty of the Rio de la Plata* (London: Athlone Press, 1958). Also see Luis Navarro García, *Intendencias en Indias* (Seville: Escuela de Estudios Hispano-Americanos, 1959).

102 Lynch, *Spanish Colonial Administration*, p. 136.

103 Miss Fisher has published some divergent opinions of contemporaries on the effectiveness of the reform. Fisher, *The Intendant System*, pp. 73–96. Also see Lynch, *Spanish Colonial Administration*, pp. 279–89.

104 Lynch, *Spanish Colonial Administration*, pp. 283–84.

CHAPTER 8: THE SINNERS AND THE SAINT

1 The two most vivid accounts of the spirit and the character of baroque culture are Irving Leonard, *Baroque Times in Old Mexico* (Ann Arbor, 1959), and Mariano Picón-Salas, *A Cultural History of Spanish America from Conquest to Independence* (Berkeley and Los Angeles, 1962), pp. 85–105.

2 Reginald Trevor Davies, *The Golden Century of Spain: 1501–1621* (London, 1961), p. 230.

3 John H. Elliott, *Imperial Spain: 1469–1716* (London, 1963), p. 295.

4 Sister María de Jesús' work *La mística ciudad de Dios* went through 49 editions in several languages. Reginald Trevor Davies, *Spain in Decline, 1621–1700* (London, 1961), pp. 58, 59, 60. F. Silvela, *Cartas de Sor María de Ágreda* (2 vols., Madrid, 1885–86).

5 George Kubler and Martin Soria, *Art and Architecture in Spain and Portugal and their American Dominions, 1500–1800* (Baltimore, 1959), p. 88. My brief discussion closely follows Kubler's account: *ibid.*, pp. 86–88, 173, 318, 320, and Harold E. Wethey, *Colonial Architecture and Sculpture in Peru* (Cambridge, Mass., 1949), pp. 18, 73, 262–63, 295. Also see the following: Pál Kelemen, *Baroque and Rococo in Latin America* (New York: Macmillan, 1951), pp. 137–50, 205 ff. José Gabriel Navarro, *Religious Architecture in Quito* (New York: Metropolitan Museum of Art, 1945). José Gabriel Navarro, *La escultura en el Ecuador* (Madrid: A. Marzo, 1939). José Gabriel Navarro, *Artes plásticas ecuatorianas* (Mexico: Fondo de Cultura Económica, 1945). Robert Stevenson, "Music in Quito: Four Centuries," *The Hispanic-American Historical Review*, XLIII (May, 1963), 246–66. Benjamin Gento Sanz, O.F.M., "The History and Art of the Church and the Monastery of San Francisco de Quito," *The Americas*, IV (1947–48), 175–94.

6 "Relación de los celebres y famosas fiestas, alegrías y de mostraciones que hiço la muy noble y muy leal ciudad de San Francisco de Quito en el Pirú al dichoissimo y feliz nacimiento del principe de España, don Baltasar Carlos," AMQ, XCV, foll. 88–92, 95. Federico González Suárez, *Historia general de la república del Ecuador* (7 vols., Quito, 1890–1903), IV, 467–70. R. de Carvajal y Robles, *Fiestas de Lima por el nacimiento del principe Baltasar Carlos*, ed. F. López Estrada (Seville: Escuela de Estudios Hispano-Americanos, 1950: 1st ed., Lima, 1632).

7 Constantino Bayle, S.J., *Los cabildos seculares en la América española* (Madrid, 1952), pp. 279, 300, 312, 317, 329, 659–70, 681–87, 689, 691–712.

8 W. E. Retana, "Estudio preliminar," in Antonio de Morga, *Sucesos de las islas filipinas* (Madrid, 1909), p. 126.

9 A partial text of the will is in Morga, *Sucesos*, pp. 163–67. The full text can be found in "Autos hechos por el señor don Alonso de Castillo . . . sobre los bienes de doctor Antonio de Morga," AGI/AQ 12.

10 José María Vargas, O.P., *Historia de la iglesia en el Ecuador durante el patronato español* (Quito, 1962), pp. 225–30.

11 *Ibid.* Bishop to king: April 20, 1618, AGI/AQ 77. González Suárez, *Historia*, IV, 73–79. Also see Cedula: October 19, 1600, AGI/AQ 427, Bk. 30, fol. 383.

12 For a discussion of Solórzano's regalism, see José María Ots Capdequí and Javier Malagón, *Solórzano y la Política indiana* (Mexico and Buenos Aires, 1965), pp. 68 ff.

13 Retana, "Estudio," pp. 44, 95.

14 Morga sentence, AGI/AQ 12, and Retana, "Estudio," pp. 148 ff.

15 Oidor Manuel Tello de Velasco to king: February 18, 1626, *ibid.* 61. "Interrogatorio presentado por el oidor D. Manuel Tello de Velasco y de las respuestas de algunos testigos, referentes al Dr. Antonio de Morga," 1625, AGI/EC 919. Retana, "Estudio," pp. 131–34.

16 See note 15.

17 The originals are in the AGI/EC 921. Retana has published the six love notes in Spanish. Retana, "Estudio," pp. 139–41.

18 Lic. Juan de Mañozca to king: December 9, 1626, AGI/EC 921.

19 "Limpieza de sangre de doña Catalina de Alcega," 1609, Archivo General de la Nación (Mexico), Inquisición 286. Retana, "Estudio," pp. 120–26.

20 *Calendar of Philippine Documents in the Ayer Collection of the Newberry Library,* ed. Paul Lietz (Chicago, The Newberry Library, 1956), No. 23. Retana, "Estudio," p. 146.

21 See Chapter 10, notes 29–31.

22 Tello de Velasco sentence: November 14, 1637, AGI/EC 921a.

23 Sentences of Melchor Suárez de Poago, Diego de Valencia León, and Andrés de Orozco Guzmán, *ibid.*

24 Metcalfe in Delhi is an obvious example. Philip Mason, *The Men Who Ruled India* (2 vols., London, 1953), I, 266–78.

25 On the clergy's failure to observe the vow of chastity the documentation is copious. Fiscal Blas de Torres Altamirano to king: April 17, 1602, and April 9, 1604, AGI/AQ 9. The diocesan synod of 1596 found it necessary to prohibit priests from attending in person the baptisms, the weddings, or the funerals of their own children and grandchildren on pain of a fine of 20 ducats. Luis Lopes de Solís, "Constituciones sinodales del Quito," ms., Univ. of Wisconsin Library, Ch. 59. The regular clergymen were often accused of avarice as well as violations of celibacy. See Chapter 7, notes 86–90. No more forthright and better documented indictment of the short-comings of the clergy can be found than in the writings of González Suárez, the historian, who also became archbishop of Quito. González Suárez, *Historia,* IV, 48–61, 138–56, 169–73, 196–204, 351–63, 421 ff. Archbishop González Suárez' candor aroused vehement criticism in clerical and conservative circles. Adam Szászdi, "The Historiography of the Re-public of Ecuador," *Hispanic-American Historical Review,* XLIV, No. 4 (November, 1964), 511–14. González Suárez is the founder of modern scientific historiography in Ecuador. The Church had as much difficulty in enforcing compliance of sacerdotal celibacy in the Philippines as it did in Quito. See my *Hispanization of the Philippines: Spanish Aims and Fili-pino Responses, 1565–1700* (Madison, 1959), pp. 35–40.

26 Frances Parkinson Keyes, *The Rose and the Lily* (New York, 1961), pp. 213–14. Mrs. Keyes has a useful bibliography: *ibid.,* pp. 243 ff. The most important primary source is Jacinto Morán de Butrón, *Vida de Santa Mariana de Jesús* (Quito, 1955); the first edition was published in 1697. Alonso de Rojas, S.J., *Oración funebre* (Lima, 1646), and reprinted in Diego de Córdoba y Salinas, O.F.M., *Crónica franciscana de las provincias*

del Perú, ed. Lino G. Canedo, O.F.M. (Washington, D.C., 1957; 1st ed., Lima, 1651), pp. 959–66. *Proceso informativo, 1670–78,* in *Documentos para la historia de la Beata Mariana de Jesús* . . . (Quito: Imprenta del Clero, 1902). In addition, there are 30 volumes of testimony taken in the eighteenth century which are in the archives of the archdiocese of Quito. Among the secondary sources, the most useful are the following. González Suárez, *Historia,* IV, 219–23. Aurelio Espinosa Pólit, *Santa Mariana de Jesús, hija de la compañía de Jesús, según los procesos* (Quito, 1957). Wilfrido Loor, *Santa Mariana de Jesús según los procesos* (Quito: La Prensa Católica, 1954). Augusto Arias, *Mariana de Jesús* (Quito: Talleres Gráficos del Ministerio de Educación, 1944).

27 For the events leading up to her canonization, see Keyes, *The Rose and the Lily,* pp. 223–30.

28 *Ibid.,* p. 183.

29 Vargas, *Historia de la iglesia,* p. 225. González Suárez, *Historia,* IV, 283. For efforts to reform the convents under the Bourbons, see Asunción Lavrin, "Ecclesiastical Reform of Nunneries in New Spain in the Eighteenth Century," *The Americas,* XXII, No. 2 (October, 1965), 182–203.

30 González Suárez, *Historia,* IV, 283–95.

31 Vargas, *Historia de la iglesia,* p. 202. Throughout the Spanish and Portuguese empires, colonists did on occasion urge that the convents of nuns be closed so that the young ladies with dowries would be encouraged to become mothers of future citizens. Phelan, *Hispanization,* pp. 106–7. Charles R. Boxer, *Portuguese Society in the Tropics: The Municipal Councils of Goa, Macao, Bahia, and Luanda 1510–1800* (Madison and Milwaukee, 1965), pp. 64–65, 92–94, 145.

32 Morán de Butrón, *Vida de Santa Mariana,* pp. 389–90, 397–98.

CHAPTER 9: JUSTICE

1 John H. Parry, *The Audiencia of New Galicia in the Sixteenth Century* (Cambridge, 1948), p. 133. The ordinances of Monzón are also in the AGI/AQ 211.

2 *Recopilación de las leyes de los reynos de las Indias* (4 vols., Madrid, 1681), Bk. II, Title ii, law 58. Juan de Solórzano y Pereira, *Política indiana* (5 vols., Madrid, 1647), Bk. V, Ch. xvii.

3 Parry, *The Audiencia,* pp. 160–61. A. Esmein, *A History of Continental Criminal Procedure with Special Reference to France,* trans. John Simpson (Boston: Little, Brown & Co., 1913), pp. 228–89, 295–301.

4 My discussion of Spanish judicial procedures closely follows John Parry's authoritative treatment. Parry, *The Audiencia,* pp. 150–62.

5 One prison warden received a sentence of six years as a galley slave for allowing prisoners to escape: ACS, *Libro de acuerdos de la real audiencia, 1630–41:* October 11, 1632. For another case, see *ibid.:* July 16, 1635. The Council of the Indies reprimanded Dr. Morga in his sentence for not maintaining separate quarters in the audiencia jail for men and women.

Morga sentence, October 26, 1636, AGI/AQ 12, No. 68; and W. E. Retana, "Estudio preliminar," in Antonio de Morga, *Sucesos de las islas filipinas* (Madrid, 1909), pp. 147–53.

6 Ronald Goldfarb, "Crime, Wealth and Justice," *New Republic* (August 22, 1964), pp. 15–16.

7 Ricardo Levene commented on the absence of the death penalty but offered no explanation. Ricardo Levene, *Historia del derecho argentino* (11 vols., Buenos Aires, 1945–58), II, 141. The only death penalty that, to my knowledge, was actually enforced was that of a Negro condemned to die by hanging for homicide. ACS, *Libro de acuerdos de la real audiencia, 1630–41:* December 23, 1630. For a homicide which was not punished by the death penalty, see ACS, *Libro de acuerdos de la real audiencia, 1610–30:* June 26, 1625. Lic. Francisco Rodríquez Plaza, subsequently twice acting fiscal of the audiencia, was convicted as a young man for the murder of Domingo Agurto. The audiencia commuted the death penalty issued by a lower court to a period of exile from the kingdom and a fine. Lic. Juan de Mañozca to king: April 10, 1625, AGI/AQ 61. Although the audiencia did impose the death penalty on Nicolás de Larraspuru for the murder of Pedro Sayago del Hoyo, that was a major scandal with far-ranging political implications, which will be discussed at some length shortly. The sentence was not carried out, for the culprit fled the kingdom.

8 Thomas Gage, *The English-American, His Travail by Sea and Land: Or a New Survey of the West Indies,* 2nd ed. (London, 1648), p. 126.

9 Parry, *The Audiencia,* p. 160.

10 President Antonio de Morga to king: May 30, 1623, AGI/AQ 10.

11 Antonio Domínguez Ortiz, *Política y hacienda de Felipe IV* (Madrid, 1960), p. 282.

12 ACS, *Libro de acuerdos de la real audiencia, 1610–30:* December 1, 1630, August 27, 1626.

13 Pedro Sayago del Hoyo was not a ringleader in the disturbances of Potosí, but he was an activist who was usually there when there was a brawl. Alberto Crespo, *La guerra entre Vicuñas y Vascongados en Potosí, 1622–1625* (Lima, 1956), pp. 65, 66, 68, 101, 119, 124, 152, 154.

14 Federico González Suárez, *Historia general de la república del Ecuador* (7 vols., Quito, 1890–1903), IV, 129–33.

15 Fiscal Melchor Suárez de Poago to king: February 4, 1627, AGI/AQ 11.

16 For accounts of the crime, see *ibid.* Lic. Juan de Mañozca to king: March 20, 1627, *ibid.* 62. Audiencia to king: March 11, 1628, *ibid.* 11. Suárez de Poago to king: April 16, 1630, *ibid.* Morga to king: April 20, 1631, *ibid.*

17 ACS, *Libro de acuerdos de la real audiencia, 1610–30:* January 1, 1627. The fiscal made much of Lic. Mañozca's partiality toward Larraspuru, but he failed to note that Dr. Morga was equally friendly toward the culprit. González Suárez follows the fiscal's account too closely, and in this particular case he deals too harshly with the visitor general: González Suárez, *Historia,* IV, 129–33.

18 ACS, *Libro de acuerdos de la real audiencia, 1610–30:* January 1, 1627.

19 *Ibid.:* January 21, 1627.
20 *Ibid.*
21 Morga sentence, AGI/AQ 12, Nos. 24 and 25; and also Retana, "Estudio," pp. 147–53.
22 Morga to king: April 20, 1631, AGI/AQ 11.
23 Audiencia to king: March 11, 1628, *ibid.*
24 Larraspuru acquired his encomienda largely on the basis of his father's distinguished reputation. Consulta: January 15, 1625, *ibid.* 1. Consulta: January 19, 1627, *ibid.*
25 ACS, *Libro de acuerdos de la real audiencia, 1610–30:* January 21, 1627, October 7, 1632.
26 *Ibid.:* February 5, 1627.
27 Suárez de Poago to king: April 16, 1630, AGI/AQ 11.
28 *Ibid.*
29 *Ibid.* "Averiguaciones y informaciones por el s. d. Galdós de Valencia . . . contra don Nicolás de Larraspuru . . . 1631," *ibid.* Galdós de Valencia to king: January 14, 1632, *ibid.* Don Nicolás attempted to claim immunity from the jurisdiction of the audiencia in his capacity as a knight of the order of Santiago. The crown flatly denied any such pretension, and this particular cedula ended up in the *Recopilación: Recopilación,* Bk. II, Title xv, law 96.
30 Morga to king: April 20, 1631, AGI/AQ 11.
31 Helmut G. Koenigsberger, *The Government of Sicily under Philip II of Spain: A Study in the Practice of Empire* (London and New York, 1951), pp. 116–22.
32 President Lope Antonio de Munive to king: July 30, 1681, AGI/AQ 69; and Alberto Landazuri Soto, *El régimen laboral indígena en la real audiencia de Quito* (Madrid, 1959), p. 126.
33 *Libro primero de cabildos de la villa de San Miguel de Ibarra, 1604–1617,* ed. Jorge Garcés (Archivo Municipal, Vol. XII, Quito, 1937), pp. 31–36, 46–47. Fiscal Blas de Torres Altamirano to council: April 17, 1606, AGI/AQ 9. Suárez de Poago to king: April 29, 1622, AGI/AQ 10.
34 The charge of the fiscal and Diego de Niebla's defense, which are included in "Testimonios de las sentencias de vista y revista pronunciadas contra Diego de Niebla," are attached to Morga's letter to the king: April 15, 1620, AGI/AQ 10. For other accounts critical of Niebla, see Torres Altamirano to king: April 17, 1606, *ibid.* 9. Oidor Diego de Zorrilla to king: April 24, 1617, *ibid.* 10. Suárez de Poago to council: April 29, 1622, *ibid.* Also see ACS, *Libro de acuerdos de la real audiencia, 1610–30:* December 5, 1611, November 8, 1612, May 7, 1612.
35 Morga to king: April 15, 1620, AGI/AQ 10. Also attached is the petition of his wife of January 25, 1620.
36 Diego de Niebla to king: March 4, 1617, and April 28, 1620, *ibid.* 29.
37 Morga to king: April 25, 1621, *ibid.*
38 Morga to king: April 15, 1622, *ibid.*
39 Cedula to Morga: June 7, 1621, *ibid.* 201 (I, foll. 265–66).
40 Goldfarb, "Crime, Wealth and Justice."

41 *Recopilación,* Bk. II, Title xxix, and Bk. V, Title v, law 29.
42 As quoted in Goldfarb, "Crime, Wealth and Justice," p. 16.
43 Richard Morse, "Toward a Theory of Spanish American Government," *Journal of the History of Ideas,* XV, No. 1 (January, 1954), 72.

CHAPTER 10: THE COMING OF THE VISITA GENERAL—THE GATHERING STORM

1 Cedula to Lic. Juan de Mañozca: March 23, 1622, AGI/Audiencia de Santa Fe 244.
2 Treasury to king: March 10, 1628, AGI/AQ 20. Schäfer's figure of 29,000 pesos covers only the first 14 months of the visita general, which lasted for 32 months: Ernesto Schäfer, *El consejo real y supremo de las Indias* (2 vols., Seville, 1935–47), II, 130. The exact figure was 29,978 pesos, seven reales, and three cuartillos, according to the maliciously accurate report of the treasury. Treasury to king: February 25, 1626, AGI/AQ 61.
3 Schäfer, *El consejo,* II, 130.
4 The principal primary sources for both the residencia and the visita general are the following. Juan de Matienzo, *Gobierno del Perú* (Buenos Aires: Compañía Sudamericana de Billetes de Banco, 1910). The author was oidor in Charcas from 1560 to 1573. *Recopilación de las leyes de los reynos de las Indias* (4 vols., Madrid, 1681), Bk. II, Title xxxiv, and Bk. V, Title xv. Juan de Solórzano y Pereira, *Política indiana* (5 vols., Madrid, 1647), Bk. V, Ch. x. Pedro Pérez Landero Otáñez y Castro, *Práctica de visitas y residencias de los reynos del Perú . . .* (Naples, 1646). Jerónimo de Castillo de Bovadilla, *Política para corregidores y señores de vassallos en tiempo de paz y guerra . . .* (Barcelona, 1916). Among the principal secondary sources are the following. Clarence Haring, *The Spanish Empire in America* (New York, 1947), pp. 148–57. José María Ots Capdequí, *Manual de historia del derecho español en las Indias* (Buenos Aires, 1945), pp. 400–401. Carmelo Viñas Mey, "El régimen jurídico de responsabilidad en la América indiana," *Revista de las Españas,* III, IV (January–February, and August, 1928, January–February, 1929), pp. 17–21, 362–69, 36–54. Herbert I. Priestley, *José de Gálvez, Visitor General of New Spain, 1765–1771* (University of California Publications in History, No. 5, Berkeley, 1916), pp. 83–134. José María de la Peña Cámara, *A List of Spanish Residencias in the Archives of the Indies, 1516–1775,* with an introduction by John Finan (Washington, D.C., 1955). José María Mariluz Urquijo, *Ensayo sobre los juicios de residencia indianas* (Seville, 1952). Guillermo Céspedes del Castillo, "La visita como institución indiana," *Anuario de estudios americanos,* III (Seville, 1946), 984–1021. Enrique Ruiz Guiñazú, *La magistratura indiana* (Buenos Aires, 1916). Schäfer, *El consejo,* II, 128–57. Many of the proceedings and even the sentences of many visitas generales have been lost.
5 Priestley, *Gálvez.* Vicente Palacio Atard, *Areche y Guirior, observaciones sobre el frascaso de una visita* (Seville: Escuela de Estudios Hispano-Americanos, 1946).

6 Priestley, *Gálvez,* pp. 109–10. Hubert Howe Bancroft, *History of Mexico* (3 vols., San Francisco, 1883), III, 6–7. This is still a useful work.

7 For the sources on Olivares, see Chapter 7, notes 28 and 29. For an earlier statement of Olivares' belief that all the kingdoms of the Habsburg monarchy should share the administration on something like equal terms, see Consulta of the Council of Italy: November 12, 1592, Archivo de Simancas, Secret., Prov., legajo 985, as cited by Helmut G. Koenigsberger, *The Government of Sicily under Philip II of Spain: A Study in the Practice of Empire* (London and New York, 1951), p. 49.

8 In his celebrated letter to Philip IV of December 25, 1624, outlining the goals of his administration, Olivares only briefly touched on the New World. Several copies are in the Biblioteca Nacional, Madrid, mss. 9893, 1105, and 1164. He promised the king another letter dealing specifically with America, but I have not been able to locate a copy. The objectives of colonial policy, however, can be reconstructed from other sources.

9 Consulta: September 25, 1621, AGI/Indiferente General 754. Consulta: July 1, 1622, AGI/AL 4.

10 Cedula to Lic. Mañozca: April 30, 1622, AGI/AQ 209.

11 Philip IV to Pedro de Ledesma: June 27, 1622, AGI/Indiferente General 754. Juan de Aponte Figueroa, a retired army officer in Lima who was looking for another royal merced, wrote a circumstantial account of graft on all levels of the administration in the audiencia of Lima. This report, dated April 24, 1622, probably did not reach Spain in time to influence the consulta of July 1, 1622, but there were many other critical accounts available. Juan de Aponte Figueroa, "Memorial que trata de la reformación del reino del Pirú," Martín Fernández de Navarrete *et al.,* eds., *Colección de documentos inéditos para la historia de España* (112 vols., Madrid, 1842–95), LI, 524–62. For letters critical of the outgoing administration of Viceroy Esquilache, see audiencia to king: April 19, 1618; Oidor Juan Páez de Laguna to President Fernando Carrillo: April 19, 1619; Oidor Merlo de la Fuente: April 24, 1619, AGI/AL 96.

12 Consulta: July 1, 1622, AGI/AL 4.

13 King to council: October 21, 1622, AGI/Indiferente General 615.

14 Schäfer first suggested Olivares' interest in colonial reform, but he did not develop the theme very extensively: Schäfer, *El consejo,* II, 131.

15 This proposal was not original with Olivares. As early as 1573, Juan de Matienzo had suggested that there be a visita general of each audiencia every seven years. Matienzo to king: October 18, 1573, Juan de Matienzo, *Gobierno del Perú,* pp. viii–ix.

16 John H. Elliott found that it was impossible to write a political biography of Olivares, since his personal papers were destroyed in the fire of the Duke of Alba's palace of Buenavista in 1794. John H. Elliott, *The Revolt of the Catalans: A Study in the Decline of Spain, 1598–1640* (Cambridge, 1963), p. 579.

17 The exchange of correspondence between the king and the council— Consultas: June 23, 1627, and December 2, 1627—are in AGI/Indiferente

General 755. Some of this material is also in Schäfer, *El consejo*, II, 131, and Richard Konetzke, *Colección de documentos para la historia de la formación social de Hispanoamérica, 1493–1810* (4 vols., Madrid, 1958–62), II, 301–5.

18 For the complex causes of the riot of 1624, in which the viceroy's political ineptitude was only one factor, see Lesley Byrd Simpson, *Many Mexicos* (Berkeley and Los Angeles: University of California Press, 1961), pp. 136 ff. Chester Lyle Guthrie, "Riots in Seventeenth-Century Mexico City," *Greater America, Essays in Honor of Herbert Eugene Bolton* (Berkeley and Los Angeles: University of California Press, 1955), pp. 243–58.

19 President Antonio de Morga to king: April 15, 1620, AGI/AQ 10.

20 *Ibid.* Fiscal Melchor Suárez de Poago to king: May 8, 1620, and May 15, 1620, *ibid.*

21 Viceroy to king: April 24, 1620, AGI/AL 39. Inquiry conducted by Dr. Morga concerning the marriage of Oidor Zorrilla: 1619, AGI/EC 912.

22 Viceroy to king: April 24, 1620, AGI/AL 39. Solórzano, *Política indiana*, Bk. V, Ch. ix, No. 67.

23 Morga to king: April 15, 1625, AGI/AQ 10.

24 Morga to king: April 15, 1620; *ibid.;* king to audiencia: October 23, 1621, *ibid.* 209 (II, fol. 7).

25 See Chapter 7, note 83.

26 Among the minor posts he had held was deputy of the corregidor of Quito: *Libro de cabildos de la ciudad de Quito, 1610–1616,* ed. Jorge Garcés (Archivo Municipal, Vol. XXVI, Quito, 1955), pp. 321–22, 323–26. "Información hecha de oficio de los méritos y servicios del Lic. Francisco Rodríquez Plaza," 1618, AGI/AQ 50. Mañozca to king: March 28, 1625, AGI/AQ 61. Morga to king: April 15, 1625, AGI/AQ 10. Rodríquez Plaza to king: March 6, 1626, AGI/AQ 61. Rodríquez Plaza to king: April 19, 1627, AGI/AQ 62. Also see Chapter 11, notes 34–36.

27 Juan García de Solís to king: April 28, 1620, and Pedro de Espinosa Pacheco to king: April 25, 1620, AGI/AQ 29.

28 For the action that the audiencia took against Lic. Rodríquez Plaza, see Chapter 11, notes 34–36.

29 Testimony of Lic. Manuel Tello de Velasco: 1625–26, AGI/AQ 62.

30 Testimony of doña Francisca de Tapia y Calderón: November 22, 1625, AGI/EC 919. For the role of the Marquis of Siete Iglesias at the Court of Philip III, see Julio de Atienza, *Nobiliario español* (Madrid, 1948), pp. 918, 968.

31 Morga to king: April 15, 1623, AGI/AQ 61.

32 Morga to king: April 15, 1620, *ibid.* 10.

33 For an expression of the central authorities' skepticism of charges made in the Indies against the conduct of magistrates, see Antonio Rodríguez de León Pinelo, *Autos, acuerdos i decretos de gobierno del real i supremo consejo de las Indias . . .* (Madrid, 1658), Consulta of May 24, 1603.

34 King to Morga: October 23, 1621, AGI/AQ 209 (II, foll. 2–4). *Recopila-ción*, Bk. II, Title xviii, law 42.

35 King to Morga: October 23, 1621, AGI/AQ 209 (II, foll. 2–4).

36 Morga to king: April 15, 1622, *ibid.* 10.

37 President Manuel Ibarra to king: December 16, 1606, *ibid.* 9.

38 *Ibid.*

39 Consulta: March 7, 1608, and Consulta: December 22, 1608, *ibid.* 1.

40 Solórzano, *Política indiana*, Bk. V, Ch. x, No. 19.

41 For a concise analysis, see L. N. McAlister, "Social Structure and Social Change in New Spain," *Hispanic-American Historical Review*, XLIII, No. 3 (August, 1963), 349–70. Richard Morse, "Toward a Theory of Spanish American Government," *Journal of the History of Ideas*, XV, No. 1 (January, 1954), 71.

42 McAlister, "Social Structure," p. 357. Richard Konetzke, "La formación de la nobleza en Indias," *Estudios americanos*, III (Seville, 1951), 356. For some vivid expressions of this notion, see Treasury to king: October 25, 1626, AGI/AQ 20, and the testimony of Ana Ronquillo de Galarda (wife of Diego de Niebla): January 25, 1620, attached to Morga to king: April 15, 1620, AGI/AQ 10.

43 Antonio Rodriguez de León Pinelo, *Tratado de confirmaciones reales,* (Buenos Aires: Casa Jacobs Peuser, 1922).

44 Constantino Bayle, S.J., *Los cabildos seculares en la América española* (Madrid, 1952), pp. 142–52. For the agitation of the procuradores of the city for a restoration of the privilege of electing its magistrates, see AMQ, XIII, foll. 163–67, 168–76, 191–92.

45 James F. King, "The Case of José Ponciano de Ayarza: A Document on *Gracias al sacar,*" *Hispanic-American Historical Review*, XXXI, No. 4 (November, 1951), 640–47.

46 Konetzke, *Colección,* II, 61, 68, 99.

47 A bitter critic of the mestizos, Lic. Mañozca estimated that there were about 2,500 mestizos and mulattoes, all of whom he considered potential rebels. Mañozca to king: September 25, 1625, AGI/AQ 61.

48 Mario Góngora, *El estado español en el derecho indiano: época de fundación 1492–1570* (Santiago, Chile, 1951), p. 197.

49 Charles R. Boxer, *Portuguese Society in the Tropics: The Municipal Councils of Goa, Macao, Bahia, and Luanda, 1510–1800* (Madison and Milwaukee, 1965), pp. 7–8, 27–28, 155–58, 73–77, 179–82.

50 McAlister, "Social Structure," pp. 365–70.

CHAPTER 11: A ZEALOUS VISITOR GENERAL

1 Lic. Juan de Mañozca to king: April 10, 1625, AGI/AQ 62.

2 Ernesto Schäfer, *El consejo real y supremo de las Indias* (2 vols., Seville, 1935–47), II, 138.

3 Consulta: September 25, 1621, AGI/Indiferente General 754.

4 Mañozca to Antonio González de Legarda: February 28, 1627, AGI/AQ 62.

5 Federico González Suárez, *Historia general de la república del Ecuador* (7 vols., Quito, 1890–1903), I, 123.

6 Governor Diego Fernández de Velasco to king: July 4, 1613, Archivo Histórico Nacional (Madrid), Inquisición, Bk. 1009.

7 "Información hecha por el s. inquisitor general de vida y costumbres de Lic. Juan de Mañozca . . .": 1620, *ibid.* Also see José T. Medina, *Historia del tribunal del santo oficio de la inquisición de Cartagena de las Indias* (Santiago, Chile, 1899), pp. 125–49.

8 Sebastián de Chumillas, O.F.M. to king: May 12, 1609, Archivo Histórico Nacional (Madrid), Inquisición, Bk. 1001.

9 *Ibid.*

10 Medina, *Historia,* p. 149. For a briefer but less sharply focused account of his career in Cartagena, see Henry Charles Lea, *The Inquisition in the Spanish Dependencies* (New York, 1908), pp. 460–63, 473–76.

11 Mañozca to González de Legarda: September 4, 1626, and February 28, 1627, AGI/AQ 61 and 62.

12 Consulta: September 25, 1621, AGI/Indiferente General 754.

13 Schäfer, *El consejo,* II, 138. The only portion of his instructions that I could locate dealt with the visita general of the treasury. King to Mañozca: October 2, 1622, AGI/AQ 61. Diego de Landeras y Velasco, visitor general of Mexico, received the following instructions on March 26, 1606: (1) that he be prompt in reporting his findings to the king and the council, (2) that his salary was to come from fines imposed, (3) that he perform the visita general of both the audiencia and the treasury, (4) that magistrates under investigation were to be informed of the content of unfavorable testimony but not the names of witnesses, (5) that the final verdict be rendered by the king and the council, (6) that all magistrates from the viceroy downward were to assist and to cooperate with the visitor general, (7) that any magistrate who obstructed the work of the investigation might be suspended from office forthwith by the visitor until the king took other action, (8) that the visitor general also might suspend from office any other magistrate who, after presenting testimony in his own defense, *los descargos,* was in the opinion of the visitor general "notoriously guilty." Herbert I. Priestley, *José de Gálvez, Visitor General of New Spain, 1765–1771* (University of California Publications in History, No. 5, Berkeley, 1916), pp. 109–10. Internal evidence suggests that all of these provisions and probably others were included in the instructions to Lic. Mañozca. For a similar set of instructions to Juan Suárez, visitor general of the audiencia of Panama (January 15, 1614), see Archivo Nacional (Panama) 109–1–1, and AGI/Audiencia de Panama 109–1–1. These principles became standard policy: see Juan de Solórzano y Pereira, *Política indiana* (5 vols., Madrid, 1647), Bk. IV, Ch. x.

14 Cedula to Mañozca: October 1, 1622, and Auto of Lic. Mañozca: December 2, 1624, AGI/AQ 61.

15 Visitor General Landeras y Velasco also received anonymous complaints.

Priestley, *Gálvez*, pp. 109–10. For Solórzano's disapproval of the practice, see *Política indiana*, Bk. IV, Ch. x, No. 29.

16 John H. Parry, *The Audiencia of New Galicia in the Sixteenth Century* (Cambridge, 1948), p. 152. *Recopilación de las leyes de los reynos de las Indias* (4 vols., Madrid, 1681), Bk. II, Title xxiii, law 16.

17 ACS, *Libro de acuerdos de la real audiencia, 1610–30*. Mañozca to king: April 10, 1625, AGI/AQ 62. Mañozca to king: September 22, 1625, and February 25, 1626, AGI/AQ 61.

18 ACS, *Libro de acuerdos de la real audiencia, 1610–30:* December 7, 1624. Until the departure of Lic. Mañozca in September, 1627, the oidores even signed their signatures in full, but after that date they merely initialed each decision.

19 Mañozca to king: April 10, 1625, and September 22, 1625, AGI/AQ 61 and 62. ACS, *Libro de acuerdos de hacienda, 1601–57:* January 16, 1625. Treasury to king: April 20, 1625, AGI/AQ 61. They claimed that their more abbreviated form of bookkeeping was the style laid down by the previous visitor general, Dr. Manuel Barros, and that a larger staff would be required to follow the instructions of Lic. Mañozca.

20 ACS, *Libro de acuerdos de hacienda, 1601–57:* January 16, 1625. Also see *Recopilación*, Bk. II, Title xv, laws 116 and 119.

21 "Contra Juan de Beraín . . . sobre tener el sello real fuera de las casas reales . . . 1625," AGI/AQ 61. Mañozca to king: September 22, 1625, *ibid*. González Suárez, *Historia*, IV, 133–37.

22 Schäfer, *El consejo*, I, 217 ff. Mañozca to king: February 26, 1626, AGI/AQ 61. Antonio Rodríguez de León Pinelo, *El gran canciller de las Indias*, ed. Guillermo Lohmann Villena (Seville: Consejo Superior de Investigaciones Científicas, 1953).

23 *Recopilación*, Bk. II, Title xxi, law 1.

24 Mañozca to González de Legarda: February 28, 1627, AGI/AQ 62.

25 Mañozca to king: February 28, 1625, *ibid*. 61. Mañozca to king: April 10, 1625, *ibid*. 62. "Cuaderno de cargos contra el presidente y oidores sobre la residencia de Pedro de Vergara . . . ," 1625–26, *ibid*.

26 Cedula to audiencia: May 3, 1605, *ibid*. 209 (I, fol. 176).

27 The audiencia pointed out that no such prohibition had existed in the past and that if such a change were undertaken, it should apply to all the audiencias in the Indies and not just Quito. The audiencia indicated its lack of sympathy by suggesting that purchasable offices, such as constable and escribano, would fetch less money if the trade prohibition were enforced. Audiencia to king: April 20, 1606, *ibid*. 9.

28 Cedula: August 31, 1619, *Recopilación*, Bk. II, Title ii, law 59.

29 For the voluminous documentation, see the following: Mañozca to king: April 10, 1625, AGI/AQ 61, and Mañozca to king: April 10, 1625: *ibid*. 30, and a third letter of the same date, *ibid*. 62. Mañozca to king: February 26, 1626, AGI/AQ 61. Audiencia to king: May 8, 1626, AGI/AQ 62. April 18, 1625, *ibid*. 87. Mañozca to king: April 10, 1625, *ibid*. 30. Cedula

to Mañozca: March 3, 1626, *ibid.* 209 (II, foll. 17–18). Andrés de Orozco Guzmán to king: April 12, 1627, *ibid.* 31. ACS, *Libro de acuerdos de la real audiencia, 1630–41:* November 15, 1632. Audiencia to king: March 4, 1625, AGI/AQ 61. Fiscal Melchor Suárez de Poago to king: February 26, 1626, AGI/AQ 61. Audiencia to king: May 8, 1626, AGI/AQ 62.

30 ACS, *Libro de acuerdos de la real audiencia, 1630–41:* July 24, 1632.

31 Morga sentence: October 22, 1636, AGI/AQ 12, and W. E. Retana, "Estudio preliminar," in Antonio de Morga, *Sucesos de las islas filipinas* (Madrid, 1909), pp. 147–53.

32 Sentences of Andrés de Orozco Guzmán and Diego de Valencia León: November 14, 1637, AGI/EC 921a.

33 See Chapter 10, notes 19–26.

34 Mañozca to king: March 28, 1625, April 10, 1625, February 25, 1626, AGI/AQ 61. "Querella criminal del Lic. Francisco Rodríquez Plaza contra Diego de Valencia León . . . ," 1625–26, AGI/EC 920. Rodríquez Plaza to king: March 6, 1626, April 19, 1627, AGI/AQ 61, 62. Audiencia to king: March 4, 1625, AGI/AQ 61. Oidor Matías de Peralta: February 28, 1626, AGI/AQ 31. Audiencia to king: May 8, 1626, AGI/AQ 61.

35 Morga sentence: October 22, 1636, AGI/AQ 12, and Retana, "Estudio," pp. 147–53.

36 ACS, *Libros de acuerdos, de la real audiencia, 1610–30* and *1630–41,* contain no decisions relative to complaints of Lic. Rodríquez Plaza against the audiencia.

37 *Recopilación,* Bk. II, Title xxxiv, law 35.

38 Solórzano, *Política indiana,* Bk. V, Ch. x, Nos. 18, 20, 22, 26.

39 Mañozca to king: April 10, 1625, March 27, 1627, AGI/AQ 61, 62.

40 The authors of these fourteen complaints were Juan Serrano del Valle (ten) and Miguel de Gorrivar and Alonso García de Galarca with two apiece.

41 Solórzano, *Política indiana,* Bk. V, Ch. x, No. 43. Solórzano cited the cedula of February 11, 1593, which expressly forbade a visitor general to hear such cases. *Recopilación,* Bk. II, Title xxxiv, law 30. Solórzano evidently gave a visitor general a little more discretion than the cedula did. Also see the cedula of March 7, 1627, which ordered visitors to use embargoes of estates as the very last resort and not the first step in hearing demandas públicas. This cedula evidently reflects the displeasure of the king and the council at the procedures of Lic. Mañozca. *Recopilación,* Bk. II, Title xxxiv, law 22.

42 Suárez de Poago to Mañozca: December 14, 1626, AGI/AQ 11. Audiencia to king: March 4, 1625, May 8, 1626, *ibid.* 61. Suárez de Poago to king: March 28, 1627, *ibid.* 11.

43 Suárez de Poago to king: March 28, 1627, *ibid.* Mañozca to king: March 28, 1625, and March 27, 1627, *ibid.* 61. Although Lic. Mañozca was notorious for his stiff sentences, his Draconian verdict in the case of Juan Serrano del Valle may have been inspired more by political than strictly judicial considerations. The position of the visitor general had so deteriorated that

he was compelled to restore to office several suspended magistrates. Not only was there the possibility that the re-established audiencia might investigate the career of Juan Serrano del Valle, but also Lic. Mañozca faced the grim prospect of being dismissed as visitor general in response to the growing complaints against his conduct. That Lic. Mañozca wanted to get Juan Serrano del Valle out of Quito, lest subsequently he might provide incriminatory evidence against the visitor general and his staff, was suggested by the bitterest critic of Lic. Mañozca, the fiscal, Melchor Suárez de Poago. In spite of its highly prejudiced authorship, this explanation is indeed plausible. Suárez de Poago to king: March 28, 1627, *ibid.* 11.

44 Suárez de Poago to king: March 28, 1627, *ibid.* Audiencia to king: March 4, 1625, *ibid.* 61. Francisco Juárez Arguello to king: January 15, 1626, *ibid.* Peralta to king: February 28, 1626, *ibid.* Audiencia to king: May 8, 1626, *ibid.*

45 Mañozca to king: April 10, 1625, *ibid.*

46 Mañozca poked fun at the alarm and bitterness of the magistrates over the humble station of their opponents. Mañozca to king: March 28, 1625, *ibid.*

47 Audiencia to king: May 8, 1626, *ibid.*

48 Audiencia to king: March 4, 1625, *ibid.* Peralta to king: February 28, 1626, *ibid.* 31. Audiencia to king: May 8, 1626, *ibid.* 61. Suárez de Poago to king: March 28, 1627, *ibid.* 11. Suárez de Poago to Mañozca: December 14, 1626, *ibid.*

49 At the time of the dismissal of Lic. Mañozca, Juan de Ibarra was exercising a commission of the visitor general to inspect the treasury office in Cali. He held other commissions also in Popayán and with the probate court (*bienes de difuntos*). AGC 1943, August 4, 1627; AGC 295, August 29, 1627; AGC 1612, August 22, 1627; AGC 1623, May 11, 1628. ACS, *Libro de acuerdos de la real audiencia, 1610–30:* October 7, 1627.

50 Lic. Mañozca also found his inquisitional authority useful to invoke in dealing with the clergy, as we shall see in the next chapter. Mañozca to king: April 28, 1625, AGI/AQ 61. "Memoria de las culpas que a cometido Fr. Francisco de la Fuente," 1625–26, *ibid.* Consulta: February 11, 1628, AGI/AL 5. Cabildo of Quito to viceroy: August 1, 1628, April 4, 1629, and July 6, 1629, AMQ, XIII, foll. 197–98, 200–204, 215–16. Gerónimo Pérez de Burgales to king: [1626?], AGI/AQ 31. Pedro Ortiz de Ávila to king: 1626, AGI/AQ 31.

51 For some graphic accounts of Mañozca's investigatory technique, see audiencia to king: March 4, 1625, AGI/AQ 61, and President Antonio de Morga to king: February 26, 1626, *ibid.* The correspondence of the visitor general provides ample testimony as to his vigor and zeal as an investigator.

52 ACS, *Libro de acuerdos de la real audiencia, 1610–30:* July 22, 1625.

53 *Ibid.:* July 17, 1625.

54 Mañozca to king: September 22, 1625, September 28, 1625, and February 25, 1626, AGI/AQ 61.

55 *Recopilación,* April 17, 1606, Bk. II, Title xxxiv, law 24.

56 *Ibid.,* October 19, 1588, Bk. II, Title xxxiv, law 26. Visitors general to the audiencias of Lima and Mexico City could not suspend from office the viceroy as such, but they could suspend him, under the conditions outlined, in his role as president of the royal audiencia.

57 Suárez de Poago to king: March 28, 1627, AGI/AQ 11. Treasury to king: April 26, 1627, *ibid.* 20.

58 Consulta: February 22, 1627, *ibid.* 1.

59 Treasury to king: March 4, 1626, April 26, 1627, *ibid.* 20.

60 ACS, *Libro de acuerdos de la real audiencia, 1610–30:* February 26, 1626. An audiencia, however, could continue to function with only one oidor sitting on the bench: *Recopilación,* Bk. II, Title xv, law 181.

61 See Chapter 10, notes 32–34.

62 For the testimony, see Morga to king: April 15, 1623, AGI/AQ 61.

63 King to Mañozca: March 29, 1625, *ibid.*

64 *Ibid.* Solórzano, *Política indiana,* Bk. V, Ch. x, Nos. 18, 20, 22.

65 Audiencia to king: March 4, 1625, AGI/AQ 61.

66 Mañozca to king: February 23, 1626, and February 25, 1626, *ibid.*

67 Morga to king: February 26, 1626, *ibid.* Audiencia to king: May 8, 1626, *ibid.* Suárez de Poago to king: March 28, 1627, *ibid.* 11.

68 Mañozca to king: March 5, 1626, and October 20, 1626, *ibid.* 61 and 31.

69 See note 67.

70 Mañozca to king: February 25, 1626, AGI/AQ 61.

71 Mañozca described Arellano as "un hombre según corre noble pero jugador perdido y como de poca capacidad y atrevido . . .": Mañozca to king: February 23, 1626, *ibid.*

72 Cedula to audiencia: March 4, 1627, AMQ, XCV, foll. 1–13.

73 "Memorial de la causa de Lic. don Manuel Tello de Velasco: 1625–26," AGI/AQ 61. For the full hearings of the countersuit of Velasco see AGI/EC 920.

74 Mañozca to king: March 20, 1627, AGI/AQ 62.

75 See Ch. 8, notes 17–18.

76 Viceroy to king: March 8, 1627, AGI/AL 41. Suárez de Poago to king: March 28, 1627, AGI/AQ 11.

77 See Chapter 9, notes 13–17.

CHAPTER 12: THE BIRTH OF NATIONALISM

1 President Antonio de Morga to king: April 15, 1620, AGI/AQ 10. José María Vargas, O.P., *Historia de la iglesia en el Ecuador durante el patronato español* (Quito, 1962), pp. 39, 40, 153, 202.

2 Vargas, *Historia de la iglesia,* pp. 39, 40, 153, 202.

3 Bishop-archbishop of Quito to king: January 10, 1632, AGI/AQ 88. Also see Chapter 7, notes 86–91.

4 See Chapter 7, notes 86–91. Morga to king: April 15, 1625, AGI/AQ 10. Also see my *Hispanization of the Philippines: Spanish Aims and Filipino Responses, 1565–1700* (Madison, 1959), pp. 35–38. Jorge Juan and An-

tonio de Ulloa, *Noticias secretas de América* . . . , ed. Rufino Blanco-Fombona (Biblioteca Ayacucho, Vols. XXXI–XXXII, Madrid, 1918), XXXII, 10–29.

5 L. N. McAlister, "Social Structure and Social Change in New Spain," *Hispanic-American Historical Review*, XLIII, No. 3 (August, 1963), 363. Richard Konetzke, "La condición legal de los criollos y las causas de la independencia," *Estudios americanos*, II (Seville, 1950), 31–54.

6 Lic. Juan de Mañozca to king: February 4, 1626, AGI/AQ 61. Every letter he wrote regarding the disputed election among the Dominicans vibrates with a vitriolic prejudice against the creoles and the mestizos and mulattoes.

7 When Lic. Mañozca dismissed Juan de Vallejo as escribano público of Riobamba, he cited the mestizo origin of the latter as one of his principal justifications. Mañozca to king: March 6, 1627, *ibid.* 62.

8 The most succinct summary can be found in Antonine Tibesar, O.F.M., "The Alternativa: A Study of Spanish-Creole Relations in Seventeenth Century Peru," *The Americas*, XI, No. 3 (January, 1955), 229–82. Augustín Arce, O.F.M., "Origines de la alternativa de oficios en las provincias franciscanas del Perú," *Archivo Ibero-Americano*, VII, No. 47 (September–October, 1921), 145–62.

9 See note 8.

10 Juan de Solórzano y Pereira, *Política indiana* (5 vols., Madrid, 1647), Bk. IV, Ch. xix.

11 *Ibid.* For his unusually high opinion of the creoles, an attitude which won the favorable acclaim even of some leaders of the independence period, see *ibid.*, Bk. II, Ch. xxx. Also see José María Ots Capdequí and Javier Malagón, *Solórzano y la Política indiana* (Mexico and Buenos Aires, 1965), pp. 16–17, 60–62. But his attitude toward the castes was unfriendly and suspicious. Toward the Indians his feelings were paternalistic.

12 Tibesar, "The Alternativa," pp. 233–34.

13 The sources concerning the disputed election of 1624 and the subsequent series of events, which are the topics of this chapter, are voluminous. For Lic. Mañozca's viewpoint see Mañozca to king: September 22, 1625, and February 4, 1626, AGI/AQ 61. Upon returning to Lima, Lic. Mañozca published a pamphlet defending his conduct. The John Carter Brown Library, Brown University, has a copy without title, classified as Juan de Mañozca, *Alegatos ecuatorianos*, 1626. A more accurate date might be 1627 or 1628. Fiscal Melchor Suárez de Poago replied at length to this treatise. Suárez de Poago to king: December 16, 1629, AGI/AQ 11. Also see the fiscal's reply to the "Memorial of Fr. Francisco de la Fuente y Chaves" in Suárez de Poago to king: April 20, 1632, AGI/AQ 11. Among the principal sources critical of the conduct of the visitor general, the most important is Leonardo Araujo, O.S.A., *Relación de las cosas que svedieron en la ciudad de Quito, reyno del Pirú con las ordenes de Santo Domingo y San Augustín por mano del Lic. Juan de Mañozca, visitador de la real audiencia de la dicha ciudad* . . . (Lima, 1627), and audiencia to king:

May 8, 1626, AGI/AQ 61. All the autos of this controversy are in AGI/AQ 10. Among the primary sources of less importance are the following. Gaspar Manrique de Lara, O.P., to king: January 1626, AGI/AQ 88; viceroy to king: February 12, 1626, AGI/AL 40. Morga to king: October 20, 1628, AGI/AQ 11. Gerónimo Pérez de Burgales to king: 1626, AGI/AQ 31. The most useful secondary account is that of Federico González Suárez, *Historia general de la república del Ecuador* (7 vols., Quito, 1890–1903), IV, 137–55.

14 Morga sentence: October 26, 1636, AGI/AQ 12. For another such expression, see Oidor Diego Maldonado to king: December 17, 1628, *ibid.* 31.

15 Viceroy to king: May 15, 1628, AGI/AL 41.

16 See Chapter 11, notes 6–10.

17 ACS, *Libro de acuerdos de la real audiencia, 1610–30:* July 10, 1625.

18 Suárez de Poago to king: December 6, 1629, AGI/AQ 11.

19 Viceroy to Lic. Juan de Carvajal: November 20, 1625, AGI/AL 40.

20 Audiencia to viceroy: December 3, 1625, *ibid.*

21 Viceroy to audiencia: January 20, 1626, *ibid.*

22 Audiencia to king: May 8, 1626, AGI/AQ 61.

23 *Ibid.*

24 Solórzano, *Política indiana,* Bk. IV, Ch. xxvi, Nos. 58–66.

25 Cedula: March 25, 1617, Archivo Nacional (Panama), and AGI/Audiencia de Panama 16. Cedula: November 3, 1618, *ibid.* Consulta: January 16, 1619, AGI/AQ 1.

26 Mañozca to king: April 10, 1625, AGI/AQ 61. This is one of the first reports of the visitor general to the king in which he refers to the fiscal's strife-torn years in Panama. He flays "la terribilidad de su condición" and he describes the fiscal as "un hombre poco dueño de sus acciones."

27 For some outstanding examples of the fiscal's wrath against the visitor general, see Suárez de Poago to king: February 26, 1626, *ibid.* Suárez de Poago to king: March 28, 1627, *ibid.* 11; March 30, 1627; December 11, 1629, and April 14, 1630, *ibid.* 11.

28 Mañozca to king: February 4, 1626, AGI/AQ 61.

29 In order to prevent further collusions between two regular orders, the Holy See subsequently provided that a judge conservator, created to defend the privileges of one regular order, must be chosen from the ranks of the secular clergy. The Quito case, along with other similar ones, was a factor leading to the papal decision: Solórzano, *Política indiana,* Bk. IV, Ch. xxvi, Nos. 58–66.

30 "Memoria de las culpas que a cometido Fr. Francisco de la Fuente y Chaves de su vida y costumbres," 1626, AGI/AQ 61. For his subsequent career see Chapter 14, notes 9–11.

31 Consulta: August 25, 1623, AGI/AQ 1. Audiencia to king: April 25, 1625, *ibid.* 10. Vargas, *Historia de la iglesia,* pp. 230–34. González Suárez, *Historia,* IV, 152–53.

32 Araujo, *Relación,* fol. 11.

33 *Ibid.,* fol. 13.

34 Cedula to audiencia: April 9, 1626, AGI/AQ 61. *Recopilación de las leyes de los reynos de las Indias,* February 25, 1627, Bk. I, Title xiii, law 51. Viceroy to king: March 15, 1628, AGI/AL 41.

35 Vargas, *Historia de la iglesia,* p. 249. After being restored to office, Rosero encountered great difficulties in governing his strife-torn order. Rosero to audiencia: February 17, 1627, ANH, I, No. 74.

36 Viceroy to king: February 12, 1626, AGI/AL 40.

37 Cedula: February 13, 1627, *Recopilación,* Bk. I, Title xiv, law 58.

CHAPTER 13: THE FALL OF A VISITOR GENERAL

1 The principal reports critical of Lic. Mañozca are the following. Leonardo Araujo, O.S.A., *Relación de las cosas que svedieron en la ciudad de Quito, reyno del Pirú con las ordenes de Santo Domingo y San Agustín por mano del Lic. Juan de Mañozca, visitador de la real audiencia de la dicha ciudad* . . . (Lima, 1627). The treatise was submitted to the council of the Indies by its author in manuscript form. Subsequently it was published. The provincial superiors of the Dominican, Jesuit, Franciscan, and Merced orders wrote restrained pro-Morga and anti-Mañozca statements with dates in early and late March, 1626, AGI/AQ 88. See the letter of the suspended treasury officials of February 25, 1626, AGI/AQ 88. Fiscal Melchor Suárez de Poago to king: March 4, 1626, AGI/AQ 20. Oidor Matías de Peralta to king: February 26, 1626, AGI/AQ 31. President Antonio de Morga to king: February 26, 1626, AGI/AQ 31. Also considered by the council was the letter of the audiencia of May 18, 1626, AGI/AQ 61. I could locate no letters from the city council of Quito for that year. That they opposed the visitor general is abundantly clear from subsequent communications. Many of their members were arrested and their estates embargoed by Lic. Mañozca. The *libros de cabildo* for the years 1616–38 are missing. For the hostile attitude of the cabildo of Quito toward Lic. Mañozca, see their letters addressed to the viceroy (August 1, 1628), to the Inquisition in Lima (April 4, 1629), and to the viceroy (July 6, 1629), AMQ, XIII, foll. 197–98, 200–204, 215–16.

2 The audiencia had such authority, but their powers of enforcement left much to be desired.

3 Francisco Juárez Arguello to king: January 15, 1626, AGI/AQ 61.

4 Federico González Suárez, *Historia general de la república del Ecuador* (7 vols., Quito, 1890–1903), IV, 103–4. ACS, *Libro de acuerdos de la real audiencia, 1630–41:* April 2, 1632.

5 González Suárez, *Historia,* IV, 472–78. Viceroy to king: May 5, 1630, AGI/AQ 43. Treasury to king: April 20, 1625, March 10, 1626, April 26, 1627, AGI/AQ 20. Morga to king: April 30, 1629, AGI/AQ 11.

6 Lic. Juan de Mañozca to king: April 11, 1625, AGI/AQ 61. The visitor general seldom mentioned economic conditions in his correspondence.

7 Treasury to king: March 4, 1626, and February 25, 1626, *ibid.* 20 and 61.

8 Treasury to king: August 26, 1627, and March 10, 1628, *ibid.* 20.

9 King to Mañozca: August 19, 1627, *ibid.* 209 (II, fol. 51).

10 An *agente de negocios* had to receive a license from the council in order to practice his craft. The council would not receive his petitions unless he presented a duly notarized power of attorney from his client. How influential the agentes de negocios were as a subgroup is debatable. Their major responsibility was to get the busy council to act on the petitions of their clients. Although most corporations and individuals who had litigations pending before the council found it expedient to retain the services of an agente de negocios, major reliance was placed not on them but on the services of influential friends at Court. Lic. Mañozca, for example, had an agente, but he placed more reliance on an old personal friend, a Dominican friar, Diego de Otaola, a fellow Basque, whom he had befriended during his turbulent clash with the Dominicans in Cartagena. See Mañozca to Antonio González de Legarda: September 4, 1626, *ibid.* 61.

11 Francisco Juárez Arguello to king: January 15, 1626, *ibid.*

12 Juan de Solórzano y Pereira, *Política indiana* (5 vols., Madrid, 1647), Bk. V, Ch. x, No. 35. Solórzano was then a member of the Council of the Indies.

13 See his letters of February 4, 1626, and February 23, 1626, AGI/AQ 61.

14 Mañozca to González de Legarda: September 4, 1626, *ibid.* 61. González de Legarda was royal secretary of the Council of the Indies for the viceroyalty of Peru.

15 Juan de Salazar to king: January 22, 1627, *ibid.* 61.

16 Consulta entitled, "Sobre el mal proceder de Lic. Mañozca . . . ," February 22, 1627, *ibid.* 1.

17 John Lynch, *Spain under the Habsburgs* (2 vols., New York, 1964——), I, 342.

18 That the Inquisition intervened to protect Lic. Mañozca is merely a plausible supposition. The king wrote the viceroy on December 10, 1627, that he was planning to remove Lic. Mañozca from the Holy Office in Lima in view of his apparent incapacity to preserve harmonious relations with the regular clergy. King to viceroy: March 7, 1627, AGI/AL 41. This intention was never carried out, for Lic. Mañozca remained in the Holy Office in Lima until 1639.

19 King to audiencia and king to Mañozca: March 7, 1627, AGI/AQ 209 (II, fol. 38).

20 Audiencia to king: March 11, 1628, *ibid.* 11.

21 *Ibid.*

22 González Suárez, *Historia,* IV, 159.

23 Morga to king: April 30, 1629, AGI/AQ 11.

24 Mañozca to Morga: September 25, October 30, and November 8, 1627, AGI/AQ 11.

25 Archivo General de la Nación (Mexico), Inquisición, 274, 275, 287, contains several cases in which Dr. Morga participated.

26 Audiencia to king: March 11, 1628, AGI/AQ 11. Mañozca to king: June 8, 1628, AGI/AQ 62.

27 For Lope de Bermeo's difficulties, see ACS, *Libro de acuerdos de la real audiencia, 1610–30:* September 27, October 7, and November 8, 1627, and August 1 and December 22, 1628. For Juan de Ibarra, who eventually escaped from jail and fled to Lima, see *ibid.:* October 7, November 18, and December 16, 1627, January 17, February 14, 24, and 28, March 30, May 15, June 9, and September 12, 1628.

28 The visitor general was never allowed to see the correspondence of the magistrates being visited dealing with his conduct. *Recopilación de las leyes de los reynos de las Indias* (4 vols., Madrid, 1681), Bk. II, Title xxxiv, law 17.

29 By far the most balanced and complete coverage of the visita general of Lic. Mañozca is the account in González Suárez, *Historia,* IV, 111–68. His approach is narrative rather than analytical. Retana's account contains some useful primary sources from the AGI, but the coverage of events is quite incomplete: W. E. Retana, "Estudio Preliminar," in Antonio de Morga, *Sucesos de las islas filipinas* (Madrid, 1909), pp. 128 ff. The usefulness of Schäfer's account, one of the classic studies on the administrative history of the Spanish empire, is greatly limited by his failure to consider the second stage of the visita general under Lic. Galdós de Valencia: Ernesto Schäfer, *El consejo real y supremo de las Indias* (2 vols., Seville, 1935–47), II, 142–44. None of these accounts attempts to evaluate systematically the overall view of the Morga administration. González Suárez approaches it but he avoided the assignment.

30 The Latin edition, *De indiarum iure,* was first published in Madrid in 1629. The Spanish edition, *Política indiana,* did not come out until 1647. Solórzano left Lima for Spain in March, 1627. He was a member of the Council of the Indies when that body passed the final verdicts of the visita general of Quito in 1636 and 1637.

CHAPTER 14: A CAUTIOUS VISITOR GENERAL

1 Council to king: March 12, 1627, AGI/AQ 1. King to viceroy: March 3, 1627, *ibid.* 209 (II, fol. 42). Cedula: April 3, 1627, *ibid.* (II, foll. 42–44). Viceroy to king: March 15, 1628, and June 25, 1628, AGI/AL 41.

2 President Antonio de Morga to king: April 15, 1629, AGI/AQ 11. Audiencia to king: April 30, 1629, *ibid.* Fiscal Melchor Suárez de Poago to king: April 24, 1629, *ibid.* Viceroy to king: April 1, 1629, AGI/AL 42.

3 Ernesto Schäfer, *El consejo real y supremo de las Indias* (2 vols., Seville, 1935–47), II, 454, 460, 463, 465, 482. Years before, he was scheduled to be visitor general to Guatemala, but the king called off that inspection. Consulta: September 25, 1620, AGI/Indiferente General 615. For his appointment to Lima, see the Consulta: January 20, 1622, AGI/AL 4.

4 Oidor Galdós de Valencia to king: May 3, 1630, AGI/AQ 11.

5 King to audiencia: March 7, 1627, AGI/AQ 209 (II, fol. 38).

6 During 1627 Oidor Tello de Velasco was a minority of one in 48 votes out of a total of 273 decisions reached, 51 out of a total of 179 cases in 1628,

28 out of 133 cases in 1629, and in 1630 24 out of a total of 110 votes taken. ACS, *Libro de acuerdos de la real audiencia, 1610–30.* Several of these cases concerned Lope de Bermeo and Juan de Ibarra, don Manuel usually favoring the former staff members of Lic. Mañozca.

7 *Ibid.:* May 24, 1629.

8 *Ibid.:* August 28, 1629.

9 Suárez de Poago to king: April 20, 1632, AGI/AQ 11.

10 Suárez de Poago to king: April 15, 1630, *ibid.* Morga to king: August 20, 1631, *ibid.* 32. Suárez de Poago to king: 1635, *ibid.* 12. Also see Chapter 4, note 45. Federico González Suárez, *Historia general de la república del Ecuador* (7 vols., Quito, 1890–1903), IV, 154–56.

11 I was unable to locate a copy of Herrera's memorial. For the reply of the fiscal, see his letter to the king: April 20, 1632, AGI/AQ 11.

12 Galdós de Valencia to king: May 3, 1630, *ibid.*

13 Consulta: January 16, 1619, *ibid.* 1.

14 Galdós de Valencia to king: May 3, 1960, *ibid.* 11.

15 *Ibid.*

16 *Ibid.* Suárez de Poago to king: April 15, 1630, *ibid.*

17 Auto of Galdós de Valencia: January 13, 1631, *ibid.*

18 Suárez de Poago to king: April 15, 1630, *ibid.* Cabildo of Quito to king: April 20, 1630, AMQ, XIII, fol. 219. Morga to king: 1631, AGI/AQ 11.

19 Galdós de Valencia to king: February 3, 1631, and June 4, 1632, AGI/AQ 11.

20 *Ibid.* Morga to king: October 15, 1632, *ibid.*

21 Galdós de Valencia to king: June 14, 1632, *ibid.*

22 *Recopilación de las leyes de los reynos de las Indias* (4 vols., Madrid, 1681), Bk. II, Title xxxiv, law 26.

23 ACS, *Libro de acuerdos de la real audiencia, 1630–41:* July 24, 1632.

24 *Ibid.:* July 20, 1632.

25 Audiencia to king: February 19, 1624, *Documentos para la historia de México,* ed. J. R. Navarro (21 vols., 2nd series, Mexico, 1853–57), II, 53–54. For the background, see Lesley Byrd Simpson, *Many Mexicos* (Berkeley and Los Angeles: University of California Press, 1961), pp. 137–41.

26 Cedula to viceroy: April 3, 1627, AGI/AQ 209 (II, fol. 42). Galdós de Valencia to king: May 3, 1630, and June 14, 1632, *ibid.* 11.

27 The salary of Lic. Galdós de Valencia was 2,000 ducats annually, the same as that of Lic. Mañozca, in addition to his salary as oidor of Lima. Cedula to the visitor general: April 3, 1627, *ibid.* 209 (II, foll. 42–44). There are no available treasury reports on the expenses of this mission, but the practice of the visitor general to restrict the appointments of agents tended to keep expenses down.

28 Morga to king: October 15, 1632, *ibid.* 11. Galdós de Valencia to king: May 10, 1634, and May 30, 1635, AGI/AL 99.

29 See note 28. Also Morga to king: May 10, 1633, and April 30, 1634, AGI/AQ 11 and 12. Viceroy to king: May 23, 1635, AGI/AL 46.

30 Consulta: December 22, 1635, AGI/AQ 2.
31 See Chapter 16, notes 4–7.
32 Lic. Castillo de Herrera: printed in Lima, no date, no title, probably 1636, AGI/AL 100.
33 Galdós de Valencia to king: March 24, 1637, *ibid.*
34 Consulta: December 22, 1635, *ibid.* 2.
35 Audiencia to king: April 5, 1637, AGI/AQ 12. Suárez de Poago to audiencia: April 2, 1638, *ibid.*
36 The cedula containing the fine was dated April 26, 1639, but I was unable to locate it. Galdós de Valencia to king: May 26, 1640, AGI/AL 100.
37 Consulta: May 5, 1642, *ibid.* 6.

CHAPTER 15: THE VERDICT

1 Juan de Solórzano y Pereira, *Política indiana* (5 vols., Madrid, 1647), Bk. V, Ch. x, No. 12.
2 *Ibid.,* Nos. 18 and 22. Solórzano, as well as the future Bishop Palafox, was a member of the council that passed verdicts on this particular visita general. Both the strength and the weakness of his classic work is that Sólorzano reflected somewhat literally the attitudes of the Spanish bureaucracy. From the point of view of political theory, the *Política indiana* would have been a more exciting book if the author had abstracted more.
3 For a published version of the Morga sentence, see W. E. Retana, "Estudio Preliminar," in Antonio de Morga, *Sucesos de las filipinas* (Madrid, 1909), pp. 147–53. The original is in the AGI/AQ 12.
4 Sentence of Oidor Manuel Tello de Velasco: November 14, 1637, AGI/EC 921a. Consulta: December 25, 1637, AGI/AQ 2.
5 Sentence of Fiscal Melchor Suárez de Poago: November 14, 1637, AGI/EC 921a. Consulta: December 25, 1637, AGI/AQ 2.
6 Cedula to audiencia: April 11, 1638, AGI/AQ 209 (II, foll. 122–23).
7 Consulta: December 22, 1635, *ibid.* 2.
8 Cedula to viceroy of Mexico: February 22, 1638, *ibid.* 209 (II, foll. 120–21). *Archivo General de la Nación* (Mexico), *Reales cédulas,* I, exped. 234, foll. 440–41.
9 Sentence of Diego de Valencia León: November 14, 1637, and Sentence of Andrés de Orozco Guzmán: November 14, 1637, AGI/EC 921a.
10 Oidor Antonio Rodríquez de San Isidro Manrique to king: February 18, 1639, and May 20, 1639, AGI/AQ 12.
11 "Autos hechos por el s. lic. don Alonso del Castillo de Herrera . . . sobre los bienes de señor d. Antonio de Morga . . . ," 1637, *ibid.* Suárez de Poago to king: April 12, 1638, *ibid.* Lic. Alonso de Mesa y Ayala to king: April 22, 1638, *ibid.* The fiscal of the council expressed surprise and disappointment on September 22, 1639, as to the small amount collected: Suárez de Poago to king: April 12, 1638, *ibid.* Treasury to king: May 5, 1638, *ibid.* Autos of Mesa y Ayala *re* the fines: 1638, AGI/EC 921a. Rodríquez de San Isidro to king: February 18, May 6, and May 20, 1639, AGI/AQ 12.

Consulta: June 21, 1642, AGI/AQ 2. The collection of fines arising out of a visita general or a residencia was the statutory responsibility of the senior oidor.

12 This is an absolute minimum estimate. See Chapter 8, note 8, and Chapter 14, note 27. Lic. Mañozca spent 68,878 ducats, according to treasury reports. The sum of 12,000 ducats for the Galdós de Valencia mission, of which amount 5,000 ducats was for salary, is a conservative estimate indeed.

13 President Antonio de Morga to king: April 30, 1634, AGI/AQ 12.

14 Morga to king: April 20, 1635, *ibid.*

15 Consultas: November 12, 1635, and December 22, 1635, *ibid.* 2.

16 Consulta: July 17, 1636, *ibid.*

17 Audiencia to king: April 5, 1637, *ibid.* 12.

18 Consulta: July 17, 1636, *ibid.* 2.

19 See note 11.

20 Consulta: June 21, 1642, AGI/AQ 2. On the legal complexities of collecting fines from the estates of deceased magistrates, see Solórzano, *Política indiana,* Bk. V, Ch. xi.

21 "Autos hechos por el lic. d. Alonso Mesa y Ayala . . . sobre la cobranza de las condenaciones . . . a Diego de Valencia . . .": 1638, AGI/EC 921a. Rodríquez de San Isidro to king: February 18, 1639, AGI/AQ 12.

22 See note 11.

23 I have no documentary proof that Oidor Peralta did in fact pay his fine, but it is highly improbable that he did not, since he remained in the imperial bureaucracy for many subsequent years. See note 8.

24 Rodríquez de San Isidro to king: May 6, 1639, AGI/AQ 12. I have encountered no evidence in the AGI or in the Archivo de la Nación in Guatemala that he did pay the fine. Tello de Velasco served in Guatemala from 1639 to 1643, when his honorable retirement and death followed closely upon each other. Audiencia to king: November 23, 1643, AGI/ Audiencia de Guatemala 16.

25 *The Milwaukee Journal,* March 14, 1965, p. 4.

26 *Recopilación de las leyes de los reynos de las Indias* (4 vols., Madrid, 1681), Bk. II, Title xxxiv, law 13.

27 Solórzano, *Política indiana,* Bk. V, Ch. x, Nos. 22, 26, 27, 47–52.

28 Schäfer implies that the relatively light sentences of most visitas generales indicate the lack of abuses among the magistrates, an interpretation that I do not share. Ernesto Schäfer, *El consejo real y supremo de las Indias* (2 vols., Seville, 1935–47), II, 128 ff.

29 As cited in Helmut G. Koenigsberger, *The Government of Sicily under Philip II of Spain: A Study in the Practice of Empire* (London and New York, 1951), p. 188.

30 For a stimulating article, see that of Congressman Henry Reuss, "An Ombudsman for America," *New York Times Magazine* (September 13, 1964), pp. 30 ff.

31 Solórzano, *Política indiana,* Bk. V, Ch. x, No. 19.

CHAPTER 16: AU PLUS CELA CHANGE, AU PLUS C'EST LA MÊME
CHOSE

1 See Chapter 14, notes 31–34.
2 President Alonso Pérez de Salazar to king: May 10, 1639, AGI/AQ 12.
3 President Martín Arriola to king: August 17, 1648, *ibid*. 13. Cedula to the audiencia: June 28, 1647, *ibid*. 209 (II).
4 For that correspondence from 1639 to 1643, see the AGI/Audiencia de Guatemala 16. Furthermore, there are few references to the activity of Tello de Velasco in the Archivo General de la Nación in Guatemala City.
5 Consulta: November 23, 1643, AGI/Audiencia de Guatemala 16. "Que el lic. Alonso de Castro y de la Cerda . . . ," December 30, 1643, Archivo General de la Nación (Guatemala), Al 23, exped. 39223, legajo 4568, fol. 23. "Merecimientos y servicios del Lic. don Juan Manuel Tello de Velasco, antiguo oidor de la audiencia de Guatemala," 1647, Archivo General de la Nación (Guatemala), Al 1, exped. 5039, legajo 212, fol. 64. This is a request for a royal largesse to his widow. In citing his services in Seville, Quito, and Guatemala, Tello de Velasco makes no mention of the visita general in Quito.
6 Domingo Juarros, *Compendio de la ciudad de Guatemala*, 3rd ed. (2 vols., Guatemala: Tipografia Nacional, 1937), I, 186, 263.
7 Thomas Gage, *The English-American, His Travail by Sea and Land: Or a New Survey of the West Indies*, 2nd ed. (London, 1648), p. 126. Hubert Howe Bancroft, *A History of Central America* (3 vols., San Francisco, 1886), II, 653.
8 Manuel Tello de Velasco, hijo: 1661, Archivo General de la Nación (Guatemala), Al 2, exped. 48501, legajo 5774.
9 Oidor Matías de Peralta to king: August 1, 1651, AGI/Audiencia de México 76.
10 For the climax of his career, see the following primary sources. Gregorio Martín de Guijo, *Diario de sucesos notables, 1648–1664*, in *Documentos para la historia de México*, ed. J. R. Navarro (15 vols., 1st series, Mexico, 1853–57), I, 152, 157, 161, 166, 167, 205, 221, 276, 308. Juan Pérez de Aller to king: 1652, AGI/EC 274. King to viceroy: February 1, 1653, Archivo General de la Nación (Mexico), *Reales cédulas*, IV, exped. 108. For the secondary sources, see the following: Vicente Riva Palacio, *México a través de los siglos* (5 vols., Barcelona, 1888), II, 615. Hubert Howe Bancroft, *History of Mexico* (3 vols., San Francisco, 1883), III, 137–39. Herbert I. Priestley, *José de Gálvez, Visitor General of New Spain, 1765–1771* (University of California Publications in History, No. 5, Berkeley, 1916), pp. 111–14.
11 Archivo General de la Nación (Mexico), *Reales cédulas*, IV, exped. 116.
12 Viceroy to king: May 31, 1632, AGI/AL 43.
13 José Toribio Medina, *Historia del tribunal del santo oficio de la inquisición de Lima, 1569–1820* (2 vols., Santiago, Chile: Fondo Histórico y Biblio-

gráfico, 1956), II, 16–45, 58, 70, 77, 89, 102, 109, 141, 378–79, 397, 398–99. Henry Charles Lea, *The Inquisition in the Spanish Dependencies* (New York, 1908), pp. 421–32. The climax of this anti-Portuguese sentiment, a Spanish reaction to the Portuguese revolt of 1640, occurred in the auto-da-fé of April 11, 1649. Also see note 19.

14 I have no archival documentation about the career of Lic. Mañozca in Spain from 1639 to 1645.

15 Lic. Juan de Mañozca to Antonio González de Legarda: February 28, 1627, AGI/AQ 62.

16 Bancroft, *History of Mexico,* III, 173.

17 Gil González Dávila, *Teatro eclesiástico de la primitiva iglesia de la Nueva España en las Indias occidentales* (2 vols., Madrid: José Porrua Turanzas, 1959), I, 99–102.

18 Francisco Sosa, *El episcopado mexicano* (Madrid, 1877), pp. 99–103. Sosa has the most complete account of Mañozca's administration as archbishop.

19 *Ibid.* Sosa asserts that Mañozca was not responsible for the resurgence of activity of the Holy Office. I do not share this interpretation. Sosa, who describes the archbishop as "piadoso y benigno," adjectives that his contemporaries seldom used in describing the fiery Basque cleric, ignores the archbishop's life-long and family connections with the Holy Office. Also see Guijo, *Diario,* pp. 42–52. Lea, *The Inquisition,* pp. 230–33. Also see note 13.

20 Bancroft, *History of Mexico,* III, 104–11. Pablo González Casanova, "Aspectos políticos de Palafox y Mendoza," *Revista de historia de América,* No. 17 (June, 1944), pp. 49 ff.

21 Bishop Palafox shared the generous opinion of the capabilities of the Indians, which was characteristically held by the early missionaries but seldom expressed in the mid-seventeenth century. Juan de Palafox y Mendoza, *Virtudes de indios,* in *Colección de Libros raros o curiosos que tratan de América* (21 vols., Madrid, 1891–1928), Vol. X. He praised the Indians for their meekness, humility, and contentment with poverty, but his vision was as paternalistic as Gerónimo de Mendieta's. The Indians were children who needed guardians to protect their innocence and simplicity. Also see González Casanova, "Aspectos políticos de Palafox," pp. 47–48.

22 For background, see my *Millennial Kingdom of the Franciscans in the New World: A Study of the Writings of Gerónimo de Mendieta, 1525–1604* (University of California Publications in History, No. 52, Berkeley and Los Angeles, 1956), pp. 51–52. H. H. Bancroft's account is still useful, but more work needs to be done: Bancroft, *History of Mexico,* III, 100–101. Genaro García, *Don Juan de Palafox y Mendoza, obispo de Puebla y Osma y virrey de la Nueva España* (Mexico: Librería de Bouret, 1918), pp. 81 ff.

23 Some of the vehement opposition expressed in Quito to the expansion of the Jesuits came from the secular clergy, who feared that their income from the tithes would shrink as the Jesuits acquired more rural property. Cathedral chapter to king: 1620, AGI/AQ 80. Bishop to king: April 29,

1621, *ibid.* 77. Bishop to king: April 10, 1627, *ibid.* Cedula to audiencia: May 4, 1641, ANH, I, No. 85 (I). The other regular orders opposed the expansion of the Jesuits partially out of fear and jealousy that the better organized and more disciplined Jesuits would provide unwelcome competition. See ANH, I, No. 85 (II) and (III).

24 In the Philippines, on the other hand, the bishops never did enforce their claim to supervise the regular clergy as parish priests. See my *Hispanization of the Philippines: Spanish Aims and Filipino Responses, 1565–1700* (Madison, 1958), pp. 32–35.

25 See Chapter 12, note 29.

26 García, *Palafox,* p. 165.

27 Cedula to the judges conservator: June 25, 1648, Archivo General de la Nación (Mexico), *Reales cédulas,* III, exped. 17, fol. 42.

28 Cedula to provincial superior of the Dominican order: January 25, 1648, *ibid.,* exped. 15, fol. 40.

29 Cedula to the archbishop: January 25, 1648, *ibid.,* fol. 41.

30 Cedula to audiencia: January 25, 1648, *ibid.,* exped. 21, fol. 50.

31 The literature on the Palafox-Jesuit controversy is as voluminous as it is polemical. Some of the key primary sources are in Genaro García, ed., *Colección de documentos inéditos ó muy raros para la historia de México* (36 vols., Mexico: Vda. de C. Bouret, 1905–11), VII. González Dávila, a contemporary, avoided mentioning the controversy. For another contemporary account, see Guijo, *Diario.* Francisco Antonio de Lorenzana y Butrón, *Concilios provinciales primero y sequndo . . .* (Mexico, 1769), pp. 219, 251–69. Antoine Touron, O.P., *Histoire générale de l'Amérique . . .* (14 vols., Paris, 1769–70), VII, 316–86, VIII, 1–100. One of the classic Jesuit sources virtually avoids the subject. Andrés Cavo, S.J., *Historia de México,* ed., Ernest J. Burus, S.J., 2nd ed. (Mexico: Editorial Patria, 1949), pp. 303 ff. The ablest Jesuit defense is that of Francisco Alegre, S.J., *Historia de la compañía de Jesús de la Nueva España,* Ernest J. Burus, S.J., and Félix Zubillaga, S.J., eds. (4 vols., Rome: Institutum Historicum, 1956–60), III, 70–177. Alegre wrote his history in Italy after the expulsion of the Jesuits from the Spanish empire in 1767. Sosa's account in *El episcopado* follows very closely that of Guijo, *Diario,* pp. 99–103. García, *Palafox,* pp. 114–203. Niceto de Zamaçois, *Historia de México . . .* (22 vols., Mexico, 1878–1902), V, 336–47, 349–50. Riva Palacio, *México a través de los siglos,* II, 601–5. Bancroft, *History of Mexico,* III, 116–33. Charles P. Simmons, "Palafox and his Critics: Reappraising a Controversy," *Hispanic-American Historical Review,* XLVI, No. 4 (November, 1966), 394–408. The Jesuits came off quite poorly in the nineteenth-century accounts, most of which have more than a tinge of anticlericalism. A fresh examination of the primary sources, especially the unpublished material in the archives, might serve to restore the balance.

32 Vincencio Caraffa, S.J., to Pedro Velasco, S.J.: Rome, January 30, 1648, García, ed., *Documentos,* VII, 90–94.

33 Bancroft, *History of Mexico,* III, 132.

34 *Ibid.*, p. 133. García, *Palafox,* pp. 267 ff.

35 Richard Herr, *The Eighteenth Century Revolution in Spain* (Princeton: Princeton University Press, 1958), pp. 20, 192.

36 Cedula to archbishop: January 25, 1648, Archivo General de la Nación (Mexico), *Reales cédulas,* III, exped. 15, fol. 41.

37 Alegre, *Historia de la compañía,* III, 181.

38 The archbishop's nephew, don Juan Sáenz de Mañozca, who, as a member of the Inquisition, had taken a strong stand against Palafox, reversed his attitude subsequently while in Cuba in 1665, when "that holy prelate" appeared to him in a vision. García, ed., *Documentos,* VII, 161–65. The nephew inherited much of his uncle's temperament. In 1661 he was suspended from office for nine years and fined 1,300 pesos for the harshness and severity of his official conduct: Lea, *The Inquisition,* pp. 257–63.

Chapter 17: A Weberian Analysis of the Spanish Bureaucracy

1 My discussion of Max Weber is based on his own *The Theory of Social and Economic Organization,* transls. A. M. Henderson and Talcott Parsons (New York, 1947). Especially useful is Reinhard Bendix' lucid *Max Weber, An Intellectual Portrait* (Garden City, 1960).

2 See my *Millennial Kingdom of the Franciscans in the New World: A Study of the Writings of Gerónimo de Mendieta, 1525–1604* (University of California Publications in History, No. 52, Berkeley and Los Angeles, 1956).

3 Richard Morse, "The Heritage of Latin America," in Louis Hartz, *The Founding of New Societies: Studies in the History of the United States, Latin America, South Africa, Canada and Australia* (New York, 1964), pp. 157–58. Magali Sarfatti, *Spanish Bureaucratic-Patrimonialism in America* (Berkeley: Institute of International Studies, 1966). The analysis in this short book follows the line first suggested by Morse.

4 Weber, *The Theory of Social and Economic Organization,* p. 357.

5 S. N. Eisenstadt, *The Political Systems of Empires* (New York, 1963). My discussion in this chapter of historical bureaucratic polities closely follows Eisenstadt's analysis.

6 For an earlier formulation of mine, see my "Authority and Flexibility in the Spanish Imperial Bureaucracy," *Administrative Science Quarterly* V, No. 1 (June, 1960), 47–65. For a reprint of this article, see Howard Cline, ed., *Latin American History: Essays on Its Study and Teaching, 1898–1965* (2 vols., Austin: University of Texas Press, 1967), II, 739–49.

7 Eisenstadt, in his admirable study, minimizes the extent and the depth of the political struggle in the Spanish system. His contention that the political struggle in the Indies was limited to local matters with questions of principle decided in Spain is misleading. The audiencias and the local elites had much, perhaps too much, to do with the shaping of social relationships. The reforms of Charles III in one sense were an effort to reassert centralized control over both the bureaucracy and the local elites. Eisenstadt, *The Political Systems of Empires,* pp. 222–72.

BIBLIOGRAPHICAL ESSAY
AND LIST OF SOURCES

Archival Sources

Much of the documentation for this book came from archival sources in both Spain and Latin America. Not surprisingly, the single richest depository by far was the Archivo General de Indias in Seville. In the Audiencia de Quito section, 48 of the 608 *legajos* contained pertinent material. Among the legajos I consulted during a six-month stay in Seville in 1961 were the following: Audiencia de Quito 1, 2, 8, 9, 10, 11, 12, 13, 14, 15, 17, 19, 20, 29, 30, 31, 32, 50, 51, 61, 62, 77, 80, 87, 88, 209, and 268. The following legajos were particularly useful from Escribanía de Cámara: 274, 686, 917, 918, 921, 978, 994, and 998. The following legajos in the Audiencia de Lima section were consulted: 4, 5, 6, 15, 38, 39, 40, 41, 42, 43, 44, 45, 46, 47, 48, 49, 96, 97, 98, 99, 100, 571, and 588. In the usually interesting Indiferente General section, I consulted the following bundles: 615, 619, 620, 753, 754, 755, 760, 1151, 1152, 1153, and 1154. I also used the following legajos: Audiencia de Guatemala 1, 16; Audiencia de México 72, 73; Audiencia de Santa Fe 244; and Contaduría General 10.

The overwhelming majority of the archival sources came from the AGI. Their quantity as well as their quality are impressive. Although colonial magistrates often disregarded or evaded the instructions of the king and the Council of the Indies, they found it desirable to dispatch detailed reports to Spain justifying their courses of action or inaction. These voluminous reports were originally deposited in the Spanish national archives at Simancas, founded by the Emperor Charles V. In the late eighteenth century, Charles III set up the AGI in Seville as a colonial archive. Today this archive is the richest depository of manuscripts relating to the history of Spain's colonial empire.

The American archives, much smaller in quantity than the collection in Seville, supplement but seldom duplicate the holdings of the AGI. The business of the cabildos, correspondence between the audiencia and the viceroy, certain aspects of the judicial functions of the audiencia, some of the correspondence between the corregidores or corporate groups and the audiencia are a few of the areas that are often better covered in the archives of Quito than in the AGI.

The best organized archive in Quito is the Archivo Municipal, whose indefatigable director, Jorge Garcés, has published more than 30 volumes from his archive. Unfortunately the acts of the cabildo from 1616 to 1638 are missing. They were last used by González Suárez. Yet in spite of this important lacuna, that archive does contain some valuable material for study. Particularly useful is some of the correspondence between the cabildo and the viceroy.

The Archivo Nacional de Historia in Quito, whose director was Alfredo Chaves when I was there in 1960 and 1962, has only a few volumes on the Morga period, but the material is choice. That archive has, for example, some of the correspondence between the viceroy and the audiencia as well as some letters exchanged between the corregidores and the audiencia, none of which can be easily located in either Lima or Seville.

The Archivo de la Corte Suprema de Justicia (Quito), which is now housed in the Casa de la Cultura, was, in 1961 and 1962, so badly organized that it was difficult if not impossible to use. That archive inherited what remains of the records of the colonial audiencia. Two items, however, were priceless finds. They were the *Libro de acuerdos de la real audiencia* (1610–41) in two volumes and the *Libro de acuerdos de hacienda* (1601–57). The various religious orders and the archdiocese of Quito maintain archives, which undoubtedly contain material on the seventeenth century. A layman, however, cannot secure ready access to them.

Some useful source material on the relations between Popayán and Quito can be found in the well-organized Archivo Central de Cauca in Popayán, whose distinguished director is José María Arboleda. I also consulted the very small and much less interesting municipal archive in Cali.

For the pre-Quito or the post-Quito careers of some of the magistrates in this study, I made brief excursions to the following archives: Archivo Nacional (Panama), Archivo General de la Nación (Guatemala), and the Archivo General de la Nación (Mexico).

The Inquisition section of the Archivo Histórico Nacional in Madrid yielded useful information on certain aspects of the career of Lic. Mañozca.

The most disappointing archival center for the purposes of this book was that in Lima, where, in spite of a diligent search, I encountered nothing of interest.

LIST OF PUBLISHED SOURCES

The following list of published sources is selective rather than exhaustive. Certain items, such as the standard bibliographical works of reference, have been intentionally excluded. Some works cited only a few times have been omitted.

Alcedo, Antonio de. *Diccionario geográfico-histórico de las Indias occidentales ó América.* 5 vols. Madrid, 1786.

Araujo, Leonardo, O. S. A. *Relación de las cosas que svedieron en la ciudad de Quito, reyno del Pirú con las ordenes de Santo Domingo y San Agustín por mano del Lic. Juan de Mañozca, visitador de la real audiencia de la dicha ciudad* . . . . Lima, 1627.

Ayala, Francisco Javier de. *Ideas políticas de Juan de Solórzano.* Seville: Escuela de Estudios Hispano-Americanos, 1946.

Bancroft, Hubert Howe. *History of Mexico.* 3 vols. San Francisco, 1883.

Bayle, Constantino, S. J. *Los cabildos seculares en la América española.* Madrid: Sapientia, 1952.

Bendix, Reinhard. *Max Weber, An Intellectual Portrait.* Garden City: Doubleday, 1960.

Blunt, Sir Edward. *The Indian Civil Service.* London: Faber and Faber, 1937.

Borah, Woodrow W. *Early Colonial Trade and Navigation between Mexico and Peru.* Ibero-Americana, No. 38. Berkeley and Los Angeles: University of California Press, 1954.

————. "Representative Institutions in the Spanish Empire: The New World," *The Americas,* XII, No. 3 (January, 1956), 246–57.

————, and Sherburne F. Cook. *The Aboriginal Population of Central Mexico on the Eve of the Spanish Conquest.* Ibero-Americana, No. 45. Berkeley and Los Angeles: University of California Press, 1963.

————, and ————. *The Indian Population of Central Mexico, 1531–1610.* Ibero-Americana, No. 44. Berkeley and Los Angeles: University of California Press, 1960.

————; and ————. *The Population of Central Mexico in 1548.* Ibero-Americana, No. 43. Berkeley and Los Angeles: University of California Press, 1960.

Boxer, Charles R. *The Dutch in Brazil.* Oxford: Oxford University Press, 1957.

————. *Portuguese Society in the Tropics: The Municipal Councils of Goa, Macao, Bahia, and Luanda 1510–1800.* Madison and Milwaukee: University of Wisconsin Press, 1965.

Campbell, George. *Modern India: A Sketch of the System of Civil Government.* London, 1853.

Cánovas del Castillo, Antonio. *Historia de la decadencia de España desde el advenimiento de Felipe III al trono hasta la muerte de Carlos II.* Madrid, 1854.

Castillo de Bovadilla, Jerónimo de. *Política para corregidores y señores de vassallos en tiempo de paz y guerra* . . . . Barcelona, 1916.

Céspedes del Castillo, Guillermo. "La visita como institución indiana," *Anuario de estudios americanos,* III (Seville, 1946), 984–1021.

Chailley, Joseph. *Administrative Problems of British India.* London: Macmillan, 1910.

Chaunu, Pierre, and Huguette Chaunu. *Seville et l'Atlantique, 1504–1650.* 9 vols. Paris: École Pratique des Hautes Études, 1956–59.

Colección de las memorias ó relaciones que escribieron los virreyes del Pirú acerca del estado en que dejaron las cosas generales del reino. 2 vols. Madrid: Imprenta del Asilo de Huérfanos del S.C. de Jesús, 1921–30.

Consejo Real de las Indias. *Sobre que se debe escusar el de cámara en que se ha de tratar de formar.* Madrid, 1644(?).

Córdoba y Salinas, Diego de, O.F.M. *Crónica franciscana de las provincias del Perú.* Lino G. Canedo, O.F.M., ed. Washington, D.C.: Academy of American Franciscan History, 1957. 1st ed., Lima, 1651.

Curry, J. C. *The Indian Police.* London: Faber and Faber, 1932.

Domínguez Ortiz, Antonio. *Política y hacienda de Felipe IV.* Madrid, 1960.

Eisenstadt, S. N. *The Political Systems of Empires.* New York: Free Press of Glencoe, 1963.

Elliott, John H. *Imperial Spain: 1469–1716.* London: Edward Arnold, 1963.

————. *The Revolt of the Catalans: A Study in the Decline of Spain, 1598–1640.* Cambridge: Cambridge University Press, 1963.

Espinosa Polit, Aurelio. *Santa Mariana de Jesús, hija de la compañía de Jesús, según los procesos.* Quito: La Prensa Católica, 1957.

Frykenberg, Robert E. *Guntur District, 1788–1848: A History of Local Influence and Central Authority in South India.* Oxford: Clarendon Press, 1965.

Gage, Thomas. *The English-American, His Travail by Sea and Land: Or a New Survey of the West Indies.* 2nd ed. London, 1648.

Garcés, Jorge, ed. *Libro de cabildos de la ciudad de Quito, 1610–16,* and *1638–46.* Vols. XXVI and XXX of the Archivo Municipal de Quito. Quito, 1955, and 1960.

Gerhard, Peter. *Pirates on the West Coast of New Spain, 1565–1742.* Glendale, Calif.: A. H. Clark, 1960.

Geyl, Pieter. *The Netherlands in the Seventeenth Century.* 2 vols. New York: Barnes and Noble, 1961–64.

————. *The Revolt of the Netherlands.* New York: Barnes and Noble, 1958.

Gibson, Charles. *The Aztecs under Spanish Rule: A History of the Indians of the Valley of Mexico, 1519–1810.* Stanford: Stanford University Press, 1964.

Góngora, Mario. *El estado español en el derecho indiano: época de fundación, 1492–1570.* Santiago: Universidad de Chile, 1951.

González Suárez, Federico. *Historia general de la república del Ecuador.* 7 vols. Quito: Imprenta del Clero, 1890–1903.

Haring, Clarence. *The Spanish Empire in America.* New York: Oxford University Press, 1947.

Jaramillo Alvarado, Pío. *Historia de Loja y su provincia.* Quito: Casa de la Cultura Ecuatoriana, 1955.

Jiménez de la Espada, Marcos, ed. *Relaciones geográficas de Indias.* 4 vols. Madrid, 1881–97.

Jouanen, José, S.J. *Historia de la compañía de Jesús en la antigua provincia de Quito, 1570–1696.* 2 vols. Quito: Editorial Ecuatoriana, 1941.

Juan, Jorge, and Antonio de Ulloa. *Noticias secretas de América* . . . . Rufino Blanco-Fombona, ed. Biblioteca Ayacucho, Vols. XXXI–XXXII. Madrid: Editorial América, 1918.

Keyes, Frances Parkinson. *The Rose and the Lily.* New York: Hawthorn, 1961.

Koenigsberger, Helmut G. *The Government of Sicily under Philip II of Spain: A Study in the Practice of Empire.* London and New York: Staples Press, 1951.

————. "Patronage and Bribery during the Reign of Charles V," *Anciens pays et assemblées d'états,* XXII (Louvain and Paris, 1961), 168–75.

Konetzke, Richard. *Colección de documentos para la historia de la formación social de Hispanoamérica, 1493–1810.* 4 vols. Madrid: Consejo Superior de Investigaciones Científicas, 1958–62.

Kubler, George. "The Quechua in the Colonial World," *Handbook of South American Indians,* Julian Steward, ed. 7 vols. Washington, D.C., 1946–59, II, 331–410.

————, and Martin Soria. *Art and Architecture in Spain and Portugal and their American Dominions, 1500–1800.* Baltimore: Penguin, 1959.

Landazuri Soto, Alberto. *El régimen laboral indígena en la real audiencia de Quito.* Madrid: Aldecoa, 1959.

Lea, Henry Charles. *The Inquisition in the Spanish Dependencies.* New York: Macmillan, 1908.

León Pinelo, Antonio Rodríguez de. *Autos, acuerdos i decretos de gobierno del real i supremo consejo de las Indias* . . . . Madrid, 1658.

Leonard, Irving. *Baroque Times in Old Mexico.* Ann Arbor: University of Michigan Press, 1959.

Linke, Lilo. *Ecuador, Country of Contrasts.* London: Oxford University Press, 1960.

Lohmann Villena, Guillermo. *El corregidor de indios en el Perú bajo los Austrias.* Madrid: Cultura Hispánica, 1957.

Lopes de Solís, Luis. "Constituciones sinodales del Quito." MS (18th century copy of 1596 original), University of Wisconsin Library.

López de Velasco, Juan. *Geografía y descripción universal de las Indias.* Madrid, 1894.

Lynch, John. *Spain under the Habsburgs.* 2 vols. New York: Oxford University Press, 1964————.

McAlister, L. N. "Social Structure and Social Change in New Spain," *Hispanic-American Historical Review,* XLIII, No. 3 (August, 1963), 349–70.

Maconochie, Sir Evan. *Life in the Indian Civil Service.* London: Chapman and Hall, 1926.

Mañozca, Juan de. *El lic. Mañozca . . . con los señores doctores d. Andrés de Reuda Rico . . . sobre la precedencia que pretendo me toca en el asiento y demás actos como más antiguo.* Madrid, 1640.

Marañón, Gregorio. *El conde-duque de Olivares, la pasión de mandar.* 4th ed., Madrid: Espasa-Calpe, 1959.

Maravall, José Antonio. *La teoría española del estado en el siglo xvii.* Madrid: Instituto de Estudios Políticos, 1944.

Mariluz Urquijo, José María. *Ensayo sobre los juicios de residencia indianas.* Seville: Escuela de Estudios Hispano-Americanos, 1952.

Mason, Philip. *The Men Who Ruled India.* 2 vols. London: Jonathan Cape, 1953.

Matienzo, Juan de. *Gobierno del Perú.* Buenos Aires: Compañía Sudamericana de Billetes de Banco, 1910.

Medina, José T. *Historia del tribunal del santo oficio de la inquisición de Cartagena de las Indias.* Santiago, Chile, 1899.

Memorias de los virreyes que han gobernado el Perú durante el tiempo del coloniaje español. 6 vols. Lima, 1859.

Miranda, Luis. "Primera historia de Filipinas," and "Sucesos de las islas Filipinas," *Boletín bibliográfico,* Nos. 155 and 156 (May 15, 1959, and June 10, 1959), pp. 2 and 6, and pp. 2 and 8.

Misra, B. B. *The Central Administration of the East India Company, 1773–1834.* Manchester: Motilal Banarsidass, 1959.

Morán de Butrón, Jacinto. *Vida de Santa Mariana de Jesús.* Quito: Imprenta Municipal, 1955.

Morga, Antonio de. *Recopilación de cédulas despachadas en diferentes tiempos por S. M. . . . para la real audiencia . . . del Quito del Pirú, 1589–1632.* MS (1632), Biblioteca Nacional, Mexico City.

———. *Sucesos de las islas filipinas.* W. E. Retana, ed. Madrid: Librería General de Victoriano Suárez, 1909.

Morse, Richard. "The Heritage of Latin America," in Louis Hartz, *The Founding of New Societies: Studies in the History of the United States, Latin America, South Africa, Canada, and Australia.* New York: Harcourt, Brace & World, 1964.

———. "Some Characteristics of Latin American Urban History," *American Historical Review,* LXVII, No. 42 (January, 1962), 317–38.

Olano, Antonio. *Popayán en la colonia, bosquejo histórico de la gobernación y de la ciudad de Popayán en los siglos xvii y xviiii.* Popayán: Imprenta Oficial, 1910.

O'Malley, L. S. *The Indian Civil Service, 1601–1930.* London: J. Murray, 1931.

Ots Capdequí, José María. *España en América: Las instituciones coloniales.* 2nd ed., Bogotá: Universidad Nacional de Colombia, 1952.

———. *El estado español en las Indias.* 3rd ed., Mexico: Fondo de Cultura Económica, 1957.

————. *Manual de historia del derecho español en las Indias.* Buenos Aires: Editorial Losada, 1945.

————, and Javier Malagón. *Solórzano y la Política indiana.* Mexico and Buenos Aires: Fondo de Cultura Económica, 1965.

Parry, John H. *The Audiencia of New Galicia in the Sixteenth Century.* Cambridge: Cambridge University Press, 1948.

————. *The Sale of Public Office in the Spanish Indies under the Habsburgs.* Berkeley and Los Angeles: University of California Press, 1963.

————. *The Spanish Seaborne Empire.* New York: Alfred A. Knopf, 1966.

Pelsmaeker é Ibáñez, Francisco de. *La audiencia en las colonias españolas de América.* Madrid: Revista de Archivos, 1925.

Peña Cámara, José María de la. *A List of Spanish Residencias in the Archives of the Indies, 1516–1775.* Washington, D.C.: Library of Congress, 1955.

Pérez, Aquiles R. *Las mitas en la real audiencia de Quito.* Quito: Ministerio del Tesoro, 1947.

Pérez Landero Otáñez y Castro, Pedro. *Práctica de visitas y residencias de los reynos del Perú* .... Naples, 1646.

Phelan, John L. "Authority and Flexibility in the Spanish Imperial Bureaucracy," *Administrative Science Quarterly,* V, No. 1 (June, 1960), 47–65.

————. *The Hispanization of the Philippines: Spanish Aims and Filipino Responses, 1565–1700.* Madison: University of Wisconsin Press, 1959.

————. *The Millennial Kingdom of the Franciscans in the New World: A Study of the Writings of Gerónimo de Mendieta, 1525–1604.* University of California Publications in History, No. 52. Berkeley and Los Angeles, 1956.

————. "The Road to Esmeraldas, The Failure of a Spanish Conquest in the Seventeenth Century," *Essays in History and Literature Presented by the Fellows of the Newberry Library to Stanley Pargellis.* Heinz Bluhm, ed. Chicago: The Newberry Library, 1965.

Picón-Salas, Mariano. *A Cultural History of Spanish America from Conquest to Independence.* Berkeley and Los Angeles: University of California Press, 1962.

Pike, Frederick. "The Municipality and the System of Checks and Balances in the Spanish American Colonial System," *The Americas,* XV, No. 2 (October, 1958), 139–58.

Pike, Ruth. *Enterprise and Adventure: The Genoese in Seville and the Opening of the New World.* Ithaca: Cornell University Press, 1966.

Priestley, Herbert I. *José de Gálvez, Visitor General of New Spain, 1765–1771.* University of California Publications in History, No. 5. Berkeley, 1916.

Recopilación de las leyes de los reynos de las Indias. 4 vols. Madrid, 1681.

Retana, W. E. "Estudio Preliminar," in Antonio de Morga, *Sucesos de las islas filipinas.* Madrid, 1909.

Rosenblat, Ángel. *La población indígena de América desde 1492 hasta la actualidad.* Buenos Aires: Institución Cultural Espanola, 1945.

Ruiz Guiñazú, Enrique. *La magistratura indiana.* Buenos Aires: Facultad de Derecho y Ciencias Sociales, 1916.

Rumazo González, José. *Documentos para la historia de la audiencia de Quito.* 8 vols. Madrid: Afrodisio Aguado, 1948–50.

——. *La región amazónica del Ecuador en el siglo xvi.* Seville: Consejo Superior de Investigaciones Científicas, 1946.

Ruthnaswamy, M. *The Political Theory of the Government of India.* Madras, 1928.

——. *Some Influences that Made the British Administrative System in India.* London: Luzac & Co., 1939.

Sarfatti, Magali. *Spanish Bureaucratic-Patrimonialism in America.* Berkeley: Institute of International Studies, 1966.

Sarkar, Jadunath. *Mughal Administration.* Calcutta: M. C. Sarkar, 1952.

Schäfer, Ernesto. *El consejo real y supremo de las Indias.* 2 vols. Seville: Universidad de Sevilla, 1935–47.

Schurz, William L. *The Manila Galleon.* New York: Dutton, 1959.

Silva Santisteban, Fernando. *Los obrajes en el virreinato del Peru.* Lima: Museo Nacional de Historia, 1964.

Simmons, Charles P. "Palafox and his Critics: Reappraising a Controversy," *Hispanic-American Historical Review,* XLVI, No. 4 (November, 1966), 394–408.

Sluiter, Engel. "Dutch Maritime Power and the Colonial Status Quo, 1585–1641," *The Pacific Coast Historical Review,* XI (March, 1942), 29–41.

——. "The Dutch on the Pacific Coast of South America: 1598–1621." Ph.D. thesis, University of California, Berkeley, 1937.

Solórzano y Pereira, Juan de. *Política indiana.* 5 vols. Madrid, 1647.

Spear, Percival. *Twilight of the Mughuls.* Cambridge: Cambridge University Press, 1951.

Stevenson, William B. *Historical and Descriptive Narrative of Twenty Years' Residence in South America.* 3 vols. London, 1829.

Steward, Julian, ed. *Handbook of South American Indians.* 7 vols. Washington, D.C.: Government Printing Office, 1946–59.

Tibesar, Antonine, O.F.M. "The Alternativa: A Study of Spanish-Creole Relations in Seventeenth Century Peru," *The Americas,* XI (January, 1955), 229–82.

Tobar Donoso, Julio, and Alfredo Luna Tobar. *Derecho territorial ecuatoriano.* Quito: Editorial La Unión Católica, 1961.

Trevelyan, G. O. *The Competition Wallah.* 2nd ed., London, 1866.

Trevor Davies, Reginald. *The Golden Century of Spain, 1501–1621.* London: Macmillan, 1961.

——. *Spain in Decline, 1621–1700.* London: Macmillan, 1961.

Vargas, José María, O.P. *El arte quiteño en los siglos xvi, xvii y xviii.* Quito: Casa de la Cultura Ecuatoriana, 1949.

——. *Historia de la iglesia en el Ecuador durante el patronato español.* Quito: Editorial "Santo Domingo," 1962.

Vásquez de Espinosa, Antonio. *Compendio y descripción de las Indias occidentales.* Washington, D.C.: Government Printing Office, 1948.

Velasco, Juan de, S.J. *Historia del reino de Quito en la América meridional*. 3 vols. Quito, 1841–44.

———. *Historia moderna del reyno de Quito de la provincia de Jesús del mismo reyno*. Vols. IX and X of the Biblioteca Amazonas. Raul Reyes y Reyes, ed. Quito: El Comercio, n.d.

Viñas Mey, Carmelo. "El régimen jurídico de responsabilidad en la América indiana," *Revista de las Españas,* III and IV (January–February, and August, 1928, and January–February, 1929), 17–21, 362–69, 36–54.

Weber, Max. *The Theory of Social and Economic Organization*. A. M. Henderson and Talcott Parsons, transls. New York: Oxford University Press, 1947.

West, Sir Edward. *Bombay in the Days of George IV: Memoirs of Sir Edward West*. F. Dawtrey Drewitt, ed. London: Longmans, Green, and Co., 1907.

West, Robert C. *The Pacific Lowlands of Colombia: A Negroid Area of the American Tropics*. Baton Rouge: Louisiana State University, 1957.

Wethey, Harold E. *Colonial Architecture and Sculpture in Peru*. Cambridge, Mass.: Harvard University Press, 1949.

Whitten, Norman E., Jr. *Class, Kinship, and Power in an Ecuadorian Town, The Negroes of San Lorenzo*. Stanford: Stanford University Press, 1966.

Zook, David H. *Zarumilla-Marañón: The Ecuador-Peru Dispute*. New York: Bookman Associates, 1964.

INDEX